THE ENCYCLOPEDIA OF
Witches and Witchcraft

THE ENCYCLOPEDIA OF
Witches and Witchcraft

Rosemary Ellen Guiley

Facts On File
New York • Oxford

Facts On File, Inc.   or Facts On File Limited
460 Park Avenue South   Collins Street
New York, New York 10016   Oxford OX4 1XJ
USA   United Kingdom

Library of Congress Cataloging-in-Publication Data

Guiley, Rosemary.
  The Encyclopedia of witches and witchcraft.

  Bibliography: p.
  Includes index.
  1. Witchcraft—Dictionaries.   2. Witches—Biography—
Dictionaries. I. Title.
BF1566.G85 1989   133.4'3'03   89-11776
ISBN 0-8160-1793-X
    0-8160-2268-2 (pbk)

British CIP data available on request.

Facts On File books are available at special discounts when purchased in bulk quantities for businesses, associations, institutions or sales promotion. Please contact the Special Sales Department of our New York office at 212/683-2244 (dial 800/322-8755 except in NY, AK or HI).

Text Design by In-house Graphics
Jacket Design by Cathy Hyman
Composition by Maple-Vail Book Manufacturing Group
Manufactured by Maple-Vail Book Manufacturing Group
Printed in the United States of America
Front cover artwork: Courtauld Institute Galleries,
London (Wih Collection No. 4533).

10 9 8 7 6 5 4 3 2 1

This book is printed on acid-free paper.

Contents

Acknowledgments

In my work for this encyclopedia, I was aided by numerous persons, who granted interviews, shared resources, opened doors, conducted research and provided advisory help. The first and most important thanks of all goes to Cato Ealy, who conceived the idea for this book and helped make it a reality. Cato saw a need for a comprehensive encyclopedia on Witchcraft and related subjects that would span both past and present. I also am deeply indebted to Joanne P. Austin, a most able fellow writer and researcher who applied her talent to the subjects of possession, obsession, exorcism, Vodoun, Santería, Macumba and African witchcraft; and to Margaret Guiley, who devoted countless hours to source and information searches in libraries.

I received a great deal of help and support from persons in the Craft or neo-Paganism. I was invited into homes, granted lengthy interviews and given a wealth of material in the form of journals, articles, pamphlets, manuscripts, photographs and the like. Phone calls and referrals were made on my behalf. I received many lengthy letters with detailed answers to questions. I am grateful for the generosity of the following persons, who appear in this book: Margot Adler, Charles Arnold, Isaac Bonewits, Raymond Buckland, Z. Budapest, Laurie Cabot, Patricia C. Crowther, Scott Cunningham, Stewart and Janet Farrar, Ed Fitch, Selena Fox, Gavin and Yvonne Frost, Dr. Leo Louis Martello, Herman Slater, Starhawk, Doreen Valiente, Marion Weinstein, Carl Weschcke and Otter and Morning Glory Zell. I am particularly grateful to Isaac Bonewits, Ed Fitch and Selena Fox for their overviews on neo-Paganism and the Craft; to Patricia C. Crowther for information on Gerald B. Gardner; to Stewart and Janet Farrar for information on Alexander Sanders; and to Carl Weschcke for his hospitality. In addition, Valerie Voigt of the Pagan/Occult/Witchcraft Special Interest Group of Mensa provided information on Victor Anderson and the Faery Tradition and gave me numerous referrals. Don Frew of the Covenant of the Goddess also gave me referrals. Andraste of Forever Forests provided information on Gwydion Pendderwen. Leonora James of the Pagan Federation provided information on John Score and the Pagan Federation. There are others who provided help but wish to remain anonymous for reasons of privacy.

The following persons also provided invaluable assistance: Australian author Nevill Drury, who gave me details about Rosaleen Norton; Brian Hayden, Ph.D., professor in the Department of Arachaeology, Simon Fraser University, Burnaby, British Columbia, who gave me an interview and articles pertaining to Paleo-Paganism; Nancy Mostad of Llewellyn Publications, who provided information on Lady Sheba and helped me reach persons I wished to interview; and Carolyn J. Weekly, director of the Abby Aldrich Rockefeller Folk Art Center in Williamsburg, Virginia, who provided information and suggestions for research. Marion Zimmer Bradley granted me a much appreciated interview to explain her involvement in occultism and her views on the Craft.

Much of the research was conducted at the library of the American Society for Psychical Research, New York City, whose collection includes many fine books on witchcraft and magic. My thanks to the staff of the A.S.P.R., and especially to James G. Matlock, librarian and archivist, for his expert assistance. I also was aided by the library staff of the Essex Institute, Salem, Massachusetts, under the direction of Eugenia A. Fountain, research librarian, and by many persons at the U.S. Library of Congress in Washington, D.C.

I would like to thank Doreen Valiente and Robert Hale, Ltd., for permission to use Valiente's "Charge of the Goddess," as it appears in *The Witches' Way* by Janet and Stewart Farrar.

I also would like to express heartfelt thanks to my editor, Kate Kelly, who provided support, guidance and resources, and to my husband, Bruce S. Trachtenberg, for his love.

Introduction

To most persons in the modern day, witchcraft remains a dark and mysterious subject. It is often regarded with fear. Popular ideas about witchcraft have been shaped largely through the media, which perpetuates stereotypes based on the gross exaggerations of centuries past. To complicate matters, the Witchcraft of today is connected in name only to the witchcraft of the Inquisition.

The purpose of this book is to provide information pertaining to the evolution of witchcraft in Western civilization: its history, beliefs, practices and adherents. Many of the popular beliefs about witchcraft and witches are derived from a period in European, and to a small extent, American, history, from about 1450 to 1700. During these years, witchcraft was a matter of social, political, and religious conflict and perceptions of evil: witches were portrayed as heretics who worshipped the Devil and worked harmful magic against their God-fearing neighbors. It was said that witches were ugly, flew through the air, attended orgiastic sabbats and had the power to become invisible and metamorphose into animals. They raised storms, concocted poisons and conjured evil spirits. Hundreds of thousands of persons were persecuted, tried and executed as ''witches.''

A form of modern Witchcraft, often called Wicca or the Craft, largely a product of the 20th century, is much different. It is a religion that emphasizes worship of the Goddess and the practice of a magical craft that is to be used for beneficial purposes, not to harm. Modern Witches view themselves as healers and helpers. Their religion has a diverse heritage of pagan religions, the Western esoteric tradition, folk magic, and, more recently, shamanism and tribal religions. It is part of the broader neo-Pagan movement. It has no connection with Devil-worship or Satanism.

Not all contemporary Witches are Witches in the religious sense; many are simply practitioners of sorcery, ceremonial magic or folk magic.

A major portion of this encyclopedia covers the history of the witch persecutions, underlying beliefs, major trials and witch-hunters and cases of demonic possession that were believed to be related to or caused by witchcraft. Another large portion concerns the modern religion of Witchcraft, its history, beliefs, major organizations, rituals, holy days and prominent followers. I have included a number of entries on pagan goddesses and gods and on neo-Paganism and neo-Pagan organizations, followers, history and beliefs.

The encyclopedia also covers various aspects of folk magic, sorcery, divination, ceremonial magic, occultism and shamanism as they relate to Witchcraft.

Because many persons lump ''witchcraft'' with Satanism and religions such as Vodoun, Santería and Macumba, and with tribal sorceries, I have included some entries on those subjects to distinguish the differences.

When referring to religions, I have capitalized the appropriate terms: Witchcraft, Wicca, Witch, Craft, neo-Pagan and neo-Paganism. There is no evidence that those who were persecuted during the Inquisition were practicing witchcraft as a pagan religion; consequently, when dealing with those matters, I have used the lower case for witchcraft and witch. I also have used the lower case in discussing witchcraft and witches in tribal societies.

Finally, it is my intent that this book will help illuminate the reader's understanding of witchcraft and Witchcraft and put present practices in proper perspective with the past.

abracadabra A magical spell consisting of a single word, which was popular in medieval times to get rid of illness, misfortune or DEMONS. The word is inscribed on an amulet (see AMULETS) or written out on paper in a magical inverted triangle, in which one letter of the word is dropped in each succeeding line, until nothing is left. The evil is supposed to fade away just as the word does. The diminishing word technique is used in many other SPELLS for the same purposes.

In medieval times, *abracadabra* was believed to ward off the plague. The triangle was written on a piece of paper, which was tied around the neck with flax and worn for nine days, then tossed backwards over the shoulder into a stream of water running toward the east.

Theories of the word's origin differ. It is said by some to have been invented around 208 A.D. by Quintus Serenus Sammonicus, physician to the Roman Emperor Severus, as a cure for fever. Some hold that Sammonicus merely borrowed a formula that was much older.

According to other theories, the word comes from the old Aramaic phrase, *abhadda kedhabhra*, "disappear like this word," or the Hebrew phrase, *abreq ad habra*, "hurl your thunderbolt even unto death." It is also said to be derived from the name Abraxas, the Gnostic god who appears on charms against the evil eye dating from the 2nd century. Another possibility is that it is the name of some long-forgotten demon. INCREASE MATHER dismissed it as a "hobgoblin word" that had no power at all. ALEISTER CROWLEY, on the other hand, said it is a magical word of great power and that its true form is *abrahadabra*.

See also CHARMS.

abrahadabra See ABRACADABRA.

Abramelin the Mage (1362–1460) A Jew from Würzburg, Germany, Abraham, or Abramelin (also spelled Abra-Melin), created a body of magical works that for centuries influenced magicians, including ALEISTER CROWLEY. An expert on the KABBALAH, Abramelin said he learned his magical knowledge from angels, who told him how to conjure and tame DEMONS into personal servants and workers, and how to raise storms (see STORM RAISING). He said that all things in the world were created by demons, who worked under the direction of angels, and that each individual had an angel and a demon as FAMILIARS. The basis for his system of magic, he said, may be found in the Kabbalah.

According to lore, Abramelin created 2,000 spirit cavalrymen for Frederick, elector of Saxony. He also is said to have aided an earl of Warwick in his escape from jail and helped save the antipope John XXIII (1410–1415) from the Council of Constance (see POPES AND SORCERY).

The magic of Abramelin allegedly is contained in a manuscript, *The Sacred Magic of Abramelin the Mage*, actually a collection of three books. The manuscript was written in French in the eighteenth century but claims to be a translation of Abramelin's original manuscript in Hebrew, dated 1458. It was translated into English around the turn of the 20th century by S. L. MacGregor Mathers, one of the early and most influential members of the HERMETIC ORDER OF THE GOLDEN DAWN. Crowley borrowed from the book for his own rituals to master demons.

Abramelin magic is similar to that found in *The Key of Solomon*, considered the leading magical grimoire (see GRIMOIRES). It is based on the power of numbers and sacred names and involves the construction of numerous magical squares for such purposes as invisibility, FLYING, commanding spirits,

NECROMANCY, shape shifting (see METAMORPHOSIS) and scores of other feats. Rituals for conjuring spirits, creating magic squares and making seals and SIGILS are elaborate and must be followed exactly in accordance with astrological observances.

See also MAGIC.

Adler, Margot (1946–)

American Pagan and journalist, Adler is the first writer to chronicle in detail the emergence of NEO-PAGANISM in the United States. The results of her research, *Drawing Down the Moon* (1979; revised edition 1986), comprise a landmark study of a highly complex and diversified religious movement.

Adler's interest in Paganism began with an early fascination with ancient Greek deities. Born April 16, 1946, in Little Rock, Arkansas, she grew up in New York City in a nonreligous household (her father is an atheist and her mother a Jewish agnostic). Psychiatry was a significant influence: her father and an aunt are psychiatrists; her grandfather was renowed psychiatrist Alfred Adler.

At age 12, Adler became acquainted at grammar school with the pantheon of ancient Greek deities. She was particularly drawn to Artemis and Athena for their images of strength and power. While a

Margot Adler (photo by Stan Barouh; courtesy National Public Radio)

student at the High School of Music and Art, Adler made a religious search, visiting different churches. Religion then took a backseat to politics for a few years. From 1964 to 1968, Adler attended the University of California at Berkeley, where she earned a bachelor's degree in political science and became increasingly involved in political activities. She participated in the free-speech movement, civil rights activities in Mississippi in 1965 and demonstrations at the Democratic convention in Chicago in 1968.

In 1968 she entered broadcast journalism, first as a volunteer for the radical/alternative radio stations in Berkeley and New York, owned by Pacifica Foundation. From 1969 to 1970 she earned a master's degree in journalism from the Graduate School of Journalism at Columbia University in New York, and then went to work for WBAI, Pacifica's station in Manhattan. In 1971 WBAI sent Adler to Washington, D.C., to manage its news-bureau operation there.

In Washington politics and religion came together for Adler. She devoted extensive coverage to environmental issues, which stimulated her interest in nature writers such as Thoreau. She saw a connection between environmental issues and religion: the Judeo-Christian view that it is mankind's right to have dominion over the earth seemed flawed and had led to exploitation of nature and the earth. In contrast, Paganism and animistic religions viewed mankind as a part of nature equal with all other creatures and parts.

On a trip to England, Adler investigated the history of the DRUIDS and in the process discovered numerous neo-Pagan organizations. She became a subscriber to a Pagan journal, *The Waxing Moon*, which led to her introduction to WITCHCRAFT.

WBAI relocated Adler back to New York, where she worked as a producer and then hosted her own live program, "Hour of the Wolf," which aired for two hours in the early morning five days a week. She received a letter from two Essex Witches who were selling tapes of rituals to *Waxing Moon* subscribers. At first, the idea of Witchcraft rituals on tape struck Adler as a joke. She replied that she might air them on her radio program.

The first tape she received was of the DRAWING DOWN THE MOON ritual and the CHARGE OF THE GODDESS, a poetic address. It evoked childhood memories of beautiful Greek goddesses, and in a powerful moment, Adler realized that the idea of becoming the GODDESS as an empowering image was not only permissable but was being done by others. She began to search for such people.

In the early 1970s neo-Pagan Witchcraft was rapidly gaining in the United States. Imported from England under the aegis of Raymond and Rosemary

Buckland (see RAYMOND BUCKLAND), followers of GERALD B. GARDNER, the Craft was modified by numerous American covens. Adler joined a study group in Brooklyn run by the New York Coven of Welsh Traditional Witches. Another group hived off from that coven to observe the Gardnerian tradition, and Adler followed. She was initiated as a first-degree Gardnerian priestess in 1973 (see INITIATION).

Adler stayed in the coven about three years, then formed a PAGAN WAY grove in Manhattan, which became an informal recruiting center for persons interested in Witchcraft and neo-Paganism. She also traveled around the country, interviewing about 100 persons and groups involved in the neo-Pagan community to research a book, *Drawing Down the Moon*. To her surprise, Adler discovered that the Pagan movement was not an integrated spiritual movement with environmental concerns. Some segments do fit that image, while others are quite different, being more concerned with political agendas or artistic and visionary traditions. Adler also observed that neo-Pagan Witchcraft was becoming aligned with the women's spirituality movement.

Though she acknowledges that she is a Witch in the Wiccan religion (see WICCA), Adler prefers to call herself a Pagan. She feels the term "Witch" has so many negative associations that it may never be reclaimed as a term of female power and independence. Furthermore, what is now practiced as Witchcraft has nothing to do with the heretical witchcraft of the Inquisition and witch hunts.

In 1977, two years into the book project, Adler left WBAI. Upon completing *Drawing Down the Moon*, she worked as a freelance reporter for National Public Radio (NPR) in Manhattan, then joined the NPR staff in 1979. She was priestess of a Gardnerian coven for five years until 1981, when she was awarded a one-year Neiman fellowship to Harvard University. Following the Neiman, she returned to NPR in New York but did not rejoin a coven or Pagan group. She lectures, participates in rituals and festivals and gives numerous workshops on women's spirituality.

On June 19, 1988, Adler married her long-time companion, Dr. John Gliedman, in a handfasting officiated by SELENA FOX. The wedding was the first Wiccan handfasting to be written up in society pages of *The New York Times*.

African witchcraft Although the countries of Africa continue to move rapidly into 20th-century technology, politics, religion and warfare, many people still identify the "dark continent" with WITCHCRAFT. First colonial and now independent authorities have banned the practice of many traditional witchcraft practices, including the use of POISONS to identify witches. Yet ancient tribal customs die hard; modern Africans who wear Western clothing and drive big cars still ask the local WITCH DOCTOR to bless their homes and petition the gods for safety.

Study of African tribal religions illustrates the African ancestry of modern VODOUN, SANTERIA and Candomblé cults. There is a fairly universal belief in a supreme God, who manifests himself in light and brightness: a shining, snowcapped mountain, or the light streaming through a sacred grove of trees. But such a God is remote, accessible only to the priests or elders. God inspires great awe in his people, causing them to fear and avoid his symbols, such as thunder and lightning. The birth of twins is also a sign from God, creating reverence for the twins' divinity and their isolation from the rest of the community.

The spirits of the dead, or the "shades," however, are regarded as alive and able to communicate the needs of humans to the divines. They are always about, participating in daily living, evident in the rustling of leaves, dust spirals in the earth, currents in the river. Southern Africans divide the shades into two categories: the deceased relatives of any particular family and the founding heroes, male or female, who define a community, chiefdom or region.

To keep the ancestors happy, living relatives offer food, drink and animal sacrifice. Offering feasts must be attended by the ancestor's kin, since the meal itself is a communion between the living and the dead. Family members air and resolve any quarrels before the offering, since Africans believe that festering, unspoken anger is the root of witchcraft.

For the tribal African, the power of evil is everywhere, abetted by witches and their FAMILIARS but brought on by anger, hate, jealousy, envy, lust and greed—all the vices men observe in themselves and their neighbors. It can even be brought on by laziness, as certain evil persons raise the dead to do their work for them (see ZOMBIE). Evil does not come from the shades, nor do the shades possess a living person. Both are outside influences caused by witchcraft.

Members of the Nyakyusa tribes describe witchcraft as a "python in the belly," while the Pondo people call it a "snake of the women." As in Europe, most witches come from the ranks of women, poor men and young people. Others depict witchcraft as a baboon, and members of the Xhosa tribes see it as a fantastic hairy beast with exaggerated sexual organs. People accused of witchcraft within a tribe often confess, attributing their evil to quarrels with wives, children or co-workers. If witchcraft has caused sickness, no recovery is possible without the witch's confession and subsequent goodwill toward the victim.

In his groundbreaking studies of the Azande tribes in the late 1920s, Professor E. E. Evans-Pritchard found that the Azande believe witchcraft, or *mangu*, is a hereditary trait found in the stomach of a witch. Such an abdominal condition results in an oval, blackish swelling or sac containing small objects located near the bile tract. The Azande admit not seeing this sac while a person is alive but claim to have extracted it in autopsy. Professor Evans-Pritchard speculated that the Azande were describing the gallbladder.

Nevertheless, the Azande attribute any misfortune, however, small, to *mangu*. Many people who possess *mangu* do not know it; since the spirit of witchcraft leaves the witch at night to attack the victim's spirit, such dirty work could occur while the perpetrator is asleep and unaware. Nightmares are considered witch attacks. Sons of male witches inherit the condition from their fathers, while daughters receive *mangu* from their mothers. Children's *mangus* are small and inexperienced, so children cannot be accused of witchcraft until they are older. The Azande also believe that witchcraft emits a small, bright light, similar to that of fireflies or sparks, which is invisible except to other witches or to witch doctors, who are trained witch-hunters (see WITCHES' LIGHT).

Interestingly, the Azande attribute little witchcraft activity to SORCERY. Sorcery is possible, but unlikely unless a man has seen an *adandala*—a species of wildcat associated with witchcraft, the sight of which is fatal—or has touched his wife's menstrual BLOOD or seen her anus.

Witches among the Azande call each other to meetings where they learn each other's techniques, discuss crimes and rub their bodies with a special ointment called *mbiro mangu*. A particularly successful supernatural killing may be celebrated by feasting on the revived body of the victim. Their familiars, both animal and human, accompany them and goad them on to greater evil. Whereas European witches preferred cats, dogs and toads as familiars, African witches choose owls, bats, hyenas, baboons, zombies or, among the Xhosa, "hairy dwarves."

To identify a witch, relatives of the sick first consult the *iwa* oracle, a rubbing board operated with a wooden instrument (see ORACLES). The names of possible suspects are placed before the *iwa*, and the oracle selects the culprit and his or her accomplices. Then the family verifies the witch's name via the *benge* oracle: chickens are given poison while a list of names is read aloud. If a chicken dies while a particular person's name is called, that person is guilty.

At that point, a wing from the unlucky chicken is cut off and attached to a stick like a fan. One of the sick man's relatives takes it to a deputy of the neighboring chief, to maintain impartiality, and the deputy carries the fan to the home of the suspected witch. The suspect's reaction and apparent sincerity are most important; if the suspect claims innocence and begs his *mangu* to stop bothering the sick person, recovery may occur. If not, the procedure is repeated. If the suspect is a respected figure in the community, the relatives may announce they know witchcraft is behind their relative's illness without naming names. Their discretion in the affair appeals to the pride and honor of the suspected witch, and he may stop the spell in appreciation.

According to Isaac Schapera in his 1952 study of Bechuanaland, now Botswana, members of the Tswana peoples deny the possibility of an uncontrollable *mangu*; for them, all witchcraft involves malice aforethought. They do, however, distinguish between "night witches" and "day sorcerers." Day sorcerers, called *baloi ba motshegare*, use magic to inflict harm through the use of herbs and other medicinal preparations on a specific enemy and do not practice witchcraft habitually.

Night witches, or *baloi ba bosigo*, are mainly elderly women who gather at night in small groups and then travel about the countryside bewitching the unfortunate. Instead of wearing clothes, they smear their bodies with white ashes or the blood of the dead. Admission is open to anyone, but the applicant must profess her zeal by causing the death of a close relative, usually a firstborn child. Initiates receive an ointment that allows them to wake instantly and join their colleagues when called. Some tribes say that a special medicine is injected into the witch's thumb, and when her thumb itches, she will awake and depart.

Among their activities is the exhumation of newly buried corpses, which the night witches accomplish by using a special magic that makes the body float to the surface. The witches then take whatever body parts they need for their spells and medicines. Walls and locked doors cannot keep a witch from entering a victim's house; once inside, the witch cuts her victim and inserts small stones or fragments of flesh that will sicken him and eventually cause death unless treated.

Night witches choose OWLS as their familiars and ride on hyenas to cover great distances, with one foot on the hyena's back and one on the ground. Members of the BaKgatla tribe say that the witches make their own hyenas from porridge and then activate them with special medicines.

Although beliefs in night witches are widely held,

many Africans take such stories lightly, acknowledging that no one has seen *baloi ba bosigo* at work. But the activities of day sorcerers are taken seriously, as many people have seen the results of *go jesa* ("to feed"), or the practice of putting poison in food or drink. In some accounts the poison changes into a miniature crocodile, gnawing away at the victim's insides until he dies in pain. But most Africans describe true poison, acting so slowly that suspicions are not aroused until the victim is seriously ill or dying, and making identification and indictment of the poisoner very difficult.

Agrippa (Henry Cornelius Agrippa von Nettesheim) (1486–1535)

A natural mystic, Agrippa was one of the most important occultists of the 16th century. His writings on MAGIC and the occult influenced generations of thinkers that followed. Like PARACELSUS, he was far ahead of his time, which made him very unpopular with his contemporaries. He spent most of his life in trouble with the authorities of Church and state.

Agrippa was born on September 14, 1486, in Cologne, and was educated at the University of Cologne. Some biographers say he was born into a noble family, but the prevailing view is that he adopted the name von Nettesheim himself, after the founder of Cologne.

As a young man, he excelled in his studies. He became proficient in eight languages and was a voracious reader. He was fascinated by alchemy and magic and delved into the KABBALAH and Hermetic literature (see HERMETICA), attracted by the idea of achieving a spiritual union with the Godhead.

His first job was an appointment as court secretary to Maximilian I, Holy Roman emperor and king of Germany, who sent him to Paris as a spy. In what would become a hallmark of his career, Agrippa became embroiled in local political trouble and was forced to leave.

By the time he was 24, he had collected a vast store of knowledge, which he set down in a three-volume work, *On Occult Philosophy (De Occulta Philosophia)*, which was a summation of all the magical and occult knowledge of the time. Agrippa maintained that magic had nothing to do with the DEVIL or SORCERY but depended upon natural psychic gifts such as second sight. He believed in the ultimate power of will and imagination to effect magic and in the power of mind over body; a jilted lover, he said, could truly die of grief. He said that man could achieve his highest potential by learning the harmonies of nature.

Agrippa embraced ASTROLOGY, DIVINATION, the magic of numbers (see NUMEROLOGY) and the power

Agrippa von Nettesheim (J. Schliebe, *Das Kloster*, 1846)

of gems and stones. He described the astral body as the "chariot of the soul" and said it could leave the physical body like a light escaping from a lantern. It was said that he practiced NECROMANCY for divination and conjured various DEMONS.

After writing *On Occult Philosophy*, more than 20 years passed before it was published. Meanwhile, Agrippa weathered one storm after another in his life. In 1509, at the University of Dole, France, he earned a doctorate of divinity and lectured on the Kabbalah. He tried to win the patronage of Maximilian's daughter, Margaret of Ghent, with a flattering work, *The Nobility of Women*, but the local monks denounced him as a heretic, and he was forced to flee to England the same year.

Agrippa spent years drifting around Europe, forming secret societies, holding various jobs until his temper or his occult views caused him to be run out of town. He was frequently at odds with the Church, for he considered many monks to be ignorant and narrow-minded. He was unlucky in marriage: two wives died and the third ruined him emotionally and financially.

In Lyons he was appointed physician to Louise of Savoy, the queen mother of the king of France. She was slow to pay him and kept him confined to Lyons, impoverished, from 1524 to 1526. Finally, he was able to quit his job and leave for Metz, where he undertook the defense of a woman accused of witchcraft. The chief evidence against the woman was that her mother had been burned as a witch. Agrippa destroyed the case against her with the theological argument that man could be separated from Christ only by his own sin, not that of another. As REGINALD SCOT describes in *Discoverie of Witchcraft* (1584), Agrippa triumphantly "delivered her from the clawes of the bloodie moonke, who with hir accusers, were condemned in a great summe of monie to the charter of the church of Mentz, (sic) and remained infamous after that time almost to all men." The humiliated inquisitor threatened to prosecute Agrippa for being a supporter of heretics and witches. Ever after that, Agrippa was suspected of witchcraft himself and was considered an enemy of the Church.

Many fantastic tales surround the life of Agrippa, who was widely regarded as a black magician. He was said always to be accompanied by his familiar, who took the shape of a large black dog (see FAMILIARS). On his deathbed, he renounced his magic works and the familiar by saying, "Begone, wretched animal, the entire cause of my destruction," whereupon the familiar ran out and threw himself in a river.

Agrippa conjured demons and spirits, sometimes using magic MIRRORS. He supposedly conjured the spirit of Tully to deliver an oration for him; the spirit was so effective that it reduced the audience to tears. It was also said that when Agrippa traveled, he paid innkeepers in gold coins that later turned into seashells (see MONEY). He became associated with the story of FAUST, the legendary doctor who sold his soul to the Devil.

The most famous occult legend about Agrippa tells of an unfortunate young man who poked about in his study. Agrippa, who was living in Louvain, Belgium, at the time, rented out a room to this young man. Once when Agrippa was out of town, the youth asked the magician's wife for a key to his study, saying he was interested in reading some of the books. At first the wife refused, but the youth begged her until she relented and gave him the key.

In the study, the youth found a book of magic SPELLS lying on a table and began to read aloud. Suddenly there was a knocking at the door, and a demon appeared. The demon demanded to know why he had been summoned. The young man was so terrified that he could not reply, whereupon the demon seized him by the throat and strangled him.

When Agrippa returned home, he was horrified to find the corpse. If he called the authorities or tried

to get rid of the body, he would be accused of murder. He summoned the demon to restore the corpse to life. The demon did, and Agrippa sent the reactivated corpse to walk up and down the marketplace, and then collapse in an apparent natural death. But the marks of strangulation were found, and Agrippa was accused of murder. Once again, he had to flee town.

Agrippa secured the patronage of Charles V, who appointed him to chronicle history. By then, he was disillusioned with magic and considered it a waste of time. Theology, he said, was the only thing worth studying. Around 1530 he had published *On the Vanity of Sciences and Arts,* an attack on all sciences and the occult, in which he took the view that knowledge only makes man aware of how little he really knows. The book angered the king, who had Agrippa jailed for a year on charges of heresy.

After his release, *On Occult Philosophy* was published, and it appeared to contradict everything Agrippa had said in *Vanity.* The apparent inconsistency further blackened his reputation.

Agrippa went to Cologne, where he got into trouble with the inquisitor. Not only was he thrown out of Cologne, he was banished from all Germany. He went back to France, but his uncomplimentary remarks about his former employer, the queen mother, led him again into jail.

Upon his release, he went to Grenoble, where he died in 1535. His first work, *On Occult Philosophy,* survived to have a profound impact upon the development of Western occult thought.

aiguillette A knotted loop of thread, also called a *ligature,* which witches were said to use to cause impotence, and perhaps even castration, in men; barrenness in women; and general discontent in marriage. The *aiguillette* also served to bind couples in illicit amatory relationships.

The phobia of the ligature, or fear of satanic castration, was widespread in 16th century France. It was believed that at the instant when a priest blessed a new marriage, the witch slipped behind the husband, knotted a thread and threw a coin on the ground while calling the Devil. If the coin disappeared, which all believed to mean that the Devil took it and kept it until Judgment Day, the couple was destined for unhappiness, sterility and adultery.

Couples living in Languedoc were so fearful of satanic castration that not 10 weddings in 100 were performed publicly in church. Instead, the priest, the couple and their parents went off in secret to celebrate the sacrament. Only then could the newlyweds enter their home, enjoy the feasting and go to bed. At least one physician, Thomas Platter, concluded that the panic was so bad that there was a local danger of depopulation.

See also MALEFICIA.

Aix-en-Provence Possessions

The burning alive of Father Louis Gaufridi for bewitchment of the nuns at Aix in 1611 formed the legal precedent for the conviction and execution of Urbain Grandier at Loudun (see LOUDUN POSSESSIONS) more than 20 years later. This case was one of the first in France to produce a conviction based on the testimony of a possessed demoniac. Prior to the 17th century in France, accusations from a demoniac were considered unreliable, since most clerics believed that any words spoken by one possessed by the Devil were utterances from "the father of lies" (John 8:44) and would not stand up to accepted rules of evidence. As in Loudun, sexual themes dominated the manifestations of the nuns' possession (see DEMONIC POSSESSION).

In his book *The World of the Witches* (1961), historian Julio Caro Baroja comments that "in the history of many religious movements, particularly those which have to struggle against an Established Church, an important part is played by men who have a physical and sexual power over groups of slightly unbalanced women in addition to strong spiritual powers." By the 17th century, the Catholic Church was fighting mightily to stem the tide of Reformation through miraculous cures and demonstrations of faith and by the TORTURE of heretics and WITCHES. Baroja continues: "At a later stage [in the religious movement] we find such people formally accused of being sorcerers and magicians . . . and causing the women they had abused [or seduced] to be possessed by the Devil." Baroja finds Father Gaufridi to be the perfect example, concluding that if he indeed was guilty of sexual crimes, he certainly was not a satanist (see SATANISM).

Nevertheless, Father Gaufridi was convicted by his own confession following torture and the accusations of two nuns: Sister Madeleine Demandolx de la Palud and Sister Louise Capel. Gaufridi recited his DEVIL'S PACT for the inquisitors, in which he renounced all spiritual and physical goodness given him by God, the Virgin Mary and all the saints, giving himself body and soul to Lucifer. Sister Madeleine also recited her pact, renouncing God and the saints and even any prayers ever said for her. Gaufridi was burned alive, and the two nuns were banished from the convent.

Two years later, in 1613, the possession epidemic at Aix spread to nearby Lille, where three nuns accused Sister Marie de Sains of bewitching them. Most notable about Sister Marie's testimony, in many ways a copy of Sister Madeleine's earlier pact, was her detailed description of the witches' sabbat: The witches copulated with devils and each other in a natural fashion on Mondays and Tuesdays, practiced sodomy on Thursdays and bestiality on Saturdays and sang litanies to the Devil on Wednesdays and Fridays. Sunday, apparently, was their day off (see SABBATS).

Albertus Magnus (1193 or 1206–1280)

Also called St. Albert the Great, a Dominican scholar, theologian and scientist who believed in natural MAGIC and practiced alchemy. He also believed in ASTROLOGY and in the psychic link between man and the forces of nature. THOMAS AQUINAS was among his pupils.

Albertus Magnus was born in Swabia, Germany, in either 1193 or 1206; authorities disagree on the date. He entered the Dominican order in 1223, advancing until he was named Bishop of Ratisbon in 1260, but resigned in 1262 in order to teach. He wrote extensively on Aristotle, and he acquired and recorded a vast store of knowledge on natural phenomena, including magic.

Albertus Magnus has at times been called a sorcerer, though he did not cast SPELLS or conjure DEMONS and spirits. He saw natural, good magic in herbs, plants, stones and gems. He believed that the pursuit of knowledge could not be done without the study of magic.

He described at length the magical properties of various STONES and plants; amethyst, for example, strengthened concentration, he said, while the plant betony could enhance clairvoyance. Like Aristotle, he believed that man and nature were controlled by the stars and planets.

Albertus Magnus is credited with a number of firsts in alchemy: the production of arsenic in free form; the discovery of the chemical composition of cinnabar, minium and white lead; and the preparation of caustic potassium. He believed in the transmutation of base metals into gold. Legend has it that he discovered the Philosopher's Stone, though there is no record of that in his own writings. In his work *On Alchemy*, he advised other alchemists to live a life of isolation, patience and discretion, and to have enough money to support themselves in case their experiments to create gold failed. He advised discretion because once word of success leaked out, especially to the royalty and nobility, the alchemist's work could be destroyed.

Stories of incredible magic are attributed to Albertus Magnus. According to one tale, he once invited some guests, including William II, the Count of Holland, for dinner at his home on New Year's Day,

1249. The count owned a piece of land which Albertus Magnus wanted to purchase for the site of a monastery; the count did not want to sell. When the guests arrived, they were astonished to see that Albertus Magnus had set up a meal in the garden outdoors. Everything was covered with snow and the temperature was freezing. He assured them that everything would be all right. Despite their misgivings, the guests sat down to eat. As soon as they had done so, the snow melted, the sun came out, flowers burst into bloom and birds flew about and sang. When the meal was over, the summery scene vanished, and the shivering guests had to go inside to warm themselves by the fire. The impressed count agreed to sell Albertus Magnus the land he wanted.

In another legend, Albertus Magnus, using natural magic and astrology, created a man-shaped android that could talk. The android was his servant. But its jabbering so disturbed Thomas Aquinas in his studies that Aquinas smashed it to pieces.

Albertus Magnus died on November 15, 1280, and was buried in Cologne. He was beatified in 1622 and was canonized in 1932 by Pope Pius XI.

allotriophagy The vomiting or disgorgement of strange or foul objects, usually associated with someone possessed by or obsessed with the DEVIL or other DEMONS (see DEMONIC POSSESSION). Such actions also once were seen as illusions or SPELLS caused by witches or as attempts at suicide by the mentally deranged. Most treatises on possession written during the Middle Ages included the vomiting of unusual objects as an indication that the Devil had entered a person's body. The objects vomited by the victim could be anything from live animals, such as toads, snakes, worms or butterflies, to pieces of iron, nails, small files, pins, needles, feathers, stones, cloth, shards of glass, hair, seaweed or foam.

In the demonic possession case of JOSEPH AND THEOBALD BRUNER, two small boys living in Illfurth, Alsace, France, in the mid-1860s, the boys often vomited yellow foam, feathers and seaweed. During his exorcism, Theobald is reported to have drooled a steady stream of yellow froth (see DEMONIC EXORCISM).

Simon Goulart, a 15th-century historian, tells of a young girl whose abdomen continually swelled, as if she were pregnant. Upon receiving drugs, the girl began vomiting a huge mass of hair, food, wax, long iron nails and brass needles. In another account, Goulart says a man named William, succumbing to the fervent prayers of his master's wife, Judith, began vomiting the entire front part of a pair of shepherd's trousers, a serge jacket, stones, a woman's peruke (hairpiece), spools of thread, needles and a peacock feather. William claimed that the Devil had placed the items in his throat. Finally, Goulart relates the case of 30 children in Amsterdam in 1566 who became frenzied, vomiting pins, needles, thimbles, bits of cloth and pieces of broken jugs and glass. Efforts by doctors, exorcists and sorcerers had no effect, and the children suffered recurrent attacks.

Alrunes In German and Scandinavian myth, the Alrunes are sorceresses or female DEMONS who can change shape; they are believed to be the mothers of the Huns. As late as the 19th century in some rural areas, they were personified by small statues, which were kept in the home, clothed and made offerings of food and drink. It was believed that the Alrunes could divine the future by responding to questions with motions of the head. If the statues were not properly cared for, they were said to cry out, which would bring great misfortune to the household.

altar Elevated place where religious ceremonies are conducted and where offerings are made to a deity or deities. The altar has ancient associations with the GODDESS and Mother Earth, who rule the wheel of birth-death-rebirth.

In neo-Pagan WITCHCRAFT, the altar is always placed within a MAGIC CIRCLE. It usually faces either east or north, depending on the tradition and practices of the COVEN. If it can rest on a ley, a line of invisible power traversing the earth, so much the better (see LEYS). There are no set rules in the Craft for the construction of the altar. If the ceremonies take place out of doors, rocks or tree stumps may be used. Indoors, the altar may be a table, a wooden box or a board placed on boxes or bricks. Whatever the form or materials, the altar should not contain conductive metals such as iron or steel, since they could interfere with the energy of the ritual tools made of iron or steel (see WITCHES' TOOLS). Since many covens meet in homes or apartments where space is at a premium, the altar may not be permanent but erected only during ceremonies.

The objects of ritual and worship placed on the altar vary, depending upon the practices of the coven and the rituals to be performed. They are: an athame (a black-handled knife that is the Witch's primary magical tool), a white-handled knife, a sword, a wand, CANDLES, a cup or goblet of wine, anointing OILS, dishes for SALT and WATER, a necklace without beginning or end, a censer, BELLS, scourges (whips), dishes for offering food and drink to the deities and images of the deities, such as figurines, wax statues or drawings (see WITCHES' TOOLS). If a broom (see

BROOMS) and CAULDRON are needed in rituals, they are placed on either side of the altar.

The altar is never used for blood SACRIFICE, as none are performed in neo-Pagan Witchcraft.

In the GREAT RITE, which is actual or symbolic ritual sex, the naked body of the high priestess is considered an altar of the sacred forces of life, which echoes back to the ancient connection of altar to the Mother Goddess. This is not to be confused with, nor equated with, other practices, such as Satanism, in which a naked woman sometimes serves as an altar, as an object of degradation. Naked girls and women also served as altars in the BLACK MASS in 17th-century France.

During the witch-hunts of the Middle Ages and Renaissance, it was commonly believed that at witches' SABBATS, the woman who was high sorceress or high priestess served as both living altar and sacrifice to the DEVIL. "On her loins a demon performed Mass, pronounced the *Credo*, deposited the offertory of the faithful," observes historian Jules Michelet in *Satanism and Witchcraft*. According to Michelet, the eucharist at these sabbats consisted of a cake baked upon the altar of the woman: "It was her life, her death, they ate. The morsel was impregnated already with the savour of her burning flesh."

Most of these accounts of sabbats, however, come from confessions extracted under TORTURE by inquisitors and must be viewed as highly unreliable.

amber A yellow gold, fossilized resin with electrical properties, highly prized since prehistoric times and worn as JEWELRY to protect against WITCHCRAFT, SORCERY and POISONS. Only the pearl is older than amber in use as jewelry and AMULETS. Amber was heavily traded by the Phoenicians. The ancient Romans used it to cure headaches and throat infections, and considered a phallus made of amber to be the ultimate protection against the EVIL EYE.

Amber also is considered a bringer of good luck and a protector of health. It is believed to help women in labor, to keep a person cool in the hot sun and to remedy failing eyesight, earaches and a host of intestinal and kidney ailments. Jet, or black amber, has similar properties. In Iceland, jet serves as a protective amulet. In medieval Europe, jet was burned to drive away evil spirits.

American Witches, Council of See COUNCIL OF AMERICAN WITCHES.

amulets Man's desire to protect himself against bad luck, illness and evil is as old as man himself. From the days of the earliest cave dwellers, the amulet, an object imbued with mysterious and magical properties, has offered a sense of protection. Amulets are universal. The objects themselves may come and go in fashion, but their purpose endures, no matter how "civilized" a society may be.

Amulets are answers to age-old needs: to be healthy; to be virile and fertile; to be powerful and successful; to have good fortune. To ancient man, these needs were controlled by the invisible forces of good and evil. PRAYERS, SACRIFICES and offerings induced the good spirits to grant blessings; amulets prevented the evil spirits from taking them away.

Originally, amulets were natural objects whose unusual shapes or colors attracted attention. The magical properties of such objects were presumed to be inherent. As civilization advanced, amulets became more diverse. They were fashioned into animal shapes, symbols, RINGS, seals and plaques, and were imbued with magical power with inscriptions or SPELLS (see ABRACADABRA).

The term *amulet* comes from either the Latin word *amuletum* or the Old Latin term *amoletum*, which means "means of defense." The Roman naturalist, Pliny, defined three basic types of amulets: those offering protection against trouble and adversity; those providing a medical or prophylactic treatment; and substances used in medicine. Within these three general categories are many subdivisions, for no one amulet is broadly multipurpose. Amulets with inscriptions are also called CHARMS. An amulet typically is worn on the body—usually hung around the neck—but some amulets guard tombs, homes and buildings.

The ancient Egyptians, Assyrians, Babylonians, Arabs and Hebrews placed great importance in amulets. The Egyptians used them everywhere. The frog protected fertility; ANKHS were linked to everlasting life and generation; the *udjat*, or eye, was for good health, comfort and protection against evil; the scarab beetle was for resurrection after death and protection against evil magic. Some Egyptian amulets are huge: a stone beetle mounted on a pedestal at Karnak (now at the British Museum) measures five feet long by three feet wide, and weighs more than two tons.

The Assyrians and Babylonians used cylinder seals which were imbedded with semiprecious and precious stones, each stone having its own unique magical powers (see STONES). Various animal shapes served as amulets; for example, the ram for virility, and the bull for virility and strength.

The Arabs gathered dust from tombs and carried it in little sacks as protection against evil. They also wore pieces of paper on which were written prayers, spells, magical names or the highly powerful attributes of God, such as "the compassionate," and "the forgiver."

Hebrews wore crescent moons to ward off the EVIL EYE and attached BELLS to their clothing to ward off evil spirits.

The natives of the west coast of Africa carry amulets which Western explorers named fetishes (see FETISH). A fetish consists of a pouch or box of "medicine" such as plants, fruits or vegetables, animal hair, paws, dung or livers, snake heads, SPITTLE and URINE. Natives believe that the fetish also contains a god or spirit who will help the wearer of the fetish obtain his or her desire.

Two amuletic symbols that are nearly universal throughout history are eyes and phallic symbols. Eyes protect against evil spirits and are found on many tombs and walls, and on utensils and JEWELRY. The phallic symbol, as represented by horns and hands, protects against the evil eye.

The names of God and gods, and magical words and numbers, have provided amuletic protection since antiquity; they were particularly popular from the Renaissance to the early 19th century, when the GRIMOIRES, books of instruction, were written for magicians. In MAGIC, using the name of a deity is equivalent to tapping into divine power. In the Old Testament, the Hebrews gave the personal name of God as a four-letter word called the tetragrammaton, transliterated as YHWH and pronounced "Yahweh." This name appeared in different spellings on many amulets and TALISMANS to help magicians conjure DEMONS and protect them from attack by the spirits (see NAMES OF POWER).

Some magical words and numbers are arranged in patterns of squares. One of the best known of these is the "Sator square":

$$
\begin{array}{ccccc}
S & A & T & O & R \\
A & R & E & P & O \\
T & E & N & E & T \\
O & P & E & R & A \\
R & O & T & A & S
\end{array}
$$

Although numerous attempts have been made to translate the Sator square into something that makes sense, it remains nonsensical. It was inscribed on walls and vessels as early as ancient Rome and was considered an amulet against SORCERY, poisonous air, colic and pestilence, and for protecting cow's milk from WITCHCRAFT.

In all cultures, holy books such as the Koran, Torah and Bible are considered to have protective powers. Bits of parchment with scripture quotes, carried in leather pouches or silver boxes, are amulets in various religions. Ancient pagans wore figurines of their gods as amulets. This custom was absorbed into the Catholic Church.

In neo-Pagan Witchcraft, the most powerful amulet is the silver pentacle, the religious symbol of the Craft (see PENTACLE AND PENTAGRAM). SILVER in general is held to have amuletic properties and is used in jewelry along with various crystals and gems. The sign of the pentacle, called a *pentagram*, is traced in the air in rituals done to protect sacred sites, homes and other places. Other amulets are made from herbs and various ingredients, which are placed in a charm bag (also called a GRIS-GRIS).

Anderson, Victor   The cofounder of the Faery Tradition of WITCHCRAFT was born shortly after the turn of the 20th century in New Mexico. When he was a young child, his family moved to Bend, Oregon. An uncorrected condition or ailment left him nearly blind for life.

In Oregon, Anderson met and was initiated at about age nine into the Craft by WITCHES who called themselves faeries. He came upon a small, old woman sitting naked in the center of a circle alongside brass bowls filled with herbs (see MAGIC CIRCLE). She told him he was a Witch. Instinctively, he took off his clothes and was sexually initiated. He experienced a vision, which he could see clearly despite his near-blindness, in which he floated in black space, holding on to the woman (who became the GODDESS), until he suddenly found himself in a junglelike setting under a vast sky filled with stars and a green moon. Coming toward him was the HORNED GOD, a beautiful and powerful man, yet effeminate, with an erect phallus. His head was horned, and from his head came a blue flame. After some communications with the deities, the vision vanished and Anderson returned to the present. He sat in the circle with the old woman and was taught the ritual use of the herbs and teas in the brass bowls. She washed him in butter, oil and SALT. He dressed and returned home.

Anderson worked in a COVEN; most of the coveners hailed from the American South and practiced a type of Witchcraft (there were no "traditions" then) that was not so much a religion but more a "devotional science," a way of living that emphasized harmony with nature, MAGIC, celebration, music and ecstatic dancing. They revered Pagan deities, which they called "The Old Gods" and "The Old Powers," but did not have the developed theologies of more modern Craft traditions.

Anderson married a northern Alabama woman, Cora, who came from a family of Christians who practiced folk magic. In the 1950s the Andersons broke up a fistfight between their only son and a neighbor boy. The boy, who years later changed his name to GWYDION PENDDERWEN, became a good friend of the family and was initiated into Witchcraft by the Andersons. The publication of GERALD B. GARDNER's book, *Witchcraft Today*, inspired Anderson to form his own coven. He and Pendderwen cofounded and wrote most of the rituals for the Faery Tradition, named after the Faery Witches Anderson worked with as a child. After Pendderwen's meeting with Alexandrian-tradition Witches in England, he and Anderson incorporated material from the Alexandrian BOOK OF SHADOWS into the Faery Tradition.

Anderson, who has lived with his wife in the Bay Area of California since the 1960s, is the author of a book of Craft poems, *Thorns of the Blood Rose.*

ankh The Egyptian symbol of life, the universe and immortality is the *tau* or looped cross called the *ankh,* which means both "life" and "hand mirror." It is a symbol of regeneration, an AMULET against bad luck, and a TALISMAN for good fortune. It also represents the union of the male principle (the staff) and the female principle (the closed loop). In ancient Egypt, the House of Life was a building or group of buildings that housed the temple library, the repository of all magical lore available to the magicians, priests and laymen. Egyptian art shows the ankh being carried as a scepter in the right hand of deities and being applied to the nostrils of the dead in order to bring them back to life. Ankh amulets were made of faience, semiprecious and precious stones, WAX, metal and wood. Tutankhamen had a hand mirror in the shape of an ankh.

Egyptians who converted to Christianity in the 1st century A.D. used both the ankh and the Christian cross as their signs. The ankh is worn as JEWELRY by many neo-Pagans, Witches and occultists.

See also CROSSES.

anointing oils See OILS.

Apollonius of Tyana (d. ca. 2nd century?)

Greek philosopher reputed to possess supernatural powers. FRANCIS BARRETT (*The Magus*, 1801) called him "one of the most extraordinary persons that ever appeared in the world." Apollonius's birthdate in Tyana, now part of Turkey, is not known. At age 16 he became a follower of Pythagoras. He cured sick persons and did not speak for a six-year period.

Apollonius went to Rome and gained prominence during the reign of Nerva (96–98) as a magician, healer, miracle worker and prophet. He claimed to rid cities of pests and pestilence; banish a vampire

Apollonius of Tyana (Jacques Boissard, *De Divinatione et Magicis*)

from Corinth; eliminate the plague from Ephesus by telling residents to stone the spirits who brought disease; and banish scorpions from Antioch by burying a bronze scorpion in the city in a magic rite. He also claimed to communicate with birds (see MAGIC).

In Rome, Apollonius enjoyed great prestige and popularity. Many legends grew up around him, including one story in which he revealed that one of his students had married a LAMIA, a type of vampire. Apollonius used magic to make the lamia disappear. According to another legend, an Indian magician made seven RINGS of the seven planets and gave them to Apollonius, one of which he wore every day, and which reputedly helped him to maintain a youthful vigor well into old age.

Apollonius eventually fell out of favor with Emperor Severus, who put him on trial and had his hair cut in an effort to destroy his magical power. According to legend, Apollonius simply vanished from the courtroom and was never seen again. A temple was built for him in Tyana, and several statues of him were erected in temples elsewhere.

In the 19th century, magician ELIPHAS LEVI attempted to conjure the spirit of Apollonius in a necromantic ritual. A spirit appeared and scared Levi half to death; he never acknowledged whether the shade was really Apollonius (see NECROMANCY).

apples   Apples, cultivated in Britain as early as 3000 B.C., have had a long association with MAGIC, WITCHES and GODDESS deities. Magic apple lands, whose fruit gave eternal life, were cultivated by various Western pagan goddesses, among them the Greek Hera, the Scandinavian Idun (Idhunn), the Teutonic FREYA and the Norse Hel, Queen of the Underworld. In Iroquois myth, the apple is the central tree of heaven. In Christianity, the apple offered Eve by the serpent is really the fruit of life, not sin, according to scholar Robert Graves.

To Witches and GYPSIES, the apple is magical; cut crosswise, the shape of core is the "PENTACLE of Kore," a star hidden within DEMETER, or Mother Earth.

Games and DIVINATION with apples were part of the Celtic/Druidic harvest festival of Samhain (All Hallow's Eve), now celebrated on October 31 (see DRUIDS; SABBATS). A surviving custom is the dunking for apples on this night. According to another custom, peeling an apple in front of a candlelit mirror on Samhain will reveal an image of one's future spouse.

Magical fermented cider may have been used in other pagan rites. In parts of England, another name for strong cider is *witches' brew*. Apples and apple peel are used in divination methods common in the British Isles.

In English lore, the apple tree is synonymous with enchantment and associated with figures in the Arthurian legends. Arthur, upon being mortally wounded, was spirited by three fairy queens to the magical place of Avalon, "Isle of the Apples" or "appleland," ruled by MORGAN LE FAY, the crone or Mother Death aspect of the Triple Goddess. Arthur's knight Lancelot fell asleep under a grafted apple tree and was carried off by four fairy queens. Queen Guinevere gave an apple to St. Patrick, who died; she was accused of WITCHCRAFT and condemned to burn at the stake, but was rescued by Lancelot.

Witches who wished to bewitch or poison others were often said to use apples, as in the folktale of Snow White, who was put to sleep by the poisoned apple of the black witch-queen. In 1657 Richard Jones, a 12-year-old boy in Shepton Mallet in the county of Somerset in England, was said to be bewitched by a girl who gave him an apple. Jones suffered fits, and neighbors said they saw him fly over his garden wall. The girl, Jane Brooks, was charged with witchcraft, convicted and hanged on March 26, 1658.

According to English folklore, it's bad luck to pick all the apples in a harvest: some must be left for the FAIRIES.

The apple is a love charm in VODOUN, and in English, Danish and German folklore (see DEMONIC POSSESSION).

Aquinas, St. Thomas (1226–1274)

A Dominican and one of the greatest theologians of the Christian church, Thomas Aquinas had a profound effect on the witch-hunts of the Inquisition (see WITCHCRAFT). His revolutionary philosophy was cited by demonologists and inquisitors for centuries as a basis for their persecutions.

Born at his family's castle near Roccasecca, Italy, Aquinas was educated by the Benedictines at Monte Cassino. He studied liberal arts at the University of Naples and then entered the Dominican order. He was sent to Paris and Cologne for training. It was in Cologne that he met the famous alchemist, ALBERTUS MAGNUS, and became his pupil in 1244. Aquinas believed in the verity of alchemy and sought to discover the Philosopher's Stone.

Various legends exist purporting to his magical feats accomplished while under Albertus Magnus's tutelage. He is said to have assisted Magnus in the creation of an animated, humanoid brass statue that could talk. The statue worked as a servant, but its chattering so annoyed Aquinas that he took a hammer and smashed it to pieces. According to another legend, Aquinas became greatly annoyed by the clatter of horses' hooves outside his study window as grooms led their animals on daily exercises. He created a talisman (see TALISMANS) of a small bronze statue of a horse, inscribed with cabalistic symbols (see KABBALAH), and buried it at midnight in the middle of the road. The next morning, the horses refused to pass over the spot where the statue was buried, rearing up on their hind legs and showing great fright. The grooms were forced to find another place for daily exercises, and Aquinas was left in peace.

In 1252 Aquinas returned to Paris to the Dominican St. James Convent. In 1256 he was appointed professor of theology at the University of Paris. In 1259 he traveled to Italy, where he spent nine years teaching, writing and lecturing at the papal court. He was recalled to Paris in 1268, then back to Italy in 1272. In 1274 Pope Gregory X appointed him consultant to the Council of Lyons, but Aquinas died en route, on February 7, at the Benedictine monastery of Fossanova.

During the course of his career, Aquinas produced voluminous works which revolutionized Christian theology, most notably *Summa Contra Gentiles* and *Summa Theologica*. His philosophy had a major impact on the Church's view of witchcraft and on the transformation of SORCERY into the heresy of witchcraft: heresy, even if the product of ignorance, was a sin because ignorance is the product of criminal negligence. Aquinas also stated that the practice of MAGIC was not virtuous and was practiced by "men of evil life."

He believed in the DEVIL as a tangible person with the senses of man. While he did not believe in formal pacts with the Devil, he did believe in implicit pacts (see DEVIL'S PACT). A heretic, just by virtue of being a heretic, could be assumed to have somehow given himself over to the Devil, whether or not the thought had even crossed his mind. He also believed in transvection, METAMORPHOSIS, STORM RAISING and ligatures (see AIGUILLETTE). He was among the clerics and demonologists who refuted the CANON EPISCOPI, which attributed such phenomena to delusion.

DEMONS, Aquinas said, do assail man and do so with the explicit permission of God. Demons and the Devil tempt man with pseudomiracles and are responsible for all sin and sexual impotence. Witchcraft, he declared, is permanent in the world, not to be remedied by more witchcraft, but only by the cessation of sin and sometimes by exorcisms performed by the Church (see DEMONIC EXORCISM).

See also THE MALLEUS MALEFICARUM.

ÁR NDRAÍOCHT FÉIN Irish Gaelic for "Our Own Druidism," *Ár nDraíocht Féin* (ADF) is an American-based neo-Pagan Druid religious fellowship. It has no direct links to the ancient DRUIDS but is a reconstruction of Druidic and Indo-European pagan rituals and religions (see NEO-PAGANISM). It was founded in 1983 by P.E.I. (ISAAC) BONEWITS, former Archdruid of several groves within the Reformed Druids of North America. Bonewits serves as the organization's only Archdruid, and Shenain Bell as Vice-Archdruid.

ADF integrates religion with alternate HEALING arts, ecology-consciousness, psychic development and artistic expression. It is organized in groves, many of them named after TREES. The oak tree is sacred, as it was to the ancient Druids. The groves observe eight seasonal High Days (the SABBATS in WITCHCRAFT) and conduct regular study and discussion groups and a wide range of artistic activities. Through study and training, members advance through a series of five circles, the fourth of which is the equivalent of a master's degree, and the fifth the equivalent of a doctorate. The idea of the circle structure was borrowed from the CHURCH OF ALL WORLDS.

Worship and rituals usually are conducted outdoors. ADF is polytheistic, and recognition of various deities depends on the individual grove and the purpose of individual rites. The one deity who is worshipped at every ritual is the Earth-Mother (Mother Nature). Deities, ancestors and nature spirits of the Three Worlds—Land, Sea and Sky—are invoked. The Waters of Life, passed or asperged (sprinkled) in rites, represent the spark of immanent deity.

Liturgy and rituals are based on scholarly research into old Indo-European religious, folk magic, art and social customs. While little is known about the Druids themselves, scholars say it is likely that Druidism had much in common with other Indo-European religions of the time. The research is ongoing and involves translation of numerous foreign and archaic language texts.

Bonewits has identified five phases of liturgical design common in the religions of related Indo-European cultures:

1. The consecration of time and space; the psychic centering, grounding and unifying of the participants into a "groupmind."
2. The opening of the Gates between the Worlds and the starting of a flow of energy back and forth between participants and deities.
3. The raising and sending of the major part of the congregation's energy to the deities being worshipped.
4. The returning of power from the deities to the congregation.
5. The reversing of the rite's beginnings, and closing down of the psychic, magical and spiritual energy fields that were created.

Sacrifices made to the deities include tree branches, fruits, flowers and vegetables. Although animal, and even human, sacrifices were performed in most paleo-pagan religions, they are strictly forbidden in ADF rituals, as well as in neo-Paganism in general (see SACRIFICE).

Clergy wear long white robes; members of the congregation are encouraged to dress in paleo-pagan garb. Bonewits has introduced the white beret as a signature of ADF; the berets and any other headcoverings are removed upon entrance to a ritual site, except during very hot weather. The ADF's sigil (see SIGILS), a circle pierced by two vertical parallel lines, was first associated with neo-Pagan Druidism by David Fisher, the founder of the Reformed Druids of North America (inactive). The sigil may have been taken from the shape of a foundation of an old Roman-Catholic temple. The logo, a branch sprouting from an oak tree stump, is a Celtic rendition inspired by the badge of the Scottish MacEwen clan.

The journal of ADF is *The Druid's Progress*, edited by Bonewits and published twice yearly. *News from the Mother Grove* is a newsletter published bimonthly.

Aradia The Tuscan legend of Aradia, daughter of the moon goddess DIANA who was dispatched to earth to establish WITCHCRAFT and teach it to WITCHES, was made public by the American folklorist, CHARLES GODFREY LELAND, in 1889. Leland said the legend had been passed on to him by a hereditary Etruscan witch named Maddalena. Godfrey said the name *Aradia* is a corruption of *Herodias*, or Queen Herodias, the wife of Herod, with whom Diana came to be identified by the 11th century.

The manuscript that Leland published, *Aradia, or the Gospel of the Witches*, is considered unreliable by some historians. Leland said he had first learned of the existence of the manuscript in 1866, while staying in Italy. He later said he had never seen such a manuscript but had heard the story orally from Maddalena, who had also given him some handwritten notes. Leland never produced either Maddalena or the notes for the academic world. In his preface, he acknowledged drawing from other, unspecified sources.

Aradia recounts the story of Diana's daughter and of Diana's rise to become Queen of the Witches. Diana is created first among all beings and divides herself into light and darkness. She retains the darkness and makes the light into Lucifer (whose name means "light-bearer"), her brother and son. She falls in love with him and seduces him by changing herself into a cat. Their daughter from that union, Aradia, is destined to become "the Messiah of witches." Aradia lives for a while in heaven and then is sent to earth by Diana to teach the arts of witchcraft, especially poisoning and malevolent acts against "oppressors":

> And thou shalt be the first of witches known;
> And thou shalt be the first of all i' the world;
> And thou shalt teach the art of poisoning,
> Of poisoning those who are the great lords of all;
> Yea, thou shalt make them die in their palaces;
> And thou shalt bind the oppressor's soul (with power);
> And when ye find a peasant who is rich,
> Then ye shall teach the witch, your pupil, how
> To ruin all his crops with tempests dire,
> With lightning and with thunder (terrible),
> And with the hail and wind . . .
> And when a priest shall do you injury
> By his benedictions, ye shall do to him
> Double the harm, and do it in the name
> Of me, *Diana*, Queen of witches all!

When Aradia's task is finished, Diana recalls her daughter to heaven and gives her the power to grant the desires of the meritorious witches who invoke Aradia. Such requests include success in love, and the power to bless friends and curse enemies, as well as:

> To converse with spirits.
> To find hidden treasures in ancient ruins.
> To conjure the spirits of priests who died leaving treasures.
> To understand the voice of the wind.
> To change water into wine.
> To divine with cards.
> To know the secrets of the hand [palmistry].
> To cure diseases.
> To make those who are ugly beautiful.
> To tame wild beasts.

The invocation for Aradia is given as follows:

> Thus do I seek Aradia! Aradia! Aradia! At midnight, at midnight I go into a field, and with me I bear water, wine, and salt, *I bear water, wine, and salt,* and my talisman—*my talisman, my talisman,* and a red small bag which I ever hold in my hand—*con dentro, con dentro, sale,* with salt in it, *in it.* With water and wine I bless myself, *I bless myself* with devotion to implore a favor from Aradia, Aradia.

It is possible that Leland may have adapted the Aradia legend to fit his own views that the victims of the witch-hunts were oppressed rebels against feudalism.

In neo-Pagan Witchcraft, Aradia is considered a moon goddess and is invoked in many rituals.

See also BOOK OF SHADOWS.

Arianrhod See ARIANROD.

Arianrod (also Arianrhod) Welsh goddess of the dawn, famed for her beauty, whose name means "silver wheel" or "silver circle." Arianrod was worshipped as a virgin/fertility goddess and as a lunar goddess. She was the mistress of GWYDION THE WIZARD and bore twin sons, Llew Llaw Gyffes (the counterpart to the Irish LUGH), and Dylan, a god of the sea. She is associated with the constellation Corona Borealis, which also is known as Caer Arianrod.

See also GODDESS.

Arnold, Charles (1947–) In December 1987, WICCA gained legal recognition as a religion for the first time in Canada, the result of a lengthy and highly publicized religious discrimination case fought by Charles Arnold, a second-degree Wiccan high priest of Toronto. Arnold's case centered on his request to his employer, the Humber College of Applied Arts and Technology, to be granted paid leave to observe two major religious holidays, Beltane (observed April 30) and Samhain (observed October 31) (see SABBATS). The case was arbitrated by a Ministry of Labor arbitration board.

Arnold, a secretary in the Equine Center at Humber, applied for leave for Beltane in 1986. The college's contract with the Ontario Public Service Employees Union, of which Arnold is a member (and as of 1987, a vice-president of his local), states that time off with pay may be granted for religious reasons and may not be unduly withheld. Arnold initially applied for leave without pay but altered his application to bring it in line with the terms of the contract. He was rejected and filed a grievance, which also was rejected.

Arnold's next step was to meet with a vice-president of the college, who told him that his grievance would be turned down again but would be reconsidered if Arnold could provide a statement from the Canadian Council of Churches recognizing Wicca as a religion; a statement from Revenue Canada recognizing Wicca as a church; and a letter from the "head" of Wicca saying that the holidays in question should be observed. Arnold could not provide these statements for the following reasons: the Canadian Council of Churches does not formally recognize any religion; Revenue Canada recognizes charitable corporations that have made application; and there is no "Witch Pope" head of Wicca. Backed by his union, Arnold decided to take his grievance to arbitration. While he waited for a hearing, Samhain passed, and he filed another grievance, which was combined with his first.

The union provided legal counsel; as a result, Arnold did not seek the aid of the Canadian Civil Liberties Association.

In 1987 the arbitrators gave the case two days of hearings several months apart, in which Arnold was asked to prove that Wicca was a religion, that he was a believer of the religion and that Wicca celebrated Beltane and Samhain. While Arnold could not reveal secrets of the Craft, he did provide testimony about the Goddess, the Horned God, the fundamentals of the Craft and its holidays and his own involvement in the religion.

Born in Washington, D.C., Arnold, a Vietnam War veteran, moved to Canada after his discharge from the U.S. Army. He began practicing the Craft as a SOLITARY in the late 1970s, intuiting rituals and sensing innately that he had always been a Witch. He later was initiated in several traditions (see COVEN; INITIATION). Arnold became involved in the Wiccan Church of Canada for about two-and-a-half years, serving on its board of directors and as secretary-treasurer. He left that organization in 1984 to found the Spendweik Coven, of which he later was named Elder. He resigned from that to help found, and serve as executive director of, Wicca Communitas, a nonprofit support and network organization for Wiccans and Pagans in southern Ontario. Wicca Communitas oversees the Temple of the Elder Faith, a

public organization of which Arnold was high priest until 1988. His pastoral responsibilities, he told the arbitrators, were similar to those of a pastor or priest in any other religion, including planning and conducting worship services, teaching and counseling.

Arnold also refuted common misconceptions about Witchcraft, pointing out that it has no links to SATANISM and does not involve Devil worship, or animal or human SACRIFICE.

Supporting testimony was given by Rev. Donald Evans, an ordained minister with the United Church of Canada and a teacher of philosophy of religion at the University of Toronto. Evans told the commission that Wicca met his definition of a religion, as "a set of beliefs and practices of a community pertaining to a spiritual dimension in the cosmos and the practice of rituals designed to enable the participants to live their daily lives in relation to that spiritual dimension."

The college presented a weak case that attempted to make light of the issue and deride sabbats as parties.

On December 9, 1987, the arbitrators found in favor of Arnold, issuing a 21-page statement that declared, "Wicca is obviously a religion. We are of the view that it would be unreasonable for the employer to continue its refusal to grant religious leave." The ruling noted that Wicca is "the modern survival of the ancient pagan religions of Western Europe which were suppressed following the conversion, in Roman times, to Christianity." It is secret and misunderstood, "which is not surprising," the ruling said, given "the well-known persecution to which its adherents were subjected by Christianity."

The ruling further said that "had the parties [to the college's collective bargaining agreement] intended to restrict this provision to leave for the purposes of majority or well-established religions, it is our view that they should have said so in much clearer language." That, however, probably would have violated human-rights laws, the ruling observed.

The arbitrators said further that Arnold was entitled to two religious holidays each year with paid leave. They awarded him only one day's back pay, stating that he did not initially provide the college with sufficient information in his application for leave and that the college did not act unreasonably in turning him down.

License to marry. Prior to the arbitration board's ruling, Arnold pursued another legal quest in applying to the Ministry of Consumer and Commercial Relations for a license to perform marriages. That was turned down on March 15, 1988, on the grounds that the application did not satisfy a criterion of the

Marriage Act: the denomination or tradition of the applicant must have been in existence for at least 25 years. Though Arnold provided information on his tradition and initiation as a high priest, the ministry said it did not sufficiently demonstrate "that his denomination had been permanently established both as to the continuity of its existence as well as its rites and ceremonies."

The organization under which Arnold filed is The Temple of the Elder Faiths, a Communitarian organization founded in 1986 as a noninitiatory, public temple whose rituals and services are based largely on the PAGAN WAY. Its priests come from diverse traditions, including the well-established Gardnerian and Alexandrian traditions.

The province of Ontario grants marriage licenses only to those who have been ordained in approved faiths, as well as justices of the peace and judges. Arnold decided not to seek status as a justice of the peace, because those individuals may perform marriages only within their offices; most Wiccans and pagans prefer to have their handfastings in other settings, including outdoors (see HANDFASTING). Arnold filed complaints about the application procedures with the Ontario Human Rights Commission and the Office of the Ontario Ombudsman but did not expect the matter to be resolved for several years.

By 1988, Arnold had resigned from all offices and positions he held in various organizations across North America, in order to devote his time to his studies, and his spiritual and private life. He continues to conduct workshops and seminars on a variety of subjects throughout North America and to appear at major psychic fairs as a TAROT and intuitive reader.

Arras witches　A mass witch-hunt took place in Arras, in northern France, in 1459–60, mounting to hysterical proportions. The accused were brutally tortured and promised their lives, then cruelly burned at the stake. The entire affair roused the ire of the Duke of Burgundy, and eventually those executed were posthumously exonerated.

The witch-hunt was one of the earliest in the region, and the inquisitors seemed to have only vague ideas about WITCHCRAFT. Witches were loosely lumped with the Waldenses, or VAUDOIS, a religious sect being persecuted and burned for heresy. The Arras affair began at Langres in 1459, when a hermit, who may have been suspected of being one of the Vaudois, was arrested. Under TORTURE, he admitted attending the sabbat (the Vaudois were said to hold nocturnal revelries in worship of the Devil; see SABBATS) and named a prostitute and an elderly poet of Arras as his companions. The hermit was burned at the stake, and the inquisitors arrested and tortured

his accomplices. They, in turn, confessed and named others.

A widening pool of accusations, arrests, tortures and confessions spread through Arras, including not only poor and feebleminded women but persons of importance. The inquisitor of Arras was spurred on by his zealous superiors, two Dominican monks. The Dominicans believed that one-third of the population of Europe were secret WITCHES, including numerous bishops and cardinals in the Church. Anyone who was against burning witches was also a witch.

The accused were put on the rack and tortured. The soles of their feet were put into flames, and they were made to swallow vinegar and oil. They confessed to whatever the judges wanted, specifically, to attending the sabbat, where they bowed to the devil and kissed his backside (see KISS OF SHAME), and then indulged in a sexual orgy. They also named others in accordance with the inquisitors' leading questions. The inquisitors lied to them, promising that in exchange for their confessions, they would be spared their lives and given only the mild punishment of a short pilgrimage. Instead they were sent to the stake, where they were publicly denounced and burned alive. As they died, some of them shrieked out to the onlookers, protesting their innocence and how they had been framed, but to no avail.

Some of the richer prisoners bribed their way out, but most were not so lucky. Their estates and possessions were seized. Eventually, the witch-hunt took a severe toll on the commerce of the city. Arras was a trading and manufacturing center, and many ceased doing business there, out of fear that the merchants they dealt with would be arrested and have their monies seized.

By the end of 1460, Philip the Good, the Duke of Burgundy, intervened, and the arrests stopped. In 1461 the Parlement of Paris demanded the release of some of those imprisoned; the remainder were freed by the Bishop of Arras, who had been absent during the hysteria. Thirty years later, in 1491, the Parlement of Paris condemned the cruelty of the tortures and said the Inquisition had acted without due process.

Artemis　See DIANA.

Ashtart　See ASTARTE.

Ashtoreth　See ASTARTE.

Astarte (also Ashtart, Ashtoreth)　In ancient Phoenicia, the great goddess of fertility, motherhood and war. She is the counterpart to the Babylonian goddess ISHTAR and is one of the oldest Middle Eastern aspects of the GODDESS, dating to the Neolithic and Bronze Ages. Tammuz is identified as her son/consort, as he is with Ishtar. According to myth, Astarte descended to earth as a fiery star, landing near Byblos in a lake at Alphaca, the site where the original Tammuz is said to have died.

The Phoenicians portrayed Astarte with cow horns, representing fertility. Ancient Assyrians and Babylonians portrayed her caressing a child. She was associated with the moon and called the Mother of the Universe, giver of all life on Earth. She was ruler of all spirits of the dead, who lived in heaven in bodies of light and were visible on earth as stars. Her other counterparts are ISIS and Hathor of Egypt, KALI of India and Aphrodite and DEMETER of Greece.

The first recoded mention of Astarte's name dates back to 1478 B.C., but her cult was already well established by then. The cult of Astarte spread westward from Phoenicia into ancient Greece, Rome and as far as the British Isles. The goddess was worshipped with sexual rituals that were condemned by the prophets of the Old Testament. Sacrifices made to her included firstborn children and newborn animals.

Christians turned Astarte into a male demon, Astaroth (also Ashtaroth; see DEMONS).

astrology Perhaps the oldest system of DIVINATION and prophecy, astrology is based on the Hermetic belief that the physical world is a reflection of the cosmos ("as above, so below"). In astrology, the positions of the planets, sun and moon in the Zodiac constellations exert influences on the lives of mankind and the world below. A complex art, astrology is used by some modern WITCHES as a divinatory and spiritual development tool.

The beginnings of astrology perhaps go back to the earliest primitive man, who looked up at the sky and noticed the shift of patterns throughout the night and the seasons. The Chaldeans were the first to develop astrology into a system, around 3000 B.C. It was either the Chaldeans or the Babylonians, another civilization of heaven-watchers, who first identified the belt of 12 constellations—the ecliptic—through which the sun, moon and planets travel. Today it is known by its Greek name, the Zodiac, which means "circus of animals." Over the centuries, the Chaldeans, and then the Greeks, developed astrology, correlating a person's destiny with the positions of heavenly bodies at his time of birth. The system of astrology practiced in the West in modern times has been inherited from the Greek system of nearly 2,000

Arab astrologers (Macrobius, *In Somnium Scipionis*, 1513)

years ago, as developed by Ptolemy in his book, *Tetrabiblios* ("Four Books on the Influence of Stars"). The Greeks democratized astrology, disseminating it among the masses.

Other civilizations also developed astrology. The ancient Chinese were using it as early as 2000 B.C., and it also was in early use by Hindus, Tibetans and Mayans. Oriental astrology developed somewhat differently than Western astrology, in that it takes into account earthly influences as well as celestial ones.

In the West, from about the 12th to the 16th centuries, astrology was considered a science, and was integrated with alchemy, medicine, natural magic and ceremonial magic. It was used for political purposes as well as private ones. With the Age of Reason in the 17th century, astrology began to fall out of favour with the intellectual elite. This transition perhaps was best exemplified by Restoration England. In 1641, a year before the start of the Civil War (1642–1648), official censorship collapsed, resulting in a burst of publications and public politics. Astrologers were much in demand to interpret celestial signs and predict the future, and the Society of Astrologers reached its zenith. The leading astrologer was William Lilly, who espoused a magical, divinatory branch of astrology called horary. By this method, questions were answered according to celestial configurations at the time the question was asked. Horary astrology had merit, for many people of the time did not know their birth information. But Lilly's astrology, as well as all types of astrology, barely survived the Restoration, which began in 1660. The new government of England imposed a strict censorship, and publishers of all manner of censored material, including astrological, were jailed. Astrology was denounced as a "disgrace to Reason" by Thomas Sprat, a founding fellow of the Royal Society. Gradually, astrology became seen as a pursuit of "the ignorant and vulgar mob." It disappeared into private parlors and the provinces in the 18th century and made a middle-class comeback in the 19th century. In the 20th century, throughout the West, astrology has regained greater popular favor.

The key to astrology is one's natal chart or horoscope, the map of the heavens at the exact time and place of birth. Based on the horoscope, the celestial patterns are interpreted at any given time concerning events or proposed actions in one's life. Modern astrologers also say the horoscope can be used to discover past lives, karmic lessons to be learned in the present, and hidden talents and skills. It is used in counseling as a means to discover the self and one's potential.

Avebury   The most important and oldest megalithic henge in Britain, predating the DRUIDS with active use between 2600 and 1600 B.C. It is also said to be the largest henge in the world, covering 28.5 acres and including most of the village of Avebury, located six miles west of Marlborough in Wiltshire, in southern England. The site may have served Neolithic GODDESS worship and is considered a center of earth and psychic power by modern WITCHES, Pagans and others.

The Avebury henge is surrounded on three sides by the Marlborough chalk downs and consists of a 15-foot-high bank, 1,200 feet in diameter, encircling an outer ditch. The bank is intersected by four roads, three of which, and possibly a fourth, are thought to be have been causeways, and provide access to and egress from the henge. From the air, Avebury looks like a Celtic, or circled, cross.

Within the large outer circle stand the ruins of two and perhaps three smaller circles. The outer Great Stone Circle once contained about 100 upright sarsen stones—hard, sandstone rocks found in the downs. Only 27 remain, as a result of massive destruction by the Puritans in the 17th and 18th centuries. The largest of these weigh about 60 tons and stand around 25 feet tall.

The exact purpose of Avebury is not known, but excavations have uncovered human remains, suggesting it was a burial site. West Kennet Long Barrow, located near Avebury, is a burial mound 350 feet long, dating to ca. 2700 B.C. Windmill Hill, 1.5 miles northwest of Avebury, has an earthwork on the top that was built around 2500 B.C. Animal bones uncovered here suggest it may have been a cattle market, trading post and ritual site.

William Stukely, 18th-century antiquarian, believed Avebury was a serpent temple used by the Druids, a theory that has fallen out of favor. The most widely accepted theory holds that Avebury was built by Bronze Age beaker folk, so named for the pottery and metal beakers they produced, over a period of five centuries. Beaker pottery has been found in the area, and timber buildings were uncovered at the site, suggesting that Avebury might have once been a settlement of huts. The name Avebury, however, implies that at some time in its history it was a burial site; indeed, it was referred to as such in the 10th-century charter of King Athelstan.

In his book *The Avebury Cycle*, British archaeologist Michael Dames suggests that the stones were related to one another and were built by the Beakers as a setting to stage a religious play that took a whole year to perform, with each site used for celebration of a particular event in the farming year. Neolithic farmers worshipped the Great Goddess, whose seasonal aspects were celebrated with dancing, processions along Avebury's avenues and the offerings of nuts and other objects, and perhap even animal or human SACRIFICE. The alternating shapes of many of the stones—tall pillars and diamonds—suggest male and female fertility aspects. Silbury Hill may be an image of the pregnant Goddess, another fertility symbol. Still another symbol is the Devil's Chair, a huge stone that measures 14 feet wide by 13 feet high, and that contains a ledge. As late as the beginning of the 20th century, Avebury village girls would sit on Devil's Chair on Beltane (May Eve) to make wishes.

The stones of Avebury are widely believed to be the collectors and repositories of earth energy and psychic energy over the millennia, which was known to the original users of the site. It is theorized that Avebury was the leading power center from which other power centers could be contacted through tapping the energy held within the stones. During the building of large new power centers, a call for additional labor could be made to other major power centers all over ancient Britain.

See also MEGALITHS.

B

Baba Yaga In Russian folklore, a female witch who loved to roast and eat people, preferably children. She was as likely to pop a niece in the oven as she was a stranger. She lived in a little hut beyond a river of fire in the "thrice tenth kingdom." The hut was ringed with stakes topped by human heads. It stood on chicken's legs and dog's heels and turned on command. Those who were brave enough to enter the hut usually found Baba Yaga lying on the floor with her right leg in one corner and her left leg in another, sometimes with her nose growing into the ceiling.

The Bony-Legged One, as Baba Yaga often was called, would cackle at her guests, "Fie! Fie! I smell a Russian bone!" If she didn't try to get them into the oven, she gave them advice.

Baba Yaga possessed a magic wand and flew in an iron mortar (CAULDRON) that she spurred on with a pestle as she swept away her tracks with a broom (see BROOMS). She had two or three sisters, also called Baba Yaga.

Babylonian devil trap A terra-cotta bowl inscribed with CHARMS or magical texts, used by ancient Hebrews in parts of Babylonia to drive away evil. The bowls were inverted and buried under the four corners of the foundations of houses and buildings. Their magic was believed to protect against an assortment of evils, including male and female DEMONS, illness, CURSES, and the EVIL EYE. Babylonian devil traps were common between the 3rd to 1st century B.C. and 6th century A.D. They were a pagan custom and technically were forbidden by the Hebrew religion, which proscribed MAGIC in general. Some inscriptions invoked God or quoted from Hebrew scriptures, perhaps in an attempt to circumvent religious law. One bowl from the 3rd century B.C. proclaims a "bill of divorce" to the DEVIL and all his night-monsters, ordering them to leave the community.

See also AMULETS.

Bamberg Witches The TORTURE and execution of at least 100,000 WITCHES in Germany during the 16th and 17th centuries can only be described as a holocaust. The witch-hunts were led by obsessed rulers, who used barbaric tactics, inflicting horrendous torture and condemning victims to horrible deaths. Some of the worst witch trials occurred in the 1620s in Bamberg, a small state ruled by Gottfried Johann Georg II Fuchs von Dornheim. The *Hexenbischof* (Witch Bishop) von Dornheim, as he was known, ruled the state from 1623 to 1633 and established an efficient witch-burning machine.

By the time von Dornheim reached power, witch-hunting had already been established in Bamberg, and at least 400 persons had been executed since 1609. Von Dornheim established an operation of lawyers, full-time torturers and executioners, led by Suffragan Bishop Friedrich Forner. A witch prison, a *Drudenhaus*, was built, with a capacity of 30 to 40 prisoners. A network of informers was encouraged, and the hunts began afresh in 1624. Accusations were not made public, and the accused were denied legal counsel.

Torture was the rule, not the exception, and was rigorously applied to all suspects. No one subjected to torture avoided confessing to attending SABBATS, descecrating the cross, having intercourse with DEMONS, poisoning persons (see POISONS) and other crimes. Victims were put in thumbscrews and vises, dumped in cold baths and in scalding lime baths, whipped, hung in the strappado (see TORTURE), burned with feathers dipped in sulphur, put in iron-spiked stocks and subjected to other forms of excruciating abuse. The torture did not stop even after condemnation. As they were led to the stake, prisoners had their flesh ripped with hot pincers or had their hands cut off.

Many prominent persons in Bamberg fell victim to the "machine," including all the burgomasters. Von Dornheim, meanwhile, confiscated their property and lined his own coffers. Anyone who showed sympathy for the victims or expressed doubt about their guilt became a victim as well, including the vice-chancellor of the diocese, Dr. George Haan. Haan tried to check the trials but was himself tried as a witch and burned at the stake along with his wife and daughter in 1628.

In 1627 von Dornheim built a *Hexenhaus* (Witch House), a larger, special prison for witches that contained both cells and torture chambers.

Some managed to escape Bamberg and went to appeal to Emperor Ferdinand for help. The Emperor made an effort to intercede in one case but was defied by von Dornheim. Finally, political pressure forced Ferdinand to issue mandates opposing the persecutions in 1630 and 1631. The situation also was changed by the deaths of Forner in 1621 and von Dornheim in 1632.

As a result of the Bamberg trials, Ferdinand's son, Ferdinand II, decreed that in future trials, the accusations were to be made public, the defendants were to be allowed attorneys and no property could be confiscated.

Von Dornheim's cousin, Prince-Bishop Philipp Adolf von Ehrenberg, ruled over Würzburg, another small state, and subjected his citizens to the same type of terror. Between 1623 and 1631, when he died, von Ehrenberg tortured, beheaded and burned 900 persons, including at least 300 children three to four years of age.

See also JOHANNES JUNIUS.

Baphomet   The symbol of the satanic goat, usually portrayed as a half-human, half-goat figure, or a goat head. It is often misinterpreted as a symbol of WITCHCRAFT in general. It is used by satanists, who worship the DEVIL, but is not used by neo-Pagan witches, who do not worship the Devil (see SATANISM).

The origin of the name *Baphomet* is unclear. It may be a corruption of *Mahomet* (Mohammed). The English witchcraft historian MONTAGUE SUMMERS suggested it was a combination of two Greek words, *baphe* and *metis*, meaning "absorption of knowledge." Baphomet has also been called the Goat of Mendes, the Black Goat and the Judas Goat.

In the Middle Ages the Baphomet was believed to be an idol, represented by a human skull, a stuffed human head or a metal or wooden human head with curly black hair. The idol was said to be worshipped by the Order of the KNIGHTS TEMPLAR as the source of fertility and wealth. In 1307 King Philip IV of France accused the Order of the Knights Templar of heresy, homosexuality and, among other things, worshipping this idol and anointing it with the fat of murdered children. However, only 12 of the 231 knights interrogated by the Church admitted worshipping or having knowledge of the Baphomet. Novices said they had been instructed to worship the idol as their god and savior, and their descriptions of it varied: it had up to three heads and up to four feet; it was made of either wood or metal, or was a painting; sometimes it was gilt.

In 1818 a number of idols called *heads of Baphomet* were discovered among forgotten antiquities of the Imperial Museum of Vienna. They were said to be replicas of the Gnostic divinity, Mete, or "Wisdom."

Perhaps the best-known representation of Ba-

Baphomet, by Eliphas Levi

phomet is the drawing by the 19th century French magician, ELIPHAS LEVI, called "the Baphomet of Mendes." Levi combined elements of the TAROT Devil card and the he-goat worshiped in antiquity in Mendes, Egypt, which was said to fornicate with its women followers (as the Church claimed the Devil did with witches). Levi's Baphomet has a human trunk with rounded, female breasts, a caduceus in the midriff, human arms and hands, cloven feet, wings and a goat's head with a pentagram (see PENTACLE AND PENTAGRAM) in the forehead and a torch on top of the skull between the horns. The attributes, Levi said, represented the sum total of the universe— intelligence, the four ELEMENTS, divine revelation, sex and motherhood and sin and redemption. White and black crescent moons at the figure's sides represent good and evil.

ALEISTER CROWLEY named himself Baphomet when he joined the Ordo Templis Orientalis, a secret sexual magic order formed around 1896 in Germany.

The Church of Satan, founded in 1966 in San Francisco, adopted another rendition of Baphomet to symbolize SATANISM. The symbol is a goat's head drawn within an inverted pentacle, enclosed in a double circle. In the outer circle, Hebraic figures at each point in the pentagram spell out *Leviathan*, a huge water serpent associated with the Devil. In Church of Satan rituals, the symbol of Baphomet is hung on the wall behind the alter (see ALTAR). The Baphomet may also be worn as a medallion.

Barrett, Francis (19th century)

Little is known about Francis Barrett beyond his authorship of *The Magus*, a landmark compendium of occult and MAGIC published in London in 1801. Barrett, an Englishman, billed himself as a student of chemistry, metaphysics and natural occult philosophy. He was an eccentric man, giving lessons in the magic arts from his apartment, and spending long hours meticulously translating Kabbalistic and ancient texts into English (see KABBALAH). He was passionately interested in reviving interest in the occult; while he is likely to have influenced Bulwer-Lytton, the English occult novelist, *The Magus* went largely unnoticed for several decades, until ELIPHAS LEVI was swayed by it.

The Magus deals with the natural magic of herbs and STONES; magnetism; talismanic magic; alchemy and ways to create the Philosopher's Stone; NUMEROLOGY; the ELEMENTS; ceremonial magic; and biographies of famous adepts from history.

Concerning WITCHES, Barrett believed their power to torment or kill by enchantment, touch or wax effigy was not derived from Satan. If the Devil wanted to kill a man who was guilty of deadly sin, he would

Francis Barrett (Francis Barrett, *The Magus*, 1801)

do it and would not need a witch as an intermediary, Barrett claimed:

> That magical power, therefore, is in the inward man . . . since there is a certain proportion of the internal man towards the external in all things, glowing or growing after its own manner, which is an appropriated disposition, and proportioned property.

Barrett included in *The Magus* an advertisement, seeking students and interested persons to form a magic circle. It is not known whether or not he accomplished this, although the English historian MONTAGUE SUMMERS maintains that he did, and turned Cambridge into a center of magic.

Bayon John See DOCTOR JOHN.

bees According to the demonologists of the Inquisition, WITCHES or sorceresses who managed to eat a queen bee before they were arrested would be able to withstand TORTURE and trial without confessing. This is one of the many ready explanations witch-hunters had for victims who refused to buckle under, thus enabling them to condemn the accused to death without confessions.

bells Bells are associated with the divine: their sound is symbolic of creative power, their shape a symbol of the female force and the celestial vault. The sound vibrations created by the ringing of bells have been believed for centuries to possess magical and/or spiritual power. The ancient Egyptians, Assyrians, Babylonians, Peruvian aborigines and Hindus all used bells in various religious rites, and bells continue to play important roles in Hinduism and various forms of Buddhism. In neo-Pagan Witchcraft, small hand bells are rung in rituals to enhance harmony and augment power. In African religions and VODOUN, bells and dancing are used to invoke the gods and *loas* (see AFRICAN WITCHCRAFT). Shamans have long used magical bells in their rituals to chase away evil spirits (see SHAMANISM).

In folk magic, the ringing of bells drives away evil spirits, witches and the DEVIL himself, and wards off the EVIL EYE. Bells have been attached to clothing, worn as AMULETS, tied to children and hung from the necks of horses, camels, cows, asses and other animals important to a community.

As fertility CHARMS, bells have been worn on human phalluses in certain rites. Bells are sometimes said to have curative powers; medicine is drunk from them. In the Middle Ages, bell ringing was believed to clear the air of disease and was prescribed by some doctors. Bells also have been used to raise the spirits of the dead and FAIRIES. Fairies are said to wear bells on their garments. Bells are rung in numerous rain-making rites in diverse cultures around the world.

Since the 5th century A.D., bells have been part of many Christian rites and beliefs. Church bells acquired a special magical potency in combating evil and in chasing off the wicked spirits that lurked on every church threshold. In the Middle Ages, on nights when witches were believed to be about, such as Samhain (All Hallow's Eve) and Beltane (also known as WALPURGISNACHT), church bells were rung to keep the WITCHES from FLYING over a village. The townspeople also turned out and added to the noise by banging on pots and pans and ringing their own bells. In witch trials, accused witches testified to being transported through the air to SABBATS on the backs of DEMONS or the Devil, and to being thrown off to fall to the ground when a church bell sounded in the night.

Thunder and lightning storms were believed to be the work of witches and demons, and church bells also would be rung at an approaching storm in an attempt to dispel it. At someone's death, the tolling of the church bells helped the departing soul on its way to heaven and prevented evil spirits from interfering with the journey.

Church bells were baptized, named for saints and in some cases, ascribed human characteristics. Some were said to talk, ring on their own and sweat blood at the invasion of their community. Medieval Europeans believed that their church bells traveled to Rome on Good Friday; everyone stayed inside so as not to witness their flight from the belfries. A bell that missed the Good Friday pilgrimage brought bad luck to the community.

Shopkeepers hung bells over their thresholds, not so much to alert them to the entry of customers but to keep evil spirits from entering their premises.

The Necromantic Bell of Giradius. Bells have been used in rituals for summoning the dead. One such necromantic bell is that of Giradius. Eighteenth-century French instructions specified that the bell be cast from an alloy of GOLD, SILVER, fixed mercury, tin, IRON and lead at the exact day and hour of birth of the person who intends to use it. The bell was to be inscribed with various astrological symbols and the magical words of Adonai, Jesus and the Tetragrammaton (see NAMES OF POWER).

Then, the bell was to be wrapped in green taffeta and placed in the middle of a grave in a cemetery. It was to be left for seven days, during which time it absorbed certain vibrations and emanations. At the end of a week, the bell was properly "cured" for NECROMANCY rituals.

bell, book and candle A phrase from the Roman Catholic ritual for excommunication that sometimes is used to denote a witch or witchcraft. Excommunication, or exclusion from the religious fellowship of the Church, represents a condemnation to spiritual darkness, with repercussions in society. The excommunicated becomes an outcast in secular as well as religious life.

The rite is the equivalent of a curse (see CURSES) and involves a bell (see BELLS), the holy Book, and a candle or CANDLES. The priest reads the following sentence:

> We exclude him from the bosom of our Holy Mother the Church, and we judge him condemned to eternal fire with Satan and his angels and all the reprobate, so long as he will not burst the fetters of the demon, do penance and satisfy the Church.

The priest then closes the book, rings a bell—a symbolic toll for death—extinguishes the candle and throws it down, which symbolizes the removal of the victim's soul from the sight of God.

The phrase "bell, book and candle" is associated with WITCHES because the Church believes them to be Devil-worshipping reprobates, incompatible with the Church.

Bell Witch, The   See GHOSTS, HAUNTINGS AND WITCHCRAFT.

benandanti

Participants in the lingering remnants of an ancient agrarian cult in northern Italy, which came to the attention of inquisitors in the late 16th century because of the cult's nocturnal battles with WITCHES and WARLOCKS over the fertility of the crops and livestock.

The term *benandanti* means "good walkers." The cult flourished in the Friuli region of Italy, an isolated area where Italian, German and Slavic traditions met and mingled. The *benandanti* were comprised of men and women "born of the caul," that is, with the inner fetal membrane still covering the body, especially the head. This was a sign not only of the *benandanti* but of supernatural powers of HEALING the bewitched and the power to see witches. Some *benandanti* saved their cauls and wore them about their necks as AMULETS or TALISMANS.

The *benandanti* were compelled to serve their villages during the Ember Days, the changing of the seasons marked by the solstices and equinoxes. At midnight, usually on Thursday but sometimes on Friday or Saturday of the Ember Days, they were summoned, sometimes by drums or, tradition has it, by angels. If they did not respond promptly and were late, they were severely beaten. They left their bodies, and their spirits assumed the shapes of butterflies, mice, cats and hares (see METAMORPHOSIS). They went to the valley of Josaphat in the center of the world, where they met the army of witches and warlocks, also in spirit guises. The *benandanti* would be armed with stalks of fennel, renowned for its healing properties; the witches would be armed with sorghum stalks, a type of millet perhaps identified with BROOMS.

For an hour or several hours, the opposing spirit armies engaged in battle, beating each other with their stalks. If the *benandanti* won, the year's crops would be abundant. If the witches won, storms would plague the growing and harvesting seasons, and famine would ensue. After the "games," as the battles were called, the *benandanti* and the witches passed by houses looking for clean water to drink. If they found none, the witches entered the cellars and either overturned the wine casks, or drank the wine and urinated in the casks.

The spirits had to return to their bodies by cock's crow. If they did not, or if their bodies had been turned over onto their stomachs while their spirits were gone, they either had great difficulty re-entering them, or could not get back in at all. The spirits then were forced to wander the earth until their bodies' destined time of death arrived.

The origins of the *benandanti* cult are unknown; the roots are probably ancient. The leaving of the body and doing battle in spirit, in the guise of animals, is shamanic in nature. The *benandanti* may be an offshoot of the cult of DIANA, which was known in Italy from the end of the 14th century. Followers of Diana held peaceful SABBATS at night and were not associated with diabolical rites until later by the Church. The rites of the *benandanti* had no similarities to the celebrated witches' sabbat but were entirely agricultural in intent, and were emotionally intense. The *benandanti* considered themselves soldiers of the good fight, preserving their crops and protecting their villages from the evildoing of witches. The cult persisted in spite of the magical/holy measures provided by the Church to protect crops, such as the sprinkling of holy water over the fields, the erection of a cross and the processions and prayers on Rogation Days. Apparently, the *benandanti* believed their ways were more effective.

Though pagan, the cult had acquired Christian elements by the late 16th century. The *benandanti* went out in the service of Christ and God, to battle the agents of the Devil.

The *benandanti* came to the attention of the Church in 1575, when a priest in Brazzano heard rumors of a man in Civdale, Paolo Gasparutto, who could cure bewitched persons and who "roamed about at night with witches and goblins." Summoned and questioned by the priest, Gasparutto admitted the Ember Days' outings, adding that in addition to fighting, there was leaping about, dancing and riding of animals. To the priest, this sounded ominously like a witches' sabbat, and he involved the inquisitors.

Various interrogations and trials of *benandanti* were conducted in the region from 1575 to 1644. The Church inquisitors made efforts to associate the *benandanti* with witches and to get them to confess that they participated in witches' sabbats (said to occur every Thursday night, not just during the Ember Days), were forced to abjure Christ and gave their souls to the Devil.

With few exceptions, the *benandanti* staunchly deflected these efforts. They also insisted that being *benandanti* did not at all interfere with their regular churchgoing and Christian prayers. They said they were forced to go out in service because they had been born with the caul. They were initiated at maturity, and after some 10 or 20 years in service, were relieved of their obligations. While some *benandanti* claimed to go out during each of the Embers Days, others said they went out only once every few years. Still others said they were called out whenever witches "did evil." Some said they knew who were other *benandanti* and who were witches, while others said they did not know anyone but recognized the spirit forms as one side or the other. Most protested that they could not reveal names or even details about the battles, lest they be severely beaten in punishment. The inquisitors, however, often succeeded in eliciting names of both factions.

One aspect of the *benandanti's* nocturnal travels that puzzled inquisitors the most was the leaving behind of the body. By the late 16th century, inquisitors and demonologists were beginning to question the actuality of the witches' sabbat, contending instead that it was all hallucinatory. But the *benandanti* insisted that their spirit battles were very real; that they did leave the body and travel in spirit, and could assume the shapes of animals. They did not feel pain in the fighting, they said. Some said they left the body after rubbing on an ointment or oil, while others fell into a faint that resembled a cataleptic state. Beyond that, the peasants were at a loss to explain. One description of the spirit travel to the valley of Josaphat, offered in 1591 by Menechino della Nota as a dream in order to dodge the inquisitors, is described in *Night Battles* by Carlo Ginzburg:

> . . . I had the impression there were many of us together as though in a haze but we did not know one another, and it felt as if we moved through the air like smoke and that we crossed over water like smoke . . . everyone returned home as smoke . . .

No inquisitors could accept that the soul could leave the body while it was living, and return. That the *benandanti* took the shapes of animals led the inquisitors to believe that they were physically led off on animals, and they tried to ascertain that the Devil did the leading.

Until the Church inquisitions, little had been known about the secretive *benandanti*, even in their own villages. Some who were known for their healing and spell-breaking abilities were sought out. The public attention, plus the persistent efforts of the Church to ally the *benandanti* with witches, eventually did lead to increasing association of the *benandanti* with witches. By 1623 the Church had obtained confessions from *benandanti* that they participated in the witches' sabbats. This led to more damning confessions of Devil's pacts (see DEVIL'S PACT), desecration of the cross, vampirism and abjuration of the Christian faith. What had once been a purely agricultural rite became transformed into a rite of Devil-worship.

Despite its success, the Church put little effort into prosecuting the *benandanti*. Many trials were never concluded, and TORTURE was not used. Punishment,

when meted out, was mild—prison sentences or banishment. The *benandanti* apparently came to light when skepticism about witches was gaining ground in parts of Europe. The last major *benandanti* trial took place in 1644. A few scattered inquisitional efforts occurred into the late 1600s, but trials were abandoned.

See also LYCANTHROPY; WILD HUNT.

Berkeley Witch   In English folklore, the Berkeley Witch was a wealthy woman who lived during the time of the Norman Conquest in the town of Berkeley in England's heartland. She was wealthy and well liked, and lived luxuriously. Her secret, kept until she was close to death, was that her wealth was given her by the DEVIL, in a pact for her soul (see DEVIL'S PACT). Apparently, she earned the name *witch* simply because she sold her soul to the Devil, which reflects the once-common belief that all WITCHES made diabolic pacts.

One evening, as the Berkeley Witch ate at her dining table, her pet raven gave a single, harsh note and dropped dead. The woman recognized this as a sign that her end was near and that she would have to live up to her end of the bargain with the Devil. The beginning of the end was an onslaught of bad news, the first being the death of her oldest son and his entire family. She was so overwhelmed that she took to bed and grew weaker by the day. She confessed her pact to her two other children, who were a monk and a nun. It was determined that the only way to keep her out of the Devil's clutches was to wrap her body in a stag's skin, place it in a stone coffin bound with three magic IRON chains—for iron drives away the Devil and his hordes—and place the coffin upright in church. Psalms and masses were to be sung and said over the coffin for 40 days and 40 nights. Meanwhile, if the coffin were not violated by the Devil by the third day, her body could be buried in the church's graveyard.

On the first night after her death, a horde of DEMONS appeared and broke one iron chain. They reappeared on the second night and broke a second chain. But the third chain remained impervious to the demons' efforts, despite the fact that the very church shook on its foundation, and doors splintered on their hinges.

Then a hideous figure appeared—the Devil himself—and bade the Berkeley Witch follow him. From inside the coffin she replied she could not, for she was bound. "I will unbind you, to your great loss," the Devil answered. He tore away the chain, smashed the coffin and seized the living corpse of the witch. He strode outside, where there waited a huge, demonic black horse covered with spikes. He threw the witch on the horse, and her corpse was pierced through with spikes. Her screams reportedly could be heard for miles, but for naught: the Devil leaped up on the horse and rode away into the night.

Bibliomancy The use of the Bible for purposes of divination. The Bible served as an important instrument of magical DIVINATION, particulary during medieval and Reformation times in Britain and parts of Europe. It was believed that the Bible, opened at random, would reveal one's fortunes or answer questions. Bibles laid on a child's head would induce sleep. Reading from the Bible to a pregnant woman would give her a safe delivery. Persons accused of WITCHCRAFT and SORCERY were weighed against the great Bible in the local church. If the accused weighed less than the Bible, she or he was innocent. A method of Bibliomancy to determine guilt in a crime was the "key and book" method, still used in some rural parts of Britain as late as the 19th century. In that procedure, a key was placed randomly within the pages of the Bible. The names of the suspects were written on small pieces of paper and inserted up the hollow end of the key. When the paper bearing the name of the guilty party was inserted, the Bible would fall out of the grasp of the person holding it.

Black Goat See BAPHOMET.

Black Mass An obscene parody of the Catholic Holy Mass, the Black Mass is firmly entrenched in the popular notion of Devil-worship. Black Masses are erroneously associated with all WITCHES. They are not performed by modern Witches, who do not worship the DEVIL, and it is doubtful that they were ever performed, at least in any significant numbers, by witches of centuries past. The Black Mass exists more in fiction and film than it does in reality, though it is performed by various modern satanic groups that worship the Devil (see SATANISM).

There is no one Black Mass ritual. The general idea of the mass is to parody the Catholic Holy Mass by performing it or parts of it backwards, inverting the cross, stepping or spitting on the cross, stabbing the host and other obscene acts. URINE is sometimes substituted for the holy water used to sprinkle the attendees; urine or WATER is substituted for the wine; and rotted turnip slices, pieces of black leather or black triangles are substituted for the host. Black CANDLES are substituted for white ones. The service may be performed by a defrocked priest, who wears vestments that are black or the color of dried BLOOD, and embroidered with an inverted cross, a goat's head (see BAPHOMET), or magical symbols.

The magical significance of the Black Mass lies in the belief that the Holy Mass involves a miracle: the transubstantiation of the bread and wine into the body and blood of Christ. If the priest, as magician, can effect a miracle in a Holy Mass, then he surely can effect MAGIC in a mass used for other purposes. Priests who attempted to subvert the Holy Mass for evil purposes, such as cursing a person to death (see CURSES), were condemned by the Catholic church as early as the 7th century.

One such famous form of the Black Mass is the Mass of St. Secaire, said to have originated in the Middle Ages in Gascony. The purpose of the mass is to curse an enemy to death by a slow, wasting illness. MONTAGUE SUMMERS provides a colorful description of it in *The History of Witchcraft and Demonology*:

> The mass is said upon a broken and desecrated altar in some ruined or deserted church where owls hoot and mope and bats flit through the crumbling windows, where toads spit their venom upon the sacred stone. The priest must make his way thither late, attended only by an acolyte of impure and evil life. At the first stroke of eleven he begins; the liturgy of hell is mumbled backward, the canon said with a mow and a sneer; he ends just as midnight tolls.

The Mass of St. Secaire requires a triangular, black host and brackish water drawn from a well in which the corpse of an unbaptized baby has been tossed.

The beginnings of the Black Mass as it is known in modern times date back to the 14th century, when the Church was persecuting heretics. Most of the Black Mass cases centered in France. In 1307 the KNIGHTS TEMPLAR were accused of conducting blasphemous rites in which they renounced Christ and worshipped idols made of stuffed human heads. They also were accused of spitting and trampling upon the cross, and worshipping the Devil in the shape of a black cat. Through arrests and trials, the order was destroyed.

In the 15th century, GILLES DE RAIS, a French baron, was arrested and accused of conducting Black Masses in the cellar of his castle in order to gain riches and power. He was accused of kidnapping, torturing and murdering more than 140 children as sacrifices, and was executed in 1440 (see SACRIFICE).

In the 16th and 17th centuries numerous priests in France were arrested and executed for conducting Black Masses. In 1500 the cathedral chapter of Cambrai held Black Masses in protest against their bishop. A priest in Orleans, Gentien le Clerc, tried in 1614–15, confessed to performing a "Devil's mass" which was followed by drinking and a wild sexual orgy. In 1647 the nuns of Louviers said they had been bewitched and possessed, and forced by chaplains to participate nude in masses, defiling the cross and trampling upon the host (see LOUVIERS POSSESSIONS).

During the same period, the Black Mass was associated with witchcraft. Witches tortured and tried by witch-hunters and inquisitors confessed to participating in obscene rituals at SABBATS, in which the cross was defiled and the Devil served as priest. It is unlikely that most of these incidents were Black Masses; rather they were probably pagan rites that inquisitors twisted to fit the prevailing beliefs about witches and their obeisance to the Devil. It is possible, however, that some groups of pagans, clinging to their beliefs in the face of oppression by the Church, might have performed rites celebrating the Devil, as a way to fight back.

The height of the Black Mass was reached in the late 17th century, during the reign of Louis XIV, who was criticized for his tolerance of witches and sorcerers. It became fashionable among nobility to hire priests to perform erotic Black Masses in dark cellars. The chief organizer of these rites was Catherine Deshayes, known as "La Voisin," said to be a witch who told fortunes and sold love philtres. La Voisin employed a cadre of priests who performed the masses, including the ugly and evil Abbé Guiborg, who wore gold-trimmed and lace-lined vestments and scarlet shoes.

The mistress of Louis XIV, the Marquise de Montespan, sought out the services of La Voisin because she feared the king was becoming interested in another woman. Using Montespan as a naked altar, Guiborg said three Black Masses over her, invoking Satan and his demons of lust and deceit, Beelzebub, Asmodeus and Astaroth, to grant whatever Montespan desired. It was said that while incense burned, the throats of children were slit and their blood poured into chalices and mixed with flour to make the host. Whenever the mass called for kissing the altar, Guiborg kissed Montespan. He consecrated the host over her genitals and inserted pieces in her vagina. The ritual was followed by an orgy. The bodies of the children were later burned in a furnace in La Voisin's house.

When the scandal of the Black Masses broke, Louis arrested 246 men and women, many of them among France's highest-ranking nobles, and brought them to trial. Confessions were made under torture. Most of the nobility got off with jail sentences and exile in the countryside. Thirty-six of the commoners were executed, including La Voisin, who was burned alive in 1680.

The Black Mass continued as a decadent fashion into the 19th century, when it began to wane. The Hellfire Club, a fraternal group in London in the late 19th century, was said to perform a Black Mass regularly in worship of the Devil, though it is likely that the rites were little more than sexual escapades with liberal quantities of alcohol. In 1947 a Black Mass was performed at the graveside of ALEISTER CROWLEY, the renowned occultist who believed he was the Antichrist. When the Church of Satan was founded in 1966, a Black Mass was not included among the rituals; it was the opinion of the church's founder, Anton Szandor LaVey, that the Black Mass was outmoded. Nevertheless, other satanic groups perform their own versions of Black Masses, said to include deviant sexual acts and orgies, necrophilia, cannabalism of sacrificial victims (including humans) and the drinking of the victims' blood.

Black Shuck Various forms of black demon dogs populate the legendary lore of parts of England, particularly in East Anglia, a region steeped in WITCHCRAFT. These dogs are generally called Black Shuck, and sometimes Old Shuck, from the Anglo-Saxon term *scucca*, which means "demon." Like ghosts that haunt a particular location, Black Shuck lurks about a graveyard, a lonely country road, a misty marsh or the hills around a village. Like the spectral hounds of HECATE, he is a creature of the night, as big as a calf, with eyes that glow red or green. His bone-chilling howls can be heard above the fiercest storms. He follows travelers, breathing an icy breath upon their necks. He is an omen of death; to see Black Shuck means that one or a member of one's family will soon die. In Suffolk, it is believed that Black Shuck is fairly harmless as long as he is not bothered (see DEMONS).

Spectral black dogs played a prominent role in the witchcraft beliefs of the Middle Ages and Renaissance. The DEVIL was believed to appear as a black dog. Witches could transform themselves into one or send demon FAMILIARS in the form of black dogs to bewitch or torment victims. In the Chelmsford witch trial of 1566, Joan Waterhouse was accused of sending a familiar in the form of a black dog with a short tail, the face of an ape, a pair of horns on his head and a silver whistle about his neck (see CHELMSFORD WITCHES). In 1577, during a storm in East Anglia, a demonic black dog tore through a church in Bungay, leaving behind two persons strangled and a third "as shrunken as a piece of leather scorched in a hot fire." In 1945 a phantom black dog was associated with the alleged witchcraft murder of CHARLES WALTON in the Cotswolds. Walton himself had seen such a dog, which metamorphosed into a headless woman, as an omen of death (see METAMORPHOSIS).

Nocturnal travelers in parts of England today still claim to see Black Shuck, leaping across the road in front of them.

blasting A medieval term for the ability of WITCHES to interfere with or destroy the fertility of man, beast and crop. This malicious destruction was considered a common activity among witches, and remedies and preventive actions circulated in folklore and MAGIC. Blasting is the antithesis of pagan rituals to enhance fertility, and accusations of it date back as early as the 2nd century A.D. Witches also were credited with the power to produce abundant harvests and ensure healthy offspring of livestock and humans, but this ability was largely ignored in favor of MALEFICIA; witches could not be prosecuted by inquisitors for good acts (see WITCHCRAFT).

Since fertility was vital to prosperity, it was believed that a witch who wanted to harm a neighbor would cast a spell (see SPELLS) on his generative ability or that of his livelihood. If cows didn't calve, if the corn failed to sprout, if the wife miscarried, then the household had been bewitched. The bewitchment could be done with a look (see EVIL EYE) or touch but usually involved incantantions and magic powders. According to the Church, God allowed the DEVIL to have power over the generative act because the first sin of corruption was sex; a serpent tempted Eve; therefore, witches—the alleged agents of the devil—could use snakes to impair fertility.

To blast crops, witches were said to take a flayed cat, toad, lizard and viper and lay them on live coals until they were reduced to ashes. From this, they made a powder and sowed it in the crop fields. To disrupt conception and cause miscarriages, stillbirths and the births of deformed young, they placed serpents under barns, stables and houses. A medieval male witch named Stadlin in Lausanne, France, confessed (perhaps with the aid of TORTURE) that he had for seven years caused miscarriages in the wife and animals of a certain household simply by placing a serpent under the threshold of the outer door of the house. Fertility, he said, could be restored by removing it. But the serpent had long since decayed into dust, and so the owners excavated an entire piece of ground. After that, fecundity was restored to humans and animals alike.

In a story recounted in the *MALLEUS MALEFICARUM* (1486), a pregnant noblewoman in Reichshofen was warned by her midwife not to speak to or touch any witches if she ventured outside her castle. She did go out and after awhile sat down to rest. A witch came up and put both hands on her stomach, causing her immediately to begin aborting the fetus. She returned home in great pain. The fetus did not come out whole, but in little pieces.

Witches reportedly could blast generations of a family with such CURSES as "a heavy pox to the ninth generation" or "pox, piles and a heavy vengeance."

With regard to humans, the Devil and witches also were believed to interfere with fertility by obstructing the sex act in several ways: by preventing bodies from coming together by interposing a demon in a bodily shape; by destroying desire; by preventing an erection, and by shutting off the seminal ducts so that no ejaculation occurred. These bewitchments were directed mostly at men because, it was said, most witches were women who lusted after men. The Devil preferred to work through witches rather than directly because that offended God more and increased the Devil's power.

The "removal" of the male organ by a witch was explained as illusion, though the Devil was said to have the power actually to take the organ away physically. A spurned mistress, for example, might be a witch who cast a spell to make her lover believe he had lost his member—he couldn't see or feel it. The only way to restore it was to get the witch to remove the curse; if she didn't or couldn't, the effect was permanent. One story attributed to a Dominican priest tells of a young man who came to confession and proved to the father that he was missing his member by stripping off his clothes. The priest could scarcely believe his eyes. The young man convinced the witch who'd bewitched him to remove her curse, and his penis was restored.

This type of bewitchment allegedly affected only those persons who were "sinful" fornicators and adulterers. The Devil, apparently, could not disturb the organs of the pious.

Some witches were said to collect male organs and keep them in boxes, where they wiggled and moved and ate corn and oats. The *Malleus Maleficarum* also tells of a man who lost his member and went to a witch to ask for it back:

> She told the afflicted man to climb a certain tree, and that he might take which he like out of a nest in which there were several members. And when he tried to take a big one, the witch said: You must not take that one; adding, because it belonged to a parish priest.

Given the prevalence of folk magic in daily life in centuries past, and given the jealous and vengeful aspects of human nature, it is likely that individuals cast or paid to have cast blasting spells against neighbors and competitors. The Inquisition used blasting to its own ends, as one of many justifications for the crushing of pagans, heretics and political enemies of the Church.

In neo-Pagan Witchcraft, blasting and all other acts of harmful magic are considered unethical, a violation of the Craft law, "An' it harm none, do what ye will." According to tenets of the Craft, Witches must use their powers for good, to help others and work in harmony with nature (see WICCAN REDE).

In many tribal cultures, however, such ethical distinctions are not made, and blasting continues to be among the acts of SORCERY carried out against people, animals, crops and possessions.

blessed be In neo-Pagan WITCHCRAFT and NEO-PAGANISM, "blessed be" is a widely used salutation and parting in conversation and correspondence. A common variation is "bright blessings."

blood Called the "river of life," blood is identified with the soul and is the vehicle that carries the vital energy of the universe through the body. In MAGIC, blood is revered and feared for the miraculous power it possesses and confers. Blood that is let is believed to unleash power: sacrificial blood scattered on the earth regenerates the crops. Animals, fowl and humans are sacrificed in religious and some magical rites (see SACRIFICE). The blood of executed criminals is said to be a powerful protector against disease and bad luck, because of the energy of resentment and fury that is released upon execution.

Blood is used to bind oaths and brotherhood, either by mingling or in signing. Blood oaths are considered inviolate. According to lore, Devil's pacts are always signed in blood (see DEVIL'S PACT).

In folklore, it was once commonly believed that the magical power of WITCHES could be neutralized or destroyed by burning their blood in fires—hence the common European method of execution by burning at the stake—or a practice called "blooding." Witches were "scored above the breath" (cut above the mouth and nose) and allowed to bleed, sometimes to death. Shakespeare made use of the blooding custom in Part I of *King Henry VI,* when Talbot sees Joan of Arc:

> Devil, or devil's dam, I'll conjure thee;
> Blood will I draw from thee, thou art
>   a witch,
> And straightway give thou soul to him
>   thou serv'st.

A few drops of blood of a person used in magical CHARMS and SPELLS, sprinkled in potions and WITCH BOTTLES or on effigies, is said to give a witch or magician power over that person, in the same manner as do HAIR AND NAIL clippings. Animal blood also is used in folk charms and spells. The blood of a black cat is said to cure pneumonia.

Menstrual blood. Menstrual blood is particularly potent and is sacred in matriarchies and cultures in which the GODDESS has reigned supreme or is rec-

ognized as part of the male-female polarity of the universe. Menstrual flow is linked to the phases of the moon. The blood of the Goddess, also called "wine," "milk," "mead" and "wise blood," appears universally in mythologies; it is drunk for wisdom, fertility, regeneration and immortality. The menstrual blood of the Goddess is valued as a healing charm. The blood of IRIS, symbolized in an ambrosia drink, conferred divinity on pharaohs. According to Taoism, red yin juice, as menstrual blood was called, confers long life or immortality. A pagan custom that has survived Christianity is the carrying of seeds to the field in a cloth stained with menstrual blood. In some shamanic cultures, menstrual periods are said to be accompanied by prophetic dreams that guide the shamaness-to-be to her path of power (see SHAMANISM).

In patriarchies, such as Christianity and Judaism, men traditionally feared menstrual blood, which was associated with uncleanliness and evil. Contact with menstrual blood, or even being in the presence of a menstruating woman was considered dangerous, even fatal. In some societies, menstruating women are still shunned or isolated, lest they pollute the earth and harm others with their blood. In the 1st century A.D., ancient Romans believed the touch of a menstruating woman could blunt knives, blast fruit (see BLASTING), sour wine, rust iron and cloud mirrors.

In the Old Testament, Leviticus 18:19 states, "You shall not come near a woman while she is impure by her uncleanness to uncover her nakedness." In orthodox Judaism, the Talmud specifies that husband and wife are to be sexually separated, and sleep in different beds, for 12 days a month (an average of five days for menstruation, followed by seven "clean days" to make sure the woman is free of every drop of pollutant). Sex may be resumed after a ritual bath, called a *mikveh,* in which the woman is to scrub every part of her body. It is still the custom among some orthodox Jews not to shake hands with a woman, lest she be menstruating, and never to use the same wash water as a woman, for the same reason.

In Christianity, menstrual blood has been similarly scorned and feared. Early Church scholars shamed women for their uncleanliness. At various times, up to the late 17th century, menstruating women were forbidden to partake in communion, or in some cases, even to enter church. Menstrual blood was believed to spawn demons. Some factions within the Catholic church continue to believe menstruating women would defile an altar, one reason why they should not be admitted into the priesthood.

In many magical ceremonies practiced in neo-Paganism and neo-Pagan Witchcraft, menstruating women are barred from participation, because it is believed their flux interferes with the raising of psychic power and the effectiveness of spells.

In folk magic, menstrual blood is believed to be a powerful ingredient in love PHILTRES and charms. A few drops of menstrual blood mixed in a man's meal supposedly will secure his undying love. Conversely, menstrual blood also is used in charms to cause impotency.

bloodstone A variety of semi-precious stones with magical or healing properties. Perhaps the best known is green jasper with red flecks, used in rituals and CHARMS by sorcerers and witches. It is considered an enabling stone, bringing about the wishes of the user. It protects health, drives away night demons (see LAMIA), guards against deception and pacifies. It is also used in the DIVINATION of natural disasters, such as storms, earthquakes and floods. Powdered, it has been used in medicines throughout history, particularly by women as an aid to pregnancy and lactation.

Bloodstone also refers to red coral, red marble, red jasper, carnelian, red agate and heliotrope. The ancient Egyptians associated red jasper with the blood of ISIS. Ancient Greeks believed bloodstones fell from heaven and could stop internal and external bleeding.

In Europe, especially in the Mediterranean area, bloodstones have long been regarded as protection against the EVIL EYE.

See also HEALING; RED.

Blymire, John (1895?–   ) In the secret world of Pennsylvania Dutch witchcraft, John Blymire became the central figure in a celebrated murder trial in York, Pennsylvania, in 1929. Blymire, a witch of mediocre repute, and two other men were charged with the murder of a well-known witch, Nelson Rehmeyer, known as "The Witch of Rehmeyer's Hollow." After a trial that attracted journalists from all over the world—much to the consternation of the quiet, rural residents—all three men were found guilty. The trial was colored by the deliberate suppression of evidence in a collusion between the judge and district attorney, which, in more modern times, would have resulted in a mistrial.

Blymire was born in York County, an area of Pennsylvania steeped in the superstition and lore of the Pennsylvania Dutch folk. His family and neighbors were primarily farmers, descendants of early German settlers who brought their own culture and language with them from the Old World.

In the "hex belt," as this part of the state is still called, belief in WITCHES, WITCHCRAFT and folk magic runs strong. At the turn of the century, many persons ran profitable businesses as witches or "powwow-ers," curing illnesses by faith healing and magical powders, potions and charms; hexing people; and removing hexes (see HEX; POWWOWING). The country folk often preferred to consult a local witch rather than a medical doctor for such things as warts, flu, colds, minor disorders and even serious illnesses. Every powwower consulted as the bible of the craft a book by John George Hohmar called *Pow-wows, or Long Lost Friend,* which was a grimoire of sorts, containing remedies and charms for all sorts of afflictions (see GRIMOIRES).

Blymire was born into a family of witches. Both his father and grandfather were skilled in powwowing. True to lore, little John inherited their supernatural ability. Blymire gradually absorbed knowledge about his family's peculiar powers from his father and grandfather. When the older men could not cure one of their own family of an illness, they took them to a neighbor witch who lived eight miles away. The witch, Nelson Rehmeyer, was a brooding giant of a man who reportedly could conjure Beelzebub, one of the major DEMONS of hell. Blymire's first visit to Rehmeyer took place the winter when he was five and was suffering from *opnema,* a wasting away that was often believed to be the result of a hex but usually was due to malnutrition.

Rehmeyer took the sick boy off to his dark basement and emerged half an hour later. He told John's father to make the boy urinate into a pot before sunrise, then boil an egg in the urine. They were to take a needle and punch three small holes in the egg, then leave it on an anthill. John would be cured when the ants ate the egg, Rehmeyer promised. The elder Blymire followed the instructions, and the boy was cured by the following spring.

At age seven, the boy successfully "tried for" his first cure, enabling his grandfather to overcome difficulty in urinating. At age ten, he was sent back to Rehmeyer not as a patient but as an employee, digging potatoes for 25 cents a day.

As he grew older, Blymire had modest successes as a witch. He was a dull boy, however, of limited intelligence. He was homely, with a long, pointy nose, and he was extremely twitchy and nervous. All of these factors caused others to shun him except when seeking out his ability as a witch. Blymire was thus extremely lonely.

In 1908, at age 13, he left school and took a job in a cigar factory in York. He lived by himself in a series of rooming houses. He kept to himself, but word gradually got around that he could heal. A co-worker who suffered from a wheal in his right eye had heard that Blymire's family did powwowing and asked him if someone could help cure the wheal. Blymire offered to do it himself. He instructed the co-worker,

Albert Wagner, to bring a dirty supper plate to work, which Wagner did the next morning. Blymire pressed the dirty side against the inflamed eye while he muttered something unintelligible. Then he threw the plate to the ground and stomped it to pieces. He made the sign of the cross three times on Wagner's eye and stated it would be better the next day. To Wagner's astonishment, the eye was healed when he awoke the following morning.

Others started coming to Blymire with their health problems. As was customary in powwowing, Blymire charged no fees but accepted whatever "voluntary" offerings his clients cared to give him.

One hot summer day in 1912, at quitting time, Blymire and the other men were heading out of the factory onto the streets of York. All of a sudden, someone screamed, "Mad dog!" A rabid collie, foaming at the mouth, was charging straight for them. Everyone scrambled to get back inside the factory, but they were blocked by the men who were coming out. But Blymire put himself in front of the collie, murmured an incantation and made the sign of the cross over the collie's head. The dog stopped foaming at the mouth. Miraculously, it seemed cured of rabies. Blymire patted its head. The dog licked his hand and followed him down the street, wagging its tail.

That incident should have clinched Blymire's fame as a powwower. Instead, it plummeted him into poor health and financial ruin, and an obsession that followed him for nearly 20 years. Shortly after his glory with the dog, Blymire began suffering from opnema. He lost his appetite and couldn't sleep. Already thin, he lost even more weight. He became convinced that someone had put a hex on him, perhaps an envious competitor who didn't want him to become too popular as a powwower.

In Pennsylvania Dutch belief, a hex cannot be removed until the identity of the one who cast the hex is discovered. Neither Blymire's father nor his grandfather was able to unmask the hexer and break the spell. Blymire consulted other witches, spending all of his meager pay but failing to get rid of the hex. The longer he was unable to break the mysterious curse, the more obsessed he became with doing so. He spent more and more time consulting witches further and further afield of York.

In the winter of 1913, shortly before he turned 18, he quit his job at the cigar factory in order to devote more time to breaking the hex on him. He moved from rooming house to rooming house, eking out a living with his own powwowing and odd jobs as a janitor, busboy and assistant to the sexton in a Presbyterian church. He spent all of his money on "voluntary offerings" to other witches, some of whom took him for hundreds of dollars before giving up. By the time he was 19, Blymire was a wreck. He weighed less than 100 pounds and suffered from real and imagined pains and illnesses, and nearly constant headaches.

At one rooming house, he fell in love with Lily Halloway, the landlord's 17-year-old daughter. They were married in 1917, and the relationship seemed to provide the cure he sought. Blymire's health improved, he gained weight, he got a steady job and his powwowing clientele increased.

The illusion was broken with the birth of their first child, a son who died within five weeks. A second child was born prematurely and lived only three days. Blymire was convinced the hex was back. His health declined, the headaches returned and he lost his job. He vowed he would not stop until he discovered his unknown hexer and removed the curse.

By 1920 Blymire had consulted more than 20 witches, none of whom was able to help him. One of them was Andrew C. Lenhart, a powerful witch who struck fear into the hearts of the police, who gave him a wide berth. It was said that if Lenhart hexed someone, only the Devil himself could remove the spell. Lenhart was known to advise his clients to take violent action in order to break spells cast by enemies. He told Blymire he had been hexed by someone "very close." Blymire, half out of his mind by this time, immediately suspected his wife. Lily began fearing for her life. Her father hired a lawyer and was able to get Blymire examined by a psychiatrist. He was evaluated as a "borderline psychoneurotic" and was committed to the state mental hospital in Harrisburg. After 48 days, Blymire escaped by walking out the door. He returned to York, and no one made an effort to have him recommitted. Lily divorced him.

In 1928 Blymire went back to work at the cigar factory in York. He met 14-year-old John Curry, who had suffered a harsh childhood, with an apathetic mother and an abusive stepfather. Curry thought he himself had been hexed. In misfortune, he and Blymire had something in common, and became friends.

In June of 1928, Blymire consulted Nellie Noll, a witch of formidable reputation in her nineties, who lived in Marietta. At their sixth session, Noll identified Nelson Rehmeyer as the villain who had hexed Blymire. At first he didn't believe it. To prove it, Noll told him to take out a dollar bill and stare at George Washington's picture. He did and saw Washington's face dissolve into that of Rehmeyer. Noll told him there were only two ways to break Rehmeyer's hex: to take Rehmeyer's copy of the *Long Lost Friend* and burn it, or to cut a lock of his hair and bury it six to eight feet in the ground.

About this time, a farmer named P. D. Hess, who was convinced he was hexed, consulted Blymire for help. Hess and his family, their crops and livestock all were wasting away. Blymire tried to identify the source of the hex but failed. So as not to lose Hess as a client, Blymire secretly consulted Noll, who named Rehmeyer as the hexer not only of Hess but of John Curry as well.

Blymire recruited Curry and Hess's son, Wilbert, to accompany him to Rehmeyer's isolated cabin, where they would somehow wrest away his copy of the *Long Lost Friend* or a lock of his hair. It was a rainy, pitch-black November night, and all three men were nervous about confronting Rehmeyer.

Rehmeyer was not at home. The men went next to the cabin of his estranged wife, who told them he was probably at the home of a woman he was seeing. The three returned to Rehmeyer's Hollow, and by this time—close to midnight—a light was on inside. They knocked, and Rehmeyer invited them inside.

The four men sat up for hours making small talk. Blymire was too frightened to reveal his real purpose in coming, sensing the greater power possessed by Rehmeyer, and fearing that Rehmeyer was able to guess what he wanted. At last Rehmeyer excused himself and went upstairs to bed, telling the others they could spend the night. In the morning, he fed them breakfast, and they left.

Hess returned to his father's farm. Blymire and Curry hitched a ride to York. Blymire had already hatched a new plan of attack. The two went straight to a hardware store, where Blymire bought rope. They took it to Curry's room, where they cut it into 14 foot-and-a-half lengths. Then they went to the Hess farm, where they fetched Wilbert for a return visit to Rehmeyer's Hollow. It was the night of November 27, clear and bright under a full moon.

Once again, Rehmeyer invited them inside. Blymire immediately demanded "the book." Rehmeyer acted as though he didn't know what they meant. He denied having "the book," which incited Blymire to violence. Blymire shrieked and grabbed at Rehmeyer, and Curry and Hess joined in the fight. It took all three of them to hold down the huge, strong man. Curry got out a length of rope and struggled to tie up Rehmeyer's legs.

Rehmeyer then offered to give them "the book" if they would let him up. They did, and he threw out his wallet. That made Blymire even angrier, and he attacked Rehmeyer once again. The three of them managed to get Rehmeyer down, and Blymire tied a piece of rope around his neck and began choking him and beating him. Hess kicked and beat him. Curry picked up a block of wood and hit him three times on the head until blood poured out his ear.

The men continued to kick and pummel Rehmeyer until his face was beaten beyond recognition. No one ever admitted who dealt the fatal blow, but at last Rehmeyer groaned and died. It was just after midnight. Blymire exulted, "Thank God! The witch is dead!" They ransacked the house and divided up what little money they found, which ranged from 97 cents, according to Wilbert, to $2.80, as the district attorney claimed later.

Rehmeyer's body was discovered on November 30 by a neighbor who heard his hungry mule braying and went to check to see what was wrong. It didn't take the authorities long to trace the deed to Blymire and his accomplices, through information supplied by Rehmeyer's estranged wife. Blymire, Curry and Hess were arrested. Blymire readily confessed, bragging that he had killed the witch who had hexed him.

The press had a field day with the case, dubbing it "voodoo murder" and writing about the backward ways and superstitions of the private Pennsylvania Dutch folk. The case came before Judge Ray P. Sherwood, a man who thought witches, powwowing and hexes constituted a lot of nonsense. He was greatly disturbed at the negative publicity generated by the case. Sherwood instructed all the attorneys involved that the case would be dispensed with as quickly as possible, and under no circumstances would he entertain any evidence or discussions about witchcraft. The motive for the murder was to be nothing more than robbery, a ridiculous notion considering that Rehmeyer's poverty was widely known. In an area where $100,000 estates were common, he had left an estate of only $500 to $1,000. The entire amount taken by his murderers was less than $3.00.

Sherwood appointed the attorneys for Curry and Blymire, who were too poor to afford their own, but the Hess family was able to hire their own counsel. The trials began on January 9, 1929. As a result of Sherwood's instructions, all references to witchcraft and hexes were edited out of the confessions before they were admitted into the record. All of the defense attorneys' efforts to circumvent the judge were defeated. The jury of peers, who undoubtedly believed in witchcraft and would have understood Blymire's motive, and perhaps even sympathized with him, did what the judge wanted and found all three guilty—Blymire and Curry of murder in the first degree and Hess of murder in the second degree.

They were sentenced on January 14. Blymire and Curry were given life in prison. Hess was given 10 to 20 years. In 1934 Curry and Hess were paroled. Both resumed quiet, respectable lives in the York area. Curry died in 1962. Blymire petitioned for parole several times and was refused. Finally, in 1953, at the age of 56 and after 23 years and five months in prison, he was released. He returned to York and got a job as a janitor. He bought a modest house with the money he had saved in prison, determined to live quietly for the rest of his life.

Bodin, Jean (1529–1596) French demonologist and political theorist who encouraged the vicious persecution of WITCHES and helped fan the fires of the Inquisition throughout Europe. He declared that people who denied the existence of WITCHCRAFT were witches themselves and said that, with rare exceptions, no accused witch should go unpunished.

Bodin was born in Angers, France. For a time, he served as a Carmelite monk. He left the monastery to go to the University of Toulouse, where he became a professor of Roman law. Bodin possessed a brilliant intellect and distinguished himself in his studies of philosophy, law, classics and economics. In 1561 he left Toulouse for Paris, where he worked in the service of the king. But his book *Six Livres de la Republique,* published in 1576, caused him to fall out of favor with the king because of its concept that sovereign power belonged to the people.

Bodin wrote other works of political theory, but he is best known for his treatise on witchcraft, *De la Demonomanie des Sorciers (The Demonomania of Witches),* published in 1580. The book was an immediate success and was reprinted frequently throughout Europe. Like The MALLEUS MALEFICARUM published nearly 100 years earlier, it served as a guide to witch-hunters and judges in the matters of identifying, prosecuting and executing witches. Bodin drew on his own experience as a judge at numerous witchcraft trials.

Demonomanie describes witches, their methods of diabolic acts and their abilities, such as pacts with Satan (see DEVIL'S PACT), FLYING through the air to their SABBATS, copulating with incubi and succubi and casting evil SPELLS. It also acknowledges that there are good daemons as well as evil DEMONS, and that good daemons can communicate with man and provide inspiration. He himself had such a daemon, who whispered instructions in his ear.

Bodin believed that authorities were too soft in prosecuting witches, whom he saw less as heretics than as social deviants. He condoned convicting the accused on the basis of lies by informants, confessions made under TORTURE, secret accusations and false promises of leniency. He urged local authorities to encourage secret accusations by placing a black box in the church for anonymous letters.

He was adamant about torturing and punishing witches, saying that God would reject those who did not do so:

Those too who let the witches escape, or who do not punish them with the utmost rigor, may rest assured that they will be abandoned by God to the mercy of the witches. And the country which shall tolerate this will be scourged with pestilences, famines, and wars; and those which shall take vengeance on the witches will be blessed by him and will make his anger cease.

Even children and invalids were not to be spared torture, as Bodin demonstrated time and again by his own example as judge. Children, he said, should be forced to testify against their accused parents. One of his favored methods was cauterizing flesh with a red-hot iron and then cutting out the putrefied flesh. That torture, he said, was mild compared to the hell that awaited the condemned witch.

Bodin took exception with DEMONIC EXORCISM, however, which he said was both ineffective and dangerous to the exorcist. Music was preferable as a form of exorcism; in the Old Testament, Saul's possession had been calmed by music. Bodin did not believe that a person could cause another to become possessed (see DEMONIC POSSESSION).

Bodin savagely criticized JOHANN WEYER, a Lutheran physician and contemporary, who opposed the burning of witches and maintained they were helpless victims. Bodin said Weyer's books should be burned.

Except for *Demonomanie,* which served the purpose of the Church, all of Bodin's other books on political theory were condemned by the Inquisition. Bodin died in Laon, a victim of the bubonic plague.

See also NICHOLAS REMY.

Bonewits, P. E. I. (Isaac) (1949–   ) One of the brightest and most colorful figures of the neo-Pagan movement, Philip Emmons Isaac Bonewits is best known for his leadership in modern Druidism (see NEO-PAGANISM). He is a priest, magician, scholar, author, bard and activist, and has dedicated himself to reviving Druidism as a "Third Wave" religion aimed at protecting "Mother Nature and all Her children."

Bonewits was born on October 1, 1949, in Royal Oak, Michigan—the perfect place, he likes to joke, for a future Archdruid. The fourth of five children (three girls, two boys), he spent most of his childhood in Ferndale, a suburb of Detroit. When he was nearly 12, the family moved to San Clemente, California.

From his mother, a devout Roman Catholic, Bonewits developed an appreciation for the importance of religion; from his father, a convert to Ca-

P. E. I. (Isaac) Bonewits (Photo by George Tipton, courtesy Samuel Weiser)

tholicism from Presbyterianism, he acquired skepticism. He bounced back and forth between parochial and public schools, largely due to the lack of programs for very bright students—his I.Q. was tested at 200.

His first exposure to MAGIC came at age 13, when he met a young Creole woman from New Orleans who practiced VODOUN. She showed him some of her magic and so accurately divined the future that he was greatly impressed. During his teen years, he read extensively about magic and parapsychology. He also read science fiction, which often has strong magical and psychic themes.

In ninth grade, Bonewits entered a Catholic high-school seminary. He soon realized, however, that he did not want to be a priest in the Catholic faith. He returned to public school and graduated a year early. After spending a year in junior college to get foreign-language credits, he enrolled at the University of California at Berkeley in 1966. At about the same time, he began practicing magic, devising his own rituals by studying the structure of rituals in books, and by observing them in various churches.

His roommate at Berkeley, Robert Larson, was a Druid, an alumnus of Carleton College, where the Reformed Druids of North America (RDNA) had been founded in 1963. Larson interested Bonewits in Druidism and initiated him into the RDNA. The two established a GROVE in Berkeley. Bonewits was ordained as a Druid priest in October 1969. The Berkeley grove was shaped as a neo-Pagan *religion,* unlike other RDNA groves, which considered the order a *philosophy.* The neo-Pagan groves became part of a branch called the New Reformed Druids of North America (NRDNA).

During college, Bonewits spent about eight months as a member of the Church of Satan, an adventure that began as a lark. The college campus featured a spot where evangelists of various persuasions would lecture to anyone who would listen. As a joke, Bonewits showed up one day to perform a satirical lecture as a Devil's evangelist. He was so successful that he was approached by a woman who said she represented Anton Szandor LaVey, the founder of the Church of Satan. Bonewits attended the church's meetings and improved upon some of their rituals but dropped out after personality conflicts with LaVey. The membership, he found, consisted largely of middle-class conservatives who were more "rightwing and racist" than satanist (see SATANISM).

Bonewits had intended to major in psychology but through Berkeley's individual group-study program fashioned his own course of study. In 1970 he graduated with a bachelor of arts degree in magic, the first person ever to do so at a Western educational institution. He also was the last to do so in the United States. College administrators were so embarrassed over the publicity about the degree that magic, WITCHCRAFT and SORCERY were banned from the individual group-study program.

The fame of his degree led to a book contract. In 1971 *Real Magic* was published, offering Bonewit's views on magic, ritual and psychic abilities. A revised and updated edition was published in 1979 and reissued in 1988.

In 1973 Bonewits met a woman named Rusty, a folksinger in the Berkeley cafés. They moved to Minneapolis, where they were married, and where Bonewits took over the editorship of *Gnostica,* a neo-Pagan journal published by CARL WESCHCKE of Llewellyn Publications. He gave *Gnostica* a scholarly touch and turned it into the leading journal in the field. But the job lasted only 1 1/2 years, for the editorial changes resulted in the loss of many non-Pagan readers, who found the magazine too high brow.

Bonewits remained in Minneapolis for about another year. While there he established a Druid grove called the Schismatic Druids of North America, a splinter group of the RDNA. He also joined with several Jewish pagan friends and created the Hasidic Druids of North America, the only grove of which existed briefly in St. Louis, where its membership overlapped with that of the CHURCH OF ALL WORLDS. In 1974–75, Bonewits wrote, edited and self-published *The Druid Chronicles (Evolved)*, a compendium of the history, theology, rituals and customs of all the reformed Druid movements, including the ones he invented himself.

He also founded the Aquarian Anti-Defamation League (AADL), a civil liberties and public relations organization for members of minority belief systems, such as the Rosicrucians, Theosophists, neo-Pagans, WITCHES, occultists, astrologers and others. Bonewits sought to convince such persons that they had more in common with each other than they realized. By banding together, they could effectively fight, through the press and the courts, the discrimination and harassment of the Judeo-Christian conservatives.

Bonewits served as president of the AADL and devoted most of his income—from unemployment insurance—to running it. The organization scored several small victories in court, such as restoring an astrologer to her apartment, after she had been evicted because a neighbor told her landlord that her astrology classes were "black magic séances." In 1976 Bonewits and Rusty divorced, and he decided to return to Berkeley. The AADL disintegrated shortly after his departure.

In Berkeley, Bonewits rejoined the NRDNA grove and was elected Archdruid. He established *The Druid Chronicler* (which later became *Pentalpha Journal*) as a national Druid publication in 1978. He attempted to make the Berkeley grove as neo-Pagan as the groves in Minneapolis and St. Louis, which caused a great deal of friction among the longtime members. After a few clashes, Bonewits left the organization. *Pentalpha Journal* folded.

In 1979 he married for a second time, to a woman named Selene. That relationship ended in 1982. In 1983 he was initiated into the New Reformed Order of the Golden Dawn. The same year, he married again, to Sally Eaton, the actress who created the role of the hippie Witch in the Broadway musical, *Hair*. They moved to New York City in 1983 where Bonewits met Shenain Bell, a fellow neo-Pagan, and discussed the idea of starting a Druidic organization. The fellowship, ÁR NDRAÍOCHT FÉIN ("Our Own Druidism" in Irish Gaelic), was born as a fresh neo-Pagan religious organization with no ties to the ancient Druids or to the RDNA, which by this time was apparently defunct. Bonewits became Archdruid, and Bell became Vice-Archdruid.

In 1986 Bonewits and Eaton separated, and he moved to Kansas City for several months, where he worked as a computer consultant. He then returned to Berkeley but could not find work in Silicon Valley, which was in a slump. He moved back to the East Coast, to Nyack, New York, near Manhattan, in November 1987, with his intended fourth wife, Deborah, a Wiccan high priestess. He continued work as a computer consultant and worked on the building of Ár nDraíocht Féin. He also began work on a book on the creation, preparation and performance of effective religious rituals.

The "10-year gap." Bonewits has discovered, he says, a "10-year gap" between many of his views and their acceptance among neo-Pagans. In 1973 he was the first neo-Pagan to state publicly that the alleged antiquity of neo-Pagan Witchcraft (Wicca) was "hogwash." The Craft, he said, did not go back beyond GERALD B. GARDNER and DOREEN VALIENTE. Bonewits was held in contempt by many for that, yet by 1983, neo-Pagans generally acknowledged that neo-Pagan Witchcraft was a new religion, not the continuation of an old one. The Aquarian Anti-Defamation League was also ahead of its time. In 1974–75, neo-Pagans were not ready to admit that they needed public relations and legal help. By a decade later, a number of such organizations were in existence.

Around 1985 Bonewits began regularly discussing the need to provide social services for domestic and personal problems and drug dependencies. Neo-Pagans, he points out, represent a cross section of the population, and such problems cut across religious lines. Bonewits estimates that as many as 80 percent of neo-Pagans come from "nonfunctional family" backgrounds. Neo-Pagans, he observes, are brighter and more artistic than average, but also, therefore, "more neurotic." The community has been quick to address these social issues with programs.

Bonewits also began lobbying for financial support for full-time neo-Pagan clergy (the priesthood is essentially a volunteer job), but the idea fell on uninterested ears. In 1988 Bonewits was pursuing a goal of buying land and establishing an academically accredited Pagan seminary.

book of shadows A book of beliefs, rituals, WITCHCRAFT laws and ethics, herbal and HEALING lore, incantations, chants, dances, SPELLS, DIVINATION methods, SABBAT rites and miscellaneous topics, which serves as a guide for WITCHES in practicing their Craft and religion. There is no definitive book of shadows for Witchcraft in general; each tradition may have a standard book of shadows, which may be added to or adapted by separate covens (see COVEN). In addition, individual Witches add their own personal material. The book is to be kept secret, but some Witches have gone public with their books of shadows over the years.

Traditionally, only one copy should exist for an entire coven, kept by the high priestess or high priest, but that rule has proved unfeasible, and it is commonplace for all Witches to have their own copies. Ideally, a newly initiated Witch copies the coven's master copy, held by the high preistess or high priest, in her or his own handwriting. In fact, books of shadows are sometimes impersonally distributed via computer disk.

Material is limited according to the Witch's position in the hierarchy. As a Witch advances in skill and in the hierarchy—the most common system is one of three degrees—more material is provided. The book of shadows cannot be kept by a Witch if he or she leaves the coven.

Little is known about the existence of books of shadows prior to the renaissance of modern Witchcraft in the mid-20th century. In earlier times, folk magic and lore generally were handed down orally through the generations. Some hereditary Witches, however, say their ancestors recorded their secret spells and lore in little books. One of the first prototypical books of shadows to be published in English was CHARLES GODFREY LELAND's *Aradia, or Gospel of the Witches* (1899), which set down Witch lore Leland said was passed to him by an Etruscan Witch.

When GERALD B. GARDNER, the English Witch who is considered the father of modern Witchcraft, was initiated into a coven of hereditary Witches in 1939, he received a book of shadows in fragmentary form (see INITIATION). He published the basic rituals in a pseudonymous novel, *High Magic's Aid*, in 1949. Gardner filled out his book of shadows with extracts from the writings of ALEISTER CROWLEY. DOREEN VALIENTE, whom Gardner initiated in 1953, helped him revise the rituals and write additional ones. Valiente removed most of the Crowley material and substituted simpler wording, including some of her own poetry.

The Gardnerian book of shadows in turn was used by ALEXANDER SANDERS in the formation of the Alexandrian traditon and has inspired the books of shadows of other traditions as well.

A book of shadows reflects the practices and beliefs of each individual coven and the interests or specialties of the individual Witch. It can be a dynamic collection of information, with additions being made as necessary.

According to tradition, a Witch's book of shadows is destroyed upon her death. Gardner's original book of shadows, however, was passed to Valiente after his death. Most likely, other books of shadows are passed on as keepsakes and documents of historical significance.

Bradley, Marion Zimmer (1930–) Her best-selling science fiction and mainstream novels carry such Wiccan themes (see WICCA) as the power of women and worship of the Earth Goddess; as a result, author Marion Zimmer Bradley is sometimes called a Witch (see WITCHES) or Wiccan priestess. She is an occultist, has studied ceremonial MAGIC and has worked with Witches, but she is not, and never has been, a Witch. "That is not my path in this life," states Bradley, who is an ordained priest in the New Catholic Church. "I myself am unalterably Christian."

Bradley has been interested in and involved with the occult for most of her life. She was born on June 3, 1930, in Albany, New York, to a Lutheran family. She had an early interest in poetry and writing and dictated poetry to her mother before she could write. At age 11, she started an alternative school newspaper, *The Columbia Journal*, because she did not like the official school paper. She also had an early and intense interest in classical history, classical ceremonial magic, the mystery religions and the Arthurian legends.

Bradley spent three years at New York State Teachers College in Albany (now part of the State University of New York) but did not graduate. In October 1949, she married Robert A. Bradley, a railroad man, and had a son. The Bradleys moved to Texas, living in what Bradley terms "a succession of small towns and smaller towns," including Levelland and Rochester. For a period in the early 1950s, Bradley joined the Rosicrucians, which gave a structure to her interest in the occult.

Bradley started her writing career in the 1950s by producing short stories for the pulp and confession magazines, and then original paperback novels, most of them science fiction. Her first novel was *Seven from the Stars*, published in 1955.

In 1959 Bradley left her husband and went to Abilene, where she finished college at Hardin Simmons University, majoring in education, psychology and Spanish, and earning a teaching certificate. She financed her tuition by writing confessional and romance novels, which were selling so well by the time she graduated that she never had to use her teaching certificate.

In 1963 Bradley moved to Berkeley, where she presently resides. She undertook graduate work in psychology at the University of California at Berkeley from 1965 to 1967 but did not complete a degree.

In February 1964 she married Walter Breen, a leading authority on rare coins. Breen became the first member of an occult order Bradley had conceived while still in Texas, the Aquarian Order of the Restoration. The purpose of the order was to restore worship of the GODDESS, long before it became fashionable to do so. At its height, the order had about 18 members. The order eventually dissolved, feeling that its purpose had been accomplished. The last meeting took place in 1982.

Of Bradley's novels, the one that identified her most closely with Witchcraft is *The Mists of Avalon*, published in 1983. Bradley began work on the book in 1978. It tells the story of Arthur through the viewpoints of the women around him. *Mists*, which eloquently portrays the ancient ways of the Goddess, the mysterious world of Faerie (see FAIRIES) and the conflict between paganism and Christianity, gained a wide following in the neo-Pagan/Witchcraft community.

Bradley herself became involved in that community in the late 1970s. She joined a women's group (which was not a coven but included STARHAWK as one of the leaders). She and other women formed the Dark Moon Circle, of which she was a member for about four to five years. The group was described as "part coven, part women's consciousness-raising, and part sewing circle." The Dark Moon Circle continues to exist, but Bradley dropped out shortly after *The Mists of Avalon* was published. She found herself besieged by people who wanted her to speak on female consciousness, crystals and how much of the book had been "channeled" (none). Also, some of the members of the Dark Moon Circle wanted to open it to men. Bradley had joined because of her interest in learning how to relate better to women.

Bradley remains interested in ceremonial magic and has many friends who are Witches. She takes exception with some of the values and aspects of the Craft that she feels are "intellectually dishonest." For example, modern WITCHCRAFT is a fertility religion, yet many feminist Witches lobby for abortion rights. Bradley feels strongly that "Witchcraft is too tied up in people's minds with the medieval witchcraft, which is a form of Satanism. Witches do not even believe in, let alone worship, Satan." Also, she says, trying to return to the old Earth religions in a society that is irrevocably high technology does not make sense (see SATANISM).

brass In folk magic, brass is considered to be effective in repelling WITCHES and evil spirits. It has been used in the making of numerous kinds of AMULETS. Brass BELLS hung on the necks of horses, cows and other animals protect them from the EVIL EYE.

See also IRON.

bright blessings See BLESSED BE.

brooms In folklore, brooms were the primary means of travel for WITCHES, who mounted them and soared through the air at tremendous speed. The witch

Witches flying up chimney on broomsticks (Thomas Erastus, *Dialogues touchant le pouvoir des sorcières et de la punition qu'elles meritent*, 1579)

riding her broomstick has become a popular cultural stereotype. There are different theories as to why brooms are associated with witches. The most likely explanation is that brooms are a symbol of female domesticity, a tool of every woman, and most witches were women. In earlier centuries, it was customary for a woman to prop her broom outside the door or push it up the chimney as a sign to neighbors and callers that she was away from the house. From there, it was an easy step to believe that witches, who purportedly could fly, would use their most common tool and soar up the chimney on it (see FLYING). Another theory holds that the association between witches and brooms goes back to ancient times, when pagans performed fertility rites to induce their crops to grow high. They mounted brooms, poles and pitchforks and rode them like hobbyhorses in the fields, dancing and leaping high into the air.

In medieval and Renaissance times, the belief that witches traveled by broom was more prevalent on the European continent than in the British Isles. English witchcraft laws never specifically outlawed flying, and brooms are mentioned only once in English witch trials.

Accused witches on trial said they were able to fly thanks to magical OINTMENTS they rubbed on themselves or on chairs or brooms. If they wished, they could travel invisibly. However, not all authorities agreed that this was possible. JEAN BODIN, a 16th-century French demonologist, maintained that only a witch's spirit could fly, not her physical body.

The broom was not always the "steed of the Devil." In early 16th-century German woodcuts, witches are shown astride forks, sticks, shovels and DEMONS in the forms of animals. By the late 16th and early 17th centuries, witches were more often shown riding either brooms or demon-animals. The position of the faggot, the bound bundle of twigs, changed over time. Initially, the faggot was held down, so that the witch could sweep her tracks from the sky; this is the image that has prevailed into the 20th century. But by the late 17th century, witches often were depicted in art riding with the faggot-end up. The faggot held a candle to light the way.

Some lore had it that the DEVIL gave every newly initiated witch a broom and flying ointment; other lore had it that he dispensed those items only to weak witches who needed help.

Before mounting their broomsticks, witches first had to anoint themselves or their sticks with the flying ointment, a vile concoction that typically included hallucinogenic and/or toxic ingredients. If they were inside a house, they supposedly rose up through the chimney, though few witches brought to trial actually acknowledged doing so. Sorcerers as well as witches flew on brooms, though men were more often depicted riding on pitchforks.

According to lore, witches flew their brooms to the SABBATS, sometimes carrying along demons or their FAMILIARS in the shapes of animals. They also rode their brooms to fly out to sea in order to raise up storms (see STORM RAISING). Legend had it that novices sometimes fell off. On witch festival nights such as WALPURGISNACHT, townspeople laid out hooks and scythes to kill any witches who fell off their brooms. They also rang church BELLS, which had the power to ground broomsticks and knock witches off them.

ISOBEL GOWDIE, a famous Scottish witch of the 17th century, claimed to use her broom not for travel but to deceive her husband. Prior to going to a sabbat, she substituted her broom for herself in bed. He never knew the difference, she said, which might have been more of a comment on their marriage than a confession of witchcraft.

The broom is used in some neo-Pagan Witchcraft rituals. It is placed at the altar with other tools and objects (see WITCHES' TOOLS). A COVEN's high priestess or maiden uses a broom symbolically to sweep away evil, as in clearing the space for a MAGIC CIRCLE or sweeping bad fortune away from a newly handfasted couple (see HANDFASTING). In a handfasting, the bride and groom traditionally jump over a broom, which is similar to an old Welsh custom that calls for newlyweds to enter their new home by stepping over a broom. In some sabbat rites, the broom is taken around the circle DEOSIL to sweep away the old and worn.

Brossier, Marthe (1573–?) The possession of Marthe Brossier in the late 16th century probably ranks as the most famous case of fraud throughout the entire period of demonic hysteria. Undoubtedly used as a vehicle for raising money from the gullible, Marthe's alleged possession by the demon Beelzebub (see DEMONIC POSSESSION) also served as another means of undercutting Huguenot religious reform. The case also stands as the first where accusations of fraud were backed up by detailed physical evidence.

Reported as both the eldest and the youngest of four daughters of a poor draper in the town of Romorantin, France, Brossier first showed signs of unusual behavior at the age of 25 in 1598. Still without a husband, she cut her hair, wore men's clothing, screamed and contorted her body. She attacked her friend Anne Chevion (also known as Chevreau) in a fit of jealousy, accusing the latter of bewitching her. Although no records exist detailing Anne's fate, other "possessed" persons in Romorantin successfully used the witchcraft defense. Brossier's career as a demoniac also may have been influenced by an account of the MIRACLE OF LAON. In any case, she demanded exorcism by her local priest and began the usual demoniacal routine: fits, impossible body contortions, a psychosomatic pregnancy and, as in Laon, ravings by Beelzebub against the heresy of the Huguenots (see DEMONIC EXORCISM).

Realizing the celebrity potential of her possession, Brossier and her family traveled the Loire Valley, stopping in various towns for an exorcism and drawing large audiences. Physician Michel Marescot, who examined Brossier in 1599, unkindly described her tours as "fifteen months spent in carrying of her too [sic] and fro, like an Ape or a Beare, to Angers, Saulmur, Clery, Orleans and Paris." In Orleans Brossier obtained a certificate of genuine possession from the local priest. Not everyone was fooled, however, as administrators in Clery and Orleans posted documents forbidding any priest to exorcise "that fictitious spirit." At Angers, Bishop Charles Miron tested Brossier on her reactions to holy water and sacred Latin texts, and she failed both examinations: she did not react to real holy water but to ordinary water, and the Latin, which caused more convulsions, was merely a line from Virgil's *Aeneid*. Bishop Miron ordered Brossier and her family to return to Romorantin and stop playing tricks.

Instead, in early March 1599, Marthe and her father went to Paris. Just a few days earlier, the Parlement of Paris had passed the Edict of Nantes, giving official tolerance to both Catholic and Huguenot beliefs. The Brossiers sought refuge in the Capuchin monastery of Ste. Geneviève, where the monks began to exorcise Marthe immediately and broadcast Beelzebub's anti-Huguenot diatribes. The exorcisms attracted huge crowds, and by the end of March, public feeling was so high that Henri De Gondy,

Bishop of Paris, intervened to verify Brossier's possessed state. Both theologians and physicians examined Brossier, including Marescot, and all agreed on March 30 that Marthe was not possessed but merely ill; her symptoms were mostly counterfeit.

On March 31, two of the doctors re-examined Brossier and found an insensitive spot between her thumb and index finger. Believing it to be a DEVIL'S MARK, they asked for a postponement of the earlier report and began to exorcise her on April 1. The Capuchins brought in another group of doctors on April 2, and on April 3 they proclaimed her genuinely possessed.

But their efforts were too late. Fearing a breakdown of the Edict, King Henri IV ordered a halt to the public exorcisms. Brossier was imprisoned for 40 days, and her copy of the Miracle of Laon was confiscated. Her convulsions gradually ceased. On May 24, Parliament ordered Brossier and her father to return to Romorantin, where the local judge was to check on her every two weeks. All was quiet until December, when Alexandre de la Rochefoucauld, the Prior of St. Martin-de-Randan in Auvergne and a believer in Marthe's possession, kidnapped her and took her to Avignon and finally to Rome to see the Pope, all the while encouraging her anti-Huguenot performances. They arrived just in time for the Papal Jubilee of 1600, where Brossier contorted and was exorcised for the edification of the tourists.

On the advice of Henri IV and other clerics, the French Cardinal d'Ossat stopped the Prior's exhibitions, although Brossier continued to perform. According to an account by Palma Cayet in 1605, Marthe was still staging possessive fits in Milan as of 1604 and acting as Beelzebub's mouthpiece.

brownies See GOBLINS.

bruja, brujo The feminine and masculine names, respectively, for the WITCHES of Mexico, Meso-America and Hispanic communities in the United States. Of the two, the *bruja*, the woman, is more prevalent and considered the more powerful. In the superstitious culture of Mexico, the *bruja* holds a visible, important function: she is sought for remedies for physical illness, and SPELLS and CHARMS to remedy emotional, romantic and social problems. *Brujas* may be found in many open-air markets in Mexico, selling herbs, charms and other objects from which customized AMULETS and charms may be made. Many of their remedies for physical ailments are based on folk cures handed down through the centuries.

One of their most popular magical objects is a dead hummingbird, which the *bruja* wraps in embroidery threads of brilliant colors, leaving only the beak, feet and some tail feathers uncovered. The charm is used to reveal the identities of those who are suspected of casting spells on, or gossiping about, the owner of the charm. To make the charm work, the owner wraps it in a piece of clothing or a lock of hair from the suspected offender (see HAIR AND NAILS). The bird is then held in the palm of the hand and meditated upon; it is supposed to reveal the answers telepathically.

See also CURANDERO, CURANDERA; DEVIL FISH; GARLIC.

brujo See BRUJA, BRUJO.

Bruner (also known as Burner), Theobald (1855–1871) and Joseph (1857–1882) The case of the Bruner boys in Illfurt (also Illfurth), Alsace, France, stands as a classic example of DEMONIC POSSESSION and DEMONIC EXORCISM. The boys exhibited all the accepted signs of diabolic interference—contortions, blasphemies, levitation, speaking in unknown languages, revulsion toward holy objects and clairvoyance—and the DEVIL was exorcised by ritual.

Theobald (also Thiebaut) and Joseph first began displaying unusual and frightening behavior in September 1865. Confined mostly to their beds for the next two years, the boys would entwine their legs, sometimes every two or three hours, in knots so tight that no human pressure could entangle them. They would stand on their heads for hours, bend completely backwards, become rigid and undergo attacks of vomiting, expelling great quantities of yellow foam, seaweed and foul-smelling feathers (see ALLOTRIO-PHAGY).

The boys levitated in their beds as well (see LEVITATION). Sometimes their mother, seated on the bed while it rose off the floor, would be thrown into the corner. Their room was unbearably hot, although no stove was on; only when holy water was sprinkled on the bed did the room's temperature return to normal. Furniture flew about the room, the drapes would come down by themselves and the windows would burst open. The entire house shook, as if from an earthquake.

More disturbing was the boys' increasing fascination with the DEVIL and their hatred of holy objects. They would draw devilish faces on the walls by their bed and talk to them. Rosaries or sacred relics placed on or under their bed would send the boys into hysterical fits, in which they would hide under the covers and scream blasphemies. The blessed host was particularly loathsome, and pictures of the Virgin Mary—even the mention of her name—enraged the boys. According to the records kept by the local priest, Father Karl (also Charles) Brey, if a ''clergyman or pious Catholic visited the house, the possessed children crawled hastily under a table or bed, or jumped out the window." But when someone of less fervent faith came in, the boys were delighted, proclaiming, "That one is one of ours. They should all be like that!"

The final proof of their possession was the boys' ability to speak in foreign languages—English, Latin and various Spanish dialects—unknown to them, and to display paranormal, or clairvoyant, knowledge of outside events. Father Brey reported that two hours before one woman died, Theobald knelt in his bed and acted as if he were ringing a mourning bell. On another occasion, Theobald rang his imaginary mourning bell for an entire hour, claiming it was for the death of one Gregor Kunegel. Kunegel's daughter happened to be in the house and angrily denied her father's death, protesting that he was not even ill working as a mason on a new seminary building. Theobald answered that the man had fallen, as indeed he had, and broken his neck.

It took about four years for the Bruners and Father Brey to agree on a diagnosis of demonic possession and convince Father Brey's bishop to approve an exorcism. Finally, Theobald was sent to the St. Charles Orphanage at Schiltigheim, near Strasbourg, on October 3, 1869. Held by three strong men and forced to stand before the altar, Theobald remained silent for three days (other accounts say two), only drooling a thick yellow froth. On the fourth day, he roared in a horrible voice that he had come and was furious. When the nun asked who had come, Theobald answered, "I am the Lord of Darkness!" At that point, Theobald was placed in a straightjacket, as he began tearing his clothes and breaking everything in reach. Finally, after the exorcist Father Stumpf again called upon the Virgin, Theobald screamed in agony and pitched forward in a deep sleep. When he came to, he was himself again and had no memory of the previous three days.

Father Brey himself exorcised Joseph, also in the orphanage, on October 27, after only three hours of frantic struggling and screaming. Like Theobald, Joseph was surprised to find himself in church and did not remember his ordeal.

Unfortunately, the boys did not live long, peaceful lives. Theobald died two years later, at age 16, while Joseph died in 1882 at age 25.

Buckland, Raymond (1934–   )

The introduction of contemporary WITCHCRAFT into the United States was accomplished primarily through the efforts of Raymond Buckland, an Englishman who moved to America in 1962. Buckland also founded a new tradition of Witchcraft, Seax-Wica, and for more than

Raymond Buckland (courtesy Raymond Buckland)

two decades served as a leading spokesperson for Witchcraft.

Buckland was born in London on August 31, 1934. His father's Gypsy heritage makes him a *poshrat*, or half-blooded Gypsy (see GYPSIES). He was raised in the Church of England, but around age 12, a Spiritualist uncle interested him in Spiritualism and the occult, and the interest expanded over time to include Witchcraft and MAGIC.

Buckland was educated at King's College School in London and served in the Royal Air Force from 1957 to 1959. He married his first wife, Rosemary, in 1955. The couple immigrated to the United States in 1962 and settled in Brentwood, Long Island. Buckland went to work for British Airways (then BOAC).

His decision to embrace Witchcraft as his religion was greatly influenced by two books, *The Witch-cult in Western Europe* by MARGARET A. MURRAY, and *Witchcraft Today*, by GERALD B. GARDNER, which helped him realize that witchcraft was the religion for which he had been searching. Buckland wrote to Gardner, who was living on the Isle of Man, and struck up a mail and telephone relationship. He became Gardner's spokesperson in the United States; whenever Gardner received a query from an American, he forwarded the letter to Buckland.

Buckland met Gardner shortly before the latter's death in 1964, upon his INITIATION into Witchcraft by Gardner's high priestess, Lady Olwen. The initiation took place in Perth, Scotland, where Lady Olwen lived. Rosemary was initiated at a later time.

Interest in Witchcraft caught on quickly in America, but the Bucklands built their own COVEN slowly and cautiously. They were later criticized for their caution; people who did not want to wait to be witches by traditional initiation simply started their own covens. Initially, Buckland kept his real name and address out of the media. The information eventually was published, which focused more attention on him as a spokesperson for the Craft.

Buckland was inspired by Gardner's Museum of Witchcraft and Magic on the Isle of Man, and began collecting pieces for his own museum, the first Museum of Witchcraft and Magic in the United States. The collection began in a bookcase, spilled out into the Bucklands' basement and eventually into a separate building.

In 1969 Buckland published his first book, *A Pocket Guide to the Supernatural,* followed in 1970 by *Witchcraft Ancient and Modern* and *Practical Candleburning Rituals.* Also in 1970, he published a novel, *Mu Revealed,* written under the pseudonym Tony Earll, an anagram for "not really." It was a tongue-in-cheek novel inspired by the successful books on the lost continent of Mu by James Churchward.

The year 1973 was transitional. The museum collection was big enough to fill a rented building, and Buckland quit his job to run it full-time. But the Bucklands' marriage broke up, and they turned the leadership of their coven over to Theos and Phoenix, a high priestess and high priest, respectively, of Long Island. Buckland moved to New Hampshire, where he married Joan Helen Taylor, and reopened the museum.

At about the same time, Buckland left the Gardnerian tradition and founded Seax-Wica, a new tradition that is based on a Saxon heritage and is open and democratic in nature. He had two primary reasons for making this move: Gardnerian witchcraft no longer met his religious needs, and he had been dismayed at some of the ego and power trips exhibited within the Craft.

Four years later, the couple moved to Virginia, where they established the Seax-Wica Seminary, a correspondence school that grew to have more than 1,000 students worldwide. Plans to establish a campus, however, fell through due to lack of finances.

After nearly 10 years of marriage, Buckland and Taylor divorced. Buckland married Tara Cochran of Cleveland. They moved to Charlottesville, Virginia, where they ran the seminary school and Taray Publications. In December 1984 they moved to San Diego, and the seminary correspondence course was phased out. Seax-Wica covens remain established around the world.

In San Diego, Buckland withdrew from his high-profile position in Witchcraft, practicing with his wife as solitaries (see SOLITARY). In 1986 his 11th and presumably final book on Witchcraft was published, *Buckland's Complete Book of Witchcraft,* which comprises everything Buckland feels he has to say on the subject. Some WITCHES criticized him for revealing too much. While the book does not reveal Gardnerian secrets, it does reflect his view that the Craft should be more open.

In the late 1980s Buckland turned to new creative avenues, writing a book on Gypsies, as well as screenplays and novels. None of the fiction is occult, but is instead comedy, mystery and Tolkien-style fantasy. The Bucklands also developed a workshop program, "Basics of Wica," a study-group format for persons who have already accepted Witchcraft as their religion but need to learn more of its fundamentals.

Buckland has not operated the Museum of Witchcraft and Magic since leaving New Hampshire but still has the exhibits in his possession.

His other books include *Witchcraft from the Inside* (1971); *Amazing Secrets of the Psychic World* (1975); *The Tree: The Complete Book of Saxon Witchcraft* (1974); *Here Is the Occult* (1974); *Anatomy of the Occult* (1977); *The Magic of Chant-O-Matics* (1978); and *Practical Color Magick* (1983).

In addition, Buckland has written numerous magazine and newspaper articles on Witchcraft. He has appeared on talk shows and lectured at universities. He also served as technical advisor for Orson Welles' movie, *Necromancy,* and for a stage production of *Macbeth,* and worked with William Friedkin, the director of *The Exorcist.* He holds a doctorate in anthropology from Brantridge Forest College in Sussex, England.

Buckland, Rosemary   See RAYMOND BUCKLAND.

Budapest, Z (1940–   )   The dynamic founder and leader of the main branch of feminist Dianic WICCA hails from a Hungarian family whose roots in Paganism and WITCHCRAFT, she says, date back to 1270. Z Budapest (her feminist name) took what she learned from two revolutions—the Hungarian uprising of 1956 and the feminist movement in America—to create a feminist Wiccan tradition.

She was born Zsusanna Mokcsay in Budapest on January 30, 1940, the day on which Candlemas is celebrated in Europe. The recorded history of the family, which is part Transylvanian on her father's side, includes a long line of women herbalists and

Z Budapest (courtesy Z Budapest)

healers and male military leaders and bishops. Some of the latter also served as pagan priests in the double life many Europeans lived after Christianization. According to Budapest, her grandmother, Ilona, was an herbalist and healer, a suffragette who campaigned for the liberation of Transylvania, which Hungary lost in World War I. Her mother, Masika, was a ceramics artist whose work depicted the GODDESS and whose psychic gifts included trance mediumship, psychometry and palmistry. Masika communicated with the dead, delivering messages to the living, and also channeled a spirit who spoke in a foreign language, which eventually was identified by University of Budapest scholars as an ancient Egyptian dialect.

At age three, Budapest had her first psychic experience, an apparitional vision of Ilona, who manifested to say good-bye upon her death. (She later learned that Ilona died of starvation while saving a red apple, tucked beneath her pillow, for her favored grandchild; her last words were Zsusanna's name.) According to Hungarian tradition, a death apparition means the departed one will take on the role of guardian spirit to the living one. Ilona has served in that capacity throughout her life, Budapest claims. As Budapest grew older, she remained close to Ilona's spirit, praying to her for guidance and protection.

At age 12, Budapest met Tom, a 14-year-old boy whom she immediately knew would someday be her husband. But the Hungarian revolt of 1956 shattered her ordered world. After the Russians squelched the revolt, Budapest consulted with Ilona and her mother and decided to leave Hungary. She petitioned Ilona for protection, helpers and the cloak of invisibility. At the full moon on November 19, 1956, Budapest made her way successfully to Austria through various checkpoints. In Innsbruck, she was taken in by a wealthy family and continued her schooling.

Tom located her through relatives, and the two were engaged by the time Budapest was 18. She was awarded a scholarship to the University of Chicago. Three weeks after her arrival there, she and Tom were married. Budapest had two sons, Làszò and Gàbor, by the time she was 21.

Life as an immigrant, student, wife and mother was a series of difficult adjustments. One saving grace was her involvement in the Second City school for improvisation acting, where Budapest studied for about two years. After moving to New York in 1964, Budapest enrolled in the American Academy of Dramatic Arts and Tom took a teaching job as a mathematics professor.

Difficulties, including marital trouble, left Budapest so unhappy that she became severely depressed. On an afternoon bicycle trip to the ocean with her sons, she decided to ride her bike off the edge of the sea cliffs. Before she could act, she hit a sandpile and was thrown from her bike and knocked unconscious. She experienced a pulsating pink vision of utter peace and happiness. When she awoke, she said, she was filled with renewed hope, and was determined to live and find the happiness that she now knew was inside of her.

In 1970 her marriage broke up and she hitchhiked to California, praying to Ilona once again for protection and guidance. (In Hollywood, she took a studio apartment, appropriately numbered 13 [see THIRTEEN].) When a rally was held in Los Angeles to commemorate the anniversary of women winning the right to vote, Budapest attended out of curiosity and was immediately drawn to the feminist movement. She worked on the staff of a local women's center, which acquainted her, she says, with "women's pain." Budapest saw a need to develop a female-centered theology that not only would help women but would answer opponents of the feminist movement who claimed that feminism was "against God." Drawing on her own heritage and her improvisational skills, she collected six friends and began holding SABBATS. A COVEN was born on the winter solstice, 1971, named the Susan B. Anthony Coven after the leader of the women's suffrage movement.

The sabbats were uplifting and empowering, and word-of-mouth quickly drew more participants. The expanding group was moved to the beach, a location that drew too many onlookers, and then to a mountaintop in Malibu. For 10 years, Budapest led sabbats and full-moon circles, initiating priestesses (see INITIATION) and teaching women to bless each other and connect with the GODDESS through Mother Nature. One of Budapest's pupils was STARHAWK. In addition, Budapest opened a shop, The Feminist Wicca, in Venice, and self-published a book that became a basic text of Dianic Wicca, *The Feminist Book of Lights and Shadows,* a collection of rituals, SPELLS and lore. The book later was sold to a publisher and was issued as the two-volume *The Holy Book of Women's Mysteries.*

During the 1970s, the Dianic Wicca movement (also called by some "wimmin's religion") grew to be a major force both in witchcraft and feminism. By 1976 the core of the Susan B. Anthony coven consisted of 20–40 women; up to 300 participated in some of the activities. Related covens were formed in at least five other states.

In the early 1980s, Los Angeles's air pollution caused Budapest to close the shop, turn the Susan B. Anthony coven over to another leader and move to Oakland. She formed a new coven, the Laughing Goddess, but was dismayed to see it fail, due partly to internal politics and friction.

Budapest did not form or join another coven but turned her attention to speaking engagements and counseling on ritual skills. For a time, she hosted a radio program in the Bay Area, then became director of the Women's Spirituality Forum in Oakland. She organizes lectures, Spiral Dances, annual conferences, camping festivals and retreats, and has formulated plans to train advanced students as priestesses and work on platforms for national conferences. She also works on a cable television program about the Goddess, "Thirteenth Heaven," a title she says was suggested by her deceased mother in a dream.

Budapest believes Witches should use their powers to stop or prevent evil by hexing perpetrators of crime so that they are caught (see HEX). One celebrated hexing she led took place in 1980 in the Bay Area, against the Mt. Tam Murderer, a serial killer who ambushed and shot joggers, most of them women. Budapest and other Witches conducted a public hexing ritual, calling for the murderer, who had been at large for nearly three years, to bring himself down through his own evil and mistakes. Within three months, the killer made enough mistakes to lead to his arrest; he was later convicted and given the death sentence.

The impact of Dianic Wicca may be seen in the increase of literature and college courses devoted to the Goddess and women's spirituality. Religion, says Budapest, is the "supreme politics" because it influences everything people do. Patriarchal monotheism, she believes, has worked to the detriment of women; it has glorified war and has permitted suffering for all. Her vision for the future is one of peace and abundance, expressed in female values, dominating the world's consciousness. Then, Budapest says, "both sexes will be free to flourish according to their natural inclinations and abilities. Global Goddess Consciousness means acknowledging the oneness of all as children of one Mother, our beloved blue planet, the Earth."

Burner, Theobald and Joseph   See THEOBALD AND JOSEPH BRUNER.

burning times   A term used by neo-Pagan WITCHES and other neo-Pagans to refer to the period in Western history of intense witch-hunting and executions, generally the mid-15th to early 18th centuries. That burning, one of the most extreme forms of execution, should be decreed for witches originates with St. Augustine (354–430), who said that pagans, Jews and heretics would burn forever in eternal fire with the DEVIL unless saved by the Catholic Church. During the Inquisition (see WITCHCRAFT), witches fell into the category of "heretics" who had renounced God and formed a compact with the Devil (see DEVIL's PACT). Fire itself is the element of purification, and nothing less than fire could negate the evil that was said to be witches. JEAN BODIN, 16th-century demonologist, stated in *De la Demonomanie des Sorciers:*

> Even if the witch has never killed or done evil to man, or beast, or fruits, and even if he has always cured bewitched people, or driven away tempests, it is because he has renounced God and treated with Satan that he deserves to be burned alive . . . Even if there is no more than the obligation to the Devil, having denied God, this deserves the most cruel death that can be imagined.

Not all witches were burned at the stake; hanging was the preferred means of execution in England and the American colonies. In France, Scotland and Germany, it was customary to strangle (worry) condemned witches first, as an act of mercy, by either hanging or garroting, and then burn them to ashes. Nonetheless, many were burned alive, especially if they recanted their confession at the last moment or were unrepentant for their "crimes." The expenses of the burning—along with all the expenses of the trial and the stay in jail—were billed to the deceased's relatives or estate. Witch lynchings and burnings continued sporadically into the late 19th century in England, Europe and Latin America. There are no reliable figures on the numbers of persons who have been burned and hanged for witchcraft; estimates range from about 30,000 (during only 150 years of the Inquisition) to a minimum of 100,000 in Germany alone, where the most virulent witch-hunts took place.

The burning of a witch was usually a great public occasion. The execution took place shortly after the sentencing, just long enough to hire an executioner, construct the execution site and gather the fuel. In

Scotland, a witch burning was preceded by days of fasting and solemn preaching. The witch was strangled first, and then her corpse—or sometimes her unconscious or semiconscious body—was tied to a stake or dumped into a tar barrel and set afire. If the witch was not dead and managed to get out of the flames, onlookers shoved her back in. Records of trials in Scotland report that burning a witch consumed 16 loads of peat plus wood and coal. In 1608 witches in Brechin, Scotland were executed in the following manner, according to original records as cited in *Enemies of God: The Witch-hunt in Scotland* (1981) by Christine Larner:

> . . . they were brunt quick [alive] eftir sic ane crewell maner, than sum of thame deit in despair, renunceand and blasphemeand; and utheris, half brunt, brake out of the fyre, and wes cast quick in it agane, quhill they wer brunt to the deid.

The term *burning times* also refers to any threatened return of prejudice against or persecution of Witches and neo-Pagans by other religious groups, law enforcement agencies, employers, politicians and others (see HELMS AMENDMENT).

Bury St. Edmonds Witches   Of the various witch trials of Suffolk, England, conducted in Bury St. Edmonds during the 17th century, two episodes stand out. In 1645, 68 WITCHES went to their deaths on the gallows, victims of the witch-hunting zeal of MATTHEW HOPKINS and John Stearne. Seventeen years later, in 1662, Sir Matthew Hale presided over trials that led to the condemnation and execution of two witches based on the flimsy spectral evidence of hysterical, "possessed" children. The 1662 trials heavily influenced officials of the Salem witch trials in 1692–93, the worst witch incident in the history of America (see SALEM WITCHES).

The Hopkins trials. In 1645 Matthew Hopkins, England's most notorious witch-hunter, and his associate, John Stearne, a rigid Puritan, were storming about the countryside routing out "witches" in exchange for exorbitant fees. Using unscrupulous methods to extract confessions, the witch-hunters, according to surviving records, charged at least 124 Suffolk men and women of WITCHCRAFT, who were tried at Bury St. Edmonds in August. (There probably were more persons charged than surviving records indicate.) Most of the "confessions" concerned the possession by evil imps (see IMP), the making of compacts with the Devil (see DEVIL'S PACT) and having carnal relations with the Devil, the latter of which was guaranteed to inflame Puritan outrage. Some of the witches also were charged with murder of livestock and people.

Victims were thoroughly searched for witch's marks (see WITCH'S MARK), a most humiliating ordeal for women, since the "marks" usually were found in or on the genitals. These marks, which were said to be supernumerary teats from which imps sucked, were discovered in the folds of the labia or were sometimes the clitoris itself. Stearne had a particular fondness for searching for witch's marks and boasted that 18 of the Bury St. Edmonds witches "all were found by the searchers to have teats or dugs which their imps used to suck. . . . And of these witches some confessed that they have had carnal copulation with the Devil, one of which said that she had conceived twice by him, but as soon as she was delivered of them, they ran away in most horrid, long and ugly shapes."

John Bysack confessed that he had been compromised 20 years earlier by the DEVIL, who came in through his window in the shape of a sandy-colored, rugged dog and demanded that Bysack renounce God, Christ and his baptism. Bysack agreed, and the Devil used his claw to draw blood from Bysack's heart. The Devil gave him six imps in the forms of snails, who sustained themselves by sucking Bysack's blood. Each snail was an assassin with a particular assignment: Atleward killed cows, Jeffry pigs, Peter sheep, Pyman fowls, Sacar horses and Sydrake Christians. Stearne claimed he found snail marks on Bysack's body.

Margaret Wyard confessed to having seven imps, including flies, dogs, mice and a spider. She had only five teats, however, which forced her imps to fight "like pigs with a sow." Wyard said the Devil had come to her seven years earlier in the likeness of a calf, saying he was her husband. She would not submit sexually to him (a comment, perhaps, on the state of her marriage) until the Devil returned as "a handsome young gentleman." Imps of other accused witches included a chicken named Nan; two "heavy and hairy" mice; and three imps "like chickens."

Stearne recorded that 68 witches were executed; one who was tried at Ipswich instead of Bury St. Edmonds reportedly was burned to death. Dozens more may have been hanged—records are uncertain—and still others died in prison.

Ironically, Parliament had established a special commission to oversee witch-hunting activities, in response to reports of excesses. The commission, however, benignly accepted the "evidence" for Devil's pacts and the existence of imps, leaving Hopkins and Stearne free to wreak their havoc for another two years.

The hysterical children of 1662. Rose Cullender and Amy Duny of Lowestoft, Suffolk, were two old widows who were accused of bewitching seven children, one of them to death, and performing various other malicious acts upon their neighbors over a period of years. Sir Matthew Hale (later Chief Justice), who heard the trials, was a believer in witchcraft and did nothing to discourage the most outrageous accusations. The trials of the two unfortunates were recorded by COTTON MATHER in *On Witchcraft: Being the Wonders of the Invisible World* (1692).

Duny's fate as a witch was sealed when she was hired as a baby-sitter by Dorothy Durent for her infant. Duny tried to nurse the baby, William, contrary to Durent's instructions, and was reprimanded, much to her (obvious) displeasure. Not long after, the baby began having fits that went on for weeks. Durent took it to a "white witch" doctor (a man), who told her to hang the child's blanket in a corner of the chimney for a day and a night, then wrap the infant in it and burn anything that fell out. According to Mather:

. . . at Night, there fell a great Toad out of the Blanket, which ran up and down the Hearth. A Boy catch't it, and held it in the Fire with the Tongs: where it made a horrible Noise, and Flash'd like to Gun-Powder, with a report like that of a Pistol: Whereupon the Toad was no more to be seen.

The child recovered. The next day, Duny reportedly was seen with burn marks. Now labeled a witch, Duny was accused of causing fits in other children who had had contact with her. The Durents's 10-year-old daughter, Elizabeth, fell into fits, complaining that the specter of Duny plagued her. The girl became lame in both legs and died within three days. Mrs. Durent herself went lame and had to walk about with crutches. Another Durent child, Ann, suffered fits and swooning spells and vomited pins (see AL-LOTRIOPHAGY), blaming her maladies on the specter of Rose Cullender.

The nine- and 11-year-old daughters of Samuel Pacy, Deborah and Elizabeth, suffered fits that included lameness, extreme stomach pain as though being stabbed with pins and "shrieking at a dreadful manner, like a Whelp, rather than a rational creature." They also vomited crooked pins and a two-penny nail. These girls cried out against Duny and Cullender, claiming to see them as specters, and saying that the witches threatened them not to talk, lest they be tormented 10 times greater than before. The Pacy girls could not pronounce the names of Lord, Jesus or Christ without falling into fits. But the names of Satan or the Devil made them say, "This bites, but it makes me speak right well!"

The Pacy children also saw invisible mice, one of which they threw on the fire, and it "screeched like a Rat." Another invisible mouse thrown on the fire "Flash'd like to Gun-Powder" just like the toad of

Durent. The specter of Duny, meanwhile, tempted one of the girls to destroy herself.

Jane Bocking was so afflicted with fits and pain caused by the specters of Duny and Cullender that her mother had to testify in her place.

Another girl, Susan Chandler, said Cullender would come into her bed, and that she was accompanied by a great dog. Chandler had fits and vomited pins. Cullender was searched for a witch's mark. According to Mather:

. . . they found on her Belly a thing like a Teat, of an inch long; which the *said Rose* ascribed to a strain. But near her Privy-parts, they found Three more, that were smaller than the former. At the end of the long Teat, there was a little Hole, which appeared, as if newly Sucked; and upon straining it, a white Milky matter issued out.

To bolster the testimony of the girls and their families, the court heard "evidence" from others. John Soam testified that one day, while he was bringing home his hay in three carts, one cart wrenched the window of Cullender''s house. She flew out in a rage, shouting threats against Soam. The cart that wrenched the window later overturned two or three times the same day. The men had such difficulty with the carts—one got stuck in a gate, so that the gateposts had to be cut down—and were so exhausted that their noses bled.

Robert Sherringham testified to a similar incident, in which the axle-tree of his cart broke off a part of Cullender's house. (Perhaps Cullender's house was in an unfortunate position on a roadway; if these accidents happened regularly, it is understandable that she would lose her temper.) In an angry fit, Cullender told him his horses should suffer for it. Within a short time, his four horses died, followed by many of his cattle. Sherringham also was afflicted with lameness and was "so vexed with Lice of an extraordinary Number and Bignes, that no Art could hinder the Swarming of them, till he burnt up two Suits of Apparel."

As for other testimony against Duny, she was said to have been overheard saying the Devil would not let her rest until she revenged herself on the wife of one Cornelius Sandswel. The Sandswels's chimney collapsed and their chickens died suddenly.

Sir Thomas Browne, a respected physician, testified that the victims were bewitched and commented that witches discovered in Denmark afflicted their victims in the same manner, with fits and vomitings of pins.

Mather wrote of Hale's instructions to the jury:

He made no doubt, there were such Creatures as Witches; for the Scriptures affirmed it; and the Wisdom of all Nations had provided Laws against such persons. He pray'd the God of Heaven to direct their Hearts in the weighty thing they had in hand; for, *To Condemn the Innocent, and let the guilty go free, were both an Abomination to the Lord.*

The jury took exactly half an hour to convict Duny and Cullender on 19 counts of witchcraft. The next morning, the children were miraculously restored to good health. Duny and Cullender confessed nothing, and were hanged.

When the witch hysteria broke out in Salem in 1692, the authorities took their cue from the 1662 Bury St. Edmonds trials. Hale, after all, was respected as a judge who would not convict a person without solid evidence. As Mather wrote in *Wonders of the Invisible World:*

It may cast some Light upon the Dark things now in *America,* if we just give a glance upon the *like things* lately happening in *Europe.* We may see the *Witch-crafts* here most exactly resemble the *Witchcrafts* there; and we may learn what sort of Devils do trouble the World.

Butters, Mary (late 18th–early 19th centuries)

An attempt to cure a cow of bewitchment with white MAGIC ended in disaster for Mary Butters, the "Carmoney Witch," who nearly escaped a trial in Carricfergus, Ireland, in March 1808. Butters was a reputed wise woman, skilled in herbal knowledge and various SPELLS.

In August 1807 Butters was hired by Alexander Montgomery, a tailor who lived in Carmoney, to cure a cow that gave milk from which no butter could be made. Montgomery's wife was convinced that the cow was bewitched. On the appointed night of the exorcism (see SPIRIT EXORCISM), Butters arrived with her charm bag of magical ingredients. She ordered Montgomery and an onlooker, a young man named Carnaghan, out to the barn, where they were to turn their waistcoats inside out and stand by the cow's head until she sent for them. Butters, Mrs. Montgomery, the Montgomery's son and an old woman named Margaret Lee remained with her in the house.

Montgomery and Carnaghan waited until dawn, growing increasingly worried. They returned to the house, where they were shocked to find all four persons collapsed on the floor. The smoky air smelled of sulphur; on the fire was a big pot containing milk, needles, PINS and crooked nails. The windows and door were sealed tight, and the chimney was covered. The wife and son were dead, and Butters and Lee were close to death; Lee died moments after the men arrived. In a fury, Montgomery threw Butters out onto a dung heap and began kicking her to consciousness.

On August 19 an inquest was held in Carmoney, at which it was determined that the victims had died of suffocation from Butters's "noxious ingredients" and smoke. Butters, terrified, claimed that during her spell-casting, a black man appeared inside the house wielding a huge club. He knocked everyone down, killing the other three and stunning Butters to unconsciousness.

Butters was put forward for trial at the Spring assizes, but the charges against her were dropped. The community's reaction to the tragedy was one of derision. The incident was made the subject of a humorous ballad.

C

Cabala See KABBALAH.

Cabot, Laurie (1933–) Salem, Massachussetts, site of the greatest witch tragedy in America in the years 1692–93 (see SALEM WITCHES), has finally come to comfortable terms with WITCHCRAFT, thanks in part to the efforts of Laurie Cabot, "the Official Witch of Salem." Cabot cuts a dramatic figure about town, dressed in flowing black garments, openly displaying her gold pentacle pendant. Her life revolves around being a public, city Witch, which enables her to spread her particular vision of the Craft and work against public misconceptions (see WITCHES).

Laurie Cabot (her family name) was born March 6, 1933, in Wewoka, Oklahoma, during a family move from Boston to Anaheim, California. Her father, a businessman, was descended from a line of Cabots from the Isle of Jersey off the coast of England, a place renowned for witchcraft. From an early age, Cabot, an only child, felt an affinity with Witches. She says she is descended from a long line of Witches, including a mysterious woman who lived some 4,000–5,000 years ago, whose memory Cabot feels she possesses nearly intact. (In Cabot's view of REINCARNATION, the personality itself does not survive intact and reincarnate; rather, an individual possesses attributes and aspects that are drawn from the reincarnational genetic memory pool.)

By age six, her psychic gifts became apparent, and she constantly got herself into trouble for discussing information she picked up through extrasensory perception. From her father, a science-oriented man who did not believe in the Devil, Cabot developed a lifelong interest in science, which she dovetailed with her interest in Witchcraft, the occult and the paranormal.

Laurie Cabot (courtesy Laurie Cabot)

From Anaheim, Cabot returned to Boston at age 14 with her mother in order to finish high school. She embarked on a comparative study of religions and spent much time in the library. There she met a woman on the staff who encouraged her to look beyond Christianity for information on paranormal phenomena. The woman eventually revealed that she was a Witch, and she introduced Cabot to two

47

other female Witches, one of them elderly. The three women helped to school Cabot in the Craft. When she was 16, the Witches initiated her in a profoundly transformational experience (see INITIATION). She was anointed with oil and dubbed with a sword. She took the sword, impaled it in the earth and said, "I return to earth my wisdom and I call myself Witch."

Cabot made a life's projection for herself, in which she asked the GODDESS and God to enable her to teach Witchcraft as a science to the masses. At the time, she never dreamed she would do just that—in Salem, of all places.

After high school, Cabot did not follow through on plans to attend Smith College, but instead became a dancer in Boston's Latin Quarter. She had two marriages, one to an Italian and one to a Greek, each of which produced a daughter: Jody in 1963 and Penny in 1965. After her second divorce, in the late 1960s, Cabot and her daughters moved to the North End of Boston. She made a vow that she would live her life "totally as a Witch": she would wear nothing but traditional Witch clothing (which she believes is long black robes), would wear her pentacle out (see PENTACLE AND PENTAGRAM) and would emulate the Goddess by outlining her eyes in black makeup, according, she says, to an ancient tradition.

She admits she was naive in not realizing how such attire would provoke people and in thinking that as soon as she explained herself, others would understand and accept her. Over the years, she has had to deal with jokes, aversion and accusations that she dresses that way for commercial exploitation.

A friend whom she met in north Boston, Patty, also a divorcée and mother, told Cabot that as a Witch, she belonged in Salem; Cabot demurred. They decided to pool their funds to rent a house together. Cabot cast a MAGIC CIRCLE, and Jody saw a vision of their future house—which Patty found in Salem. The house was the first house built on Salem's historic Chestnut Street and had been home to NATHANIEL HAWTHORNE for a year. Three years earlier, Cabot had gone through a past-life regression, to the life of a woman, Susan Sarah Prescott, who supposedly had lived in Salem during the 1700s. Cabot believes she picked up on traces of a genetic memory. She discovered that Prescott had indeed existed and that her father had been the builder of their house. (She stayed in the house one year, then moved two times, eventually settling in her present house.)

Cabot also discovered that Salem had little idea of what to think of modern Witches. Members of the public derided her for believing "in all that," and other Witches criticized her for her appearance. Through a new friend, she began teaching "Witchcraft As a Science" classes in the continuing educa-

tion program at Wellesley High School, forming the beginnings of her tradition by the same name (see WITCHCRAFT). She also taught classes for seven years in the Salem State College continuing-education program, gave TAROT readings, diagnosed illnesses by aura readings, consulted for an oil company and occasionally worked with police around the country in solving crimes.

She opened The Witch Shop in Salem, which did not do well and closed; a second venture, Crow Haven Corner, is much more successful and has become one of the major tourist attractions of Salem. Cabot turned the shop over to her daughter, Jody, in the late 1970s.

In 1973 Cabot established the annual Witches' Ball, a costume party to celebrate Samhain (All Hallow's Eve) in Salem, which each year draws an international crowd of participants and media.

Since 1971 Cabot had sought to be named "the Official Witch of Salem" but was turned down by local government; then-Mayor Samuel Zoll was quoted as saying he thought it would be "improper" and that "the historical recognition of the city would be internationally demeaned by allowing a commercial capitalization by one individual." In 1977 Michael Dukakis, then governor of Massachusetts, signed a citation granting Cabot the title. The "Paul Revere" citation, as it is called, is recognition given to various citizens courtesy of members of the legislature. Cabot received hers for her work with dyslexic children. The title has served both Cabot and Salem well.

In 1987 Cabot entered the Salem mayoral race, after incumbent Anthony V. Salvo made derogatory comments about Witchcraft in the press. One of Salvo's opponents, Robert E. Gauthier, a friend of Cabot's, was rumored to be a "warlock," an unfavorable term not used by Witches of either sex (see WARLOCKS). Gauthier denied this and blamed the Salvo camp for spreading the rumors. Salvo denied the accusation, saying he discounted Witchcraft and that no one with "average intelligence" believed in it. Cabot jumped into the race "to prove that Witches have civil rights" and ran a spirited campaign that attracted much local support and national media attention. But on August 11, the deadline for returning nominating papers, she dropped out of the race, citing business commitments, including work on a book. Cabot continues to serve Salem as a member of the executive board of the Chamber of Commerce, which she joined in 1980.

In 1988 Cabot established the Temple of Isis, a chapter of the National Alliance of Pantheists. She no longer teaches in public-school programs. She established her own school with a broad, "New Age" curriculum, located above Crow Haven Corner in quarters also planned to house the Temple of Isis library. Through the National Alliance of Pantheists, she was ordained Reverend Cabot and may perform legal marriages. She continues to give psychic counselings and aura readings.

Cabot feels that Witches should take a stronger stand for their civil rights and public image. In 1986 she founded the WITCHES LEAGUE OF PUBLIC AWARENESS to protest filming in Massachussetts of John Updike's novel, THE WITCHES OF EASTWICK, which she feels exploits negative stereotypes about Witches. The League expanded to take up other causes, including civil-rights issues and harassment of Witches by police and Fundamentalists.

Cagliostro, Count Alessandro (1743–1795)

Sicilian magician, alchemist, psychic and healer who dazzled many of Europe's nobility before running afoul of the Catholic Church. Historians disagree over whether Cagliostro was nothing more than an occult scam artist, or whether he was a truly gifted humanitarian. He pulled frauds to make a fast dollar, yet he also healed many sick people for free by a laying on of hands. He was supported by numerous wealthy patrons, and he gave away huge sums of money to the poor. Shallow cheat or magnanimous magician, he was at the very least a most colorful man.

Cagliostro was born Giuseppe Balsamo to a poor Sicilian family in Palermo. As a child, he was quick and bright and had big dreams that transcended his family's poverty. He was drawn to the occult and demonstrated an innate and remarkably accurate talent for predicting the future. At age 23 he journeyed to Malta, a center of SORCERY and alchemy, where he gained the sponsorship of the Grand Master of the Order of the Knights of Malta. The young Balsamo dabbled in alchemy, searching for the Philosopher's Stone, and studying the KABBALAH and the occult theories of Pythagoras. He changed his name to Count Alessandro Cagliostro, taking the name of his godmother, Countess Cagliostro, a member of Sicily's poor nobility.

In Rome, Cagliostro met the beautiful Lorenza Feliciani, and married her. They traveled around Europe and England, never lacking admirers and willing customers for alchemic secrets such as the Elixir of Life and the Philosopher's Stone. They reportedly met the Count de Saint-Germain, court magician to Louis XV of France. In England, Cagliostro was admitted into the Freemasons.

Cagliostro practiced crystal-gazing (see SCRYING), HEALING, conjuring spirits and predicting winning lottery numbers. The latter made him so much in demand that he had to quit playing the lottery. He

Cagliostro (Paul Christian, *Histoire de la magie*)

sold magic potions, held seances, practiced NECROMANCY, cast out DEMONS and hypnotized people. Cagliostro's precognitive ability served him well, and in Paris he was hailed as "The Divine Cagliostro."

All of this success was certain to attract enemies. Resentful physicians denounced him; the Catholic clergy began to look askance at his "miracle" cures. In 1785 events took a downward turn for Cagliostro and Lorenza. In Paris, they became victims, ironically, in a royal fraud not of their doing: the "Queen's Necklace Affair." The Cardinal de Rohan, an ambitious man who wanted to be First Minister to Louis XVI, was out of favor with Queen Marie Antoinette. The cardinal was "set up" by a Countess de Lamotte, who convinced him he would be back in favor if he cosigned a note for 1,600,000 livres so that the queen could purchase a diamond necklace she desired. De Rohan did so, and the countess got the necklace for herself. When the first installment of the note came due, the cardinal realized he had been had, and went to the king. De Rohan was arrested. The countess accused Cagliostro of the theft, and he, Lorenza and some others who were also accused were arrested, jailed and put on trial. Cagliostro talked his way out of trouble by spinning a fantastic story of his life and times, and he and his wife were released. They left for England. There, Cagliostro wrote a letter to the public of France, predicting the French Revolution. Shortly afterwards, a London newspaper exposed his "real" life, and Cagliostro's reputation was ruined.

The two went to Rome, where Cagliostro foolishly tried to establish an "Egyptian Freemasonry" order in the face of the Catholic Church. The Church brooked no tolerance of this, and in 1789, arrested and imprisoned Cagliostro. After 18 months of inquisition, Cagliostro was found guilty of "impiety, heresy and crimes against the Church" and was sentenced to death on April 7, 1791. Pope Pius VI commuted his sentence to life imprisonment.

Cagliostro was placed in solitary confinement in San Leo prison, in a cistern cell devoid of light and fresh air. After nearly four years, he was removed to a cell above ground, where he died, allegedly of apoplexy, on March 7, 1795.

Lorenza was sentenced by the Church to life imprisonment in a convent in Rome. She is believed to have died in 1794.

For decades after his death, rumors circulated in Europe, Russia and even America that "The Divine Cagliostro" was still alive and wandering the earth.

In the late 19th and early 20th centuries, a Swiss medium who went by the pseudonym Helénè Smith (1861–1929) claimed to be able to summon Cagliostro's spirit to her séances. Cagliostro, who appeared with other ghostly luminaries such as Marie Antoinette, supposedly used Smith's vocal chords to speak. When the count appeared, Smith seemed to acquire a double chin and her eyelids drooped. She spoke in a bass voice with an Italian accent.

LEO LOUIS MARTELLO, an American Witch of Italian descent, claims Cagliostro as a distant ancestor.

cakes-and-wine (also cakes-and-ale)

In most traditions of neo-Pagan WITCHCRAFT, every ESBAT, or "circle," ends with cakes-and-wine, a relaxed sharing of food and drink, and conversation. The food, usually cakes, biscuits or cookies, and the drink, usually wine but also beer, ale, mead or fruit juice, are consecrated and blessed by the high priest and priestess. An offering is made to the deities as a thanks for the basic necessities of life. The high priest and high priestess sample the food and drink, then share them with the coveners. Some of the refreshments may be scattered upon the earth as an offering or be left for the FAIRIES or ELEMENTALS. Cakes-and-wine are also part of SABBATS, HANDFASTINGS, rites of passage and INITIATIONS. Customs vary according to tradition.

Calling Down the Moon See DRAWING DOWN THE MOON.

candles

Candles have a long history in religious worship, magic and folklore. Candles provide light, thus illuminating the darkness and repelling evil spirits while attracting benevolent ones. In liturgy, they are offerings of fealty to a deity. In magic, candles are used in various rituals and SPELLS. In folklore, candles are associated with the dead.

The origin of candles is not known, though there is evidence that beeswax candles were used in Egypt and Crete as early as 3000 B.C. Other early candles consisted of tapers made of a fibrous material, such as rushes, saturated with tallow. The late Egyptians of about the 3rd century A.D. used lamps, and possibly candles, in a magic ritual for "dreaming true," or obtaining answers from dreams. The individual retired to a dark cave facing south, and stared into a flame until he saw a god. He then lay down and went to sleep, anticipating that the god would appear in his dreams with the answers he sought.

Ancient pagans used candles and lamps in religious observances, a practice which the Roman Christian theologian Tertullian (ca. 200 A.D.) vehemently protested as "the useless lighting of lamps at noonday." By the fourth century A.D., both candles and lamps were part of Christian rituals, but it was not until the latter part of the Middle Ages, from the 12th century on, that candles were placed on church altars. The Catholic Church established the use of consecrated holy candles in rituals of blessings and absolving sins, and in exorcising demons (see DEMONIC EXORCISM). Medieval farmers used holy candles to protect their livestock from danger and bewitchment. During the witch-hunts of the Middle Ages and Renaissance, inquisitors' handbooks such as the MALLEUS MALEFICARUM (1486) prescribed holy candles as among those consecrated objects "for preserving oneself from the injury of witches."

According to the prevailing lore during the witch-hunts, witches were said to light candles at their sabbats as offerings of fealty to the Devil, who was often portrayed as wearing a lighted candle between his horns. The witches lit their candles from the Devil's candle; sometimes he lit the candles and handed them to his followers. Witches also put lighted candles in the faggots of their brooms, which they rode through the air to their sabbats.

It was believed that witches made perverse use of holy candles in putting curses on individuals. According to an English work, *Dives and Pauper* (1536), "it hath oft been known that witches, with saying of the Paternoster and dropping of the holy candle in a man's steps that they hated, hath done his feet rotten of."

In Western folklore, candles have a strong association with the dead, perhaps dating back to old

Jewish customs, later adopted by Christians, of lighting candles for the dying and dead. A lit candle placed by the bedside of a dying person was believed to frighten away demons. One Jewish custom calls keeping a lit candle for a week in the room where a person had died, perhaps to purify the air. In American folklore, however, a candle burning in an empty room will cause the death of a relative. Superstitions about candles hold that a guttering candle means someone in the house is about to die, and a candle that burns blue means a ghost is nearby.

Candles made of human fat allegedly contain life energy, and were used in the BLACK MASS in the 17th century, and in other black magic rituals. The *Petit Albert*, an 18th century grimoire (see GRIMOIRES), claims that a "Magic Candle" made of human tallow would disclose buried treasure. The treasure-seeker took the candle into a cave or other subterranean location. When the candle began to sparkle brightly and hiss noisily, treasure was at hand. The nearer the treasure, the more intensely burned the candle, until it went out at the exact spot. Treasure-hunters were advised to carry along lanterns with consecrated candles, not only for light, but to conjure the spirits of dead men who were said to guard buried treasure. The spirits were to be summoned in the name of God and promised anything in order to help them find "a place of untroubled rest."

At the turn of the 19th century, FRANCIS BARRETT, author of *The Magus* (1801), wrote that candles made of "some saturnine things, such as a man's fat and marrow, the fat of a black cat, with the brains of a crow or raven, which being extinguished in the mouth of a man lately dead, will afterwards, as often as it shines alone, bring great horror and fear upon the spectators about it."

Candles are lit in necromantic rituals to conjure the dead in cemeteries (see NECROMANCY). In VODOUN necromancy practiced in Haiti, three lighted candles are placed at the foot of a cross of the grave selected for corpse-raising.

In modern WITCHCRAFT, consecrated white candles are placed on altars and at the four quarters of a MAGIC CIRCLE. If a ritual calls for it, candles are placed at the points of a pentagram (see PENTACLE AND PENTAGRAM). Candles are burned in all religious ceremonies. Colored candles are used in magical SPELLS; each color has its own vibration, attribute, symbolism and influence. In addition, colors correspond to signs of the Zodiac; some signs have more than one color.

In preparation for casting a spell, a Witch may dress, or rub, the candle with anointing oil while concentrating on the purpose of the spell. The formula of the oil depends upon the purpose of the spell (see OILS). Or, a Witch may scratch a wish on a candle. Procedures vary and may contain elements of folk and ceremonial magic.

Color symbolisms and associations are:

White: Spiritual truth and strength; breaking of curses; meditation; household purification.

Yellow: Persuasion; confidence and charm; aid to memory and studying; Virgo; Gemini.

Green: Healing; money and prosperity; luck; fertility; Sagittarius.

Pink: Love and friendship; entertaining; morality; overcoming evil; Cancer.

Red: Sexuality; strength, physical health and vigor; passion; protection; Scorpio; Aries.

Orange: Courage; solving of legal problems; concentration; encouragement; Taurus.

Blue: Psychic and spiritual awareness; peace; prophetic dreams; protection during sleep; Aquarius; Virgo.

Purple: Ambition; reversing a curse; speeding healing in illness; extra power; Pisces; Libra (lavender).

Brown: Protecting pets; solving household problems; attracting help in financial crises; Capricorn.

Gold: Intuition; protection; Leo.

Gray: Stalemate; neutrality; cancellation.

Black: Evil; loss; sadness; discord.

Black candles are used only in cursing magic and in the rituals of Satanists (see SATANISM).

(See also HAND OF GLORY.)

Candomblé See MACUMBA.

Canewdon Witches According to a prophecy by the famous 19th-century cunning man (see WIZARD), James Murrell, the Essex village of Canewdon, located in England's "witch country" of East Anglia, would be populated with WITCHES "forever." Indeed, the village and the surrounding area have been steeped in witch lore since at least 1580, when a woman named Rose Pye was accused of WITCHCRAFT, tried and acquitted. Legend has it that every time a stone falls from the tower of St. Nicholas Church, one witch will die but another will take her place. At midnight, a headless witch sometimes materializes near the church and floats down to the river. Anyone who encounters her is lifted into the air and let down in the nearest ditch.

Many of the witches of Canewdon were said to keep white mice FAMILIARS, or imps (see IMP). A blacksmith, who became a witch when he sold his soul to the DEVIL, was given mice familiars. When he reached the end of his life—in fear of his eventual fate—he confessed on his deathbed that he could not die until he had passed on his powers to a successor. All of his imps climbed up on the bed and sat before him as he spoke. His wife refused them, but at last he was able to persuade his daughter to accept them, and he died.

Canewdon witches were usually described as old, ugly women with unpleasant personalities, true to the HAG stereotype. In the late 19th century, their bewitchments were countered by a white witch, known as Granny, with such folk-magic CHARMS as a knife or pair of scissors under the doormat, which would keep witches out, and potions made for WITCH BOTTLES that would break bewitchments.

See also OLD GEORGE PICKINGILL.

Canon Episcopi The   One of the most important ecclesiastical documents of the Middle Ages was the *Canon Episcopi*, recorded ca. 900, which defined WITCHCRAFT as Devil-worship but declared it to be nothing more than a foolish delusion. The origin of the cannon is unknown. When it was made public at the beginning of the 10th century by Regino of Prüm, Abbot of Treves, it was erroneously presented as an ancient authority dating back to the fourth century. Around 1140, the Italian monk, Gratian, incorporated the *Canon Episcopi* into his authoritative text of canon law, the *Concordance of Discordant Canons* (usually called the *Decretum*). Thus the *Episcopi* became entrenched in the highest canonical law.

The *Canon Episcopi* denied that WITCHES had the ability to fly through the air and metamorphose themselves into animals and birds (see FLYING, METAMORPHOSIS). Whoever was "so stupid and foolish" as to believe such fantastic tales was an infidel. While such *physical* feats were impossible, the canon acknowledged that they could be accomplished *in spirit*.

The *Canon Episcopi* presented a dilemma for the demonologists of the 12th century and later, who accepted the physical reality of metamorphosis and transvection. Convoluted theories were put forth in order to skirt the *Canon Episcopi*. It was reasoned that, even if witches flew with DIANA and DEMONS in spirit or imagination only, they were just as guilty as if they had done so in the flesh. It was then easy to propose that all heretics (including witches) were guilty of having pacts with the Devil (see DEVIL'S PACT) just by virtue of being heretics.

With its portrayal of hordes of women riding upon beasts through the air at night, following their goddess Diana, the *Canon Episcopi* helped promote the idea of the demonical sabbat, the descriptions of which became increasing lurid in the writings of demonologists (see SABBATS).

The text of the *Canon Episcopi* is as follows:

> Bishops and their officials must labor with all their strength to uproot thoroughly from their parishes the pernicious art of sorcery and malefice invented by the Devil, and if they find a man or woman follower of this wickedness to eject them foully disgraced from their parishes. For the Apostle says, "A man that is a heretic after the first and second admonition avoid." Those are held captive by the Devil who, leaving their creator, seek the aid of the Devil. And so Holy Church must be cleansed of this pest. It is also not to be omitted that some wicked women, perverted by the Devil, seduced by illusions and phantasms of demons, believe and profess themselves, in the hours of the night, to ride upon certain beasts with Diana, the goddess of pagans, and an innumerable multitude of women, and in the silence of the dead of the night to traverse great spaces of earth, and to obey her commands as of their mistress, and to be summoned to her service on certain nights. But I wish it were they alone who perished in their faithlessness and did not draw many with them into the destruction of infidelity. For an innumerable multitude, deceived by this false opinion, believe this to be true, and so believing, wander from the right faith and are involved in the error of the pagans when they think that there is anything of divinity or power except the one God. Wherefore the priests throughout their churches should preach with all insistence to the people that they may know this to be in every way false and that such phantasms are imposed on the minds of infidels and not by the divine but by the malignant spirit. Thus Satan himself, who transfigures himself into an angel of light, when he has captured the mind of a miserable woman and has subjugated her to himself by infidelity and incredulity, immediately transforms himself into the species and similitudes of different personages and deluding the mind which he holds captive and exhibiting things, joyful or mournful, and persons, known or unknown, leads it through devious ways, and while the spirit alone endures this, the faithless mind thinks these things happen not in the spirit but in the body. Who is there that is not led out of himself in dreams and nocturnal visions, and sees much when sleeping which he has never seen waking? Who is so stupid and foolish as to think that all these things which are only done in spirit happen in the body, when the Prophet Ezekiel saw visions of the Lord in spirit and not in the body, and the Apostle John saw and heard the mysteries of the Apocalypse in the spirit and not in the body, as he himself says "I was in the spirit"? And Paul does not dare to say that he was rapt in the body. It is therefore to be proclaimed publicly to all that whoever believes such things or similar to these loses the faith, and he who has not the right faith in God is not of God but of him in whom he believes, that is, of the Devil. For of our Lord it is written "All things were made by Him." Whoever therefore believes that anything can be made, or that any creature can be changed to better or to worse or be transformed into another species or similitude, except by the Creator himself who made everything and through whom all things were made, is beyond doubt an infidel.

By the mid-15th century, inquisitors and demonologists had begun to dismiss the *Canon Episcopi*. Its influence, however, lingered for at least another 200 years.

Cape Cod Cranberry, Legend of the   See LEGEND OF THE CAPE COD CRANBERRY.

Carmoney Witch   See MARY BUTTERS.

Cassandra
In Greek mythology, a seer whose prophecies, including the fall of Troy, were ignored. She was the daughter of Priam and also was called the daughter of HECATE. Cassandra received the gift of clairvoyance by sleeping in the temple of Apollo and allowing snakes to lick her ears. When Apollo tried to seduce her, she rebuffed him, and he punished her by declaring that no one would pay attention to her forecasts. In another version of the myth Apollo fell in love with her and gave her the gift of prophecy in return for her promise of giving herself to him. She reneged. Apollo begged for a kiss, to which she consented. By breathing into her mouth, he gave her the gift of prophecy but took away her power of persuasion.

After the fall of Troy, Cassandra was taken prisoner by Agamemnon, whose death she prophesied, and which came to pass with his slaying by his wife, Clytemnestra. Another version of Cassandra's tale says she was killed in the fall of Troy.

She also was able to understand the language of animals.

See also ORACLE.

cats
Cats have been associated with the supernatural since ancient times. In various cultures, cats are associated with either good or bad luck, HEALING or harm. In folklore, the cat is one of the favored animal companions of WITCHES, sorcerers (see SORCERY) and fortune-tellers. Superstitions about cats abound.

The cat was sacred to the ancient Egyptians, who associated it with the MOON and Bast, the goddess of marriage. It also was associated with the Mother Goddess, ISIS. In Egyptian art, the sun god, Ra, was personified as a cat slaying the Serpent of Darkness. Black cats were associated with darkness and death.

According to lore, virtually every sorcerer, witch and Gypsy fortune-teller was supposed to have a cat—and sometimes an owl and a toad as well (see OWLS; TOADS). Cats were FAMILIARS; they embodied DEMONS who performed the witches' tasks of *MALEFICIA* against their neighbors. Elizabeth Francis of Chelmsford, England, convicted as a witch in 1556, said she kept a white spotted cat named Sathan, which, whenever it performed a job for her, de-

manded a reward of a drop of her BLOOD (see CHELMSFORD WITCHES).

Witches were said to be able to assume the shape of a cat nine times, presumably because a cat has nine lives. Black cats were said to be the DEVIL himself. Throughout medieval Europe, black cats were routinely hunted down and burned, especially on Shrove Tuesday and Easter. A cat accused of being a witch's familiar usually was killed by being burned alive. Cats were also used in witches' SPELLS. In the trial of JOHN FIAN, Scotland's most famous witch, in 1590–91, Fian and his COVEN were accused of trying to drown JAMES VI and Queen Anne on their voyage to Denmark. The witches christened a cat, tied it to a dismembered human corpse and threw the bundle into the sea while they recited incantations. A great storm arose and forced the royal ship to return to Scotland, but the king and queen were unharmed.

In the lore of the Scottish Highlands, a large breed of wild cats, called Elfin Cats, are said to be witches in disguise. The Elfin Cats are about the size of dogs and are black with a white spot on the breast. They have arched backs and erect bristles—the stereotypical Halloween cat.

Though the black cat is associated with WITCHCRAFT, it is nevertheless considered good luck to own one in parts of Europe, England and the United States. But having one's path crossed by a black cat is always bad luck. In other folklore, if a cat jumps over a corpse, the corpse will become a vampire. To prevent this, the cat must be killed. Cats are fertility CHARMS—a cat buried in a field will ensure a bountiful crop.

The cat plays a role in VODOUN in the southern United States. Cat charms, particularly those made with cats' whiskers, can bring bad luck, disease and death to the victim. Conversely, in folklore cats have many healing properties. A broth made from a black cat is said to cure consumption. In the 17th century, a whole cat boiled in oil was held to be good for dressing wounds. Illnesses could be transferred to cats, who were then driven from homes.

Cats' eyes are supposed to be able to see ghosts. In Western Asia, a stone called the Cat's Eye—dull red with a white mark—has an evil reputation and is associated with trouble.

Among modern Witches, the cat remains a favored familiar, valued for its psychic sensitivity.

cauldron
Usually an iron pot, the cauldron is a tool of WITCHES and sorcerers (see SORCERY). In the witch lore of the Middle Ages and Renaissance, the cauldron was the receptacle in which POISONS, OINTMENTS and PHILTRES were brewed. Neo-Pagan Witches still use cauldrons, but today they use them for

Witches stirring up brew in cauldron (Abraham Saur, *Ein Kurtze Treue Warning,* 1582)

burning fires and incense in rituals, or for decoration in the home. Magical "brews" most likely are herbal preparations for healing or positive magic. If used in rituals, the cauldron is placed on the witches' altar (see ALTARS) inside the MAGIC CIRCLE. As a vessel, it is a feminine symbol and is associated with the womb of the Mother GODDESS.

The cauldron has had a magical significance in many cultures throughout history. In the lore of ancient Ireland, magic cauldrons never ran out of food at a feast. The early Celts associated cauldrons with fertility and abundance, and revival of the dead. Cauldrons were used in human SACRIFICE—the victims had their throats slashed over the bowls, or were drowned or suffocated in them. The Cauldron of Regeneration, of death and rebirth, the receptacle of souls and the source of inspiration, is associated with the Celtic goddesses CERRIDWEN and Branwen and with the Babylonian fate-goddess, Siris, who stirred the mead of regeneration in the cauldron of the heavens. Cerridwen's cauldron was said to provide the mead of wisdom and inspiration. Among the Celts, the priestess of the moon goddess was required to sacrifice human victims by cutting off their heads over a SILVER cauldron. The BLOOD was boiled to produce a magical drink of inspiration. The Celtic god, CERNUNNOS, identified with the HORNED GOD, was torn apart and boiled in a cauldron, to be born again. Decorations on the Gundestrup cauldron, fashioned out of silver in about 100 B.C. and recovered from a peat bog in Gundestrup, Denmark, depict victims being plunged headfirst into a sacrifical cauldron. Sacrificial cauldrons also appear in some shamanic traditions (see SHAMANISM). In Norse mythology, the patriarch god, ODIN, drank magic blood from a cauldron of wisdom to obtain divine power. In Greek mythology, the witch goddess, Medea, could restore people to youth in a magic cauldron. The cauldron is linked to the chalice of the Holy Grail, which became incorporated into Christian myth.

In medieval art, literature and folktales, the cauldron was in every witch's house, set over a blazing fire. Witches supposedly stirred up vile brews made with ingredients such as bat's blood, decapitated and flayed toads, snakes and baby fat. Before a sabbat (see SABBATS), witches prepared their flying ointments and drugs in cauldrons. They often carried their pots to their sabbats, where they used them to boil small children for the feast. Witches could cause storms at sea by dumping the contents of their cauldrons into the ocean (see STORM RAISING). One of the more bizarre cauldrons allegedly belonged to Lady ALICE KYTELER, an accused Irish witch of the 14th century. Lady Alice reportedly used the skull of a beheaded robber for mixing up her poisons and potions.

According to one tale with an ironic twist, a 14th-century Scottish WIZARD was executed in a cauldron. William Lord Soulis, described as a pernicious wizard and perpetrator of "the most foul sorceries," was convicted for various evil crimes and boiled to death in a cauldron.

The cauldron also was an important tool of the alchemist in the search for formulas to change lead into gold or silver, and mold small gems into big ones.

Cernunnos The HORNED GOD of the Celts, associated with the hunt and with fertility. He was sometimes portrayed with serpent's legs, a man's torso and the head of a bull or ram; or he was shown with stags or wearing stag antlers. Cernunnos was ruler of the underworld or otherworld, the opener of the gates between life and death. He also was worshipped by the Romans and Gauls, who sometimes portrayed him as triple-headed. The name *Cernunnos* means simply "the horned."

The famous Gundestrup CAULDRON, a large, gilt silver cauldron dated ca. 100 B.C. and recovered from a bog near Gundestrup, Denmark, depicts a stag-horned Cernunnos in several scenes: as an antlered man attended by animals, including a boar, and grasping a ram-headed serpent; and grasping a stag in each hand. The cauldron is believed to be Celtic in origin, though some scholars say it is Gallic.

In neo-Pagan WITCHCRAFT, the Horned God is most often addressed as "Cernunnos" in rituals.

Cerridwen (also Keridwen) Celtic goddess of wisdom, intelligence, MAGIC, DIVINATION and enchantment. She possessed the gifts of prophecy and shape-shifting (see METAMORPHOSIS) and presided over the mysteries of the DRUIDIC bards (see DRUIDS). She was associated with water and the MOON, which represent the emotions, the unconscious and intuition. Her primary symbol was the CAULDRON, in which she made a magical brew of herbs, roots and the foam of the ocean, prepared according to the movements of the heavenly bodies. The brew boiled

for a year and a day to yield three drops, which bestowed knowledge, inspiration and science.

According to the *Book of Taliesin* (ca. 1275), a collection of poems and songs, some of which may be the works of the 6th-century Welsh bard, Taliesin, Cerridwen prepared her magic-cauldron brew for her ugly son, Avaggdu. She put a youth named Gwion in charge of stirring the contents. Gwion consumed the three magical drops and gained the wisdom meant for Avaggdu. The rest of the brew turned to poison and split the cauldron open. In a rage, Cerridwen pursued Gwion, intent on destroying him, but he possessed the wisdom to evade her. He changed into a hare, a fish, an otter and a bird, but she shape-shifted accordingly and kept up the pursuit. At last Gwion turned himself into a grain of wheat and hid himself among other grains. Cerridwen turned into a black hen and ate Gwion. Nine months later, she gave birth to a beautiful baby boy, Taliesin, whom she bound up in a leather sack and threw into the sea. Taliesin was rescued by Gwyddno and Elphin, who found the sack while fishing.

Cerridwen is recognized in NEO-PAGANISM and neo-Pagan WITCHCRAFT and plays a key role in the initiatory and mystery rites of Celtic magic.

See also GODDESS.

chanting The rhythmic repetition of words or phrases, usually done in conjunction with dancing, drumming, rattling and hand-clapping, is a primitive way to alter consciousness and raise power. The chants, along with the dancing, drumming, hand-clapping or other accompaniment, are gradually speeded up in tempo until a peak state is reached.

Since ancient times around the world, chanting has been part of religious, ceremonial and magical rites. In ancient Greece, female sorcerers were said to howl their magical chants. Early and medieval sorcerers and magicians also chanted their incantations in howls and forceful voices, a practice carried into the 20th century by magicians such as ALEISTER CROWLEY, who believed that the sound of words profoundly affects both man and universe (see MAGIC; SORCERY). Modern WITCHES and neo-Pagans chant to raise power for magical spells (see CONE OF POWER). The chants may be names of the GODDESS or HORNED GOD, rhymes, alliterative phrases or CHARMS. Charms to chant may be obtained from books on folk and ceremonial magic; many Witches create their own charms to suit the purpose at hand. Chanting usually is done in conjunction with a ring dance around the MAGIC CIRCLE, or while working with cords (see WITCHES' TOOLS). The Witches' Rune, composed by English Witch DOREEN VALIENTE, is a common power-raising chant, the refrain of which is:

Eko Eko Azarak
Eko Eko Zomelak
Eko Eko Cernunnos
Eko Eko Aradia

Shamans chant power songs that follow rhythms and melodies that have been passed down through generations. The words vary according to the individual. Power songs help a shaman achieve an altered state of consciousness for healing or divining. The chanted songs are monotonous, short refrains and have different purposes. Every shaman has at least one chant to summon his power animal or guardian spirit, which provide the source of his shamanic powers (see SHAMANISM).

Native American Indians have chants for the undertaking of many activities, such as hunts, battles and weather control, and for the rites of funerals and initiations. Curing chants are important in Navaho ceremonies. The chants are long texts in which are entwined myths about how the chants were performed for the first time by deities or supernatural beings. The chanters must chant the texts perfectly, or else the cures will be nullified. Incorrectly rendered chants also will strike the chanter with the illness they are supposed to cure. The chants may go on for many days and nights. A chanter is assisted by helpers, all of whom are paid for their work. If a chanter of great repute does not err yet fails to cure an illness, he usually blames witchcraft as the reason. If sickness has been caused by a witch's spell, only Evil Way chants will be effective. Navaho chanters take care not to perform the same chant more than three times a year, lest they suffer the illness they cure.

Charge of the Goddess   In modern WITCHCRAFT, a poetic and inspiring address given by the GODDESS to her worshippers through her intermediary, the COVEN high priestess. The Charge of the Goddess is used primarily in the Gardnerian and Alexandrian traditions, but is not limited to them. It was authored in the 1950s by GERALD B. GARDNER and DOREEN VALIENTE, and is one of the best-loved and most oft-quoted writings in the Craft. It customarily is delivered in DRAWING DOWN THE MOON, a ritual in which the high priest invokes the Goddess into the high priestess, who enters an altered state of consciousness and allows the Goddess to speak through her.

Gardner wrote the first version of the Charge, in which he adapted Tuscan witches' rituals as recorded by CHARLES GODFREY LELAND in *Aradia: The Gospel of the Witches* (1889), and added extracts from ALEISTER CROWLEY's writings. Valiente rewrote Gardner's version in verse, retaining words from *Aradia* because they were traditional, but eliminating much of the Crowley material. The verse version begins "Mother darksome and divine . . ." and its first verse continues to be given by the high priestess in the Drawing Down the Moon ritual.

Aradia includes a "Charge of the Goddess," which consists of instructions given to mortal witches by Aradia, daughter of DIANA and Lucifer. Leland maintained that the legend possibly dated back to the Middle Ages and had been handed down orally from generation to generation. According to the legend, Diana charges Aradia with coming to earth to teach witchcraft to mortals. When Aradia is finished, Diana recalls her to heaven. As she prepares to leave earth, Aradia tells her witches:

When I have departed from this world,
Whenever ye have need of anything,
Once in the month, and when the moon is full,
Ye shall assemble in some desert place,
Or in a forest all together join
To adore the potent spirit of your queen
My mother, great *Diana*. She who fain
Would learn all sorcery yet has not won
Its deepest secrets, them my mother will
Teach her, in truth all things as yet unknown.
And ye shall all be freed from slavery,
And so ye shall be free in everything;
And as a sign that ye are truly free,
Ye shall be naked in your rites, both men
And women also: this shall last until
The last of your oppressors shall be dead; . . .

After writing her verse version of the Charge, Valiente found that most persons preferred a prose Charge. She wrote a final prose version which retains bits of *Aradia*, as well as phrases from Crowley's writings, such as "Keep pure your highest ideal," from *The Law of Liberty*, and "Nor do I demand [aught in] sacrifice," from *The Book of the Law*.

The following prose text of the Charge is as it appears in *Eight Sabbats for Witches* (1981) by Janet and Stewart Farrar. The Farrars, who call the Charge a "Wiccan Credo," made small changes in Valiente's wording, such as substituting "witches" for "witcheries":

The High Priest says:
"Listen to the words of the Great Mother; she who was of old also called among men Artemis, Astarte, Athene, Dione, Melusine, Aphrodite, Cerridwen, Dana, Arianrhod, Isis, Bride, and by many other names."
The High Priestess says:
"Whenever ye have need of any thing, once in the month, and better it be when the moon is full, then shall ye assemble in some secret place, and adore the spirit of me, who am Queen of all witches. There shall ye assemble, ye who are fain to learn all sorcery, yet have not won its deepest secrets; to these will I

teach things that are yet unknown. And ye shall be free from slavery; and as a sign that ye be really free, ye shall be naked in your rites; and ye shall dance, sing, feast, make music and love, all in my praise. For mine is the ecstasy of the spirit, and mine also is joy on earth; for my law is love unto all beings. Keep pure your highest ideal; strive ever towards it; let naught stop you or turn you aside. For mine is the secret door which opens upon the Land of Youth, and mine is the cup of wine of life, and the Cauldron of Cerridwen, which is the Holy Grail of immortality. I am the gracious Goddess, who gives the gift of joy unto the heart of man. Upon earth, I give the knowledge of the spirit eternal; and beyond death, I give peace, and freedom, and reunion with those who have gone before. Nor do I demand sacrifice; for behold, I am the Mother of all living, and my love is poured out upon the earth."

The High Priest says:

"Hear ye the word of the Star Goddess, she in the dust of whose feet are the hosts of heaven, whose body encircles the universe."

The High Priestess says:

"I who am the beauty of the green earth, and the white Moon among the stars, and the mystery of the waters, and the desire of the heart of man, call unto thy soul. Arise, and come unto me. For I am the soul of nature, who gives life to the universe. From me all things proceed, and unto me all things must return; and before my face, beloved of Gods and of men, let thine innermost divine self be enfolded in the rapture of the infinite. Let my worship be within the heart that rejoiceth; for behold, all acts of love and pleasure are my rituals. And therefore let there be beauty and strength, power and compassion, honor and humility, mirth and reverence within you. And thou who thinkest to seek me, know thy seeking and yearning shall avail thee not unless thou knowest the mystery; that if that which thou seekest thou findest not within thee, thou wilt never find it without thee. For behold, I have been with thee from the beginning; and I am that which is attained at the end of desire."

(See also: ARADIA; DRAWING DOWN THE MOON.)

charms Magical words, phrases, chants (see CHANTING) and incantations to protect against or cure disease and ward off evil, disaster and WITCHCRAFT. Charms have been common since ancient times and are still used in folk MAGIC. Some charms are verbal only—a phrase, formula or PRAYER—while others are inscriptions on paper, parchment, wood or other materials and are worn on the body. Still other charms combine phrases with actions, such as spitting (see SPITTLE). Charms exist for virtually every desire and purpose: to secure or lose a lover; ensure chastity, fertility and potency; gain victory, riches and fame; and exact revenge. Other charms protect crops and farm animals, milking and churning butter and get rid of rats, vermin and weeds. The most common charms concern health and illness, and witchcraft.

Some of the oldest charms are magical words or phrases written on parchment and worn around the neck. The term ABRACADABRA, which dates back at least to 2nd-century Rome, and probably is older than that, is supposed to cure fever.

The medieval Church promoted the use of numerous holy charms, including rosaries and holy relics. The most common charm was the *agnus dei*, a small wax cake, originally make out of paschal CANDLES, bearing images of the lamb and the flag. When blessed by the Pope, the *agnus dei* protected the wearer against attacks by the DEVIL, thunder, lightning, fire, drowning, death in childbed and other dangers. In the 17th century, rosaries were similarly blessed as AMULETS against fire, tempest, fever and evil spirits.

Medieval WITCHES and WIZARDS who were renowned as healers employed many charms. These "charmers," as they were often called, used Christian prayers spoken or written in Latin, or debased Christian prayers. The Church approved the use of prayers and the Scriptures as cures and as protection against evil but disapproved of the prescription of them by sorcerers and charmers—a rather contradictory position that blurred the line between religion and magic. In the 17th century, a Nottingham sorcerer, for example, sold copies of St. John's Gospel as a charm against witchcraft. To break witches' SPELLS, he prescribed herbs plus the recitation of five Paternosters, five Aves and one Creed.

Some charms were simple little verses, such as this 19th-century English charm against witchcraft:

He who forges images, he who bewitches
the malevolent aspect, the evil eye,
the malevolent lip, the finest sorcery,
Spirit of the heaven, conjure it! Spirit of the earth
conjure it!

Even witches had their good-luck charms, according to this old folk-magic verse:

The fire bites, the fire bites; Hogs-turd over it, Hogs-turd over it, Hogs-turd over it; the Father with thee, the Son with me, the Holy Ghost between us both to be: ter.

After reciting this verse, the witch spit once over each shoulder and three times forward.

Charms are recited during MAGIC-related activities, such as the gathering of medicinal herbs, the consecration of tools (see WITCHES' TOOLS) and the boiling of a pot of URINE to break a witch's spell.

With the advance of science in the late 17th century, the efficacy of magic charms was challenged, and folk magic in general began to diminish, especially in urban centers. Charms, though, are still part of folk culture. Some linger even in the industrialized West, such as the popular charm to divine love, "He/she loves me, he/she loves me not . . . ," spoken while pulling petals out of a daisy.

In neo-Pagan Witchcraft, the term *charm* is obsolete, replaced by such terms as *chant, incantation* and rune. Some Witches carry "charm bags," little drawstring pouches containing items used in spells (see GRIS-GRIS).

In SHAMANISM, charms are used to conjure spirits, destroy enemies, create talismans and exorcise disease.

Chelmsford witches   In the 16th and 17th centuries, the assizes in Chelmsford, Essex, England, was the site of four major witch trials, all of which demonstrated the deplorable means by which innocent people were executed on the basis of flimsy evidence of WITCHCRAFT.

The first trial occurred in the summer of 1566, under the rule of Queen Elizabeth, whose Parliament had passed the second of England's three witchcraft acts in 1563. The Act of 1563 tightened penalties for witchcraft, making it a felony to invoke evil spirits for any purpose, regardless of whether or not harm resulted (see EVOCATION AND INVOCATION). It provided for mandatory jail sentences but did not provide for the death penalty unless a human being died because of MALEFICIA. Thus, the 1566 Chelmsford trials became the first significant witch trials to be tested under the new law. The outcome of the trials took on further weight because of the prestigious judge and prosecutors: John Southcote, a justice of the Queen's Bench; Rev. Thomas Cole, a rector of a church near Chelmsford; Sir John Fortescue, who later became chancellor of the Exchequer; and, most notably, Sir Gilbert Gerard, attorney general. The records of the trials were written up and distributed in pamphlets, which became popular reading.

Three women were charged with witchcraft: Elizabeth Francis, Agnes Waterhouse and Agnes's daughter, Joan Waterhouse. All lived in the little village of Hatfield Peverell. Their only connection was a white-spotted cat named Sathan, which was alleged to be a familiar that talked (see CATS; FAMILIARS). The most damning testimony in the two-day affair was given by a malicious 12-year-old girl. Francis and Agnes Waterhouse "confessed" to their charges, while Joan Waterhouse threw herself on the mercy of the court.

Francis was the first to be tried, on July 26. The wife of Christopher Francis, she was charged with

Hanging of three Chelmsford witches (English pamphlet, 1589)

bewitching the baby of William Auger, which "became decrepit." She confessed to that crime and also to some doings far racier and more nefarious, including illicit sex, murder and abortion.

Francis said she had been taught the art of witchcraft at age 12 by her grandmother, Mother Eve, who counseled her to renounce God and give her blood to the DEVIL. Mother Eve delivered the Devil to Francis in the likeness of a white-spotted cat, which was to be named Sathan, fed bread and milk and kept in a basket. According to the trial records:

. . . this Elizabeth desired first of the said Cat (calling it Sathan) that she might be rich and to have goods, and he promised her that she should—asking her what she would have, and she said sheep (for this Cat spake to her as she confessed in a strange hollow voice, but as such she understood by use) and this Cat forthwith brought sheep into her pasture to the number of eighteen, black and white, which continued with her for a time, but in the end did all wear away she knew not how.

Item, when she had gotten these sheep, she desired to have one Andrew Byles to her husband, which was a man of some wealth, and the Cat did promise her that she should, but that she must first consent that this Andrew should abuse her, and she so did.

And after when this Andrew had thus abused her he would not marry her, wherefore she willed Sathan to waste his goods, which he forthwith did, and yet not being content with this, she willed him to touch his body which he forthwith did whereof he died.

Item, that every time he did anything for her, she said that he required a drop of blood, which she gave him by pricking herself, sometime in one place and then in another, and where she pricked herself there remained a red spot which was still to be seen.

Item, when this Andrew was dead, she doubting [believing] herself with child, willed Sathan to destroy it, and he bade her take a certain herb and drink it, which she did, and destroyed the child forthwith.

Item, when she desired another husband he promised her another, naming this Francis whom she now hath, but said he is not so rich as the other, willing her to consent unto that Francis in fornication which she did, and thereof conceived a daughter that was born within a quarter of a year after they were married.

After they were married they lived not so quietly as she desired, being storred (as she said) to much unquietness and moved to swearing and cursing, wherefore she willed Sathan her Cat to kill the child, being about the age of half a year old, and he did so, and when she yet found not the quietness that she desired, she willed it to lay a lameness in the leg of this Francis her husband, and it did in this manner. It came in a morning to this Francis' shoe, lying in it like a toad, and when he perceived it putting on his shoe, and had touched it with his foot, he being suddenly amazed asked of her what it was, and she bad him kill it and he was forthwith taken with a lameness whereof he cannot be healed.

After Elizabeth Francis had kept Sathan for 15 or 16 years, she grew tired of him. One day, she encountered Agnes Waterhouse en route to the oven and asked Waterhouse for a cake, in exchange for which she would give her "A thing that she should be the better for so long as she lived." Waterhouse agreed and gave her a cake. Francis then delivered Sathan to her and taught Waterhouse what she had been taught by Mother Eve, including feeding the cat her blood, bread and milk.

The records do not indicate whether or not testimony was given by William Auger, father of the bewitched child, nor do they explain why the confessions to murder did not lead to a death sentence. Francis was found guilty of bewitching the child and was sentenced to a year in prison.

The following day, July 27, Agnes Waterhouse, a 63-year-old widow, went on trial on the charge that she had bewitched one William Fynee, who deteriorated and died in November 1565. Agnes confessed to her guilt and acknowledged that she had also willed her cat to destroy her neighbors' cattle and geese. When she fell out with the widow Gooday, Agnes drowned the woman's cow. She also caused another neighbor to lose her curds when the woman denied Agnes's request for butter. At Agnes's command, Sathan caused another neighbor man to die. After all these acts of *maleficia*, Agnes said she rewarded Sathan, whom she kept at home as a toad. She denied that she gave the cat her blood, but court officials examined her and found numerous telltale spots on her face and nose (see WITCH'S MARK).

Agnes testified that she dispatched her daughter, Joan, to the home of Agnes Brown, a 12-year-old girl, to ask for bread and cheese. The girl refused the request. Angry, Joan went home and, in the words of her mother,

. . . remembered that her mother was wont to go up and down in her house and to call Sathan Sathan she said she would prove the like, and then she went up and down the house and called Sathan and then there came a black dog to her and asked her what she would have, and then she said she was afraid and said, I would have thee to make one Agnes Brown afraid, and then he asked her what she would give him and she said she would give him a red cock, and he said he would have none of that, and she asked him what he would have then, and he said he would have her body and soul . . ."

Agnes Brown was called to the stand. The girl testified that on the day in question she was churning butter at home when she saw "a thing like a black dog with a face like an ape, a short tail, a chain and a silver whistle about his neck, and a pair of horns on his head (see BLACK SHUCK). The dog carried the key to the milk-house door in his mouth. She asked the creature what he wanted, and he answered, "Butter," but she said no. The dog then took the key and opened the milk-house door and laid the key on a new cheese. After a while, he came out and told the girl he had made flap butter for her, and left.

Brown told her aunt, who immediately sent for a priest. The priest advised Brown to pray and call on the name of Jesus.

The next day, the dog reappeared carrying the milk-house key. Brown said, "In the name of Jesus what hast thou there?" The dog replied that she spoke "evil words" in using the name of Jesus, and left.

In subsequent visits, the dog came bearing a bean pod in its mouth and then a piece of bread. Each time, Agnes said, "In the name of Jesus what hast thou there?" and the dog spoke of "evil words" and left.

Finally, the dog showed up with a knife in its mouth and asked Agnes if she were not dead. Agnes replied she was not and thanked God. Then, she testified,

> . . . he said if I would not die that he would thrust his knife to my heart but he would make me to die, and then I said in the name of Jesus lay down thy knife, and he said he would not depart from his sweet dame's knife as yet, and then I asked of him who was his dame, and then he nodded and wagged his head to your house Mother Waterhouse . . .

The court asked Agnes Waterhouse to produce the dog and offered to let her go if she could, but the old woman claimed to have no more power over the animal.

Joan Waterhouse, 18, was tried on the charge of bewitching Brown, who claimed to become "decrepit" in her right leg and arm on July 21. Joan was found not guilty, but her mother was sentenced to die by hanging. Agnes was executed on July 29.

Just before she went to the gallows, she made a final confession:

> . . . that she had been a witch and used such execrable sorcery the space of fifteen years, and had done many abominable deeds, the which she repented earnestly and unfeignedly, and desired almighty God's forgiveness in that she had abused his most holy name by her devilish practises, and trusted to be saved by his most unspeakable mercy.

Waterhouse confessed she had sent Sathan one last time to destroy a neighbor and his goods, a tailor by the name of Wardol, but the cat returned saying Wardol's faith was so great he could not be harmed. She also admitted that she always prayed in Latin, not in English, which seemed to upset the townspeople more than her alleged witchcraft crimes, for it was considered "God's word" that prayers could be said in "the English and mother tongue that they best understand." Waterhouse replied that Sathan would not allow her to pray in English.

While Joan remained free of trouble after the trial, Elizabeth Francis encountered more difficulty with the law. She was later indicted for bewitching a woman, who fell ill for 10 days. Francis pleaded innocent but was found guilty and sentenced to another year in jail plus four confinements to the public pillory.

The second and third mass trials at Chelmsford. In 1579 four women were charged with bewitchment; one case involved another evil black dog. One woman was a repeat offender: Elizabeth Francis, who was charged with causing the slow death of one Alice Poole in 1578. Francis pleaded innocent, but this time the court was out of patience. She was hanged.

Ellen Smith was charged with bewitching a four-year-old child, who cried out, "Away with the witch!" as she died. The child's mother then saw a large black dog go out the door of her house. Smith, whose mother had been hanged as a witch, threw herself on the mercy of the court and was hanged.

A third accused witch, Alice Nokes, was also hanged, but the fourth, Margery Stanton, accused of bewitching a gelding and a cow to death, was released because of the weakness of the case against her.

Ten years later, in 1589, nine women and one man were brought up on charges of bewitchment. The bulk of the evidence against them came from children, and once again, testimony as to the existence of familiars was accepted by the court. Trial records indicate the fate of only seven of the 10: four were hanged for bewitching others to death, and three were found not guilty on charges of bewitching persons and property.

Matthew Hopkins comes to Chelmsford. The fourth major trial took place in 1645, at the instigation of England's most notorious witch finder, MATTHEW HOPKINS. Hopkins made a substantial living traveling about the countryside whipping up antiwitch hysteria. He promised to find witches, bring them to trial and get them convicted—the last was most important, for his fees were based on numbers of persons convicted. His methods relied heavily upon establishing the existence of familiars and finding witch's marks, and he relied as well on TORTURE, such as walking and sleep deprivation, to extract confessions.

It is not known exactly how many people were charged by Hopkins at Chelmsford, but the jail calendar and pamphlets published after the trials listed 38 men and women, of whom Hopkins claimed 29 were condemned. Most were hanged; several died in jail. Hopkins amassed evidence against them from 92 persons. Much of the testimony was coaxed from witnesses with plenty of suggestion added by Hopkins. For example, a child who spoke of nightmares and being bitten in bed was not bitten by fleas, which were in the bed, but by a witch's familiar, Hopkins suggested. Once the possibility of a familiar was established, Hopkins ordered a search of the suspect's premises and body. Any animal, from a toad to a rat to a cat, was immediately declared the said familiar, while any unusual marks upon the suspect's body added further proof.

For example, Hopkins succeeded in getting one Margaret Landish to admit that, while lying ill, "something" had come to her and "sucked her on her privy parts and much pained and tormented her." Landish was encouraged to speculate who sent this IMP, and she pointed the finger at Susan Cock, another defendant. The familiars soon multiplied to include a rat, mice, kittens, toads, cats, rabbits, dogs and frogs, which were alleged to have tormented many and killed children and adults. Margaret Moone admitted to harboring an army of 12 imps, which she dispatched to destroy bread in a bakery and to upset brewing. When her landlord evicted her in favor of a man who would pay a higher rent, Moone said she got her revenge by sending a plague of lice to the landlord's household. Anne Cate signed a confession admitting to sending her four mice familiars to bite the knees of a man who then died.

Hopkins went into great detail regarding the descriptions and activities of these malevolent imps, perhaps because he once claimed to have been frightened by a familiar, which he described as "a black thing, proportioned like a cat oneley it was thrice as big." It stared at him and then ran away, followed by a greyhound.

Of the 38 known accused in the Chelmsford trials, 17 were hanged; six were declared guilty but reprieved; four died in prison; and two were acquitted. The fate of the remainder is not certain.

Church and School of Wicca Founded in 1965 by Gavin and Yvonne Frost, the Church of Wicca is the oldest recognized church of WITCHCRAFT (see also WICCA) in the United States and achieved federal recognition in 1972. Located in New Bern, North Carolina, the Church runs a survival community and has a teaching arm, the School of Wicca. The Frosts have steadfastly followed their own path in the Craft, and whenever that took them out of mainstream views, it brought them much criticism from others in the neo-Pagan community. Though the Frosts are WITCHES, they do not consider themselves Pagans, because they do not worship nature or named deities. They are open about their Craft and view their work as a needed "information booth" to neo-Pagans and non-neo-Pagans alike.

Backgrounds of the Frosts. Gavin Frost was born in 1930 in Staffordshire, England, to a Welsh family. The seeds of his interest in Witchcraft were planted in childhood, during which time he spent holidays in Wales, a country steeped in folk MAGIC, witchcraft and the occult. From 1949 to 1952, he attended London University, graduating with a bachelor of science degree in mathematics and then a doctorate in physics and math. While working on infrared missiles in the Salisbury Plain for an aerospace company—a job

that required nighttime hours—Frost had ample time to explore STONEHENGE and the environs during the day. He became intrigued about the MEGALITHS and their mysterious builders and was led to the Craft.

Yvonne Frost was born Yvonne Wilson in 1931 in Los Angeles, into a "foot-washing Baptist" family. After struggling through her childhood and teen years to come to terms with the Baptist faith, Yvonne began a comparative study of religions in her early adult years to find a more compatible faith. She married in 1950, and when the marriage ended 10 years later, enrolled in Fullerton Junior College in Fullerton, California, to earn an A.A. degree in secretarial skills. She graduated in 1962.

Meanwhile, Gavin's career in the aerospace industry had taken him to Ontario, Canada, and then to California. He and Yvonne met in the 1960s in the halls of their mutual employer, a major aerospace company in Anaheim. She was involved in spiritualism, and he was involved in Witchcraft. Together they studied psychic development with a spiritualist teacher. A career move took them to St. Louis, where they pursued the Craft and were initiated into the Celtic tradition (see INITIATION).

Establishment of the School and Church. With their initiations, Gavin and Yvonne decided to espouse the Craft as well as study and practice it. They coauthored a book, *The Witch's Bible,* but could not find a publisher for it. As an alternative, they organized the material in the form of a correspondence course and advertised the "School of Wicca" in magazines. The establishment of the Church quickly followed. The Frosts married in 1970; they have one daughter.

In 1972 Gavin left his aerospace career to devote himself full-time, along with Yvonne, to the numerous activities of the Church and School. They moved to Salem, Missouri, and then to New Bern, North Carolina, in 1974–75. Both Gavin and Yvonne have doctor of divinity degrees from the Church of Wicca. Gavin serves as Archbishop and Yvonne as Bishop. They have taken vows of poverty. Fees for courses and products offered by the school cover administrative and operational expenses.

Beliefs and tenets of the Church. The roots of the Church are Welsh Celtic, coming from Gavin Frost's own Welsh heritage. Its early philosophy, as expressed in *The Witch's Bible* (finally published in 1975), created much controversy in the Craft. The Church held that the Ultimate Deity is not definable, thus downplaying the emphasis given the GODDESS by most other Witches, and maintained that the Craft is agnostic, as well as both monotheistic and polytheistic. Gods and goddesses exist in animal and vegetable

Yvonne Frost (courtesy Gavin & Yvonne Frost)

Gavin Frost (courtesy Gavin & Yvonne Frost)

form; lower-level polytheistic deities, or "stone gods," can be created in anthropomorphic form as storehouses of energy for use in magic rituals. In addition to the controversy, the Church's early view that homosexuals did not fit into the Craft, a fertility religion, was criticized as prejudiced.

Over the years, the Church's position has grown and changed. Elements of Eastern, Native American Indian and Afro-American practices have been recognized for their overlap with the Welsh Celtic tradition; and, the Church is now open to people of all sexual orientations. The Church's view of the Ultimate Deity is still genderless; God is impersonal, treating all persons alike, transcending human emotions.

The Church espouses five basic tenets of the Craft:

1. The Wiccan Rede—"If (An') it harm none, do what you will."
2. Reincarnation as an orderly system of learning. This is not a tally of "sins" and punishments. Rather, human experiences are comparable to term papers: a way of learning.
3. The Law of Attraction—What I do to other living creatures I will draw to myself. Shakespeare called this "measure for measure." It can also be expressed as "birds of a feather."
4. Power through Knowledge—Each living creature has the power (energy) within its body. The skill of directing that power can be taught and learned. Whether the power is "good" or "evil" depends on the intent in the mind of the worker.
5. Harmony—There are perceptible rhythms in the patterns of the sun, the moon and the seasons. It makes sense to learn those rhythms and to live in harmony with them.

The Church's view of REINCARNATION is that it is a steadily upward development of the soul. The Frosts feel that excessive and careless sex has led to the incarnation of numerous ill-prepared souls, one of the reasons for the increase in poverty, crime, warfare and other societal troubles around the world. They personally advocate more judicious contraception.

The use of "stone gods"—Yvonne Frost calls them "mascots"—continues to be taught for magic ritual. These anthropomorphic deities are objects temporarily charged with psychic power; the specific object chosen depends on the purpose of the ritual and/or the choice of the practitioner. Yvonne Frost often uses her Volkswagen ignition key, because of the charge-holding capability of the metal.

Craft observances in the Church are held on full-moon nights. The four great SABBATS are observed: Samhain, Imbolc, Beltane and Lugnasadh. The Church occasionally conducts services that are open to the public, but these do not include power-raising rituals.

The Church has chartered 28 independent subsidiary churches around the world. In the late 1970s the Celtic Heritage Investigation Foundation was created under the auspices of the Church to conduct "an archaeology of ideas, beliefs and practices that were lost in the BURNING TIMES when the books of shadows were destroyed." The foundation runs a survival community in the countryside, which offers land for sale to Wiccans "who want to live in a nondestructive way," and provides the site for regular Church services. Community members have worked together to build steel boats. In the event of a nuclear holocaust, the survival community believes one of the safer places on the planet will be in steel boats, from which survivors can live off the sea. By 1988, eight lots had been sold and several households established in the survival community; the Church owns 20 acres.

Other major activities of the Church include working for Wiccan rights and bringing Craft teachings to those in the military, and to prisoners in state and federal penitentiaries. The Church was among the Wiccan and Pagan organizations that fought against the HELMS AMENDMENT, an attempt by Congress to strip Wiccan and Pagan churches of their tax-exempt status. The Church publishes a bimonthly periodical, *Survival*.

The School of Wicca. The largest Witchcraft correspondence school in the United States, the School of Wicca offers numerous courses, among them Celtic Witchcraft, sorcery, Tantra, astrology, developing psychic ability, healing, use of herbs, dreams, the KABBALAH, Western sex magic, SPELLS and rituals, sacred and mysterious sites, Ufology, Egyptian and Native American Indian magic and travel in the astral realm, called *Side*.

An average of 25,000 queries about the School pour in yearly. The School has enrolled nearly 50,000 students since its beginning; it keeps its student body limited to about 5,000 on an ongoing basis. Fewer than 250 graduate each year; 10 or fewer are initiated by the Church as a result of "extremely rigorous requirements."

The School also sponsors special-interest groups, such as groups for gay Wiccans and Wiccans in the military. It markets the dozen-plus books written by the Frosts, video and audio cassettes and other special services and products, such as astrological natal charts (see ASTROLOGY), biorhythm charts and occult jewelry.

Students of the School, as well as followers of the Church, are encouraged to keep their own BOOK OF SHADOWS—or, rather, "book of lights," as Yvonne Frost prefers to call these personal handbooks, because they represent a reaching up to the deity and the light of spiritual knowledge.

Church of All Worlds One of the most important religious organizations of NEO-PAGANISM in America is the Church of All Worlds (CAW). Under the leadership of Tim Zell (who later changed his name to OTTER ZELL), CAW played a key role in the 1970s in the networking of diverse Pagan and Wiccan groups and interests, and in the defining of a Pagan as a nature lover.

Formation of the Church. The genesis of CAW began in 1961 with a group of high-school friends, led by Richard Lance Christie of Tulsa, Oklahoma, who became immersed in the ideas of Ayn Rand and the "self-actualization" concepts of Abraham Maslow. After enrolling at Westminster College in Fulton, Missouri, Christie met fellow student Zell; together, they began experiments in extrasensory perception. The Christie group, which Zell joined, read Robert A. Heinlein's science fiction novel, *Stranger in a Strange Land* (1961), which became a catalyst and inspiration for CAW.

In the novel, Valentine Michael Smith is an Earthman born on Mars and raised by Martians. He eventually returns to Earth, where he finds that his upbringing renders him literally a "stranger in a strange land." Smith forms the Church of All Worlds, organized in nests. The Church teaches "grokking," or the intuiting of the "fullness" of all things and beings, and joyful, coequal love between the sexes. God is immanent in all things; Church members greet each other with "Thou art God." In a ceremony called the "waterbrotherhood," members share water and "grok" the divine that exists in each other.

Heinlein's book had a profound impact on the Christie-Zell group. They related it to Maslow's self-actualizers, whom Maslow described as being alienated from their own culture. In 1962, following a watersharing between Zell and Christie, the group formed a waterbrotherhood called Atl, a term derived from an Aztec word for "water," and also meaning "home of our ancestors." Atl remained a loose organization dedicated to innovative political and social change and attracted up to about 100 members.

From Atl, Zell founded CAW and it evolved under

his leadership. The Church filed for incorporation in 1967 and was formally chartered on March 4, 1968, making it the first of the neo-Pagan earth religions in the United States to obtain full federal recognition as a church. It also was the first neo-Pagan organization to apply the term *Pagan* to the emerging, ecology-conscious "Earth Religions" of the 1960s.

In 1968, CAW began publishing *Green Egg* under the editorship of Zell. The journal, one of three membership newsletters (the other two, *Scarlet Flame* and *Violet Void*, were short-lived) gained a reputation as one of the leading Pagan periodicals, providing a thought-provoking forum for the exchange of ideas in the broad neo-Pagan community.

CAW initially was refused recognition as a church by the state of Missouri because of its lack of dogma concerning God, the hereafter, the fate of souls, heaven and hell, and sin and its punishment, among other matters. That decision was reversed in 1971.

Early organization and beliefs. Like Heinlein's fictional Church, the early CAW was organized around nests. The Church had nine circles of advancement, each named after a planet. One advanced by fulfilling reading and writing requirements, and participating in psychic training systems such as a martial arts discipline. The process was intended to be continuous.

The basic dogma of the CAW was that there was no dogma; the basic belief was the lack of belief. The only sin was hypocrisy, and the only crime in the eyes of the Church was interfering with another. The unofficial goal of CAW was to achieve union with all consciousness. To this end, the Church absorbed some of the concepts of an early neo-Pagan group, Feraferia, including the adoption of the word *ecopsychic*, Feraferia's term for harmony with the Earth and all things.

By 1970, CAW was placing greater emphasis on ecology and nature. The term *Pagan* was used less to identify non-Christians or anti-Christians, and more to identify nature-lovers. In 1970 Zell formulated and published what he called "the thealogy [sic] of deep ecology," concerning the interconnection of all living things to each other and to Mother Earth, a sentient being in her own right (see GAIA). Zell views mankind's reconnection with nature as critical to the survival of the planet as a whole.

Zell expresses great impatience with contemporary religions, because the sole interest of their followers is personal salvation, something so insignificant as to be unworthy of attention. In Zell's own words:

Religion means relinking. It should be about connecting one with everything else, integrating the individual into the greater scheme of things, the life

flow, the universe, the cosmic vision. The connectedness of each individual with the whole of everything is in essence the religious quest, and this is what a religion should be about. This is what the Church of All Worlds is about.

Rather than personal salvation, people should be concerned with salvation of the planet and endangered species.

Evolution of the Church. The move toward nature-consciousness eventually led to a dissolution of the relationship between CAW and Atl. Atl continues on a small scale with private groups. CAW and Feraferia formed a brief collaboration in the formation of the Council of Themis, an ecumenical alliance of neo-Pagans dedicated to achieving eco-psychic potential. After a short life, the council disbanded due to internal dissension.

By 1974 CAW had nests in more than a dozen states around the country. The same year, Zell remarried. In 1976 he and his wife, MORNING GLORY ZELL, left St. Louis, eventually settling in Eugene, Oregon, and then at the Coeden Brith land in northern California, adjacent to GWYDION PENDDERWEN'S Annwfn. With Zell gone from the central leadership, CAW suffered a great deal of internal conflict, and in large part dissolved. The *Green Egg* ceased publication in 1976, after 80 issues over nine years. The nine-circle structure was revamped. By 1978 CAW was significantly changed and no longer had the role of catalyst in the neo-Pagan movement.

CAW eventually disbanded in St. Louis. A few nests remained for awhile in other cities, such as Chicago and Atlanta; a group called the New Reformed Church of All Worlds, which had nothing in common with CAW, sprang up in Milwaukee. The focus of CAW shifted with the Zells to California, where for several years it served as an umbrella organization for subsidiaries.

CAW subsidiaries. In 1977 Morning Glory Zell founded the Ecosophical Research Association (ERA) to research arcane lore and legends. The premise of the ERA is that all life on the planet originated from a single cell and is thus integrated, and that human archetypes are often reflected in material things, animals or places. Morning Glory coined the term *ecosophy*, meaning "wisdom of the home," to define research aimed at relating such archetypes to Earth.

The first project of note for the ERA was the creation of living unicorns in 1980. In their research, the Zells noted that in early art, unicorns resembled goats more than horses. They discovered the work of W. Franklin Dove, a biologist at the University of Maine who researched horn development in the 1930s and created a "taurine," or bull unicorn. The Zells reconstructed what they said was an ancient uni-corning procedure, and applied it to baby goats. During the first week of life, the horn buds of kids are not attached yet to the skull, but are loose tissue beneath the skin. The tissue may be manipulated surgically so that the two buds become fused together and grow out as a single massive horn perpendicular to the forehead. The procedure is performed with local anesthetic.

The Zells created several unicorns, including pets Lancelot and Bedivere, and made appearances at Pagan festivals and medieval fairs. In 1984, the Zells signed a contract to lease four unicorns to Ringling Brothers/Barnum and Bailey Circus. The animals caused a great deal of controversy and were denounced by the Association for the Prevention of Cruelty to Animals (ASPCA), an accusation some consider ironic, as the Zells are animal lovers and volunteer for a wildlife rescue organization. Under the terms of their contract, the Zells were prohibited from publicly discussing the unicorns for a number of years.

Another ERA project was an expedition in 1985 to search for *ri*, supposedly unknown sea creatures associated with legends of the mermaids, off the coast of Papua New Guinea. They discovered *ri* is the local term for dugong, a type of marine mammal, and concluded that the mermaid legends relate to dugongs.

In 1978 CAW merged with Nemeton, the neo-Pagan organization founded by Pendderwen and Alison Harlow; Nemeton became CAW's publishing arm. In 1987 CAW also absorbed Forever Forests, another of Pendderwen's organizations. Annwfn, Pendderwen's 55-acre parcel in Mendocino County, was deeded to CAW, which operates it as a wilderness retreat. Lifeways, a teaching order founded and directed by ANODEA JUDITH, who also has served as president of CAW since 1986, is an outgrowth of Forever Forests, and focuses on healing, bodywork, magic, psychic development, dance, ritual, music and religion.

Another subsidiary is the Holy Order of Mother Earth (HOME), a group of individuals dedicated to magical living and working with the land.

Renaissance of CAW. By 1988 CAW had all but ceased to exist outside of Ukiah, California, where the Zells had relocated in 1985. Membership was an estimated 100–200 persons, including four active priestesses and five active priests. The Zells began implementing plans to restore CAW as a national organization, with rural and urban nest meetings, new publications, a correspondence course, summer training courses, tree plantings and new rituals and songs. Publication of the *Green Egg* was resumed in 1988.

Under the revamped circle structure, the First and Second Circles are introductory and general; the Third Circle is for those who regularly attend and begin to assist in activities; the Fourth Circle includes regular workers in the meetings, festivals and day-to-day business affairs; the Fifth Circle is for those who have advanced to some decision-making functions; the Sixth Circle is for those who are leaders and decision-makers, and who are preparing for the priesthood; and the Seventh Circle includes the priesthood. The only person to achieve the Eighth Circle is Otter Zell, who did so after a vision quest in 1976. No one has achieved the Ninth Circle, and in the eyes of CAW, it is unlikely that anyone will. The minimum requirement at each level is the traditional one year plus one day, though most members spend much longer in each circle. CAW is governed by a Council of the Third Ring, which consists of the priesthood plus representatives of the Orders, the four subsidiary organizations.

CAW sees itself as a spiritual and physical eclectic Mother for the celebration of life and Nature. Its purpose is to "weave into the web of life the development of 'Evolutionary Theologies,' " defined as "theologies that focus on evolution [which] serve to connect people to a constantly changing and evolving model of existence. These theologies create mythological frameworks that enable people to not only understand but also assist worldwide changes as they occur."

CAW recognizes the Earth Mother GODDESS and the HORNED GOD, who represent the plant and animal kingdoms, respectively. It is dedicated to the "celebration of life, the maximum actualization of human potential and the realization of ultimate individual freedom and personal responsibility in harmonious eco-psychic relationship with the total Biosphere of Holy Mother Earth." It celebrates the eight seasonal festivals recognized throughout neo-Paganism and the Craft (see SABBATS).

See also OTTER ZELL.

Church of Circle Wicca   See CIRCLE SANCTUARY.

Church of Wicca   See CHURCH AND SCHOOL OF WICCA.

Circe   In Greek mythology, a sorceress renowned for her enchantments, who turned Odysseus's men into swine. Described by Homer as fair-haired, she was sometimes said to be the daughter of HECATE, patron goddess of WITCHCRAFT and MAGIC. Homer said she controlled fate and the forces of creation and destruction with braids in her hair (see KNOTS). She is seen both as a moon goddess—because she lived in the west of the isle of Aeaea—and as a goddess of degrading love.

Circe was married to the king of Sarmaritans, whom she poisoned. She was exiled to Aeaea, which means "wailing," built herself a palace and learned magic. She cast a spell over the entire island so that anyone who came there would be turned into an animal (see SPELLS).

Odysseus's men were turned into swine, but Odysseus escaped with the help of a magical herb, *moly*, given to him by HERMES. He forced Circe to restore his men to their human form. Nevertheless, he was so taken with her that he spent a year with her. She was slain by Telemachus, who married her daughter, Cassiphone.

Circle See CIRCLE SANCTUARY.

circle, magic See MAGIC CIRCLE.

Circle Sanctuary (also known as Circle; formerly known as the Church of Circle Wicca)
One of the most active and well-established ecumenical neo-Pagan centers in America is Circle, a Wiccan church with headquarters on a nature preserve and herb farm between Mt. Horeb and Barneveld, Wisconsin (see NEO-PAGANISM; WICCA; WITCHCRAFT). Circle was formed in 1974 in Madison, Wisconsin, by SELENA FOX with the help of Jim Alan and a small group of neo-Pagans. Fox continues to direct its activities with her husband, Dennis Carpenter.

Circle originally was formed as an informal COVEN, after Fox conceived the idea, name and logo in a meditation. Fox and Alan drew on their musical backgrounds to create a body of Pagan ritual chants and songs, which continue to be used by Wiccan and neo-Pagan groups around the country. Circle took an active, leadership role in the growing neo-Pagan community, providing a national and international contact service, organizing and coordinating gatherings and disseminating information to individuals and groups within the movement, the general public and the media.

The networking activity led to the formation of Circle Network and to the incorporation in 1978 of Circle Sanctuary as a nonprofit religious organization and a legally recognized church at the state level. A newsletter, *Circle Network News*, was started, and it remains the largest neo-Pagan journal. In 1980 Circle was recognized as a church at the federal level.

In the fall of 1980 Circle organized the Pagan Spirit Alliance, a special network within Circle Network that is devoted to fostering friendship among Wiccans and other neo-Pagans through the mail. Beginning in 1981 Circle began sponsoring the Inter-

national Pagan Spirit Gathering, held each year at summer solstice at a private campground in Wisconsin. The church also coordinates or assists other Pagan gatherings held around the United States.

During its early years, Circle was based in the various homes of Fox and Alan. In 1983 the church used its own funds to purchase a 200-acre nature preserve in rural hill country west of Madison. The land has a rich spiritual heritage and includes sites once used by ancient Indians. The region is said in local legends to be enchanted with trolls, FAIRIES and nature spirits. Sightings of ghosts, spirits, Bigfoot, UFOs and other unusual phenomena are often reported.

Numerous religious, educational, therapeutic and spiritual training activities take place on, or are coordinated from, the Circle Sanctuary land. As ministers, Fox, Carpenter and others perform weddings (see HANDFASTING), child blessings, funerals and other "life passage" ceremonies at Circle and all over the United States. Wiccan SABBATS, full-moon ceremonies and new-moon healing circles take place on the land.

Educational activities include week-long training programs—a school for Priestesses for women and WICCAN SHAMANISM training for women and men. Both programs include all-night vision quests on Circle land. Fox and Carpenter give numerous lectures, workshops and media programs, both on the land and around the country.

The church also sponsors organic farming, gardening and wild-plant foraging activities.

Over the years, Circle Network, which includes "Wiccans, Neo-Pagans, Goddess Worshippers, Shamans, Druids, Seers, Eco-Feminists, Native American Medicine People, Norse Religionists, Gnostics, Mystics, Hermetic Magicians, Pantheists and others," has grown to include thousands of individuals and hundreds of groups. Members come from the United States, Canada and more than 50 other countries.

The Pagan Strength Web network includes Pagan religious freedom activists who help Pagans who are being harassed or discriminated against because of their religion. Fox and Circle played leading roles in 1985 in a lobbying campaign against the HELMS AMENDMENT, which would have prohibited Wiccan churches from having nonprofit, tax-free status.

Zoning Challenges. Zoning laws and codes have been used against various neo-Pagan organizations by local people who object to the organizations' presence and/or activities. Circle Santuary has fought one of the most visible legal battles against such zoning. In 1984 the county zoning administrator paid a visit to Circle Sanctuary as a result of calls from local citizens claiming that Circle was a cult of "Devil-worshippers" and was operating a commercial print shop on the land. Neither rumor was true. In an attempt to dispel community fears, Fox and Alan met with local government officials.

Two years later, in 1986, zoning issues were raised by local government. The county zoning administrator informed Circle that the zoning code had been violated by remodeling done to the barn—despite the fact that Circle had been told by local government in 1983 that no permit was needed to remodel the barn as long as it was an existing structure. Circle decided to hire an attorney and apply for a conditional-use permit for a church in an agricultural district. Circle was aided by the Wisconsin branch of the American Civil Liberties Union.

A lengthy fight ensued, involving hearings and negotiations. Because of the religious overtones—some local folk seemed determined to cling to the idea that Circle was a satanic organization—the hearings became known as "the Witch Trials of Barneveld" and attracted a gread deal of media attention.

In January 1988 the county and town boards granted Circle a conditional-use permit to operate as a church, marking the first time in the United States that a local government legally recognized a Witchcraft organization in a public hearing. Other zoning issues were raised, however, leaving Circle Sanctuary facing more protracted legal battles.

Cleary, Bridget   See FAIRY WITCH OF CLONMEL.

Clonmel, Fairy Witch of   See FAIRY WITCH OF CLONMEL.

Clutterbuck, Old Dorothy (1880–1951)   High priestess of a COVEN of hereditary WITCHES in the New Forest of England, who initiated GERALD B. GARDNER into WITCHCRAFT in 1939. Little was known about Clutterbuck for many years, prompting some outside observers to speculate that she had never existed at all but was fabricated by Gardner. In 1980 DOREEN VALIENTE, English high priestess and an early initiate to Gardner's coven, undertook a search of records to prove that Old Dorothy Clutterbuck had indeed lived and died.

Clutterbuck was born January 19, 1880, in Bengal, to Thomas St. Quintin Clutterbuck, a captain (later major) in the Indian Local Forces, and Ellen Anne Clutterbuck. The Clutterbucks had been married in Bengal in 1877 at the ages of 38 and 20, respectively.

Virtually nothing is known about Clutterbuck's early years. At some point, she went to live in England, where she enjoyed an affluent life. Gardner became acquainted with her through the Fellowship of Crotona, a group that opened "The First Rosicrucian Theatre in England" in 1938 in the New Forest region, and performed plays with occult themes. Some of the members of the Fellowship revealed themselves to Gardner as Witches. In 1939, just after the start of World War II, Clutterbuck initiated Gardner in her home (see INITIATION). She was considered "a lady of note in the district" and had a large house, and a pearl necklace valued at 5,000 pounds, which she liked to wear often.

Clutterbuck died in 1951, leaving a considerable estate of more than 60,000 pounds.

Valiente began her search near Samhain (All Hallow's Eve), 1980. On the actual night of Samhain, Valiente reports that she and three other Witches met in a wood in southern England and called upon Clutterbuck's spirit to show a sign that she wished Valiente to succeed in her search. An answer interpreted as affirmative came when the lantern at the south quarter of the MAGIC CIRCLE suddenly tipped over and broke its glass. Valiente also heard the deceased Gardner calling her name. It took Valiente two years to trace the documents proving the existence of Clutterbuck.

cocks   Symbols of light and goodness, cocks have been favored birds of SACRIFICE to the gods in various religions throughout history. In many cultures, the cock is sacred and is associated in particular with sun deities; it has the power to banish evil. The cock is a bird of omen (see ORACLES), both of luck (in Wales) and death and evil (in Hungary). It is also a symbol of fertility and has been used in DIVINATION for centuries around the world.

In surviving customs of paganism, the cock is one embodiment of the corn-spirit, who guards the corn crop until it can be harvested. The last sheaf of corn is variously called the cock-sheaf, cock, harvest-cock, autumn-hen and harvest-hen. Traditionally, a cock is sacrificially killed at the end of harvest, in order to ensure a bountiful crop the following season. According to some customs, the cock is bound up in the cock-sheaf and then run through with a spit. Sometimes it is buried in the fields up to its neck and then beheaded. Or, it is whipped, beaten or stoned to death. It is either cooked, or the flesh is thrown out and the skin and feathers saved to be sprinkled on the new fields in the spring.

During the witch-hunts, WITCHES were said to sacrifice cocks as an offense to God. The cock represented God, light and goodness, the very things that the Devil's legions hated. Accused Irish witch Dame ALICE KYTELER in the 14th century supposedly sacrificed cocks to her familiar (see FAMILIARS) at a CROSSROADS. Witches also were said to sacrifice cocks over

Witches sacrificing cock and snake to raise hailstorm (Ulrich Molitor, *De Ianijs et phitonicius mulieribus*, 1489)

their cauldrons as part of their spells to raise rain and storms (see STORM RAISING).

The witches' SABBATS went on all night until cockcrow, at which point the revelers scattered. MONTAGUE SUMMERS observes in *The History of Witchcraft and Demonology* (1926):

> That the crowing of a cock dissolves enchantments is a tradition of extremest antiquity. The Jews believed that the clapping of a cock's wing will make the power of demons ineffectual and break magic spells . . . . The rites of Satan ceased [at dawn] because the Holy Office of the Church began. In the time of S. Benedict Matins and Lauds were recited at dawn and were actually often known as *Gallicinium*, Cock-crow.

NICHOLAS REMY, 16th-century French demonologist and witch prosecutor, said that a witch confessed to him that cocks were hated by all witches and sorcerers. The cock heralds the dawn, which brings light to the sins of the night and rouses men to the worship of God.

Cocks were said to crow at the birth of Christ and at his death. During the Middle Ages, the cock became an important Christian symbol of vigilance and resurrection, and earned a place at the top of church steeples, domes and buildings.

Cocks are sacrificed in VODOUN, SANTERÍA, MACUMBA, various animistic religions and SATANISM, but *not* in NEO-PAGANISM or neo-Pagan WITCHCRAFT, which do not condone sacrifice.

Cole, Ann (17th century)   The curious possession in 1662 of Ann Cole of Hartford, Connecticut, astonished her townspeople and led to the execution of an accused witch. Cole suddenly seemed to acquire preternatural knowledge of the malicious activities of the accused witch, who was a stranger to her. INCREASE MATHER described Cole as "a person of real piety and integrity" in his account of the tale, in *An Essay for the Recording of Illustrious Providences* (1684).

In 1662 Cole was living in the house of her father—described as "a godly man"—when she began having bizarre fits, "wherein her Tongue was improved by a *Daemon* to express things which she herself knew nothing of," Mather wrote. Sometimes the discourses went on for hours. Cole named persons and described how they intended to carry out "mischievous designs" against herself and others, by afflicting bodies and spoiling names.

At times Cole lapsed into gibberish. Then she began speaking English with a precise Dutch accent, describing how a woman who lived next to a Dutch family had been afflicted by a strange pinching of her arms at night.

One of the persons named by Cole was a "lewd and ignorant" woman named Greensmith, who was in jail on suspicion of WITCHCRAFT. Greensmith had denied the charges against her, but when confronted by a written account of Cole's discourses, she was astonished and confessed everything.

Greensmith said the DEVIL had first appeared to her in the form of a deer or fawn, skipping about her so that she would not be afraid, gaining her confidence. She had sex with the Devil on numerous occasions and had often accompanied him to SABBATS. She denied entering into a DEVIL'S PACT but said that the Devil had told her they would attend a merry sabbat at Christmastime, during which she would sign a pact with him. Greensmith also said that WITCHES had met at a place not far from her house and that some of them arrived in the shapes of animals and crows.

The confession was sufficient to convict Greensmith, and she was executed, probably by hanging.

Her husband was also put to death, even though he said he was not guilty of any wrongdoing. The court apparently felt that since he was the woman's husband, he could not help but be involved in her evil activities.

A man and a woman also named by Cole were given the SWIMMING test of being bound and thrown into water. They neither floated nor sank but bobbed like buoys, half in and half out of the water. A witness, protesting that anyone bound with their hands to their feet would not sink (and therefore be guilty), underwent the test himself. He was lowered gently into the water, not thrown in as were the accused, and promptly sank.

It is not known how many others named by Cole were tried and executed for witchcraft; some fled Hartford and were never seen again. Cole eventually recovered and had no more fits. She resumed her life as "a serious Christian."

cone of power   In neo-Pagan WITCHCRAFT, psychic energy that is raised and directed in MAGIC and HEALING.

Raising a cone of power is done within a MAGIC CIRCLE. It calls for coveners to focus on a desired goal, which is visualized in a symbol or image upon which everyone agrees. The power is raised usually through dancing, CHANTING, hand-clapping, drumming or cord magic (see KNOTS). As the coveners dance around the circle, the tempo increases, and the cone of power begins to rise over the circle, which forms the base of the cone. To those with developed psychic ability, the energy is visible as a shimmering silver or blue-silver light. When the high priestess or high priest senses that the energy is at its peak, she or he instructs the coveners to release it in a burst toward the goal. Timing is crucial; otherwise, the spell misfires. According to GERALD B. GARDNER, the cone of power was one of the "old ways" of WITCHES. He described it as a COVEN dancing in a circle around a fire or candle (see CANDLES), then linking hands and rushing toward the fire until everyone was exhausted or someone fainted, which indicated the energy had been sent off successfully. It is not certain exactly how old the cone-of-power custom is, but projection of magical energy toward a desired goal by a variety of means is an ancient, universal practice.

The cone shape itself has symbolic significance in Witchcraft. In parts of ancient Syria, the cone was the symbol of ASTARTE, the Phoenician goddess of motherhood, fertility and war. Tall, conical hats are traditionally associated with magicians and Witches (see HATS). The cone also is associated with the circle, symbol of the sun, unity, eternity and rebirth, and with the triangle, which has associations with the ELEMENTS and pyramids, and represents the upward spiritual aspirations of all things. The triangle also represents the number three, an important number in Witchcraft for its association with the Triple Goddess.

According to Gardner, perhaps the most famous use of a cone of power took place in England in 1940 on Lammas Day, August 1, one of the most important Witches' SABBATS. In 1940 there was a great deal of fear in England that Hitler's armies would invade British soil. On that day, all the covens in southern England gathered in the New Forest for "Operation Cone of Power," to send Hitler a telepathic message to stay out of England. Hundreds of Witches, among them Gardner and his high priestess, OLD DOROTHY CLUTTERBUCK, assembled skyclad (nude) and chanted against Hitler and his generals, trying telepathically to implant the thoughts, "you cannot cross the sea" and "not able to come." The Nazis did not invade, but whether or not the cone of power had any influence on that will never be certain.

It is also said that the same method worked in the 1700s against Napoleon, and in 1588 against the Spanish Armada. The Armada, launched by Philip II to invade England, consisted of 130 ships, which were repeatedly buffeted by storms. Storms delayed the launching of the fleet. Then, after the English fleet inflicted serious damage on the ships and scattered them, the Spaniards fled north, sailing around Scotland and Ireland in heavy storms. The Armada suffered the loss of about half its ships (see STORM RAISING).

conjure men   See WITCH DOCTORS.

corpse light   See JACK-O'-LANTERN.

Council of American Witches   An alliance of WITCHES from different traditions, which was active in 1973–74 in an effort to define the principles of WICCA. The effort was spearheaded by CARL WESCHCKE, a Wiccan priest and president of Llewellyn Publications in St. Paul, Minnesota. Weschcke believed that the formulation of a common set of principles and definitions would help dispel myths about WITCHCRAFT and distinguish it from SATANISM in the eyes of the public and press.

Under the sponsorship of Llewellyn Publications, 73 witches from various Witchcraft traditions convened in Minneapolis in the fall of 1973 and formed the Council. Weschcke was named chair. A newsletter, *Touchstone*, was inaugurated, and the Council began collecting statements of principles from Wiccan traditions around the country. Differences were many, but by April 1974 the Council was able to unify them into a general set of 13 principles. Weschchke drafted "The Principles of Wiccan Belief," which many Witches continue to endorse, and which were later incorporated into one or more editions of the handbook for chaplains in the U.S. Army.

In adopting the principles, the Council stated:

> In seeking to be inclusive, we do not wish to open ourselves to the destruction of our group by those on self-serving power trips, or to philosophies and practices contradictory to those principles. In seeking to exclude those whose ways are contradictory to ours, we do not want to deny participation with us to any who are sincerely interested in our knowledge and beliefs, regardless of race, color, sex, age, national or cultural origins or sexual preference.

Shortly after this landmark action, the Council disbanded, due in part to continuing differences among traditions.

The principles of Wiccan belief are as follows:

1. We practice rites to attune ourselves with the natural rhythm of life forces marked by the phases of the Moon and the seasonal Quarters and Cross Quarters.

2. We recognize that our intelligence gives us a unique responsibility toward our environment. We seek to live in harmony with Nature, in ecological balance offering fulfillment to life and consciousness within an evolutionary concept.

3. We acknowledge a depth of power far greater than that apparent to the average person. Because it is far greater than ordinary it is sometimes called "supernatural," but we see it as lying within that which is naturally potential to all.

4. We conceive of the Creative Power in the universe as manifesting through polarity—as masculine and feminine—and that this same Creative Power lies in all people, and functions through the interaction of the masculine and the feminine. We value neither above the other, knowing each to be supportive of the other. We value sex as pleasure, as the symbol and embodiment of life, and as one of the sources of energies used in magickal practice and religious worship.

5. We recognize both outer worlds and inner, or psychological, worlds sometimes known as the Spiritual World, the Collective Unconsciousness, Inner Planes, etc.—and we see in the inter-action of these two dimensions the basis for paranormal phenomena and magickal exercises. We neglect neither dimension for the other, seeing both as necessary for our fulfillment.

6. We do not recognize any authoritarian hierarchy, but do honor those who teach, respect those who share their greater knowledge and wisdom, and acknowledge those who have courageously given of themselves in leadership.

7. We see religion, magick and wisdom in living as being united in the way one views the world and lives within it—a world view and philosophy of life which we identify as *Witchcraft—the Wiccan Way.*

8. Calling oneself "Witch" does not make a Witch—but neither does heredity itself, nor the collecting of titles, degrees and initiations. A Witch seeks to control the forces within her/himself that make life possible in order to live wisely and well without harm to others and in harmony with nature.

9. We believe in the affirmation and fulfillment of life in a continuation of evolution and development of consciousness giving meaning to the Universe we know and our personal role within it.

10. Our only animosity towards Christianity, or towards any other religion or philosophy of life, is to the extent that its institutions have claimed to be "the only way" and have sought to deny freedom to others and to suppress other ways of religious practice and belief.

11. As American Witches, we are not threatened by debates on the history of the Craft, the origins of various terms, the legitimacy of various aspects of different traditions. We are concerned with our present and our future.

12. We do not accept the concept of absolute evil, nor do we worship any entity known as "Satan" or "the Devil," as defined by Christian tradition. We do not seek power through the suffering of others, nor accept that personal benefit can be derived only by denial to another.

13. We believe that we should seek within Nature that which is contributory to our health and well-being.

coven   The formal organization and working unit of WITCHES. The purpose, structure and activities of a coven have differed at different times in history. The origin of the word *coven* is not clear. Most likely, it derives from the verb *convene*, which includes in its variants *convent*, which once referred both to a religious meeting and the place of a religious meeting. Chaucer used the term *covent* in *Canterbury Tales* to refer to the meeting of 13 people. The term *covine* was used in 1662 in the trials of the Auldearne, Scotland, witches to describe the witches' organizations. One of the witches, ISOBEL GOWDIE, likened the covines to squads. The witches were divided into these subdivisions because there were so many of them, Gowdie said.

Sir Walter Scott, in *Letters on Demonology and Witchcraft* (1830), notes that the term *Covine tree* was the common name for the tree that usually stood in front of a castle, probably so named because the lord of the castle met his guests there:

> He is the lord of the hunting horn
> And king of the Covine tree;
> He's well loo'd in the western waters
> But best of his ain minnie.

MONTAGUE SUMMERS referred to covens as *conventicles*, from the Latin *coventus*, (assembly or coming together) and also includes *covey, coeven* and *curving* as variations of the word.

Historical Beliefs about Covens

The existence of covens. References in literature to covens of witches date back as early as the 12th century. In *Polycraticus*, John of Salisbury describes organized groups of witches carrying on at wild SABBATS but adds the caveat that they are merely deceptions created by the DEVIL and are not to be believed. A story popular in the late Middle Ages concerns an episode in the life of St. Germain, the bishop of Auxerre (390–448), in which he encounters villagers preparing a dinner for "the good women who walked about at night." St. Germain, expressing the dominant view of the Catholic Church, discredited these sabbats of covens as deceits of the Devil.

It was not until the Renaissance that the existence of covens was taken more seriously. Accused witches were tortured into confessing that they were members of secret, subversive organizations, and were forced to implicate others (see TORTURE).

British anthropologist MARGARET A. MURRAY held that covens were far more prevalent and organized than the Church was willing to believe, though there is little evidence to support that contention. It is possible that witches included worshippers of the old pagan religions, who still clung together in secret groups, but many accused witches brought down by the Inquisition were solitary old women, outcasts from society, who probably possessed special healing or clairvoyant powers.

The earliest reference to a coven in a witch trial occurred in 1324 in Kilkenny, Ireland, when Dame ALICE KYTELER was accused of being part of a 13-member group. In the 16th and 17th centuries, more witches, though not a great number of them, confessed to having joined covens. Most such confessions probably were led by the inquisitors, who automatically sought to cast as wide a net as possible. By the time witch-hunting died down in the early 1700s, the concept of the coven was firmly established.

Among modern neo-Pagan Witches, it was once commonly believed that WITCHCRAFT had descended unbroken from prehistoric times as a Pagan religion. The existence of the Cave of Bats, discovered in Spain in the 19th century, was cited as evidence of this theory. An inner cavern appears to have been a Neolithic burial chamber, in which 58 skeletons were found. Most interesting was a female skeleton, seated against one wall, surrounded by a neat semicircle of 12 skeletons. The central female had been clothed in a tunic skin and a necklace of seashells with a boar's-tusk pendant. Beside the 12 skeletons were bags of woven esparto grass, perhaps prehistoric charm bags. Scattered about on the floor were the remains of poppy heads. The scene suggests some sort of ritual activity, and possibly a covenlike organization.

Some Witches claim to be members of covens that date back generations. SYBIL LEEK's New Forest coven claimed to be 800 years old. Some covens may indeed be old, but there is little evidence to indicate that covens have existed in unbroken lines throughout history. As of the 1980s, most Witches had abandoned the unbroken-tradition theory in favor of the view that modern Witchcraft reflects a resurrection of old beliefs and practices.

Number in a coven. Traditionally, the number of Witches in a coven is supposed to be 13: 12 followers plus a leader. Murray stated this unequivocally in *The God of the Witches* (1931), concerning medieval covens:

> The number in a coven never varied, there were always thirteen, i.e., twelve members and the god . . . . In the witch-trials the existence of covens appears to have been well known, for it is observable how the justices and the priests or ministers of religion press the unfortunate prisoners to inculpate their associates, but after persons to the number of thirteen or any multiple of thirteen had been brought to trial, or had at least been accused, no further trouble was taken in the matter.

The leader was believed to be either the Devil himself or a person, usually a man, who, witch-hunters said, represented the Devil and dressed himself in animal skins and horns at sabbats.

The evidence for a constancy of 13 members is slim, however, and is referenced in only 18 trials (see THIRTEEN). At her trial in 1662 Isobel Gowdie stated, "Ther ar threttein persons in ilk Coeven." In 1673 accused witch Ann Armstrong of Newcastle-on-Tyne stated she knew of "five coveys consisting of thirteen persons in every covey," and of a large meeting or sabbat of many witches, and "every thirteen of them had a divell with them in sundry shapes."

Structure and activities of a coven. In *The History of Witchcraft and Demonology* (1926), Summers defined covens as:

> . . . bands of men and women, apparently under the discipline of an officer, all of whom for convenience' sake belonged to the same district. Those who belonged to a coven were, it seems from the evidence at the trials, bound to attend the weekly Esbat. The arrest of one member of a coven generally led to the implication of the rest.

COTTON MATHER, in writing on the Salem witchcraft trials of 1692, said "the witches do say that they form themselves much after the manner of Congregational Churches, and that they have a Baptism, and a Supper, and Officers among them, abominably resembling those of our Lord."

Murray also drew on witch trials to portray the alleged organization of a coven. According to old testimony, the titular head of each coven was the *grandmaster*, or deity worshipped. Most likely, this was a pagan deity with horns (see HORNED GOD), but in the INQUISITION, it became the Devil himself. Usually, the god/Devil was represented by a substitute man or woman who conducted rituals in the god/Devil's name. At sabbats, when the god/Devil was present in person, the grandmasters then became *officers*.

Each coven also had a *summoner*, a person who secretly gave notice to members regarding the next meeting time and location. Sometimes the officer and summoner were the same person; not uncommonly, this person was a Christian priest who still participated in pagan ceremonies. The duties of the officer/summoner included keeping attendance records, scouting for recruits and presenting initiates to the god/Devil.

Covens also had a high-ranking position called *maiden*, a comely young lass with primarily ceremonial duties. The maiden served mostly as consort and hostess at the right hand of the grandmaster, or Devil, at sabbats and led the dance with him. The witches of Auldearne, Scotland, in 1662 claimed to have a "Maiden of the Covine," described in Sir Walter Scott's *Letters on Demonology and Witchcraft* as "a girl of personal attractions, whom Satan placed beside himself, and treated with particular attention, which greatly provoked the spite of the old hags, who felt themselves insulted by the preference." In some accounts, this maiden was also called the *Queen of the Sabbat*.

Murray contended that JOAN OF ARC was a witch and that her appellation "the Maid" therefore had special significance.

Each coven was independent yet supposedly was linked to other covens in a region through a cooperative network. In the trial of the North Berwick witches in Scotland in 1591, three covens allegedly worked together to try to murder King James VI of Scotland (see NORTH BERWICK WITCHES). There is scant other historical evidence for formal networks of covens.

The Coven in neo-Pagan Witchcraft

Existence and formation of covens. Many modern Witches belong to covens, although it is estimated that many more practice alone as solitaries (see SOLITARY). The number of covens is unknown, for most exist quietly, some even secretly, in order to avoid harassment and problems.

Witches do not proselytize or seek converts; prospective joiners must seek out a coven and ask for admission. Novices are admitted at the coven's discretion; not everyone who wants to join a coven is admitted. Applicants are screened and trained in a "training circle" or PAGAN WAY group, traditionally for a year and a day. They are evaluated as to their reasons for wanting to enter the Craft and how well they fit with the group. A coven is a close working group, the effectiveness of which depends heavily upon the rapport and trust of its members. Persons who are interested in using magic for manipulation or for evil purposes, or who are entranced by the "shock effect" of being able to say they are Witches, generally are rejected. Successful candidates are those who are interested in using the powers of the Craft for healing and who are seeking spiritual development through worship of the Goddess and other Pagan beliefs. Candidates who are accepted are formally initiated into the Craft and the coven.

Sybil Leek was of the opinion that American covens have not screened applicants as carefully as covens in England and Europe, which has resulted in many "pseudo-covens." In the 1960s and 1970s, it was faddish in America to start or belong to a coven. Some were based on solid foundations, but many were little more than social groups. With the 1980s, this fad passed, and most covens now in existence are serious religious and/or magical working groups.

Most covens follow a tradition, which is similar to a denomination in Christianity. A tradition has its own BOOK OF SHADOWS, which is a set of rules, ethics, beliefs, rituals, songs and administrative procedures for running a coven. The dominant traditions are Gardnerian and Alexandrian, named after English Witches GERALD B. GARDNER and ALEXANDER SANDERS. It is customary for new covens to be formed by "hiving off" from existing covens. Some witches start their own eclectic covens.

Modern Witchcraft is fluid, and virtually any witch can start a new tradition, as well as a coven. Smaller ones abound, even one-coven traditions. Some of them are short-lived. Some covens choose to be eclectic, blending various traditions together or incorporating elements of SHAMANISM or other religions. Even within traditions, covens vary in the emphasis given to aspects of the Craft (see WITCHCRAFT).

Sometimes covens and traditions are started by those who are denied entrance into an existing coven. Sanders apparently started his own coven after failing to gain entry to a number of established covens.

Even though part of a tradition, each coven is an

autonomous unit. Some covens join together and incorporate in organizations that serve as sources for networking or as advocates in legal issues (see COVENANT OF THE GODDESS).

The regular, working meeting of a coven is the ESBAT or *circle,* which usually occurs at the full moon but may be set at other lunar phases. Covens also meet to celebrate eight seasonal sabbats. The *coven-stead* is the location of a coven's temple and the place where a coven meets. It may be an outdoor site or the basement or spare room in the home of one of the coven members. The covenstead is the epicenter of a circular area called the *covendom,* which extends out one league, or three miles, in all directions, and in which all coven members are supposed to live. Traditionally, covendoms are not to overlap, but this rule is not strictly observed.

Number in a coven. Gardner considered 13 to be the ideal number of a coven, which would include six "perfect couples" of men and women, plus a leader. Ideally, the couples would be married or be lovers, in order to produce the best harmony and results in magic. Leek also said that all New Forest covens had 13 members: six men and six women plus a high priestess.

Thirteen is traditional, but not a rigid rule. Many covens vary in size from three to about 20 members. Size is important, for too few members means ineffective magic. Too many become unwieldy. Some Witches consider nine to 13 the ideal range. Much depends upon the group rapport and harmony.

Most covens have both male and female members, which is in keeping with the male-female polarity required for a fertility religion. Some covens are politically feminist or gay and are all-women or all-men.

History of a coven. Members of a coven are called *coveners.* All are priests and priestesses, save the leaders, who are the high priestess and/or high priest. Most traditions have a three-degree system of advancement that calls for a minimum of a year and a day at each degree. As the Witch advances, she or he learns more secrets of the Craft and is entrusted to perform higher-level duties and rituals. Third-degree Witches are eligible to become high priestesses and high priests.

In most covens, the high priestess is the ranking leader of a coven and represents the GODDESS. In England, the high priestess is sometimes called the *magistra.* If a coven has both male and female members, the high priestess shares leadership with a high priest; however, she is still viewed as the titular head of the coven. A Witch may become high priestess by leaving a coven to start her own, or by group consensus, should a high priestess leave a coven or step down. The high priestess is responsible for the smooth running of the coven, which can only be accomplished when all members work in spiritual harmony with one another. Besides good leadership qualities, the high priestess is supposed to possess strong psychic powers and sharp intuition. Much of a coven's magic work involves the sensitive use of psychic abilities. The high priestess must be able to build and shape the group psychic powers and sense when they are at their peaks. In addition, she helps individual coveners develop their own psychic abilities. It is usually the role of the high priestess to cast and purify the MAGIC CIRCLE and invoke the Goddess and the spirits of the four quarters and ELEMENTS. She also directs the chants, rituals and magic work. The high priestess may "pass the wand" or delegate these duties from time to time to other coveners, as part of their training.

The high priest represents the Horned God, who is the consort to the Goddess and performs certain rituals with the high priestess. In most traditions, only high priests and high priestesses may initiate others into the craft; men initiate women and women initiate men (see INITIATION).

There are no appointed or elected "kings" and "queens" of Witches, though some individuals have adopted those titles. A high priestess from whose coven others have hived off is entitled to be called a *Witch Queen,* which is entirely different.

Many covens have a maiden, who is at least a second-degree Witch and is the personal assistant of the high priestess. The maiden can substitute for the high priestess in certain tasks; she also handles various administrative duties. She is likely to be in charge of a "training circle" of potential initiates. According to tradition, the office of maiden is held by one woman, until she succeeds the high priestess or leaves to form her own coven. In some covens, the position may be rotated as a means of training for third degree.

Many covens have a summoner, also called a *fetch,* who is in charge of scheduling meetings and notifying members.

Covenant of the Goddess A nonprofit federation of autonomous covens (see COVEN) and SOLITARY witches based in Berkeley, California, which works to foster good relations in the neo-Pagan and Craft community; to gain recognition of WITCHCRAFT as a legitimate religion; and to end harassment and persecution of WITCHES. The Covenant of the Goddess (COG) was formed in 1975 by 13 covens and a number of solitaries. By the 1980s it had become national in focus, with members in at least 15 states. COG recognizes the autonomy of each coven and the variations in Craft law among various traditions. The organization does not shape or direct policy. It does have a code of ethics, which states, among other things that witches must follow the WICCAN REDE: "An' it harm none, do what ye will"; that witches may not charge fees for initiations or initiate training (see INITIATION); that Witches may charge "reasonable fees" to the public; and that Witches must respect the autonomy of other Witches. COG has a governing council and conducts an annual members' meeting. Membership is open to all covens and individual Witches.

cowan In neo-Pagan WITCHCRAFT, the term for a non-Witch, a person who has not been initiated into the Craft (see INITIATION). The word is an old Scottish term for a mason who has learned the trade without serving an apprenticeship. Cowans generally are not allowed to attend circles, or ESBATS, the regular meetings of covens in which magical work is performed. Cowans may be invited to attend SABBATS, the seasonal festivals.

Craft name It is customary in neo-Pagan WITCHCRAFT to adopt a new name upon INITIATION, which reflects one's new identity as Witch (see WITCHES). A Witch may keep a Craft name secret and use it only in silent meditation or may disclose it only to members of the COVEN. Some Witches choose to use their Craft names publicly, while others have both private and public Craft names. Some covens have strict rules against disclosing Craft names to outsiders.

There are two main reasons for the secrecy surrounding Craft names: lingering prejudice against Witches, and age-old beliefs about the power of names (see NAMES OF POWER). In many cultures, it is believed that knowing a person's name gives another magical power over that person. Many old SPELLS involve the writing of the victim's name upon paper or an object.

During the witch hysteria, witch-hunters and inquisitors spread the notion that witches were given new names by the DEVIL after he had signed them to pacts and baptized them. In neo-Pagan Witchcraft, Craft names have nothing to do with the Devil, who is neither recognized nor worshipped by Witches.

Craft names are highly individualistic. They may reflect personal aspirations, ethnic heritage or an aspect of a deity with whom the Witch identifies. A Witch selects a Craft name through meditation, study or oracular DIVINATION. Some use trances to receive a name bestowed by the GODDESS. Others are given names by their high priestess. Witches may change their Craft names as they advance from first degree to third degree, the levels of knowledge in major traditions, or as their sense of identity and purpose changes.

crosses Crosses are among the oldest AMULETS in the world, predating Christianity by many centuries.

In the commonest form of a cross, all four arms are of equal length rather than in a T-shape. Crosses have been associated with sun deities and the heavens, and in ancient times they may have represented divine protection and prosperity. Crosses also are represented by the Y-shaped Tree of Life, the world-axis placed in the center of the universe, the bridge between the earth and the cosmos, the physical and the spiritual.

In Christianity, the cross transcends the status of amulet to become symbolic of the religion and of the suffering of Christ's crucifixion; yet, it still retains aspects of an amulet, protecting against the forces of evil. Even before the crucifixion of Christ, the cross was a weapon against the dark forces. According to legend, when Lucifer declared war upon God in an attempt to usurp his power, his army scattered God's angels twice. God sent to his angels a Cross of Light on which were inscribed the names of the Trinity. Upon seeing this cross, Lucifer's forces lost strength and were driven into hell.

Early Christians made the sign of the cross for divine protection and as a means of identification to each other. In the 4th century, Christ's wooden cross was allegedly found in excavations in Jerusalem by Empress Helena, mother of Constantine I. It is said that Helena found three buried crosses at the site of the crucifixion but did not know which belonged to Christ. She tested all three with the corpse of a man. Two crosses had no effect upon the body, but the third caused it to come to life. Helena sent part of the cross to Constantine, who sent a portion to Rome, where it is still preserved in the Vatican. The rest of the cross Helena reburied. Bits of the cross that were fashioned into amulets became highly prized.

As the Church grew in power, so did its symbol, the cross. According to belief, nothing unholy can stand up to its presence. The cross, and the sign of the cross, will help exorcise DEMONS and devils (see DEMONIC EXORCISM), ward off incubi and succubi, prevent bewitchment of man and beast, protect crops from being blasted by WITCHES (see BLASTING), and force vampires to flee. During the Middle Ages, inquisitors often wore crosses or made the sign of the cross while in the presence of accused witches, in order to ward off any evil SPELLS they might cast. People crossed themselves routinely, before the smallest task, just in case an evil presence was near. The cross in a hot cross bun is a remnant of a medieval custom of carving crosses in the dough of bread to protect it against evil.

In cases of DEMONIC POSSESSION, victims have been known to suffer stigmata in the shape of a cross. Other victims recoil from the cross, as in the case of a 16-year-old girl, Clara Germana Cele, in 1906. Cele reportedly could not stand to be in the presence of even a small piece of a cross, even if it had been wrapped and concealed. In the Catholic rite of exorcism, the priest protects himself and the victim with the sign of the cross. The rite requires numerous signs of the cross to be made on the victim's forehead.

See also: ANKH; SWASTIKA. Compare with PENTACLE AND PENTAGRAM.

Crossing the Bridge See RITE OF PASSING.

crossroads The intersection of roads is a customary site of religious and magical ritual. Since antiquity, the junctions of roads have been considered to have magical significance. The Greek goddess of WITCHCRAFT, HECATE, was also goddess of the crossroads, and animals were sacrificed to her at such locations. It was believed that Hecate appeared at crossroads on clear nights, accompanied by spirits and howling dogs. Offerings were placed there to propitiate her and ask for her intercession in cases of madness, which was believed to be caused by departed souls. In Celtic Ireland and Wales, it was traditional on Samhain (All Hallow's Eve), the Druidic new year, to sit at a crossroads and listen for the howling of the wind, which would prophesy the year to come.

From antiquity through the Middle Ages, sorcerers (see SORCERY) and WITCHES were said to frequent crossroads to conjure the DEVIL or his DEMONS or make sacrifices to them. (It is likely that many such persons were practicing rites to pagan deities, which Christians viewed as demons and the Devil; see SACRIFICE.) In the sixth century, the sorcerer Salatin conjured the Devil for THEOPHILUS at a crossroads. In 1324 Dame ALICE KYTELER, an accused Irish witch, was said to sacrifice COCKS to her familiar at a crossroads.

According to Carl G. Jung, a crossroads is a mother symbol; in that respect, it corresponds to the emphasis placed on the Mother GODDESS in neo-Pagan WITCHCRAFT. The crossroads also represents the intersection of positive, neutral and negative forces. It is a place of flux and of change.

Crowley, Aleister (1875–1947) The most controversial and perhaps least understood magician and occultist of his time, Aleister Crowley has been both vilified and idolized. He was a man of both low excesses and high brilliance. He considered himself to be the reincarnation of other great occultists: Pope Alexander VI (see POPES AND SORCERY), renowned for his love of physical pleasures; Edward Kelly, the notorious assistant to JOHN DEE in Elizabethan England; CAGLIOSTRO; and ELIPHAS LEVI, who died on the day Crowley was born. Crowley also believed he

had been Ankh-f-n-Khonsu, an Egyptian priest of the XXVIth dynasty.

Crowley was born in Warwickshire, England. His father was a brewer and a preacher of Plymouthism, the beliefs of a sect founded of the Plymouth Brethren in 1830 that considered itself the only true Christian order. As a child, Crowley participated in the preaching with his parents, then rebelled against it. His behavior inspired his mother to call him "the Beast" after the Antichrist. Later, he called her "a brainless bigot of the most narrow, logical and inhuman type." His father died when he was 11.

As Crowley grew older, he became interested in the occult. He also discovered he was excited by descriptions of TORTURE and BLOOD, and he liked to fantasize about being degraded by a Scarlet Woman who was both wicked and independent.

He entered Trinity College at Cambridge, where he wrote poetry and pursued, on his own, his occult studies. He loved to climb rocks and mountains and attempted some of the highest peaks in the Himalayas. In 1898 he published his first book of poetry, *Aceldama, A Place to Bury Strangers in. A Philosophical Poem. By a Gentleman of the University of Cambridge,* 1898. In the preface, he described how God and Satan had fought for his soul: "God conquered—now I have only one doubt left—which of the twain was God?"

Crowley wanted to become known as a great person. He was led to choose MAGIC as a vocation rather than avocation after reading Arthur Edward Waite's *The Book of Black Magic and of Pacts,* which hints of a secret brotherhood of adepts who dispense occult wisdom to certain initiates. Intrigued, Crowley wrote to Waite for more information and was referred to *The Cloud upon the Sanctuary,* by Carl von Eckartshausen, which tells of the Great White Brotherhood. Crowley determined he wanted to join this brotherhood and advance to the highest degree.

On November 18, 1898, Crowley joined the London chapter of the HERMETIC ORDER OF THE GOLDEN DAWN, which was the First or Outer Order of the Great White Brotherhood. He discovered he had a natural aptitude for magic and rose quickly through the hierarchy. He began practicing Yoga, in the course of which he discovered his earlier incarnations (see REINCARNATION). He left Trinity College without earning a degree, took a flat in Chancery Lane, named himself Count Vladimir and pursued his occult studies on a full-time basis. He advanced through the First Order and sought entry into the Second Order of the Great White Brotherhood, a Rosicrucian order also called the Order of the Red Rose and the Golden Cross. Beyond this was the top order, the Silver Star, or A∴ A∴ (*Argentum Astrum*), which had three grades: Master of the Temple, Magus and Ipissimus. The latter could be achieved only by crossing an unknown and uncharted abyss.

Crowley was intensely competitive with S. L. MacGregor Mathers, the chief of the Hermetic Order of the Golden Dawn and a magician. Mathers taught Crowley Abra-Melin magic (see ABRAMELIN THE MAGE) but had not attained any of three grades in the A∴ A∴. The two quarreled, and Mathers supposedly dispatched an army of ELEMENTALS to attack Crowley. Crowley also argued with other members of the Golden Dawn as well and as a result was expelled from the order. He pursued the attainment of Ipissimus on his own.

Around 1899 or 1900 Crowley may have briefly joined one of OLD GEORGE PICKINGILL's covens in Essex, according to Witch lore. If he did, he makes no mention of it in his autobiography, *The Confessions of Aleister Crowley*.

Crowley traveled widely. He studied Eastern mysticism, including Buddhism, Tantric Yoga and the *I Ching*. For a time he lived in Scotland, in an isolated setting near Loch Ness. In 1903 he married Rose Kelly, who bore him one child. Rose began to receive communications from the astral plane, and in 1904 she told Crowley that he was to receive an extremely important message. It came from Aiwass, a spirit and Crowley's Holy Guardian Angel, or True Self. Crowley also later identified Aiwass as a magical current or solar-phallic energy worshiped by the Sumerians as Shaitan, a "devil-god," and by the Egyptians as Set. On three consecutive days in April 1904, from noon until 1 P.M., Aiwass reportedly manifested as a voice and dictated to Crowley *The Book of the Law*, perhaps the most significant work of his magical career. It contains the Law of Thelema: "Do what thou wilt shall be the whole of the law." Though some have interpreted it to mean doing as one pleases, it actually means that one must do what one must and nothing else. Admirers of Crowley say the Law of Thelema distinguishes him as one of the greatest magicians of history.

Aiwass also heralded the coming of a new Aeon of Horus, the third great age of humanity. The three ages were characterized as Paganism/Christianity/Thelema, represented, respectively, by ISIS/OSIRIS/Horus. Crowley considered himself the prophet of the New Aeon.

From 1909 to 1913, Crowley published the secret rituals of the Golden Dawn in his periodical, *The Equinox*, which also served as a vehicle for his poetry. Mathers tried but failed to get an injunction to stop him. By 1912 Crowley had become involved with the *Ordo Templi Orientis*, a German occult order that practices sex magic.

In 1909 Crowley explored levels of the astral plane with his assistant, poet Victor Neuberg, using ENOCHIAN MAGIC. He believed he crossed the Abyss and united his consciousness with the universal consciousness, thus becoming Master of the Temple. He described the astral journeys in *The Vision and the Voice*, published first in *The Equinox* and posthumously in 1949.

Crowley kept with him a series of "scarlet women." The best known of these was Leah Hirsig, the "Ape of Thoth," who indulged with him in drinking, drugs and sexual magic and who could sometimes contact Aiwass. Crowley apparently made several attempts with various scarlet women to beget a "magical child," none of which was successful. He later fictionalized these efforts in his novel, *Moonchild*, published in 1929.

From 1915 to 1919 Crowley lived in the United States. In 1920 he went to Sicily and founded the Abbey of Thelema, which he envisioned as a magical colony.

In 1921, when Crowley was 45, he and Hirsig conducted a ritual in which Crowley achieved Ipissimus and became, according to his cryptic description, a god ("As a God goes, I go"). He did not reveal attaining Ipissimus to anyone, only hinting at it in his privately published *Magical Record* much later, in 1929. After the transformation, however, Hirsig found him intolerable. Crowley later discarded her and acquired a new scarlet woman, Dorothy Olsen.

In 1922 Crowley accepted an invitation to head the *Ordo Templi Orientis*. In 1923 the bad press that he routinely received led to his expulsion from Sicily, and he had to abandon his abbey. After some wandering through France (where he suffered from a heroin addiction), Tunisia and Germany, he returned to England.

In 1929 he married his second wife, Maria Ferrari de Miramar, in Leipzig.

In his later years he was plagued with poor health, drug addiction and financial trouble. He kept himself afloat by publishing his writings, both nonfiction and fiction. In 1945 he moved to a boardinghouse in Hastings, where he lived the last two years of his life, a dissipated shadow of his former vigorous self. During these last years, he was introduced to GERALD B. GARDNER, an English Witch (see WITCHES), by ARNOLD CROWTHER. He died in 1947 in Hastings.

Crowley's other published books include *The Diary of a Drug Fiend*; *Magick in Theory and Practice*, still considered one of the best books on ceremonial magic; *The Strategem*, a collection of fiction stories; *The Equinox of the Gods*, which sets forth *The Book of the Law* as mankind's new religion; and *The Book of Thoth*, his interpretation of the TAROT. *Confessions* originally was intended to be a six-volume autohagiography, but only the first two volumes were published. Typically, he argued with the publishing company, which was taken over by his friends and then went out of business. The remaining galleys and manuscripts—he had dictated the copy to Hirsig while under the influence of heroin—were lost or scattered about. They were collected and edited by John Symonds and Kenneth Grant and published in a single volume in 1969.

Crowley referred to himself in some of his writings as "the Master Therion" and "Frater Perdurabo." He spelled *magic* as *magick* to "distinguish the science of the Magi from all its counterfeits." Some modern occultists continue to follow suit.

See also DEMONS.

Crowther, Arnold (1909–1974).

English Witch (see WITCHES) and skilled stage magician, friend of GERALD B. GARDNER and husband of PATRICIA C. CROWTHER. According to Patricia, Crowther, like Gardner, was an "old" soul who had lived many earthly lives. He discovered a past life as a Tibetan monk, and he experienced vivid dreams in which the secrets of ancient MAGIC were revealed to him.

Crowther was born on October 7, 1909, in Chestham, Kent, one of a pair of fraternal twin brothers.

Arnold Crowther (courtesy Patricia C. Crowther)

His mother was Scottish and his father, an optician, was from Yorkshire.

Crowther was fascinated with sleight-of-hand, magic tricks, ventriloquism and puppeteering. From the age of about eight on, he practiced tricks in secret in his bedroom. Both he and his twin planned to follow their father's footsteps as opticians, but magic led Crowther in another direction. By his early twenties, he was touring his professional magic act. He had a good stage persona and was very clever at sleight-of-hand.

He worked in cabaret, and in 1938–39, he entertained the then-Princesses Elizabeth and Margaret Rose at Buckingham Palace, which led to numerous engagements to entertain the titled gentry of England. He was a founder member of the Puppet Guild and made more than 500 puppets. He lectured on "curios of the world" to various societies and clubs and was himself a collector of odd items from around the world. An African witch doctor gave him the title, "White Witch Doctor." Crowther was a Freemason and was interested in Buddhism, until he entered the Craft.

Crowther met Gerald B. Gardner and Gardner's wife, Donna, shortly before the start of World War II, probably at a lecture, and struck up a friendship with them. Crowther became very interested in the Craft but was not initiated into it for about 18 years (see INITIATION). Gardner's coven was wary of adverse publicity and felt that Crowther might use the Craft in his act. Gardner assured Crowther that the time would come when a "very special person" would initiate him into the Craft. The Gardners kept a flat in London, and Crowther frequently met them there, especially at the Caledonian Market, an antique market where Gardner loved to browse. Crowther was often out of town during the summer season, but upon his return, he would drop by the Caledonian Market and often find Gardner, who would greet him as though he'd never been gone: "Oh, hello, old man, did I tell you . . . ?"

During the war, Crowther was in the Entertainers National Services Association and toured throughout Europe entertaining troops with his show, "Black Magic." The show's name derived from its African Basuto choir. Crowther performed wherever required, including in a DC 3 plane at 4,000 feet, en route from Tripoli to Malta on November 10, 1943.

While stationed in Paris, he learned of his past life as a beggar Tibetan monk when he and an officer visited a palmist, Madame Brux, who invited them to a séance and introduced them to a medium. The medium went into trance and began communicating with a masculine spirit who said he had been Crowther's teacher in a previous life and was his guide in the present life. The medium reported that Crowther had been a young student in a Tibetan lamasary and had been killed. She spoke the name "Younghusband," but Crowther knew no one of that name. "Your possessions will be returned to you," the medium said. With that, an object fell on the séance table. It was a Tibetan prayer wheel inscribed with the most holy of mantras, *"Om mani padme hum."* The medium said it was an apport (see REINCARNATION).

After the war, other Tibetan articles found their way into Crowther's possession: a butter lamp, a trumpet made of a human thigh bone, a drum made of a human skull and a small rattle hand-drum. An expert told Crowther such articles were used by the *Z'i-jed-pa,* "The Mild Doer," a homeless medicant class of Yogi regarded as a saint, who should attain Nirvana after death and not have to be born again.

If he had indeed been such a monk in a previous life, then he would not have reincarnated as Crowther, he reasoned. He discovered, however, that if he, as the monk, had killed someone, he would have had to be reincarnated to balance the karma. At an exhibition of Tibetan curios in London, Crowther discovered that a Colonel Younghusband had led a military attack against Tibet in 1904. Crowther believed he had killed one of the soldiers in the attack before being killed himself.

During his wartime travels Crowther also met ALEISTER CROWLEY. He introduced Gardner to Crowley in 1946.

After the war, Crowther returned to the public stage. Just as Gardner had predicted, he met a fair-haired woman, Patricia Dawson, who initiated him into the Craft. After their marriage in 1960, he and Patricia made their home in Sheffield and achieved prominence as spokespersons for the Craft.

Crowther died on Beltane (May 1), 1974. He was given the Passing Rite of the Old Religion at his funeral (see RITE OF PASSING). A piper played a lament, as he had requested before his death. When the music ended, the sound of a running brook could be heard: the Brook of Love, according to DION FORTUNE, from the other side.

In addition to two books, numerous articles for a wide variety of magazines, and a radio series on Witchcraft written in collaboration with Patricia, Crowther's published credits include: *Let's Put on a Show* (1964), a how-to book of magic which he illustrated himself; *Linda and the Lollipop Man* (1973), a book on road safety for children; *Yorkshire Customs* (1974); and *Hex Certificate* (late 1970s), a collection of cartoons he drew on themes of Witchcraft. His autobiography, *Hand in Glove,* was not published but

was serialized on B.B.C. Radio in Bristol, Sheffield, Medway and Leeds between 1975 and 1977.

Crowther, Patricia C. A Witch and high priestess of Sheffield, Yorkshire, England, Patricia Crowther has, since the 1960s, been a leading spokesperson for the Old Religion in books, the media and lecture appearances (see WITCHES; WITCHCRAFT). Initiated formally into the Craft by GERALD B. GARDNER, she is regarded by many as Gardner's spiritual heir and has worked to help the renaissance of the Old Religion in order to benefit and enlighten humankind. She has formed flourishing covens all over the United Kingdom.

She was born Patricia Dawson in Sheffield. Her great-grandmother of Brittany was an herbalist and clairvoyant, who also told fortunes. Her grandmother, Elizabeth (Tizzy) Machon (her maiden name) was a very small woman whose surname means "fairy" (see FAIRIES).

The Dawsons lived next door to a palmist, Madame Melba, who accurately predicted that Patricia would develop great clairvoyant powers. During childhood, she experienced synchronistic associations with fairies and the Craft: at a children's birthday party, she was chosen to be Fairy on the Moon, and was wheeled around seated on a huge, illuminated crescent moon (the GODDESS with crescent moon is often symbolic of DIANA); for a birthday present, she was given a gold snake bangle, symbol of wisdom, life and rebirth; she performed as Robin Hood in pantomime, and performed in a revue entitled *The Legend of the Moon Goddess.*

When Patricia was 30, a hypnotist regressed her to previous lives, including one as a Witch, Polly, an old crone of about 66 in the year 1670. Polly revealed that she lived in a hut with a cat, frog, goat and hen, and worked spells for people, most of whom she held in contempt. Polly freely recited numerous spells, all in rhyme, with instructions on how to use them. Patricia had no knowledge of such spells, which experts determined were authentic. The regression proved to her that she had been a Witch in a previous life and that, in accordance with Witch lore, she would find her way back into the Craft in the present life. Since that experience, she has recalled, in numerous clairvoyant visions, another past life in which she served as a priestess of the Goddess who had great power. She identifies more strongly with the spiritual priestess than with the spell-casting crone.

Patricia's parents had trained her in singing, dancing and acting for the stage, and she toured all over the United Kingdom. While playing a theater in Birmingham in 1954, she met a fortune-teller who

Patricia C. Crowther (courtesy Patricia C. Crowther)

predicted she would meet her future husband, a man named Arnold, two years later over water. The prediction seemed utterly fantastic, but it was borne out. In 1956 Patricia took a summer job on the Isle of Wight, where she met ARNOLD CROWTHER, a stage magician and ventriloquist who was performing in the same show as she. When Arnold discovered her interest in Witchcraft, he offered to introduce her to Gardner, a personal friend. Several years earlier, Gardner had predicted that Arnold would meet a fair-haired woman who would initiate him into the Craft. This prediction proved to be true as well.

After several meetings with Gardner, Patricia was initiated by him on June 6, 1960 (see INITIATION). The initiation took place in Gardner's private Magic Room, the top floor of a barn, at his home in Castletown on the Isle of Man. Patricia in turn initiated Arnold. Gardner presented them with ritual tools and jewelry, including a coral necklace for Patricia.

During the rite, Patricia had a profound and powerful trance experience in which she saw herself being reborn into the priesthood of the Moon Mysteries, initiated by a line of howling, naked women who passed her, gauntlet-style, through their spread legs. Gardner posited that she had gone back in time to another previous life and relived an ancient initiation ceremony.

A few weeks later, on November 8, 1960, Patricia and Arnold were married in a private HANDFASTING officiated by Gardner. The ceremony took place in a circle; participants were skyclad (nude). The following day, November 9, the Crowthers were married in a civil ceremony which the press found out about in advance and publicized heavily. The Crowthers established their home in Sheffield. They took the second-degree initiation on October 11, 1961; Patricia became high priestess on October 14.

The Crowthers often were sought out by the media for interviews. One interview inadvertantly led to the gradual formation of a COVEN. Asked by a reporter if she wanted to meet others who were interested in the Craft, Patricia answered yes. The reporter's story was headlined, "Witch Seeks Recruits for Coven," which prompted many inquiries from interested persons. The Crowthers initiated the first member of their coven in December 1961, with others following gradually over time.

The Crowthers continued their instruction in the Craft with Gardner. Patricia was taught a 300-year-old secret, inner tradition by an old woman who lived in Inverness, who saw Patricia on a television program and wrote to her. Her name was Jean, and she told Patricia she considered her worthy of inheriting this knowledge, which she imparted over the course of a two-year correspondence.

The Crowthers' media exposure generated requests for more interviews and speaking engagements. Together, they authored two books, *The Witches Speak* (1965, 1976) and *The Secrets of Ancient Witchcraft* (1974). For Radio Sheffield, the Crowthers produced the first radio series in Britain on Witchcraft, *A Spell of Witchcraft*, which debuted on January 6, 1971. They performed numerous services for people, including casting SPELLS and exorcising ghosts (see SPIRIT EXORCISM). They wrote rituals for the seasons of the year and introduced new music and poetry into the Craft.

Patricia's books include *Witchcraft in Yorkshire* (1973); her autobiography, *Witch Blood!* (1974); *The Witches Speak* (1976); and *Lid Off the Cauldron* (1981, 1985). In addition, she has written articles for numerous periodicals, including *Prediction, Gnostica, New Dimensions, Zodiac,* and *The Lamp of Thoth*. She is a frequent guest on radio and television shows and lectures as well, working to dispel sensational misconceptions associated with the Old Religion and with the modern Craft. She is unhesitant in answering religious bigots and critics, defusing many with cool self-assurance and a sense of humor. In 1978 she represented Wicca in the United Kingdom at an international occult conference in Barcelona.

Patricia has been instrumental in bringing the Great Goddess back into consciousness on a racial level, in order to foster a greater harmony on spiritual levels of thought, and in furthering the equality and prominence of women in general.

In addition to her activities on behalf of the Craft, Crowther continues to work professionally as a singer, magician and puppeteer.

cunning men/cunning women   See WIZARD.

Cunningham, John   See JOHN FIAN.

Cunningham, Scott (1956–)   Prolific Wiccan author and expert on earth and natural MAGIC, best known for his books on magical herbalism, earth power, crystals, gems and metals and "the truth about Witchcraft." Born June 27, 1956, in Royal Oak, Michigan, Cunningham has lived in San Diego since 1961. He began practicing WICCA in 1971. A full-time writer, he has authored more than two dozen fiction and nonfiction books and has written scripts for occult videocassettes.

Cunningham was introduced to the Craft (see WITCHCRAFT) in 1971 through a book purchased by his mother, *The Supernatural,* by Douglas Hill and Pat Williams. Early on in life, Cunningham had had a strong interest in plants, minerals and other natural earth products, and the book piqued his curiosity. He read it and was particularly fascinated by the book's descriptions of Italian hand gestures used to ward off the EVIL EYE.

In the next two days, two other incidents added impetus to his interest in the Craft: a movie about Witchcraft shown on television; and a female classmate in high school who was involved in an occult and magic study group. Meeting on the first day of drama class, the two began talking, and Cunningham unconsciously made the evil-eye hand gestures. The classmate recognized them and asked, "Are you a Witch?" "No," said Cunningham, "but I'd sure like to be one." The classmate introduced him to Wicca. Learning magic intensified his interest in the power of nature. Since then, Cunningham has been initiated into several covens of various traditions (see INITIATION) but eventually opted to practice as a SOLITARY.

In 1974 he enrolled in San Diego State University and studied creative writing, intending to become a professional writer like his father, Chet, who has authored more than 170 nonfiction and fiction books. He wrote truck and automotive trade articles and advertising copy on a freelance basis. After two years

Scott Cunningham (photo by Chet Cunningham; courtesy Scott Cunningham)

in college, he realized he had more published credits than most of his professors, and decided to drop out and begin writing full-time.

The first book he wrote was *Magical Herbalism,* though it was not his first to be published. That book, *Shadow of Love,* an Egyptian romance novel, appeared in 1980. *Magical Herbalism* was published in 1982. Between 1980 and 1987, Cunningham wrote and had published 21 novels in various genres, six nonfiction occult books and one nonfiction booklet. Besides *Magical Herbalism,* his credits include *Earth Power: Techniques of Natural Magic* (1983); *Cunningham's Encyclopedia of Magical Herbs* (1985); *The Magic of Incense, Oils and Brews* (1987); *The Magical Household* (1987; coauthored with David Harrington); and *Cunningham's Encyclopedia of Crystal, Gem and Metal Magic* (1987).

Cunningham anonymously wrote a booklet, *The Truth About Witchcraft,* which explains folk magic as well as the Wiccan religion. An expanded, book-length version of *The Truth About Witchcraft,* as well as a second title, *Wicca: A Guide for the Solitary Practitioner,* were published in 1988. He also wrote *The Magic of Food,* a book about the magical properties within foods, as well as instructions on selecting foods to create specific changes in life.

Cunningham lectures and teaches to groups around the country and occasionally makes media appearances on behalf of the Craft. He views Wicca as a modern religion, created in the 20th century. Though Wicca incorporates elements of pagan folk magic, it is not a continuation of the ancient pagan religion. Cunningham feels Wicca should be stripped of its quasi-historical and mythological trappings and presented to the public as a modern religion sprung from primeval concepts. The purpose of Wicca is to facilitate human contact with the GODDESS and God; the differences between traditions, he maintains, are petty and detracting.

Like others in the Craft, Cunningham believes in reincarnation, but he feels many people place too much importance on exploring past lives. He says the present is what counts, and one's attention should be given to learning the lessons of the here and now.

curandera See CURANDERO, CURANDERA.

curandero, curandera The Spanish terms for the medicine men and women of Mexico, Meso-America and the Hispanic communities of the United States. The *curandero* and *curandera* have a different healing function than their counterparts, the *brujo* and *bruja* (male and female WITCHES). *Curanderos* (most are men) function primarily as folk psychiatrists, providing magical cures for mental and emotional problems; a *curandero*, for example, will "clean the soul," which may involve exorcising of spirits believed responsible for problems. Both *curanderos* and *brujos* use herbal and folk remedies.

See also BRUJA, BRUJO.

curses In MAGIC, SPELLS intended to bring misfortune, illness, harm or death to a victim. The most dreaded form of magic, curses are universal. They are "laid" or "thrown" primarily for revenge and power but also for protection, usually of homes, treasures, tombs and grave sites. A curse can take effect quickly or may be dormant for years. Curses have been laid upon families, plaguing them for generations.

The word HEX is sometimes used synonymously with *curse*. Among the Pennsylvania Dutch WITCHES, however, *hex* is used for both good and evil spells. In neo-Pagan WITCHCRAFT, some Witches use the term *hex* to describe a binding spell, which is different from a curse.

Any person can lay a curse simply by expressing a desire that a particular person come to some kind of harm. However, the efficacy of a curse depends upon the curser's station and condition. Curses are believed to have more potency—and therefore more

danger—when they are laid by persons in authority, such as priests, priestesses or royalty; persons of magical skill, such as Witches, sorcerers and magicians; and persons who have no other recourse for justice, such as women (in most societies), the poor and destitute and the dying. Deathbed curses are the most potent, for all the curser's vital energy goes into the curse.

If a victim knows he has been cursed and believes he is doomed, the curse is all the more potent, for the victim helps to bring about his own demise. This is called *sympathetic magic*. However, Witches and sorcerers say curses work without such knowledge on the part of the victim. In fact, many say they would never let the victim know a curse has been laid, lest he find another Witch to undo the spell.

Like a blessing, a curse is a calling upon supernatural powers to effect a change. Intent makes the difference between benefit and harm. With the exception of neo-Pagan Witches, witches and sorcerers in most societies throughout history have performed both blessings and curses as services to others, either to clients in exchange for fees, or in carrying out judicial sentences. As Plato noted in the *Republic*, "If anyone wishes to injure an enemy, for a small fee they [sorcerers] will bring harm on good or bad alike, binding the gods to serve their purposes by spells and curses."

Persons who feel they've been cursed will hire the same Witch or sorcerer to break the curse, for an additional fee, of course, or go to another Witch to have the curse broken. In the case of the latter, the opposing Witches may engage in a magical battle to see whose power is stronger.

Perhaps the most universal method of laying a curse is with a figure or effigy that represents the victim. Waxen effigies were common in ancient India, Persia, Egypt, Africa and Europe, and are still used in modern times. Effigies are also made of clay, wood and stuffed cloth (*poppets*). They are painted or marked, or attached with something associated with the victim—a bit of hair, nail clippings (see HAIR AND NAILS), excrement, clothing, even dust from his footprints—and melted over, or burned in, a fire. As the figure melts or burns, the victim suffers, and dies when the figure is destroyed. The Egyptians often used wax figures of Apep, a monster who was the enemy of the sun. The magician wrote Apep's name in green ink on the effigy, wrapped it in new papyrus and threw it in a fire. As it burned, he kicked it with his left foot four times. The ashes of the effigy were mixed with excrement and thrown into another fire. The Egyptians also left wax figures in tombs.

Waxen images were popular during the Middle Ages and Renaissance in Europe, and numerous witches were accused of cursing with them. JAMES I of England, writing in his book, *Daemonologie* (1597), described how witches caused illness and death by roasting waxen images:

> To some others at these times he [the Devil], teacheth how to make pictures of wax or clay. That by the roasting thereof, the persons that they beare the name of, may be continually melted or dried away by continual sicknesses.
>
> They can bewitch and take the life of men or women, by roasting of the pictures, as I spake of before, which likewise is verie possible to their Maister to performe, for although, as I said before, that instrument of waxe has no vertue in that turne doing, yet may he not very well, even by the same measure that his conjured slaves, melts that waxe in fire, may he not, I say at these times, subtily, as a spirite, so weaken and scatter the spirites of life of the patient, as may make him on the one part, for faintnesses, so sweate out the humour of his bodie. And on the other parte, for the not concurrence of these spirites, which causes his digestion, so debilitate his stomacke, that this humour radicall continually sweating out on the one part, and no new good sucks being put in the place thereof, for lacke of digestion on the other, he shall at last vanish away, even as his picture will die in the fire.

As an alternative to melting, effigies may be stuck with pins, thorns or knives. Animal or human hearts may be substituted for effigies. Hearts, animal corpses or objects which quickly decompose, such as eggs, are buried with spells that the victim will die as the objects deteriorate.

In Ireland, "cursing stones" are stones that are stroked and turned to the left while a curse is recited. Gems and crystals are often said to have the power to hold curses; the Hope Diamond, purchased by Louis XVI from Tavernier in 1668, is deemed cursed because its owners have suffered illness, misfortune and death.

One of the most famous alleged curses is the "mummy's curse" on the tomb of Tutankhamen. When the Earl of Carnarvon and Howard Carter excavated Tutankhamen's burial chamber in 1922, legend has it that they found in the antechamber an inscribed clay tablet that read:

> Death will slay with his wings whoever disturbs the peace of the pharaoh.

Six months later, Carnarvon was dead of an infected mosquito bite. Altogether, six of the seven principal members of the excavation team were said to have died strange and sudden deaths, all as a result of the curse. The tablet was never photographed and mysteriously disappeared from the collection of artifacts. It probably never existed, according to Bob Brier, American parapsychologist and Egyptologist. Brier notes in *Ancient Egyptian Magic* (1980) that it is not typically Egyptian to write on clay tablets or to refer to death as having wings. Also, no other reliable sources exist that cite the curse.

Numerous legends exist in the United Kingdom and Europe about curses laid on families, especially the aristocracy. One of the worst curses was that of childlessness or death to heirs, so that a family lineage died out.

Curses in modern Witchcraft. In the various traditions of neo-Pagan Witchcraft, it is against the ethics and laws of the Craft to lay curses (see WICCAN REDE). Most Witches abide by this and believe that a curse will come back on the curser in some form (see THREEFOLD LAW OF RETURN). SYBIL LEEK was a notable exception, for she believed cursing was justified against one's enemies. Witches from ethnic cultures, such as the Italian STRIGA, the Mexican BRUJA and the *brauchers* of the Pennsylvania Dutch (see POWWOWING), also believe curses are justified.

Repelling curses. Just as many methods exist to break curses as to make curses; in neo-Pagan Witchcraft, "banishing rituals" are performed. AMULETS that have been made according to various formulas are said to repel curses, as is dragon's blood, which is used in herbal mixes for protection. A cloth poppet stuffed with nettles, inscribed with the name of the curser (if known), then buried or burned, also breaks a curse. Nettles sprinkled about a room add protection. The OILS of rosemary and van-van, and various mixed VODOUN oils, placed in baths or used to anoint the body, are other remedies. Burning a purple candle while reciting a spell is yet another method (see CANDLES). Hindu sorcerers turn curses in the opposite direction, "upstream," sending them back to slay their originators.

Traditionally, the most propitious time for both laying and breaking curses is during the waning moon. (See also WELLS.)

D

Danu (also Dana)   In Irish mythology, the mother goddess of the Tuatha de Danaan ("people of the Goddess Danu" or FAIRIES), the divine race of Old Irish myth. In some legends, she was the daughter of the Dagda, the solar god. Danu is often transposed with Anu, goddess of plenty, and Brigid (Brigit), goddess of fertility, cattle, crops, fire, wisdom, poetry, household arts and smithing.

See also GODDESS.

Darrell (also Darrel), Reverend John (16th century)   The Puritan minister John Darrell, caught in religious infighting between moderate Catholics, English Anglicans and Puritans, was convicted of fraud in May 1599, as a result of exorcising the DEVIL from the demoniac William Sommers of Nottingham (see DEMONIC EXORCISM). Darrell was called to exorcise nine other people before Sommers: Katherine Wright in 1586, Thomas Darling in 1596, and seven possessed children in Lancashire in 1597. He was unsuccessful in dispossessing Wright, and although a witch (see WITCHES) was accused of causing the possession, the Justice in charge refused to commit her and warned Darrell to desist from exorcisms or face imprisonment. In the case of Thomas Darling, Darrell advised fasting and PRAYER but was not present so as to avoid personal "glory."

The possession of the seven Lancashire children had already led to the execution of Edmund Hartley—originally brought in to cure the children but eventually found to be the witch responsible—but the children were still having fits and convulsions. Assisted by Derbyshire minister George More, Darrell exorcised the children in one afternoon, emphasizing that the greatest value of such Puritan exorcisms was in refuting the claim by the Papists that theirs was the only true Church, since they could cast out devils.

Darrell's last case, the dispossession of William Sommers, began in November 1597. Sommers, aged 20, suffered fits and had a lump the size of an egg which ran about his body. His behavior was obscene, including bestiality with a dog in front of onlookers. Darrell exorcised him in front of 150 witnesses, but Sommers suffered repossessions, eventually naming witches responsible. Although Sommers did not react consistently to the various witches' presence, Darrell had all 13 arrested. All but two were released, but Darrell claimed that Sommers's accusations were correct, and that Sommers could probably find all the witches in England. Eventually, one of the accused witch's powerful families charged Sommers with WITCHCRAFT, and Sommers confessed to having simulated his fits.

Fearful of the effect that talk of witchcraft had on the people, as well as the increasing power of the Puritans, or Calvinists, the Archbishop of Canterbury moved against Darrell. Katherine Wright and Thomas Darling were summoned as witnesses against Darrell and joined Sommers in confessing fraud. Wright and Sommers even accused Darrell of teaching them how to contrive fits. Based mainly on Sommers's detailed accusations, the ecclesiastical court found Darrell to be a counterfeit and deposed him from the ministry in May 1599. Darrell languished in prison for several months but was never really sentenced.

As a result of Darrell's conviction, the Anglican Church of England passed Canon 72 of the Episcopal Church, forbidding exorcism as a formal ritual. Although there are Anglican priests today practicing exorcism on an informal basis with the approval of their bishops, most Anglicans—as well as other Protestants—have adopted the belief of Martin Luther: that the Devil can best be driven from a tortured soul by prayer alone.

See also DEMONIC POSSESSION.

Dee, John (1527–1608)

Alchemist, mathematician, astronomer and astrologer, sometimes called "the last royal magician" because of his astrological services to Queen Elizabeth I. Dee was a scholarly man—some say he was the most learned man in Europe of his time—who was fascinated by the occult and MAGIC. He was an adept in Neoplatonic, Hermetic and Kabbalistic philosophy (see HERMETICA; KABBALAH) and devoted most of his life to trying to communicate with spirits, for which he relied on mediums due to his professed lack of psychic ability. His occult writings are believed to have influenced Shakespeare, who may have used him as the model for Prospero in *Tempest*.

Dee was born in London on July 13, 1527. His father, a Welshman, was a low-ranking official in the court of Henry VIII. Dee entered St. John's College in Cambridge at age 15, vowing that he would spend the rest of his life studying for 18 hours a day, eating for two hours and sleeping for four. (It is not known how well he adhered to this rigorous schedule throughout his 81 years, but he did pursue a lifelong quest for mystical knowledge.) Magic and alchemy intrigued him; at that time, these fields were closely related to science. Finding Cambridge stifling, Dee went to the Continent to study and lecture. He was heavily influenced by the occult writings of AGRIPPA and also by his meeting of Jerome Cardan, a self-professed witch who apparently possessed genuine clairvoyant ability and could experience out-of-body (astral) projection (see WITCHES).

Dee was plagued with money problems and decided that alchemy could provide the solution. He was determined to contact spirit forces that would help him find the Philosopher's Stone or discover buried treasure. He paid great attention to his dreams and tried SCRYING. Except for a few instances during his life, Dee was unable to see or hear spirits. Dee considered himself a resolute Christian; the spirits he sought were angels, not DEMONS. He believed the magic he pursued was pure and good, and not demonic or evil.

After the death of Henry VIII, Dee returned to England and was granted a pension by the 10-year-old successor, Edward VI. But Edward died at 16, and with him Dee's hopes for a financially secure future. His prospects brightened when Queen Mary gained the throne and asked him to cast her horoscope. He also visited Mary's half-sister, Elizabeth, whom Mary had imprisoned, and cast a horoscope for her to determine when Mary would die (see ASTROLOGY). For this, Dee was accused of attempting to murder Mary by black magic, and he was imprisoned. He was also accused of murdering children by sorcery (of which he was acquitted) and for being "a companion of hellhounds and a caller and conjurer of wicked and damned spirits." He was released in 1555.

Mary died in 1558 and Elizabeth ascended the throne. Much more superstitious and interested in astrology than her sister, she consulted Dee for an auspicious day for her coronation. His horoscope casting gained favor in court, and he also gave Elizabeth lessons in mystical interpretations of his writings. But Elizabeth never granted him the generous pension he sought, and his income from horoscope casting was meager. Dee spent years traveling around the Continent, some believe as a spy for Elizabeth. He also aided navigators to the New World.

Dee built up a considerable library of books on magic, the occult and WITCHCRAFT. In Antwerp in 1563, he found a rare copy of *Stenographia*, written about 100 years earlier by the German Benedictine abbott, Johann Trimethius, on magic, numbers, cyphers and symbols. This inspired Dee to write his own book on the subject, *Monas Hieroglyphia*. In all, Dee wrote 79 manuscripts, but few were published by the time of his death.

Dee was married three times. His first marriage, to Katherine Constable, took place in 1565. Little is known about her, but evidently she died by 1575, when Dee married for the second time. His unknown second wife died in 1576 of the plague, and in 1578, he married Jane Fromond, who was much younger than he. They lived in his mother's house in Mortlake; she eventually bore him eight children.

In his diary, Dee recorded his dreams, alleged spirit rappings and the few times he thought he saw spirits. He possessed a "magic glass," a mirror (see MIRRORS) of black obsidian obtained by Cortés in Mexico in the 1520s. But his overall lack of success in communicating with spirits on his own drove him to seek out collaborations with psychics. His first partnership was with a young man named Barnabas Saul, who got into trouble with the law after a few months. Then Dee met Edward Kelly, a roguish Irishman who had lost his ears as punishment for forgery. Kelly said he could communicate with spirits, and for seven years, the two had an uneasy partnership. Kelly was hot-tempered, impetuous and opportunistic; Dee was reserved, serious and scholarly, an easy target for manipulation. In 1582 Kelly moved into the Dee house in Mortlake. Dee's wife took an instinctive and immediate dislike to Kelly, who was rumored to be a necromancer and to ·be inhabited by an evil spirit (see NECROMANCY). Several hundred years later, in the early 20th century, ALEISTER CROWLEY expressed reverance for Kelly, while he described Dee as a humorless old man.

Kelly held the upper hand in his strange relationship with the studious Dee. Kelly would gaze into a crystal and summon spirits with incantations or "calls" in a complex and secret language, Enochian (see ENOCHIAN MAGIC). He said he could see and hear the spirits, and he acted as intermediary for Dee, who would pose questions to them. Dee identified one cherubistic spirit as Uriel, the angel of light in the Kabbalah. Another major being was a childlike creature who said her name was Madimi; Dee named one of his daughters after her. Shortly after Kelly arrived on the scene, Dee recorded one of his few psychic experiences, in which he saw Uriel floating outside his window, holding a pale pink crystal about the size of an orange. Then the archangel Michael appeared and told Dee to use it. This crystal, along with Dee's "magic mirror" and other instruments, is on display in the British Museum.

Dee and Kelly provided their mediumistic services to a variety of noblemen, including Count Albert Laski of Poland, who urged them to come to Poland. In 1585 Dee, Kelly and their wives and families set off on a four-year journey around the Continent, performing for royalty and nobility. They had some success but were thrown out of Prague because the Pope accused Dee of necromancy. Dee and Kelly had numerous quarrels, and Kelly would quit scrying for periods of time. The breaking point came when Kelly informed Dee that Madimi had ordered them to share wives, which Dee reluctantly agreed to do. Jane was hysterical but acquiesced. It is not recorded whether or not Kelly actually slept with her, but shortly after that, the strange partnership between Dee and Kelly broke up and the Dees returned to England. Kelly remained in Europe. He was killed in 1595 while trying to escape from prison in Prague.

Back in England, Dee found his Mortlake house ransacked by his enemies, and a good number of his books and scientific instruments destroyed. Elizabeth reimbursed him for some of the 2,000 pounds in damages he claimed, and he was able to salvage some 3,000 books, most of which are in British museums. Elizabeth made him warden of Christ's College in Manchester in 1595, but Dee did not find the job fulfilling. Jane died of the plague. Elizabeth died in 1603, and her successor, James I, was an opponent of magic and witchcraft. Dee retired to Mortlake. He found a new partner, Bartholomew Hickman, who said he could communicate with the angel Raphael. The spirit offered Dee vague promises of discovering the secrets of God and the universe he had pursued

for so many years, but none were realized. He died in poverty and obscurity in 1608.

deiseal See DEOSIL.

Delphi, Oracle at See ORACLE AT DELPHI.

Demeter The Greek goddess of the fertile soil and agriculture, who is an important aspect of the GODDESS deity worshipped in contemporary WITCHCRAFT. As a goddess of nature, Demeter also represents women, marriage, harmony and health. She controls the seasons, the dying of the earth in winter and its rebirth in spring. She is acknowledged in the spring and autumn equinox SABBATS observed by WITCHES, just as she was worshipped in ancient times.

Cults of Demeter were particularly strong in ancient Eleusinia, and she was a central figure in the Eleusinian Mysteries of death and rebirth. According to myth, Demeter is the daughter of Cronos and Rhea, and the sister of Zeus and Poseidon. In an incestuous union with Zeus, she bore a daughter, Kore, "the maiden," also know as Persephone. Hades, the god of the underworld, lusted after Kore, and Zeus promised the maiden to him without telling Demeter.

Hades raped Kore and kidnapped her to his underworld kingdom. When Demeter learned of this, she went into profound mourning, donning black clothing and searching nine days for her daughter. On the tenth day she encountered HECATE, the patron goddess of witchcraft, who had heard Kore cry out. The two went to Helios, who had witnessed the abduction.

Upon hearing the entire story from Helios, Demeter went into a rage. She resigned from the company of the gods and neglected her duties. Crops failed and famine spread throughout the lands. The situation grew worse and worse, but Demeter could not be persuaded to act. Finally, HERMES succeeded in convincing Hades to let Kore go. But the crafty god of the underworld tricked Kore into eating part of a pomegranate before she left; this partaking of food in the underworld doomed her to spend at least part of her time with Hades forever. A compromise was struck: each year she would spend six months above the earth, six months below. The coming and going of Kore is signaled by the equinoxes.

Demeter was so grateful to have her daughter back at least part of the year that she initiated mankind into her mysteries and taught him agriculture, symbolized by corn. Many of the secret rites of her cults were practiced only by women, because of their power to bring forth life. In Attica, the rituals were performed by both men and women.

Abduction of Proserpine (Persephone) on a unicorn (Albrecht Dürer, 1516)

Demeter and Kore were sometimes considered as two aspects of the Corn Mother and were called the "Two Goddesses" or the "Great Goddesses." Sacrifices of fruit, honey cakes, bulls, pigs and cows were made to them.

The Romans identified Demeter with Ceres, the goddess of the earth, and incorporated Demeter's aspects into their own goddess. The concept of the earth goddess who governs the fertility of the earth exists around the world.

demonic exorcism The expulsion of evil spirits in a religious setting differs from a SPIRIT EXORCISM: instead of talking to possessing spirits and asking them to depart, DEMONS are commanded to leave in the name of Jesus Christ, to return to their hellish home. However powerful the DEVIL may be, he ultimately must yield to the power of the Lord. The exorcist also calls upon all the saints, the Virgin Mary and the angels, especially the archangel Michael, an ancient foe of the Devil.

The word *exorcism* comes from the Greek *exousia*, meaning "oath," and translates as *adjuro*, or *adjure*, in Latin and English. To "exorcize," then, does not really mean to cast out so much as it means "putting the Devil on oath," or invoking a higher authority to compel the Devil to act in a way contrary to its wishes. Such compulsion also implies binding. The Anglican pamphlet *Exorcism* (1972) states, "Christian exorcism is the binding of evil powers by the triumph of Christ Jesus, through the application of the power demonstrated by that triumph, in and by his Church." Exorcism rituals often begin with the Latin words, *"Adjure te, spiritus nequissime, per Deum omnipotentem,"* which translates as "I adjure thee, most evil spirit, by almighty God." Jesus, who cast out devils, did not exorcise, because he did not need to call on any higher authority than Himself.

Violence both physical and spiritual, often dominates a demonic exorcism. Furniture bangs and breaks, waves of heat and cold pour over the room, horrible cries emanate from the victim and often the victim suffers real physical pain and distress. The Devil seems to revel in spitting, vomiting (see ALLOTRIOPHAGY) and other, more disgusting bodily functions as well. Spiritually, the Devil and the exorcist battle for the soul of the victim, and while the Devil hurls invectives, the exorcist counters with the strongest demands for the demon's departure, vowing pain and penalty if it does not comply.

Exorcisms may also include the physical beating of a sufferer to force the demon to depart, or throwing stones at the possessed person. In extreme cases, such as that of the unfortunate Urbain Grandier in Loudun, the possessed person is killed and burned,

or even burned alive, to remove all traces of the Devil's evil (see LOUDUN POSSESSIONS). Such punishments imply that the exorcist does not believe the victim suffered innocently at the hands of the Devil, but rather that in some say he or she invited trouble. As late as 1966, members of a fanatic cult in Zurich, Switzerland, ritually beat a young girl to death for being "the Devil's bride."

Priests and ministers perform most demonic exorcisms, but clairvoyants and spiritualists also expel evil spirits. Rev. J. C. Neil-Smith, an Anglican priest and exorcist in England, claims that the ritual is not nearly as important as the exorcist himself (or herself); such talent is a gift that should be developed. The exorcist must be convinced of the victim's possession and have faith in the power of the Lord to work through the exorcist.

In his book *Hostage to the Devil* (1976), former Jesuit professor Dr. Malachi Martin describes the typical exorcist:

Usually he is engaged in the active ministry of parishes. Rarely is he a scholarly type engaged in teaching or research. Rarely is he a recently ordained

Priest exorcising demon from possessed woman (Pierre Boaistuau, *Histoires prodigieuses*, 1597)

priest. If there is any median age for exorcists, it is probably between the ages of fifty and sixty-five. Sound and robust physical health is not a characteristic of exorcists, nor is proven intellectual brilliance, postgraduate degrees, even in psychology or philosophy, or a very sophisticated personal culture. . . . Though, of course, there are many exceptions, the usual reasons for a priest's being chosen are his qualities of moral judgment, personal behavior, and religious beliefs—qualities that are not sophisticated or laboriously acquired, but that somehow seem always to have been an easy and natural part of such a man.

Pope John Paul II has performed exorcisms and receives gibing for his talk about Satan from more worldly colleagues.

The exorcist as victim. Although most accounts of demonic exorcism concentrate on the sufferings of the victim and the machinations of the Devil, little has been said about the effect on the exorcist. Yet an exorcist assumes a heavy risk when fighting evil. Not only can the ordeal go on for weeks, maybe months, but the exorcist must be prepared to have his entire life bared by the paranormal knowledge of the Devil. Secret sins are blurted out and ridiculed, and the demons may even mimic the voices of long-lost loved ones.

Becoming possessed himself ranks as the greatest danger to the exorcist, especially if he suffers from guilt and secretly feels the need to be punished.

Father Jean-Joseph Surin, Jesuit exorcist to the nuns at Loudun, became possessed while ministering to Jeanne des Anges after the death of Grandier. Reared in a cloister, Surin practiced self-denial during his early years as a priest, denying himself food, sleep and social contact. By the time he went to Loudun, Surin suffered from poor health, severe headaches, muscle pain, melancholy and attacks of depression and confusion. Unlike many of his fellow Jesuits, Surin firmly believed that Sister Jeanne and the others were truly possessed.

On January 19, 1635, Surin experienced his first possession, and by January 7 of the next year, the demon Isacaaron—devil of lust and debauchery—had left Sister Jeanne and entered Father Surin. Leviathan and other demons also tortured the priest. In May 1635 Father Surin wrote of his torments to his friend Father Datichi, a Jesuit in Rome:

Things have gone so far that God has permitted, for my sins, I think, something never seen, perhaps, in the Church: that during the exercise of my ministry, the Devil passes from the body of the possessed person, and coming into mine, assaults me and overturns me, shakes me, and visibly travels through me, possessing me for several hours like an energumen.

. . . Some say that it is a chastisement from God upon me, as punishment for some illusion; others say something quite different; as for me, I hold fast where I am, and would not exchange my fate for anyone's, being firmly convinced that there is nothing better than to be reduced to great extremities.

Surin continued ill and tormented throughout 1637 and 1638, and by 1639 he could no longer dress himself, eat without difficulty, walk or read and write. Author Aldous Huxley, who wrote about Surin's plight in *The Devils of Loudun* (1952), noted that Surin's "pathological illiteracy" continued until 1657. In 1645 Surin attempted suicide. He would have probably died had not the kindly Father Bastide taken over as head of the Jesuit College at Saintes, where Surin lived, in 1648. He brought Surin back to health step by step, giving him the love and attention Surin had never experienced. Eventually Father Surin was able to walk again, and to read and write; he even attained enough inner strength to preach and hear confession. He wrote of his experiences at Loudun in his memoirs, *Science Experimentale*, and finally died, peacefully, in 1665.

The setting of an exorcism. Dr. Martin carefully describes the scene of an exorcism, noting that there is a special connection between the spirit and its possessing location, most often the victim's bedroom or personal place. Anything that can be moved is taken out, such as rugs, lamps, dressers, curtains, tables and trunks, to minimize flying objects. Only a bed or couch remains, accompanied by a small side table to hold a crucifix, candle, holy water and prayer book. Doors and windows are closed but cannot be nailed shut as air must be allowed to enter the room. Doorways must be kept covered, even if the door is open, or else the evil forces inside the room could affect the vicinity outside. Late-20th-century exorcists also employ a small tape recorder to validate the procedure. The priest-exorcist wears a white surplice and a purple stole.

Few exorcists choose to work alone; they are usually assisted by a junior priest chosen by the diocese and in training to be an exorcist himself. The assistant monitors the exorcist, trying to keep him to the business at hand and not be misguided by the perversions of the demons, and provides physical aid if necessary. If the exorcist collapses or even dies during the ritual, the assistant takes over.

Other assistants include a medical doctor and perhaps a family member. According to Dr. Martin, four assistants are normal. Each must be physically strong and be relatively guiltless at the time of the exorcism, so that the Devil cannot use their secret sins as a weapon against the exorcism. Dr. Martin continues:

The exorcist must be as certain as possible beforehand that his assistants will not be weakened or overcome by obscene behavior or by language foul beyond their imagining; they cannot blanch at blood, excrement, urine; they must be able to take awful personal insults and be prepared to have their darkest secrets screeched in public in front of their companions.

Rites of exorcism. Rituals vary from a more spiritual laying-on of hands by a clairvoyant exorcist, taking the entity into his or her own body and then expelling it, to the formal procedure outlined in the Catholic *RITUALE ROMANUM.* Salt, which represents purity, and wine, which represents the blood of Christ, figure prominently in exorcisms as well as strong-smelling substances such as hellebore, attar of roses and rue.

Members of many faiths—Hasidic Jews, Muslims, Hindus, Protestant Christians and Pentecostal Christians—practice exorcism, but only the Roman Catholic church offers a formal ritual. In India, Hindu priests may blow cow-dung smoke, burn pig excreta, pull their or the victim's hair, press rock salt between their fingers, use copper coins, recite mantras or prayers, cut the victim's hair and burn it or place a blue band around the victim's neck to exorcise the demonic spirits. Trying another tack, the exorcist may offer bribes of candy or other gifts if the spirit leaves the victim. Early Puritans relied solely on prayer and fasting.

The official exorcism ritual outlined in the *Rituale Romanum* dates back to 1614, with two small revisions made in 1952. Cautioning priests to make sure a victim is truly possessed before proceeding, the rite includes prayers and passages from the Bible and calls upon the demons, in powerful Latin, to depart in the name of Jesus Christ.

While no two exorcisms are exactly alike, they tend to unfold in similar stages:

1. The Presence. The exorcist and his assistants become aware of an alien feeling or entity.
2. Pretense. Attempts by the evil spirit to appear and act as the victim, to be seen as one and the same person. The exorcist's first job is to break this Pretense and find out who the demon really is. Naming the demon is the most important first step.
3. Breakpoint. The moment where the demon's Pretense finally collapses. Dr. Martin describes such a moment as a scene of extreme panic and confusion, accompanied by a crescendo of abuse, horrible sights, noises and smells. The demon begins to speak of the possessed victim in the third person instead of as itself.
4. The Voice. Also a sign of the Breakpoint, the Voice

is, in the words of Dr. Martin, "inordinately disturbing and humanly distressing babel." The demon's voices must be silenced for the exorcism to proceed.
5. The Clash. As the Voice dies out, there is tremendous pressure, both spiritual and physical. The demon has collided with the "will of the Kingdom." The exorcist, locked in battle with the demon, urges the entity to reveal more information about itself as the exorcist's holy will begins to dominate. As mentioned above, there is a direct link between the entity and place, as each spirit wants a place to be. For such spirits, habitation of a living victim is preferable to Hell.
6. Expulsion. In a supreme triumph of God's will, the spirit leaves in the name of Jesus, and the victim is reclaimed. All present feel the Presence dissipating, sometimes with receding noises or voices. The victim may remember the ordeal or may have no idea what has happened.

While exorcism may be the final answer for demonic possession, most exorcists and spiritualists advise prevention rather than cure. The most important measure is to refrain from dabbling in the supernatural, especially with ouija boards. If possession has begun, one should try forcing the mind to expel the spirits by strongly concentrating on other things and ideas—even watching television to drown out the voices inside. And most important, one should call upon one's Supreme Being, however that idea manifests itself, for guidance.

See also DEMONIC POSSESSION.

demonic possession A person who is demonically possessed suffers from a complete takeover of his or her personality by a diabolical entity, allowing the entity to dominate; the victim becomes, even somewhat physically, that demonic being. In the past, apparent demonic possession commonly was blamed on bewitchment, when in fact the causes often were hysterical fantasies, physical and mental disorders and repressed sexual desire. In modern times, demonic possession is still sometimes attributed to WITCHCRAFT; however, it is against the religious principles of neo-Pagan Witchcraft to cause harm of any sort, including demonic possession, to any living thing.

Christian theology in the Middle Ages considered the idea of spirit possession heretical, so anyone found showing signs of unusual behavior or a different personality was automatically possessed (*energumenus;* the possessed person is an *energumen*) by the DEVIL. Early Christians enjoyed a much more intimate relationship with Christ and God, so con-

Hanging of farm woman convicted of being possessed by demons (*Rappresentatione della assione,* 1520)

sequently they feared personal, active intervention by the forces of evil. PRAYERS, CHARMS and AMULETS were employed to keep the Devil at bay, since he was constantly on the prowl for unsuspecting victims.

There are two ways to become possessed by the Devil: either the Devil passes directly into a person, or someone—usually said to be a witch or wizard—working with the Devil sends a demon into a victim through bewitchment (see WITCHES; WIZARDS). Many medieval unfortunates found themselves branded as witches or evil ones simply because they were old, ugly or on the social fringe (see HAG). Notes Julio Caro Baroja in *The World of the Witches* (1961):

> there is a deep-rooted belief in various parts of Europe in the existence of people who quite involuntarily bring "bad luck" (*mal fario*) . . . or have the "evil eye." . . . Spanish writers of the 16th and 17th centuries worked out theories that the "evil eye" was the result of the presence of certain harmful properties in the eye or in other parts of the body of certain types of people . . . more particularly through those of elderly spinsters, cripples and certain types of sick people.

Such evil body parts were not necessarily the result of the unfortunate's own free will (see EVIL EYE). Terrible deformities, especially of the face, also led the general populace to believe the sufferer was marked by the Devil, much as the Elephant Man of nineteenth-century London was feared and mocked.

Most medieval thinkers, however, firm in their belief in man's sinfulness, assumed that the Devil used one of his human henchmen to torment the innocent. Every time a child sickened or had seizures—which now probably would be diagnosed as epilepsy—or livestock died, or crops failed, sufferers looked for a witch responsible. The witch usually was a poor old woman, angry with her station in life, argumentative with her neighbors and quite likely a midwife.

The witch was believed to transmit the demon through some tangible object, often a potion, charm or amulet. The most common means of sending the Devil to an innocent victim was through food. In his *Dialogues,* Pope Gregory the Great tells the story of a possessed servant girl. She apparently ate some lettuce leaves from the garden, and a devil had been sitting on one when she consumed it. The demon complained about such treatment of an innocent bystander, but he was exorcised anyway.

Henri Boguet, a great demonologist and witch judge in 17th-century France, found that apples, a treat in which the Devil could easily hide and that raised no alarm in the eater, were the best food for transmission. "In this, Satan continually rehearses the means by which he tempted Adam and Eve in the earthly paradise," Boguet comments in *Discours des sorciers* (1602), his authoritative legal textbook on demonology. He reports an incident at Annecy, Savoy, in 1585 where townspeople pushed an apple that was giving out a "great and confused noise" into the river. Boguet says confidently that the apple was no doubt full of devils and that the citizens had successfully foiled a witch's attempt to possess someone.

Modern occultists and exorcists believe that people become possessed by evil spirits today by toying with the supernatural, such as by playing with an ouija board, a DIVINATION device in which entities are invited to spell out messages on a board with a pointer operated by the human medium. The spirits that are attracted by the ouija usually take unpleasant shapes.

The Jesuit professor Dr. Malachi Martin, in *Hostage to the Devil* (1976), outlines the stages of possession: the actual entry point, when the evil spirit first enters the victim; a stage of erroneous judgments by the possessed in vital matters, perhaps including the making of unethical choices; the voluntary yielding of control by the possessed person to the invading spirit, even though he knows the spirit is alien to his personality; and finally, perfect possession. Although Dr. Martin acknowledges the original innocence of the victim, he stresses that possession cannot occur without the consent, however subliminal, of the possessed.

The Catholic Church defines the true signs of possession as displaying superhuman strength, often accompanied by fits and convulsions; having knowledge of the future or other secret information; being able to understand and converse in languages previously unknown to the victim; and revulsion toward sacred objects or texts. Early Puritan ministers and later Protestant clergy agree on these same signs, adding the complete ignorance of the possessed person about his fits and behaviors. In a treatise written in Rouen in 1644, in response to the possession at Louviers convent (see LOUVIERS POSSESSIONS), the author lists 11 indications of demonic possession, which would alert a priest to look for the sure signs:

1. To think oneself possessed.
2. To lead a wicked life.
3. To live outside the rules of society. (Many accused witches led mildly scandalous lives.)
4. To be persistently ill, falling into heavy sleep and vomiting strange objects (see ALLOTRIOPHAGY). Some theologians described such symptoms as merely illusions caused by a witch, not signs of possession.
5. To blaspheme.
6. To make a pact with the Devil. (Most demonologists found pact-makers were accused witches, not possessed victims; see DEVIL'S PACT.)
7. To be troubled by spirits.
8. To show a frightening and horrible countenance. (The thinking was that since God and his angels were beautiful, man made in God's image, and not the Devil's, would be beautiful, too.)
9. To be tired of living (and probably contemplating suicide, a sin).
10. To be uncontrollable and violent.
11. To make sounds and movements like an animal. (Many medieval sufferers believed they were vicious animals, most often wolves. Some resorted to running on all fours and even tearing at their victims with their teeth. From such stories arose the myths of LYCANTHROPY, or werewolves.)

To this list may be added the practice of lewd and obscene acts—or even just sexual thoughts—and the classic picture of a possessed person emerges. Many possessed victims smelled horrible as well, either of foul bodily odors or of sulphur, associated with the Devil's fiery home.

Other signs of possession include a complete change in body features, such as a distended stomach, wrenching of the face into horrible expressions or rapid weight loss. The victim may seem so wasted that death appears inevitable. The voice usually changes also, to a deep, rasping, menacing, guttural croak. Sometimes the evil spirit expresses itself through automatic writing. Other possessed victims, like ANNA ECKLUND, levitated.

Examined in the light of 20th-century medicine, the convulsions and seizures, the manifestations of another personality and even the paranormal experiences are most likely symptoms of epilepsy, hysteria, schizophrenia or some other psychological problem. Demonic possession is not the automatic answer for unexplained behavior, nor is exorcism the preferred treatment (see DEMONIC EXORCISM). For the Catholic Church, only when the indications of possession are accompanied by striking paranormal phenomena and extreme revulsion toward sacred objects should they be considered manifestations of the Devil.

Even during the height of witchcraft and possession hysteria in the 16th and 17th centuries, debate raged over the existence of witches and whether they could cause people to be possessed by the Devil. "Celebrity" possession victims like Jeanne des Anges in Loudun (see LOUDUN POSSESSIONS) and the infamous MARTHE BROSSIER were sometimes tricked into convulsing at the sight of a "holy" relic, when in fact the item was just a piece of wood or plain water. Ten years after Urbain Grandier's death for his role at Loudun, a Frenchman named Monconys visited Jeanne des Anges at the convent and found that the "blood" of her stigmata was merely red paint.

Famous cases of demonic possession in the 16th and 17th centuries include Nicole of Laon (see MIRACLE OF LAON), who used her possession by Beelzebub to indict French Huguenots; the possessions of nuns at the convents of Aix-en-Provence (see AIX-EN-PROVENCE POSSESSIONS), Louviers, Lille and Loudun; the WITCHES OF WARBOYS, or the possession of the Throckmorton children in England; the fraud Marthe Brossier; and the witchcraft hysteria in Salem (see SALEM WITCHES). The possession of the BRUNER brothers in Alsace; the Watseka Possession, or Lurancy Vennum; and the case of Anna Ecklund stand out as notorious instances of possession in the 19th and 20th centuries. Many other, smaller incidents have been documented, and exorcism of possessing demons continues today.

See also SPIRIT POSSESSION.

demons Any of a wide range of lesser intermediary spirits between their world and the physical world. Demons usually are associated with evil, but in pre-Christian and non-Christian cultures, demons were, and are, not necessarily good or evil. There are good and bad demons, and demons capable of both kinds of behavior. The study of demons is called *demonology.*

The term *demon* means "replete with wisdom;" good demons once were called *eudemons,* and evil demons were called *cacodemons. Demon* is derived from the Greek term *daimon,* or "divine power," "fate" or "god." In Greek mythology, *daimons* included deified heroes. *Daimons* were intermediary spirits between man and the gods. A good *daimon* acted as a guardian spirit, and it was considered lucky to have one for guidance and protection. A guardian *daimon* whispered advice and ideas in one's ear. Evil *daimons* could lead one astray. Socrates claimed he had a *daimon* his entire life. The *daimon's* voice warned him of danger and bad decisions but never directed him what to do. Socrates said his guardian spirit was more trustworthy than omens from the flights and entrails of birds, two highly respected forms of divination at the time.

Historically, demons have been controlled by magicians and sorcerers. Solomon commanded the DJINN to work for him. Demons have been exorcised as the causes of disease, misfortune and possession (see DEMONIC POSSESSION). In ancient Egypt, it was believed that a magician who exorcised a demon responsible for a possession would be just as likely to use the same demon to other ends. To the present day in many tribal societies, demons are blamed for a wide range of misfortunes and illnesses.

Jewish systems of demonology have long and complex histories and distinguish between classes of demons. According to the KABBALAH, evil powers emanate from the left pillar of the Tree of Life, especially from Geburah, the sephira (sphere) of the wrath of God. By the 13th century, the idea had developed of ten evil sephiroth to counter the ten holy sephiroth of the Tree. Another system of demons distinguishes those born of night terrors, and yet another system describes the demons that fill the sky between the earth and the moon. There are demons who, with angels, are in charge of the night hours, and interpretations of diseases, and those who have seals that may be used to summon them.

In the development of Christian demonology, demons have come to be associated only with evil; by virtue of being demons, they are agents of the DEVIL. Good Christian spirits belong to the ranks of angels of the Lord. In the Bible, demons are linked to the fallen angels who followed Lucifer when he was cast out of heaven by God. In early Christianity, by the end of the New Testament period, demons were synonymous with fallen angels, all under the general direction of Satan. Their sole purpose was to tempt humankind into immoral acts and come between humans and God. It is an oft-said truism that when one culture gains dominance over another, the gods of the old become the demons of the new. As Christianity spread, the ranks of demons swelled to include the gods and demons of the ancient Middle Eastern and Jewish traditions, and all pagan deities and nature spirits.

As agents of the Devil, demons became associated with WITCHES during the Middle Ages and Renaissance, an association perpetuated well beyond the Reformation. INCREASE MATHER, writing in *Cases of Conscience* (1693), said, "The Scriptures assert that there are Devils and Witches and that they are the common enemy of Mankind." George Giffard, an Oxford preacher of about the same period, said that witches should be put to death not because they kill others but because they deal with devils: "These cunning men and women which deale with spirites and charme seeming to do good, and draw the people into manifold impieties, with all other which haue [have] familiarity with deuils [devils], or use conjurations, ought to bee rooted out, that others might see and feare."

Sex between Humans and Demons

Demons with sexual appetites for intercourse with humans exist in the demonologies of the ancient Hebrews, Egyptians, Greeks, Romans, Assyrians, Persians and other cultures. In *The Zohar* ("Book of Splendor"), the principal work of the Kabbalah, any pollution of semen results in the birth of demons, including intercourse with the night-terror demons such as LILITH. Demons in the shape of human males (*incubi*) prey on women, while demons in female shapes (*succubi*) prey on men. In Christianity, the possibility of intercourse with demons was denied prior to the 12th century. But as the Inquisition began and gained force, intercourse with demons became accepted in theological dogma by the 14th century. In particular, witches and other heretics—enemies of the Church—were said not only to have sex with demons but also to copulate wildly and frequently with them, especially at SABBATS, and to worship them in their rites. In many cases, the distinction between the Devil himself and demons was blurry, and witches said to copulate with "the Devil" probably were accused of having sex with an incubus or succubus.

Sex with demons invariably was portrayed as unpleasant and painful. Sometimes demons appeared to persons in the forms of their spouses or lovers. After copulation, they would reveal their true identities and blackmail the victims into continuing the sexual liaison.

Incubi were especially attracted to women with beautiful hair, young virgins, chaste widows and all "devout" females. Nuns were among the most vulnerable and could be molested in the confessional as well as in bed. While the majority of women were forced into sex by the incubi, it was believed that some of them submitted willingly and even enjoyed the act. Incubi had huge phalluses, sometimes made of horn or covered with scales, and they ejaculated icy semen. When they appeared as demons and not as human impostors, they were described as ugly, hairy and foul-smelling.

Incubi were believed to have the ability to impregnate women. They did not possess their own semen but collected it from men in nocturnal emissions, masturbation or in coitus while masquerading as succubi. The demons preserved the semen and used it later on one of their victims. The children that resulted were considered the child of the man who unwittingly provided the semen; some horror stories held that the children came out half human and half beast.

In a small number of cases, claims of molestation by incubi were dismissed as the products of female melancholia or vivid imaginations. False pregnancies that arose from this state were chalked up to flatulence.

The wild copulation between witches and demons was lamented in the MALLEUS MALEFICARUM (1486), which noted that "in times long past the Incubus devils used to infest women against their wills [but] modern witches . . . willingly embrace this most foul and miserable servitude." Some incubi served as FAMILIARS to witches, who sent them to torment specific individuals.

Since sex with incubi was expected of witches, many accused witches were tortured until they confessed to this crime (see TORTURE). In 1485 the Inquisitor of Como sent 41 such women to their deaths at the stake. Their "confessions" were corroborated, incredibly, by eye-witness accounts, as well as by hearsay evidence "and the testimony of credible witnesses."

Incubi were believed to be always visible to witches but only occasionally visible to others—even the victims. Reports exist of people observed in the throes of passion with invisible partners. Husbands, however, commonly saw incubi as they copulated with their wives but thought they were other men.

The Church prescribed five ways to get rid of incubi and succubi: 1) by making a Sacramental Confession; 2) by making the sign of the cross; 3) by reciting the Ave Maria; 4) by moving to another house or town; and 5) by excommunication of the demon by holy men. Sometimes the LORD'S PRAYER worked, as did a sprinkling of holy water.

Succubi could appear in the flesh as beautiful, voluptuous women (perhaps an indication of male fantasies). They usually visited men in their sleep—especially men who slept alone—and their sexual activities caused erotic dreams and nocturnal emissions.

Succubi were not as prevalent as incubi. Because of the inherent evil of women, in the view of Christianity, women were morally weak and therefore more licentious than men. If a man were assaulted by a succubus, it was most likely not his fault.

The sex act itself with a succubus was often described as penetrating a cavern of ice. There are accounts of men being forced to perform cunnilingus on succubi, whose vaginas dripped urine, dung and other vile juices and smells.

Succubi appeared often in the records of witchcraft trials. Men accused of witchcraft sometimes were tortured until they confessed having sex with demons, among other diabolical crimes. In 1468 in Bologna, Italy, a man was executed for allegedly running a brothel of succubi.

It should be noted that cases of sexual molestation by demons did not die with the witch-hunts; they continue to be reported to the present time, often in connection with poltergeist activities and demonic possession. *The Haunted,* by Robert Curran (1988), tells of the Smurl family of Wilkes-Barre, Pennsylvania, who say they have been tormented by a hideous demon for several years. The demon has manifested in various forms, including a hag with scraggly, long white hair, scaly skin and vampirelike fangs, which sexually molested the husband. (See also NIGHTMARE.)

Demons in Modern Witchcraft

Demons play no role in neo-Pagan Witchcraft. Demons are invoked in satanic rituals (see SATANISM), which have no connection with neo-Pagan Witchcraft.

Demons in Ceremonial Magic

Ceremonial magicians view demons as powerful intelligences that may be summoned and controlled in rituals. They also work with other spirits, including god-forms, elementals, angels, planetary and Zodiacal spirits and thought-forms. The GRIMOIRES give detailed instructions for conjuring and controlling demons. The rituals are tedious, but modern magicians say they work. Demons are dangerous; hence the magician takes great care to be precise. Demons appear in ingenious disguises to try to tempt magicians out of the protective MAGIC CIRCLE, shriek obscenities, spit on the magicians and threaten to go out of control. (See also MAGIC.)

A dramatic example of the dangers of conjuring demons occurred in 1909 and involved ALEISTER CROWLEY and his student, Victor Neuberg. Crowley routinely conjured demons in his exploration of the Aethyrs of ENOCHIAN MAGIC. The two went into the desert south of Algiers, where they cast a magic circle to protect Neuberg and a triangle in which Crowley would conjure a manifestation of the Abyss of the eleventh Aethyr. They slit the throats of three pigeons, one at each point of the triangle, "that their blood might be a basis whereon the forces of evil might build themselves bodies," according to Crowley. Dressed in a hooded black robe, Crowley went through a ritual in which he allowed himself to become possessed by the Dweller of the Abyss, Choronzon. The demon, he said, was not an individual but an evil and malignant force that longed to become real.

Crowley saw Choronzon appear in his SCRYING topaz, blustering, raging and laughing wildly. From within the triangle, it manifested to Neuberg and tried to entice him out of his circle so that it could take control of him. To do so, it flattered him and promised to serve him; took the form of a woman Neuberg loved; appeared as a serpent with a human head; and took the form of a naked Crowley begging for water to slake his thirst. Neuberg attempted to control the demon with the Names of God and the pentagram, to no avail (see NAMES OF POWER). Choronzon began dictating a long speech, and while Neuberg wrote furiously, the demon threw sand from the triangle and broke the magic circle. It rushed in, flung Neuberg to the ground and tried to tear out his throat with froth-covered fangs. Neuberg once again invoked the Names of God and struck at the demon with his magic dagger. Cowed, the demon writhed back into the triangle, where it continued to rave and attempted another seduction as the woman Neuberg loved. But the blood of the pigeons was spent and could no longer sustain the manifestation of form, and Choronzon vanished.

During this episode, Crowley had remained in trance, astrally identifying with the demon and experiencing all of the emotions it exhibited. When it was over, he took his magic ring and wrote the holy name of Babalon in the sand. He and Neuberg lit a fire to purify the site and destroyed the circle and triangle. The two-hour ordeal left both men exhausted. Some say that Crowley was obsessed by Choronzon for the rest of his life.

The Hierarchies and Functions of Demons

Demons have been catalogued, ranked and classified since at least 100–400 A.D. the period in which the *Testament of Solomon* appeared, describing Solomon's magic ring for commanding the DJINN and listing the names and functions of various Hebrew, Greek, Assyrian, Babylonian, Egyptian and perhaps Persian demons. Christian demonologists of the 16th and 17th centuries catalogued demons into hierarchies of hell and ascribed to them attributes and

Asmodeus, demon of lust and anger (L. Breton, in Collin de Plancy's *Dictionnaire Infernal,* 1863)

duties, including ambassadorships to various nations. JOHANN WEYER, who devised the most complex hierarchy, estimated that there were 7,405,926 demons serving under 72 princes. The grimoires of ceremonial magic also give their own hierarchies. Some of the major demons are:

Asmodeus. The demon of lechery, jealousy, anger and revenge. His chief objectives are to prevent intercourse between husband and wife, wreck new marriages and force husbands to commit adultery. He is also one of the chief demons involved in cases of possession. Throughout history, he has been regarded as one of the most evil of Satan's infernal demons. He is usually portrayed as having three heads, those of an ogre, a ram and a bull, all sexually licentious creatures; having the feet of a cock, another sexually aggressive creature; and having wings. He rides on a dragon and breathes fire.

Asmodeus has his roots in ancient Persia. He is identified with the demon Aeshma, one of the seven archangels of Persian mythology. The Hebrews absorbed him into their mythology, where he attained the highest status and most power of all demons in Hebrew legends. According to the Hebrews, he is the son of Naamah and Shamdon. He was part of the Seraphim, the highest order of angels, but fell from grace. In other Hebrew legends, he is either associated with or is the husband of Lilith, the demon queen of lust. Sometimes he is said to be the offspring of Lilith and Adam.

Asmodeus migrated into Christian lore, becoming one of the Devil's leading agents of provocation. Witches in the Middle Ages were said to worship him, and magicians and sorcerers attempted to conjure him to strike out at enemies. The medieval grimoires sternly admonish anyone seeking an audience with Asmodeus to summon him bareheaded out of respect. Weyer said Asmodeus also ruled the gambling houses. He was one of the infernal agents blamed for the obscene sexual possession of the Louviers nuns in 17th-century France (see LOUVIERS POSSESSIONS).

Astaroth (also Ashtaroth). A male demon who evolved from the ancient Phoenician mother goddess of fertility, ASTARTE or Ashtoreth. In his male incarnation, he has little to do with man's sexual nature. He is a teacher of the sciences and a keeper of the secrets of the past, present and future and is invoked in necromantic rituals of DIVINATION. He appears as an angel in human form, by some accounts ugly and by other accounts beautiful. He does, however, possess a powerful stench. Weyer said Astaroth was a grand duke of hell and commanded 40 legions of demons. Astaroth is listed as one of the three supreme evil demons, with Beelzebub and Lucifer, in the *Grimoire Verum* and *Grand Grimoire,* which date from about the 18th century.

The demon is said to instigate cases of demonic possession, most notably that of the Loudun nuns in France in the 16th century. The nuns accused a priest, Father Urbain Grandier, of causing their possession. At Grandier's trial, a handwritten "confession" of his was produced detailing his pact with the Devil, witnessed and signed by Astaroth and several other demons (see LOUDUN POSSESSIONS).

Baal. Many small deities of ancient Syria and Persia carried this name, which means "the lord" (from the Hebrew *ba'al*), but the greatest Baal was an agricultural and fertility deity of Canaan. The son of El, the High God of Canaan, Baal was the lord of life and ruled the death-rebirth cycle. He engaged in a battle with Mot ("death") and was slain and sent to the underworld. The crops withered, until Baal's sister, Anath, the maiden goddess of love, found his body and gave it a proper burial. The Canaanites worshipped Baal by sacrificing children by burning. As a demon in Christianity, Baal was triple-headed, with a cat's head and a toad's head on either side of his human head. He imparted visibility and wisdom.

Beelzebub. Known as "Lord of the Flies," Beelzebub was the prince of demons in Hebrew belief at the time of Jesus. The Pharisees accused Christ of exorcising demons in Beelzebub's name. In medieval

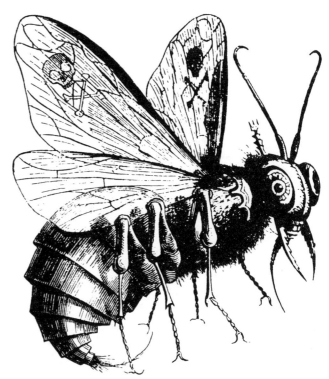

Beelzebub, "Lord of the Flies" (L. Breton, in Collin de Plancy's *Dictionnaire Infernal,* 1863)

times, Beelzebub was regarded as a demon of great power. A sorcerer conjured him at his own risk of death by apoplexy or strangulation; once conjured, the demon was difficult to banish. When he manifested, it was as a gigantic, ugly fly.

Beelzebub was said to reign over witches' sabbats. Witches denied Christ in his name and chanted it as they danced. There are many stories of his copulating with witches in wild orgies; to do this, he apparently appeared in other than fly form. When Black Masses were fashionable in high society in the 17th century, Beelzebub's name was chanted during the rites (see BLACK MASS).

Beelzebub was among the demons blamed for the demonic possession cases of the nuns of Loudun and Aix-en-Provence in 17th-century France, forcing the nuns into lewd behavior (see LOUDUN POSSESSIONS; AIX-EN-PROVENCE POSSESSIONS).

Belial. One of Satan's most important and evil demons, who is deceptively beautiful in appearance and soft in voice, but full of treachery, recklessness and lies. He is dedicated to creating wickedness and guilt in mankind, especially in the form of sexual perversions, fornication and lust.

Belial's name probably comes from the Hebrew phrase *beli ya'al,* which means "without worth." The ancient Hebrews believed Belial was the next angel created after Lucifer and was evil from the start, being one of the first to revolt against God. After his

Belial (Jacobus de Teramo, *Das Bach Belial*, 1473)

fall from heaven, he became the personification of evil.

Weyer believed Belial commanded 80 legions of demons (at 6,666 demons per legion) and served as infernal ambassador to Turkey. Magicians of that time believed that sacrifices and offerings were necessary to invoke him. Belial was reputed to break his promises to magicians, but those who managed to gain his true favor were handsomely rewarded.

Belial's name is sometimes used as a synonym for Satan or the Antichrist. In the Old Testament, the phrase "sons of Belial" refers to worthlessness and recklessness. Belial also is known as Beliar.

Lucifer. In Latin, his name means "light-bringer," and he originally was associated with Venus, the morning star. His rebellion against God caused him and his followers to be cast from heaven. The fallen angels lost their beauty and power and became "fiendes black." The name "Lucifer" was sometimes applied to Christ, as the light-bearer, but in the Middle ages, both "Lucifer" and "Satan" were used as names for the Devil. Lucifer could apply to the Devil in either his pre-fall or post-fall state. In the

hierarchies of demons, Lucifer is emperor of hell and ranks above Satan, one of his lieutenants (ranks and distinctions not made in theology). When conjured, he appears as a beautiful child. Lucifer was said to rule Europeans and Asiatics.

deosil (also deiseal) Clockwise circular movement which in MAGIC and WITCHCRAFT is used in casting positive SPELLS and in casting the MAGIC CIRCLE. The clockwise rotation is associated with the movement of the sun across the heavens and with blessings and good fortune. *Deiseal* is the Irish term for "a turning to the right," or the "holy round." Deosil dances and circuits are done not only around magic circles but around sabbat fires (see SABBATS), holy objects such as sacred STONES, crops, fields, homes and buildings. The opposite of deosil is WIDDERSHINS.

Descent of the Goddess See RITE OF PASSING.

Devil Christianity's Prince of Supreme Evil, the Devil, or Satan, is not a god of neo-Pagan WITCHES.

Lucifer reigning over souls of sinners (John Baptist Medina for John Milton's *Paradise Lost*, 1688)

The notion that witches worshipped the Devil arose in the Middle Ages and Reformation, when belief in a personal Satan as the agent of all evil was particularly strong. Accusations of Devil-worship were not limited to witches. Christians charged the same of Jews, Muslims, pagans, Cathars, Albigenses, Waldenses, "Red Indians" and other heretics, and Protestants and Catholics accused each other of it as well. Even Martin Luther was said by Catholics to have given himself over to the Devil.

The term *Devil* comes from the Greek *diabolos* ("slanderer" or "accuser"), translated from the Hebrew *satan*. The concept of the Devil as archfiend of evil developed slowly over many centuries, becoming a composite of Lucifer, the fallen angel whose pride and ego get him expelled from heaven; Satan, the tempter of man; and various pagan deities such as PAN and CERNUNNOS. The religion of the early Hebrews was, like pagan and Eastern religions, monistic, in that the one Supreme Being, God, or Yahweh, was both good and bad. Satan plays a minor role in the Old Testament as the opponent of man, dispatched

by God to test man's faith. He is not evil and is an angel in the kingdom of heaven. In Job, Satan follows God's instructions to destroy Job's family and possessions and cover him with running sores in an effort to tempt him into cursing God. In the New Testament, Satan becomes more personal and is the great antagonist of God as well as man. Revelations forecasts that Christ, in his second coming, will bind the Devil for 1,000 years, at which time the Devil will reappear one final time, as the Antichrist, before being destroyed. The dualism of Christianity became firmly established, with a god of light and goodness and a god of evil and darkness.

By the Middle Ages, Satan, the Devil, was a real, potent being who possessed terrible supernatural powers and was intent upon destroying man by undermining his morals. In this pursuit, he was aided by an army of evil DEMONS (a corruption of the Greek term *daimon* or *daemon*, meaning "guardian spirit"). This army expanded to include heretics and sorcerers, whose MAGIC posed a threat to the divine miracles of the Church. Witches were included first as associates of sorcerers (see SORCERY), then as heretics.

Preachers in the Middle Ages and Reformation pounded fear of the Devil into their followers by constantly inveighing against his attempts to pervert people and turn them away from God. Satan's kingdom was the material world. He would tempt people with false riches, luxuries and carnal pleasures, only to claim their souls for eternal damnation in the end. His chief means of attacking others was through demonic possession. Pacts with the Devil, which date back to the 6th century, became implied; any consort with the Devil automatically meant one had entered into a diabolic pact (see DEVIL'S PACT). John Stearne, the assistant to MATTHEW HOPKINS, England's notorious witch-hunter of the 17th century, was of the opinion that the preachers' obsession with Satan encouraged witches to worship him. Undoubtedly, there must have been some persons so beaten down by poverty that worship of such a powerful being as the Devil offered the only hope of relief. Agnes Wilson, an accused witch of Northampton in 1612, was asked how many gods she believed in and replied, "Two—God the Father, and the Devil." Her answer was no surprise in light of the prevailing social-religious climate, but it was taken by her prosecutors as an admission of Devil-worship.

The Devil was said to appear in many guises in order to fool people. His most common human shape was that of a tall black man or a tall man, often handsome, dressed in black. Black is universally associated with fear, evil, the dark and chaos. Henri Boguet (1550–1619), a jurist in witch trials, stated in *Discourse des sorciers* (1602) that:

Whenever he [the Devil] assumes the form of a man, he is, however, always black, as all witches bear witness. And for my part I hold that there are two principal reasons for this: first, that he who is the Father and Ruler of darkness may not be able to disguise himself so well that he may not always be known for what he is; secondly, as proof that his study is only to do evil; for evil, as Pythagoras said, is symbolized by black.

The Devil also could appear as a saint, the Virgin Mary, comely young women and preachers. He could appear in a multitude of animal shapes, most commonly a dog, a serpent or a goat (see METAMORPHOSIS). He also had ugly appearances: as the alleged god of witches, he was portrayed as half human, half animal, like Pan, with horns, cloven feet, hairy legs, a tail, a huge penis, glowing eyes and Saturnine features.

In folklore, the Devil was often portrayed in a lighter fashion, perhaps to mitigate the fear inspired by the clergy. He was often buffoonish and called by nicknames such as Jack, Old Nick, Old Horny and Lusty Dick. He could be easily tricked, as in the numerous versions of the DEVIL'S BRIDGE story.

Witches attending Satan (Pierre Boaistuau, *Histoires prodigieuses*, 1597)

In both theology and folklore, the distinction between the Devil as Prince of Evil and his hordes of demons often blurs. The phrase "the devil" referred to both. Joseph Glanvil observed in *Saducismus Triumphatus* (1689) that "The Devil is a name for a body politic, in which there are very different orders and degrees of spirits, and perhaps in as much variety of place and state, as among ourselves."

Images of the Devil have remained largely unchanged to present times. The New Age movement, which gained momentum in the 1960s as the Age of Aquarius, has been termed the "Devil's plan for world domination" by certain Fundamentalist Christians. The worship of Satan as a god of power and materialism is practiced by numerous groups. Neo-Pagans and neo-Pagan Witches do not worship the Devil. Pagan deities, and the HORNED GOD of Witches, are often confused in the public mind with the Devil.

See also INITIATION; SABBATS; SATANISM; SIX-SIX-SIX.

devil fish A type of ray fish used by Mexican witches (*brujas* or *brujos*) in the casting of SPELLS. When dried, the devil fish resembles a man with a horned head, tail and webbed arms. It is considered effective in quieting up gossipy neighbors.

Devil's bridge Numerous old bridges in England and Europe are called "Devil's bridge" because of folkloric belief that the DEVIL or his DEMONS helped in their construction. According to ancient legends, demons were master architects and builders. The legendary King Solomon commanded legions of them and the DJINN to build his temples. It was believed in the Middle Ages that whenever engineers and architects needed help or ran out of resources, the Devil and his demons stepped in to lend a helping hand. The infernal beings were called upon most often for bridges but also assisted with the construction of castles.

Devil's bridges are particularly common in Britain, Spain, Germany, Switzerland and France. There is a Devil's bridge in Einsiedeln, Switzerland, near the birthplace of PARACELSUS. In France, the Pont de Valentre bridge at Cahors was believed to be entirely constructed by the Devil.

The Devil's price for this service was the soul of the first creature who crossed the bridge. Folktales tell of local townsfolk tricking the Devil by sending a cat or dog across first. In the legend of the Devil's bridge across the Afon Mynach near Aberystwyth, Wales, an old woman spotted her cow on the opposite side of a chasm, unreachable. The Devil appeared in disguise and offered to create a bridge if she would give him the first living thing that crossed

St. Cado and Devil bargaining over Devil's bridge (French print)

Satan marking witch with claw (R. P. Guaccius, *Compendium Maleficarum*, 1626)

over it. She agreed, though she knew she was dealing with the Devil, because she had spotted his cloven hooves. When the bridge was completed, she threw a crust of bread across and sent her dog to fetch it.

Devil's Dandy Dogs See WILD HUNT.

Devil's mark According to medieval witch-hunters, the DEVIL always permanently marked the bodies of his initiates to seal their pledge of obedience and service to him. He marked them by raking his claw across their flesh or using a hot iron, which left a mark, usually blue or red, but not a scar. Sometimes he left a mark by licking them. The Devil supposedly branded WITCHES at the end of INITIATION rites, which were performed at nocturnal SABBATS.

The marks were always made in "secret places," such as under eyelids, in armpits and in body cavities. The mark was considered the ultimate proof of being a witch—all witches and sorcerers (see SORCERY) were believed to have at least one. All persons accused of WITCHCRAFT and brought to trial were thoroughly searched for such a mark. Scars, birthmarks, natural blemishes and insensitive patches of skin that did not bleed qualified as Devil's marks. Experts firmly believed that the mark of Satan was clearly distinguishable from ordinary blemishes, but in actuality, that was seldom the case. Protests from the victims that the marks were natural were ignored.

Accounts of being marked by the Devil were obtained in the "confessions" of accused witches, who usually were tortured to confess (see TORTURE). Inquisitors routinely stripped off the accused witch's clothes and shaved off all body hair so that no square inch of skin was missed. Pins were driven deeply into scars, calluses and thickened areas of skin (see PRICKING). Since this customarily was done in front of a jeering crowd, it is no surprise that some alleged witches felt nothing from the pricks.

Fortunately for medieval inquisitors, the Devil also left invisible marks upon his followers. If an accused witch had no likely natural blemishes that could be called a Devil's mark, pins were simply driven into her body over and over again until an insensitive area was found.

British anthropologist MARGARET A. MURRAY theorized that Devil's marks were actually tattoos, marks of identification, which she offered as support of her contention that witchcraft as an organized pagan religion had flourished in the Middle Ages. Murray's controversial theories are now discounted.

Devil's marks were sometimes called WITCH'S MARKS.

Devil's pact A pledge to serve the DEVIL or one of his satellite DEMONS, sometimes oral but traditionally written on virgin parchment and signed in BLOOD. The pact provides that in exchange for allegiance and

one's soul, the Devil will grant whatever a person wishes. Pacts with the Devil or demons for personal gain appear in many cultures.

From the earliest days of Christianity, a pact with the Devil was tacitly understood to be part of any MAGIC, SORCERY or DIVINATION performed by an adept. Pacts also involved ordinary people: in legends, the Devil routinely appeared to people in distress and bartered love, money or power in exchange for souls. In the witch hysteria of the Middle Ages and Renaissance, the pact took on new significance as proof of heresy and became grounds for prosecution and condemnation of accused WITCHES. (Pacts with Satan are not part of neo-Pagan Witchcraft; see WITCHCRAFT.)

The definition of a Devil's pact has altered somewhat over the course of history, depending upon its perceived role in magic, sorcery and witchcraft. The collaboration between men and demons, which implies a pact, predates Christ by thousands of years. King Solomon, son of David, acquired his wisdom and riches with the help of an army of demons (see DJINN).

The Bible does not expressly deal with satanic pacts, but Christian theologians have always assumed them to exist and have condemned them. If the worship of God required a pledge of service and the soul, then surely those who followed God's opposite, Satan, would do the same. The prevailing view of the Church was that worldly goods and the like could not be obtained without crime except by appealing directly to God, or to Him through one of his saints.

One of the earliest Christian stories of a pact with Satan concerns THEOPHILUS, treasurer of the church of Adana, who allegedly sold his soul to the Devil around 538 in order to become bishop.

Two major early Christian theologians, Origen (185–254) and St. Augustine (354–430) claimed that divination and the practices of magic and sorcery required demonic pacts. Much later, this was affirmed by the influential theologian THOMAS AQUINAS (ca. 1227–1274), who stated in *Sententiae,* "Magicians perform miracles through personal contracts made with demons."

Using the ritual instructions in a grimoire (see GRIMOIRES), the magician or sorcerer evoked various satellite demons for the purpose of attaining wealth, the power of invisibility, love or political power—but seldom to harm enemies. The belief was that sooner or later such demonic favors sucked the magician into selling his soul to Satan in return. If Satan himself was invoked instead of a lower-ranking demon, he always demanded the magician's soul as payment "up front."

The Key of Solomon, one of the major medieval grimoires whose authorship is attributed to King Solomon, offered the following instruction for making a pact with a demon:

Exactly at dawn, use a new knife to cut a fork-shaped wand from the twig of a wild nut tree that has never borne fruit. Take the wand, a magic bloodstone and consecrated candles to the site of the ritual, preferably a ruined castle or deserted house, where one will be undisturbed and receive whatever treasures the demon produces. With the bloodstone, draw a triangle on the ground or floor, and place the candles on the side of it. Stand in middle of the triangle, hold the wand and recite the required invocation. When the work is finished, recite another incantation to dismiss the demon.

Stories of Devil's pacts were common from the Middle Ages to the 16th and 17th centuries. Typically, the victim was not a witch but an ordinary person who was vulnerable to temptation. Satan or a demon would appear, sometimes as a man and sometimes as an animal, and offer to help. The pact would last for a specified number of years, at which time Satan would collect: the victim would die and his soul would go to hell. Perhaps the best-known tale is the story of FAUST, a scientist and alchemist who sells his soul to the demon Mephistopheles in exchange for youth and lust. These moralistic stories were publicized through pamphlets and portrayed Satan as a trickster. The victim, despite his or her supernatural favors, usually came to a dreadful demise. Sometimes the Virgin Mary would intercede for the victims and snatch the pacts away from the Devil.

In the medieval persecution of witches, the Devil's pact took on new resonance. Witches were said to derive their powers from Satan, which required entering into a pact with him. The purpose of the pact was portrayed less as personal gain than as the deliberate and malicious intent to harm others, and a renunciation of God and the Christian faith. Christian demonologists created a substantial body of literature on Devil's pacts and the alleged rituals surrounding them—and the punishment that should be meted out for such acts. A representative view was expressed by Johann Trithemius (1462–1516), abbot and scholar, in his work, *Liber Octo Quaestionum:*

Witches are a most pestiferous class, who enter on pacts with demons, and, after making a solemn profession of faith, dedicate themselves, in lasting obedience, to some particular demon. No one can describe the evils of which this class of beings is guilty. Hence they must nowhere be tolerated, but utterly and everywhere exterminated.

Demonologists and witch-hunters distinguished between two kinds of pacts: the private pact and the solemn public pact. The private pact was a vow made by a witch, sometimes with the help of another witch. It was assumed that eventually the initiate would declare his or her allegiance to the Devil publicly. The details of these pacts were obtained from accused witches through TORTURE.

The public pact was made in a ceremony, either in a Christian church or at a sabbat, which always took place outdoors (see SABBATS). If held in a church—an act of sacrilege—the Devil himself was not always present; at a sabbat, he was.

According to demonologists, the initiates renounced their Christian faith and baptism, swore allegiance to Satan and promised to sacrifice to him unbaptized children, pledged an annual tribute to him and gave him a token piece of their clothing. They signed a written pact in their own blood. The Devil gave them new names and marked them with his claw (see DEVIL'S MARK). In some accounts, the Devil stripped off the initiates' clothing and forced them to pay homage to him by kissing him on the anus (see KISS OF SHAME).

Typically, all aspects of the ceremony were done in reverse, since Satan is the reverse of God. Crosses were held upside down and then trampled, pacts were written backwards, the initiates signed their names with their left hands and the Devil made his mark on the left side of the body.

Until the 14th century most witches were prosecuted only for the alleged harm they did to people and their animals—not just for worshipping and making a pact with the Devil. The Church began to press the idea that witches should be prosecuted for heresy as well. This view received a powerful impetus from the Bull of POPE INNOCENT VIII (1484), which, in addition to citing various MALEFICIA done by witches, adds, ''. . . over and above this, they blasphemously renounce that Faith which is theirs by the Sacrament of Baptism . . .''

In order to prove this heresy in a witch trial, the existence of a formal pact with the Devil had to be established. Most inquisitors had little trouble with this—they simply tortured the accused until he or she confessed to anything. Seldom was a document actually produced; the Devil conveniently took most of his pacts with him in order to protect his servants.

One notable exception to this was the trial of Father Urbain Grandier, parish priest of St.-Pierre-du-Marche in Loudon, France, in 1633. Grandier was accused of causing the nuns in Loudon to become possessed. At his trial, a Devil's pact, allegedly written backwards in Latin in his own hand and signed in blood,

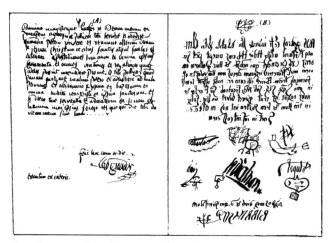

Devil's pact allegedly signed by Father Urbain Grandier of Loudun, countersigned by Lucifer, Beelzebub, Satan, Elimi, Leviathan, Astaroth and Baalbarith

was produced and introduced as evidence. The pact stated:

> We, the all-powerful Lucifer, seconded by Satan, Beelzebub, Leviathan, Elimi, Astaroth, and others, have today accepted the pace of alliance with Urbain Grandier, who is on our side. And we promise him the love of women, the flower of virgins, the chastity of nuns, worldly honors, pleasures, and riches. He will fornicate every three days; intoxication will be dear to him. He will offer to us once a year a tribute marked with his blood; he will trample under foot the sacraments of the church, and he will say his prayers to us. By virtue of this pact, he will live happily for twenty years on earth among men, and finally will come among us to curse God. Done in hell, in the council of the devils.
>
> [Signed by] Satan, Beelzebub, Lucifer, Elimi, Leviathan, Astaroth.
>
> Notarized the signature and mark of the chief devil, and my lords the princes of hell.
>
> [Countersigned by] Baalberith, recorder.

Grandier was convicted and burned (see LOUDUN POSSESSIONS).

Louis Gaufridi, a man who confessed to being a witch in 1611, recited his pact verbally for the inquisitors:

> I, Louis Gaufridi, renounce all good, both spiritual as well as temporal, which may be bestowed upon me by God, the Blessed Virgin Mary, all the Saints of Heaven, particularly my Patron St. John-Baptist, as also S. Peter, S. Paul, and S. Francis, and I give myself body and soul to Lucifer, before whom I stand, together with every good that I may ever possess (save always the benefits of the sacraments touching those who receive them). And according to the tenor of these terms have I signed and sealed.

One of Gaufridi's victims was a woman named Madeleine de la Paud (see AIX-EN-PROVENCE POSSESSIONS) who also confessed her Devil's pact:

> With all my heart and most unfeignedly and with all my will most deliberately do I wholly renounce God, Father, Son and Holy Ghost; the most Holy Mother of God; all the Angels and especially my Guardian Angel, the Passion of Our Lord Jesus Christ, His Precious Blood and the merits thereof, my lot in Paradise, also the good inspirations which God may give me in the future, all the prayers which are made or may be made for me.

The prosecution of witches solely for having pacts with the Devil increased slowly on the European continent, though convictions still required evidence of *maleficia*. Witch-hunting handbooks such as the MALLEUS MALEFICARUM (1486) discussed pacts in great detail.

In Protestant England, Devil's pacts were acknowledged to exist but apparently did not play a major role in most trials, according to surviving records. The public cared little about pacts and more about what harm a witch did to her neighbors. Such *maleficia* was presumed possible without a pact. Of the three Parliamentary Witchcraft Acts to be passed, only the third (1604) outlawed pacts "with any evil or wicked spirit." The first oral Devil's pact was recorded in 1612, and Elizabethan witches in general were believed not to be in direct contact with Satan.

In 1645 MATTHEW HOPKINS began his infamous hunt of witches in England and obtained sworn evidence of written pacts. Some of his 230-plus victims may have been condemned largely on the basis of such "evidence."

In modern SATANISM, the practices of which vary widely, followers generally pledge to serve Satan, a form of pact. Some satanic groups may have more formal pacts with the Devil. The Church of Satan does not, holding that a pact is not necessary to become a satanist. Anton Szandor LaVey, founder of the Church of Satan, states in *The Satanic Bible* (1969) that the Devil's pact is a threat "devised by Christianity to terrorize people so they would not stray from the fold."

Neo-Pagan Witches, who do not worship the Devil, have nothing to do with Devil's pacts.

See also CHRISTOPHER HAIZMANN; STACKER LEE.

Diana (Artemis) Classical goddess of the MOON and the hunt, Diana is one of the most important aspects of the GODDESS in modern WITCHCRAFT. Diana (counterpart to the Greek Artemis) personifies the positive attributes of the moon, which is the source of Witches' magical power, as well as independence,

Apollo and Diana (Albrecht Dürer, 1502)

self-esteem and fierce aggressiveness. A virgin goddess and maiden warrior, she is the eternal feminist, owned by no man, beholden to none. As a moon goddess, Diana shares the lunar trinity with SELENE and HECATE and serves as patron goddess of witches. In the trinity, she represents power over the earth.

Diana's origins as Artemis comprise a rich mythology. Her cult flourished throughout the Mediterranean region during the Bronze Age. The Amazons build a beehive-shaped temple to her at Ephesus circa 900 B.C., and it is considered the Seventh Wonder of the ancient world. The temple contained a statue of Black Diana, on which was implanted a magical stone. Emperor Theodosius closed the temple in 380, allegedly because he despised the religion of women. Early Christians sought to destroy the cult as Devil-worshippers, and Black Diana was smashed ca. 400.

According to myth, Artemis was born of Zeus and Leto, a nature deity and the twin sister of Apollo, who became the god of oracles and of the sun. As soon as she was born, Artemis was thrust into the role of protector and helper of women. Though Artemis was born without pain, Apollo caused Leto great suffering. Artemis served as midwife. As a result, women have traditionally prayed to her to ease childbirth.

As a youth, Artemis exhibited a boyish taste for adventure and independence. At her request, Zeus granted her a bow and a quiver of arrows, a band of nymph maidens to follow her, a pack of hounds, a short tunic suitable for running and eternal chastity, so that she could run forever through the wilderness. She was quick to protect wildlife and animals, as well as humans who appealed to her for help, especially women who were raped and victimized by men.

She was equally quick to punish offending men. Actaeon, a hunter who spied Artemis and her nymphs bathing nude in a pool, was turned into a stag and torn to pieces by his own hounds. She killed Orion, whom she loved, with an arrow shot to the head. In one version, she was tricked into killing Orion by Apollo, who did not like Orion; in another version, she killed him out of jealousy over his feelings for Dawn. She sent a boar to ravage the countryside of Calydon as punishment to King Oeneus, because he forgot to include her in the sacrifice of the first fruits of harvest. (None of the bravest male warriors of Greece could slay the boar. It took another woman, Atalanta, to do it.)

In British myth, Diana directed Prince Brutus of Troy to flee to Britain after the fall of that city. Brutus, who then founded Britain's royalty, is said to have erected an altar to Diana at the site where St. Paul's Cathedral is located today. A surviving remnant of that altar is the London Stone.

As late as the fifth and sixth centuries, a Dianic cult flourished among European pagans. With the slow Christianization of Europe, Diana became associated with evil and Satan. In the early Middle Ages, she was believed to be the patroness of sorcery (an evil) and to lead witches' processions and rites. Historian Jeffrey B. Russell notes that Dianic witches' processions were not known in classical times but probably grew out of the Teutonic myth of the Wild Hunt, a nocturnal spree of ghosts who destroyed the countryside. Clerical scholars may have substituted Diana, a familiar deity, for the Teutonic goddesses, Holda and Berta, who sometimes led the WILD HUNT and who were identified by the Church as followers of the Devil.

The CANON EPISCOPI, an ecclesiastical law written ca. 900, reinforced the portrayal of a devil Diana who leads the witches:

> It is not to be omitted that some wicked women, perverted by the Devil, seduced by illusions and phantasms of demons, believe and profess themselves, in the hours of the night, to ride upon certain beasts with Diana, the goddess of pagans, and an innumerable multitude of women, and in the silence of the dead of the night to traverse great spaces of earth, and to obey her commands as of their mistress, and to be summoned to her service on certain nights.

Diana also became associated somehow with Herodias, wife of Herod, who was responsible for the execution of John the Baptist. Herodias took on the aspects of a demon, condemned to wander through the sky forever but allowed by God to rest in trees from midnight to dawn. In Italian lore, the name *Herodias* became ARADIA. In the 19th century, CHARLES GODFREY LELAND recorded oral legends told to him by witches of Etruscan heritage concerning Aradia, the daughter of Diana and her brother Lucifer. Diana dispatched Aradia to earth to teach witches their craft.

British anthropologist MARGARET A. MURRAY theorized that an organized Dianic cult of witches had existed throughout the Middle Ages and the witch-hunt centuries, though scant evidence survives to prove it. Murray relied heavily upon the *Canon Episcopi* in developing this theory. It was adopted by GERALD B. GARDNER, a key figure in the revival of witchcraft in the 1950s in Britain.

Diana in Modern Witchcraft. Though most modern witches no longer believe in Murray's medieval Dianic cult, they do revere Diana as an ancient Pagan deity and an archetype. As part of the Triple Goddess aspect of the moon, Diana holds sway over the new and waxing moon, a two-week period that is auspicious for magic related to new beginnings, growth and achievement. Diana is invoked as nurturer and protector. At the full moon, she turns her power over to Selene.

As an archetype, Diana serves as a role model for feminist Witchcraft, called the Dianic tradition. She is a free spirit, an achiever, who knows what she wants and scores the mark with a single arrow shot. She is neither dependent upon nor subjugated by men. Though a lunar goddess, she walks the earth, and her domain is the wild; she is one with nature.

divination The act of foretelling the future, finding objects and people and determining guilt by means of information obtained from signs, omens, dreams, visions and divinatory tools. Divination is one of the primary skills of WITCHES, WIZARDS, wise women, cunning men, medicine men, sorcerers and shamans (see SORCERY; SHAMANISM). In some civilizations throughout history, divination has been performed only by special classes of priests or priestesses, who were trained in their methods and interpretations.

Since the earliest times in all known civilizations, man has looked to supernatural sources for help and advice, in personal affairs and particularly in matters of state. Historically, methods of divination involve either interpretation of natural patterns in the environment or patterns that are formed by the tossing of objects such as sticks, stones or bones. Information is obtained from the way smoke curls from a fire, the shape of an animal bone, the formation of clouds and the markings on organs and entrails of sacrificed animals. The ancient Romans favored *augury*, the interpretation of the flight pattern of birds, and *haruspicy*, the examination of the livers and entrails of sacrificed animals. The augurs were a special caste of priests who read the signs to determine whether the gods approved or disapproved of coming events.

The ancient Egyptians and the DRUIDS relied on dreams and SCRYING. The Druids also read the death throes and entrails of sacrificial victims. The Hebrews used scrying. The Greeks relied on oracles, usually priestesses who went into trances and became mouthpieces for deities (see ORACLE).

Popular in the Middle Ages was the tossing of grain, sand or peas onto the earth to see what could be read from the patterns. Similarly, the Japanese traditionally set out characters of their writing system in a circle, then scatter rice around them and let a cock pick at the rice. Whatever characters are nearest the grain picked up by the cock are used to puzzle out messages. As far back as 1000 B.C., the Chinese have used the *I CHING*, an oracle that involves tossing and reading long and short yarrow sticks. Another ancient Chinese divinatory method, which is still in use, is *feng-shui*, or geomancy, the siting of buildings, tombs and other physical structures by determining the invisible currents of energy coursing through the earth (see DOWSING; LEYS).

Finding the guilty. Throughout history, divination has been used to identify guilty parties in crime. Despite the true psychic ability no doubt employed by many diviners, it is certain that many innocent people have been punished along with the guilty. In the Pacific Islands, medicine men claim they can identify murderers by examining the marks of a beetle crawling over the grave of a victim. The Lugbara of western Uganda fill small pots with medicines that represent the suspects. The pot that does not boil over when heated reveals the culprit. In other methods, suspects are forced to eat or drink various substances and concoctions, such as the gruesome stew made from the boiled head of an ass. Whoever is unfortunate enough to choke or suffer indigestion—even a rumbling stomach—is guilty by divination.

During the witch-hunts of the Middle Ages and Renaissance, suspected witches were bound and thrown in lakes and rivers to see if they would float (guilty) or sink (innocent). If the sinking innocent drowned, that was simply an unfortunate consequence (see SWIMMING).

Divinatory methods favored by modern Witches. Most Witches use a favored tool in divining. The tool acts as a prompt to intuition and the tuning-in to psychic forces and vibrations. The divined information comes in a variety of ways, depending on the individual. Some persons "hear" it with the inner ear; others visualize images. Divinatory information comes through other senses, including taste, smell and touch.

Among modern Witches, the most popular divinatory tool is the TAROT deck of cards. Other popular tools are crystals, MIRRORS or bowls for scrying; ASTROLOGY; the I CHING; NUMEROLOGY; and RUNES and STONES for casting. Many Witches also use psychometry, which is the reading of objects by handling them. Personal objects are believed to be imbued with the energy of their wearers. By handling them, the Witch or psychic picks up on the vibrations of and gets information about the owner. Psychometry is particularly useful in finding missing persons and is frequently employed by psychic detectives. Photographs may also be psychometrized. Pendulums, made out of coins, crystals or other objects suspended on a cord or string, are used to divine yes-no answers to questions. Many Witches also use "dreaming true," the use of dreams to answer questions.

Some Witches divine by reading auras, the layers of invisible energy that surround all living things. The colors and fluxes of the aura are interpreted; often images form in the aura, which may be perceived clairvoyantly.

PALMISTRY, the reading on lines on the hand, and TASSEOMANCY, the reading of tea leaves, are used by some Witches.

Divinatory trance mediumship and channeling are not part of modern Witchcraft, though some Witches have experimented with these methods.

In divining the future, most Witches hold the view that the information obtained reveals a likely—not a fixed—outcome based upon the direction of events and the circumstances in force at the time of the reading. The future may be changed by choice. Divination is useful in helping a person make better choices.

Divination is both art and skill, and a Witch's proficiency depends on his or her natural psychic gifts and regular practice. For some, divination comes fairly easily, while others must work harder and longer to attune the psychic faculties. Most covens offer training in developing psychic abilities and divinatory skills (see COVEN). Many Witches feel that the best time to divine is between midnight and dawn, when the psychic currents are supposed to be at their strongest.

See also NECROMANCY.

djinn In Arab and Muslim folklore, the djinn are DEMONS, usually ugly and evil, who possess supernatural powers and serve those who know the correct MAGIC. The Western term is *genie*.

In pre-Islamic folklore, the djinn roamed the deserts and wilderness. They were malicious. Though usually invisible, they had the power to take on any shape—insect, animal, or human (see METAMORPHOSIS). They were adopted into Islamic lore and modified; some were allowed to become beautiful and good-natured. Solomon tamed them and became their ruler with the help of his magic ring, which was set with a gem—probably a diamond—that had a living force of its own and protected him from evil. He carried them on his back when he traveled and directed them to make statues, gardens and palaces (see RINGS).

Djinn appear in tales such as "Aladdin's Lamp" in *Arabian Nights*, in which they carry out the wishes of a master who learns the magic that will command them. There are five kinds of djinn with varying degrees of power. The most important individual *djinnee* is Iblis, the prince of darkness.

Djinn are born of fire and are not immortal. They live with other supernatural beings in the Kaf, a mythical range of emerald mountains that encircles the earth.

Doctor John Nineteenth-century WITCH DOCTORS in the United States, also called *conjure men*, were all men, while the leaders of black religions were all women. One of the most famous American witch doctors was Doctor John (also called Bayou John and Jean Montaigne), a free black man who owned slaves in antebellum New Orleans.

A huge man, Doctor John claimed he was a prince in his homeland of Senegal, sent into slavery by the Spaniards and taken to Cuba. There he became an excellent cook and convinced his master to grant his freedom. Next he worked as a sailor, returning to Senegal, where he no longer felt at home. Returning to sea, he ended up in New Orleans, where he found work as a cotton roller on the docks. He noticed he had the "power," and his bosses made him overseer.

Doctor John's fame spread, and he found he could get money for his tricks and services. He built a house on Bayou Road and bought female slaves. He married some of them, performing his own ceremonies, eventually boasting 15 wives and more than 50 children. New Orleanians stared at him in public, for he rode in a carriage with horses as fine as any white man. When Doctor John rode horseback alone, he wore a gaudy Spanish costume. Later he affected an austere black costume with a white, frilly shirt and grew a beard.

Leaving the Voodoo (see VODOUN) meetings to the administration of the queens, Doctor John specialized in fortune-telling, healing and making GRIS-GRIS. His house was filled with snakes, lizards, toads, scorpions and human skulls stolen from graveyards. Blacks and whites came to him for advice, love potions and the placing or lifting of CURSES. Others followed his commands out of fear of Doctor John's secret knowledge. Most of his wisdom did not come from the spirits, however, but from a huge network of black servants placed all over town. He either bought or took information from them, thereby giving him an

Belial and demons presenting their credentials to King Solomon (Jacobus de Teramo, *Das Buch Belial*, 1473)

advantage when thickly veiled white girls came to him desiring to know if their lovers were faithful.

One of Doctor John's specialties was the starting or stopping of poltergeist phenomena, usually showers of rocks and stones on the victim's home (see LITHOBOLY). Policemen stood baffled as the rocks rained down, apparently from nowhere. Naturally, Doctor John could stop such harassment, for a fee. One case reports that the slaves of a Samuel Wilson paid $62 to stop a shower of rocks, but Wilson took Doctor John to court to retrieve the $62. A few days later, the rock showers began again.

Unable to read or write, Doctor John supposedly amassed a fortune, even burying $150,000 on his property, according to local stories. He never forgot his poorer neighbors, however, dispensing food to anyone who needed it. But by the end of his life, his poor business sense caused his financial demise. He didn't trust banks, convinced that once he gave a bank his money he would never see it again. His investments turned sour, and his wives and children were continually leaving with part of his assets. Others cheated him outright. Finally, Doctor John employed a young black to teach him to read and write, and he spent long hours learning to sign his name. One day, a con artist had him sign his name at the bottom of a long paper, and Doctor John lost all his Bayou Road property.

Doctor John tried to regain his prestige, but younger people—principally his protégée, MARIE LAVEAU, then her daughter of the same name—had taken over the voodoo business. At age 80, he was forced to move in with children from his white wife, though he despised mulattoes. New Orleanians gossiped that Doctor John was "fixed," or the victim of spells greater than his. He died in August 1885 at age 82, four years after the death of the first Marie Laveau.

dowsing Sometimes called "water witching," dowsing is a DIVINATION method for finding water, metals, coal, gold, treasures, people and animals, using a forked rod of wood or metal. It is especially associated with locating objects and substances below the ground. Since the Middle Ages, dowsing has been unfairly associated with SORCERY and the DEVIL, perhaps because some psychically gifted persons—WITCHES, in the medieval view—are adept dowsers. Modern dowsers include Witches; SYBIL LEEK once noted that the witches of New Forest, England, were experts at it.

Dowsing has been in use for about 7,000 years and was known to the ancient Egyptians and Chinese. It was used extensively in the Middle Ages in Europe to help miners find coal deposits and to find water. Martin Luther condemned it as WITCHCRAFT, which

Dowsing in 16th-century mines (Sebastian Munster, *Cosmographia universalis*, 1544)

was equated with Devil-worship at the time. Nevertheless, dowsing continued to be a popular form of divination until the 19th century, when scientists cast a cloud over it as invalid and "occult." Sir William Barrett, a professor at the Royal College of Science in Dublin, stated in 1897 that "few subjects appear to be as unworthy of serious notice and so utterly beneath scientific investigation as that of the divining rod."

Dowsing was revived in the 20th century and has been applied in geological and archaeological work, in missing person and murder investigations and by utilities companies in locating damaged cables and pipes. Dowsing also is used in medical diagnosis in Europe and Great Britain but is prohibited for that purpose in the United States. Ley hunters use dowsing to locate lines of earth energy and power spots (see LEYS).

The traditional dowser's tool is a forked rod made of HAZEL, a wood that has a long reputation as having powerful magical properties. Ash, rowan and WILLOW, other woods considered excellent for magical wands, also are used. Some rods are made of aluminum or copper or of simple coat hangers. Many dowsers, especially in medical diagnosis, prefer to work with a pendulum suspended on a string.

Before beginning, a dowser "attunes" her- or himself to what is being sought. Methods include visualization or exposing the rod or pendulum to a location, personal belonging or type of material sought, such as ore. The dowser grasps the forked ends of the rod with palms turned up and walks over terrain until the rod begins to tremble and dip down, sometimes jerking violently. At one time, it was thought that mysterious vibrations picked up by the dowser caused the rod to twitch. Many dowsers, however, never go into the field but work with a pendulum and maps. The pendulum is hung from a string over the map and rotates as the dowser scans the map. When they score a hit, some dowsers also get mental images of what they have found. A good dowser can be highly accurate—sometimes more so than a scientist.

Drawing Down the Moon

An important ritual in some traditions of neo-Pagan WITCHCRAFT in which a COVEN's high priestess enters a trance and becomes the GODDESS, who is symbolized by the MOON. The transformation is accomplished with the help of the high priest, who invokes, or draws down, the spirit of the Goddess into the high priestess.

The origins of Drawing Down the Moon can be found in classical times. Ancient Thessalian WITCHES were believed to control the moon, according to an old tract: "If I command the moon, it will come down; and if I wish to withhold the day, night will linger over my head; and again, if I wish to embark on the sea, I need no ship, and if I wish to fly through the air, I am free from my weight."

In the modern rite, the high priestess may recite the CHARGE OF THE GODDESS, a poetic address written by DOREEN VALIENTE, high priestess in the Gardner-

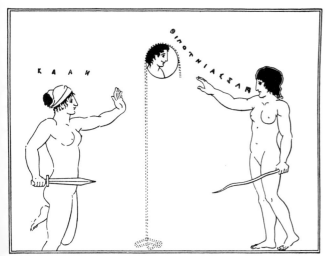

Greek vase ca. second century B.C. depicts Drawing Down the Moon ceremony (New York Public Library)

ian tradition (see GERALD B. GARDNER), or she may deliver a spontaneous address.

Drawing Down the Moon is one of the most serious and beautiful of all rituals in neo-Pagan Witchcraft. Depending upon the high priestess's altered state of consciousness and the energy raised, the words that come forth can be moving, poetic and inspiring. Through Drawing Down the Moon, many women connect with the power of the Goddess and therefore with the power within themselves.

A similar rite for invoking the HORNED GOD into the high priest is called Drawing Down the Sun or Drawing Down of the Horned God. A similar neo-Pagan ritual is called Calling Down the Moon.

Druids

An exalted caste of priests of the Celts, a barbaric, tribal people who spread through Gaul, Britain, Ireland, Europe, Asia Minor and the Balkans by the 5th century B.C. In the 1st century A.D. the Romans launched a series of suppressions of the Celts, and their religion eventually was replaced by Christianity.

The rituals and teachings of the Druids were highly secret and were passed on by oral tradition. Little is known about the Druids, who have been the subject of much research and speculation. Most of what is known comes from the writings of the Greeks and Romans, the opinions of the latter of whom, as the conquerors, must be viewed with some skepticism; from archaeological evidence obtained from graves, shrines and temples; and iconography. The writings span the 2nd century B.C. to the 4th century A.D. and are scanty at best.

The exact role of the Druids in Celtic society is open to interpretation and seems to vary according to geography. In the 3rd century, Diogenes Laertius said that the Druids were an ancient institution in the 4th century B.C., during the time of Aristotle. Julius Caesar said the Gaulish Druids were one of the two highest castes, along with the knights, and were organized under a single titular head. In Ireland, the Druids were the second highest of three castes, below the nobility and above the plebes, or landless ones. By most accounts, the Druids were the keepers of traditional wisdom who were concerned with moral philosophy, natural phenomena and theology. They were skilled in the interpretation of omens (see ORACLE), the correct rites of SACRIFICE, the construction of a calendar, the medicine of herbs, the science of astronomy and the composition of poems. Ammianus, Roman historian (ca. 330–395 B.C.), said Druids "are uplifted by searchings into things most secret and sublime." Gaulish Druids were said to administer law and justice, though it is not known how they did so without circumventing

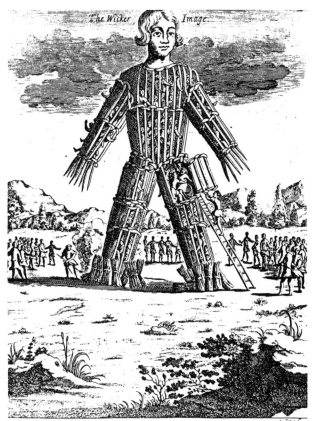

Artistic concept of Druidic human sacrifice (Aylett Sammes, *Britannia Antiqua Illustrata*, 1676)

the authority of their tribal chiefs. Irish Druids were described as men of learning and art, who included seers, wise men, bards and jurists. The Druids of Gaul and Britain were said to be separate from others in the priesthood, including diviners (see DIVINATION), bards and seers. There seems to have been some overlap, however, as Druids were said to read omens and prophesy the future. Druids included both men and women, for women had a place of importance in Celtic society.

Dio Chrysostomus, Greek philosopher (ca. 40–112 A.D.), equated the Druids with Hindu Brahmins, Persian magi and Egyptian priests. In more recent times, writers such as occultist Lewis Spence (1920) and historian Ward Rutherford (1978) have theorized that the Druids were shamans (see SHAMANISM). Rutherford says they also were a possession cult, which is typical of societies that practice human sacrifice. Customs that can be traced to the Druids include night fires, drumming, chanting and ecstatic dancing.

As members of the priesthood, the Druids certainly played a key role in the sacred and secular life of the Celts. They conducted religious ceremonies, served as mediators between the people and gods,

exercised influence over the moral, ethical and spiritual fabric of Celtic society through their teachings and divination and made political and judicial decisions. Their teachings included moral philosophy, ethics, astronomy, the law of nature, the power of the gods and the concept of immortality.

Certain TREES, plants and animals were believed to be endowed with sacred and curative powers, and the Druids used them in religious ceremonies and for remedial purposes. The MISTLETOE, believed to be a sign from heaven, was used as a remedy against poisons and infertility, even for animals. The robur oak tree was thought to have come from the sacred forest, and its foliage was used in ceremonies. The term *Druid* means "knowing the oak tree" in Gaelic.

Religious ceremonies were conducted in sacred woods or oak groves which served as temples. These sacred enclosures were also assembly sites where the Druids made decisions and administered justice in civil and criminal disputes. Other meetings took place at river sources and lakes because the Celts worshipped water gods and believed water to be sacred.

Ceremonies included prayers, libations and human and animal sacrifices. Victims were burned alive in wickerwork cages, stabbed, impaled on stakes and shot with arrows. It was the sacrifice of humans that so outraged the Romans, who had outlawed the practice as barbaric by Senatorial decree in 97 B.C. Later writers tried to excuse the Druids' participation in sacrifices, saying they did not do the actual killing. This is highly unlikely, given their role as a priest caste of religion.

The only extant detailed account of a Druid ceremony comes from Pliny and concerns the harvesting of mistletoe. On the sixth day of the moon, a Druid garbed in a white robe climbed an oak tree and, with his left hand, cut the mistletoe with a gold sickle (or, more likely, a gilded bronze sickle, since gold is too soft to cut mistletoe). The mistletoe, which was not supposed to fall to the ground, was caught in a white cloth. Two white bulls were sacrificed and a feast was held.

In interpreting omens, the Druids observed the hare or birds such as the crow and eagle to foretell events. They practiced divination by observing the death throes and entrails of their sacrificial victims. During religious festivals, the Druids divined by dreams. A man would be put to sleep with Druids chanting over his body. Upon awakening, the man described his dream and the Druids interpreted it.

Classical writings make references to the Druids' MAGIC, including CHARMS with herbs and mistletoe, and belief in a magical egg made from the SPITTLE of angry snakes, which would ensure success in court and guarantee favors from princes.

The Druids believed in the immortality of the soul and life after death, which some writers have equated with Pythagoras's belief in metempsychosis. The dead were cremated with all their possessions. Sometimes relatives committed religious suicide by jumping into the fire and holding the corpses so as to be with them in the next world. The Celts wrote letters to the dead and advanced loans that would be repayable after death. Caesar said that this belief in immortality sustained the legendary Celtic courage in battle.

The Romans feared and were repulsed by the Celts, and in 43 A.D., Claudius banned Druidism throughout the empire. In 60 or 61 A.D., the Romans sacked and destroyed their holy stronghold on the island of Mona (also called Mon or Anglesey). According to Tacitus, black-clad Druidesses leaped among the Celtic warriors, howling to the gods and screaming curses at the Romans. The Romans were victorious and not only slayed the warriors but killed all the Druids and laid waste to the sacred groves. The loss sent Druidism into a permanent decline; within several generations, the venerated and powerful priesthood was on a par with common sorcerers.

Modern Druidic movements. In the 16th and 17th centuries, interest in the Druids revived. Translators of the classical texts romanticized them and turned them into stock folklore characters. John Aubrey, 17th-century British antiquarian, suggested the Druids had constructed STONEHENGE, a theory that has since been refuted as inaccurate. Aubrey's views were endorsed in the 18th century, however, by William Stukeley, who became known as the "Arch Druid" and the founder of modern Druidism. A meeting of "British Druids" is said to have taken place in 1717, organized by John Tolan and led by Stukeley. In 1781 the Ancient Order of Druids was founded by Henry Hurle, a carpenter. This order was inspired by Freemasonry and also was a benefit society (charitable organization). The issue of charity split the organization in 1833. The United Ancient Order of Druids continued purely as a benefit society, while the Ancient Order of Druids retained its mystical underpinnings. By the early 20th century there were at least five modern Druidic organizations, including the Druidic Hermetists and the British Circle of the Universal Bond, but most did not survive more than a few decades. In 1963 the Order of Bards, Ovates and Druids split away from the Ancient Order of Druids,

drawing members away from that group and the British Circle of the Universal Bond.

Before 1915 Stonehenge was privately owned, but modern Druids were allowed to assemble there. In 1900 a stone was knocked over, and the owner fenced the henge and began charging admission. At the next solstice ceremony, some of the Druids objected to the fee. The police were called and the Druids were thrown out. They ritually cursed the owner (see CURSES). In 1915 Stonehenge was sold to Cecil Chubb, who turned it over to the government. Modern Druids were allowed to hold festivals at Stonehenge until 1985, when the monument was placed off limits to all such festivals, because of vandalism by the spectators who were attracted to the gatherings.

In the United States, another modern Druidic movement with no connection to the ancient Druids or to the modern Druids in England, was formed in 1963. The Reformed Druids of North America (RDNA) initially was conceived as a hoax by a group of students at Carleton College in Northfield, Minnesota, who were protesting a school requirement that students attend religious services. The requirement was dropped in 1963–64, but the Reformed Druids decided to take themselves seriously and continue as an organization of autonomous "groves." Rituals were reconstructed from anthropological material and included nonbloody sacrifices. The founders of the RDNA did not intend for it to become a religion but rather viewed it as a philosophy. Some groves split off to form a separate branch, the New Reformed Druids of North America (NRDNA), which emphasized neo-Pagan religion. Among these groves was the Berkeley grove, which was led by Archdruid P. E. I. (ISAAC) BONEWITS in the mid-1970s. Bonewits left the organization around 1978–79. In 1983 he formed his own Druidic organization, *ÁR NDRAÍOCHT FÉIN* ("Our own Druidism").

By 1985 modern Druidic activity in the United States had declined. The Reformed Druids of North America was no longer active as an organization, though individual groves remained scattered around the country. *Ár nDraíocht Féin* had approximately 400 members as of 1988.

Modern Druids observe the eight seasonal Pagan holidays (see SABBATS), holding their rites outdoors. American Druids gather at a Stonehenge replica in Washington State.

E

Ecklund, Anna (ca. 1882–?) One of the best-documented and most notorious DEMONIC POSSESSION cases in the 20th century. The possession of Anna Ecklund is unusual for its combination of both devils and demonic entities within one victim.

Ecklund was born in the Midwest about 1882 and was raised a devout and pious Catholic. She first began showing the symptoms of possession—revulsion toward holy objects, inability to enter a church and disturbing thoughts about unspeakable sexual acts—at age 14, finally becoming totally possessed in 1908. In the account of Ecklund's travails, *Begone Satan!*, written in German by Rev. Carl Vogl and translated into English by the Rev. Celestine Kapsner, O.S.B., Anna's aunt Mina, a reputed witch (see WITCHES), caused her possession by placing SPELLS on herbs used in her food. Father Theophilus Riesinger, a native Bavarian and a Capuchin monk from the community of St. Anthony at Marathon, Wisconsin, successfully exorcised her on June 18, 1912, only to have her fall prey to the Devil again after her father heaped CURSES on her and wished her possessed. In 1928, when Ecklund was 46 years old, Father Theophilus tried to exorcise her again (see DEMONIC EXORCISM).

Seeking a place where she was unknown, Father Theophilus approached his old friend, Father F. Joseph Steiger, parish priest in Earling, Iowa. With great reluctance, Father Steiger agreed that the exorcism could take place in the nearby convent of the Franciscan Sisters; Ecklund arrived in Earling on August 17, 1928. Trouble started immediately; sensing that someone had sprinkled holy water on her evening meal, she threw a fit, purring like a cat, and refused to eat until unblessed food could be brought.

After that, the devils within her always knew if one of the nuns had tried to bless the food or drink, and they always complained.

The ancient ritual began in earnest the next morning. Father Theophilus had several of the strongest nuns hold Ecklund onto a mattress laid upon an iron bed, and her clothes were bound tightly around her to keep her from stripping herself. With the first exhortations, Ecklund's mouth clamped shut and she fell into unconsciousness, followed almost immediately by an extraordinary feat of LEVITATION: rising swiftly from the bed, she hung onto the wall above the door like a cat, and it took great effort to pull her down. Although she was completely unconscious and her mouth never moved throughout the sessions, voices came from within her, accompanied by screams, howls and unearthly animal noises. Earling citizens, alarmed by the outcries, gathered at the convent, ruining Father Theophilus's hopes of keeping the exorcism secret.

Totaling 23 days, the exorcism comprised three sessions: August 18 to 26, September 13 to 20 and December 15 to 23. Through it all, Ecklund's physical state deteriorated to the point of death. She ate no food but only swallowed small amounts of milk or water. Nevertheless, she vomited enormous quantities of foul-smelling debris, often resembling tobacco leaves, and spit prodigiously (see ALLOTRIOPHAGY). Her face became horribly disfigured and distorted, often suffusing with blood as her head swelled and elongated, her eyes bulged and her lips grew, reportedly, to the size of hands. Her abdomen would swell to the point of bursting, only to retract and become so hard and heavy that the iron bedstead would bend under the enormous weight.

In addition to these physical changes, Ecklund understood languages previously unknown to her, recoiled at holy words and objects and revealed clairvoyant knowledge by exposing secret childhood sins of the other participants. The nuns and Father Steiger were so frightened and troubled that none of them could stay in Ecklund's room throughout the entire exorcism but instead worked in shifts. Father Steiger, taunted by the devils for having agreed to the exorcism in his parish, was especially harassed and suffered an auto accident that the devils had predicted and apparently arranged. Only Father Theophilus, confident of his powers, remained steadfast.

Hordes of lesser devils and avenging spirits, described as "a swarm of mosquitoes," possessed Ecklund, but her principal tormentors were the devil Beelzebub (see under DEMONS), Judas Iscariot and the spirits of her father Jacob and his mistress, Ecklund's aunt Mina. Beelzebub revealed himself first, engaging Father Theophilus in sarcastic theological conversations and acknowledging that the curses of Jacob, Anna's father, sent the devils into her at age 14. Father Theophilus tried to reach Jacob, only to be answered by a spirit identifying himself as Judas Iscariot, who admitted he was there to torment Anna into committing suicide and thereby going to hell.

Jacob eventually spoke and said that he had cursed Ecklund for not submitting to his incestuous advances, calling upon the Devil to tempt her with every unspeakable sin against chastity. He took Anna's aunt Mina as mistress while he was still married and repeatedly tried to seduce Ecklund. Whether Anna's virginity really remained intact, even at age 46, or whether she had repressed her sexual contact with her father is unknown.

Ecklund remained pious throughout her ordeal. Sensing his eventual triumph, Father Theophilus continued to exhort the devils to depart, and by the latter part of December 1928 they began to weaken and moan, rather than scream, against his efforts. Father Theophilus demanded that when they returned to hell, each should call out his name as a sign of his or her departure, and the devils agreed.

On December 23, 1928, at about 9 P.M., Anna suddenly jerked up and stood erect in bed, looking as if she were about to rise to the ceiling. Father Steiger called for the nuns to pull her down, while Father Theophilus blessed her and roared, "Depart ye fiends of hell! Begone Satan, the Lion of Juda reigns!" Ecklund crumpled back onto the bed as a terrible shout of "Beelzebub, Judas, Jacob, Mina" followed by "Hell, hell, hell" filled the room, repeated several times until the sound seemed to fade into the distance. Ecklund opened her eyes and smiled, while tears of joy ran down her face and she cried, "My Jesus, mercy! Praised be Jesus Christ!"

The departing devils left a terrible stench behind. The windows were opened and the ordeal was over.

egg tree A charm (see CHARMS) against WITCHES once common in the Ozark mountain region of the United States but infrequently used since the 1930s. The egg tree is a dead bush with the limbs cropped, decorated with dozens or perhaps hundreds of blown eggs. The bush is set in the ground near a cabin and is said to ward off witches.

elder In neo-Pagan WITCHCRAFT, a Witch who has attained a high level of respect for his or her experience and skill in the Craft. An elder does not necessarily have to be of the third, or highest, degree of rank; she or he may be a first-degree Witch (see INITIATION; WITCHES). Most elders, however, are third-degree Witches who have been in the Craft a long time. Elders are consulted in policy decisions and interpretations of Craft laws and traditions.

See also: COVEN.

elementals Low-level spirits that personify the four ELEMENTS—earth, air, fire and water. The term also is applied to NATURE SPIRITS, which are said to exist in all things in nature, such as animals, insects, birds, rocks and plants. Ruled by devas or archangels (called in modern WITCHCRAFT the Lords of the Watchtowers, the Guardians or the Mighty Ones), elementals serve as the life force and may be summoned by WITCHES to assist in MAGIC, such as weather control.

Salamander (Michael Majer, *Scrutinium Chymicum*, 1687)

Earth elementals are known as gnomes; fire as salamanders; water as undines; and air as sylphs. They may be seen by psychically gifted persons who are close in spirit to nature. Numerous elemental sightings have been reported at the CIRCLE SANCTUARY at Mt. Horeb, Wisconsin. The pioneers of the Findhorn community in northern Scotland have achieved remarkable gardening results reputedly by communicating with elementals.

Some elementals are said to be malicious and unpredictable, tricking human beings into accidents, setting traps for them and killing them. Most Witches who work with elementals, however, prefer to work with friendly ones in the creation of positive magic.

Artificial elemental is a term occasionally used for *thought-form*, a being of energy ritually created through intense will, which is programmed to carry out assignments and disintegrate once the work is done.

elements   The four elements of nature—earth, air, water and fire—form the foundation of natural MAGIC. Modern WITCHES and Pagans revere these forces. The elements are associated with the cardinal points of the MAGIC CIRCLE and with a hierarchy of spirits— lower-level beings called ELEMENTALS, who in turn are governed by higher beings, devas, also called the Lords of the Watchtowers, the Mighty Ones and the Guardians.

In Western occultism, the four elements are considered the basis of all life, not only on the planet but throughout the universe as well, linking mankind to nature, the heavens and the divine, and governing mankind's well-being. In the ancient Mysteries, the rays of celestial bodies become the elements when they strike the crystallized influences of the lower world. The elements figured prominently in the magic of the ancient Egyptians and Greeks, who ascribed to each one various attributes and characteristics. Plato divided all beings into four groups based on the elements—air/birds, water/fish, earth/pedestrians and fire/stars—all of which are interrelated. The magicians and alchemists of the Middle Ages ascribed elements to external and internal parts of the human body; various gems, minerals and metals; planets and constellations; the Four Horsemen of the Apocalypse; various species of the animal and plant kingdoms; human personality traits; and geometrical shapes. Roger Fludd (1574–1637), alchemist and astrologer, related the elements to harmonics, while another Renaissance alchemist, Sisismund Bactrom, believed that if all the elements could be harmonized and united, the result would be the Philosopher's Stone.

The Mithraic Mysteries hold that man must rule the elements before he can attain spiritual wisdom;

accordingly, he must successfully undergo the initiations of earth, air, water and fire, each of which test a different aspect of his nature and being.

Some of the major correspondences of the elements are:

Earth: The north; the pentacle; female principle; fertility; darkness, quiet; practicality; thrift; acquisition; patience; responsibility; boredom; stagnation; the materialization of cosmic powers; the color green; the metal gold.

Air: The east, the wand (in some witchcraft traditions, the sword and athame); male principle; intellect, energy, endeavor; sociability; squandering, frivolity; the expression of the magician's will; the color yellow; the metal silver.

Water: The west; the cup, challice and cauldron; female principle; fecundity; body fluids; magical brews; the rhythms of nature; emotions, sensitivity, receptivity; instability, indifference; the color blue; the metal silver.

Fire: The south; the sword or athame (in some traditions, the wand); male principle; action, courage, defense against hostile forces; struggle, animosity, jealousy, anger; the color orange; the metal gold.

In working magic, Witches summon the subtle forces of the elements and their guardian spirits. FAMILIARS are considered sources of vital elemental energy. Both Witches and ceremonial magicians consecrate their working tools and ritual objects with the four elements, by placing them on or touching them with a pentacle, passing them over a candle flame and a censer (air) and sprinkling them with salted water (see WITCHES' TOOLS). When a magic circle is cast, it is consecrated and purified with the elements. Each element or its symbol is taken to its corresponding quarter, and its guardian spirit is invoked.

elf arrows   Arrowhead-shaped flints from the Stone Age found in many parts of the British Isles, Europe and northern Africa, which medieval witches supposedly used as weapons against animals and people. Elf-arrow superstitions predominate in Celtic areas such as Ireland, Scotland and parts of England, where fairy lore is strong (see FAIRIES). According to lore, many witches learn their craft from fairies and elves.

Elf arrows are said to be fatal to cattle, a common target of WITCHES. Stricken cattle can be saved by touching them with the arrow, then dipping the arrow into water and giving the water to the cattle to drink. In some Celtic areas, the term *elf-shot* is still applied to sick animals.

A person shot with an elf arrow supposedly comes

down with mysterious and fatal supernatural illnesses. The use of elf arrows was among the accusations of WITCHCRAFT brought in 1560 against a Scottish woman, Catherine Ross, Lady Fowllis, and her son-in-law, Hector Munro. The two were part of a group of witches who conspired to kill Ross's husband and Marjory Campbell, Lady Balnagowan, so that Ross and Lord Balnagowan could marry. The witches were charged with "the making of two clay pictures, one for the destruction of the young Lady Balnagowan, and getting them enchanted, and shooting of elf-arrow heads at the said persons." Apparently the witches' plot was uncovered before the victims were killed.

See also ISOBEL GOWDIE.

elfin cat   See CAT.

Emerald Tablet, The   See HERMETICA.

Endor, Witch of   See WITCH OF ENDOR.

Enochian Magic   A system of MAGIC that teaches communication with angels and spirits, and travel through various planes, or *aethyrs,* of consciousness. Enochian magic apparently originated with JOHN DEE and Edward Kelly in the 16th century. Dee, who was royal astrologer to Elizabeth I, joined in an odd partnership with Kelly in attempts to communicate with the spirits through SCRYING. Dee is said to have recorded their proceedings and rituals, thus creating the Enochian system of magic.

The communication with spirits, or angels, was done in the Enochian language, a complex language of unknown origin. It is a real language with a solid grammar and syntax; it has a melodic sound similar to Sanskrit, Greek or Arabic. Some maintain that Kelly, who had a reputation for fraud, invented Enochian and that it was a secret code that he and Dee used in espionage activities for Queen Elizabeth I. If Kelly did this, he was a master of magic, cryptography, ASTROLOGY and mathematics, the elements of which are all embodied in the language. Each letter of the Enochian alphabet has a numerical value, or GEMATRIA, and corresponds to elemental (see ELEMENTS), planetary and TAROT properties.

Dee and Kelly conjured the angels with the Nineteen Calls, or Keys, of Enochian, or incantations. The first two keys conjured the element Spirit, and the next 16 keys conjured the four ELEMENTS, each subdivided into four. The Nineteenth Key invoked any of 30 "aethyrs" or "aires" which have never been precisely defined but probably represent levels of consciousness.

When the angels appeared in Kelly's crystal, he communicated with them in Enochian, using a complicated procedure. He set up charts which were squares either filled with letters or left blank. The angels would spell out messages by pointing with a rod to various squares, which Kelly dictated to Dee.

Kelly claimed the messages were always dictated backwards, because to communicate them directly would unleash dangerous and powerful forces beyond control. When the messages were finished, he and Dee rewrote them in reverse order.

Following the deaths of Dee and Kelly, Enochian sank into virtual oblivion, until it was revived in the 19th century by the HERMETIC ORDER OF THE GOLDEN DAWN. It also was studied at length by ALEISTER CROWLEY, who said the Keys were genuine. ". . . Anyone with the smallest capacity for Magick finds that they work," he stated in his autobiography, *The Confessions of Aleister Crowley.* His most extensive commentary on the magic of the keys was published in *The Vision and the Voice* in 1911.

Crowley subscribed to the definition of the aethyrs as " 'Dominion extending in ever widening circles without and beyond the Watch Towers of the Universe,' these Watch Towers composing a cube of infinite magnitude." He maintained that only properly initiated adepts could invoke all of the aethyrs in the Nineteenth Key, and he claimed to be able to do so himself. The results produced visions of spirits and astral beings, and Crowley recorded his communications with them.

Enochian magic continues to be practiced. There are two primary types of magical operations: (1) invoking spirits and (2) traveling to the aethyrs in the astral body, the mental body and mystical states of consciousness akin to *samadhi* (Hindu term for the highest state of yogic meditation, which leads to self-realization). Some of the aethyrs have sexual energies. Most involve an initiatory experience, such as "death" of the old personality and rebirth of the new.

esbat   The regular meeting of a COVEN of WITCHES at which religious worship is conducted, business is discussed and MAGIC and HEALING work is done.

The frequency of esbats depends on the coven. Most covens meet at the full moon, which occurs 13 times a year (see MOON). They may also meet at the new moon. Some meet weekly.

The esbat may take place indoors or outdoors. A coven may have a regular meeting place or rotate it among the homes of coveners. The coveners may wear loose clothing such as robes, or they may be skyclad (nude), as is the practice in Gardnerian, Alexandrian and other traditions of neo-Pagan WITCHCRAFT.

Animals belonging to coveners usually are allowed to be present at an esbat and to come and go as long as they do not disturb the energy flow of the rituals and magic work. In neo-Pagan Witchcraft, animals are not used or sacrificed in the rituals themselves (see SACRIFICE).

At the end of the esbat, coveners share food and drink (see CAKES AND WINE).

The term *esbat* has come into popular use in the 20th century; it may have been coined by MARGARET A. MURRAY, a British anthropologist who wrote about medieval witchcraft as an organized pagan religion. Most modern Witches use the term *circle* rather than *esbat* for their regular meeting; *esbat* is used formally. In the Middle Ages and Renaissance, the gatherings of witches were referred to as SABBATS, a term that now refers only to the major festivals celebrated by Witches.

evil eye   The causing of illness, misfortune, calamity and death by the looks of strangers and by envious looks. AMULETS and incantations (see CHARMS) ward it off.

The evil eye exists in virtually every culture around the world, dating back to ancient times. The oldest recorded references to it appear in the cuneiform texts of the Sumerians, Babylonians and Assyrians, about 3000 B.C. The ancient Egyptians believed in it and used eye shadow and lipstick to prevent the evil eye from entering their eyes or mouths. The Bible makes references to it in both the Old and New Testaments. It is among ancient Hindu folk beliefs. Evil-eye superstitions have remained strong into the 20th century, especially in Mediterranean countries such as Italy and in Mexico and Central America.

There are two kinds of evil eye: involuntary and deliberate. Most cases of evil eye are believed to occur involuntarily; the person casting it does not mean to do it and probably isn't even aware of it. No revenge is sought for this hazard.

Malevolent evil eye is called "overlooking" and is a form of WITCHCRAFT that can bring about misfortune or catastrophe: illness, poverty, injury, loss of love, even death. In the Middle Ages, witches were said to give anyone who crossed them the evil eye and to use it to bewitch judges from convicting them.

The evil eye typically occurs when someone, especially a stranger, admires one's children, livestock or possessions, or casts a lingering look on anyone. Unless immediate precautions are taken, the children get sick, the animals die, the possessions are stolen or good fortune in business turns sour. If the evil eye cannot be warded off, the victim must turn to an initiate—usually an older woman in the family—who knows a secret cure.

Besides envious glances, the evil eye comes from strangers in town, or anyone who has unusual or different-colored eyes—a blue-eyed stranger in a land of brown-eyed people, for example. Some unfortunate souls are said to be born with permanent evil eye, laying waste to everything they see. High-ranking people such as noblemen or clergy are often believed to be afflicted like this. Pope Pius IX (1846–1878) was branded as having the evil eye shortly after his investiture as Pope in 1869. Driving through Rome in an open car, he glanced at a nurse holding a child in an open window. Minutes later, the child fell to its death, and from then on, it seemed that everything the Pope blessed resulted in disaster. Pope Leo XIII (1878–1903) was also said to possess the *mal occhio*.

The evil eye is most likely to strike when one is happiest; good fortune, it seems, invites bad fortune. Small children and animals are especially vulnerable. In many villages, it is considered unwise to show children too much in public or to call attention to their beauty. Likewise, it is not advisable to display possessions or brag about successes.

In 19th-century Ireland, animals who were under the influence of the evil eye were said to have been "blinked." In order to save such animals, local wise women were sought for ritual cures.

The primary defense against the evil eye is an amulet, which may be fashioned from almost any kind of material. Common shapes are frogs and horns, the latter of which suggests both the powerful Mother Goddess (a bull is her consort) and the phallus. Another popular amulet is the "fig," a clenched fist with thumb thrust between the index and middle fingers, which also suggests a phallus.

The roots of the phallus amulet go back to the ancient Romans and their phallic god, Priapus. Another name for him was Fascinus, from *fascinum*, which means "witchcraft"; the evil eye is sometimes called "fascination." Romans employed phallic symbols as their protection against the evil eye. Today in Italy, it is common for men to grab their genitals as a defense against the evil eye or anything unlucky.

The ancient Egyptians used an eye to fight an eye. The *udjat eye*, also called the Eye of God and Eye of Horus, appears on amulets, pottery and in art, warding off the forces of darkness.

Other defenses include BELLS and RED ribbons tied to livestock, horse harnesses and the underwear of children, which divert the attention of the evil eye. Gardens are surrounded by protective jack beans. Other plants act as amulets—the SHAMROCK in Ireland and GARLIC in Greece. In Hindu lore, barley, a universal remedy supplied by the gods and the symbol of the thunderbolt of Indra, god of war, thunder and storms, will avert the evil eye.

Without an amulet, quick action is important when

the evil eye strikes. One should make gestures such as the "fig" or "horns" (holding up the index and little finger). Spitting is a powerful remedy, a holdover from the ancient Romans and Greeks.

Cures for the evil eye usually involve reciting secret incantations, which typically are passed on from mother to daughter within a family. In Italy, an initiate diagnoses the evil eye and performs the cure with a bowl of water, olive oil and, occasionally, salt. A few drops of oil are dropped into the water (sometimes salted). The oil may scatter, form blobs or sink to the bottom. These formations are interpreted to determine the source of the attack. The initiate drops more oil into the water while reciting incantations and making the sign of the cross on the forehead of the victim. If that fails, the victim is sent to a sorceress for further treatment.

evocations and invocations
Two methods of calling forth spirits and deities in magical and/or religious rites.

Evocations are used in ceremonial MAGIC and SORCERY. An evocation is a command, a summons, to an entity to appear and do the bidding of the magician. In ceremonial magic, spirits are evoked to appear in a triangle outside the magician's protective MAGIC CIRCLE, lest they cause him harm. Evocation is an elaborate ritual, and procedures are detailed in the many magical GRIMOIRES. The magician purifies himself through fasting and prayer, dons his garb, purifies his magical tools and casts the circle and triangle. To evoke the spirit, he must have perfect knowledge of it and the purpose it is to serve. He must visualize it, for once evoked, the spirit will reappear in the same form in subsequent evocations. The evocation comprises words and gestures with ritual tools. The magician speaks in a commanding tone of voice and may even shriek the evocation to intimidate unruly spirits.

Invocations are used in religious ceremonies and some magic rites, especially in neo-Pagan WITCHCRAFT. An invocation is an invitation to an entity or deity to be present. When a magic circle is cast in modern Witchcraft, invocations are made to the Guardians of the Watchtowers, the spirits that rule the cardinal points, to witness the rites and protect the circle. In various rites, the GODDESS and/or HORNED GOD are invoked, or drawn down into the high priestess or high priest (see DRAWING DOWN THE MOON).

Invocations to deities also are used in VODOUN to effect a trance possession, in which worshippers are ridden by the *loas*. Invocation enables the invoker to tap into the powers of a spirit.

Rituals of invocation vary. Spirits and deities are summoned by name and by visual and sensory perceptions associated with the entity.

exorcism, demonic   See DEMONIC EXORCISM.

exorcism, spirit   See SPIRIT EXORCISM.

Exorcist, The
This frightening novel by William Peter Blatty (1971), allegedly based on a true story, brought the horrors of DEMONIC POSSESSION and DEMONIC EXORCISM to a mass audience.

The prologue describes a brief encounter in Iraq, where an archaeologist and cleric is finishing a dig of ancient Assyrian ruins. No names are given, but the reader receives a teaser of evil to come: the cleric, apparently familiar with the ways of the Devil, senses that the Assyrian demon Pazuzu has been disturbed by the digging and plans revenge.

The reader then begins the real story, which opens in a townhouse in the Georgetown section of Washington, D.C., where divorced actress Chris McNeil and her 11-year-old daughter, Regan, are staying while Chris finishes filming a movie. Strange noises and incidents, most of them in Regan's room, annoy Chris, but she doesn't pay too much attention to them.

Portrayed as a bright, happy, affectionate young girl, Regan succumbs slowly to her possession. Alone at home, Regan plays more and more with a ouija board, talking to a Captain Howdy. At first, the house suffers from what is described as *infestation*: attack by the DEMONS through the victim's surroundings. Chris hears rapping noises on the ceiling; Regan's room is always cold; the girl's clothing often ends up in a wadded pile on the floor; someone moves her furniture; there is a foul, burning smell in her room. Other petty incidents occur: books and objects disappear, a stuffed mouse is found in the rat traps.

Now Captain Howdy not only talks to Regan but tells her awful, horrible things, threatening pain and illness. Her bed shakes violently. Then Regan's personality changes; she becomes introverted, argumentative, eventually becoming hostile, disgusting and obscene. She begins to exhibit superhuman strength, contorting her body in jerking, twisting movements. Strange voices come out of her body, which is distended and unrecognizable. She slithers like a snake. Her conversations center around sexual and bodily functions.

Frantic to find out what torments her daughter, Chris takes Regan from one doctor to another, abandoning her career. The doctors test Regan for everything but find no physical reason for her troubles. Under hypnosis, one psychiatrist tries to talk to what he sees as Regan's other personality. The personality—or demon—identifies himself as Nowonmai, from Dogmorfmocion. Although an agnostic, perhaps an atheist, Chris believes firmly that her daughter has become possessed and needs a Catholic exorcism. She meets a priest, Father Damien Karras of Georgetown University, who agrees to help her.

Before Father Karras can obtain permission for an exorcism, Chris's friend, Burke Dennings, left alone in the house with Regan, dies mysteriously by falling out the girl's second-story bedroom window and over a steep cliff below. His head is turned completely around, a feat practically impossible, even in a severe fall. The demons in Regan eventually admit to killing Dennings, explaining that turning his head around was common practice in the murder of witches.

As Regan's condition worsens, she exhibits all the classic signs of true possession. Besides the terrible contortions, foul smells, horrible voices, obscene behavior and poltergeist phenomena (shaking bed, moving furniture, banging windows, breaking pottery), Regan suffers from incessant hiccuping and skin irritations, eventually displaying stigmata on her chest. In her own handwriting, the words *help me* appear. She recoils from religious objects or uses them blasphemously, often employing a crucifix for masturbation. She taunts Father Karras with paranormal knowledge, impersonating the voices of his mother and an early lover. She uses the clipped British accents of Dennings as well. And most importantly for the Church, Regan speaks languages previously unknown: French, German, Latin and perhaps Russian. The gibberish she mouths constantly is found to be English, backwards. "Nowonmai," the name of her demon, is "I am no one (won);" "Dogmorfmocion" is "I come from God."

When it seems Regan will die from her ordeal, the Church gives its permission for an exorcism. Father Karras is to assist Father Lankester Merrin, an old hand at fighting the Devil and the one who senses the evil of Pazuzu in the book's prologue. The devil in Regan had been calling "Marin" for quite some time, but until Father Merrin arrived no one had made the connection. The exorcism proceeds according to the ancient RITUALE ROMANUM with Regan spitting, vomiting and urinating all over the priests as they demand that the demon depart. He goads both men, flinging their pride, their secret sins and their guilt in their faces.

Father Merrin cannot survive this final encounter and dies during the exorcism, leaving Father Karras to fight alone. The demon believes he has won, for Father Karras's soul is not strong enough to overcome his guilt. At the climax, Father Karras orders the demon to leave Regan and come into him: complete possession as a fitting punishment for his sins. The window crashes open, and Father Karras is found dead below. The reader must decide whether the demon accepted Father Karras's offer, but in any case, Regan regains herself.

In the film version, released in 1973, young actress Linda Blair gives a wrenching performance as Regan, with Ellen Burstyn as her mother, Chris, and Max von Sydow as Father Merrin.

eye-biters   During the reign of Queen Elizabeth I (1558–1603), an epidemic illness spread among cattle in Ireland which rendered them blind. WITCHES automatically were accused of causing the blindness by malevolent SPELLS. Many of the eye-biters, as the witches were called, were arrested, tried and executed. Eye-biting was considered an involuntary form of EVIL EYE.

Faery Tradition She VICTOR ANDERSON; GWYDION PENDDERWEN.

fairies A host of supernatural beings and spirits who occupy a limbo between earth and heaven. Both good and evil, fairies have, at various times in history, been blended and confused with WITCHES. During the witch-hunts in Europe and the British Isles, accused witches often sought to save their lives by claiming they were taught their witch arts by fairies, which seemed less malevolent than if they had been taught by the DEVIL. For the most part, fairies have remained in a category of their own, though when convenient, the clergy allied them with the Devil.

Belief in fairies is universal and ancient, dating back to pagan deities. Fairies come in all shapes and sizes and are known by scores of names, among them brownie, elf, dwarf, troll, gnome, pooka, kobold, leprechaun and banshee. They exist in virtually all cultures but are most common in Europe and the British Isles. In the colonization of America, fairy beliefs were transported across the Atlantic, where they still survive in the Appalachians, the Ozarks and other remote mountainous areas.

The word *fairy* comes from the Latin term, *fata*, or "fate." The Fates were supernatural women who liked to visit newborn children. The archaic English term for fairy is *fay*, which means enchanted or bewitched; the state of enchantment is *fayerie*, which gradually became *faerie* and *fairy*.

There are four principle theories as to the origins of fairies:

1. *Fairies are the souls of the pagan dead.* Being unbaptized, the shades are caught in a netherworld and are not bad enough to descend into hell nor good enough to rise into heaven.

2. *Fairies are fallen angels.* When God cast Lucifer from heaven, the angels who were loyal to Lucifer plunged down toward hell with him. But God raised his hand and stopped them in midflight, condemning them to remain where they were. Some were in the air, some in the earth and some in the seas and rivers. This belief is widespread in the lore of Ireland, Scotland and Scandinavia.

3. *Fairies are nature spirits.* Somewhat similar to the fallen-angel theory, this belief holds that fairies are among the many spirits that populate all things and places on the planet. (See also NATURE SPIRITS.)

4. *Fairies are diminutive human beings.* Evidence exists that small-statured races populated parts of Europe and the British Isles in the Neolithic and Bronze Ages, before the spread of the Celts. In Ireland, they were known as the Thuatha de Danaan. They lived in barrows and in shelters burrowed under hills and mounds. They were shy and hard-working, and, as stronger races invaded and conquered with their iron weapons, they retreated into the woodlands to live secretive lives. They were pagan and continued to worship pagan deities. They were close to nature and had keen psychic senses. Some were skilled in metals and mining, and some were herdsmen, keeping stocks of diminutive cattle and horses. Some maintained a guerilla warfare against the invaders: witness the legends of Robin Hood and his band of twelve, and of Rob Roy.

The elusive fairy races were regarded with suspicion and superstition by the larger races and gradually became endowed in popular belief with magical attributes and characteristics. These races, such as the Lapps, Picts and Romano-British-Iberian peoples, were not so small as to be unable to mingle with the Celts, Normans and Saxons. Many were made into servants and serfs, while some married and mixed bloodlines. Prior to the 13th century, having fairy blood was admired.

Of the four main theories, the latter two are most likely: the small races became identified as fairies and were ascribed the supernatural abilities and characteristics of nature spirits in lore.

Fairy lore. Physical characteristics of fairies vary. Some are tiny, winged, gossamer creatures a few inches tall, who can alight on a drop of water and barely make it tremble. Some are dwarfs and "little people" barely smaller than mortals. Others are huge giants. Fairies are both ugly and beautiful. They are usually mischievous and unpredictable and must be placated by gifts of food and spotlessly clean houses. The superstitious refer to them as "the good people" or "the good neighbors" in order to stay in the fairies' good graces.

When won over by a mortal, fairies may be very generous with gifts, both material and psychic. Some are evil and malevolent. Most are lascivious and enjoy seducing mortals; some even marry mortals. In general, it is considered bad luck to talk about fairies and their activities. To do so invites a beating and the instantaneous disappearance of all the gifts bestowed by the fairies, such as wealth and possessions, and even the fairy lovers or spouses themselves.

Fairies are nocturnal creatures and like to drink, dance and sing. Their music is exquisite. Their color is green, which is also identified with witches. Green clothing perhaps helps them to blend into their forests; some are said to have green skin. They keep many animals, including dogs, cattle and sheep, which usually are red and white in color, but they do not keep cats or fowl. In Ireland, cats are regarded as fairies, generally as evil ones. The crowing of COCKS drives away fairies, as well as witches and DEMONS.

Like the Fates, fairies love to visit the newborn babies of mortals and will not hesitate to steal those that are unbaptized, or "little pagans," substituting in their place changelings—wizened fairy children. Fairies particularly desire fair-haired children, to improve their own hairy stock. To protect infants against kidnapping by fairies, an open pair of iron scissors traditionally was hung over them in the cradle—for iron is believed to repel fairies—or an iron PIN was stuck in their clothes. Other measures included laying the trousers of the child's father across the cradle; drawing a circle of fire around the cradle; making a sign of the cross over the child; sprinkling it and the cradle with holy water; and giving it a nickname. The latter relates to beliefs in the magic power of names (see NAMES OF POWER). If fairies do not know the true name of a child, they will not be able to cast a magical spell over it. In lore, witches were often said to collude with fairies to steal babies or children for money. From the Middle Ages through the 17th century, when fairy beliefs peaked, infants who were ugly, retarded or unruly were written off as changelings. It was believed that the changelings could be induced to confess if they were set afire, and many babies undoubtedly died that way.

In the early Middle Ages, fairies were said to be visible to all. As time went on, they acquired more and more supernatural powers and became invisible to all but those with second sight. Fairies who were captured by mortals were said to pine away and die quickly if they could not escape. Mortals who visited Fairyland, an enchanted land beneath the ground, discovered that time passes very slowly for fairies: what seemed like a few days translated into years when the mortals returned to the physical world.

Some fairies were said to suck human blood like vampires. On the Isle of Man, it was believed that if water was not left out for them, they would suck the blood of the sleepers in the house or bleed them and make a cake with the blood. The fairies would then leave some of the blood cake hidden in the house; it had to be found and given to the sleepers to eat, or they would die of a sleeping sickness (see HORNED WOMEN for a description of blood cakes attributed to witches.)

Fairies and witches. According to British anthropologist MARGARET A. MURRAY and other historians, real "little people" gradually became identified with witches. In the 16th and 17th centuries, when fairy beliefs were at their height, fairies and witches were often blended together. Both could cast and break SPELLS, heal people and divine lost objects and the future. Both danced and sang beneath a full moon—often together—and trafficked with the Devil. Both could change shape, fly, levitate and cause others to levitate (see METAMORPHOSIS; FLYING; LEVITATION). Both stole unbaptized children and poisoned people. Both stole horses at night and rode them hard to their SABBATS, returning them exhausted by dawn. Both avoided SALT and both were repelled by IRON. JAMES I of England, in *Daemonologie*, his book about witches, called DIANA, the goddess of witches, the "Queen of Faerie." Oberon, the name of the King of Fairies, was also the name of a demon summoned by magicians. Fairies were said to be the FAMILIARS of witches. It is no surprise, then, that fairies figured in numerous witch trials. Those richest in detail took place in the British Isles.

In 1566 John Walsh of Dorset was accused of witchcraft. He admitted being able to tell if a person was bewitched, a gift bestowed upon him partly by fairies, he said. The fairies, he claimed, lived in great heaps of earth in Dorsetshire and could be consulted for one hour, at either noon or midnight. Walsh also defined three kinds of fairies: green, white and black, and said the black were the worst.

Bessy Dunlop, a wise woman healer of Ayrshire, was accused of witchcraft and sorcery on November 8, 1576. She suddenly became a successful herbalist and healer and gained second sight, which helped her predict the recovery or death of patients and the location of lost objects.

In her trial, Dunlop testified that she had been taught these abilities by a phantom fairy named Thorne or Thome Reid. Reid told her that he had been ordered to be her attendant by the Queen of Elfhane. Many years before, when Dunlop was in childbirth, the Queen appeared before her as a stout woman, asked for a drink and was given one. Reid explained to Dunlop that afterwards, he had been killed in the battle of Pinkie on September 10, 1547 and had gone to Fairyland. He now served the Queen of Elfhane.

The ghostly Reid appeared many times before Dunlop, beseeching her to go away with him to Fairyland or to deny the Christian faith, in exchange for which he would grant her every wish. She denied him repeatedly, she testified. One day, Reid appeared with a company of eight women and four men. Reid explained that they were "good wights" (fairies) who lived in Elfland. They asked Dunlop to accompany them. When Dunlop remained silent, they left "with a hideous ugly howling sound, like that of a hurricane."

Reid continued to visit Dunlop, offering his assistance in healing sick animals and people. Eventually, he gave her herbal ointments and taught her how to use them and predict their effectiveness.

Dunlop would see Reid in town from time to time, though he remained invisible to others. He always appeared if she summoned him thrice. On every occasion, he begged her to come with him to Fairyland, sometimes tugging at her apron, but she always refused, which sometimes put him in an ill humor.

These supernatural visits went on for four years before Dunlop was brought down on charges of witchcraft. The fact that Dunlop had always used her new skills for good did not help her case; neither did her testimony that her benefactor was a fairy and not the Devil. Dunlop was convicted and burned at the stake.

A few years later, in 1588, Alison Pearson of Byrehill was charged with invoking the spirits of the Devil. She also was said to have a fairy familiar: her cousin, William Sympson, a physician who had been kidnapped by a Gypsy and had died. One day while Pearson was traveling, she felt ill and lay down. A green man (Sympson) appeared and said he would do her good if she would be faithful to him. The green man vanished and reappeared with a band of fairies, who cajoled Pearson into accompanying them and taking part in their drinking and merrymaking.

Pearson gradually became comfortable with her fairy friends. If she talked about their activities, however, she was tormented with blows that left insensitive spots on her skin. Sympson advised her of when the fairies were coming to her and of the fact that they usually arrived in a whirlwind. Sympson also taught her how to use herbal remedies and told her that every year, the Devil took one-tenth of the fairies away to hell as a tithe.

Like Dunlop, Pearson's confession only worsened her case. She also was convicted and burned.

ISOBEL GOWDIE, Scotland's renowned witch who voluntarily confessed in 1662, said she had frequent doings with fairies. Gowdie went often to Fairyland, entering through various caverns and mounds. The entrance of Fairyland was populated with elf-bulls, whose "roaring and skoilling" always frightened her. She often met with the King and Queen of Fairy, who were finely dressed and offered her more meat than she could eat. Gowdie, her fellow witches and the fairies would amuse themselves by metamorphosing into animals and destroying the homes of mortals.

Gowdie said the fairies manufactured their poisonous elf-arrow heads (see ELF-ARROWS) in their caverns, and she had seen the Devil working alongside them, putting the finishing touches on the flints. Fairies taught her how to fly, by mounting corn-straws and beanstalks and crying, "Horse and Hattock, in the Devil's name!"

As late as 1894 beliefs in fairies and witches in Ireland caused the murder of Bridget Cleary of Clonmel, who was accused by her own husband and family of being a changeling wife. The trials of Michael Cleary and Bridget's relatives were Ireland's last involving witchcraft (see FAIRY WITCH OF CLONMEL).

Neo-Pagan Witches believe in fairies and some see them clairvoyantly. Some Witches say their Craft was passed down from fairies through the generations of their families.

fairy light   See JACK-O'-LANTERN.

fairy ring   A natural mushroom fungus that grows in dark rings on grass and turf. In folklore it is said to be the site where FAIRIES and WITCHES meet at night to dance and sing. The mushroom is edible—though animals tend to shun it—and has a reddish, buff or tawny cap. It is common in Europe, the British Isles and North America and often appears after heavy rains. In Britain, fairy rings also are known as *hag tracks,* in the belief that they are created by the dancing feet of witches.

Because fairies are associated with MAGIC, fairy rings have magical superstitions attached to them. It is said that if one stands in the center of a fairy ring under a full MOON and makes a wish, the wish will come true. If one wishes to see and hear the fairies, who often are beyond the awareness of the five senses, one can run around a fairy ring nine times under a full moon. However, superstition holds, it is dangerous to do so on Samhain (All Hallow's Eve) or Beltane (May Eve), two major festivals of fairies (and witches), as the fairies may take offense and carry the mortal off to Fairyland.

Fairy rings are still associated with natural magic and are used by contemporary Witches as sites for meetings and SABBATS.

Fairies also are said to dance around stone circles.

Fairy Witch of Clonmel
In Ireland, belief in WITCHES traditionally has been tied closely to belief in FAIRIES. In folklore tales, witches and fairies mingle and collaborate, and sometimes one is said to be the other. In 1894 in Clonmel in County Tipperary, a young woman named Bridget Cleary was tortured and burned to death because her husband believed the fairies had spirited her away and substituted in her place a witch changeling.

Changelings customarily are sickly fairy infants that fairies leave in the place of the human babies they are said to kidnap. However, many stories exist of fairies kidnapping mortal men and women—especially women—to be spouses of fairies in Fairyland.

Sometime in March 1894 Michael Cleary, a man who may have suffered from mental disturbances, began to think something was strange about his 26-year-old wife, Bridget. She seemed more refined. She suddenly appeared to be two inches taller. Cleary, whose mother had acknowledged going off with fairies, immediately suspected foul play by the "little people." He confronted his wife and accused her of being a changeling. When she denied it, he began to torture her with the help of three of her cousins, James, Patrick and Michael Kennedy; her father, Patrick Boland; her aunt, Mary Kennedy; and two local men named John Dunne and William Ahearne.

The townsfolk of Clonmel noticed that Bridget was missing for several days. Hearing that Bridget was sick, a neighbor, Johanna Burke, tried to pay a visit but found the door to the house barred. She encountered William Simpson and his wife, neighbors who also were attempting to pay a visit but were not admitted to the house. The three looked in a window and eventually convinced Cleary to let them in.

The neighbors were aghast to see Bridget, clad only in nightclothes, held spread-eagled on the bed by the Kennedy boys and Dunne, while Boland, Ahearne and Mark Kennedy looked on. Michael Cleary was attempting to coerce his wife into drinking a mixture of milk and herbs (probably a fairy antidote), saying, "Take it, you witch." Cleary repeatedly asked her, "Are you Bridget Boland, wife of Michael Cleary, in the name of God?" Bridget kept crying, "Yes, yes," but Cleary did not seem to believe her. Dunne suggested holding her over the kitchen fire, which Cleary and Patrick Kennedy did, while Bridget writhed and screamed and begged the visitors in vain for help. In fairy lore, setting fire to someone is considered a failproof way to expose changelings and induce the fairy parents to return the stolen human.

Bridget continued to insist that she was Bridget Boland, wife of Michael Cleary, and finally was put to bed. Everyone except Cleary seemed satisfied that Bridget was not a witch changeling.

The next day, Cleary approached William Simpson and asked to borrow a revolver, explaining that Bridget was with the fairies at Kylegranaugh Hill, a fairy fort, and he was going to go "have it out with them." Cleary also claimed that Bridget would ride up to the house at midnight on a big gray horse, bound with fairy ropes, which had to be cut before she could return as a mortal. Simpson told Cleary he had no revolver. Later, he saw Cleary heading for Kylegranaugh Hill, carrying a big knife.

That night, Johanna Burke returned to the Cleary house to find Bridget sitting by the fire talking to Boland, Cleary and Patrick Burke, Johanna's brother. Cleary flung his wife to the ground and forced her to eat bread and jam and drink tea—fairies do not have to eat mortal food—and threatened her with more punishment if she did not. He again demanded to know her true identity, and she insisted she was Bridget, not a witch changeling.

Cleary's rage increased. He tore off her clothes and grabbed a hot brand from the fire and held it up to her mouth. He refused to let anyone out of the house until he got his wife back. Then he threw lamp oil over Bridget and set her afire. Later Burke described what happened:

> She lay writhing and burning in the hearth, and the house was full of smoke and smell . . . she turned to me and screamed out, "Oh Han, Han". . . . When I came down Bridget was still lying on the hearth, smoldering and dead. Her legs were blackened and contracted with the fire. . . . Michale [sic] Cleary screamed out, "She is burning now, but God knows

I did not mean to do it. I may thank Jack Dunne for all of it."

Cleary and Patrick Burke put Bridget's remains in a sack and buried them in a shallow grave about a quarter of a mile away. The remains, with the legs, abdomen, part of the back and the left hand nearly burned away, were found on March 22. Witnesses came forward. Cleary, Boland, the Kennedy boys and aunt, Ahearne and Dunne were charged with willful murder. In the investigation, two more men were charged: William Kennedy, another cousin, and Dennis Ganey, an herb doctor. The trial lasted two weeks.

A jury found all defendants guilty of manslaughter, a lesser charge, and the judge sentenced all to jail. Cleary received the harshest sentence: 20 years of hard labor. Even as he was sentenced, he still believed the fairies had stolen his wife and left a changeling witch in her place.

familiars   Historically, low-ranking DEMONS in constant attention to WITCHES for the purpose of carrying out SPELLS and bewitchments. Familiars usually assumed animal forms—CATS, TOADS, OWLS, mice and dogs were the most common—though virtually any animal or insect could be suspected. In WITCHCRAFT trials, if so much as a fly buzzed in the window while a witch was being questioned or tried, it was said to be her familiar. The inquisitors took the Bible to heart: those who had familiars were "an abomination unto the Lord" (Deut. 23:10–12) and should be "put to death: they shall stone them with stones: their blood shall be upon them" (Lev. 20:27).

Familiars—also called imps (see IMP)—were said to be given to witches by the DEVIL or bought or inherited from other witches. A witch could have several of them. Cats were the favored forms, especially black ones. The fear that all cats were witches' familiars was one of the reasons for the cat massacres that swept through medieval Europe.

Familiars were given names like any household pets, which most of them undoubtedly were. One 16th-century Essex woman accused of witchcraft admitted that she had three familiars in the form of mice: Littleman, Prettyman and Daynty. Another had four mice named Prickeare, James, Robyn and Sparrow. Elizabeth Clark, the first victim of MATTHEW HOPKINS, England's great witch-hunter of the 17th century, confessed to having five familiars, including unearthly ones: Holt, a kitten; Jamara, a fat, legless spaniel; Sack and Sugar, a black rabbit; Newes, a polecat; and Vinegar Tom, a long-legged, greyhoundlike creature with an ox's head and broad eyes, which could turn itself into a headless four-year-old child. Other familiars named in trials included Grizel, Greedigut, Peck in the Crown and Elemauzer. Perhaps the best-known familiar name is Pyewackett, the moniker of the witch's cat in the movie *Bell, Book and Candle,* and a name that dates back to Renaissance England. Pyewackett, Hopkins stated, was a name "no mortal could invent."

Witches were said to take great care of their familiars. According to Grillot de Givry in *Witchcraft, Magic and Alchemy* (1931) "they baptized their toads, dressed them in black velvet, put little bells on their paws and made them dance." Familiars were dispatched to bewitch people and animals into sickness and death. They also protected their witches. In return, witches gave them what they craved: BLOOD. ALICE KYTELER of Kilkenny, Ireland, convicted as a witch in 1324, confessed (or perhaps was made to confess) that she sacrificed red COCKS to her familiar. It was common for witches to allow familiars to suck blood from their fingers or any protuberance or unnatural spot on the skin. The existence of WITCH'S MARKS was proof of suckling familiars and therefore of being a witch—enough evidence to get witches hanged.

Familiars also were said to assume more than one shape. Agnes Waterhouse, an Englishwoman accused of witchcraft in 1566, had a cat familiar named Satan that could change into a dog (see METAMORPHOSIS). Familiars also could vanish at will. It should be noted that the appearance of the Devil himself as an animal was not the same as the appearance of a familiar.

If a witch was arrested, she was often tied up and left in a cell, while inquisitors watched secretly to see if her familiars came to her aid. Even an ant or cockroach crawling toward her was called a familiar.

Religion was a charm against the familiar's infernal power. Waterhouse was said to be unable to harm one man through her cat because of his religious beliefs (see CHARMS).

During the witch hysteria of the Middle Ages and Renaissance, the obsession with familiars was confined mostly to England and Scotland, where they are mentioned in numerous trial records, especially those related to Hopkins. The Witchcraft Act of 1604 made it a felony to "consult, covenant with, entertain, employ, feed, or reward any evil and wicked spirit to or for any intent or purpose." But the *MALLEUS MALEFICARUM* (1486), the major witch inquisitor's handbook, offers no instructions concerning familiars in the interrogation and trial of witches. The book does acknowledge that an animal familiar "always works with her [witch] in everything." It also advises inquisitors never to leave witch prisoners unattended, because the Devil "will cause her to kill herself." The Devil might accomplish that through a familiar.

There is scant evidence of familiars in early American witch trials. In the Salem trials in 1692, John Bradstreet was indicted for "inciting a dog to afflict." The dog was tried and hanged as a witch (see SALEM WITCHES).

Outside of witch trials, more benevolent familiars were believed to exist, serving wizards and wise men and women who were magicians or village healers. The familiars helped diagnose illnesses and the sources of bewitchment and were used for divining and finding lost objects and treasures. Magicians conjured them with rituals, then locked them in bottles, RINGS and STONES. They sometimes sold them as charms, claiming the spirits would ensure success in gambling, love, business or whatever the customer wanted. This sort of familiar technically was not illegal; England's Witchcraft Act of 1604 specifically prohibited only evil and wicked spirits.

Some familiars were said to be FAIRIES. *Oberon* was a popular name for fairy familiars in 15th- and 16th-century England.

Familiars in neo-Pagan Witchcraft. Many modern Witches have animal familiars, usually cats, which are their magical helpers. Some also have dogs, birds, snakes or toads. Witches do not believe the familiars are "demons" or spirits in animal form but simply animals whose psychic attunement makes them ideal partners in MAGIC. Some Witches say it is possible to endow pets with magical powers and turn them into familiars, though others don't believe it should be done. Still others believe familiars are never pets (and should not be treated as such) but are animals who volunteer to work as familiars and are karmically attracted to Witches. Witches who do not have familiars send out psychic "calls" to draw in the right animal.

Familiars reputedly are sensitive to psychic vibrations and power and are welcome partners inside the MAGIC CIRCLE for the raising of power, the casting of SPELLS, SCRYING, spirit contact and other magical work. They also serve as psychic radar, reacting visibly to the presence of any negative or evil energy, whether it be an unseen force or a person who dabbles in the wrong kind of magic. Familiars are given psychic protection by their witches.

Some Witches also use the term *familiar* to describe thought-forms created magically and empowered to carry out a certain task on the astral plane.

Familiars in sorcery and shamanism. Virtually all sorcerers and shamans in cultures around the world have helpers in the form of spirits (see SORCERY, SHAMANISM). Dispatching them on errands to harm or kill is sometimes called *sending*. The physical shape of a familiar varies. New Guinea sorcerers rely on snakes and crocodiles, while in Malaya, the familiar is usually an owl or badger passed down from generation to generation.

Throughout Africa, the wild creatures of the bush are said to be witches' familiars: for the Lugbara, they are the toad, snake, lizard, water frog, bat, owl, leopard, jackal and a type of monkey that screeches in the night; for the Dinka, they are black cobras and hyenas. The Zulus' familiars are said to be corpses dug up and reanimated with magic; they are sent out on night errands to scare travelers with their shrieking and pranks. The Ndembu of Zambia believe that evil men create spirit familiars out of the blood of their victims and send them out to kill others. The Pondo witches, also of Africa, are women who are said to have sex with their light-colored spirit familiars (see AFRICAN WITCHCRAFT).

In shamanism, a novice shaman acquires his familiar spirits, usually manifested in animal, reptile or bird shapes, when he completes his initiation. He may send them out to do battle in his place, but if they die, so does the shaman. Familiars usually stay with their shaman until death, then disappear. Among certain Eskimos, the familiar is embodied in an artificial seal, not a live animal.

See also WITCH OF ENDOR.

Farrar, Janet (1950–   ) and Stewart (1916–   )

The writings of English WITCHES Janet and Stewart Farrar have done much to explain modern WITCHCRAFT to a curious public and to illuminate the Craft to its practitioners. Both were initiated by the flamboyant ALEXANDER SANDERS but were able to transcend the showmanship that surrounded Sanders and his COVEN; they went on to form their own covens in England and Ireland. Their Craft has been called "reformed Alexandrian" and "post-Alexandrian," but the Farrars have steadfastly avoided applying a sectarian label to their approach to WICCA. They prefer to call themselves simply "Witches."

Pre-Wiccan backgrounds. Janet Farrar was born Janet Owen in Clapton, London, on June 24, 1950. Her father, Ronald Owen, came from an English and Welsh background; her mother, Ivy (née Craddock), was an immigrant Irishwoman. Both parents were hospital workers and followers of the Church of England. Ivy Owen died when Janet was five.

Janet attended Leyton Manor School in London and Royal Wanstead High School for Girls in Sawbridgeworth, Hertfordshire. After graduation, she worked as a model and receptionist. In 1970 she was initiated into Alex and Maxine Sanders's coven, which led to her meeting Stewart Farrar the same year.

Stewart Farrar was born on June 28, 1916, in Highams Park, Essex. His father, Frank Farrar, an Englishman, worked as a bank official, and his mother,

Agnes, (née Picken), a Scotswoman, worked as a schoolteacher. Stewart was raised a Christian Scientist, but by the time he turned 20, in 1936, he turned agnostic. He remained an agnostic until 1970, when he was initiated into the Craft.

Stewart was educated at City of London School and University College, London, where he studied journalism. He served as president of the London University Journalism Union and as editor of London Union Magazine. He graduated in 1937.

In 1939 Stewart volunteered for the Army and became an instructor in Gunnery, Anti-Aircraft. He served until discharged in 1946 with the rank of major. Following military service, he worked until 1947 as a civilian public relations and press officer for the Control Commission for Germany.

In 1947 he embarked on a long and varied career as journalist, author and scriptwriter. From 1947 to 1950, he worked as sub-editor and then deputy night editor in the London office of Reuters, and from 1953 to 1954 as a reporter for the Communist Party's *Daily Worker*. Disillusioned, he left it and the party in 1954. From 1956 to 1962, Stewart was a scriptwriter for Associated British-Pathe, where he worked on television documentaries and a feature film, and on television dramas for the company's associate, A.B.C. Television, now known as Thames Television. As a freelance writer, Stewart authored radio drama scripts for the British Broadcasting Corporation, short stories for magazines, and books. His first book, a detective novel, *The Snake on 99*, was published in 1958.

From 1969 to 1974 Stewart worked as a feature writer for the weekly *Reveille*, a job that led to his introduction to Witchcraft. Late in 1969 Stewart was sent to a press preview of the film *Legend of the Witches*. Alexander and Maxine Sanders, who had given technical advice for the film, were to be present, and *Reveille* was interested in a story. Stewart was skeptical about Witchcraft but was impressed with Sanders upon meeting him. Sanders invited Stewart to attend a Witch's INITIATION, which Stewart did, and found it both dignified and moving. He wrote a two-part feature for the magazine, which gained him Sanders's trust. Sanders told him the publisher of his biography, *King of the Witches*, was looking for an author to write another book on modern Witchcraft. Stewart got the contract for *What Witches Do* and began attending the Sanders's training classes. At first, he was a sympathetic but skeptical outsider. What he learned, however, struck a positive, personal chord, and on February 21, 1970, Maxine Sanders initiated him into the coven, where he met Janet Owen.

Wiccan activities. On December 22, Stewart and Janet left the Sanders's coven to form their own coven in London. The Sanderses separated shortly after that; the last time Stewart and Janet ever saw Alex again was in 1971. The same year, *What Witches Do* was published. Despite its inclusion of Sanders's fabricated stories about himself—and Stewart's assertion that Sanders ranked above GERALD B. GARDNER and alongside ALEISTER CROWLEY and ELIPHAS LEVI in terms of magical achievement—the book helped to establish Stewart as a clear voice in the Wiccan community. Though Stewart later candidly admitted he had been too credulous and that he no longer put Sanders on the same or better footing with Crowley, Levi and Gardner, he refused to disparage "the *enfant terrible* of British Witchcraft." Sanders, he said, nevertheless made a significant contribution to the Craft.

From 1970 to 1976 Stewart and Janet built up their coven. On January 31, 1974, they were handfasted, with Stewart's two sons and two daughters from a previous marriage attending and participating in the ceremony (see HANDFASTING). They were legally married in a civil ceremony on July 19, 1975. In 1974 Stewart left *Reveille* to work full-time as a freelance writer.

In 1976 the Farrars turned their coven over to Susan and David Buckingham and moved to Ireland, where they built up a new coven. Several Irish covens eventually hived off it. In 1988 they returned to Britain.

What Witches Do brought an unending stream of mail from persons seeking help in joining the Craft. After nine years of running a coven and being sought for advice, the Farrars jointly authored two books of ritual and nonritual material, *Eight Sabbats for Witches* (1981) and *The Witches' Way* (1984). In the United States the books were combined and published as *A Witches Bible Compleat* (1984). The books include rituals created by the Farrars plus a wealth of material relating to the religion of the Craft. *The Witches' Way* provides the first thorough reconstruction of the evolution of the Gardnerian BOOK OF SHADOWS, as developed by Gardner and DOREEN VALIENTE, and includes contributions from Valiente. Like other Witches who have written on the Craft, the Farrars have been criticized for revealing too much. They counter that the false secrecy mandated in the Craft leads inevitably to distorted information. They do not feel they have revealed essential secrets but merely clarified and illuminated material that already has reached the public.

The Farrars are also the coauthors of *The Witches' Goddess* (1987); *Life & Times of a Modern Witch* (1987); and *The Witches' God* (1989), a companion to *The Witches' Goddess*.

Stewart Farrar's other fiction works include two additional detective novels, *Zero in the Gate* (1960) and *Death in the Wrong Bed* (1963); a romance novel, *Delphine, Be a Darling* (1963); and seven occult novels: *The Twelve Maidens* (1974); *The Serpent of Lilith* (1976); *The Dance of Blood* (1977); *The Sword of Orley* (1977); *Omega* (1980); *Forcible Entry* (1986); and *Backlash* (1988).

Faust   The most famous legend of a man who succumbs to the temptation of making a DEVIL'S PACT for personal gain is that of Faust. In the hundreds of stories that grew up around the legend, Faust was an old and scholarly man who sold his soul to the DEVIL in exchange for infinite knowledge and wisdom, youth and the pleasures of the flesh. In some of the stories, Faust met his tragic end when the Devil claimed his soul in death; in other stories, he repented and was redeemed.

The legend of Faust is based loosely on a real Dr. George (later Johannes) Faustus, a German who lived circa 1480–1539 or 1540. What is fact and what is fiction concerning the real man is unclear. It is believed that he may have been one of the charlatan magicians who traveled around Europe during the Renaissance, entertaining at fairs and at royal courts. Stories began to circulate that Dr. Faustus had sold his soul to the Devil in exchange for incredible powers of MAGIC. He was said to be accompanied by a familiar in the form of a dog with red eyes (see FAMILIARS). He allegedly rode through the air on bales of hay and on beer or wine barrels (see FLYING), and conjured the spirits of the dead. His infernal servant was the high-ranking demon, Mephistopheles, who did his bidding for the 24 years of Faust's pact with the Devil.

The stories of Faust incorporated many elements of other pact-with-the-Devil tales, which were popular during the Renaissance. Faust was said to enjoy youth, the seduction of young women and the finest food and wines. Mephistopheles taught him the secrets of the universe and all the magic he cared to know. Using Mephistopheles as a demonic steed, Faust flew wherever he wanted on the earth and to other planets as well. Nothing was denied him, even indulgences in pranks. At the Vatican, Faust made himself invisible and slapped the Pope across the face with a dead fish and stole his dinner.

After about 16 years of such escapades, Faust became jaded and bored with entertaining himself with silly magical pranks, usually illusions that suddenly vanished on people. For example, he sold a fine horse to man who, after Faust was long gone with the money, found himself astride a bale of hay. Faust also amused himself with conjuring the dead, including Helen of Troy. But as the deadline of his pact approached, he became increasingly worried about his fate.

The Tragicall Historie of the Life and Death of Doctor Faustus.

With new Additions.

Written by CH. MAR.

Printed at London for *Iohn Wright*, and are to be fold at his fhop without Newgate. 1631.

Title page of Christopher Marlowe's *The Tragicall Historie of the Life and Death of Doctor Faustus*, 1631

According to one tale, when the term of the contract was up, the Devil came to collect Faust's soul one night after midnight. A terrible wind howled around Faust's house. Neighbors heard him scream for help, but no one went to his aid. In the morning, his twisted body was found outside in a pile of dung, and his blood, brains and teeth were splattered about his house. His eyes were stuck to one wall.

Faust inspired many literary and musical works of fiction. The first book, *Dr. Faust, the Notorious Magician and Necromancer*, appeared in 1587 in Germany and was an immediate success. Notable works include Marlowe's play, *The Tragical History of Doctor Faustus*, published between 1589 and 1592, and Goethe's play, *Faust*, which was published in two parts in 1808 and 1833. Three operas, all based on Goethe's version of the Faust legend, have remained in popular repertoire around the world since their composition in the 19th century: Gounod's *Faust*, Berlioz's *La Damnation de Faust* and Boito's *Mefistofele*.

In 1962 a grimoire (see GRIMOIRES) titled *Great and*

Powerful Sea Ghost was published in Amsterdam and attributed to the authorship of Dr. Faust. The introduction tells of Faust's dealings with Beelzebub and how the demon agreed to send Mephistopheles to Faust to be his servant.

fetish   An object, usually a West African wooden doll, that is possessed by spirits and represents those spirits to the fetish owner. Fetishes may also be animals' teeth, snake bones, beautiful stones or even the huts where WITCH DOCTORS commune with spirit guides. They are often worn as ornamental AMULETS or carried on the body.

A fetish is supposed to possess magical powers and be capable of bringing about the owner's designs or preserving him from injury (see MAGIC). Some scholars trace the evolution of the West African world *juju*, meaning "fetish," to the French *joujou*, or "doll."

Possession of a fetish by a slave in the New World was punishable by sadistic torture and death. Not only were the fetishes graven images of a god other than the Catholic one, they represented tribal ways feared by white masters.

See also AFRICAN WITCHCRAFT.

Fian, John (?–1591)   A young schoolmaster in Saltpans, Scotland, in the late 16th century, Dr. John Fian was the central figure in Scotland's most famous witch trials, which involved JAMES VI himself. Fian, also known as John Cunningham, was accused of leading a COVEN of WITCHES in North Berwick who, among other charges attempted to assassinate the king. Fian was brutally tortured until he confessed and was burned at the stake in 1591.

The downfall of Fian was brought about by a young servant girl named Gillis Duncan, whose gift for natural HEALING was suspected by her master as the Devil's MAGIC. Under TORTURE, she accused several persons of WITCHCRAFT, including Fian (see NORTH BERWICK WITCHES). Fian, who had a reputation as a conjurer, was arrested on December 20, 1590, and charged with 20 counts of witchcraft and high treason.

The most important charge was that of the attempted murder of King James as he sailed to Denmark to fetch his bride-to-be. The witches allegedly raised a terrible storm at sea by tossing a charm of a dead cat with human limbs tied to its paws into the ocean and crying "Hola!" On the return voyage, Satan then cast a "thing like a football" into the sea, raising a mist. The king's vessel was battered about but returned safely with no casualties (see STORM RAISING). Other charges against Fian included acting as secretary at the coven meetings, at which he recorded the oaths of allegiance to Satan; kissing the

Devil's anus (see KISS OF SHAME) and making a DEVIL'S PACT; falling into ecstasies and trances, during which his spirit was transported to various mountains; bewitching a man to have a spell of lunacy once every 24 hours because he loved the same woman as Fian; attempting to seduce the woman by bewitching her, but instead bewitching a heifer that followed him about "leaping and dancing . . . to the great admiration of all the townsmen of Saltpans;" robbing graves for body parts to use as CHARMS; and various acts of magic, such as FLYING through the air. He was also accused of putting magical CANDLES on the legs of his horse and upon his staff, which enabled him to turn night into day as he rode.

Upon his arrest, Fian was imprisoned. He refused to confess and was subjected to severe torture. After having his head "thrawed" with a rope (bound and twisted in various directions), he still denied the charges. Fian was then given a torture described as "the most severe and cruell paine in the world," the "boots," a vise that went around the legs from knee to ankle, and that was progressively tightened with blows from a hammer. Fian was given three hammer blows while in the boots, and passed out. His torturers "found" two pins under his tongue, thrust in up to their heads. The court declared that the pins were a witch's charm to prevent him from confessing.

Fian was released from the boots and taken before King James. Broken, he confessed in his own writing. He renounced the DEVIL and vowed to lead the life of a Christian. He was taken back to jail.

The following day, the jailors found Fian greatly distressed. He said the Devil had appeared before him in the night, dressed in black and carrying a white wand, and had demanded that he continue his service in accordance with his pact. Fian said he stood firm in his renunciation, but the Devil reminded him that he still would possess Fian's soul upon death. The Devil broke the wand and vanished.

All that day, Fian languished in depression. That night, he stole the key to the prison door and fled to Saltpans. The king had the area scoured. Fian was soon arrested and brought again before James. He recanted his confession.

James was convinced that Fian had entered into a new pact with the Devil. He had Fian's body searched for a new DEVIL'S MARK, but none could be found. Determined to get another confession out of the schoolmaster, James ordered more brutal torture, described as follows in a pamphlet, *Newes from Scotland* (1591):

His nailes upon all his fingers were riven and pulled off with an instrument called in Scottish a turkas, which in England wee called a payre of pincers, and under everie nayle there was thrust in two needles over, even up to the heads; at all which tormentes, notwithstanding, the Doctor never shronke anie wit, neither woulde he then confess it the sooner for all the tortures inflicted upon him.

Then was hee, with all convenient speed, by commandement, convaied againe to the torment of the bootes, wherein he continued a long time, and did abide so many blowes in them, that his legges were crusht and beaten together as small as might bee, and the bones and flesh so bruised, that the blood and marrow spouted forth in great abundance, whereby they were made unserviceable for ever.

Fian still would not confess, "so deeply had the devill entered into his heart." The enraged king nevertheless condemned him to die. Fian was put into a cart and taken to Castle Hill in Edinburgh, where a great bonfire was prepared. On a Saturday at the end of January, 1591, he was strangled and thrown immediately into the flames.

Firth, Violet Mary   See DION FORTUNE.

Fitch, Ed   American Wiccan (see WICCA; WITCH-CRAFT) high priest and key founder of the PAGAN WAY, an organization whose rituals have been in widespread use since 1970. Born in Roxboro, North Carolina, to a family with Russian roots, Fitch grew up in various locations around the country because of the moves required of his father, who worked in the construction trade. At age nine, he and his father sighted a UFO over their ranch in northern California. Fitch remembers that a circular object about 50 feet in diameter, with an aura of orange flames, rose up from a nearby mountain and cruised silently over the ranch.

Fitch spent four years at the Virginia Military Institute, where he began a lifelong research into the paranormal. After graduation, he entered the Air Force and was sent to Japan, where he ran a courier station, carrying secret documents from a spy organization that evesdropped on Soviet activities in Siberia. While there, he delved into Buddhism and Shinto.

After three years, Fitch returned to civilian life in the United States, working as a technical writer and electronics engineer in Washington, D.C. It was now the 1960s, and modern Witchcraft and neo-Paganism were spreading around the country. Fitch was initiated into the Gardnerian tradition of Witchcraft by Raymond and Rosemary Buckland (see RAYMOND BUCKLAND), and eventually rose to the rank of high priest. He also was trained in trance channeling by Spiritualist mediums from the CHURCH OF ALL WORLDS.

The Air Force called him back to duty during the Vietnam war and stationed him in Thailand, which provided him with another opportunity to learn about Eastern religions and mysticism. He obtained a black belt in Tae Kwon Do, which introduced him to Zen thought and action, a discipline that has stuck with him throughout life.

In Thailand, Fitch wrote two books that were never formally published but that later circulated in the Pagan community and became "underground classics": *The Grimoire of the Shadows*, a book of magical training techniques, and *The Outer Court Book of Shadows*, which reconstructs the magical and seasonal rituals of ancient Crete, Greece and Druidic Europe (see also BOOK OF SHADOWS). Twenty years later, material from these books was still surfacing in new traditions and rituals, sometimes being labeled as an "ancient Celtic tradition from Ireland and Scotland."

After Thailand, Fitch was reassigned to North Dakota to work on the redesign of Minuteman rockets. During this time he became part of a informal group that created the Pagan Way. Fitch composed introductory and background materials and public rituals and was instrumental in the forming of the first Pagan Way grove, in Chicago.

The Air Force sent Fitch next to southern California. He left the military as a captain and obtained a master's degree in systems management from the University of Southern California. He went to work for a major aerospace firm as a research and development engineer.

In the growing Pagan movement, Fitch helped to organize and chair two Pagan Ecumenical Councils, which established the COVENANT OF THE GODDESS as an international umbrella organization for Pagans in 1975. Fitch also published for a time *The Crystal Well*, a magazine of neo-romantic Paganism, which resulted in a published book, *Magical Rites from the Crystal Well* (1984).

In the 1980s Fitch remained active as a Gardnerian high priest and became involved in Odinism, a form of Norse Paganism that stresses conservative, family-oriented values. In the late 1980s his projects included books on the Odinist traditions of northern, central and eastern Europe; dance magic; and geomancy (see ODIN). He also worked on videotapes on magic, metaphysics and dance.

Fitch lives in the outskirts of Los Angeles with his wife and two sons.

fivefold kiss   A ritual kissing of five parts of the body, done in certain rites and ceremonies, such as HANDFASTING, in some traditions of neo-Pagan WITCHCRAFT. It is always done within a MAGIC CIRCLE and is symbolic of the homage paid by the God and the GODDESS to each other. The fivefold kiss can be done man to woman or woman to man. The kisses may be given on the parts of the body which, with arms and legs outstretched, correspond to points of a pentacle: head, arms or hands; legs or feet. Or, eight kisses may be given in five body points: on each foot; on each knee; above the pubic hair; on each breast; on the lips. Each kiss is accompanied by a blessing, such as the following:

> Blessed by thy feet that have brought thee in these ways; blessed be thy knees that shall kneel at the sacred altar; blessed be thy womb [phallus], without which we should not be; blessed be thy breasts, formed in beauty [strength]; blessed be thy lips that shall utter sacred names.

flying   A prevailing believe in the Middle Ages and Renaissance held that the DEVIL, his DEMONS and WITCHES could transport themselves and others through the air. Flying (also called *transvection*) usually was done with the aid of a broomstick, fork or shovel, according to lore (see BROOMS); some witches were said to ride demons who were transformed into animals such as goats, cows, horses and wolves (see METAMORPHOSIS). The Devil had the power to pick people up and whisk them through the air with no visible means of transport or support.

While a popular belief, flying was not accepted universally during the centuries of witch-hunting in Europe. As early as the 10th century, flying was disputed as impossible. The *CANON EPISCOPI* said that if witches flew, it was in their imaginations. But in the late 15th century, the *MALLEUS MALEFICARUM,* the bible of witch-hunters and judges, lamented this "erroneous" view, saying it allowed witches to go unpunished.

The Devil reputedly could transport whomever he pleased at whim. Stories tell of children and adults being picked up in their sleep and flown through the air for miles. One 15th-century German priest claimed he saw a man "borne on high with his arms stretched out, shouting but not whimpering." The fellow, the priest said, had been drinking beer with friends. One of the men went to fetch more beer, but upon opening the door of the tavern, saw a mysterious cloud, became frightened and refused to go. The man who was picked up and flown said he would go instead, "even if the Devil were there."

Witches, sorcerers and necromancers were said to be able to fly with the help of magical ointments consisting mostly of baby fat that had been boiled off the limbs of a young child who had been killed before baptism. Such ointments also contained various herbs and drugs, which doubtless put witches into hallucinatory states in which they really believed they were flying (see OINTMENTS). One witch in Italy in 1560 rubbed herself with ointment and went into a trance. When she came out of it, she said she had been flying over mountains and seas. In 14th-century Italy, necromancers (see NECROMANCY) made beds fly with magical INCANTATIONS.

The speed of flight was great, and novices were prone to fall off their forks or broomsticks. Sometimes the demons who rode with them pushed them off. One story tells of a German man who convinced a sorcerer to fly him to a sabbat (see SABBATS). En route, the sorcerer threw him off the broom. The man fell into a strange country that was so far away, it took him three years to get home.

Church bells were supposed to be able to ground brooms, and in some towns, the church bells were run constantly during witch festivals to prevent witches from flying overhead (see BELLS).

While some demonologists and inquisitors did not believe that witches could actually fly, they accepted confessions of it, reasoning that if witches *thought* they could fly, it was just as incriminating as if they actually did so. Many witches did confess to flying. Some said it was possible to fly either bodily or by imagination. If a witch wanted to observe a sabbat without actually being there, all she had to do was lie down on her left side and breathe out a blue vapor, in which she could watch the activities—a medieval version of clairvoyance.

Flying is not mentioned much in English cases of witches. The various witchcraft acts in effect between 1542 and 1736 outlawed many witchcraft practices but did not prohibit flying.

Magical and mystical flight. Various magical and spiritual disciplines place importance on the ability to fly. It is not the act of flying that is important but what the flying signifies: the soul's breaking free of the bonds of earth and soaring into the cosmos, accessing realms that others reach only through death. Flying is a transcendent experience, a flight of the spirit. In some cases, the ecstasy may actually manifest in a form of corporeal flying, or LEVITATION; Christian hagiography records numerous instances of saints levitating and moving about in the air. Eastern avatars and adepts also are said to levitate.

Magical and mystical flight is attributed to alchemists, mystics, sorcerers, shamans, medicine men, yogis and fakirs, as well as Witches. In many shamanic rites, the shaman identifies with, or becomes, a bird in order to take flight. Each magical/spiritual system has its own techniques for achieving the ecstasy of flight, though breathing, meditation, contemplation, dancing, drumming, chanting and/or hallucinogenic drugs (see SHAMANISM).

Mystical flight is attained by many modern Witches, many of whom blend Eastern and shamanic spiritual elements into neo-Pagan Witchcraft. It is possible that incidents of flying in earlier centuries were linked to the Devil in order for the Church to have better control over the populace. If all personal salvation was to be placed in the hands of the Church, it was not to the Church's advantage to allow individuals the freedom to discover spiritual truths through their own transcendent experiences.

footprints   Footprints are widely reputed to contain the essence of a person and may be used in magical CHARMS and SPELLS. Dust or dirt taken from a footprint may be used to obtain power over the person who made the print, just as clippings of HAIR AND NAILS, bits of clothing, URINE and excrement are believed to have magical potential. In the lore of Lithuania, footprint dirt buried in a graveyard will cause someone to fall fatally ill. Australian aborigines believe they can magically cause lameness by placing bits of glass or sharp stones in a footprint. In European folk MAGIC, lameness is caused by putting some earth from a footprint, a nail, a needle and broken glass into a kettle, and boiling the mixture until the kettle cracks. In VODOUN magic, dirt from a footprint placed in a GRIS-GRIS, or charm bag, will cause a person to follow one. In parts of Africa, great care is taken to obliterate footprints, lest a witch or sorcerer use them for harmful magic.

FAIRIES also are associated with the magic of footprints. In Irish lore, if you are passed by fairies on All Hallow's Eve, you should throw the dirt from your footprint after them, which will force them to surrender any humans they have taken captive.

In cases of DEMONIC POSSESSION and poltergeist hauntings, strewing ashes about the house will help identify the demon, as it is believed the demon will leave his clawprint in the ashes.

Fortress of Dumbarton   According to legend, the fortress at Dumbarton, Scotland, near Glasgow on the Clyde River, was created by a band of angry WITCHES in pursuit of St. Patrick. Around the year 388, the DEVIL became so offended at the piety of St. Patrick that he incited "the whole body of witches in Scotland" against the saint. In an army, the witches attacked St. Patrick, who fled toward the Clyde. At the mouth of the river, he found a little boat, leaped into it and set off for Ireland. The witches were unable to cross running WATER—another folk belief— and in anger, they ripped off a huge chunk of rock from a nearby hill and hurled it after the saint. Their aim was so bad that the rock fell harmlessly to the ground. Later, the rock was turned into a fortress.

Fortune, Dion (1891–1946)   The magical name of Violet Mary Firth, British occultist and author whose books continue to have an impact on modern WITCHCRAFT and NEO-PAGANISM. Considered one of the leading occultists of her time, Fortune was an adept in ceremonial MAGIC and was perhaps one of the first occult writers to approach magic and hermetic concepts from the psychology of Jung and Freud (see HERMETICA). Some Witches and neo-Pagans consider her fiction more important than her nonfiction, for her novels contain Pagan themes and are a rich source for rituals.

Fortune was born into a family of Christian Scientists and displayed mediumistic abilities in her teen years. In her early twenties, she worked as a law analyst at the Medico-Psychological Clinic in London. Her interest in exploring the human psyche resulted from an unpleasant episode in 1911, when, at age 29, she went to work in a school for a principal who took a great personal dislike to her. When Fortune went to see the woman to announce she was leaving her job, she was subjected to invective that she had no self-confidence and was incompetent. Fortune said later that the principal also conveyed this by psychic attack, using yogic techniques and hypnotism that left Fortune a "mental and physical wreck" for three years.

As a result, she studied psychology, delving into the works of both Freud and Jung. She preferred the ideas of Jung but eventually concluded that neither Freud nor Jung adequately addressed the subtleties and complexities of the mind. The answers, Fortune felt, lay in occultism.

In 1919 Fortune joined the Alpha and Omega Lodge of the Stella Matutina, an outer order of the HERMETIC ORDER OF THE GOLDEN DAWN, and studied under J. W. Brodie-Innes. She experienced clashes with the wife of S. L. MacGregor-Mathers, one of the founders of the Golden Dawn, which she again felt were forms of psychic attack. She felt Stella Matutina in 1924 and founded her own order, the Community (later Fraternity) of Inner Light. The order initially was part of the Golden Dawn but later separated from it.

Fortune worked as a psychiatrist, which brought her into contact with other cases of psychic attack. She was a prolific writer, pouring her occult knowledge into both novels and nonfiction. Her pen name was derived from the magical motto she adopted upon joining the Stella Matutina, "Deo Non Fortuna," ("by God, not chance"), which became shortened to Dion Fortune. Her books are considered classics and continue to enjoy wide readership.

For a time she lived in Glastonbury and became deeply interested in the Arthurian legends and magical-mystical lore centered there. She wrote about Glastonbury in *Avalon of the Heart.*

Fortune used her experiences with psychic attack to conclude that hostile psychic energy can emanate both deliberately and unwittingly from certain people and that one can mentally fend off such energy. Her book *Psychic Self-Defense* (1930) remains the best guide to detection and defence against psychic attack.

Perhaps her most famous book is *The Mystical Qabbalah* (1936), in which she discusses the Western esoteric tradition and how the Qabbalah (also KAB-BALAH) is used by modern students of the Mysteries. The true nature of the gods, she said, is that of magical images shaped out of the astral plane by mankind's thought, and is influenced by the mind.

Her other major nonfiction works include *Sane Occultism* (1929); *The Training and Work of an Initiate* (1930); *Through the Gates of Death* (1932); *Applied Magic; Aspects of Occultism;* and *Spiritualism in the Light of Occult Science. Machinery of the Mind* (1922) was published under her given name. But it is her novels that have captured the most interest among modern Witches and Pagans. In particular, *The Goat-Foot God* (1936) concerns the powers of Pan, a HORNED GOD, and offers a wealth of details on LEYS; *The Sea-Priestess* (1938) concerns the powers of ISIS, the moon goddess, and has been used by modern witches as an inspiration for creating rituals and invocations. Her other novels are *The Secrets of Dr. Taverner* (1926), about an adept who runs an occult nursing home; *The Demon Lover* (1927); and *The Winged Bull* (1936).

Fortune was married to a Dr. Evans. She died in January 1946.

The Fraternity of Inner Light remains based in London and now is known as The Society of Inner Light. It offers techniques in the Western esoteric tradition. The Fraternity stresses that Fortune was not a Witch and was not involved with any COVEN, and that the Fraternity is not connected with Witchcraft in any way.

fox fire   See JACK-O'-LANTERN.

Fox, Selena (1949–)   American Wiccan (see WICCA; WITCHCRAFT) high priestess renowned for her leadership role in the Wiccan-Pagan community and for founding CIRCLE SANCTUARY (also know as Circle), a legally recognized Wiccan church with a worldwide Pagan ministry.

Born October 20, 1949, in Arlington, Virginia, Fox was raised in a fundamentalist Southern Baptist family. As a child, she began having mystical experiences, out-of-body travel and psychic visions. Upon reaching her teens, she pursued her interest in dreams,

Selena Fox (photo by Lynnie Johnston; courtesy National Film Board of Canada)

the psychic and parapsychology and learned how to give psychic readings with TAROT cards. She left the Southern Baptist church while in high school, citing a number of reasons, including the church's disapproval of dancing and its refusal to allow women to become pastors.

Fox attended the College of William and Mary in Virginia, graduating *cum laude* in 1971 with a bachelor of science degree in psychology. At the age of 21 she led her first Pagan ritual as president of Eta Sigma Phi, the classics honor society. She led the society in a re-enactment of a Dionysian rite of spring, which took place outdoors in the center of campus.

After college, she worked on an archaeological dig in nearby Hampton, Virginia, where she met a woman who was an hereditary Witch. Realizing her own spiritual orientation had much in common with her friend's CRAFT, Fox embraced the Wiccan religion and later became initiated as a high priestess in several traditions.

Following the archaeological work, Fox spent several years in various jobs, including work as a photographer and as publications editor for a large corporation.

In October 1974 Fox conceived the name, logo and central spiritual focus for Circle. Fox, along with her partner, Jim Alan, and a group of friends, formed the beginnings of Circle with periodic meetings at the Fox-Alan home in Sun Prairie, near Madison, Wisconsin. In 1978 Fox decided to devote herself full-time to the Wiccan ministry. The same year, Circle Sanctuary was incorporated as a Wiccan church.

In 1979 Fox and Alan were evicted from their Sun Prairie farmhouse by a prejudiced landlord. After several moves to other farmhouses in the Madison area, they settled on land near Barneveld and Mt.

Horeb, Wisconsin. The site, owned by Circle Sanctuary, is a nature preserve, organic herb farm and church headquarters.

Fox and Alan ended their common-law relationship in 1984, and Alan eventually left Circle Sanctuary to devote himself to a writing career. In 1986 Fox married Dennis Carpenter, a Wiccan priest and former school psychologist. Fox and Carpenter work together to coordinate Circle Sanctuary's diverse activities and responsibilities.

Fox usually prefers to be called a Wiccan priestess rather than a Witch, because she feels it more accurately describes what she does. She travels extensively throughout North America, giving lectures, workshops and seminars on Paganism, spiritual growth and psychology to all kinds of audiences in colleges and universities, learning centers, conferences, churches and Pagan gatherings. She does nature therapy, psychic healing, Tarot readings, dream work, guided creative visualizations and other types of spiritual HEALING services. She is a leading spokesperson on Wicca and Paganism to the media. She also has been involved in local and international networking efforts and from time to time speaks in Christian and other mainstream religion churches. She has participated in many ecumenical efforts to foster world peace.

Fox has been one of the leading religious freedom activists in the Pagan movement. She has worked successfully on cases involving the right of Wiccans and Pagans to worship; allowing Wiccan priestesses to minister as clergy in prisons; securing paid Pagan holidays for a Canadian employee (see CHARLES ARNOLD); and helping Native American Indians protect sacred burial grounds in Kentucky. In 1985 Fox was a leader in the effort to defeat the HELMS AMENDMENT in Congress, which sought to strip Wiccan Churches of their tax-exempt status.

Fox founded WICCAN SHAMANISM, an ecumenical blend of the Wiccan religion, shamanic practices from tribal societies around the world and humanistic psychology.

Freya (also Freyja) In Norse mythology, blonde and blue-eyed Freya was the goddess of love, procreation and fecundity. The hare was her companion. She was the wife of Odur, god of sunshine, and the daughter of Njord, a Van or sea goddess, and Nerthus. Both Njord and Nerthus were members of the Vanir, deities of the earth, fertility and death. Freya also was a fierce warrior, leading the Valkyries to the battlefields to recover slain heroes and take them to Valhalla.

Freya is often confused with Frigga, wife of ODIN and goddess of marital love and marriage. Like Frigga, she loved jewelry and ornaments. She is frequently identified with Gefjon, "the Giver," a fertility goddess. Freya was condemned as a witch (see WITCHES) by early Christians and banished to the mountains, where she was said to convene and dance with her DEMONS on WALPURGISNACHT (Beltane), April 30.

In NEO-PAGANISM, Freya is worshipped in the pantheon of Norse and Teutonic deities. With her combination of sexuality, fruitfulness, aggression and bravery, she has strong feminist appeal.

See also GODDESS.

Frost, Gavin See CHURCH AND SCHOOL OF WICCA.

Frost, Yvonne See CHURCH AND SCHOOL OF WICCA.

Fuchs von Dornheim, Gottfried Johann Georg II See BAMBERG WITCHES.

G

Gaea See GAIA.

Gaia (also Gaea) In Greek mythology, the Mother Earth goddess. Gaia, or the "Deep-Breasted One," is the oldest of deities. Born from the dark abyss of Chaos, she married her son, Uranus (Ouranos), Father Heaven, and produced the first creatures, the Titans and Cyclops. At the height of her cult, she was served by the pythonness priestess at the ORACLE AT DELPHI. Gradually, she was absorbed by the deities Rhea, probably of Cretan origin, whose name derives from a term for earth, and Cybele, goddess of caverns.

Gaia corresponds to all other Earth Mother deities in other cultures, who have been variously known as the Great Goddess, the White Goddess and Mother Nature: the deity who nurtures all beings upon the planet, and the planet itself, and who rules the birth, death and regeneration cycles of all living things.

The Gaia Hypothesis. In the 1970s, media attention began to focus on the theory that all organic and nonorganic matter on Earth comprise a complex and single organism, which is capable of regulating itself to stay healthy. The Gaia Hypothesis, or Gaia, as it is simply called, developed independently in the scientific and neo-Pagan communities and evolved in separate directions. It captured the interest of the environmental movement. News reports into the late 1980s that the atmosphere was losing its ozone due to pollution, which in turn was disrupting weather patterns and causing droughts, renewed interest in Gaia.

In the scientific community, most of the credit for the development of Gaia has gone to James Lovelock, a British specialist in gas chromatography. Lovelock acknowledges he was not the first to conceive the idea: as early as 1958, Alfred Redfield put forward the hypothesis that the chemical composition of the atmosphere and oceans was biologically controlled. Lovelock surmised that many other scientists had theorized about Gaia, but the idea had never caught on in mainstream science. The name *Gaia* for the hypothesis was proposed to Lovelock by novelist William Golding.

Lovelock's own quest for Gaia began in the early 1960s, when he worked as a consultant to the Jet Propulsion Laboratories of the California Institute of Technology on the Viking mission sent to Mars to look for life. Lovelock published papers on Gaia in 1974 (with Lynn Margulis) and 1975 (with Sidney Epton). In 1979 he published his book *Gaia: A New Look at Life on Earth.*

According to Gaia, mankind is but one part of the complex biosphere organism. Life did not emerge on the planet because conditions were right; rather, Gaia created the conditions deemed necessary to support life. Gaia works to maintain optimum conditions for all terrestial life, but mankind is upsetting the balance through industrial pollution, which began in Britain in the late 18th century and has spread steadily around the globe. The more the human population increases, draws upon the earth for sustenance and in turn pollutes it, the greater is our responsibility to maintain homeostasis, which is a state of constancy in the face of changes in the environment. Otherwise, Gaia will regulate itself to compensate for the damage being done, which might mean the extinction of the problem: man.

In *Gaia*, Lovelock theorizes that the collective intelligence of humans constitutes a Gaian brain and nervous system which can anticipate environmental changes. The result may be that in the future, na-

131

tionalism will disappear in the face of the need "to belong to the commonwealth of all creatures which constitute Gaia." Another species perhaps capable of the role of Gaian brain and nervous system is the whale, which has a brain many times larger than the human brain. Since functionless tissues decrease in size or disappear over the course of evolution, it is possible that whales make use of their huge brains in ways humans cannot comprehend.

In the neo-Pagan community, Gaia, or Gaea, as it is sometimes spelled to differentiate it from Lovelock's version of the hypothesis, has more of a religious basis, focus and importance. Since antiquity, Pagan religions have emphasized the need for mankind to be in harmony with the forces of nature, which are personified as spirits and deities.

The Gaea hypothesis was developed by OTTER ZELL (formerly Tim Zell), founder and high priest of the CHURCH OF ALL WORLDS in Ukiah, California. Zell describes Gaea as the archetypal image of the Great Mother Goddess (see GODDESS), a living, sentient being with a soul-essence that can be perceived by humans.

The genesis of Gaea was a profound vision experienced by Zell on September 6, 1970, in St. Louis, Missouri, the original location of the Church of All Worlds. In the vision, Zell reported that he saw Earth as a single biological organism that has evolved from a single original cell, making all life forms on the planet a "single vast creature."

Zell named the planetary organism *Terrebia* and preached a sermon, "Theagenesis: The Birth of the Goddess," to the Church of All Worlds on September 11, 1970. He developed "Theagenesis" in a series of articles published in *Green Egg,* the journal of the Church of All Worlds, between 1971 and 1972. Zell said humans function as cells of Terrebia and therefore are Her ("Thou art God(dess)"). Mankind serves as the brain and nervous system, to ensure the optimal functioning of Terrebia, a maturing system, and to prevent damage and disruption to her vital systems.

Zell envisioned mankind awakening Terrebia to Goddess by achieving telepathic union with the consciousness of all living beings. The telepathic union is a neo-Pagan version of the Apotheosis or Omega Point of Pierre Teilhard de Chardin (1881–1955), French paleontologist and philosopher. Teilhard de Chardin saw man as the key to the universe, whose evolution would lead to the Omega Point at which all consciousness merges and Christ makes his second coming.

When the awakening of Terrebia occurs, Zell said, a new planetary biosphere will be born, and mankind will evolve to its next and glorious stage of colonizing other worlds. However, the awakening is being threatened by a polluting "cancer of the nervous system," mankind itself. In 1970 Zell theorized that nuclear holocaust would be one way to control this cancer. Years later he revised that view, noting that "nuclear winter" studies indicated the planet itself would have little chance of surviving a major nuclear war. Instead, Zell said, the planet would do her own healing through plagues, droughts, famines, floods and other natural phenomena.

Zell also created a mandate for the neo-Pagan community to become involved in the ecology movement. The Omega Point awakening can be accomplished through an end to environmental exploitation and the development of alternative, nature-conscious life-styles and communities.

Another view that Zell changed over time was that of mankind as the planetary brain and nervous system. That role, he said, belongs to the whales and dolphins. Mankind serves as "peripheral neurons and planetary stewards," and retains the role of extraterrestial colonizer.

After hearing about Lovelock's views in 1975, Zell corresponded briefly with the scientist and shared some of his "Theagenesis" material. Zell also changed *Terrebia* to *Gaea.*

Zell's Gaea has been largely ignored by the media in favor of Lovelock's Gaia. To most neo-Pagans, regardless of spellings and nuances, the basic message is one of urgent need to curb pollution and restore a harmonious balance between mankind and the planet. Environmental consciousness runs high in neo-Paganism. "Gaia Lives" is a watchword. Neo-Pagans and Witches cast frequent spells for ecological healing. Some are environmental activists and demonstrate against industrial polluters and nuclear facilities.

Gallows Hill   The execution site of those condemned as WITCHES in the infamous witch trails in Salem, Massachusetts, it has been believed to be haunted ever since the trials in 1692–93. Nineteen men and women were hanged from the trees at Gallows Hill. The site was long considered the meeting grounds for witches at annual festivals (see SABBATS). It also was oracular: young persons who wished to know their future in marriage, and the identities of their future spouses, would go to Gallows Hill at night and listen for the answers to be revealed to them by the ghosts of the dead witches. Whenever an important event was about to happen, the neighborhood would be filled with the screechings and screamings of the haunting witches (see GHOSTS,

HAUNTINGS AND WITCHCRAFT). Gallows Hill is now a residential area.

See also SALEM WITCHES.

Gardner, Gerald B(rousseau) (1884–1964)

The man chiefly responsible for reviving WITCHCRAFT in the modern West was born into a well-to-do family in Blundellsands, near Liverpool, England, on Friday, June 13, 1884. His father was a justice of the peace, a member of a family that had made money in the timber trade. Of Scottish descent, the family roots could be traced to a woman, Grissell Gairdner, who was burned as a Witch in 1610 in Newburgh (see WITCHES). Gardner's grandfather married a woman reputed to be a Witch, and some of Gardner's distant relatives were purported to have psychic gifts. Gardner's ancestral family tree also included mayors of Liverpool, and Alan Gardner, a naval commander and later vice admiral and peer, who distinguished himself as commander-in-chief of the Channel Fleet and helped to deter the invasion of Napoleon in 1807.

The middle of three sons, the young Gerald Gardner suffered severely from asthma. His nurse, Josephine "Com" McCombie, convinced his parents to let her take him traveling during the winters to help alleviate his condition. Com roamed about Europe, leaving the young Gardner to spend much time by himself reading. When Com married a man who lived in Ceylon, Gardner traveled there with her and worked on a tea plantation. Later, he moved to Borneo and then Malaysia to work.

In the Far East, he became acquainted with the natives and studied their spiritual beliefs, which left more of an impact on him than had Christianity. He became fascinated by ritual daggers and knives, so much so with the Malaysian *kris,* a dagger with a wavy blade, that he wrote a book about it, *Kris and Other Malay Weapons,* published in Singapore in 1939. The book established him as the world authority on the *kris* and remains the standard work on the subject. It was reprinted posthumously in England in 1973.

From 1923 to 1936, Gardner worked in the Far East for the British government as a rubber plantation inspector, customs official and inspector of opium establishments. He made a considerable sum of money in rubber, which enabled him to dabble in a field of great interest to him, archaeology. He said he found the site of the ancient city of Singapura.

In 1927 he married an Englishwoman, Donna. The two returned to England upon his retirement from government work in 1936. Gardner spent much time on various archaeological trips around Europe and Asia Minor. In Cyprus he found places he had dreamed about previously, which convinced him he had lived there in a previous life (see REINCARNATION).

His second book, *A Goddess Arrives,* a novel set in Cypress and concerning the worship of the GODDESS as Aphrodite in the year 1450 B.C., was published in 1939.

In England Gardner became acquainted with the people who introduced him to the Craft. Before World War II, the Gardners lived in the New Forest region, where Gardner became involved with the Fellowship of Crotona, an occult group of Co-Masons, a Masonic order established by Mrs. Besant Scott, daughter of Theosophist Annie Besant. The group had established "The First Rosicruciain Theater in England," which put on plays with occult themes. One of the members told Gardner they had been together in a previous life and described the site in Cyprus of which Gardner had dreamed.

Within the Fellowship of Crotona was another, secret group, which drew Gardner into its confidence. The members claimed to be hereditary Witches, who practiced a Craft passed down to them through the centuries, unbroken by the witch hunts of the Middle Ages and Renaissance. The group met in the New Forest. Just days before World War II began in 1939, Gardner was initiated into the coven by OLD DOROTHY CLUTTERBUCK, the coven's high priestess (see INITIATION).

Gardner and his coven joined other Witches in southern England on July 31 (Lammas Eve), 1940, to perform a ritual to prevent Hitler's forces from invading England (see CONE OF POWER). Five coveners died soon afterwards, and their deaths were blamed on the energy drain of the ritual. Gardner himself felt his health was adversely affected.

In 1946 Gardner was introduced to ALEISTER CROWLEY by ARNOLD CROWTHER, a stage magician who later joined the Craft with his wife, PATRICIA C. CROWTHER. Crowley made Gardner an honorary member of the Ordo Templi Orientis (OTO), a Tantric sex magic order at one time under Crowley's leadership. Crowley had once been involved in Witchcraft—allegedly in one of OLD GEORGE PICKINGILL's covens. Some believe that Gardner asked Crowley for information concerning the Craft rituals, and incorporated that material into his own. While Gardner admired and was influenced by Crowley, there is no evidence to suggest that Crowley provided him specifically with Craft material, according to Patricia C. Crowther.

Gardner wanted to write publicly about the survival of Witchcraft; however, Witchcraft at that time was still against the law in England. Instead, Gardner wrote about Witchcraft in a novel, *High Magic's Aid*, published in 1949 under the pseudonym, Scire. The novel included rituals he had learned from his coven, and concerned worship of the Horned God. The Goddess was not mentioned.

The law against Witchcraft was repealed in 1951, and Gardner broke away from his New Forest coven and formed his own coven. The same year, he went to Castletown on the Isle of Man, where a Museum of Magic and Witchcraft had been set up by Cecil Williamson in a 400-year-old Craft farmhouse. Williamson originally named it the Folklore Centre, and intended it to be an international center for modern-day practicing Witches. Gardner became the "resident Witch," and added his own considerable collection of ritual tools and artifacts. He bought the museum from Williamson.

In 1953 Gardner initiated DOREEN VALIENTE into his coven. The coven's rituals were virtually identical to those Gardner had included in *High Magic's Aid*. The material Gardner had inherited from his original coven was fragmentary, and he fleshed out the rituals with his own material and quotations and extracts from Crowley's works. Valiente advised him Crowley's writings were inappropriate because they were "too modern," and most of the Crowley material was taken out in subsequent rewrites. From 1954 to 1957 Gardner and Valiente collaborated on writing ritual and nonritual material, a body of work which continues to stand as the authority for what became known as the Gardnerian tradition (see BOOK OF SHADOWS).

Gardner's first nonfiction book on the Craft, *Witchcraft Today*, was published in 1954. It supports anthropologist MARGARET A. MURRAY's theory that modern Witchcraft is the surviving remnant of organized Pagan religion which existed during the witch hunts. (Murray wrote the introduction for Gardner's book.) The immediate success of *Witchcraft Today* led to new covens springing up all over England, and vaulted Gardner into the public spotlight. He made numerous media appearances, and the press dubbed him "Britain's Chief Witch," a title he did not seek. He remained uninterested in exploiting his fame for money or personal glory. In 1959 Gardner published his last book, *The Meaning of Witchcraft*.

In 1960 he was invited to a garden party at Buckingham Palace in recognition of his distinguished civil service work in the Far East. The same year, his wife died, and he began to suffer again from asthma. In 1963, shortly before he left for Lebanon for the winter, he met RAYMOND BUCKLAND, an Englishman who had moved to America, and who would introduce the Gardnerian tradition to the United States.

Gardner's high priestess, MONIQUE WILSON (Lady Olwen), initiated Buckland into the Craft.

On Gardner's return home from Lebanon by boat in 1964, he suffered heart failure and died at the breakfast table on board the ship on February 12. He was buried ashore in Tunis on February 13.

In his will, Gardner bequeathed the museum, his ritual tools and objects, notebooks and the copyrights of his books to Wilson. Other beneficiaries of his estate were Patricia C. Crowther and Jack L. Bracelin, author of an authoritative biography on Gardner, *Gerald Gardner: Witch* (1960). Wilson and her husband operated the museum for a short time and held weekly coven meetings in Gardner's cottage. They then closed the museum and sold much of the contents to the Ripley organization, which dispersed the objects in various museums.

Valiente describes Gardner as a man "utterly without malice," who was generous to a fault and who possessed some real, but not exceptional, magical powers. Those in the Craft who knew him called him "G.B.G."

During his life, Gardner sought to attract young people to the Old Religion, as the Craft also is called. He saw the Craft as appealing primarily to older persons who, when they died, would let the Craft die with them. Science, he said in *Witchcraft Today*, was displacing reliance on the old ways:

> . . . I think we must say good-bye to the witch. The cult is doomed, I am afraid, partly because of modern conditions, housing shortage, the smallness of modern families, and chiefly by education. The modern child is not interested. He knows witches are all bunk . . .

Gardner died before he could see the full results of his writings. Rather than dying out, the revival of Witchcraft continued to grow and spread far more than he had ever envisioned. The "Gardnerian tradition," a name coined after his death, continues to be the dominant tradition of modern Witchcraft.

Gardnerian Witchcraft   See GERALD B. GARDNER.

garlic   This pungent species of the onion has for thousands of years been used as a protection against WITCHES, DEMONS, vampires, the EVIL EYE and other dark supernatural forces and as an ingredient in HEALING remedies. Garlands of garlic worn around the neck or hung in a house are said to ward off evil spirits, creatures and SPELLS. In Mexico, the *ajo macho* is a huge garlic, sometimes as big as a baseball, used exclusively as an amulet (see AMULETS) against evil in general, but not against specific CURSES, which require their own special remedies. According to custom, the *ajo macho* will work only if it is given as a gift, not if it is bought. In Europe, the phrase "here's garlic in your eyes" is said to ward off the evil eye.

In times past, garlic was used to prove guilt. Suspects tossed garlic cloves into a fire; the one whose clove popped was guilty.

In healing folklore, garlic is widely reputed for its ability to cure and prevent colds and other ailments. It is baked in bread, ground into powder and made into liniment. Ancient Roman soldiers wore garlic into battle for extra courage. In ancient Greece and Rome, garlic was placed at crossroads as an offering to HECATE, the goddess of WITCHCRAFT and the night. Odysseus used garlic as protection against the witchcraft of CIRCE, who turned his men into swine.

garters   Ornaments with magical properties, and in neo-Pagan WITCHCRAFT, worn in various rituals and as badges of rank. Garters may have been used in rituals in Paleolithic times: an ancient cave painting in northeastern Spain portrays nine women, wearing pointed headdresses, dancing in a circle around a naked man, who wears a cord or garter tied under each knee.

Garters are prominent in folklore and folk MAGIC. The color of a garter carries special meaning. Green, for example, is the color of FAIRIES and Robin Hood. Garters are worn by Morris dancers, and "Green Garters" is the name of an old tune used in MORRIS DANCING. RED is protection against bewitchment; SILVER is associated with the moon.

In the Middle Ages and Renaissance, garters, or "pointes," were associated with the DEVIL. Accused witches often described the Devil's clothing as being tied with garters, as in this description by Margaret Johnson of Lancashire in 1633: ". . . a spirit or divell in the similtude and proportion of a man, apparelled in a suite of black, tyed about with silke pointes." MARGARET A. MURRAY, British anthropologist, theorized that the garter was a secret symbol of identification among medieval WITCHES; however, no evidence exists that witches were widely or uniformly organized.

In modern Witchcraft, garters have nothing to do with the Devil, who is neither recognized nor worshipped by neo-Pagan Witches. Rather, the garter is considered the ancient emblem of the high priestess of the CRAFT. Some garters are made of green snakeskin or leather, or green or blue velvet, and decorated with a silver buckle. In some traditions of the Craft, a high priestess who becomes a Witch Queen over more than one COVEN adds a silver buckle to her garter for each coven under her.

See also ORDER OF THE GARTER.

Gaufridi, Father Louis   See AIX-EN-PROVENCE POSSESSIONS.

gematria   A system for discovering truths and hidden meanings behind words, using numerical values for letters of the alphabet. Each letter corresponds to a number. The numerical values of words are totaled and interpreted in terms of other words with the same numerical value.

The first known use of gematria dates back to the ancient Babylonian king Sargon II in the 8th century B.C., who built the wall of Khorsabad exactly 16,283 cubits long, because that was the numerical value of his name. The ancient Greeks used gematria to interpret dreams; the system also appears in the literature of the Magi. The Gnostics applied it to the names of the deities Abraxas and Mithras, equating them because they both added up to 365, the number of days in a year. The ancient Hebrews used gematria as a form of DIVINATION. Early Christians borrowed the technique to come up with the dove as the symbol of Jesus: the Greek word for dove, *peristera*, adds up to 801, and so do the Greek letters of alpha and omega, which represent the Beginning and the End.

It was the Kabbalists, however, who delved deeply into gematria and raised it to an art form (see KABBALAH). The early Kabbalists of the 13th century believed the Old Testament to be written in code and inspired by God. Gematria was one of the key means to decipher the code. For example, Jer. 9:9, "From the fowl of the heavens until the beasts are fled and gone" was interpreted to mean that no travelers passed through Judea for 52 years, because the Hebrew word for beast, *behemah*, has a numerical value of 52. Entire verses were added up and interpreted in this fashion. The German Kabbalistic scholar, Eleazar of Worms, did extensive gematric commentaries on the Bible in the 13th century.

Gematria was also used to search for and interpret the secret, holy names of God, which were believed to carry incredible power (see NAMES OF POWER). Ceremonial magicians used these Kabbalistic writings to create new words of power used in conjuring and incantations.

Opinion among Kabbalists was divided over the efficacy of gematria. Two schools of thought emerged, one that advocated it and one that cautioned against it, pointing out that gematria should not be used simply to reinforce one's conclusions. Various methods of gematria were developed; one Kabbalistic tract lists 72 of them.

Two other decoding methods related to gematria are *notarikon* and *temurah*. In notarikon, the first and last letters of a word or phrase are put together to create a new word, or to turn a word into a phrase. Temurah is the creation of anagrams through systematic letter substitutions.

See also NUMEROLOGY.

genie   See DJINN.

ghosts, hauntings and witchcraft   Hauntings
by ghosts and poltergeists are sometimes blamed on WITCHES and WITCHCRAFT, particularly in areas where belief in, and fear of, MAGIC runs high. In Brazil, for example, where fear of magic is strong among the working class, many cases of poltergeist activity are attributed to witches' CURSES laid on families.

The notion that witches were responsible for ghosts and hauntings took root on the Continent and in the British Isles after the Protestant Reformation of the 16th century. The belief that dead men walk the earth as ghosts has been universal since ancient times. The Catholic church used ghosts to its own ends, teaching that they were the souls of those stuck in purgatory, who could not rest until they atoned for their sins, and that they were sent by God to roam the realm of the living. The Reformation rejected the concept of purgatory and said all souls went straight to heaven or hell, from which they never emerged. This required a new explanation for ghosts. In general, the Protestant church denied their existence, claiming that ghosts were a Catholic fraud used to manipulate the masses. Those who did see ghosts were led to think that they were caused by the DEVIL, DEMONS and witches, who also were manipulating the populace in a battle for souls. Two camps formed: those who dismissed ghosts as foolishness and those who saw ghosts as proof of demonic forces.

JAMES I of England, who said there existed a "fearful abounding" of witches in the land, gave credit to the Devil for all ghosts. Witches, being viewed as the servants of the Devil, were automatically connected to apparitions and hauntings. During the 17th century, hauntings often were blamed on the witchcraft of malicious neighbors or relatives. It was not uncommon to call upon the services of another witch or wizard to exorcise the haunting (see SPIRIT EXORCISM).

The Drummer of Tedworth. One of the most famous cases of alleged witchcraft-caused hauntings was a poltergeist case, the Drummer of Tedworth, which took place in England in 1661. In March of that year,

Manifestations of the Devil (Joseph Glanvil, *Saducismus Triumphatus*, 1689 ed.)

the drummer had been annoying the town of Ludgarshall, Wiltshire, with his drum beating. John Mompesson, of the neighboring town of Tedworth (formerly Tidworth), had the man taken before the justice of the peace. The drum was confiscated, and given to Mompesson to secure in his own home. The drummer persuaded the constable to release him, and he left the area.

In April, during Mompesson's absence, a violent storm of poltergeist activity erupted in his house, frightening his wife, children and servants. It began with a drumming noise heard outside the house and on top of it, which then moved indoors to the room where the confiscated drum was kept. For more than two years, this and other bizarre phenomena occurred at irregular intervals, creating widespread interest and drawing curious visitors. The children and servants saw apparitions, and the younger children were levitated in their beds. Some of the lesser phenomena—scratchings and pantings heard near the childrens' beds—were heard by Joseph Glanvil, who chronicled the case in *Saducismus Triumphatus* (1668).

Glanvil also reported the following: chairs walked about the room by themselves; a servant was chased by a stick of wood, while another was held by an invisible force; sulphurous and other foul odors filled the air, which became hot; clothing and children's shoes were thrown about; the sounds of coins jingling were heard; doors opened and shut violently by themselves; blue, glimmering lights were seen; footsteps and the rustling of invisible, silklike clothing were heard; clawlike marks were found in ashes, along with unintelligible letters and numerous circles; lighted candles floated up the chimney, and singing was heard in the chimney; a horse was found with its hind leg stuffed into its mouth so firmly that it took several men to pry it out with a lever; a servant saw "a great Body with two red glowring, or glaring eyes" standing at the foot of his bed; chamber pots were emptied onto beds, and a knife was found in one bed; and pocket money mysteriously burned black. The telltale phenomenon, however, was the words, "A Witch, A Witch," heard "for at least a hundred times" one morning in the children's room. The Mompesson household believed itself to be in the grip of a witch-sent demon or the Devil himself. Mompesson was approached by a wizard, who said the disturbances were caused by a "rendezvous of witches" and offered to perform an exorcism for 100 pounds. Mompesson apparently did not accept.

The vagrant drummer eventually surfaced in court again, this time at the Salisbury assizes where he was tried on theft charges, convicted and sent to the Gloucester goal. When a Wiltshire man visited the drummer, the drummer asked for news and was told there was none. The drummer reportedly replied, "No, do you not hear of the Drumming at a gentlemen's house in Tedworth? I have plagued him (or to that purpose) and he shall never be quiet, till he hath made me satisfaction for taking away my Drum." The drummer was swiftly charged with witchcraft and tried at Sarum. Numerous witnesses to the poltergeist activities testified against him.

The court banished the drummer and he left the area. Rumors surfaced later that in his wanderings he raised storms and frightened seamen. As long as he was gone, the Mompesson house was quiet, but whenever he returned to the area, the disturbances began again. Glanvil does not say if the Mompessons were plagued indefinitely or if the problem eventually went away.

Neo-Pagan Witchcraft, ghosts and hauntings. As mentioned earlier, Witches are often blamed for hauntings in societies that have such expectations. In the industrialized West, only a small percentage of cases are attributed to Witchcraft. According to statistics published in 1979 by Alan Gauld, a member of the British Society for Psychical Research, a mere 7 percent of 500 firsthand poltergeist experiences dated from 1800 on were blamed on Witchcraft. Of the 500, 460 occurred in Europe and America.

Many modern Witches exorcise haunting spirits. Like psychics, clerics and "ghostbusters," they are often called into a home or building to send on the spirit of a departed animal or person. In the United Kingdom, this is called "laying a ghost." The spirit is considered the astral entity of the deceased, which has not withdrawn from the physical plane for various reasons. The Witch contacts the spirit and either persuades it to depart or uses magical words of power to send it away.

Psychic energy also may manifest in artificially created forms that some Witches term "ghosts" and others call "thought-forms." In November of 1981 the coven of STEWART AND JANET FARRAR in Ireland acted to stop the illegal slaughter of gray seal pups by fisherman. The fishermen claimed the seals, which had their pups on the Ineshka Islands off the coast of Ireland, were a threat to salmon fishing. According to the Farrars, the COVEN magically created a gray-green thought-form named Mara (Gaelic for "of the sea") and instructed it to manifest as a ghost on the islands and frighten any seal-killers; she was not to harm any hunter unless he could be stopped no other way. At each full moon, the coven psychically recharged and reinstructed Mara. The Irish Wildlife Federation also sent volunteers to guard the seals. No massacres occurred in 1982 and 1983. Certainly the presence of the volunteers was a deterrent—but stories began to circulate about sightings of a mysterious woman, clad in a gray-green mackintosh, who moved among the seals without disturbing them.

According to Witches, ghostly remnants of thought-forms may also linger in a place where a great deal of psychic and magical work has been done, such as a Witches' covenstead. Unless banished by proper ritual, such energy is believed to be capable of poltergeistlike hauntings.

Another form of haunting, which may be exorcised by ritual magic, is that of nature spirits, or ELEMENTALS. Such beings are said occasionally to haunt newly constructed homes, buildings or roads, particularly if a secluded or wooded area was freshly cleared for the construction. Elemental hauntings are characterized by the presence of strange or uncomfortable sensations; invasions of pests; malfunctions of heating and electrical equipment; the unexplained failure of plants to grow or the wild overgrowth of plants; missing objects; and the appearance that the structure is askew.

girdle measuring   An old technique of magical HEALING by wise women and men, WIZARDS and WITCHES involving the measuring of the patient's girdle or belt. Changes in girth revealed the presence of evil spirits or FAIRIES which had invaded the body to cause the illness. After exorcising the entity, usually through CHARMS, the witch took another measurement to verify that the spirit was gone. Some cures involved the recitation of charms, cutting up of the girdle and burying the pieces in the ground. Girdle measuring was a widespread practice in Europe and the British Isles through the end of the 16th century.

See also SPIRIT EXORCISM.

Glastonbury   An ancient, sacred site to both Pagans and Christians in England's West Country, Glastonbury is identified with the Holy Grail and the mythical Avalon of Arthurian legends. For centuries, it has drawn spiritual pilgrims of all types, including Pagans, WITCHES, DRUIDS, Christians and others.

Glastonbury is located on the plains of Somerset Levels, not far from the Bristol Channel. It comprises an abbey, a town and Glastonbury Tor, a terraced volcanic rock with the remains of an old church tower at its apex. The area around the town was once almost an island surrounded by marshlands—it was not dry until the 16th century—and is thought to have been inhabited by man since Mesolithic times. There is evidence that it may have been a sacred site of the Druids. The ruins of lake villages found at Glastonbury and nearby most likely date from the third or fourth century B.C. and are believed to have been deserted shortly before the Roman occupation. North Somerset was a Roman settlement, and excavations have uncovered pottery and coins in and around the Glastonbury area, near the abbey, at Chalice Well and on the Tor.

The Tor. From the 500-foot summit of Glastonbury Tor, one can see 50 to 60 miles in all directions. The terraced slopes (three of which are steep) suggest the Tor once was farmed. Another theory holds that the terraces are the remnants of a three-dimensional maze dating to the first Christian settlements and serving as a path for pilgrims.

At one time, there was a stone circle atop the Tor. In the Middle Ages, monks built St. Michael's there; it was later destroyed during an earthquake. The remains standing today are those of a later church built on the site. A six-day fair dedicated to the saint was held at the foot of the Tor each year from 1127 to 1825.

According to legend, the summit of the Tor is said to have been the location of a stronghold belonging to King Arthur and also to be the entrance to Annwn, the secret, underworld kingdom of Gwyn ap Nudd, king of the FAIRIES. The 6th-century St. Collen is said to have visited Gwyn by entering through a hidden entrance. Finding himself inside a palace, St. Collen sprinkled holy water around and the palace vanished, leaving the saint standing alone on the top of the Tor.

At the foot of the Tor stands Chalice Well, believed to be the hiding place where Joseph threw the chalice used by Jesus at the Last Supper. The Holy Grail reportedly had magical powers, and in the popular legend, the Knights of the Round Table failed to recover it after its disappearance.

According to legend, the Chalice Well, also referred to as Blood Spring, was built of large blocks of stone by the Druids. Some 25,000 gallons of reddish iron-oxide spring water, said to have magical properties, flow through the well each day.

Witches hold SABBATS at Glastonbury, including atop the Tor. The Tor also is the site of strange lights that hover about it, perhaps the effects of a mysterious magnetic earth energy, or, perhaps, as some UFO watchers believe, the lights of extraterrestrial spacecraft.

The abbey. Legend has it that Joseph of Arimathea, the rich man who wrapped the body of Jesus and carried it to his tomb, later came to Glastonbury and built England's first Christian church, "the Old Church," below the Tor. It is also believed that St. Patrick lived among the monks there and was buried there.

King Ine is believed to have founded a monastery on the site ca. 705, which became a Benedictine house in the 10th century. The abbey's 12th-century Lady Chapel replaced a former church on the site destroyed by fire in 1184, which itself had replaced the "Old Church." The standing remains are said to be from the structure built in the 13th or 14th century and destroyed in the 16th century during the reign of King Henry VIII. In the abbey ruins the Glastonbury Thorn blooms at Easter and Christmas. According to tradition, Joseph arrived by boat on Wearyall Hill and while leaning on his staff in prayer, the staff took root and the Thorn was seeded.

The abbey grounds also are the alleged burial site of King Arthur and Queen Guinevere—one of many mentioned in legend. Arthur's sword, Excalibur, which in legend was tossed into a lake by Sir Bedivere upon the dying king's instructions, may have been thrown into the now-drained lake at Pomparles Bridge near Glastonbury. A Welsh bard is said to have revealed the secret burial site to King Henry II. The abbey was destroyed by fire in 1184; during rebuilding, monks searched for the remains of Arthur and Guinevere.

In 1190 they claimed to find them in a hollow log coffin nine feet below a stone slab. The man measured seven feet in height and had a damaged skull; a bit of blonde hair was found with the woman's remains. A lead cross was inscribed, "Here lies buried the renowned King Arthur in the Isle of Avalon." The bones were reinterred in 1278 in a black marble tomb. Though investigations in the 20th century confirmed discovery of the graves, it has been impossible to identify them conclusively as those of Arthur and his queen.

The Bond excavations. In 1907 the Church of England took over the ruins of Glastonbury and began excavations under the direction of Frederick Bligh Bond. Bond located unknown chapels and parts of the abbey and concluded that the abbey had been constructed according to an ancient, sacred geometry known to the builders of the Egyptian pyramids and the Masons. He attributed his brilliant success to automatic writing, in which mediums communicated with the spirits of monks and received directions from them. A scandal ensued, and Bond was fired. Decades later, his findings were reinvestigated and appreciated in a new light.

Bond had intuited a connection between Glastonbury and STONEHENGE and AVEBURY, which has been borne out. A ley is said to pass through the Tor linking it to Stonehenge. The ley runs along an old road called Dod Lane (from the German word for "dead," *tod)*, or "Dead Man's Lane." In folklore, Dod Lane is the path of spirits; the alleged gravesite of King Arthur is on an extension of this ley. Also, the sun rises exactly in line with Avebury about 40 miles away. Glastonbury Abbey also is said to have been built according to the same secret geometry as Stonehenge (see LEYS).

The Zodiac. The Glastonbury Zodiac, an ancient Temple of the Stars, is believed to have been constructed in order to study the stars and planets. The 12 signs of the Zodiac are laid out in patterns in the earth south of Glastonbury. First discovered by the late-16th-century physician and astrologer to Queen Elizabeth I, JOHN DEE, the Glastonbury Zodiac was rediscovered in 1929 by Katherine Maltwood. Maltwood, a sculptress, was illustrating the *High History of the Holy Grail*, written ca. 1200 in Glastonbury, when she discovered the patterns made by natural earth formations, roads, ditches, paths and earthworks, covering a circle measuring 10 miles in diameter. In her book, *The Glastonbury Temple of the Stars*, she linked the figures to Arthurian legends. Arthur is Sagittarius, MERLIN is Capricorn and Guinevere is Virgo. Glastonbury itself is Aquarius, the sign of the New Age of Enlightenment.

Since then Mary Caine, an English art teacher and a member of the London Order of Druids, has filmed the Zodiac from the air and added to its symbolism. Caine discovered a Messianic face in the Gemini figure at Dundon Hill Camp, midway between the towns of Glastonbury and Somerton.

Goat of Mendes See BAPHOMET.

goblins In French folklore, wandering sprites who attach themselves to households and both help and plague the residents. Goblins commonly live in grottoes but are attracted to homes that have beautiful children and lots of wine. When they move in, they help by doing household chores at night and by disciplining children—giving them presents when they are good and punishing them when they are naughty. Goblins have an unpredictable, mischievous nature, and instead of doing chores at night will sometimes keep everyone awake by banging pots and pans, moving furniture, knocking on walls and doors and snatching bedclothes off sleeping persons. Goblins who become tiresome can be persuaded to leave by scattering flaxseed on the floor. The sprites get tired of cleaning it up every night.

Goblins are the equivalent of brownies in England and Scotland, *kobalds* in Germany, *domoviks* in Russia and other sprites in other countries. They have become associated with Halloween and are said to roam the night when the veil is thinnest between the world of the living and the world of the dead.

Goddess In neo-Pagan WITCHCRAFT, the Goddess embodies the very essence of the Craft: she is the Great Mother, whose limitless fertility brings forth all life; she is Mother Nature, the living biosphere of the planet and the forces of the elements; she is both creator and destroyer; she is the Queen of Heaven; she is the MOON, the source of magical power; she is emotion, intuition and the psychic faculty. The Divine Force is genderless but is manifest in the universe in a polarity of the male and female principles. Most traditions of neo-Pagan Witchcraft emphasize the Goddess aspect of the Divine Force, some almost to the exclusion of the HORNED GOD, the male principle. The Goddess is called by many names, each one representing a different facet or aspect. The Goddess also is recognized in neo-Pagan traditions (see NEO-PAGANISM).

Worship of the Goddess, or at least the female principle, dates back to Paleolithic times. It has been suggested by some anthropologists that the first "God" was a female, who, according to the earliest creation myths, self-fertilized and created the universe from herself and reigned alone; that early agricultural religions were dominated by Goddess worship; that gods prospered only when graced with a beneficence

The Virgin on the Crescent. The Blessed Virgin absorbed pagan elements. Here she is both Virgin and Mother, with a crescent moon, symbol of the Goddess, at her feet. Note face of the Man in the Moon. (Albrecht Dürer, ca. 1499)

parently was once a hunting shrine, dates to ca. 19,000 B.C. She is painted in red ochre—perhaps suggesting BLOOD—and is holding a bison horn in one hand. Cro-Magnon cave paintings also depict women giving birth. A naked Goddess appeared to be patroness of the hunt to mammoth hunters in the Pyrenees and was also protectress of the hearth and lady of the wild things. Female figurines also have been found from the proto-Neolithic period of 7000–9000 B.C. In the Middle Neolithic period, ca. 6000–5000 B.C., figures of a mother holding a child appear. In the High Neolithic period, ca. 4500–3500 B.C., decorated female figurines presumably were objects of worship. In black Africa, cave images of the Horned Goddess (later ISIS) date to 7000–6000 B.C. The Black Goddess was bisexual and self-fertilizing. In predynastic Egypt, prior to 3110 B.C., the Goddess was known as Ta-Urt ("Great One") and was portrayed as a pregnant hippopotamus standing on hind legs. In the Halaf culture on the Tigris River ca. 5000 B.C., Goddess figurines were associated with the cow, serpent, humped ox, sheep, goat, pig, bull, dove and double ax, symbols often connected to the Goddess in later historical periods. In the Sumerian civilization ca. 4000 B.C., the princess or queen of a city was associated with the Goddess, and the king with the God.

The Goddess took on many aspects with the advance of civilization. She acquired a husband, lover or son who died or was sacrificed in an annual birth-death-rebirth rite of the seasons. She becames creator, mother, virgin, destroyer, warrior, huntress, homemaker, wife, artist, queen, jurist, healer, sorcerer. She acquired a thousand faces and a thousand names. She has been associated with both the sun and moon, and earth and sky.

The beginning of the end of the Golden Age of the Goddess occurred between 1800 and 1500 B.C., when Abraham, the first prophet of the Hebrew God, Yahweh, is said to have lived in Canaan.

Many modern Witches feel the Goddess has been ignored and suppressed for too long in the Judeo-Christian tradition. The powerful desire to worship the Goddess may be seen in the veneration accorded the Virgin Mary. Although officially the Virgin Mary is the human mother of the incarnate God, she is virtually deified by her many worshippers, who petition her in prayer.

Despite suppression by the Church, pagan Goddess cults, particularly of DIANA, flourished in Europe into and beyond the Middle Ages. The Church associated them, and all pagan deities, with evil and the DEVIL. Diana was said to be the Goddess of witches (see THE CANON EPISCOPI). As late as the 19th century, American folklorist CHARLES GODFREY LE-

and wisdom of the Goddess; and that early societies may have been matriarchal. "From me come all gods and goddesses who exist," says Isis in Apuleius's *The Golden Ass*. Robert Graves, in *The White Goddess* (1948; 1966), made a case for a widespread earth and moon Goddess cult, especially among the Celts, but his theory has been disputed by some scholars.

Other experts argue that existing evidence does not support those claims. While women have at times held status equal to men, there is no evidence that they have ever held superior status in a matriarchy. Goddess worship has been balanced by God worship and the worship of both male and female Supreme Deities. The sacred marriage of a Sky God and Earth Mother is a common theme in societies around the world.

Among the first human images found to date are the "Venus figures," naked female forms with exaggerated sexual parts, which date to the Cro-Magnons of the Upper Paleolithic period between 35,000 and 10,000 B.C. The Venus of Laussel, carved in bas-relief on a rock shelter in southern France that ap-

LAND claimed to have discovered material relating to a Diana/ARADIA cult of Tuscany.

In modern Witchcraft the emphasis on the Goddess appears to date to the 1950s, through the efforts of GERALD B. GARDNER. Traditional and hereditary covens in Britain emphasized the Horned God. Gardner's earliest published writing, a novel about Witchcraft (*High Magic's Aid*, 1949), makes no mention of the Goddess. Some Witches say the Goddess has always been part of the Craft, but her role seems to have blossomed after Gardner formed his own COVEN in 1951. The feminist movement has given added impetus to the importance of the Goddess. Most Witches worship both the Goddess and the Horned God, who are represented by the high priestess and high priest in a coven. The union of Goddess and God in sacred marriage is one of the fundamentals of the Craft. Some Witches worship the Goddess exclusively.

In the modern Craft, the Goddess frequently is recognized in a trinity, the Triple Goddess; a personification of her three faces as virgin, mother and crone. Trinities of goddesses (and gods) have been worshipped since antiquity in various cultures. A virgin-mother-crone goddess was worshipped in parts of Anatolia in the 7th millenium B.C. THE MORRIGAN of Ireland is personified by Ana, the virgin; Babd, the mother; and Macha, the crone.

The three aspects most common in the modern Craft are three Greek goddesses of the moon: Artemis (usually called by her Roman name, Diana), SELENE and HECATE, who are represented by the new/waxing, full and waning/dark phases of the Moon, respectively. Diana, the virgin and huntress, is associated with the new and waxing moon, and rules the earth; Selene, the mother, is associated with the full moon and rules the sky; Hecate, the crone, is associated with the waning and dark of the moon, and rules the underworld. Hecate herself was said to have three death aspects: Hecate, CIRCE and Persephone (Kore), and also was part of a Greek Mother-Goddess trinity that included Hebe as virgin, Hera as mother and Hecate as crone.

Modern Witches feel worship of the Goddess restores the power of women. The American Witch STARHAWK, in *The Spiral Dance* (1979), observes that for women, the Goddess "is the symbol of the innermost self, and the beneficent, nurturing, liberating power within woman." For a man, "the Goddess, as well as being the universal life force, is his own, hidden, female self."

In 1984 American psychiatrist Jean Shinoda Bolen put forth the theory that the Great Goddess, represented by the archetypes of various Greek goddesses, continues to play a major role in the unconscious of women. The archetypes are patterns of female personalities. Each has positive and negative traits and possesses more power and diversity in personality than women have been able to exercise throughout history

See also: ARIANROD; ASTARTE; CERRIDWEN; DANU; DEMETER; INANNA; ISHTAR; KALI; KUAN YIN; LAKSHMI.

Goddess, Covenant of the See COVENANT OF THE GODDESS.

gold The metal of the sun, solar MAGIC, the HORNED GOD, the male principle, light, power, divine intelligence and spiritual insight. In neo-Pagan WITCHCRAFT, gold JEWELRY with ritual or symbolic significance is worn by more men than women, though members of both sexes wear gold for its reputed ability to enhance power. Chrysaor, the magic sword of gold, is symbolic of supreme spiritual determination.

Gold also symbolizes all that is superior. Since ancient times, it has been associated with light, and therefore divine light, and has been prized for its amuletic (see AMULETS) and HEALING properties. Medieval alchemists sought to transmute base metals into gold. The ancient Chinese used gold leaf in unguents, believing it to be a restorative to the entire body. Aristotle believed gold was most often found in south-running waters (also known for their magical and curative properties). In parts of Central America and the East Indies, gold is believed to have a soul, and the mining of it is prohibited.

See also: BRASS; SILVER.

Gospel of St. John, The Although the reading of any Scripture is supposed to send a possessing devil into a tailspin, the words of St. John seem to cause the most discomfort (see DEMONIC EXORCISM). The beginning of the book, in particular is said to have sent medieval demoniacs into howling fits and tantrums. The following text appears in the King James version, much as 16th and 17th-century exorcists would have read it:

In the beginning was the Word, and the Word was with God, and the Word was God. The same was in the beginning with God. All things were made by him; and without him was not any thing made that was made. In him was life; and the life was the light of men. And the light shineth in darkness; and the darkness comprehended it not. (John 1:1–5)

And the Word was made flesh, and dwelt among us, (and we beheld his glory, the glory as of the only begotton of the Father), full of grace and truth. (John 1:14)

If all things are made by God, then the DEVIL is also God's instrument, perhaps sent to test man's faith. But can the Devil's claims and boasts be believed? In chapter 8, St. John tells how Jesus rebuked the Pharisees for not believing in Him or His works, saying,

> If God were your Father, ye would love me; for I proceeded forth and came from God; neither came I of myself, but he sent me. Why do ye not understand my speech? Even because ye cannot hear my word. Ye are of your father the devil, and the lusts of your father ye will do. He was a murderer from the beginning, and abode not in the truth, because there is no truth in him. When he speaketh a lie, he speaketh of his own; for he is a liar, and the father of it. (John 8:42–44)

The reasoning that any words spoken by the Devil were lies acted as a defense for many witches against their accusers. Claims that some poor soul had caused another to be possessed were looked upon skeptically by early Church inquisitors, but not so by later ones.

Yet Catholic and Protestant exorcists alike believe in the ultimate power of God's word over the work of the Devil; he may be the "father of lies," but when confronted in the name of the Lord, the Devil is forced to yield and speak the truth. In the cases of such unfortunates as Urbain Grandier (see LOUDON POSSESSIONS), accusations of WITCHCRAFT made under the holy rites of exorcism were believed to be true.

Gowdie, Isobel (?–ca.1662)

The stories of Isobel Gowdie's wild sexual escapades with the DEVIL titillated and shocked her stern Scottish neighbors, and reinforced the prevailing beliefs in WITCHES as evil creatures bent on destroying their fellow man. Gowdie, an attractive woman with RED hair, a color associated with witches, voluntarily confessed to WITCHCRAFT on four occasions in April and May 1662. The confessions in themselves astonished the local folk, but what was even more astonishing was Gowdie's assertion that she had been engaging in obscene activities for an incredible 15 years. No one, apparently, had ever caught on, not even her husband.

According to her confessions, Gowdie's involvement with the Devil began in 1647, when she met him in the shape of a man in gray in Auldearne, the remote area in Morayshire where she lived. He enticed her into his service, and that very evening baptized her as a witch in the local church with her own blood, which he sucked from her. He gave her a DEVIL'S MARK on her shoulder and renamed her Janet. Much of her witchcraft, she said, was taught to her by FAIRIES.

Gowdie joined a COVEN of 13 witches—thus bolstering the myth that all witches organize in groups of 13—which met regularly for SABBATS marked by sexual orgies with demons and the Devil, feasting and dancing. She proudly explained how she sneaked away to attend these affairs without her husband knowing: she substituted a broomstick for herself in bed, and he never realized the difference.

She and her sister witches flew off to the sabbats on corn straws, beanstalks and rushes, which they charmed into flight by shouting, "Horse and Hattock, in the Devil's name!" If someone below spotted them and did not cross himself, they would shoot him down with ELF ARROWS.

Gowdie delighted in describing her intercourse with the Devil: how he plunged an enormous, scaly penis into her, causing excruciating pain, and how his semen was cold as ice. As painful as she made it sound, Gowdie also apparently enjoyed it. If she or the other witches displeased the Devil, he beat them with scourges and wool cards.

She also told how she and her coven members tormented their neighbors. They raised storms by beating wet rags upon stones while reciting incantations. They made farmland sterile by ploughing it with a miniature plough drawn by TOADS. They hexed children by sticking pins in dolls. They blasted one farmer's crops (see BLASTING) by digging up the body of an unchristened child and burying it in his manure heap. They shot elf arrows at people to injure or kill them. If they became bored with tormenting others, the witches amused themselves by metamorphosing into animals, usually hares and cats (see METAMORPHOSIS).

Stunned by these stories, the local authorities had Gowdie stripped and searched for the Devil's mark, which they found.

The records give no reason as to why Gowdie one day decided to confess these lurid tales, without any prompting or suspicion upon her. Furthermore, she welcomed punishment: "I do not deserve to be seated here at ease and unharmed, but rather to be stretched on an iron rack: nor can my crimes be atoned for, were I to be drawn asunder by wild horses."

In *Letters on Demonology and Witchcraft* (1830), Sir Walter Scott speculated that "this wretched creature was under the dominion of some peculiar species of lunacy." In *The Occult* (1971), Colin Wilson suggests she was a highly sexed woman with a vivid imagination, who turned to fantasies to alleviate the boredom of a dull existence; at some point, her fantasies became real to her. But after 15 years, the excitement of having a secret grew thin, and there was only one way to recharge it—by making a public confession.

The records also do not indicate what became of Gowdie or the other unfortunate Auldearne witches she named. In all likelihood, she and the others were executed, for her confessions were too offensive to be tolerated at that time.

Great Rite In neo-Pagan WITCHCRAFT, a powerful, magical rite of sexual intercourse that pays homage to the male/female polarity that exists in all things in the universe. It expresses the physical, mental, spiritual and astral union between man and woman as well as the God and GODDESS aspects of the Divine Force. Neo-Pagan Witchcraft is a fertility religion, a reconstruction of ancient pagan rites and beliefs, which include ritual sexual intercourse. Sex is considered sacred.

The Great Rite is associated with the *hieros gamos,* the Sacred Marriage or Holy Matrimony, which is union with a deity or godhead. The *hieros gamos* was part of pre-Christian women's mysteries in Mesopotamia and the Mediterranean, in which women sacrificed control of their feminine power to the Goddess and were renewed by her.

In neo-Pagan Witchcraft, the Great Rite releases enormous power, which may be directed for magical purposes; it is one of the "Eightfold Paths" to magical power in the Craft (see MAGIC).

The Great Rite is performed within a MAGIC CIRCLE at some SABBATS, initiations and handfastings (see INITIATION; HANDFASTING), depending on the tradition of the COVEN. Ideally, the participating couple (usually the high priest and high priestess, except for handfastings, which involve the bride and groom) are already sexually intimate as spouses or lovers. The rite is not always performed in actuality but may be done symbolically; the high priest plunges an athame, or ritual knife (the male symbol), into a cup or chalice (the female symbol) that is filled with wine, which is held by the high priestess.

If done in actuality, the sexual union usually is performed in private; the coveners leave the room until the rite is finished. In some covens, the coveners merely go to the edge of the circle and turn their backs. GERALD B. GARDNER preferred the rite to be performed with the coven watching. Gardner also favored ritual scourging (see WITCHCRAFT) as part of the rite, a practice that has fallen out of favor.

Greatrakes, Valentine (1629–1683) Famous Irish healer called "Mr Greatrix," "Mr. Greatraks" and the "stroker," who cured maladies by a laying on of hands. The son of an Irish gentleman in County Cork, Greatrakes reputedly suffered from "melancholy derangement" early in life. He served in Cromwell's army and then in the government, retiring when he lost his office of county magistrate. Shortly thereafter, he had a spiritual awakening and realized that God had given him the power to heal scrofula,

called the "king's evil," by touching. He tested himself by curing a Saltersbridge man of the king's evil in his eyes, cheek and throat. He launched a new career as a healer and attracted a huge audience of satisfied customers. He cured epilepsy, ulcers, lameness and other sicknesses and had the ability to cause and cure fits and cast out evil spirits, which he said were the cause of various afflictions. As word of his ability spread, so many persons sought him out that he worked from six in the morning until six at night.

In 1661 Greatrakes was summoned to the trial of FLORENCE NEWTON to help determine if she was a witch (see WITCHES). In 1666 he went to England, where he effected more cures but failed to cure the chronic headaches of Anne, Viscountess Conway. He also failed in a demonstration to Charles II and soon returned to Ireland.

Greatrakes always invoked the name of God when he worked and accepted no fees other than reimbursement for travel. He rejected cases that appeared to be incurable. His stroking powers apparently were limited to physical ills, for he was unable to help an earl's butler who was possessed by FAIRIES and made to levitate off the ground. INCREASE MATHER dismissed him as a fraud, claiming he attempted to effect cures by using "that hobgoblin word, *Abrodacara*" (See ABRACADABRA). Greatrakes was neither labeled a witch nor accused of WITCHCRAFT, though his healing power was similar to that possessed by others who were called witches, wise women, wise men and WIZARDS. Later, he was compared to magnetists who healed with magnets and the passing of hands around the patient's body.

See also: HEALING.

Green Man In the British Isles and Europe, a pagan deity of the woodlands usually represented as a horned man peering out from a mask of foliage, usually the sacred oak. The Green Man, also called "Green Jack," "Jack-in-the-Green" and "Green George," represents the spirits of the trees, plants and foliage. He is attributed with the powers of making rain and fostering the livestock with lush meadows. He appears often in medieval art, including carved church decorations.

In spring Pagan rites, Green George, as he is usually called then, is represented by a young man clad from head to foot in greenery, who leads the festival procession. In some festivals, Green George, or an effigy of him, is dunked into a river or pond in order to ensure enough rain to make the fields and meadows green.

As the woodlands deity, the Green Man shares an association with the forest-dwelling FAIRIES (green is the fairy color). In some locations in the British Isles, the fairies are called "Greenies" and "Greencoaties." "The Green Children" is a myth of two fairy children, a brother and a sister, whose skin is green, and who claim to be of a race with green skin.

See also NATURE SPIRITS.

grimoires   Old handbooks of MAGIC, some reputedly dating back to ancient sources, which came into common circulation in the Middle Ages and Renaissance and were particularly popular from the 17th to early 19th centuries. Grimoires still are consulted by students of ceremonial magic in modern times, though newer books have replaced them. In neo-Pagan WITCHCRAFT, some rituals may draw on ceremonial magic texts, but the Witch's personal handbook of Craft rituals and laws is called the BOOK OF SHADOWS.

The original purpose of the grimoires was to conjure and control DEMONS and spirits, who would bring the magician great wealth and power or enable him to harm or kill his enemies. Grimoires give precise and sometimes laborious instructions for various rituals, instructing the magician in what to wear, what tools to use and what PRAYERS and incantations to recite at precise astrological times and various hours of the day and night. They give recipes for incenses to burn, descriptions for the creation of MAGIC CIRCLES, AMULETS, TALISMANS, seals and SIGILS, instructions for the slaughtering and SACRIFICE of animals and ways to deal with unruly demons. They admonish the magician to prepare with periods of fasting, sexual abstinence, cleanliness and prayer and to use only virgin materials in rituals. They describe the hierarchies of demons and spirits that may be summoned with the help of the grimoire's instructions.

Grimoires, or "black books," as they were often called, came into common usage around the 13th century. They were possessed not only by magicians and sorcerers but also by physicians and noblemen—virtually anyone who thought he had something to gain with a little help from a demon. Ideally, the grimoire was copied by hand.

The material in grimoires is drawn largely from Greek and Egyptian magical texts dating back to 100–400 A.D. and from Hebrew and Latin sources. Some grimoires are devoted to *theurgy*, or magic effected with divine intervention, while others concern *goety*, or sorcery. Some include both.

The writers and users of grimoires did not consider themselves Devil-worshippers or evil. The conjuring of demons was merely one of many means to an end. Doing business with demons often meant making pacts with them. The magician's objective was to outwit the demon so that he did not have to fullfill his end of the bargain. The grimoires helped him do this (see DEVIL'S PACT).

The greatest grimoire is *The Key of Solomon*, which has provided material for many other grimoires. The book is attributed to the legendary King Solomon, who asked God for wisdom and commanded an army of demons (see DJINN) to do his bidding and build great works. A book of incantations for summoning demons, attributed to the authorship of Solomon, was in existence in the 1st century A.D. It is mentioned in literature throughout the centuries. Over the years, it grew in size and content. So many versions of this grimoire were written that it is virtually impossible to ascertain what constituted the original text; a Greek version that dates to ca. 1100–1200 is part of the collection in the British Museum. Around 1350 Pope Innocent VI ordered a grimoire called *The Book of Solomon* to be burned; in 1559 Solomon's grimoire was again condemned by the Church as dangerous. *The Key of Solomon* was widely distributed in the 17th century.

Another grimoire attributed to Solomon is the *Lemegeton*, or *Lesser Key of Solomon*, which includes both white and black magic information.

Other major grimoires are:

Grimorium Verum. Based on *The Key of Solomon* and written in French, this book probably was written in the mid-18th century, though claims were made that it was translated from Hebrew by a Dominican priest and was published by "Alibeck the Egyptian" in 1517.

Grimoire of Honorius. First published in Rome between 1629 and 1670, it gained wide circulation during the 17th century. The authorship is attributed to Pope Honorius, a reputed sorcerer, though this is doubtful. It claims to be based on the Kabbalah, but its connection is tenuous at best, and the text is filled with Christian elements. As a magical text, it is viewed as having little foundation.

The Book of Spirits (Francis Barrett, *The Magus* 1801)

The Book of Sacred Magic of Abra-Melin in the Mage. Authorship is attributed to ABRAMELIN THE MAGE, a Jewish mage of Würzburg who supposedly wrote the grimoire for his son in 1458; most likely, however, it was written in the 18th century. The book had a major influence on ALEISTER CROWLEY.

The Book of Black Magic and of Pacts. This grimoire was written in 1898 by Arthur Edward Waite, a major figure in the Hermetic Order of the Golden Dawn. In the first part of the book, Waite discusses other grimoires; the second part comprises a "Complete Grimoire of Black Magic."

True Black Magic, also called *The Secrets of Secrets.* This 18th-century grimoire draws heavily on *The Key of Solomon.*

Grand Grimoire. This French grimoire was probably written in the 17th century. A book of black magic, it includes instructions for necromancy that "only a dangerous maniac or an irreclaimable criminal" would attempt, according to occultist Waite.

Red Dragon. Published in 1822 but purported to date back to 1522, this is nearly identical to the *Grand Grimoire.*

The Magus. This grimoire was written by FRANCIS BARRETT and published in 1801. Barrett repackaged material from older grimoires in an effort to revive occultism.

The Black Pullet. Probably written in the late 18th century in Rome, *The Black Pullet* does not claim to be a manuscript of antiquity. It places particular emphasis on magic talismans and rings. It has appeared in altered versions as *Treasure of the Old Man of the Pyramids* and *Black Screech Owl.*

Verus Jesuitarum Libellus (True Magical Works of the Jesuits). This phony grimoire appeared as a "reprint" in 1845 in Germany, then in an English translation in 1875. It contains conjurations for evil spirits of all sorts and is claimed to have been originally written in Latin by a Jesuit in 1508. The anonymous author of this grimoire apparently overlooked the fact that the Jesuit order did not exist in 1508.

gris-gris   In VODOUN, CHARMS or TALISMANS kept for good luck or to ward off evil. The original gris-gris were probably dolls or images of the gods, but most gris-gris today are small cloth bags filled with herbs, OILS, STONES, small bones, HAIR AND NAIL clippings, pieces of clothing soiled with perspiration and/or other personal items, gathered under the direction of a particular god and designed to protect the owner.

The origin of the word is unclear, but many scholars trace it to *juju,* the West African name for a FETISH, or sacred object. Juju may be a European translation of the native expression *grou-grou* (hence gris-gris), or it may refer to the French word *joujou,* which meant "doll" or "plaything." Most of the African fetishes were in the shape of dolls, and early Europeans on the African West Coast may have mistaken serious religious objects for innocent-looking poppets (see AFRICAN WITCHCRAFT).

Walter Gibson, in *Witchcraft* (1973), states that *fetish* denoted any object possessed by a holy spirit, while *juju* more specifically meant a charm, something WITCH DOCTORS needed to make their medicine work, either for good or ill. Biren Bonnerjea, whose *Dictionary of Superstitions and Mythology* first appeared in 1927, defines *juju* as the West African name for a fetish, also called *grigri.*

In New Orleans, the traditional American headquarters of vodoun and a city where nearly every citizen possesses at least conversational knowledge of the cult, gris-gris are quite common. They are made to attract money and love, stop gossip, protect the home, maintain good health and achieve innumerable other ends. Even police officers have been known to carry gris-gris for protection. A gris-gris is ritually made at an altar and consecrated with the four ELEMENTS of earth (salt), air (incense), water and fire (a candle flame). The number of ingredients is always either one, three, five, seven, nine or 13 (see THIRTEEN). Ingredients can never be even in number or number more than 13. Stones and colored objects are selected for their occult and astrological properties, depending on the purpose of the gris-gris.

Legends about the famous New Orleans Vodoun queen MARIE LAVEAU tell that her gris-gris contained bits of bone, colored stones, graveyard dust (also called *goofer dust*), salt and red pepper. More elaborate gris-gris might have been made of tiny birds nests or horsehair weavings.

A red-flannel bag containing a lodestone, or magnet, was a favorite gris-gris for gamblers, guaranteed to bring them good luck. Another gambler's gris-gris was made from a piece of chamois, a piece of RED flannel, a shark's tooth, pine-tree sap and a dove's blood. The blood and sap were mixed together, then used to write the amount the gambler wanted to win on the chamois. The chamois was covered with the red flannel, with the shark's tooth placed between the layers, and the whole thing was sewn together with cat's hair. The gris-gris was to be worn in the left shoe for best, if uncomfortable, results.

Gris-gris also can be used to cause someone else bad luck, known as "putting a gris-gris" on a person. Throwing a gris-gris bag filled with gunpowder and red pepper in someone's path or on their doorstep supposedly makes that person get into a fight. To get rid of someone, Marie Laveau would write that person's name on a small balloon, tie the balloon to a statue of St. Expedite, then release the balloon. The victim would depart in whichever direction the balloon flew. Just leaving a gris-gris, usually a powder, at someone's front door tells the person he is out of favor with "the voodoos" and should watch his step.

One of Marie Laveau's more horrible *wangas,* or bad-luck charms, reputedly was a bag made from the shroud of a person who had been dead nine days. Into the bag went a dried, one-eyed toad, the little finger of a black person who had committed suicide, a dried lizard, bat's wings, a cat's eyes, an owl's liver and a rooster's heart. If such a gris-gris were hidden in a victim's pillow, the unfortunate would surely die. Many white masters in old New Orleans who mistreated their black slaves found some kind of gris-gris in their handbags or pillows, such as a little sack of black paper containing saffron, salt, gunpowder and pulverized dog manure.

In SANTERÍA, gris-gris bags are called *resquardos,* or "protectors." A typical *resquardo* under the protection of the thunder-god Chango might contain herbs, spices, brown sugar, garlic, aloes, stones or other small sacred relics, tied up in red velvet and stitched with red thread. Finally, the Santero attaches a tiny gold sword, the symbol of St. Barbara (Chango's image as a Catholic saint), and if the sword breaks, Chango has interceded on the owner's behalf.

Gurunfindas are talismans prepared by Santería's black witches, the *mayomberos,* to ward off evil from themselves and direct it magically to others. To make a *gurunfinda,* first the *mayombero* hollows out a *guiro,* a hard, inedible fruit found in the tropics, and fills it with the heads, hearts and legs of a turtle and various species of parrots; the tongue and eyes of a rooster; and seven live ants. Next, the *mayombero* adds seven teeth, the jawbone and some hair from a cadaver, along with the cadaver's name on a piece of paper, and seven coins to pay the dead spirit for his services. Then, the *mayombero* pours rum over the mixture and buries the *guiro* beneath a sacred ceiba tree for 21 days. When he disinters the *guiro,* the *mayombero* marks the outside of the fruit with chalk and then hangs the charm from a tree near his home.

grove   The meeting place, usually outdoors, of organized groups of neo-Pagans and DRUIDS (see NEO-PAGANISM). The grove is the equivalent of a church or temple, or, in neo-Pagan WITCHCRAFT, a covenstead. *Grove* also refers to the group itself.

gurunfindas   See GRIS-GRIS.

Gwydion the Wizard   In Welsh Celtic mythology, the heroic wizard (see WIZARDS) and bard of North Wales, whose tales are told in *The Mabinogion.* Gwydion the Wizard was the son of Don, the Welsh goddess who is a counterpart of the Irish Celtic

goddess DANU. He was one of three children of Don; the other two were Gofannon the Smith, and a daughter, ARIANROD, a lunar goddess of dawn and the mother of Llew. Gwydion ruled science, light and reason. He is associated with the rainbow and is described as the British Hermes.

He was a skillful magician, a bringer of cultural gifts from the gods to man and a clever thief (see MAGIC.) He is said to be the father of April Fool's Day, for on April 1 he conjured great armies to fool Arianrod into giving arms to Llew Llaw Gyffes. He helped Math, god of wealth, create a bride for Llew: Blodeuwed, the "flowerlike." Unhappily, Blodeuwed fell in love with another man and betrayed Llew to a treacherous death. The Milky Way is said to be the tracks of Gwydion searching for the dead Llew.

Gwydion used his magic against the men of southern Wales and was punished in return. He used magic illegally to acquire a herd of Pryderi's swine and was made to do penances by Math.

Gwydion eventually slew Pryderi, son of Pwyll, who was ruler of the underworld and the first husband of Rhiannon. In Celtic magic, he plays a role in initiation rites.

Gypsies   Nomadic, dark-skinned people who probably emerged out of northern India around the 10th century and spread throughout Europe, the British Isles and eventually America. Gypsy tradition has little in the way of its own religious beliefs but is steeped in MAGIC and superstition. From their earliest known appearance in Europe in the 15th century, Gypsies have been renowned practitioners of magical arts, and they undoubtedly had a profound influence on the development of folk magic. During the Renaissance, they were associated with WITCHES and WITCHCRAFT, and many were persecuted and executed as such. In addition, Gypsies were met with general hostility and suspicion from populations wherever they went, which added to their persecution, banishment and deportation. In England, it became unlawful to be a Gypsy in 1530; the law was not repealed until 1784.

The first record of Gypsies in Europe is in 1417 in Germany, although it is quite likely that they arrived in Europe much earlier. They came as Christian penitents and claimed to be exiles from a land called "Little Egypt." Europeans called them "Egyptians," which became corrupted as "Gypsies." Their language, Romany, is related to Sanskrit, and many of their customs have similarities to Hindu customs. The Gypsies also absorbed the religious and folk customs of the lands through which they traveled, and many of their practices contain strong Christian and pagan elements. Very little is known about early Gypsy practices; most of the present knowledge comes from 19th- and 20th-century observations and records.

It is not known what led the Gypsies to leave India. Various legends exist as to their origins and why they were condemned to wander the earth: They were Egyptians scattered by Yahweh (Jehovah, or God); they were survivors of Atlantis, left without a homeland; they had refused to help the Virgin Mary during her flight to Egypt; they had forged three nails for Christ's cross of crucifixion. Voltaire proposed that they were descendants of the priests of ISIS and followers of ASTARTE.

The Gypsies' lack of religious creed is explained by an interesting Turkish legend: When religions were distributed to the peoples of the earth a long time ago, they were written down to preserve them. Rather than write in books or on wood or metal, the Gypsies recorded their religion on a cabbage. A donkey came along and ate the cabbage.

The Gypsy universe is populated with various deities and spirits. *Del* is both God and "everything which is above"—the sky, heavens and heavenly bodies. *Pharaun* is a god said to have once been a great pharoah in the Gypsies' long-lost "Little Egypt." *Beng* is the Devil, the source of all evil. Like Christians, Gypsies believe the DEVIL is ugly, with a tail and a reptilian appearance, and has the power to shape-shift. Legends exist of pacts with *Beng*. Moon worship and fire worship are extensive among Gypsies; they apparently have never worshipped the sun, at least not to any significant degree. The moon is personified by the god *Alako*, defender of Gypsies and taker of their souls after death. *Alako* originally was *Dundra*, a son of God sent to earth to teach humans law, who ascended to the moon when he was finished and became a god (compare to ARADIA). Fire is considered divine, with the ability to heal, protect, preserve health and punish the evil.

The cult of *Bibi* concerns worship of a LAMIA-like goddess who strangles *gorgio* (non-Gypsy) children by infecting them with cholera, tuberculosis and typhoid fever.

Gypsies also practice phallus worship and an animistic worship of objects, such as anvils. The horse and the bear are regarded as godlike beings.

Gypsies have a strong fear of death and the dead, and numerous taboos govern the way they deal with the dead and dying. All of a dead person's possessions, including his animals, are considered polluted and will haunt the living unless they are destroyed or buried with him. This practice has dwindled since the 19th century, as a result of economic factors and the lessening of the Gypsies' nomadic life-styles. A great fear exists that the dead are angry at being dead and will return as vampires to avenge their deaths.

IRON fences sometimes are constructed around graves in order to keep the corpses from escaping. The Gypsies also seek to appease a vampire god by leaving out rice balls and bowls of milk or animal blood. The names of the dead are believed to have magical power and are used in oaths and invocations (see EVOCATIONS AND INVOCATIONS).

The Gypsy witch is almost without exception a woman; she is called a *chovihani*. She is amoral in her use of occult powers, having the ability either to bless and heal or curse and kill. Within the Gypsy community, she is not respected for her magical powers per se but only for the money she brings in by servicing the *gorgio* population. Some historians theorize that the rise in witchcraft and folk-magic activity in Europe and the British Isles in the 15th and 16th centuries was influenced by the spread of the Gypsies.

The *chovihani* is said either to inherit her ability or acquire it in childhood through intercourse with a water or earth demon while sleeping (see DEMONS). Like *gorgio* witches, Gypsy witches are said to have an odd or ugly appearance and to possess the EVIL EYE.

Of all the magical arts, the *chovihani* is best known for DIVINATION and fortune-telling, especially by crystal-gazing or reading palms, the Tarot and tea leaves (see SCRYING; PALMISTRY; TAROT; TASSEOMANCY). The *chovihani* prescribes a multitude of CHARMS to address virtually any situation; many of them involve BLOOD and URINE, two common ingredients in folk magic because of their sympathetic magic properties (see also HAIR AND NAILS). Most illness is ascribed to evil spirits, and the *chovihani* can heal by exorcising these spirits in a trance possession ritual (see SPIRIT EXORCISM).

Bird omens are important. The OWL is a harbinger of death while the swallow, cuckoo and water-wagtail are signs of good fortune.

Magical rites are performed in conjunction with baptisms, marriages and divorces. A newborn infant is unclean. Baptism removes the taboo and protects it from evil. Baptisms consist of immersion in running water, or tattooing (see TATTOO). Two names are given, one of which is kept secret in order to fool the Devil and evil spirits. Some baptisms are done within a MAGIC CIRCLE. Baptisms are often repeated for good luck. In marriage ceremonies, the newlyweds sometimes step over a broomstick (see BROOMS) and receive SALT, bread and wine. In divorce, the broomstick ritual is reversed. Another divorce ritual calls for sacrificing a horse by stabbing it in the heart and letting it bleed to death.

G'Zell, Otter See OTTER ZELL.

hag An old, ugly woman believed to be a witch or sorceress (see WITCHES; SORCERY); also, a supernatural, demonic being whose powers enable her to live an incredibly long time.

The origin of the term may be found in the ancient GODDESS beliefs and myths of the Egyptians, Greeks, Celts and pagan Europeans. The Egyptian *heq* was a matriarchal ruler in predynastic times, one who commanded the NAMES OF POWER. Many Celtic myths feature Gráinne, or "ugliness," the Old and Undying Hag. In Greek mythology, the hag is personified by HECATE, the crone and death-goddess aspect of the Triple Goddess; in Norse mythology she is the death-goddess Hel. Old Norse hags may have been sacrificial priestesses, as evidenced by the terms *hagi*, meaning "sacred grove," *haggen*, meaning "to chop to pieces," and *haggis*, meaning "hag's dish," a dish comprised of organ meats that is still popular in Scotland.

Hags appear often in folklore, where they are sometimes benevolent, wise, beautiful and perpetually young. In Irish and Scottish lore, good hags help with spinning. Supernatural hags haunt the Fen country of Great Britain, working in league with bogeys (see BOGEY), spirits of the dead and "creeping horrors" to bring harm to human beings and their animals. The Cailleach Bheur of the Highlands is a lean, blue-faced hag, a supernatural remnant of a Celtic goddess of winter who is reborn each Samhain (All Hallow's Eve, October 31) and turns to stone on Beltane Eve (April 30). The Celts erected sacred standing stones to her. Black Annis, a blue-faced cannibal with iron claws and long teeth, lives in a cave in the Dane Hills. A remnant of the Celtic mother goddess, Anu, Black Annis eats people and animals. Until the 18th century, a ritual was performed in which she was coaxed out of her cave every Easter Monday with a dead cat soaked in aniseed.

In the 16th century, the term *hag* was often substituted for FAIRY. Fairies were reputed to teach their supernatural skills to witches, and the two consorted at night at FAIRY RINGS.

In other lore, succubus hags cause nightmares by sitting on a person's chest and "riding" them through the night, sometimes killing them from exhaustion (see NIGHTMARE). Hags can be prevented from riding by the placement of a pen-knife on one's breast or a table fork under one's head. A sifter placed under the head also prevents riding, for the hag is forced to pass through every hole in it, which takes her all night. Witch-hags are believed to sneak into stables at night and steal horses, riding them all night and returning them sweaty and exhausted. To prevent this, CHARMS and AMULETS are hung in stables.

The term *hag* in relation to witches is still used in Great Britain; *hag stones* mark magic circles (see MAGIC CIRCLE), and *hag tracking* is a means of cursing.

Modern Witches consider the term uncomplimentary, a stereotype of an ugly, disagreeable woman.

hag stone In folk MAGIC, a stone with a hole in it hung in homes and stables to keep away hags (see HAG) or WITCHES, at night. Hung on the bedpost, a hag stone is believed to prevent a hag from riding one's chest and causing a NIGHTMARE. In the stables, it prevents a hag from taking the horses and riding them all night to the point of exhaustion.

See also STONES.

hair and nails Since ancient times, hair and nails have been thought to possess magical attributes that have made them important ingredients in many magic SPELLS. Hair has been associated with strength and virility, and with psychic protection. Abundant hair was considered an asset for many monarchs. The ancient Egyptians believed that a potion made of hair, nail clippings and human BLOOD would give a person absolute power over another.

In folklore, a witch's magical power is bound in her hair. By shaking her hair, the power of a spell is doubled. The shearing off of another's hair is considered an act of degradation, humiliation or punishment. Samson lost his strength when Delilah cut his hair. The Bhils of Central India tortured suspected witches, then cut off a lock of their hair and buried it, thus severing the link between the witches and their magical power. In the Middle Ages, witches were shaved in the belief that it rendered them powerless and more likely to confess; also, they were shaved to be searched for body marks that could be construed as marks of the Devil (see DEVIL'S MARK).

Nails have been associated with DEMONS and evil; some Jews keep their fingernails as short as possible, and tribes in Madagascar believe the Devil lives under unpared fingernails.

Much Western magical lore about hair and nails can be traced to the *Vendidad*, a Zoroastrian liturgy written in the mid-5th century B.C. According to the *Vendidad*, hair and nails are instruments of evil because they grow with a life of their own and can be separated from the body, to be used by witches and wizards for conjuring the dead, bewitching and casting spells. Ahura Mazda gave Zarathustra specific rituals for the safe disposing of hair clippings and nail parings:

> . . . thou shalt take them away ten paces from the faithful, twenty paces from the fire, thirty paces from the water, fifty paces from the bundles of baresma [holy twigs].
>
> Then thou shalt dig a hole, ten fingers deep if the earth is hard, twelve fingers deep if it is soft; thou shalt take thy hair down there and thou shalt say aloud these fiend-smiting words: Out of his pity Mazda made plants grow.
>
> There upon thou shalt draw three furrows with a knife of metal around the hole, or six, or nine, and thou shalt chant the Ahuna Vairya three times, or six, or nine.
>
> For the nails, thou shalt dig a hole, out of the house, as deep as the top joint of the little finger; thou shalt take the nails down there and thou shalt say aloud these fiend-smiting words: The words are heard from the pious in holiness and good thought.

The practice of burying cut hair and nails persists among many cultures. ALEISTER CROWLEY secretly disposed of his hair and nail clippings throughout his life. In Ozark lore, hair combings are buried, never thrown out. French peasants bury hair; Turks and Chileans stuff hair clippings into walls.

Throughout history, sorcerers, cunning men and women and witches in many societies have secured the cut hairs of victims to cast spells and break spells. A bewitched victim's hair thrown into a fire supposedly projects the pain of the flames back onto the witch. The hair of a dead man buried under the threshold of an enemy supposedly will cause the enemy to develop ague. In parts of Germany, a small bag of smooth human hair placed on the stomach will tell someone if they have been bewitched. The answer is yes if the hair is tangled after three days.

Hair, particularly pubic hair, is considered a potent ingredient in many love charms. According to legend, JOHN FIAN, a 16th-century Scottish wizard, attempted to make a young girl fall in love with him by making a charm from three of her pubic hairs. However, someone substituted three hairs from a cow's udder, and the lovestruck cow followed Fian all over town. It is still common for lovers to carry lockets of head hair, and in centuries past, young girls often made hair bracelets to give to their lovers to keep them faithful.

Red-haired persons are witches or sorcerers, according to one old belief. Evidence exists to indicate that some ancient pagan sorcerers dyed their hair red for certain rituals. Red hair was common among the Celts, whose traditions were steeped in magic. During the Middle Ages and Renaissance, red-haired persons were often suspected of being witches. Witches were said to shoot hairballs into animals to harm them. These hairballs supposedly lodged in the beasts' stomachs without leaving a mark on the skin.

According to superstition, the cutting of hair must be timed according to the phases of the moon, depending on how quickly one desires the hair to grow back.

See also WITCH BOTTLES.

Haizmann, Christopher (also Christoph) Joseph (?–1700)

A minor Bavarian painter, Christopher Haizmann announced publicly in 1677 that he had signed a pact with the DEVIL. Seized with an "unnatural convulsion" on August 29, 1677, Haizmann went to the police and asked for protection, claiming that nine years earlier, he had sold his soul to Satan. The police granted his request (see DEVIL'S PACT).

Haizmann wrote and illustrated the story of his infernal pact. He stated that the Devil one day had appeared to him as a burgher with a large, black dog and asked him why he was distressed and sad. "He would help me out of my distress if I were willing to subscribe myself in ink to him to be his son; he would assist and help me in every possible way," Haizmann wrote in an autobiographical account in 1677.

The painter agreed to a nine-year contract. A pact

was drawn up and signed in Haizmann's blood. Over the ensuing years, the Devil appeared to him many times in various grotesque shapes, including that of a dragon with breasts and talons (see METAMORPHOSIS). Satan also sent him visions of hell, which Haizmann described as "filled with burning flames and terrible stench. In it there was a large cauldron from which came heart-rending moans and groans of human beings; on its edge sat a hellish devil who did nothing but pour flaming resin, sulphur and pitch over them."

When the end of his contract approached, Haizmann began to grow anxious about his own fate. Sent by the local police to a holy shrine at Mariazell, Haizmann underwent several days of exorcism, during which the Virgin Mary recovered the pact (see DEMONIC EXORCISM).

Less than a year later, Haizmann, complaining of continuing torment by the Devil, reappeared at the shrine and underwent another exorcism. This time, the Virgin Mary ripped up the pact.

Haizmann committed himself to a Bavarian monastery but still could not live in peace. He spent the rest of his life tormented by visions of the Devil and his demons. He died in 1700.

The noted Viennese librarian and researcher, court councilor Dr. Rudolf Payer-Thurn, came across a document prepared at Mariazell which described the exorcism of Haizmann. He showed the document to Sigmund Freud and asked for Freud's analysis of the case. Originally appearing in *Imago* in 1923, Freud's "Eine Teufelsneurose im Siebzehnten Jahrhundert" (A Devil Neurosis of the Seventeenth Century) is considered a key document in Freudian psychoanalysis.

The Mariazell papers, including paintings made by Haizmann during his possession, led Freud to believe the following:

1. Rather feminine self-depictions of Haizmann in his paintings show him as suppressing homosexual tendencies.
2. Multiple breasts in the paintings reveal Haizmann's sexual associations with the Devil.
3. The number nine—there is a nine-year gap between Haizmann's pact with the Devil and its implementation, and nine days in which Haizmann resisted the Devil—represents pregnancy fantasies.
4. A penis is painted on the Devil in every picture. This, along with the pregnancy fantasies, show that Haizmann "recoiled from a feminine attitude toward his father which has its climax in the fantasy of giving birth to his child. Mourning for the lost father, heightened by yearning for him,

[Haizmann's] repressed pregnancy fantasy is reactivated, against which he must defend himself through neurosis and by degrading his father."
5. Haizmann's selling of himself to the Devil bought him peace of mind: "His father had died, he had become melancholy, and the devil, who came along and asked him why he was upset and mournful, promised to help him. . . . Here we have someone who gives himself to the devil in order to be free of an emotional depression."
6. Ultimately, then, the Devil was a father figure.

hand of glory   The severed hand of a hanged murderer, magically preserved, once was used as a charm (see CHARMS) in black-magic SPELLS and was believed to aid burglars in breaking into homes and buildings.

The hand of glory was the right hand of a murderer, ideally severed while the corpse still swung from the gallows, or cut during an eclipse of the moon. It was wrapped in a shroud, squeezed of blood and pickled for two weeks in an earthenware jar with salt, long peppers and saltpeter. It was then either dried in an oven with vervain, an herb believed to repel DEMONS, or laid out to dry in the sun, preferably during the dog days of August.

Once preserved, the hand was fitted with CANDLES between the fingers. The candles, called "dead man's candles," were made from the murderer's fat, with the wick being made from his hair. In another method of curing, the hand of glory was bled, dried and dipped in wax, so that the fingers themselves could be lit as candles.

With candles or fingers burning, the hand of glory supposedly had the power to freeze people in their footsteps and render them speechless. Burglars lit hands of glory before breaking into a house, confident that the charm would keep the occupants in a deep sleep while they plundered the household. If the thumb refused to burn, it meant someone in the house was awake and could not be charmed. According to lore, once a hand of glory was lit, nothing but milk could extinguish it.

As a counter-charm, homeowners made OINTMENTS from the BLOOD of screech OWLS, the fat of white hens and the bile of black CATS and smeared it on their thresholds.

Hands of glory were linked to WITCHES during the witch-hunt centuries. In 1588 two German women, Nichel and Bessers, who were accused of WITCHCRAFT and the exhumation of corpses, admitted they poisoned helpless people after lighting hands of glory to immobilize them. JOHN FIAN, who was severely tortured in his witch trial in Scotland in 1590, con-

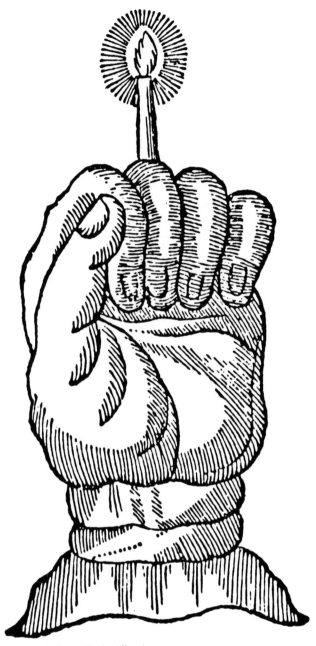

Hand of glory (*Petit Albert*)

fessed to using a hand of glory to break into a church, where he performed a service to the DEVIL.

handfasting   The rite of marriage in neo-Pagan WITCHCRAFT and NEO-PAGANISM. Handfasting is performed within a MAGIC CIRCLE, officiated by a high priestess and/or high priest. The ceremony usually is scripted by the couple. A handfasting is intended to last only as long as love does, not until death. The couple may exchange gold or silver RINGS inscribed with their Craft names in RUNES. In some ceremonies, the couple jumps over a broomstick for good luck (see BROOMS). The high priestess uses the broomstick

to sweep away all evil symbolically. The GREAT RITE of sexual union may be performed symbolically or in actuality. As in all marriage ceremonies, the handfasting ends with great feasting and merriment.

Unless the high priest or high priestess is a legally ordained minister (most are not), the handfasting is preceded or followed by a legal marriage ceremony.

Some covens also perform divorce rites, which are called "going of the ways" or "handpartings." Like most handfasting rites, they are symbolic and are not recognized legally.

handparting   See HANDFASTING.

hares   Perhaps because it is so common in the British Isles, the hare was once widely reputed to be a witch's familiar (see FAMILIARS) or a witch metamorphosed in disguise (see METAMORPHOSIS). So strong was this belief that it is still bad luck in the British Isles for one's path to be crossed by a hare.

WITCHES were said to be able to change themselves into hares and other animals with magical CHARMS: such as the following from the British Isles:

> I shall go into a hare,
> With sorrow and such and muckle care,
> And I shall go in the Devil's name.
> Ay, 'till I come home again.

The hare supposedly was the favorite disguise of ISOBEL GOWDIE, a Scottish woman who voluntarily confessed to WITCHCRAFT in 1662, astonishing her staid community of Auldearne with her wild tales. Once while in the shape of a hare, she said, she had a close call with some dogs. The DEVIL had sent her, as a hare, to carry a message to neighbors. Along the way, she encountered a man and a pack of hounds, which sprang upon her. "I run a very long time," said Gowdie, "but being hard pressed, was forced to take to my house, the door being open, and there took refuge behind a chest." The dogs pursued her into the house, and Gowdie escaped only by running into another room and uttering a "disenchanting" charm:

> Hare, hare, God send thee care!
> I am in a hare's likeness now;
> But I shall be a woman even now—
> Hare, hare, God send thee care!

Many stories exist in folklore of hunters shooting hares, only to discover they had killed old hag witches, who resumed their human forms upon death. The following Irish folktale, from W. B. Yeats's collection of *Irish Fairy and Folk Tales* (1892), tells of the wounding of a witch hare:

I was out thracking hares meeself, and I seen a fine puss of a thing hopping hopping in the moonlight, and whacking her ears about, now up, now down, and winking her great eyes, and—"Here goes," says I, and the thing was so close to me that she turned round and looked at me, and then bounced back, as well to say, do your worst! So I had the least grain of life of *blessed powder* left, and I put it in the gun—and bang at her! My jewel, the scritch she gave would frighten a rigment, and a mist, like, came betwixt me and her, and I seen her no more; but when the mist wint off I saw blood on the spot where she had been, and I followed its track, and at last it led me—whists, whisper—right up to Katey MacShane's door; and when I was at the thrashold, I heerd a murnin' within, a great murnin', and a groanin', and I opened the door, and there she was herself, sittin' quite content in the shape of a woman, and the black cat that was sittin' by her rose up its back and spit at me; but I went on never heedin', and asked the ould——how she was and what ailed her.

"Nothing," sis she.

"What's that on the floor?" sis I.

"Oh," she say, "I was cuttin' a billet of wood," she says, "wid the reaping hook," she says, "an' I've wounded meself in the leg," she says, "and that's drops of my precious blood," she says.

In Norse mythology, the hare is the companion of FREYA, goddess of fecundity.

Hawthorne, Nathaniel (1804–1864)

A native of Salem, Massachusetts, and one of the great masters of American fiction, Nathaniel Hawthorne wrote one of his best-known works, *The House of Seven Gables*, perhaps in part to atone for the role of an ancestor who played a role in the Salem witch hysteria of 1692 (see SALEM WITCHES).

The ancestor, Judge John Hathorne (an earlier spelling of the family name), was a son of Nathaniel's great-great-grandfather, Major William Hathorne. John Hathorne was a respected magistrate of Salem, who heard the trials with two other magistrates. He was not a vindictive man, and he put skeptical questions to the accusers who testified during the lengthy trials. Nevertheless, he believed in witchcraft as an evil and believed in the power to afflict others through magic with poppets. He was swayed by the testimony of spectral evidence and allowed it to be admitted in court.

As a young man, Nathaniel Hawthorne was fascinated and deeply affected by a family story that Hathorne had been cursed by one of the convicted witches. One of the condemned, Sarah Good, had issued a curse as she went to the gallows. Asked by Rev. Nicholas Noyes to confess, she replied, "I am no more a witch than you are a wizard, and if you take away my life, God will give you blood to drink." Noyes reportedly choked on his own blood in 1717. It is not known for certain whether the curse was laid on other officials responsible for the executions, but the Hathorne family apparently came to believe so. Another victim of the Salem hysteria, Philip English, a wealthy merchant and shipper, made no secret of his hate for John Hathorne and Sheriff George Corwin. As a result of the ordeal brought on by charges of witchcraft against them, the Englishes lost all their property and fortune. The health of Mary, Philip's wife, was so impaired that she sickened and died. English bore an open grudge against the authorities, particularly Corwin and Hathorne, neither of whom apparently ever expressed regret over their roles in the sufferings. English refused to forgive Hathorne until just before English died. Ironically, the Hathorne and English families eventually joined in a marriage, which produced the lineage to which Nathaniel Hawthorne was born.

Prior to the witch trials, the Hathorne family had been prosperous in shipping and farming. The family was established in America by Major Hathorne, who left England for Boston in 1630, then moved to Salem in 1636. He became the first speaker in the House of Delegates in Massachusetts colony. In the early 1700s, beginning with Nathaniel's great-grandfather, Captain Joseph Hathorne (born in 1692), the family fortunes began to decline, and the family lost social status in Salem as well.

Nathaniel was born on July 4, 1804, in a gambrel-roofed house in Salem that had been purchased in 1772 by his grandfather, Daniel Hathorne, the youngest son of Captain Joseph. Nathaniel's father, also named Nathaniel, was a sea captain who died of yellow fever while on a voyage to Surinam when the boy was six. Hawthorne spent much of his childhood in Salem and Raymond, Maine, where his mother's family owned property. He preferred to spend time alone in the woods and was described as "fragile."

His family scraped together enough money to send him to Bowdoin College. Prior to his entrance in 1821, Hawthorne wrote to his mother, "What do you think of becoming an Author, and relying for support upon my pen?. . . . How proud would you feel to see my works praised by the reviewers, as equal to the proudest productions of the scribbling sons of John Bull. But Authors are always poor Devils, and therefore Satan may take them."

After Nathaniel's graduation from college, one story goes, his older sister convinced him to restore the *w* to Hathorne, which had been dropped many generations before, in order to separate himself from the infamous Hathorne lineage.

For years, Hawthorne apparently brooded about

the witch's curse. He also was fascinated by Puritan sin and suffering. In the introduction to *The Scarlet Letter*, published in 1850, he stated:

> He [Judge Hathorne] made himself so conspicuous in the martyrdom of the witches, that their blood may fairly be said to have left a stain upon him. . . . I know not whether these ancestors of mine bethought themselves to repent, and ask pardon of heaven for their cruelties. . . . At all events, I, the present writer, as their representative, hereby take shame upon myself for their sakes, and pray that any curse incurred by them . . . may be now and henceforth removed.

Hawthorne used the curse, some real-life figures from Salem and his own gambrel-roofed house in his next novel, *The House of Seven Gables*, written in Lenox, Massachusetts, and published in 1851. Like his own family, the Pyncheon family of the novel suffers from inherited sin related to witchcraft. A piece of property owned by Matthew Maule includes a pure, sweet-water spring. Maule's jealous neighbor, Judge Pyncheon, becomes obsessed with owning it and is driven to have Maule accused of witchcraft. Maule is convicted and sentenced to be hanged. Before he is executed, he curses Pyncheon: "Pyncheon, God will give you blood to drink and quench your greed for eternity." After Maule is buried, Pyncheon buys his land and builds on it the House of Seven Gables. Pyncheon invites his friends over for a housewarming dinner, which he never gets to enjoy: he is found slumped in a chair, dead of a massive throat hemorrhage. The Pyncheon family suffers decline, then is redeemed when young Phoebe Pyncheon marries a descendant of Matthew Maule, and the land and house are restored to their rightful owner.

The malicious character of Judge Pyncheon was modeled on the Rev. Charles Wentworth Upham, mayor and minister of Salem, whose books, *Lectures on Witchcraft* (1831) and *History of Witchcraft and Salem Village* (1867), reveal malice and erroneous moral perspectives but nonetheless established him as an authority on the witch trials. Hawthorne borrowed the Maule name from Thomas Maule, a Quaker merchant who lived in Salem at the time of the trials, and who believed the witch hysteria and favored the executions. Maule's own definition of a witch was anyone who was not a Quaker.

The House of Seven Gables, as Hawthorne's house is now called, remained on its original site near the Salem harbor until 1958, when it was moved to a new location on the harbor. It was opened to the public in 1959 and remains one of Salem's biggest tourist attractions.

hazel The hazel tree is one of powerful MAGIC, according to beliefs that date back to pagan and Biblical times. Mercury's caduceus, a gift from Apollo, was made of hazel. (The caduceus is the symbol of spiritual enlightenment and the emblem of the medical profession.) The early Roman naturalist, Pliny, wrote of how to use hazel wands for divining underground springs. The rod of Moses was cut from a hazel tree by Adam in the Garden of Eden. Moses and Aaron used hazel rods to bring plagues into Egypt. In the fourth century, St. Patrick is said to have rid Ireland of snakes by drawing them together with a magic hazel rod and then casting them into the sea.

Hazel is still considered to be the best material for the magic wands used by magicians and WITCHES.

Divining rods made of forked hazel twigs are supposed to be good for finding water, criminals, metals, and buried treasure (see DOWSING).

Hazel wood and hazelnuts are believed to offer protection against WITCHCRAFT, DEMONS and fairy bewitchment (see FAIRIES). Hazel breastbands on harnesses have been used to protect horses. In Ireland, the hazel is a symbol of great mystical wisdom. Cattle are singed with hazel rods at Beltane and Midsummer fires in order to keep fairies away. In Scotland, double hazel nuts are thrown at witches.

Hazel nuts also have been used in the casting of SPELLS. In some areas, picking hazel nuts on a Sunday is believed to summon the DEVIL to appear. Hazelnuts are gathered in traditional fall fertility rites in some parts of England.

healing Modern WITCHES view healing as one of their most important functions. They use a wide range of healing techniques, including MAGIC; herbal and folk remedies; Eastern techniques that involve changing the body's energy field; Native American Indian and shamanic techniques (see SHAMANISM); and Western approaches to medicine and psychology. Some Witches are professional healers, trained in Eastern and/or Western medicine and psychology. Witches prefer holistic and natural healing methods that involve healing power of sound, breath, color, touch and movement.

Prior to the scientific age, healing commonly was the province of the village wise woman, cunning man, WITCH or WIZARD. Such individuals often were born with the mysterious gift of healing by touch; many were steeped in herbal lore that had been passed down though generations of their families. The healer diagnosed both human and animal ailments. Some were renowned for determining whether or not haunting FAIRIES or ghosts (see GHOSTS, HAUNTINGS AND WITCHCRAFT) were responsible for

Witch "inoculating" man by shooting twig through his foot (Ulrich Molitor, *De lanijs et phitonicius mulieribus*, 1489)

illness and driving them away. One common Renaissance remedy for fairy-caused illness was the recitation of Christian PRAYERS, followed by a measurement of the patient's girdle to see if the fairy had departed the body (see GIRDLE MEASURING). Other healers diagnosed the patient's urine. Healers dispensed herbal remedies in the form of powders, potions and unguents. They prescribed CHARMS, little prayers comprised of both pagan and Christian elements. They also cast SPELLS. Some folk-magic remedies required procedures on the part of the patient, such as boiling an egg and burying it in an anthill; the disease or condition would disappear when ants had consumed the egg. Healers also made use of gems and semiprecious stones, which have a long history as medicinal objects.

Herbalism. The greatest natural healing knowledge comes from herbalism, the earliest of all healing systems and one used throughout the world. In Western culture, herbalism had been developed to a high art by the ancient Egyptians, Sumerians, Assyrians, Babylonians, Greeks and Romans. Herbal sorcery was renowned in ancient Greece. The greatest collection of ancient plant lore was compiled by Pliny in *Natural History*, a 37-volume work that contains a wealth of information about the medicinal uses of plants, flowers, trees and herbs. For centuries, others built upon Pliny's work, most notably Hildegard of Bingen, a medieval Germany mystic and abbess, and Nicholas Culpeper, a 17th-century English physician

and astrologer who linked herbs to astrological signs (see ASTROLOGY).

Plants acquired numerous pagan religious associations, which the Christian church worked to replace with Christian associations. *Hypericum perforatum*, for example, blooms during the summer solstice and was an ancient totem of sun worship. The Romans burned it in bonfires in observance of the solstice, which occurs around June 21. The Christian Church associated it with the birth of John the Baptist on June 24, and the plant became known as St. John's-wort. Cunning folk, witches and healers often observed both pagan and Christian associations in their charms and recipes.

The Church attempted to discredit village healers, for their cures competed with the Church, which claimed a monopoly on miracles. Healing by SORCERY was considered fraudulent—and there were many such cases of fraud—and was a civil crime under Roman law. The laws were not strictly enforced, however, for the populace was loath to give up local healers. During the witch-hunts of the Renaissance and Reformation, healing by sorcery was considered "white" witchcraft, until demonologists began denouncing it as an evil. INCREASE MATHER stated that healing power in a witch was a diabolical gift, not a divine gift from God.

Many modern Witches become skilled in the use of herbs as part of everyday life, to maintain health as well as to cure illness. They make use of both Western and Eastern knowledge; the Chinese have been renowned herbalists for centuries. Some grow and harvest their own herbs, which they use to make salves, syrups, teas, poultices and powders. Herbs also are used in magical healing. For example, a cloth doll called a *poppet* is made to represent the patient and is stuffed with the appropriate herbal remedy. The poppet is used in the casting of a sympathetic magic spell for healing. Most modern Witches will not cast a healing spell on a person without his or her permission.

Healing by touch. The ability to heal by a laying on of hands, like healing with herbs, has primitive origins. Prehistoric cave paintings in the Pyrenees indicate that it may have been used as early as 15,000 years ago. Healing by touch has a written history dating back about 5,000 years; it was used in ancient India, China, Tibet, Egypt and Chaldea and appears in both the Old and New Testaments. Gifted individuals are born with the ability for this kind of healing, though it can be learned (see VALENTINE GREATRAKES).

The Christian Church encouraged such miraculous healing within the confines of religion. Outside the Church, it was regarded as fraudulent sorcery and witchcraft. The one notable exception, tolerated by the Church, was the king's touch, which began in England in the Middle Ages and was popular in England and France until nearly the end of the 17th century. The king's touch was the reputed ability of royalty to heal, especially a type of scrofula called the king's evil. The procedure called for the patient to kneel before the monarch, who lightly touched the face and (usually) invoked the name of God, while a chaplain read from the Gospel of Mark, "They shall lay hands on the sick and they shall recover." The king then hung a gold coin strung on a ribbon around the patient's neck; the coin was reputed to have great magical powers.

The king's touch was begun by Edward the Confessor (r. 1042–1066) and was a full ceremony by the time of Henry VII (r. 1485–1509). Charles II (r. 1660–1685) gave nearly 91,000 healings. After Charles II the procedure gradually lost favor with monarchs and royal doctors though not with the populace, who searched out wizards and the like as substitutes for the king.

To heal by touch, modern Witches blend Eastern and Western knowledge of the body's envelope of energy, called the *aura*. The aura, which is comprised of layers, is visible to clairvoyants; illness shows up as weak, cloudy or discolored spots. Some healers pass their hands over, but do not touch, a patient and detect illness by cold spots in the aura. According to ancient Hindu medicine, the aura is revitalized by *prana*, the vital force that exists in the universe. Healers have a natural abundance of *prana* and may transfer it by touch to sick patients, who are deficient in *prana*. *Prana* exists by many other names, including *ch'i* in Chinese medicine and *ki* in Japanese medicine; the Japanese call healing by touch "giving *seiki*." Healing by touch requires training and skill. The healer must learn how to diagnose illness and how to channel and transfer vital energy without absorbing the patient's illness.

Crystals and gems. Semiprecious and precious stones have enjoyed universal medicinal use since ancient times. Different stones have different healing properties. They are worn on the body, steeped in water and ground up in elixers. It is theorized that the stones emit emanations that influence the body and mind. Amber, for example, heals throat infections, while bloodstone coagulates the blood and stops heavy bleeding.

In the 1980s crystals became popular with the New Age culture, as meditational, DIVINATION and healing tools. Many modern Witches work with crystals. In some forms of crystal therapy, stones are laid in patterns on the body or over *chakra* points. In yoga, chakras are whirlpools through which *prana*, the universal life force, enters the body. There are seven major chakras, each with a different function, located near the genitals, spleen, navel, heart, throat, third eye and crown of the head.

Colors. Color is a vibration of light and has been used in healing since the time of ancient Egypt, Greece, India and China. The colors of the spectrum have specific effects on the mind and body and are used in various treatments. RED, for example, is used in blood disorders, while yellow is used in bowel and intestinal ailments. Colors are correlated with he chakras, crystals and gems, foods, metals and chemicals. The color of one's surroundings is believed to influence healing.

Witches burn colored CANDLES in magical healing spells and use colors on poppets. Another healing technique is to direct colored rays psychically to a patient, which can be done at a distance.

Magical spells. Besides candles and poppets, modern Witches use a wide variety of magical spells in healing, tailoring each spell to fit the circumstances. Some covens do a great deal of cord magic, in which healing power is tied in knots in cords and is released while a spell is chanted (see KNOTS). A sympathetic magic spell may be performed with something personal from the patient, such as a lock of hair, nail clippings (see HAIR AND NAILS), a bit of clothing or a photograph. Occasionally, a member of the coven may substitute for the patient in a spell and transmit the healing energy raised. This type of spell is considered hazardous because it exposes the stand-in to the patient's illness. A coven also can create a thought-form, (sometimes called an *artificial elemental*), which can be sent to a patient with healing energy (see ELEMENTALS).

Other healing methods. Healing by exorcism, in which a disease-causing demon or spirit is driven out of the body of a patient by an entranced healer, is common in non-Western cultures but is not often used by modern neo-Pagan Witches (see SPIRIT EXORCISM). Some Witches are trained in shamanic healing techniques, which do include exorcism. Another shamanic technique is to suck illness out of a body (see SHAMANISM). Some Witches study various Native American Indian healing techniques and other Eastern methods, such as shiatsu, acupuncture, acupressure and reflexology. Still others employ bodywork techniques, in which healing energies are said to be released through movement and deep muscle massage.

Hecate In Greek mythology, a powerful goddess who evolved into the patron of MAGIC and WITCHCRAFT. Hecate has three aspects: goddess of fertility and plenty; goddess of the moon; and queen of the night, ghosts and shades. In her moon-goddess aspect, she is often part of a trinity with SELENE and DIANA/Artemis—the Triple Goddess.

Hecate possesses infernal power, roaming the earth at night with a pack of red-eyed hell hounds and a retinue of dead souls. She is visible only to dogs, and if dogs howl in the night, it means Hecate is about. She is the cause of nightmares and insanity and is so terrifying that many ancients referred to her only as "The Nameless One."

She is the goddess of the dark of the moon, the destroyer of life but also the restorer of life. In one myth, she turns into a bear or boar and kills her own son, then brings him back to life. In her dark aspect, she wears a necklace made of testicles; her hair is made of writhing snakes which petrify, like the Medusa.

Hecate is the goddess of all CROSSROADS, looking in three directions at the same time. In ancient times, three-headed statues of her were set up at many intersections, and secret rites were performed under a full moon to appease her. Statues of Hecate carrying torches or swords were erected in front of homes to keep evil spirits at bay.

Hecate has been associated with many incantations, sacrifices (see SACRIFICE) and rituals throughout history. In ancient times, people sought to appease her by leaving chicken hearts and honey cakes outside their doors. On the last day of the month, offerings of honey, onions, fish and eggs were left at crossroads, along with sacrifices of puppies, infant girls and she-lambs. Sorcerers gathered at crossroads to pay homage to her and such infernal servants as the Empusa, a hobgoblin; the Cercopsis, a poltergeist; and the Mormo, a ghoul. One petition for her patronage was recorded in the 3rd century by Hippolytus in *Philosophumena*:

> Come, infernal, terrestrial, and heavenly Bombo (Hecate), goddess of the broad roadways, of the crossroad, thou who goest to and fro at night, torch in hand, enemy of the day. Friend and lover of darkness, thou who doest rejoice when the bitches are howling and warm blood is spilled, thou who art walking amid the phantom and in the place of tombs, thou whose thirst is blood, thou who dost strike chill fear into mortal hearts, Gorgo, Mormo, Moon of a thousand forms, cast a propitious eye upon our sacrifice.

As the goddess of all forms of magic and witchcraft, Hecate was far more important in antiquity than the mythical sorceress CIRCE, who was sometimes said to be her daughter, or the witch Medea, also sometimes said to be Hecate's daughter, who helped Jason steal the Golden Fleece.

In modern Witchcraft, Hecate is usually associated with the lunar trinity, the Triple Goddess. She rules over the waning and dark moon, a two-week period that is best for magic that deals with banishing, releasing, planning and introspection. She is invoked for justice.

See also GODDESS.

Helms Amendment   Witchcraft and neo-Pagan churches and organizations may apply for tax-exempt status in the United States, just as may other religious organizations. In 1985 two members of Congress, Senator Jesse Helms of North Carolina and Representative Robert Walker of Pennsylvania, introduced bills to remove this exemption for WITCHCRAFT and NEO-PAGANISM. Both measures failed.

The effort was begun by Helms, who queried Secretary of the Treasury James Baker about Witchcraft groups. Baker replied in a letter that several organizations that "espouse a system of beliefs, rituals and practices derived in part from pre-Christian Celtic and Welsh traditions which they label as 'witchcraft' " did indeed have tax-exempt status. Baker also pointed out that any group that is sincere in its beliefs, does not break the law and conforms to "clearly defined public policy" can qualify for tax exemption.

Of the hundreds of Witchcraft/neo-Pagan groups that rise and fade around the country, only a handful ever apply for tax-exempt status. Most operate on very slim budgets. Nevertheless, the congressmen introduced their bills. Walker's legislative assistant told the press, "If a person is praying for horrible things and sticking pins into voodoo dolls, that is not the kind of religion that should be supported by a tax exemption."

The bills were opposed by the American Civil Liberties Union and numerous Witchcraft/neo-Pagan groups, among them the COVENANT OF THE GODDESS, a Berkeley, California, organization that is tax-exempt and represents about 70 Witchcraft groups around the country; CIRCLE SANCTUARY, an international WICCA and neo-Pagan networking organization based near Mt. Horeb, Wisconsin; and the CHURCH AND SCHOOL OF WICCA, New Bern, North Carolina. The ACLU called the bill "the crudest example of First Amendment infringement." Witches, who organized a massive letter-writing and flyer campaign, termed the bills a throwback to the witch-hunts of the Middle Ages. The issue became known as the *Helms Amendment*.

Neither the Helms nor Walker measure survived to be incorporated into the sweeping tax-reform legislation passed in 1986.

Hermes   Greek messenger god, swift and cunning, portrayed with winged feet, wearing a winged helmet and carrying a caduceus, a serpent-entwined, magic wand that symbolizes spiritual illumination. Hermes also was a patron god of MAGIC, using his caduceus to cast SPELLS. As god of travelers, his image was erected at CROSSROADS; he was charged with escorting the souls of the dead to the underworld. The dog is associated with Hermes for its intelligence and devotion.

According to myth, Hermes was born of Zeus and Maia, daughter of Atlas. He was a shrewd thief from his earliest hours. Before nightfall on his first day of life, he stole most of Apollo's heifers. Zeus made him return the heifers. In contrition, Hermes invented the lyre and gave it to Apollo. Hermes continued to play malicious tricks but also was generous in his protection of others: for instance, he saved Odysseus from the magical spells of CIRCE.

Hermes appears in Greek mythology more often than any other deity. The Greeks identified him closely with the Egyptian god of wisdom and magic, THOTH. Hermes is said to have learned the mysteries of the universe, which he sought to teach others. *Hermes* is derived from *herm*, a form of *chiram*, in WITCHCRAFT the personification of the Universal Life Principle, represented by fire. Hermes has been equated with ODIN and Wotan in Norse and Teutonic mythology, and with Buddha.

Hermes, along with Thoth, is personified in HERMES TRISMEGISTUS, a mythical figure said to have written the HERMETICA texts of ancient sacred learning and lore.

Hermes Trismegistus (Jacques Boissard, *De Divinatione et Magicis*)

Hermes Trismegistus

"The thrice greatest Hermes," a mythological blend of the Egyptian god THOTH, who governed mystical wisdom, MAGIC, writing and other disciplines, and was associated with HEALING; and the Greek god HERMES, the personification of universal wisdom and patron of MAGIC, the swift, wing-footed messenger god who carried a magic wand, the caduceus. The ancient Greeks associated Hermes with Thoth so closely that the two became inseparable. "Thrice greatest" refers to Hermes Trismegistus as the greatest of all philosophers; the greatest of all kings; and the greatest of all priests.

Both Thoth and Hermes were associated with sacred writings. As scribe of the gods, Thoth was credited with all sacred books. In some Egyptian writings, he was described as "twice very great" and "five times very great." Hermes was credited with the authorship of 20,000 books by Iamblichus (ca. 250–300 B.C.), a Neo-platonic Syrian philosopher, and more than 36,000 by Manetho (ca. 300 B.C), an Egyptian priest who wrote the history of Egypt in Greek, perhaps for Ptolemy I. According to myth, both Thoth and Hermes revealed to mankind the healing arts, magic, writing, ASTROLOGY, sciences and

philosophy. Thoth recorded the weighing of souls in the Judgment Hall of OSIRIS. Hermes conducted the souls of the dead to Hades. Hermes, said Francis Barrett in *Biographia Antiqua*, ". . . communicated the sum of the Abyss, and the divine knowledge to all posterity . . ."

Hermes Trismegistus provided the wisdom of the light in the ancient Egyptian mysteries. He carried an emerald, upon which was recorded all of philosophy, and the caduceus, the symbol of mystical illumination. Hermes Trismegistus vanquished Typhon, the dragon of ignorance and mental, moral and physical perversion.

The surviving wisdom of Hermes Trismegistus is said to be the HERMETICA, 42 books that profoundly influenced the development of Western occultism and magic.

Hermetic Order of the Golden Dawn

One of the most influential Western occult societies of the late 19th century to early 20th century. Like a meteor, it flared into light, blazed a bright trail and then disintegrated. Members included W. B. Yeats, A. E. Waite, ALEISTER CROWLEY and other noted occultists.

There is some evidence that the Golden Dawn was based on a foundation of lies. The key founder was Dr. William Wynn Westcott, a London coroner and a Rosicrucian. In 1887 Westcott obtained part of a manuscript written in brown-ink cipher from the Rev. A. F. A. Woodford, a Mason. The manuscript appeared to be old but probably was not. From his Hermetic knowledge, Westcott was able to decipher the manuscript and discovered it concerned fragments of rituals for the "Golden Dawn," an unknown organization that apparently admitted both men and women.

Westcott asked an occultist friend, Samuel Liddel MacGregor mathers, to flesh out the fragments into full-scale rituals. Some papers evidently were forged to give the "Golden Dawn" authenticity and a history. It was said to be an old German occult order. Westcott produced papers that showed he had been given a charter to set up an independent lodge in England. The Isis-Urania Temple of the Hermetic Order of the Golden Dawn was established in 1888, with Westcott, Mathers and Dr. W. R. Woodman, Supreme Magus of the Rosicrucian Society of Anglia, as the three Chiefs. The secret society quickly caught on, and 315 initiations took place during the society's heydey, from 1888 to 1896.

An elaborate hierarchy was created, consisting of 10 grades or degrees, each corresponding to the 10 sephiroth of the Tree of Life of the KABBALAH, plus an eleventh degree for neophytes. The degrees are divided into three orders: Outer, Second, and Third.

One advanced through the Outer Order by examination. Initially, Westcott, Mathers and Woodman were the only members of the Second Order, and they claimed to be under the direction of the Secret Chiefs of the Third Order, who were entities of the astral plane. Mathers's rituals were based largely on Freemasonry.

In 1891 Woodman died and was not replaced in the organization. Mathers produced the initiation ritual for the Adeptus Minor rank and renamed the Second Order the *Ordo Rosae Rubeae et Aureae Crucis*, or the Order of the Rose of Ruby and Cross of Gold (R. R. et A. C.). Initiation was by invitation only.

Mathers was at the very least eccentric and possibly was a lunatic. He never consummated his marriage with his wife, Mina, who, he said, received teachings from the Secret Chiefs through clairaudience, or supernormal hearing. His finances were erratic, and in 1891 he and his wife were penniless. A rich Golden Dawner, Annie Horniman, became their benefactor. Mathers and his wife moved to Paris, where Mathers set up another lodge. He continued to write curricula materials and send them to London. He was obsessed with jealousy over West-

cott and became increasingly autocratic. He devoted a good deal of time to translating the manuscript of *The Book of the Sacred Magic of Abra-Melin the Mage*, which he claimed was bewitched and inhabited by a species of nonphysical intelligence. (The book eventually was published in 1898.)

In 1896 Horniman cut off her financial support to Mathers. The same year, Mathers claimed that the Secret Chiefs had initiated him into the Third Order. Horniman disputed his claim and was expelled from the society. In 1897 members began to discover Westcott's questionable role in "discovering" the Golden Dawn. He resigned his post and was succeeded by Florence Farr. By then, irreparable schisms were forming within the Golden Dawn.

Aleister Crowley was initiated in 1898 and rapidly rose up the ranks. In 1899 he went to Paris and insisted upon being initiated into the Second Order. Mathers complied. The London lodge, under Farr, rejected his initiation. In 1900 Crowley went to England as Mathers's "Envoy Extraordinary" and attempted to take control of the quarters of the Second Order. He appeared wearing a black mask, Highland dress and a gilt dagger, and staged a dramatic attempt, but was rebuffed.

The Crowley-Mathers alliance was an uneasy one. Crowley considered himself a superior magician to Mathers. The two supposedly engaged in magical warfare. Mathers sent an astral vampire to attack Crowley psychically, and Crowley responded with an army of demons led by Beelzebub. After Crowley's attack on the Second Order quarters, the London lodge expelled both Crowley and Mathers. Crowley retaliated by publishing some of the Golden Dawn's secret rituals in his magazine, *The Equinox*.

W. B. Yeats took over the Second Order. He attempted to restore unity, but the schisms in the Golden Dawn broke into independent groups. Followers of Mathers formed the Alpha et Omega Temple. In 1903 A. E. Waite and others left, forming a group with the name Golden Dawn but with more of an emphasis on mysticism than magic. In 1905 another splinter group was formed, the Stella Matutina, or "Order of the Companions of the Rising Light in the Morning." The Isis-Uranian Temple became defunct. In 1917 it was resurrected as the Merlin Temple of the Stella Matutina. The Stella Matutina went into decline in the 1940s, following the publication of its secret rituals by a former member, Israel Regardie, Crowley's one-time secretary.

Waite's group, which retained the Golden Dawn name and some of its rituals, declined after 1915 with Waite's departure. Some distant offshoots of the Golden Dawn continue in existence.

During its height, the Hermetic Order of the Golden

Dawn possessed the greatest known repository of Western magical knowledge. Second Order studies centered on the Kabbalistic Tree of Life. Three magical systems were taught: the Key of Solomon (see GRIMOIRES); Abra-Melin magic (see ABRAMELIN THE MAGE); and ENOCHIAN MAGIC (see also JOHN DEE). Materials also were incorporated from the Egyptian Book of the Dead, William Blake's Prophetic Books and the Chaldean Oracles. Instruction was given in astral travel, SCRYING, alchemy, geomancy, the TAROT and ASTROLOGY.

The key purpose of the order was "to prosecute the Great Work: which is to obtain control of the nature and power of [one's] own being." Some of the texts included Christian elements, such as the establishing of a closer relationship with Jesus, the "Master of Masters." Members circulated various Catholic and Anglican writings and sermons. These were omitted from the materials published by Regardie. Elements of Golden Dawn rituals, Rosicrucianism and Freemasonry have been absorbed into the rituals of modern Witchcraft.

See also: DION FORTUNE; HERMETICA; MAGIC; FRANCIS ISRAEL REGARDIE.

Hermetica

Forty-two sacred books of mystical wisdom attributed to the mythical HERMES TRISMEGISTUS, or "thrice great Hermes," the combined Egyptian and Greek deities of THOTH and HERMES, respectively. The books, which date from somewhere between the third century B.C. and first century A.D., had an enormous impact on the development of Western occultism and MAGIC. Many of the rituals and much of the esoteric symbolism contained in neo-Pagan WITCHCRAFT, are based upon Hermetic material.

The Hermetica may have been authored by one person—according to one legend, Hermes Trismegistus was a grandson of Adam and a builder of the Egyptian pyramids—but probably was the work of several persons in succession. According to legend, the books were initially written on papyrus. Clement of Alexandria, a chronicler of pagan lore, said 36 of the Hermetic books contained the whole philosophy of the Egyptians: four books on ASTROLOGY, 10 books called the *Hieratic* on law, 10 books on sacred rites and observances, two on music, and the rest on writing, cosmography, geography, mathematics and measures and priestly training. The remaining six books were medical and concerned the body, diseases, instruments, medicines, the eyes and women.

Most of the Hermetic books were lost with others in the royal libraries in the burning of Alexandria. According to legend, the surviving books were buried in a secret location in the desert, where they have survived to the present. A few initiates of the mystery

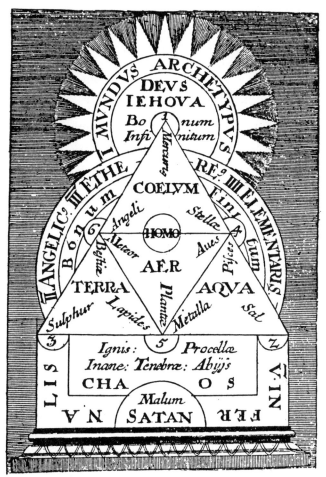

Hermetic scheme of universe (after Thomas Norton, *Musaeum Hermeticum*, 1749)

schools, ancient secret cults, supposedly know the books' location.

What little was left of the surviving Hermetic lore has been handed down through history and has been translated into various languages. The most important of these works, and one of the earliest, is *The Divine Pymander*. It consists of 17 fragments collected into a single work, which contain many of the original Hermetic concepts, including the way divine wisdom and the secrets of the universe were revealed to Hermes and how Hermes established his ministry to spread this wisdom throughout the world. *The Divine Pymander* apparently was revised during the early centuries A.D. and has suffered from incorrect translations.

The second book of *The Divine Pymander*, called *Poimandres* or *The Vision*, is perhaps the most famous. It tells of Hermes' mystical vision, cosmogony and the Egyptians' secret sciences of culture and the spiritual development of the soul.

The Emerald Tablet. Also called the *Emerald Table*, the Emerald Tablet is one of the most revered of magical documents in eastern occultism. Hermes Trismegistus was portrayed in art as holding an emerald upon which was inscribed the whole of the Egyptians' philosophy. This Emerald Tablet was said to be discovered in a cave tomb, clutched in the hands of the corpse of Hermes Trismegistus. According to one version of the legend, the tomb was found by Sarah, wife of Abraham, while another version credits the discovery to APOLLONIUS OF TYANA. The gem was inscribed in Phoenician and revealed magical secrets of the universe. A Latin translation of the Tablet appeared by 1200, preceded by several Arabic versions. No two translations are the same, and little of the Tablet appears to make sense.

The significance of the Emerald Tablet, however, lies in its opening: "That which is above is like that which is below and that which is below is like that which is above, to achieve the wonders of the one thing." This is the foundation of astrology and alchemy: that the microcosm of mankind and the earth is a reflection of the macrocosm of God and the heavens.

Herne the Hunter   A spectral huntsman of English lore, often the leader of the WILD HUNT or the nocturnal processions of the dead. As leader of the Wild Hunt, Herne has lunar associations. His name is associated with another leader of the dead, Herlechin, or Harlequin, also associated with the Devil. Herne is portrayed wearing an antlered headdress. In neo-Pagan WITCHCRAFT, he is associated with the HORNED GOD, and with CERNUNNOS and PAN. Sightings of Herne are still reported in Windsor Forest near Windsor Castle and are associated with Witchcraft activities. Similar spectral horned huntsmen exist in German and French lore.

hex   A spell (see SPELLS; CURSES) or bewitchment cast by WITCHCRAFT. The term comes from the Pennsylvania Dutch, who borrowed it from their native German word for "witch," *Hexe*, which in turn is derived from Old High German *hagazussa* or *hagzissa* ("hag"). In common usage, *hex* means an evil spell or curse, but among the Pennsylvania Dutch, for example, a hex can be either good or bad. It is cast by a professional witch whose services are sought out and paid for with a "voluntary" contribution. WITCHES also are consulted to break and protect against hexes.

See also HEX SIGNS; POWWOWING.

hex death   Also called "voodoo death," hex death is death from a HEX or curse (see CURSES) resulting from black MAGIC or the breaking of a taboo. The critical factor in hex death is belief. If a person be-

lieves that a WITCH DOCTOR or VODOUN priest can make him die by cursing him or by pointing a finger or bone at him, he probably will expire, and no amount of Western conventional medicine can save him. Hex death is largely a self-fulfilling prophecy.

In her studies on hex death, anthropologist Joan Halifax-Grof lists four causes: 1) secretly administered poisons or other physical agents; 2) the relationship between physical and emotional factors in the victim; 3) societal reactions in a particular culture; and 4) parapsychological influences. Poisons and physical agents are obvious malfacteurs; if administered "magically," with plenty of ceremony, they may kill without the victim's knowledge.

The second category refers to the fact that a person literally can die from fright. In stressful situations the adrenaline surges, preparing the body either to fight or escape. If neither is possible, the body could suffer both short- and long-term damage, such as shock, lowering of blood pressure and attacking of the body's immune system. Rage affects the body as well. Finally, if the victim believes his cursed situation to be hopeless, he begins to experience feelings of helplessness, incompetence, despair and worthlessness. Illness sets in, which the victim has no desire to fight, and eventually he succumbs. Psychologists term this situation the *giving up/given up* complex.

Cultural determinants play as large a role in hex death as the victim's own perceptions. Once cursed, the victim may be forced to withdraw from daily community life, becoming almost invisible to his neighbors. The cursed individual becomes despondent, expecting death, and his friends and relatives do not dispute such notions but corroborate them. Eventually, those not cursed see the victim as already dead, even performing funeral ceremonies over his body, which technically still lives. In Australia, aborigines actually take away food and water from the accursed, since a dead person needs no sustenance. Suffering from starvation and dehydration in the searing Australia bush, the victim indeed dies.

In many cases, however, the victim dies despite the efforts of his friends or family to save him. In such instances, Halifax-Grof speculates that the sorcerer makes a telepathic connection with the victim, somehow controlling his mind. If psychic healing can work, so, perhaps, can psychic killing. One of the most sinister acts of the *obeahman*, or witch doctor, is to steal a person's shadow. By taking a human's spirit and psychically "nailing" it to the sacred ceiba tree, the obeahman has deprived the victim of his spirit and of the need to live.

In Haiti, French anthropologist Alfred Metraux observed a phenomenon called "sending of the dead," in which Baron Samedi, god of the graveyard, possesses the *bokor,* or sorcerer, and through him commands a client to go to a cemetery at midnight with offerings of food for the Baron. At the cemetery, the client must gather a handful of graveyard earth for each person he wishes to see killed, which he later spreads on the paths taken by the victim(s). Alternatively, the client takes a stone from the cemetery, which magically transforms itself into an evil entity, ready to do its master's bidding. To start the process, the sorcerer throws the stone against the victim's house. Metraux found that whenever a person learned he was a victim of a "sending the dead" spell, he would soon grow thin, stop eating, spit blood and die.

In all these cases, only the reversal of the spell by good magic can save the victim. The mind's capacity for belief and action overpowers all other attempts at conventional logic and scientific rationality.

Sorcerers in various cultures contend that it is possible to cause a hex death without the victim being aware of the hex.

See also POINTING; SENDING.

hex signs   Round magical signs and symbols used by the Pennsylvania Dutch, primarily to protect against hexerei (WITCHCRAFT) but also to effect SPELLS. Hex signs are both amuletic and talismanic (see AMULETS; TALISMANS). Traditionally, hex signs are painted on barns, stables and houses to protect against lightning, ensure fertility and protect animal and human occupants alike from becoming *ferhexed,* or bewitched. Hex signs also are painted on cradles, on household goods such as kitchen tools and spoon racks and on wooden or metal disks that can be hung in windows.

Each hex sign has a different meaning. Some of the symbols and designs date back to the Bronze Age—such as the SWASTIKA or solar wheel, symbol of the Cult of the Sun—and to ancient Crete and Mycenae. The most common designs or symbols, all enclosed in a circle, are stars with five, six or eight points; pentagrams, or *trudenfuss* (see PENTACLES AND PENTAGRAMS); variations of the swastika; and hearts. The six-petaled flower/star, a fertility hex sign, is painted on utensils and tools relating to livestock, especially horses, and on linens, weaver's tools, mangling boards and other items. Pomegranates also are used for fertility; oak leaves for male virility; an eagle or rooster with a heart for strength and courage; hearts and tulips for love, faith and a happy marriage.

Hex signs are designed for healing, accumulating material goods and money, starting or stopping rain and innumerable other purposes. A charm or incantation is said as the hex sign is made. Little is known about hex signs, as it is a taboo for the Pennsylvania Dutch to talk about them to outsiders.

The custom of hex signs comes from the Old World and was brought from Germany and Switzerland by the German immigrants who settled in Pennsylvania in the 1700s and 1800s. In the Old Saxon religion, it was customary to paint protective symbols on barns and household items. In Germany, tradition calls for hex signs to be placed on the frames of barns, but not on houses; in Switzerland, it is customary to place the signs on houses. The Pennsylvania Dutch borrowed both practices. Among the Pennsylvania Dutch, regional customs developed in style and placement.

In the 19th century, hex signs proliferated throughout the Pennsylvania Dutch countryside. The custom began to wane in the 20th century, as magical arts in general faded.

See also POWWOWING.

hexagram   See SEAL OF SOLOMON.

hobgoblin   See BOGEY.

hocus pocus   A purported magical phrase in the style of rhyming and alliterative incantations from GRIMOIRES. It is actually nonsense. Accounts of the term's origins vary. It has been attributed to Ochus Bochus, a legendary magician and demon of the Norse. During the reign of King JAMES I of England, the term *hocus pocus* was credited to a self-styled magician, according to *A Candle in the Dark; or a Treatise Concerning the Nature of Witches and Witchcraft* (1656) by Thomas Ady:

> I will speake of one man . . . who called himself "The Kings Majesties most excellent Hocus Pocus," and so he was called, because that at the playing of every Tricke, he used to say, "Hocus pocus, tonus talontus, vade celeriter jubeo," a dark composure of words, to blinde the eyes of the beholders, to make his trick pass the more currantly without discovery.

Most likely, *hocus pocus* is a corruption and mockery of the Latin *hoc est enim corpus meum* ("this is indeed my body"), spoken by priests at Catholic Mass.

Hocus pocus has nothing to do with MAGIC or WITCHCRAFT. It is associated with trickery and stage-magic conjuring and deceit.

Holda (also Holde, Hulda)   Fierce Germanic goddess of the sky whose nocturnal rides with the souls of the unbaptized dead led to the Christian association of her with the demonic aspects of the WILD HUNT. Holda was beautiful and stately, and bold as a Valkyrie. She also was goddess of the hearth and motherhood and ruled spinning and the cultivation of flax.

As host of the Wild Hunt, Holda was said to be accompanied by WITCHES as well as the souls of the dead. They rode uncontrollably through the night sky, shrieking and crying. The land over which they passed was said to bear double the harvest.

Holda, like other pagan deities, was linked to the DEVIL by Christians. In medieval times, she was transformed from a majestic woman to an old HAG, with a long, hooked nose, long stringy hair and sharp fangs. In folklore, she has been reduced to a BOGEY and a tender of sheep or goats.

Hopkins, Matthew (?–1647?)

England's most notorious professional witch-hunter, who brought about the condemnations and executions of at least 230 alleged WITCHES, more than all other witch-hunters combined during the 160-year peak of the country's witch hysteria.

Hopkins awas born in Wenham, Suffolk, the son of a minister. Little is known about him before 1645, when he took up his witch-hunting activities. Prior to that, he made a meager living as a mediocre lawyer, first in Ipswich and then in Manningtree.

In 1645 he announced publicly that a group of witches in Manningtree had tried to kill him. He abandoned his law practice and went into business to rid the countryside of witches. He advertised that for a fee, he and an associate, John Stearne, would travel to a village and rout them out.

Hopkins knew little about witches beyond reading King JAMES I's *Daemonologie*, but he had no shortage of business. He exploited the Puritans' hatred of WITCHCRAFT, the public's fear of it and the political turmoil of the English Civil War (1642–48). Added to this volatile mixture was a rise of feminism among women who, during the Civil War, spoke up about their discontent with their station in life and the way England was being governed. It was not uncommon for politically active Royalist women to become branded as "sorceresses" and "whores of Babylon" by the Parliamentary faction. Some of the witch-hunt victims may have been singled out because they were suspected spies.

Hopkins's method of operation was to collect gossip and innuendo and turn them into formal accusations of witchcraft and Devil-worship. Since every village had at least one hag rumored to be a witch, Hopkins was enormously successful. Most of the accused, however, were merely unpopular people against whom others had grudges. Hopkins dubbed himself "Witch-finder General" and claimed to be appointed by Parliament to hunt witches. He boasted that he possessed the "Devil's List," a coded list of the names of all the witches in England.

His first victim was a one-legged hag, Elizabeth Clark. Hopkins tortured her until she confessed to sleeping with the Devil and harboring several FAMILIARS. She accused five other persons of witchcraft. The inquisitions and extorted confessions mushroomed until at least 38 persons were remanded for trial in Chelmsford. Hopkins and Stearne testified to seeing the imps and familiars of many of the accused appear and try to help them. They were aided by 92 villagers who voluntarily stepped forward to offer "evidence" and "testimony." Of the 38 known accused, 17 were hanged; six were declared guilty but reprieved; four died in prison; and two were acquitted. The fate of the remainder is not certain (see CHELMSFORD WITCHES).

With that success, Hopkins took on four more assistants and went witch-hunting throughout Essex, Suffolk, Huntingdonshire, Norfolk, Cambridge and neighboring counties. His fees were outrageously high, between four and 26 pounds and perhaps much higher; the prevailing wage was sixpence a day. To justify his fees, Hopkins argued that ferreting out witches required great skill, and he denied that he and Stearne profited from their business.

The use of TORTURE in witch trials theoretically was forbidden in England, but it was routinely applied in most cases. Hopkins was no exception, but his torture was often excessive. He beat, starved and denied sleep to his victims. His more brutal, and favored, methods included pricking the skin for insensitive spots (see WITCH'S MARK), searching for blemishes as small as flea bites, which could be interpreted as marks of the Devil, walking victims back and forth in their cells until their feet were blistered and SWIMMING. In the latter, the victims were bound and thrown into water; if they floated, they were guilty.

When the victims were worn down by torture, Hopkins plied them with leading questions such as, "How is it you came to be acquainted with the Devil?" All he required were nods and monosyllabic answers. He and his associates filled in the colorful details of the alleged malevolent activities. Most of the charges were of bewitching people and their livestock to death; causing illness and lameness; and entertaining evil spirits such a familiars, which usually were nothing more than household pets. He was particularly fond of getting victims to admit they had signed pacts with the Devil (see DEVIL'S PACT).

Not all of his victims were framed. One man, a butcher, traveled about 10 miles to confess voluntarily. He was hanged. Another man claimed to entertain his familiar while in jail; no one else could see the creature.

Later in 1645 Hopkins enjoyed another successful mass witch trial in Suffolk, in which at least 124 persons were arrested and 68 were hanged. One of them was a 70-year-old clergyman, who, after being "walked" and denied sleep, confessed to having a pact with the Devil, having several familiars and to bewitching cattle.

Throughout his witch-hunting, Hopkins constantly searched for evidence that networks of organized covens of witches existed. He found nothing to substantiate this belief (see COVEN).

In 1646 Hopkins's witch-hunting career ended almost as abruptly as it had begun. He simply over-extended himself in greed and zeal. He was publicly criticized for his excessive tortures and high fees and began to meet resistance from judges and local authorities. In the eastern counties, mass witch trials declined, though witches were still brought to trial. Hopkins began to be criticized severely for forcing the swimming test upon people who did not want to take it. He and Stearne separated, with Hopkins returning to Manningtree and Stearne moving to Lawshall.

The fate of Hopkins remains a mystery. There is no trace of him after 1647. Popular legend has it that he was accused of witchcraft and "died miserably." William Andrews, a 19th-century writer on Essex folklore, stated in *Bygone Essex* (1892) that Hopkins was passing through Suffolk and was himself accused of "being in league with the Devil, and was charged with having stolen a memorandum book containing a list of all the witches in England, which he obtained by means of sorcery."

Hopkins pleaded innocent but was "swum" (see SWIMMING) at Mistley Pond by an angry mob. According to some accounts, he drowned, while others say he floated, was condemned and hanged. No record exists of a trial, if there was one. There is a record of his burial at the Mistley Church in 1647, though there is no tombstone (not uncommon for 17th-century graves). One chronicler of the times said that the burial must have been done "in the dark of night" outside the precincts of the Church, witnessed by no one local. Hopkins's ghost is said to haunt Mistley Pond. An apparition dressed in 17th-century attire is reportedly seen in the vicinity.

According to another story circulated, Hopkins, having fallen out of favor with the public, escaped to New England.

Stearne, however, stated in 1648, "I am certain (notwithstanding whatsoever hath been said of him) he died peacefully at Manningtree, after a long sick-

enesse of a consumption, as many of his generation had done before him, without any trouble of conscience for what he had done, as was falsely reported of him."

See also BURY ST. EDMONDS WITCHES.

Horned God   In neo-Pagan WITCHCRAFT, the consort of the GODDESS and representative of the male principle of the Supreme Deity. The Horned God is the lord of the woodlands, the hunt and animals. He also is the lord of life, death and the underworld. He is the Sun to the Goddess's Moon. The Horned God alternates with the Goddess in ruling over the fertility cycle of birth-death-rebirth. The Horned God is born at the winter solstice, unites with the Goddess in marriage at Beltane (May 1) and dies at the summer solstice. His death is a sacrifice to life.

The origin of the Horned God perhaps dates back

Satyr family (Albrecht Dürer, 1505)

to Paleolithic times, as evidenced by a ritualistic cave painting discovered in the Caverne des Trois Freres at Ariège, France. One of the figures is either a stag standing upright on hind legs or a man dressed in stag costume in a dance. The wearing of animal clothes in rituals to secure game was practiced in Europe for thousands of years.

Among the deities and beings associated with the Horned God are CERNUNNOS, the Celtic god of fertility, animals and the underworld; HERNE THE HUNTER, a specter of Britain; PAN, the Greek god of the woodlands; Janus, the Roman god of good beginnings, whose two-faced visage represents youth and age, life and death; Tammuz and Damuzi, the son-lover-consorts to ISHTAR and INANNA; OSIRIS, Egyptian lord of the underworld; and Dionysus, Greek god of vegetation and the vine, whose cult observed rites of dismemberment and resurrection.

The horns of the Horned God are associated with his domain of the woodlands, and with the bull and the ram, animal consorts of the Goddess. The horns also symbolize the crescent moon, which is the symbol of the Goddess and represents increase in all things and waxing fertility. In art, the Horned God may be portrayed as half man and half animal, as were Cernunnos and Pan. There is no association between the Horned God and the DEVIL, except in the minds of confused Christians.

Neo-Pagan Witchcraft emphasizes the Goddess, though the Horned God is considered equally important in his role in male-female polarity. He is worshipped in rites, in which he is personified by the high priest, who sometimes wears an antlered headdress or a horned helmet. The Horned God represents sexuality, vitality, the hunt, logic and power, but not in an exploitative fashion. He is considered gentle, tender and compassionate yet is not effeminate.

Horned Women, The

An old Irish legend tells of 12 horned women, all WITCHES, who take over the household of a rich woman and bewitch her and her sleeping family. No reason for the bewitching is given in the story—perhaps, in times past, no reason was necessary, for witches were believed to bewitch simply because they were witches. The legend tells of how the distressed woman breaks the spell (see SPELLS).

The bewitchment began late one night, as the woman sat up carding wool while her family and servants slept. A knock came on the door, and she asked who was there. A female voice answered, "I am the Witch of the one Horn."

The woman thought it was a neighbor and opened the door. She was greeted by an ugly woman from whose forehead grew a single horn. The witch held a pair of wool carders. She sat down by the fire and began to card wool with great speed. She suddenly paused and said, "Where are the women? they delay too long."

Another knock came on the door. The mistress of the house, who seemed to be under a spell by now, felt compelled to answer it. She was greeted by another witch, who had two horns growing from her forehead, and who carried a spinning wheel. This witch also sat down by the fire and began to spin wool with great speed.

The house soon was filled with 12 frightful-looking, horned witches, each one having an additional horn, so that the last witch bore 12 horns on her forehead. They worked furiously on the wool, singing an ancient tune, ignoring the mistress, who was unable to move or call for help.

Eventually, one of the witches ordered the mistress to make them a cake, but the woman had no vessel with which to fetch water from the WELL. The witches told her to take a sieve to the well. She did, but the water ran through the sieve, and she wept. While she was gone, the witches made a cake, using BLOOD drawn from members of the sleeping family in place of water.

As she sat weeping by the well, the mistress heard a voice. It was the Spirit of the Well, who told her how to make a paste of clay and moss and cover the sieve, so that it would hold water. It then instructed her to go back to her house from the north and cry out three time, "The mountain of the Fenian women and the sky over it is all on fire." The mistress did as instructed. The witches shrieked and cried and sped off to the Slivenamon, "the mountains of women," where they lived.

The Spirit of the Well then told the mistress how to break the witches' spell and prevent them from returning. She took the water in which she had bathed her children's feet and sprinkled it over the threshold of the house. She took the blood cake, broke it into pieces and placed them in the mouths of the bewitched sleepers, who were revived. She took the woolen cloth the witches had woven and placed it half in and half out of a padlocked chest. She barred the door with a large crossbeam.

The witches returned in a rage at having been deceived. Their fury increased when they discovered that they could not enter the house because of the water, the broken blood cake and the crossbeam. They flew off into the air, screaming curses against the Spirit of the Well, but they never returned. One of the witches dropped her mantle, which the mistress took and hung up as a reminder of her ordeal. The mantle remained in the family for 500 years.

The legend of the horned women appears to be a curious blend of pagan and Christian aspects. The well is inhabited by a spirit, a common belief among the Celts. The horns of the witches symbolize the maternal and nurturing aspect of the GODDESS, who is sometimes represented by a cow. The horns also symbolize the crescent moon, another Goddess symbol. In ancient Greek and Babylonian art, the Mother Goddess often is depicted wearing a headdress of little horns. Yet the horned women of the legend are not maternal and nurturing but HAGS who cast an evil spell, fly through the air and shriek curses—the portrayal of witches spread by the Church. Twelve, the number of wholeness and perfection, may also have significance in the legend. The 12 horned women plus the mistress of the house equal 13, the number associated in Christianity with evil, COVENS and WITCHCRAFT. The cardinal point of north is associated with power, darkness and mystery in paganism, but in Christianity it is associated with the DEVIL.

horses Sacred animals since ancient times, horses are associated with fertility, MAGIC, clairvoyancy, omens, WITCHES and pagan deities. Stone Age art found in Britain depicts men wearing horse masks. The Celts believed their souls traveled on horseback to the land of the dead.

In Britain and throughout Europe, the eating of horse flesh was traditionally taboo except during an October horse feast. In ancient Rome, the feast was begun on October 15 with a chariot race on the Field of Mars; the right-hand horse of the winning chariot was killed as a sacrifice to the gods by being stabbed to death with a spear. The head was severed and decorated with a string of loaves, and fought over by two wards in a ritual battle to determine which side would get the head as a talisman (see TALISMANS). The tail was severed and taken to the king's hearth, where the BLOOD was allowed to drip onto the hearth. The rest of the blood was preserved and, the following spring, it was mixed with other blood by the vestals and given to shepherds to be burned as a purifying agent for their flocks. The entire festival was a fertility rite to ensure good crops, with the horse being a representative of the corn-spirit. In Denmark, the October horse feast was marked by the sprinkling of horses' blood toward the east and south by a priest, in observance of the incarnation of the horse as Spirit of the Solar Year. The feast was banned in the Middle Ages by the Church.

The horse as corn-spirit appears in other pagan crop-fertility rites. In Hertfordshire, England, the reaping of crops was ended with a ceremony called "crying the Mare." The last blades of standing corn were tied together to represent the Mare. The farmers threw their sickles at it, and the one who succeeded in cutting through it won blessings.

The Gallic Celts worshipped the Greek fertility goddess, Demeter, as the Mare Goddess under the name Epona, or the Three Eponae, associated with the Triple Goddess. Epona was adopted by the Roman army, which considered her the protector of horses; the goddess enjoyed a widespread cult throughout Europe. One cult that survived in Ireland until the 12th century performed a ritual in which a petty king underwent a symbolic rebirth from a white mare. He imitated a foal by crawling toward the mare naked and on all fours. The mare was slaughtered, cut into pieces and boiled in a CAULDRON. The king got into the cauldron and ate the pieces and broth. Then he stood on an inauguration stone and received a straight white wand, which he held while turning three times left and three times right, in honor of the Trinity.

Other deities with horse aspects include Athena, Aphrodite and Cronus.

Poseidon, god of the sea, whipped horses out of the waves, symbolizing the blind, primeval forces of chaos. The horse is associated with the burial rites of ancient cults of chthonian, or underworld, spirits and deities. The horse was dedicated to Mars, god of war; the unexpected appearance of a horse was an omen of war. The horse also is linked in mythology to thunder, which it creates with its hooves.

In shamanic myth and ritual, the horse is an image of death and carries the shaman through the air to the heavens on his mystical journey to ecstasy, a transformative experience of mystical death and rebirth. Hobby horses and wooden horses—some with eight hooves—and horse-headed sticks are used in various ecstatic dance rituals and shamanic séances. In shamanic horse sacrifices in central and northern Asia, the shaman ritually forces the horse's soul from its body and captures it in preparation for his own mystical flight. The horse is blessed and then killed in a cruel manner: its back is broken so that no blood falls or splashes onto the sacrificers. The skin and bones are hung from long poles, offerings are made to ancestors and the flesh is eaten in a ceremony, with the shaman taking the best portions. The shaman's ecstatic ride astride the horse soul takes place the following evening in another ceremony (see SHAMANISM).

Dreams of horses are lucky almost everywhere in the world. White horses are especially lucky.

Carl G. Jung believed the horse represents the magic, intuitive side of mankind. Throughout history, horses have been attributed with a clairvoyant power that enables them to sense unseen danger. As a result, they are considered especially vulnerable to witches' SPELLS. In times past, witches allegedly borrowed them at night in order to ride to SABBATS, driving them hard and returning them at daybreak exhausted and covered with sweat and foam. To prevent "hag riding," bewitchment and the EVIL EYE, horse owners placed CHARMS and AMULETS in their stables and attached brass BELLS to their halters. During the witch-hunts, the DEVIL and witches were believed to have the power to transform themselves into horses (see METAMORPHOSIS).

In neo-Pagan WITCHCRAFT and NEO-PAGANISM, the sanctity of all living things is recognized, and horses are not sacrificed, nor are any other animals.

See also NIGHTMARE.

horseshoe The horseshoe has long been a common folk-magic amulet (see AMULETS) against WITCHES, FAIRIES, the DEVIL, evil spirits and the EVIL EYE throughout the British Isles, Europe and Arabia. It is nailed over the doorway of a house, church, stable or building, its IRON constitution preventing evil spirits and beings from crossing the threshold. A horseshoe placed in a chimney will prevent a witch from FLYING in on her BROOM. A horseshoe nailed to one's bed will repel NIGHTMARES and DEMONS. To be effective, the horseshoe must never be removed once it is installed. In Ireland, it once was a common practice to nail a piece of a horseshoe on the threshold of a door to keep FAIRIES out of the house.

The horseshoe also is a charm for good luck, but it cannot do double duty as a luck-bringer and Devil-repellent. To protect against WITCHCRAFT, SORCERY and demons, the horseshoe should be positioned with the ends pointed downward. As a good-luck charm, the ends should point up, so that the luck that comes does not spill out.

Huebner, Louise As "The Official Witch of Los Angeles," Louise Huebner made a media splash in the late 1960s and early 1970s with various antics and SPELLS for sexual energy. Huebner, who claimed to be a hereditary witch (see WITCHES), wrote two books and made one record, all with a somewhat tongue-in-cheek tone, which portrayed witches as mean, capricious and orgiastic individuals. They included statements such as the following: "And as a witch, I can be a lot meaner than I could have been if I were Jeane Dixon"; "I always giggle when I'm excited. It's part of being a witch"; "Enchanters need orgies. The orgies will help you generate the electrical and magnetic impulses you will need to cast spells."

According to Huebner, her mother knew she was "different" by the time she was five. Her grandmother was a fortune-teller, and Huebner began practicing fortune-telling at age 10 by reading palms (see PALMISTRY).

In Los Angeles, Huebner established herself as an astrologer and psychic. She authored a newspaper column and had her own horoscope radio show from 1965 to 1969. In 1968 Los Angeles County Supervisor Eugene Debs named her "The Official Witch of Los Angeles" in connection with a Folk Day "happening" at Hollywood Bowl. Huebner, dressed in a long silver robe, passed out red candles, chalk and garlic and led a mass ritual to cast a spell over Los Angeles County to raise its "romantic and emotional vitality." The spell consisted of an incantation: "Light the flame/Bright the fire/Red is the color of desire."

When Huebner began using the "Official Witch" appellation to promote herself, Los Angeles County attempted to stop her from doing so, stating that the title was intended for Folk Day only. Huebner called a press conference and threatened to "despell" Los Angeles County. In the ensuing publicity, the county dropped the matter.

Huebner made numerous radio and television appearances around the country. She dressed in black and carried about a pet black beetle, Sandoz. She also kept a rat and a cat. In 1970 she went to Salem, Massachusetts, where she was received by Mayor Samuel E. Zoll, who gave her a broom inscribed, "May your ride be long and enjoyable." Huebner was quoted by the press as stating the reason for her visit was to forgive Salem "for what they did to those people who were not witches" in Colonial times.

Huebner's books are *Power Through Witchcraft* (1969) and *Never Strike a Happy Medium* (1971). Her record is *Seduction Through Witchcraft*.

Hulda   See HOLDA.

I

I Ching An ancient Chinese system of oracular DIVINATION popular with neo-Pagan WITCHES and neo-Pagans (see NEO-PAGANISM). The *I Ching* ("Book of Changes") does not give specific answers to questions but reveals patterns of subtle forces at work, which helps the querier to arrive at an answer through deep introspection and intuitive thought. It points out what already lies within. Answers are given in 64 hexagrams of solid lines (*yang* or male energy) and broken lines (*yin* or female energy) which represent states of being. The most common method to determine hexagrams is to toss three coins three times. The traditional, and more complicated, method is to toss a set of 50 yarrow sticks.

The *I Ching* dates back to about 2852 B.C., when Chinese Emperor Fu-hsi developed a set of trigrams. The trigrams were doubled to hexagrams around 1143 B.C. by King Wen, a founder of the Chou dynasty. The *I Ching* has inspired many great thinkers and philosophers, including Lao Tse, who drew on it for Taoism, and Confucius, who wrote 10 commentaries on it. In the late 19th century, the *I Ching* finally reached the West, through translations by James Legge and Richard Wilhelm.

imp In MAGIC and alchemy, a small demon, usually kept inside a bottle or ring and used for HEALING, DIVINATION and CHARMS. Imps are both good and evil. They are evoked by magicians in rituals of ceremonial MAGIC and commanded with incantations, words and NAMES OF POWER. The Swiss alchemist PARACELSUS (1493–1541) was believed to keep an imp trapped in the crystal pommel of his sword, because artwork shows the pommel labeled with the word *Zoth*. Apparently, this is not the name of an imp but a reference to *azoth*, the alchemists' vital mercury.

During the witch-hunts of the Middle Ages and Renaissance, witches were said to keep imps in the form of FAMILIARS, usually animals, like toads, rodents and insects. In witch trials, the term *imp* was used interchangeably with *familiar*. Witches were believed to dispatch imps to carry out their evil deeds upon innocent people. In return, they would suckle the imps with their own blood, using their fingers or protuberances on the body. Witch-hunters searched bodies for warts, discolored skin and unnatural lumps that could serve as teats or paps.

See also DEMONS; WITCH'S MARK.

Inanna Sumerian mother goddess, queen of heaven and ruler of the cycles of the seasons and fertility. She was also called *Nina;* the name *Inanna* may be a derivative of *Nina.* She was the most widely known goddess in the later periods of Sumer. The most important legend involving her is that of the sacrifice of the divine king for the fertility of the land, and his descent to the underworld. The myth is similar to that of ISHTAR, the Babylonian and Assyrian mother goddess with whom Inanna became identified.

Inanna's son-lover-consort was Damuzi (also spelled Dumuzi and Daimuz), who, after proving himself upon her bed in a rite of *hieros gamos*, or sacred marriage, was made shepherd of the land by her. Once, Inanna walked down the steps of death to the underworld, the Land of No Return, or Irkalla. She was taken captive by the Gallas, a host of demons, and was freed only by promising that she would substitute another life for her own. She returned to heaven to search for the sacrificial victim. She considered, but rejected, a loyal servant and two minor gods, Shara and Latarrek. When she entered her own temple at Erech, Inanna was shocked to find Damuzi dressed in royal robes and sitting on her throne, instead of out tending his flocks. He seemed to be celebrating her absence rather than mourning it. Enraged, she looked at him with the Eye of Death, and the Gallas dragged Damuzi off to the underworld. Each year, Inanna mourned his death, which brought winter to the land.

From about 2600 B.C. to post-Sumerian times, the kings of Sumer mystically identified themselves with Damuzi and were known as the "beloved husbands" of Inanna. At the New Year, an important rite of *hieros gamos* was performed between the king and the high priestess of Inanna, who represented the goddess.

See also GODDESS.

initiation   One of the most ancient of rites, initiation marks the psychological crossing of a threshold into new territories, knowledge and abilities. The central themes of initiation are suffering, death and rebirth. The initiate undergoes an ordeal, symbolically dies and is symbolically reborn as a new person, possessing new wisdom.

In neo-Pagan WITCHCRAFT, initiation marks entry into a closed and traditionally secret society; opens the door to the learning of ritual secrets, MAGIC and the development and use of psychic powers; marks a spiritual transformation, in which the initiate begins a journey into Self and toward the Divine Force; and marks the beginning of a new religious faith. While traditional initiation rites exist, many WITCHES and neo-Pagans feel the spiritual threshold may be crossed in many alternate ways, all of them valid. Initiation may be experienced in a group or alone. It may be formal or informal. It may be performed with an old ritual or a new one; it may come as a spontaneous spiritual awakening, in meditation or in dreams. It may occur at a festival.

Historical Beliefs about Witch Initiations

Historically, a witch's initiation was believed to be dark and diabolic, marked by obscene rituals. During the witch-hunts of the Middle Ages and Renaissance, stories of offensive initiation rituals were commonly believed. Many of them came from confessions made by accused witches who were tortured by inquisitors. The stories varied, but there were common threads to all of them. Some witches were initiated at birth or puberty, claiming their mothers had taken them to SABBATS, presented them to the DEVIL and pledged them to his service. Adult candidates were scouted

Newly initiated witches attending Satan at court (Gerard d'Euphrates, *Livre de l'histoire & ancienne cronique*, 1549)

and recruited by the local officers of covens (see COVEN). After consenting of their own free will to join, they were formally presented to the coven and initiated. Much of the rite was a parody of Christian rites, which fit the prevailing beliefs of the time.

The ceremony, at which the Devil himself was present, took place in a remote location at night. The initiates sometimes brought a copy of the Gospels, which they gave to the Devil. They renounced the Christian faith and baptism by reciting, "I renounce and deny God, the blessed Virgin, the Saints, baptism, father, mother, relations, heaven, earth and all that is the world," according to Pierre de Lancre, 17th-century French witch-hunter. The initiates then pledged a vow of fealty. Scottish witches said they placed one hand upon their crown and the other upon the sole of one foot, dedicating all between the two hands to the service of the Devil. Scandinavian witches reportedly put metal clock shavings and stones in little bags and tossed them in the water, saying, "As these shavings of the clock do never return to the clock from which they are taken, so may my soul never return to heaven."

Satan baptizing a disciple (R. P. Guaccius, *Compendium Maleficarum*, 1626)

The Devil baptized the initiates, gave them new, secret names, to be used only in the coven, and marked them permanently either by scratching them with his claw or biting them (see DEVIL'S MARK). The new witches were required to kiss the Devil's anus (see KISS OF SHAME), a parody of the kissing of the Pope's foot. Sometimes they were made to trample and spit upon the cross. The Devil cut them or pricked their fingers and had them sign pacts (see DEVIL'S PACT.) Finally, he stripped them of their clothing and assigned them one or more FAMILIARS. The coven officer or the Devil recorded their name in a "black book," a membership and attendance record for all coven meetings. Sometimes black fowl or animals were sacrificed to the Devil. After the ceremony, all the witches participated in wild dancing, copulating with the Devil or his demons and feasting upon vile things such as the flesh of roasted, unbaptized babies.

The fantastical, horrible elements of these tales may be ascribed to TORTURE or, in some cases, delusions. Some accounts may have been the result of hallucinatory drug experiences (see OINTMENTS). MARGARET A. MURRAY, a British anthropologist, theorized that witch covens were remnants of organized pagan religions. Their leader was not the Devil but a man chosen to represent the HORNED GOD, whom witch-hunters identified with the Devil. According to Murray, such pagan groups recruited followers and conducted formal initiation ceremonies, which may have included blood oaths of fealty to the god, the marking with TATTOOS, the dedication of children to the god and dancing. Drugs may have been taken, for drugs have been, and are, part of many religious rites and ceremonies around the world. Murray also said that sexual initiatory rites recognized the em-phasis on fertility in paganism. It is possible that some of the descriptions of initiations at sabbats may have been distortions of old pagan rites, but Murray's theory of the continuity of organized paganism has been refuted by most historians.

Initiations in the Modern Craft and Neo-Paganism

In neo-Pagan Witchcraft, initiatory rites bear no resemblance to the descriptions offered by those early witch-hunters and demonologists. Rites vary according to tradition but generally keep to the universal theme of suffering-death-rebirth. Despite variations, there are several things that universally are *not* part of initiation into the Craft:

1. There is no renunciation of the Christian faith or any faith.
2. There is no homage to the Devil, including kisses, oaths or pacts. Satan is not recognized by neo-Pagan Witches or neo-Pagans.
3. There is no blood sacrifice.

Traditionally, a Witch is not considered a true member of the Craft without formal initiation into a coven, after an apprenticeship period of a year and a day. Women must be initiated by a high priest, men by a high priestess. Among some hereditary Witches, mothers may initiate daughters and fathers, sons.

In the Gardnerian and Alexandrian traditions, the largest traditions in modern Witchcraft, the initiation is a formal ceremony conducted within a MAGIC CIRCLE. Both traditions have a system of three degrees of advancement, the entry to each level of which is marked by initiation. There are some differences between the two traditions, but the major aspects are similar. Advancement through the degrees is, like Masonry, advancement through the Mysteries of Western occultism; progressively, more secret teachings are revealed.

In a first-degree initiation, the candidate is blindfolded and bound with cords and challenged outside the magic circle as to the courage to continue. The initiate responds that he or she is ready with "perfect love and perfect trust" to suffer to be purified and learn. Once inside the circle, the candidate is ritually scourged (whipped lightly with cords); measured with a cord, which is tied in knots to mark the measures; and administered an oath. In the presence of the Goddess(es), God(s), Guardians, Mighty Dead and Sisters and Brothers of the Craft, the initiate vows to guard and protect the Craft, the Secrets of the Craft, and the brothers and sisters of the Craft, and, in some traditions, to render aid to said brothers and sisters.

The candidate is ritually anointed and kissed; proclaimed a Witch; and presented with a set of magical tools (see WITCHES' TOOLS). The initiate adopts a Craft name. In the Alexandrian tradition, the measure is given back to the Witch. In the Gardnerian tradition, it is customary for the initiator to keep the measure. According to GERALD B. GARDNER, the English Witch for whom the Gardnerian tradition is named, the measure serves as a sort of insurance policy that the oath will be kept. In the "old days" (Gardner did not specify how far back the "old days" go), if a Witch broke the oath of secrecy, his or her cord was buried with CURSES, so that as it rotted, so would the traitor.

In the second-degree initiation, the Witch is blindfolded and bound, and renews the oath that it is necessary to suffer to learn and be purified. A ritual scourging follows. The Witch assumes a new Craft name and is willed the magical power of the initiator. The third-degree initiation, the consummation of the Mysteries, involves the GREAT RITE, a sexual ritual that may be done in actuality or symbolically, with magical tools. All initiations end with a celebration of food and drink (see CAKES-AND-WINE).

Not all Witches follow these same procedures. Many Witches practice as SOLITARIES and do not feel they have to join covens in order to be Witches. They initiate themselves in self-designed rituals. Rites may include ritual baths (a form of baptism), anointing and pledges to serve the GODDESS and use the powers of Witchcraft for the good of others. Other Witches, as well as many neo-Pagans, have a vision quest as initiation. A Native American Indian tradition, a vision quest involves fasting and an all-night, solitary vigil outdoors, during which the initiate comes into direct contact with the gods, discovers his or her own "medicine power" and connects with tutelary, totemic or guardian spirits, which usually assume animal or bird form. Still other Witches and neo-Pagans undertake a shamanic initiation, an ecstatic journey to higher planes of consciousness (see SHAMANISM). Shamanic initiations vary around the world. In many, the initiative suffers symbolic death by gruesome dismemberment; he or she is then reassembled and imbued with magical powers of clairvoyant vision for healing the sick and seeing the future. In other initiations, the shaman makes an ascsent to the sky, where he learns the secrets of the universe and acquires his magical powers.

In shamanic cultures, shamanic initiations often involve blood sacrifices of animals and the ingestion of intoxicants. Neo-Pagan shamanic initiations eschew blood sacrifices (animal life is sacrosanct); the taking of intoxicants is an individual choice. Drugs officially are not part of neo-Pagan Witchcraft initiation rites.

See also LAURIE CABOT; PATRICIA C. CROWTHER.

Innocent VIII, Pope (1432–1492; papacy 1484–1492).

Giovanni Batista Cibo, elected pope in 1484, issued what has been termed one of the most important documents in the history of the Church's fight against witchcraft: the Bull of 1484, *Summis desiderantes affectibus* ("Desiring with supreme ardor"). Though credited with launching the Inquisition full force against WITCHES, it actually followed a long line of earlier bulls inveighing against WITCHCRAFT and SORCERY, issued since the 13th century.

The CANON EPISCOPI of 906 had relegated witchcraft to the realm of fantasy, but in the 13th century, popes began to speak out on their beliefs in the reality of witchcraft as an evil against mankind. In his first year as pope, Innocent VIII was approached by Heinrich Kramer and Jacob Sprenger, two Dominican inquisitors, who persuaded him that they were being impeded by local ecclesiastical authorities in their efforts to prosecute witches. They asked for help, and the result was the Bull of 1484, which granted them full authority to carry out their inquisitions and demanded that they receive whatever support was necessary from local officials.

The bull, noted Sir Walter Scott in *Letters on Demonology and Witchcraft* (1830), "rang the tocsin against this formidable crime [of sorcery], and set forth in the most dismal colours the guilt, while it stimulated the inquisitors to the unsparing discharge of their duty in searching out and punishing the guilty." Its chief object was to transfer the crimes of sorcery to the Waldenses, a religious sect labeled heretics, "and excite and direct the public hatred against the new sect by confounding their doctrines with the influences of the devil and his fiends."

Text of the Bull of Pope Innocent VII, 1484

Desiring with supreme ardor, as pastoral solicitude requires, that the catholic faith in our days everywhere grow and flourish as much as possible, and that all heretical pravity be put far from the territories of the faithful, we freely declare and anew decree this by which our pious desire may be fulfilled, and, all errors being rooted out by our toil as with the hoe of a wise laborer, zeal and devotion to this faith may take deeper hold on the hearts of the faithful themselves.

It has recently come to our ears, not without great pain to us, that in some parts of upper Germany, as well as in the provinces, cities, territories, regions, and dioceses of Mainz, Köln, Trier, Salzburg, and Bremen, many persons of both sexes, heedless of their own salvation and forsaking the catholic faith, give themselves over to devils male and female, and by their incantations, charms and conjurings, and by other abominable superstitions and sortileges, offences, crimes, and misdeeds, ruin and cause to perish the offspring of women, the foal of animals, the products of the earth, the grapes of vines, and the fruits of trees, as well a men and women, cattle and flocks and herds and animals of every kind, vineyards also and orchards, meadows, pastures, harvests, grains and other fruits of the earth; that they afflict and torture with dire pains and anguish, both internal and external, these men, women, cattle, flocks, herds, and animals, and hinder men from begetting and women from conceiving, and prevent all consummation of marriage; that, moreover, they deny with sacrilegious lips the faith they received in holy baptism; and that, at the instigation of the enemy of mankind, they do not fear to commit and perpetrate many other abominable offences and crimes, at the risk of their own souls, to the insult of the divine majesty and to the pernicious example and scandal of multitudes. And, although our beloved sons Henricus Institoris [Kramer] and Jacobus Sprenger, of the order of Friars Preachers, professors of theology, have been and still are deputed by our apostolic letters as inquisitors of heretical pravity, the former in the aforesaid parts of upper Germany, including the provinces, cities, territories, dioceses, and other places as above, and the latter throughout certain parts of the course of the Rhine; nevertheless certain of the clergy and of the laity of those parts, seeking to be wise above what is fitting, because in the said letter of deputation that aforesaid provinces, cities, dioceses, territories, and other places, and the persons and offences in question were not individually and specifically named, do not blush obstinately to assert that these are not at all included in the said parts and that therefore it is illicit for the aforesaid inquisitors to exercise their office of inquisition in the provinces, cities, dioceses, territories, and other places aforesaid, and that they ought not to be permitted to proceed to the punishment, imprisonment, and correction of the aforesaid persons for the offences and crimes above named. Wherefore in the provinces, cities, dioceses, territories, and places aforesaid such offences and crimes, not without evident damage to their souls and risk of external salvation, go unpunished.

We therefore, desiring, as is our duty, to remove all impediments by which in any way the said inquisitors are hindered in the exercise of their office, and to prevent the taint of heretical pravity and of other like evils from spreading their infection to the ruins of others who are innocent, the dioceses, territories, and places aforesaid in the said parts of upper Germany may not be deprived of the office of the inquisition which is their due, to hereby decree, by virtue of our apostolic authority, that it shall be permitted to the said inquisitors of these regions to exercise their office of inquisition and to proceed to the correction, imprisonment, and punishment of the aforesaid persons for their said offences and crimes, in all respects and altogether precisely as if the provinces, cities, territories, places, persons, and offences aforesaid were expressly named in the said letter. And, fore the greater sureness, extending the said letter and deputation to the provinces, cities, dioceses, territories, places, persons and crimes aforesaid, we grant to the said inquisitors that they or either of them, joining with them our beloved son Johannes Gremper, cleric of the diocese of Constance, master of arts, their present notary, or any other notary public who by them or by either of them shall have been temporarily delegated in the provinces, cities, dioceses, territories, and places aforesaid, may exercise against all persons, of whatsoever condition and rank, the said office of the inquisition, correcting, imprisoning, punishing and chastising, according to their deserts, those persons whom they shall find guilty as aforesaid.

And they shall also have full and entire liberty to propound and preach to the faithful the word of God, as often as it shall seem to them fitting and proper, in each and all the parish churches in the said provinces, and to do all things necessary and suitable under the aforesaid circumstances, and likewise freely and fully to carry them out.

And moreover we enjoin by apostolic writ on our venerable brother, the Bishop of Strasburg, that, either in his own person or through some other or others solemnly publishing the foregoing wherever, whenever, and how often soever he may deem expedient or by these inquisitors or either of them may be legitimately required, he permit them not to be molested or hindered in any manner whatsoever by any authority whatsoever in the matter of the aforesaid and of this present letter, threatening all oposers, hinderers, contradictors, and rebels, of whatever rank, state, decree, eminence, nobility, excellence, or condition they may be, and whatever privilege of exemption they may enjoy, with excommunication, suspension, interdict, and other still more terrible sentences, censures and penalties, as may be expedient, and this without appeal and with power after due process of law of aggravating and reaggravating these penalties, by our authority, as often as may be necessary, to this end calling in aid, if need be, of the secular arm.

And this, all other apostolic decrees and earlier decisions to the contrary notwithstanding; or if to any, jointly or severally, there has been granted by this apostolic see exemption from interdict, suspension, or excommunication, by apostolic letters not making entire, express, and literal mention of the said grant of exemption; or if there exist any other indulgence whatsoever, general or special, of whatsoever tenor, by failure to name which or to insert it bodily in the present letter the carrying out of this privilege could be hindered or in any way put off,—

or any of whose whole tenor special mention must be made in our letters. Let no man, therefore, dare to infringe this page of our declaration, extension, grant, and mandate, or with rash hardihood to contradict it. If any presume to attempt this, let him know that he incurs the wrath of almighty God and of the blessed apostles Peter and Paul.

Given in Rome, at St. Peter's in the year of Our Lord's incarnation 1484, on the nones of December, in the first year of our pontificate.

Immediately upon receipt of the bull, Kramer began a crusade against witches at Innsbruck. He was initially opposed by the local government, though this opposition eventually gave way not only to support but to active participation in witch-hunts. Kramer and Sprenger used the bull at the forefront of their witch-hunter's bible, the MALLEUS MALEFICARUM, published in 1486 and widely circulated throughout Europe. The worst witch-hunts and executions subsequently took place during the 16th and 17th centuries. In 1523 Pope Adrian VI enforced the Bull of 1484 with a new one, providing for excommunication of "sorcerers and heretics."

See also POPES AND SORCERY.

invocations   See EVOCATIONS AND INVOCATIONS.

iron   Iron plays a curious role in WITCHCRAFT, SORCERY and the supernatural. In folklore around the world, iron is believed to be one of the best charms against WITCHES, sorcerers, DEMONS and other evil spirits. In Europe, folklore holds that witches cannot pass over cold iron, and burying a knife under the doorstep of one's house will ensure that no witch will ever enter. In some rural locales, iron has been used to protect entire villages. In India, iron will repel the DJINN and other evil spirits; in Scotland, Ireland and Europe, iron also keeps away mischievious and malicious FAIRIES. In some parts, iron keeps ghosts away as well (see GHOSTS, HAUNTINGS AND WITCHCRAFT).

Despite these beliefs, witches and sorcerers throughout history have used iron cauldrons (see CAULDRON) and utensils for their MAGIC, with no ill effects. Similarly, some ghosts ignore the supernatural properties of iron, if one is to judge from the tales of iron-chain-clanking spirits rumbling about old castles.

In some cultures, iron has been sacred. The ancient Babylonians, Egyptians and Aztecs believed it came from heaven, perhaps because meteorites are comprised of iron and other metals.

But in ancient Greece and Rome, iron was forbidden inside temples and for use by priests. The ancient Saxons would not put iron rune wands in cemeteries because they feared the iron would scare away the departed spirits.

Iron has been a popular metal for AMULETS to protect against danger, bad luck and the EVIL EYE, as well as against evil spirits and witches. Baylonian and Assyrian men wore amulets fashioned of iron in the belief that they would enhance their virility; the women rubbed themselves with iron powder in order to attract men. Ancient Egyptians inserted iron amulets in the linen wrappings of a mummy in order to invoke the protection of the Eye of Horus. In some parts of Burma, river men still wear iron pyrite amulets as protection against crocodiles.

The 18th-century magnetist, Franz Anton Mesmer, used iron in his attempts to heal illness. Patients sat in tubs filled with water and iron fillings, with protruding iron rods. Mesmer believed the iron conducted animal magnetism, the vital energy he said was in every human body.

See also BRASS; HORSESHOE.

Ishtar   The great mother goddess of ancient Assyrian and Babylonian mythology. She was said to be either the daughter of the sky god, Anu, or the moon god, Sin. Over the course of time, Ishtar absorbed the characteristics of other goddesses and so represents different aspects. Worship of her spread throughout the Middle East, Greece and Egypt. She was an ORACLE. She ruled over fertility, sex and war and protected man against evil. As the many-breasted Opener of the Womb, she was the giver of all life; as the Destroyer and Queen of the Underworld, she also was the taker of all life. As goddess of the MOON, her waxing and waning ruled the cyclical birth and death of the planet. She was the Heavenly Cow, the Green One, the Mistress of the Field.

Her son, Tammuz, also called the Green One, became her lover upon his reaching manhood. Ishtar descended to the realm of the dead to rescue Tammuz, a myth nearly identical to an earlier Sumerian myth of INANNA and Damuzi, and similar to the myth of DEMETER and Kore. When Ishtar descended, both fertility and sexual desire went dormant, to await her seasonal return.

As Queen of Heaven, Ishtar replaced Sin as the moon deity; she rode through the sky at night in a chariot drawn by goats or lions. The Zodiac was known as the "girdle of Ishtar," which also refers to the ancient moon calendar. She was the giver of omens and prophecy through dreams, and through her magic, others could obtain secret knowledge.

Ishtar was associated with the planet Venus. The lion and dove were sacred to her.

See also GODDESS.

Isis   The ancient Egyptian Mother Goddess, the prototype of the faithful wife and fertile, protective mother. She is associated with Sirius, the dog star, the rising of which signals the vernal eqinox. Her symbol is the MOON. She is often shown crowned with a lunar orb nestled between the horns of a bull or ram. The worship of Isis was adopted by the Greeks and Romans.

The name *Isis* is the Greek word for the Egyptian hieroglyphic for "throne." She was the sister and wife of the god OSIRIS. A mortal magician, Isis acquired immortality by tricking the sun god, Ra, into revealing his secret name. She obtained some of his spit, made a snake from it and left the snake in his path. Ra was bitten and in great agony. She offered to relieve the pain if he would tell her his secret name, and he relented.

When Osiris's treacherous brother, Set (see also SETH), murdered and dismembered him, Isis scoured the land to find the body parts and used her magic to put them together and breathe life into the body so that she and Osiris could be together one last time before he left to rule the underworld. A son, Horus, was born posthumously and in a virgin birth, and Isis protected the child against Set until Horus was old enough to fight. In art, she was often depicted holding Horus in her arms. After the child was born, Set returned and cut the body of Osiris into 14 pieces, which he scattered along the Nile. Once again, Isis went in search of them, but this time she buried each piece where she found it, so that it would fertilize the land.

Isis of the mysteries and Hermetic wisdom. According to Plutarch, numerous ancient writers believed Isis to be the daughter of HERMES, while others said she was the daughter of Prometheus. Plutarch said her name meant "wisdom." She was known as the goddess of 10,000 appellations. In the Egyptian mysteries, Isis represented the female aspect of the Deity to mankind; she was the Universal Mother of all that lives; wisdom, truth and power. Statues of her were decorated with stars, the moon and the sun. Her girdle was joined together with four golden plates which signify the four elements of nature. Her priests were adept at controlling and using the Unseen Forces.

According to Hermetic wisdom, Isis, the Goddess of Women, was schooled by Hermes. With him, she invented the writings of all nations, caused men to love women, invented sailing, gave mankind its laws, ended cannibalism, made justice more powerful than GOLD or SILVER, instructed mankind in the mysteries and caused truth to be considered beautiful. An inscription at her temple at Sais read: "I am that which is, which hath been, and which shall be; and no man has ever lifted the veil that hides my Divinity from mortal eyes." The Isis of the mysteries is completely veiled by a scarlet cloth. To initiates who learn her mysteries, she lifts her veil, ·and they are to remain forever silent about what they have seen.

The Bembine Table of Isis. In 1527, after the sacking of Rome, a bronze tablet measuring 50 by 30 inches and decorated with silver and enamel inlay came into the possession of a locksmith or ironworker, who sold it to Cardinal Bembo of Italy. The Bembine Table of Isis, or Isaic Table, is covered with hieroglyphics and inscriptions concerning mystical knowledge and an occult system of sacrifices, rites and ceremonies. It apparently was once used as an altar, perhaps in the chambers where the mysteries of Isis were revealed to initiates. ELIPHAS LEVI believed the tablet was a key to the Book of Thoth (see THOTH), or the TAROT. The tablet is in the Museum of Antiquities at Turin.

Isis (Athanasius Kircher, *Oedipus Aegyptiacus*, 1652)

Isis as goddess of magic and healing. Isis possessed powerful magic that made even Anubis, god of death, subject to her whims. Therefore, people prayed to her on behalf of the sick and dying. She was goddess of healing and childbirth. At night, she visited the sick, brushing them gently with her wings as she said magical incantations to heal them.

Isis is identified as the Virgin in the constellation Virgo. In Christianity, she has been absorbed by the Virgin Mary. Her image is used in association with magical arts, the occult, thaumaturgy and sorcery.

See also GODDESS; HERMETICA.

Island Magee Witches   The last witch trial to occur in Ireland took place in 1711 and involved the mysterious death of a widow, poltergeist activities and the bizarre possession of a serving girl. The accused WITCHES were not executed but sentenced to a much milder punishment of imprisonment and public ridicule.

The incidents leading to the trial began in September 1710. Anne Hattridge (also spelled Haltridge), widow of the Presbyterian minister at Island Magee, visited the home of her son, James, and his wife. The widow was plagued every night by some unseen force which hurled stones and turf onto her bed (see LITHOBOLY), blew open the curtains, stripped off her nightclothes and snatched the pillows from under her head. Frightened, Mrs. Hattridge finally moved to another room.

But the mysterious activities continued in other forms. On December 11, as Mrs. Hattridge sat by the fire at about twilight, a strange little boy about 12 years old appeared suddenly and sat down beside her. She couldn't see his face, because he kept it covered with a worn blanket, but she observed that he had short black hair and was dressed in dirty and torn clothing. He didn't answer her questions as to who he was or where he'd come from but danced "very nimbly" around the kitchen and then ran out of the house and into the cow shed. The servants attempted to catch him, but the boy had vanished as suddenly as he had appeared.

The apparition did not manifest again until February 11, 1711, when it apparently took a book of sermons that Mrs. Hattridge had been reading. The next day, the boy appeared outside the house, thrust his hand through a glass window and held out the book to one of the servants. He declared Mrs. Hattridge would never get the book back and that the DEVIL had taught him how to read.

The servant, named Margaret Spear, exclaimed, "The Lord bless me from thee!" But the boy laughed and produced a sword, threatening to kill all the occupants of the house. They couldn't prevent him from entering, he said, because the Devil could make him any size or creature he pleased (see METAMORPHOSIS). He threw a stone through the window. When the frightened girl next looked out, she saw the boy catching a turkey cock and making off with it into the woods. The bird managed to escape his grasp.

Then the girl saw the boy begin to dig in the ground with his sword. He announced that he was "making a grave for a corpse which will come out of this house very soon." He flew off into the air (see FLYING).

All was quiet in the Hattridge household until February 15, when Mrs. Hattridge's clothes were moved about her room and then were found laid out on the bed like a corpse. By this time, the news of the supernatural activities had spread throughout town, and numerous people, including the new Presbyterian minister, had come to the house to investigate. No one was able to help. One night, Mrs. Hattridge awoke at midnight complaining of a great pain in her back, as though she'd been stabbed with a knife. The pain persisted and Mrs. Hattridge's condition began to deteriorate, until she died on February 22. During her last days, her clothing continued to be moved mysteriously about various rooms in the house. The townspeople gossiped that Mrs. Hattridge had been bewitched to death.

On February 27 a servant girl named Mary Dunbar came to stay at the house to keep the younger Mrs. Hattridge company. The night she arrived, Dunbar was plagued by supernatural trouble. She found her clothing scattered about and one of her aprons tied into five knots (see KNOTS). She undid them and found a flannel cap that had belonged to the deceased Mrs. Hattridge. On the following day she was suddenly seized with a violent pain in her thigh and suffered fits and ravings.

Dunbar exclaimed that several women were bewitching her; she described them during two fits and gave their names: Janet Liston, Elizabeth Seller, Kate M'Calmond, Janet Carson, Janet Mean, Janet Latimer and "Mrs. Ann." Accordingly, the suspects were arrested and brought to trial. Whenever one of them was brought near Dunbar (usually without Dunbar's knowledge), the young girl fell into fits, hearing and seeing visions of her tormentors and vomiting up great quantities of feathers, cotton, yarn, pins and buttons (see ALLOTRIOPHAGY). She would repeat her conversations with the alleged witches and thrash about so violently that it took three strong men to hold her down. According to testimony by Rev. Dr. Tisdall, vicar of Belfast:

In her fits she often had her tongue thrust into her windpipe in such a manner than she was like to choak, and the root seemed pulled up into her mouth.

Dunbar claimed her tormentors prohibited her from leaving her room. Whenever she attempted to do so for a while, she fell into fits. One witness claimed he saw a knotted bracelet of yarn appear mysteriously around her wrist. Dunbar also said her tormentors told her she would not be able to give evidence against them in court. During the entire trial, she was struck dumb and sat senseless as though in a trance. Later, Dunbar said she had been possessed by three of the accused witches throughout the proceedings.

According to an account of the trial in MacSkimin's *History of Carrickfergus:*

> It was also deposed that strange noises, as of whistling, scratching, etc., were heard in the house, and that a sulphureous [sic] smell was observed in the rooms; that stones, turf, and the like were thrown about the house, and the coverlets, etc., frequently taken off the beds and made up in the shape of a corpse; and that a bolster [ghost] once walked out of a room into the kitchen with a nightgown about it!

The defendants, none of whom had a lawyer, all denied the charges of WITCHCRAFT, and the "one with the worst looks, and therefore the greatest suspect, called God to witness she was wronged." According to court records,

Their characters were inquired into, and some were reported unfavorably of, which seemed to be rather due to their ill appearance than to any facts provided against them. It was made to appear on oath that most of them had received the Communion, some of them very lately, that several of them had been laborious, industrious people, and had frequently been known to pray with their families, both publickly and privately; most of them could say the Lord's Prayer . . . they being every one Presbyterians.

The trial was short, lasting from six o'clock in the morning until two in the afternoon. In Judge Upton's opinion, there was insufficient evidence to convict the defendants. He had no doubt that Dunbar's affliction was "preternatural and diabolical," but if the defendants really were witches in compact with the Devil, "it could hardly be presumed that they should be such constant attenders upon Divine Service, both in public and private." He instructed the jury that they could not reach a guilty verdict "upon the sole testimony of the afflicted person's visionary images."

The jury felt differently, however, and declared a guilty verdict for all defendants. They were sentenced to a year in jail and to stand in a pillory four times during their incarceration. While pilloried, the "unfortunate wretches" were pelted with eggs and cabbage stalks; one of them was blinded in one eye.

J

Jack-in-the-Green   See GREEN MAN.

jack-o'-lantern   A phosphorescent light seen in marsh and swamp areas, which in folklore is either the manifestation of a malicious lost soul or a death omen. Jack-o'-lantern is known by various names, including will-o'-the-wisp and corpse light (England); fairy light and fox fire (Ireland).

According to the most common legends, the jack-o'-lantern is a wandering soul who has been denied entry into both heaven and hell. Clothed in a luminous garment or carrying a lighted wisp of straw, it drifts about at night, scaring travelers and beckoning them to follow it into the marshes. CHARMS to protect oneself against the spirit include carrying an object made of IRON, which is believed to repel evil spirits, or sticking an iron knife into the ground.

In Ireland, children who are caught outdoors after dark are told to wear their jackets inside-out in order not to be lured astray by a jack-o'-lantern. In Sweden, the spirit is believed to be the soul of an unbaptized child, who tries to lead travelers to water in hopes of receiving baptism. The jack-o'-lantern also appears in American Indian and Appalachian folklore. The Penobscot Indians call it the ''fire demon,'' who has lighted fingertips which it spins in a wheel, and skims the milk at dairies during the night. In the Appalachians, mysterious, firelike balls of light appear in the hills at night and float, move and bob about the countryside. Some are quite large and rise high into the air; others light up the surroundings like daylight. In Africa, the jack-o'-lantern light is called a ''witch-fire'' and is believed to be the witch herself, flying through the air, or a light sent by the witch to scare wrongdoers. As a corpse light, the eerie glow forecasts death in a household by hovering over a rooftop or even appearing on top of the chest of the person who is about to die.

In popular American lore, the jack-o'-lantern is associated with WITCHES and the Halloween custom of trick-or-treating. It is customary for trick-or-treaters to carry pumpkin jack-o'-lanterns to frighten away evil spirits.

James I (1566–1625)   King of England from 1603 until his death in 1625, James I has been cast in a dark light by many historians on the subject of WITCHCRAFT. He is described as being overly superstitious, neurotic, paranoid and fanatical in his desire to extirpate WITCHES. He is blamed for fanning the flames of witch hysteria and for instigating passage of a tougher anti-witch statute in 1604. There is, however, evidence that such characterizations have been blown out of proportion. James's own beliefs about witchcraft reflected the popular views of the day, and while he permitted prosecutions of accused witches, he did not lead the charge against them. When public hysteria threatened to get out of hand, he moved to cool tensions down. ''James was not riding the storm like Odin,'' notes George Lyman Kittredge in *Witchcraft in Old and New England* (1929). ''He was only a mortal man, swept off his feet by the tide.''

James was born in Scotland in 1566 to Mary Queen of Scots and her second husband, Lord Henry Stuart Darnley, a vicious and dissipitated man. In 1567 Darnley was murdered by strangulation. His death was rumored to be the plot of the Earl of Bothwell, who then married Mary. The incident caused an uprising among the Scots; Mary abdicated the throne in favor of James, who ruled under regents until

1583, when he began his personal rule as James VI.

The same year, the Scottish clergy, pressured by rising public fears of witchcraft, demanded tougher enforcement of Scotland's witchcraft law, which had been enacted in 1563. James, credulous in his beliefs that witches were evil and posed a threat to God-fearing people, tolerated the increasing witch-hunts.

James was highly skeptical of the confessions made by accused witches in the North Berwick trials of 1590–92, even though the confessions involved an alleged plot by witches to murder him and his bride. In 1589 James had agreed to marry by proxy Anne of Denmark, a 15-year-old princess whom he had never met. That same year, she set sail for Scotland from Norway, but her ship was buffeted twice by terrible storms and nearly destroyed. It made port at Oslo, where the passengers were stranded for months. James sailed out to meet the ship. As a result of more storms, he and Anne were forced to remain in Scandinavia until the spring of 1590. On their return to Scotland, they were buffeted by yet more storms but managed to make land safely. The North Berwick witches claimed to have raised these storms. James, however, called them "extreme lyars," until one of the accused convinced him of their supernormal powers by repeating to him the private conversation he had had with Anne on their wedding night (see NORTH BERWICK WITCHES). James permitted brutal tortures and executions of the accused.

After the North Berwick affair, James made a study of witchcraft on the Continent and read the works of the leading demonologists. He was distressed by the counterarguments on the "witchcraft delusion" posed by REGINALD SCOT in *The Discoverie of Witchcraft* (1584) and by JOHAN A. WEYER in *De Praestigiis Daemonum* (1563). He wrote his own response, *Daemonologie*, which first appeared in 1597.

Daemeonologie has been blamed for adding to the public hysteria over witches, though Kittredge points out that it added nothing new to the prevailing beliefs about witches. Nevertheless, the book did much to reinforce prevailing beliefs. In it, James acknowledged that witches had the power to raise storms; cause illness and death by burning waxen images; and were followers of "Diana and her wandering court" (see DIANA). He stated that the DEVIL appeared in the likeness of a dog, cat, ape or other "such-like beast" and always was inventing new techniques for deceiving others (see BLACK SHUCK; METAMORPHOSIS). He defended SWIMMING as a test for witches and supported the widely held belief that more women were witches than men because women were inherently weak and predisposed to evil. He accepted the execution of a witch as the therapeutic cure for the victim. He advocated the death penalty for clients of "cunning men." He defined a witch as "a consulter with familiar spirits."

By 1597 the witch hysteria in Scotland had reached alarming proportions, and there was evidence that overzealous witch-hunters were indicting people on fraudulent evidence. James reacted by revoking all indictments, and for the remaining years of his rule on the throne of Scotland, executions for witchcraft decreased.

Upon the death of Elizabeth I in 1603, James gained the English throne as James I. His *Daemonologie* was reissued in London the same year, and he ordered copies of Scot's *Discoverie* to be burned.

In 1604 a new Witchcraft Act was passed by Parliament, which stiffened the penalties for witchcraft. The impetus for the new law had already begun years before (see WARBOYS WITCHES) and was neither the idea nor the work of James but of the ruling gentry of England.

The 1604 law closely followed the Elizabethan Witchcraft Act. Under the Elizabethan code, witchcraft, enchantment, CHARMS or SORCERY that caused bodily injury to people or damage to their goods and chattel was punishable by a year in jail with quarterly exposures in the pillory for the first offense and death for the second offense. A sentence of life in jail with quarterly pillory exposures was given for the divining of treasure and the causing of "unlawful" love and intentional hurt. Bewitching a person to death was a capital offense.

The 1604 law punished crimes of witchcraft with death on the first offense instead of a year in jail or life in jail. In addition, the conjuring or evoking of evil spirits for any purpose whatsoever was made a capital offense. Kittredge points out that the law was no tougher than the rest of England's penal code, which mandated death for stealing a sheep or a purse, or breaking into a home. Ironically, the death sentence may have been a blessing: the jails of the time were so abominable and filthy that death might have seemed infinitely preferable to life in a stinking, dank, disease-ridden hole.

Passage of the law did not evoke a wave of witch-hunts; the first trials of major importance did not occur until 1612. During James's entire reign of 22 years, fewer than 40 persons were executed for the crime of witchcraft. James pardoned some accused witches because of the weak evidence against them and exposed a number of cases of fraudulent accusations of witches, including the "possession" of a boy in Leicester that sent nine victims to the gallows in 1616. (Unfortunately, James did not uncover the fraud until after the executions. Though he was sorely displeased with the judge and sergeant, he did not punish them.)

The Witchcraft Act of 1604 remained in force until 1736, when it was repealed and replaced by a new law under George II. It was used to prosecute the accused witches in Salem, Massachusetts in 1692. Some of the worst abuses of witch-hunting in England did not occur until several decades after James's death, when MATTHEW HOPKINS terrorized the countryside in search of victims.

jewelry Necklaces, rings, bracelets and other jewelry are worn by neo-Pagan WITCHES as symbols of the Craft (see WITCHCRAFT) and for ritual or magical purposes. SILVER bracelets inscribed with coven SIGILS or Craft names in RUNES are worn for ritual; depending on a coven's practices, these may be worn by the high priestess only. High priests may also wear bracelets, of either silver, BRASS or GOLD.

Necklaces are widely worn, for according to legend, the GODDESS always wore one. One of the oldest representations of the Goddess, DIANA of Ephesus, is shown wearing a necklace of acorns; many other statues and depictions of the goddesses of various ancient cultures also show a necklace. Symbolic of rebirth, the necklace has no beginning or end and usually is made of natural materials, such as stones, beads or nuts, in multiples of nine or 13. The high priestess often wears AMBER or black jet. Many Witches wear pendants of an encircled silver or gold pentacle. Other common pendants are crystals, for their reputed healing and psychic properties; Egyptian ANKHS; moonstones; and objects or stones that are personal TALISMANS and AMULETS, or associated with nature, MAGIC and the Craft. Astrological symbols also are worn. Male Witches often wear a metal necklace called a *corq*, an incomplete choker that symbolizes death and rebirth, or a *lamen* (a thin metal plate used as a charm) with one's astrological birth sign inscribed upon it.

Silver "Goddess rings," which show the face or form of the Goddess, are worn by women, often on the pointing (index) finger, for ritual purposes. Some men wear Goddess rings, but many prefer HORNED GOD rings, which depict two touching ram heads or goat heads (see RINGS).

Other jewelry includes headbands with a crescent moon, a symbol of the Goddess, and silver rings inscribed with runes. Some Witches feel jewelry is not appropriate in the Craft and wear none.

All jewelry is consecrated and empowered in ritual prior to wearing.

See also GARTER.

Joan of Arc (1412–1431)   A French peasant girl who, spurred on by divine voices and visions, fought the English and secured the coronation of the dau-phin Charles as king of France. Contrary to popular belief, she was not executed by the English on charges of WITCHCRAFT but for being a relapsed heretic who denied the authority of the Church.

Joan was born a plowman's daughter in Domrémy, a village between the Champagne and Lorraine districts of France. Early in her life, she demonstrated exceptional piety and was hardworking and industrious. She began to hear voices and have visions at age 13 and identified them as the saints Michael, Catherine and Margaret. They told her to go to the dauphin and that she would raise the English siege of Orléans.

At that time, the crown of France was in dispute between the dauphin Charles, son of King Charles VI, and the English, who held control over portions of France. When Joan was 16, her voices led her to Vaucouleurs, a French loyalist stronghold, where she begged a captain to see the dauphin. She was refused; a year later, in 1429, she tried again. She convinced the captain that she was not a witch and that her visions were divine.

Charles received her, and she impressed the superstitious dauphin by telling him his daily personal prayer to God. Her mission, she said, was to defeat the English and get him crowned king of France. He had her interviewed by the clergy; Joan passed their inspection.

The dauphin gave Joan troops, and she led them into battle against the English. True to her visions, she raised the siege of Orléans in May 1429. The dauphin was crowned Charles VII about two months later, on July 17. He ennobled Joan and her family, and she enjoyed enormous popularity among the people as the savior of France.

France, however, was far from unified. Though the English grip was weakened, it was not broken. Paris and parts of Normandy and Burgundy remained loyal to the English. Joan attempted to take Paris but was ordered to retreat before the battle was decided.

On May 23, 1430, Joan attempted to raise a siege of Compiègne. She was unhorsed and captured, and imprisoned in a castle by the Duke of Burgundy, an ally of the English. She unsuccessfully attempted to escape by jumping out of the tower into the moat but didn't hurt herself seriously.

In exchange for 10,000 francs, the Duke of Burgundy turned Joan over to the Bishop of Beauvais, also an English ally. It was the intent of the English to execute Joan, but first they set out to discredit her as a witch and thus weaken Charles VII.

In an informal ecclesiastical hearing, Joan came through exceptionally well. It was verified that she was a virgin, which weakened the case for witchcraft, because all witches were supposed to copulate with the Devil, according to belief at the time. Character witnesses painted a shining picture of her piety and virtue. All of this testimony was repressed by the Bishop of Beauvais.

Following the informal hearings, the clergy began interrogations of Joan in her prison cell. She acknowledged that she could see, kiss and embrace her three saints.

Joan was brought to formal trial before 37 clerical judges on 70 charges, among them being a sorceress, witch, diviner, pseudoprophetess, invoker of evil spirits, conjurer and "given to the arts of magic." She was also accused of heresy. Her inquisitors did not torture her, to avoid the appearance of coercion.

The charges of sorcery and witchcraft could not be substantiated and were dropped. The 70 charges were reduced to 12, the main ones being her heresy in refusing to accept the authority of the Church, her wearing of men's clothing and her ability to see apparitions.

Joan refused to recant, even under the threat of torture or being turned over to the English secular arm for punishment, which was certain execution.

On May 24, 1431, Joan was publicly condemned as a heretic and turned over to the English, who were ready to burn her on the spot. At the last minute, she recanted and signed a hastily written confession renouncing her visions and voices as false, and swearing to return to and obey the Church. This saved her from the pyre, and she was sent to prison for life.

But in prison, she donned men's clothing—allegedly because her voices told her to, but presumably because her English guards took her women's garb and left her with nothing else to wear. On May 28 she was condemned as a relapsed heretic. She recanted her confession. On May 30 Joan was excommunicated and delivered at last to the English secular arm. She was burned at the stake the same day in Rouen. The executioner was spooked by her death, claiming that her heart refused to burn and he found it whole in the ashes. Throughout her ordeal, Charles VII, to whom she had delivered the crown of France, declined to come to her aid.

In 1450 Pope Calixtus III had her sentence annulled. Joan was canonized in 1920 by Pope Benedict XV. A national festival in her honor is held in France on the second Sunday in May.

Jones, Margaret (?–1648) The first witch to be executed in Massachusetts Bay Colony, on June 15, 1648, in Boston, was Margaret Jones, a physician who was accused of WITCHCRAFT when patients worsened under her care (see HEALING).

Jones and her husband, Thomas, were among the early settlers in Massachusetts Bay Colony, making their home in Charlestown. According to records of her trial, Jones told some of her patients that if they refused to take her medicines, they would never be healed. Her trial records state, "Accordingly, their Diseases and Hurts continued, with Relapse against the ordinary Course, and beyond the Apprehension of all Physicians and Surgeons."

While her medicines were themselves harmless, the doctor was suspected of bewitching her patients into suffering. Once that thought took hold among her neighbors, she "was found to have such a malignant Touch, as many persons were taken with Deafness, or Vomiting, or other violent Pains or Sicknesses."

Jones was arrested and jailed. A string of witnesses appeared at her trial to testify against her. A jail officer testified that he had seen a little child run from her room, but when he followed it, the child vanished. This was taken as further proof of her being a witch. Jones protested her innocence vigorously and violently, denouncing those who would condemn her, but to no avail. She was sentenced to hang. According to the records,

> . . . her Behavior at her Trial was intemperate, lying notoriously, and railing upon the Jury and Witnesses. In like Distemper, she died. . . . The same Day and Hour she was executed, there was a very great Tempest at Connecticut, which blew down many Trees, etc.

A month prior to Jones's arrest and trial, an order had been passed in Boston requiring that all husbands of accused WITCHES were to be confined to a room and watched for signs of witchcraft themselves. Accordingly, Thomas Jones was accused of being a witch and was jailed. There is no record of his fate.

Judas Goat See BAPHOMET.

Judith, Anodea (1952–) American Witch (see WITCHES), author, artist, songwriter and healer, and president of the CHURCH OF ALL WORLDS. She was born Judith Ann Mull on December 1, 1952, in Elyria, Ohio, the youngest of three children and the only daughter (one of her brothers is comedian Martin Mull).

From an early age, she was close to nature—her grandmother had a farm, where she spent much time with the animals and collecting rocks and insects. The seeds for her interest in NEO-PAGANISM and WITCHCRAFT were planted during her early teen years when she read about Greek mythology, which reconstructed her images of God. From her family Judith

Anodea Judith (courtesy Anodea Judith)

received a religious indoctrination in Christian Science, which holds that illness is an error in thinking and can be cured by a wholeness of mind, body and spirit. She learned the beneficial healing results of positive thinking and mind over matter. Mary Baker Eddy, the founder of Christian Science, could be viewed as a displaced Witch, she says. In high school, Judith was known as a healer. Christianity, however, had no appeal to her, and she looked for another system in which to apply Christian Science principles.

In 1971 Judith enrolled at Clark University to study psychology and become a therapist, but she found the courses were geared more toward academic work than therapy. She had a natural gift for art, so she changed her major to art and left for California in 1973 to paint murals. In 1974 she attended the California College of Arts and Crafts in Oakland. She also studied at John F. Kennedy University.

Her artwork led her to her first discoveries of MAGIC. She painted environmental murals—cloudscapes, sunrises, sunsets, skies and natural landscapes—which she feels help connect one to primal, racial memories. She became known for her cloudscapes on ceilings, which made rooms appear as though they were open to the sky. Judith began to

notice that after finishing a mural, she would go outside and see in the sky exactly what she had painted, as though the forces of nature had changed to reflect her creative vision.

In 1975 she underwent a spiritual transformation: she gave up smoking and meat, became bisexual, practiced Yoga daily and did numerous fastings and purifications. Her work became more creative. One day, while meditating in a lotus position in her little artist's attic in Berkeley, Judith had an out-of-body experience. She suddenly found herself looking at herself meditating. Curiously, she said, she appeared to look older than she was. She saw a book fall into her lap, which jarred her back into her body. Its title was *The Chakra System* by A. Judith Mull, the name she was still using at the time. The experience led Judith on an 11-year study and research of the chakra system, which culminated in 1987 with the publication of a comprehensive book, *Wheels of Life: A User's Guide to the Chakra System.*

In 1975–76 Judith spent much time backpacking through the wilderness to get inspiration for her artwork. She had planned to go to New York to art school but decided instead to sell her possessions and move to a five-acre piece of land on a mountaintop, which was given to her by a friend. She lived alone in a tent for two months. By then, she said, she had discovered the Goddess and Witchcraft. She became a part of nature and practiced weather magic by becoming one with the elements. It was a magical period, and Judith felt that she received direct teachings from the Goddess through nature. Her given name no longer seemed to fit; she changed it to Anodea ("one of the Goddess") Judith.

In 1977, during a severe drought, the Environmental Protection Agency commissioned her to paint a mural on canvas about the California water system. After a 10-day fast, she began work, painting rain coming down onto the mountains and flowing out to the sea. By the time she finished, rains actually were pouring, causing flooding and landslides. (The EPA cancelled its order without seeing the mural.)

At about the same time, Judith met OTTER ZELL and MORNING GLORY ZELL, of the Church of All Worlds. Judith had been conducting magical women's circles, classes in Yoga, aura readings and psychology workshops. The Zells wanted to work with her; they formed a lasting partnership and friendship.

For a time, Judith was intimately involved with GWYDION PENDDERWEN, founder of Forever Forests and cofounder of Nemeton, helping him develop the Church of All Worlds Sanctuary, known as Annwfn, the home of Forever Forests.

In 1978 she took a mural-painting job in Berkeley and moved back to urban civilization. She became involved in the Pagan community, working with P. E. I. (ISAAC) BONEWITS on *Pentalpha,* a Druidic journal (now defunct), and becoming friends with author MARION ZIMMER BRADLEY, who is goddess mother to her son. Judith joined Bradley's Aquarian Order of the Restoration, and the Dark Moon Circle, of which Bradley was a founder. Judith began a transition from artwork to bioenergetic bodywork, massage, healing and aura reading. (Bioenergetic bodywork is a process of using the bioelectric charge in the body to push through blocks and release them emotionally, and create a better sense of grounding and wholeness.) She works with many adults who were abused as children or who had alcoholic parents.

Judith had a brief marriage and bore a son, Alex, in 1982. The marriage dissolved in 1984. Judith and Alex moved to Annwfn, Pendderwen's land in Mendocino County. Pendderwen, who died in 1982, had named Judith one of five stewards of the land, now owned by the Church of All Worlds.

Judith remained at Annwfn for about 18 months, during which time she said she had profound magical experiences; from Samhain (All Hallow's Eve) to the next Samhain, she was guided by INANNA, spending six months in the stars and six months in the underworld. She returned to a city environment and finished work on her chakra book.

In 1983 she founded Lifeways, an outgrowth of Forever Forests and now a subsidiary and the teaching arm of the Church of All Worlds. Part of her ministry for the Church, Lifeways offers classes and workshops in consciousness raising, magic, ritual, psychic development, bodywork and healing. In 1986 Judith moved up from vice-president of the Church to president. In the fall of 1988 she remarried, to Richard Ely, a Pagan, Witch and geologist, who has three children from a previous marriage. In 1989 she was to receive a master's degree in metaphysical psychology from the Rosebridge Graduate School of Integrative Therapy.

Magic philosophy. Judith sees the world in terms of energy and relationships. People are energetic statements of all the things that have happened to them in their lives; the world, in turn, is also an energetic statement. Magic is the direction of energy through a sensible system that seeks balance of all things. The purpose of magic is to assist in this balancing. More energy needs to be directed to the here and now, which all people have to deal with. Judith teaches "the energetics of magic," which deals with the metaphysical principles behind magical working.

Judith defines a Witch as one who takes active control of her own life and destiny and who serves the Goddess. She identifies most strongly with the aspect of the Goddess personified by Sarasvati, the Hindu patroness of science and the arts: music, painting and writing. She lives in northern California, where she works with a coven named Vortex.

jujumen See WITCH DOCTORS.

Junius, Johannes (1573?–1628) As the burgomaster, or mayor, of Bamberg, Germany, Johannes Junius was caught, along with other local leading citizens, in one of the most vicious witch persecutions of the Inquisition. From the early 1600s to about 1630, hundreds of men and women in Bamberg were accused of WITCHCRAFT, tortured by the most barbaric means (see TORTURE) and executed. All of the burgomasters of Bamberg fell victim to the inquisitors. The trial of Junius is of historic importance for the account of his ordeal that he managed to leave behind.

Junius was 55 years old when he was accused of witchcraft by the authorities, who were led by Vicar-General Suffragan Bishop Friedrich Forner and the prince-bishop of Bamberg, Gottfried Johann Georg II Fuchs von Dornheim. Junius had been named by several persons, including the vice-chancellor of Bamberg, Dr. Georg Adam Haan.

On June 28, 1628, Junius was interrogated without torture. He protested his innocence, saying he had never renounced God and was wronged to be so accused. He called the inquisitors' bluff by saying he would like evidence of a single person who had ever seen him at the witch's sabbat (see SABBATS). The inquisitors smugly complied, producing Haan and Hapffens Elsse, who stated in the presence of Junius that they had witnessed his evil activities. Haan swore upon his life that about two years earlier, Junius had attended a witch's sabbat in the electoral council room which he had entered by the left. There, Junius, Haan and others ate and drank. Another man, Hopffens Elsse, testified that he had seen Junius on the Hauptsmoor at a witches' dance, where a holy wafer was descrated.

Junius vigorously denied the testimony, but the inquisitors told him other "accomplices" had confessed. He was given time to contemplate his situation. In all, six witnesses were brought against him, including Haan's son.

Two days later, on June 30, Junius was asked to confess, but refused. The torture began. First, he was put in thumbscrews. Still he denied renouncing God and being baptized by the Devil. The inquisitors noted that he seemed to suffer no pain in the thumbscrews. Such insensitivity to pain was often considered a sign that the Devil was aiding the witch in enduring pain.

The inquisitors then crushed his legs in legscrews.

Again Junius protested his innocence, and again the inquisitors noted that he seemed to feel no pain. After the legscrews, the inquisitors had him stripped, shaved and searched for a WITCH'S MARK, which they believed they found in a bluish patch of skin shaped like a clover leaf, which seemed insensitive to pain when pricked three times (see PRICKING).

Finally, Junius was given the strappado, a torture in which the victim's hands are bound by a rope behind his back, which is connected to a pulley. The victim is drawn up to the ceiling and allowed to drop. Junius still protested his innocence. On July 5 the inquisitors again urged him to make a full confession. Exhausted and wracked by incredible pain, Junius gave in and made up a story that he thought would satisfy his persecutors:

His dealings with the Devil began in 1624. A lawsuit he had been involved in had cost him six hundred florins. One day, he went out to sit in his orchard to contemplate, when a woman who looked like a grass-maid appeared and asked him why he was so sad. He replied that he wasn't. She spoke to him seductively, then turned into a goat which said, "Now you see with whom you have to do. You must be mine or I will forthwith break your neck." Junius became frightened. The goat grabbed him by the throat and ordered him to renounce God. "God forbid," Junius replied. The goat vanished but shortly reappeared accompanied by a host of people, who threatened him and demanded he renounce God. He did so by saying, "I renounce God in Heaven and his host, and will henceforth recognize the Devil as my God."

Junius was then baptized and christened as Krix, with a paramour named Vixen, an evil spirit. He was congratulated by the other witches, whom he named as residents of Bamberg, and was given a ducat, which later turned into a potsherd.

Whenever he wished to attend a sabbat, a large black dog appeared, and bore him through the air. Vixen promised to give him money.

This tale did not completely satisfy the inquisitors, who allowed Junius more time for "contemplation." On July 7 he was asked to confess further. He obliged them by describing a sabbat and by admitting he attempted murder at the prompting of Vixen. She ordered him to kill his younger son and gave him a gray powder. He could not bring himself to do it and killed his son's horse instead. Vixen also ordered him to kill his daughter. When he refused, she beat him.

Junius also said that the DEVIL appeared before him as a goat about a week before his arrest and told him he was going to be arrested, but not to worry, that he would be released.

Junius's implication of himself was not enough. The inquisitors took him down the streets of Bamberg, ordering him to name others who were witches. He complied but was tortured again when he did not name enough people.

After this degrading, deplorable ordeal, Junius was condemned to die at the stake in late July. Also condemned were those whom he falsely had named as Devil-worshippers, including Haan and the others who originally had accused him of the same. While in prison, Junius wrote a letter to his daughter, Veronica, which he managed to have smuggled out and delivered to her. It is written in a shaky hand; that he managed to write it at all is amazing, considering that his hands had been crushed in the thumbscrews and he had been subjected to other torture. Junius's letter provides some of the most damning testimony about the evil excesses of the witch-hunters. An excerpt follows:

Many hundred thousand good-nights, dearly beloved daughter Veronica. Innocent have I come into prison, innocent have I been tortured, innocent I must die. For whoever comes into the witch prison must become a witch or be tortured until he invents something out of his head and—God pity him—bethinks him of something. I will tell you how it has gone with me. . . . And then came also—God in highest heaven have mercy—the executioner, and put the thumb-screws on me, both hands bound together, so that the blood ran out at the nails and everywhere, so that for four weeks I could not use my hands, as you can see from the writing. . . . Thereafter they first stripped me, bound my hands behind me, and drew me up in the torture [strappado]. Then I thought heaven and earth were at an end, eight times did they draw me up and let me fall again, so that I suffered terribly agony . . .

When at last the executioner led me back into the prison he said to me: "Sir, I beg you, for God's sake confess something, whether it be true or not. Invent something, for you cannot endure the torture which you will be put to; and even if you bear it all, yet you will not escape, not even if you were an earl, but one torture will follow another until you say you are a witch . . .

And so I begged, since I was in wretched plight, to be given one day for thought and a priest. The priest was refused me, but the time for thought was given . . . at last there came to me a new idea. . . . I would think of something to say and say it. . . . And so I made my confession, as follows, but it was all a lie. Now follows dear child, what I confessed in order to escape the great anguish and bitter torture, which it was impossible for me longer to bear . . .

Then I had to tell what people I had seen [at the sabbat]. I said that I had not recognized them. "You old rascal, I must set the executioner at you. Say—was not the Chancellor there?" So I said yes. "Who besides?" I had not recognized anybody. So he said: "Take one street after another, begin at the market, go out on one street and back on the next. . . . And thus continuously they asked me on all the streets, though I could not and would not say more. So they gave me to the executioner, told him to strip me, shave me all over, and put me to the torture . . .

Then I had to tell what crimes I had committed. I said nothing. . . . "Draw the rascal up!" So I said that I was to kill my children, but I had killed a horse instead. It did not help . . .

Now, dear child, here you have all my confession, for which I much die. And they are sheer lies and made-up things, so help me God. For all this I was forced to say through fear of the torture which was threatened beyond what I had already endured . . .

Dear child, keep this letter secret so that people do not find it, else I shall be tortured most piteously and the jailers will be beheaded. So strictly is it forbidden. . . . I have taken several days to write this: my hands are both lame. I am in a sad plight . . .

Good night, for your father Johannes Junius will never see you more. July 24, 1628.

Junius added a postscript to the margin:

Dear child, six have confessed against me at once . . . all false, through compulsion, as they have all told me, and begged my forgiveness in God's name before they were executed. . . . They know nothing but good of me. They were forced to say it, just as I myself was . . .

See also BAMBERG WITCHES.

K

Kabala See KABBALAH.

Kabbalah (also Cabala, Kabala, Qabalah) A Jewish system of theosophy, philosophy, science, magic and mysticism developed since the Middle Ages, and comprising an important part of Western occultism. It has been reinterpreted in accordance with Christianity.

Kabbalah (the preferred spelling of scholars) signifies "doctrines received from tradition," specifically oral tradition and secret, mystical knowledge not revealed to the masses. According to legend, the Kabbalah was taught by God to a group of angels, who, after the Fall, taught it to man in order to provide man with a way back to God. It was passed from Adam to Noah to Abraham, who took it to Egypt, where it was passed on to Moses. Moses included it in the first four books of the Pentateuch but left it out of Deuteronomy. He initiated 70 elders into the Kabbalah who continued the tradition of passing it on orally. David and Solomon were Kabbalistic adepts. Eventually, the wisdom was written down.

The Kabbalah is a body of writings by anonymous authors. The main works are the *Sefer Yezirah*, or *Book of Creation*, and the *Zohar*, or *Book of Splendor*. The origins of the *Sefer Yezirah* date to the 8th century. The *Zohar* is believed to have been written by Moses de Leon of Guadalajara, Spain, in the 13th century.

From its beginnings, the mysticism of the Kabbalah was similar to that of Gnosticism, including concepts of MAGIC, cosmology and angels. The Kabbalah holds that God is both immanent and transcendent; God is all things, both good and evil; all things make up the whole of an organized universe; and letters and numbers are the keys to unlocking the mysteries of the universe (see GEMATRIA).

God (*En Soph* or *Ain Soph*) is boundless and fills the universe. From God come ten emanations, called *sephiroth*, of angels and men, which form the structure of the Tree of Life and represent aspects of the divine. The Tree of Life shows the descent of the divine into the material world and the path by which man can ascend to the divine while still in the flesh. Each *sephiroth* is a level of attainment in knowledge. The *sephiroth* are organized in three triangles, with the tenth *sephirah* resting at the base. The triangles represent a portion of the human body: the head, arms and legs; the tenth *sephirah* represents the reproductive organs. The triangles are aligned on three pillars, with Mercy (the male principle), on the right, Severity or Judgment (the female principle) on the left and in the middle Mildness, a balance between the two. The *sephiroth* and their names and aspects are:

1. Kether, supreme crown
2. Chokmah, wisdom
3. Binah, understanding
4. Chesed, mercy, greatness
5. Geburah, strength, rigor
6. Tiphareth, beauty, harmony
7. Netzach, victory, force
8. Hod, splendor
9. Yesod, foundation
10. Malkuth, kingdom

The cosmos is divided into Four Worlds: Atziluth, the world of archetypes, form which are derived all forms of manifestation; Briah, the world of creation, in which archetypal ideas become patterns; Yetzirah, the world of formation, in which the patterns are expressed; and Assiah, the world of the material, the plane we perceive with our physical senses. Each

The Cabala

The Tables for the calculations of the names of Spirits good & bad & under the presidency of the 7 Planets &12 militant Signes

Kabbalistic tables for calculating the names of good and evil spirits (Francis Barrett, *The Magus*, 1801)

sepirah is divided into four sections in which the Four Worlds operate.

The *sepiroth* also comprise the sacred name of God, which is unknowable and unspeakable. The Bible gives various substitutes, such as Elohim and Adonai. The personal name of God is the Tetragrammaton, YHWH, usually pronounced as Yahweh, and which appears in the Bible as Jehovah. The four letters of YHWH correspond to the Four Worlds (see NAMES OF POWER).

Magical applications of the Kabbalah were recognized as early as the 13th century. During the Renaissance, alchemists and magicians used combinations of Kabbalistic numbers and divine names in rituals and incantations. The Tetragrammaton was held in great awe for its power over all things in the universe, including DEMONS. Beginning in the late 15th century, the Kabbalah was harmonized with Christian doctrines to form a Christian Kabbalah, the proponents of which claimed that magic and the Kabbalah proved the divinity of Christ. Cornelius AGRIPPA von Nettesheim included the Kabbalah in his *De Occulta Philosophia* (1531), which resulted in its erroneous associations with witchcraft. Also in the 16th century, alchemical symbols were integrated into the Christian Kabbalah.

The Kabbalah has been regarded with much skep-ticism by many Jews. Its study and analysis peaked by the 19th century and began to decline. Interest in the Kabbalah was revived by non-Jewish Western occultists, such as FRANCIS BARRETT, ELIPHAS LEVI and Papus. It was held in great esteem by members of the HERMETIC ORDER OF THE GOLDEN DAWN, including Samuel Liddell Macgregor Mathers, ALEISTER CROWLEY and A. E. Waite, all of whom were influenced by it. DION FORTUNE called the Kabbalah the "Yoga of the West." Western occultists have linked the Kabbalah to the TAROT and ASTROLOGY, which scholar Gershom Scholem terms "supreme charlatanism." Nonetheless, such associations persist in Western occult study.

Kali   The Hindu goddess of death, destruction, fear and terror, and the wife-consort of Siva, the destroyer. As Kali Ma (the "black mother") she is one of the ten aspects of Siva's wife, a bloodthirsty and powerful warrior. Her appearance is almost always frightening: dark-complected or black, with long, disheveled hair, and is usually shown naked or wearing only a girdle and standing on the body of Siva, with one foot on his leg and one on his chest. Kali has four arms; her hands have clawlike nails. In two hands she holds a sword and the severed head of a giant, and she uses the other two to entice her worshippers. She wears a necklace of skulls and earrings of corpses. Her tongue hangs out and she has long, sharp fangs. She is spattered with BLOOD and gets drunk by drinking the blood of her victims.

Beginning in the 18th century in Bengali devotion, Kali has been worshipped as a mother goddess, particularly among the lower castes. Perhaps it was an outgrowth of a desire to control a violent world that was beyond control, especially for those in the lower castes; the deadly destroyer was sought to become the fierce protector. Or perhaps it was recognition of the multiple aspects of the Goddess, that "She Who Gives is also She Who Takes Away."

See also GODDESS.

Kelly, Edward   See JOHN DEE.

Keridwen   See CERRIDWEN.

kiss of shame   It was a common belief during the witch-hunts that all WITCHES, indeed, all heretics, paid homage to the DEVIL by kissing his posterior. The *osculum infame*, as it was called, was mentioned in virtually every recorded account of a witches' sabbat (see SABBATS), most confessions of which were extracted under TORTURE. It was generally regarded as the ultimate act of abasement, though some witches allegedly protested that the Devil had not a common posterior but a second face located there.

Witch giving ritual kiss to Satan (R. P. Guaccius, *Compendium Maleficarum*, 1626)

The kiss supposedly was given at the beginning of the sabbat, after the Devil had read the rolls of his followers. Sometimes the witches approached him backwards, in true infernal fashion, then turned, bowed and scraped and kissed his fundament. A kiss of shame was always required of new initiates (see INITIATION). Following the kiss, the witches and the Devil commenced their feasting.

Witches also kissed the posteriors of lower-ranking demons. While the kiss of shame was usually an act of homage, in one case, that of the NORTH BERWICK WITCHES in Scotland in the late 16th century, the kiss was a penance levied by the Devil. In *Newes from Scotland, declaring the damnable Life of Doctor Fian* (1592), W. Wright reports,

> . . . and seeing that they tarried over long, hee at their coming enjoyed them all to a pennance, which was, that they should kisse his buttockes, in sign of duety to him, which being put over the pulpit bare, every one did as he had enjoyned them.

Accusations of the kiss of shame were often raised in WITCHCRAFT and heresy inquisitions and trials. The Cathars and Waldenses (see VAUDUIS), religious sects persecuted for heresy, were thus accused, as were the KNIGHTS TEMPLAR in the 14th century. The Templars were said to require initiates to kiss their superiors on the anus, navel, base of the spine and phallus. Some knights also were said to worship the Devil in the form of a black cat, which they kissed beneath the tail.

In 1303 Walter Langton, the Bishop of Lichfield and Coventry in England, was accused of SORCERY and service to the Devil, which included the kiss of shame; he was able to clear himself of the charges.

But one Guillaume Edeline, a doctor of the Sorbonne in France, was not so fortunate. Accused of wizardry (see WIZARDS), he confessed to rendering the kiss of shame when the Devil appeared in the shape of a ram. Edeline was executed in 1453.

The Devil also demanded the kiss of shame in other guises besides human and ram. *Errores Haereticorum*, a medieval tract, claims the Cathars took their name "from the term cat, whose posterior they kiss, in whose form Satan appears to them." There are tales from the 12th century of Satan appearing to his followers in the form of black CATS or TOADS and demanding kisses under the cat's tail or in the toad's mouth.

Knights Templar   Also known as The Order of the Temple, the Knights Templar began with lofty ideals of chivalry, crusades and Christian faith, as practiced by an exclusive club of monastic knights. It was founded between 1119 and 1188 by Hugh de Payens of Champagne, France, and a small group of knights, who dedicated themselves to protecting pilgrims to the Holy Land and routing out the infidels from the same. The Order accumulated great wealth and power, which two centuries later brought about its downfall amid sordid accusations of heresy, DEVIL-worship, blasphemy and homosexuality.

After its inception, the Knights Templar quickly gained in reputation and respect. Their banner, a white flag with a crimson cross, became symbolic of the Christian war against the infidels, and of the highest ideals. Groups were organized throughout Europe and England, but France remained the stronghold. All members pledged their complete allegiance to a Grand Master. Knights took vows of poverty, humility and chastity, which were strictly enforced. As a religious order, the Templars were not taxed by the Crown and were not subject to the laws of the land; they were answerable only to the pope.

Despite the poverty of the individual knights, the Order solicited donations to finance its holy war. Money poured in, and the Order grew in power.

The rites of the Order were kept in deep secrecy. Over time, this gave rise to much curious speculation and rumor about what really went on in Templar strongholds. For generations, stories were told of blasphemous rites in which Christ was renounced as a false prophet and the cross was spit, urinated and trampled upon. Further, Templars were rumored to engage in homosexual rituals and to worship the Devil, who appeared in the form of a black cat, which they kissed beneath the tail (see KISS OF SHAME). They were also said to worship an idol named BAPHOMET, in some versions a stuffed human head, in others a skull or an artificial head with three faces. The Templars, it was said, roasted children and smeared their burning fat upon this idol. For years, no one acted upon these stories.

Meanwhile, in the Holy Land, the Order used its immense wealth to enter commerce. It lent money and transacted business with the enemy during times of truce. The Order's financial power, as well as its immunity to secular law, incurred increasing resentment among the nobility—in particular, King Philip IV of France, who was himself one of the Order's debtors.

The collapse of the Crusades did little to harm the Order. By the 14th century, it was at its peak of power. Then Philip, coveting the Order's vast wealth, set out to seize its riches and lands by accusing the Knights of heresy. The king's willing accomplice was Pope Clement V.

On October 13, 1307, Philip arrested Grand Master Jacques de Molay and 140 Knights in the Paris temple. More arrests followed throughout France. The Templars were subjected to TORTURE en masse. Many confessed to the blasphemies and demonic crimes of which they were accused, though the confessions were so varied that little conclusive proof was amassed. Nevertheless, Philip pursued his wholesale persecution of the Order.

On November 22, Philip pursuaded Pope Clement to issue a bull ordering all Templars to be arrested and all of their properties seized. Not all countries obeyed as zealously as Philip desired; it took a second papal bull to force King Edward II of England to torture Templars in his dominion. In other countries, leniency was shown toward the Templars, some of whom were acquitted or allowed to join other orders.

In 1310 the public trials of the Templars began in Paris. Those who had survived the brutal torture were brought forward, charged with a long list of crimes and interrogated. Some Knights defended the Order. Fifty-four who refused to confess were ordered by Philip to be taken to the suburbs and burned to death. Still, there was no definitive proof of heresy. Accounts of the idol Baphomet varied widely. Many Templars said only that they had heard of such a thing but had never seen it. Nonetheless, opponents of the Order claimed the idol was proof that the Templars had adopted the Mahometanism of the infidels. Throughout Europe, Templars were convicted of SORCERY and heresy and burned at the stake.

Clement officially dissolved the Order in 1312. The pope specified that all assets were to be turned over to a rival order, the Hospitallers, but this was not universally followed. Assets in France and England were seized by Philip and Edward, both of whom used them for personal ends or lavished them on friends. Elsewhere in Europe, other orders took the assets.

Grand Master de Molay remained in prison for seven years. In 1314 he was placed on a scaffold in Paris and ordered to make a public confession. In exchange, he would be imprisoned for life instead of being executed. To the surprise of the authorities, de Molay angrily denounced his persecution and said he had been tortured into lying. He was, he protested vigorously, innocent of all charges. Enraged, Philip ordered de Molay burned alive. He died at sunset the same day, slowly and painfully in the flames.

According to legend, the dying de Molay declared that as proof of his innocence, Philip and Clement would be summoned to meet him before the throne of God within a year. Both men died within that time.

It is possible that some of the accusations against the Templars had some basis in fact, though no doubt the stories were quite exaggerated. With their exposure to other religions in the Holy Land, the Templars may have absorbed some rites and beliefs into their own system. Some scholars believe they may have adopted aspects of Gnosticism and may have ritualized homosexuality. Many of their secrets will never be known.

knots The tying and untying of knots is used to bind and release energy in many folk-magic SPELLS and formulas. The ancient Egyptians and Greeks tied knots in cords for love spells. The "knot of Isis," a red jasper amulet (see AMULETS) wound in the shroud of royal Egyptian mummies, summoned the protection of ISIS and her son Horus for the dead in the next world. The ancient Romans believed knots could cause impotency, especially if three cords or ropes of different colors were tied in three knots while a couple recited wedding vows. According to Pliny, such marital woes could be prevented by rubbing wolf fat on the threshold of the wedding chamber (see AIGUILLETTE). Other old beliefs about knots hold that the tying of them prevents pregnancy in a woman, and the untying of them facilitates conception and childbirth. In mainstream religious practices, knotted fringe is believed to confuse and entangle evil spirits, one reason why priests wear collars with no ties, for evil spirits caught in tie knots would disrupt religious services.

Legend has it that the prophet Mohammed was bewitched by an evil man and his daughters, who tied 11 knots in a cord which they hid in a well. The spell made Mohammed ill, and he wasted away nearly to the point of death. To save him, God intervened and sent the archangel Gabriel to reveal where the cord was hidden and how to break the

Sorcerer selling wind tied in knots to sailors (Olaus Magnus, *Historia de gentibus septentrionalibus*, 1555)

spell. When the cord was brought to him, Mohammed recited 11 verses from the Koran. As he spoke each line, a knot loosened itself. When all the knots were undone, the spell was broken. In Sura (chapter) CXIII in the Koran, Mohammed calls magicians' work "the evil of [women who] are blowers on knots."

WITCHES and sorcerers (see SORCERY) were believed to be able to control wind with three knots tied into a rope, or sometimes a handkerchief. When the three knots were tied in the proper magical way, the wind was bound up in them. Sorcerers and witches sometimes sold their magic knots to sailors. The release of one knot brought a gentle, southwesterly wind, two knots a strong north wind and three knots a tempest. In the folklore of the Shetland Islands and Scandinavia, some fishermen are said to command the wind this way. The belief in controlling wind by tying it up goes back to the legends of ancient Greece. Odysseus received a bag of winds from Aeolus to help him on his journey.

In West AFRICAN WITCHCRAFT, the tying of a knot while saying a person's name gives the tier of the knot power over the person named. The power is retained as long as the knot remains tied. In the west of Ireland, an old method for healing sick cattle called for a *worm-knot*, a piece of twine tied in certain knots and dragged over the animal's back. If the twine went smoothly, the cow would recover; if it caught and hitched, the animal would die.

In MAGIC, knots are used to bind and loosen deities and power; as tools in psychic attack and defense; and in magical snares. Magic knots also have the power to kill. According to a medieval formula, a WITCH'S LADDER, made of a string with nine knots, when hidden, causes a victim to die a slow death.

Many modern Witches use knots in cord magic. In one method, the Witch ties nine knots while chanting and/or visualizing her objective, such as the success of an endeavor or a hunt for a new home. By the ninth knot, the spell is complete and the magic power is stored within the knots. According to some formulas, the spell is then effected by the untying of the knots, usually one at a time over a period of nine days; according to others, the cord is tied into a circle. Cord magic is also done by a COVEN as a group. Slip knots are worked in cords, and the magical power is released when the knots are loosened.

Kramer, Heinrich   See MALLEUS MALEFICARUM, the.

Kuan Yin   Chinese goddess of mercy and protector of women. The "Lady who brings children," she is the most universally respected and popular of Chinese deities and is a favorite among many feminist neo-Pagans and WITCHES. Prior to the 12th century, Kuan Yin was known as the male bodhisattva Avalokitesvara, the Lord gifted with complete enlightenment, who was born from a tear shed by Lord Buddha over the suffering of the world. The Chinese honored his capacity for love by endowing him with feminine characteristics.

See also GODDESS.

Kyteler, Lady Alice (?–ca. 1324)   The WITCHCRAFT case of Lady Alice is an interesting and unusual one. Lady Alice, a wealthy and respected woman, not only was the first person to be tried for witchcraft in Ireland but was among the first accused WITCHES of the Middle Ages to be accused of heresy as well. Roughly two more centuries would pass before heresy charges were routine in witchcraft trials. Lady Alice also was one of the few accused who ever successfully defied her accusers.

Family jealousies over money apparently were a major factor in the leveling of charges against her. Lady Alice was one of the richest residents of Kilkenny. Much of her wealth had come to her through a succession of husbands. Three of them had died, and Lady Alice had married for a fourth time. When her fourth husband, Sir John le Poer, fell ill with a mysterious wasting disease, he and the stepchildren became suspicious of Lady Alice. Le Poer allegedly found hidden in their home a sackful of vile ingredients for black-MAGIC potions and powders. He and the stepchildren accused her of bewitching her first three husbands to death and depriving le Poer of his "natural senses" through the use of her magical concoctions.

The accusations piqued the interest of Richard de Ledrede, the Bishop of Ossory, who may have been interested in confiscating some of Lady Alice's wealth himself. In 1324 de Ledrede made an inquisition and determined that Kilkenny was home to a band of heretical sorcerers, of whom Lady Alice was the head.

De Ledrede indicted Lady Alice and her band on the following seven counts:

1. They had denied the faith of Christ.
2. They sacrificed living animals to various DEMONS, including a low-ranking one named Robin, or son of Art. They dismembered the animals and left them at CROSSROADS. One source said a SACRIFICE consisted of nine red COCKS and the eyes of nine peacocks.
3. They used SORCERY to seek advice from demons.
4. They held nightly meetings in which they "blasphemously imitated the power of the church by fulminating sentence of excommunication, with lighted CANDLES, even against their own husbands, from the sole of their foot to the crown of their head, naming each part expressly, and then concluded by extinguishing the candles and by crying, *"Fi! Fi! Fi! Amen."*
5. They caused disease and death, and aroused love and hatred, by using evil powders, unguents, OINTMENTS and candles. Ingredients included "certain horrible worms;" dead men's nails; the entrails of cocks sacrificed to demons; the hair (see HAIR AND NAILS), brains and shreds of shrouds of boys who were buried unbaptized; various herbs; and "other abominations." While incantations were recited, the ingredients were cooked in a CAULDRON made out of the skull of a decapitated thief.
6. Lady Alice used sorcery to cause the children of her four husbands to bequeath all their wealth to her and her favorite son, William Outlawe. Also, she bewitched Sir John le Poer to the point where he was emaciated, and his hair and nails dropped off. A maid warned him that he was the victim of WITCHCRAFT. He opened some locked chests and found "a sackful of horrible and destestable things," which he turned over to priests.
7. Robin, or Son of Art, was Lady Alice's incubus demon, who appeared as a cat, a hairy black dog or a black man (see FAMILIARS). The demon was the source of her wealth.

It was also charged that Lady Alice took a broom (see BROOMS) and swept the streets of Kilkenny, raking the dirt and filth toward the home of her favorite son, muttering, "To the house of William my sonne/Hie all the wealth of Kilkennie towne."

Bishop de Ledrede sought the arrest of Lady Alice, William and the other unnamed sorcerers. William raised a ruckus, and, because of the family's status, the Bishop was blocked. He decided to handle the matter himself, and excommunicated Lady Alice and cited her to appear before him. She fled to Dublin. Not to be outdone, de Ledrede charged William with heresy.

Lady Alice brought pressure on her influential contacts and had de Ledrede arrested and jailed. He was released after 17 days. His next move was to censure the entire diocese, but he was forced to lift the ban by the Lord Justice, who sided with Lady Alice. De Ledrede tried several more times to bring a civil arrest of Lady Alice and others on charges of sorcery. Lady Alice fled again, this time to England. In Kilkenny, she was condemned as a sorceress, magician and heretic. On the same day, de Ledrede publicly burned her sackful of "abominations."

The only punishment de Ledrede was able to bring against William was a penance of hearing three masses a day for a year, feeding a certain number of poor people and covering a church chancel and chapel with lead. William failed to do these things and eventually was imprisoned.

The Bishop succeeded in arresting Lady Alice's maid, Petronilla, and having her flogged until she confessed to sorcery and orgies that involved Lady Alice. Petronilla was excommunicated, condemned and burned alive on November 3, 1324. Hers was the first death by burning for the crime of heresy in Ireland. Records say that others who were implicated by Petronilla as being members of the band of sorcerers were rounded up; some fled. Some were executed by burning, while others were merely excommunicated, whipped and banished from the diocese.

Lady Alice spent the rest of her life in comfort in England. Bishop de Ledrede was himself accused of heresy and was exiled from his diocese, and it wasn't until 1339 that he regained favor. The next witchcraft trial of record in Ireland did not occur until the 17th century.

See also ISLAND MAGEE WITCHES.

L

Lady Olwen See MONIQUE WILSON.

Lady Sheba (? –) Witch Queen who rose to prominence in American WITCHCRAFT in the late 1960s and 1970s. She set a precedent in 1971 by publishing her BOOK OF SHADOWS.

Lady Sheba was born in the mountains of Kentucky. Her family had practiced Witchcraft for seven generations, and Lady Sheba inherited her psychic gifts. When she was about six years old, her grandmother introduced her to witchcraft, beginning with stories of Irish leprechauns and little people (see FAIRIES). Every evening, Lady Sheba went with her grandmother to put out a saucer of milk for the legendary folk. As she grew older, she learned more and became aware that she was different from most other people. Though a frail child, she knew she possessed powers and knowledge that others did not.

Lady Sheba said she had been granted a "hand of power" that enabled her to protect others. The palm of her right hand was etched with symbols that could be seen only by other psychics.

Her Craft name came from an inner awareness early in life that, in addition to her family name, she had always been "Sheba," perhaps in a former life. She believed she had lived before in Northern Ireland or Scotland, though she never formally attempted to investigate her past lives.

Lady Sheba was initiated as a Witch in the 1930s (see INITIATION). She divided her time between Witchcraft and rearing a family. (She and her husband raised four sons and four daughters.) The family moved to Michigan around 1950. Lady Sheba founded her own tradition, the American Order of the Brotherhood of Wicca (see WICCA), of which she was high priestess. The tradition combined her own Celtic heritage with American Indian magic. Her rituals closely follow the Gardnerian tradition, except that coveners (see COVEN) worship robed rather than skyclad (nude).

As she influenced the forming of additional covens, Lady Sheba became Witch Queen over them all. Her covens spread over the United States, with a few overseas. Her talisman (see TALISMANS) was a large ruby ring, which she wore on her right index finger as a protector against evil and bringer of good luck. She could see visions in the stone and said others sometimes could see visions, too. She did not allow anyone to touch it, lest the protective power be broken.

Lady Sheba gained attention with the publication of *The Magick Grimoire*, a collection of excerpts from her personal workbook of SPELLS and rituals, some of them handed down through her family. Her second book, *The Book of Shadows*, published in 1971, generated a great deal of controversy in the Wiccan community. *The Book of Shadows* comprised laws, revised Gardnerian rituals and descriptions of SABBATS, information traditionally supposed to be kept secret among Witches. By making it public, Lady Sheba violated that tradition, in the eyes of some. She defended her decision to publish the book, saying she had been directed by the GODDESS to do so.

In 1973 the Twin Cities Area Council of the American Order of the Brotherhood of Wicca was formed by coven leaders, though all traditions were invited to participate. The Council took an active role in the establishment in 1973–74 of the COUNCIL OF AMERICAN WITCHES. As of the mid-1980s, only a few covens were still part of the Brotherhood.

Laksmi (also Sri, Sri-Lakshmi) One of the most popular Hindu goddesses since pre-Buddhist times, and recognized in neo-Paganism, Lakshmi is the grantor of luck, fertility, wealth, happiness and prosperity. Beautiful and perfumed, sitting on a lotus—the symbol of life and fertility—she has a regal bearing and represents ideal love and beauty. Lakshmi has been associated with various Hindu male deities, but particularly with Vishnu, as his wife and consort. With Vishnu, Lakshmi portrays marital and domestic contentment and cooperation.

See also GODDESS.

Lamia In Greek mythology, a mortal queen who became a monster and devourer of children. Desired by Zeus, Lamia was punished by Hera, who stole the queen's children. In revenge, Lamia began to steal others' children and became transformed into a hideous, flesh-eating demon who could remove her own eyes at will. Gradually, Lamia multiplied into many DEMONS, all called *lamias*, who became associated with succubi and STRIGES, sucking the blood of men and then eating them. Belief in lamias continued through the Middle Ages.

The lamias are similar to the Hindu goddesses Putana, Rasksasi, Aditi, Diti, Surabhi, Sarama, Kadru, Lohitayani and Arya, who like flesh and strong liquor, and devour children and pregnant women. They lurk in the confinement chamber, where newborn infants are kept for the first 10 days of life. The goddesses afflict children up to the age of 16, when they begin to act as positive influences instead of destructive ones.

See also LILITH.

Lancaster (also Lancashire) Witches Two of the more notable witch trials of England took place in the Pendle Forest area of Lancaster County, in 1612 and 1633. The 1612 trials are noted for the records kept by the court clerk, Thomas Potts, published as a chapbook, which set forth the HAG stereotype of WITCHES. The 1633 trials involved a boy who was coerced by his father into giving false testimony that resulted in more than 30 arrests and 17 convictions.

The 1612 trials. About 20 persons were brought under suspicion of WITCHCRAFT in the first major witch trials of northern England. The central figures were two old and decrepit women—Elizabeth Sowthern, alias "Old Demdike," who was about 80 years old, and Anne Whittle, alias "Old Chattox," who was about 60 years old—rivals in the service of wizardry and magical arts to the local population.

In March of 1612 Old Demdike was questioned by a local justice who had received reports that she was a witch. The woman, who was blind, confessed to being a witch and pointed the finger at her granddaughter, Alison Device, and Old Chattox. The three were taken into custody and held in Lancaster castle.

Old Demdike said that about 20 years before, while returning home from begging, she had been stopped in the Pendle Forest by a spirit or devil in the shape of a boy, whose coat was half black and half brown. The devil said that if she gave him her soul, she could have anything she requested. She asked the devil's name and was told, "Tibb." Old Demdike agreed. For the next five or six years, Tibb appeared to her and asked what was her bidding, but she repeatedly turned him away. At the end of six years, on one Sabbath morning, while Old Demdike had a child on her knee and was in a slumber, Tibb appeared in the likeness of a brown dog and sucked blood from beneath her left arm. The experience, she said, left her "almost stark mad" for about eight weeks.

Old Demdike also testified that her daughter, Elizabeth Device, had helped out one Richard Baldwyn at his mill just before Christmas in 1611. Led by Alison Device, Old Demdike went to Baldwyn to ask for remuneration. Baldwyn replied, "Get out of my ground, whores and witches, I will burn the one of you, and hang the other," to which Old Demdike retorted, "I do not care for thee, hang thyself." As the women were leaving, Tibb appeared and urged Old Demdike to take revenge. She agreed, and said, "Revenge thee either of him, or his." Tibb vanished and she never saw him again.

Old Chattox confessed that 14 years earlier she had entered into the "devilish abominable profession of witchcraft" through the "wicked persuasion and counsel" of Old Demdike. The Devil appeared to her in the likeness of a man, and, at Old Demdike's urging, she promised him her soul and gave him a place near her ribs to suck on. The witches were rewarded with a feast of food and drink. Old Chattox was indicted, according to Potts, for the felonious practice of "diverse wicked and devilish arts called witchcrafts, enchantments, charms and sorceries" to cause the death of one Robert Nutter of Pendle Forest.

Alison Device confessed that after the falling-out with Baldwyn, one of his daughters fell ill the next day, lingered for a year and died. She believed her grandmother bewitched the child to death. Device also was indicted for laming an old peddler.

On Good Friday in April, within a week after the women had been imprisoned in Lancaster castle, Old Demdike's daughter, Elizabeth, called a meeting of her family and that of Old Chattox to discuss a plan to free them. The meeting took place at Malking Tower, the forest home of Old Demdike, and was attended by about 21 persons, 18 of them women. The group devised a plan in which they would kill the jailer and blow up the castle with gunpowder. Following the planning, the group had a feast that included stolen mutton, and bacon and beef. When the justice, Robert Nowell, got wind of the meeting, he had arrested and sent to the castle nine of those involved: Elizabeth Device and her son, James Device; Anne Redfearne, daughter of Old Chattox; Alice Nutter; Katharine Hewit; Jane and John Bulcock, mother and son; Isabel Robey; and Margaret Pearson. Others involved managed to flee.

In all, 20 persons were brought to trial in August. They testified against each other. The principal witnesses were Elizabeth Device's children, Alison, James, who was in his twenties, and Jennet (also given as Jannet), a girl of nine. Both testified against their mother. Jennet said that Elizabeth had an IMP named Ball, which she dispatched to murder anyone who displeased her. James said he had seen Ball in the shape of a brown dog and also had seen his mother making clay images. With the testimony of her children, Elizabeth then confessed. Jennet then implicated James, saying he used another imp in the shape of a dog, Dandy, to bewitch persons to death. James confessed.

Anne Redfearne was acquitted on charges of bewitching Robert Nutter to death. This verdict was so unpopular that Redfearne was retried for bewitching Nutter's father, Christopher Nutter, to death. This time, she was convicted. Alice Nutter, Christopher's wife, was charged with killing one Henry Mytton and was named by the three Devices.

Ten persons were sentenced to hang: Old Chattox, Elizabeth, James and Alison Device; Anne Redfearne; Katherine Hewit; Jane and John Bulcock; and Isabel Robey. Old Demdike died in prison before her trial, and Margaret Pearson was sentenced to a lesser punishment of the pillory and a year in jail. The rest were found not guilty.

In his account of the trials, court clerk Potts described the defendants as the most wretched of hags. Elizabeth Device was an "odious witch," a "barbarous and inhumane monster, beyond example," who was "branded with a preposterous marke in nature, even from her birth, which was her left eye, standing lower then (sic) the other; the one looking down, the other looking up, so strangely deformed, as the best that were present in that honorable assembly, and great audience, did affirm, they had not often seen the like." Old Chattox was "a very old withered spent and decrepit creature, her sight almost gone." Old Demdike was "the rankest hag that ever troubled daylight."

Twenty-one years later, Jennet Device became involved in the second major witch trials of the Pendle Forest area.

The 1633 trials. This episode in witch-hunting history began with a farmer's son, Edmund Robinson, about 10 or 11 years of age, who seemed to have a vivid imagination. According to his story, he was out at the edge of the forest one day and saw two greyhounds, which he thought belonged to a neighbor. He tried to set them on a hare, but when they refused to course, he drew a switch and started to beat them. They turned into a little boy, and a woman he knew, Mother Dickenson. Dickenson offered him money to sell his soul to the Devil, but he refused. She took a bridle out of her pocket and put it on the little boy, who turned into a horse. Grabbing Edmund, Dickenson sprang up on the horse and rode over the terrain until they came to a large barn. It was a witches' sabbat (see SABBATS), and there were about 50 to 60 persons gathered for a feast. Edmund observed six ugly witches pulling ropes tied to the ceiling of the barn, which brought down meat, butter, bread, milk that fell into basins, hot puddings and other delicacies. Edmund was so frightened that he managed to escape home.

Edmund's father made the boy give a deposition to the authorities. Since Edmund did not know the names of all those present at the sabbat, he was sent around the countryside to churches and public places to identify them by sight. For every witch identified, he would be paid a fee. Such an incentive must have been impossible to resist, and, prodded by his father, Edmund accused more than 30 persons—including Jennet Device. Seventeen of them were found to bear the WITCH'S MARK, were tried and convicted. Among them was Mother Dickenson, a young woman who confessed she had sold her soul to the Devil for money which later vanished and another who was accused of making a pail of water run uphill. The latter apparently was in the habit of rolling her pail downhill and running ahead of it.

The local justices suspected that something foul besides witchcraft was afoot and referred the cases to the King's Council. An investigation by the Bishop of Chester revealed that the elder Robinson had been willing to accept bribes for withholding evidence against the accused. Four prisoners were sent to London, where they were examined for witch's marks, but none were found. Questioned, Edmund finally admitted that during the alleged sabbat, he had been out picking plums. He had been coerced into making up the story by his father, who had sought to make quick money. The prisoners were released (some had died in jail), and Robinson senior was jailed.

Lancre, Pierre de (1550?–1631?)   Infamous French witch-trial judge who terrorized the Basque region, sent an estimated 600 persons to their deaths at the stake (see WITCHES) and compiled detailed accounts of alleged infernal activities at witches' SABBATS. Jules Michelet, who relied heavily upon the writings of de Lancre for his own classic work, *Satanism and Witchcraft*, called Lancre "something of a Gascon, boastful and vain of his own achievements . . . a man of wit and perspicacity, and being manifestly in relations with certain young witches, was in a position to know the whole truth." Julio Caro Baroja, in *The World of Witches* (1961), says de Lancre was "[a man] obsessed with the desire to uncover criminal activities, who accepted religion as the basis for the penal code."

Pierre de Lancre was born Pierre de Rosteguy, Sieur de Lancre, between 1550 and 1560. His father

was a wealthy winegrower who adopted the surname "de Lancre" upon becoming a royal official. Pierre was given a Jesuit education. He studied law at Turin and in Bohemia, and became a lawyer.

In 1609 two men of Labourd petitioned the French Parlement to ask Henry IV to send judges to deal with witches who were plaguing the region. One of the petitioners was the Siegneur de Saint-Pei, Urtubi, who had attended a sabbat and believed a witch was sucking his blood. Henry IV agreed and appointed de Lancre and a man named d'Espaignet (also spelled d'Espagnet). They were given plenary powers subject to no appeal.

De Lancre took his job most seriously. He viewed the people of the Basque country as an irresponsible and immoral lot, easy prey for the DEVIL. By virtue of their geographic locale and their separate language, the Basques were viewed as mysterious and

Witches' sabbat according to Pierre de Lancre (Pierre de Lancre, *Tableau de l'inconstance des mauvais anges,* 1612)

isolated. The men were primarily sailors, who would go off on long fishing expeditions to Canada and Newfoundland, leaving their women behind to run the villages and support themselves and their family. Upon their return, the men would waste their earnings on festivities, wild dancing and drinking. Furthermore, superstitions and beliefs in magic ran high among the Basques. It was no wonder, then, that WITCHCRAFT had infested the population.

De Lancre seemed both fascinated and repulsed by the Basque women. Says Michelet, "the very judge that burns them is all the while charmed by their fascinations." In his writings, de Lancre himself described the Basque women as follows:

> When you see them pass, their hair flying in the wind and brushing their shoulders, so well adorned and caparisoned are they, as they go, with their lovely locks, that the sun glancing through them as through a cloud, makes a flashing aureole of dazzling radiance. . . . Hence the dangerous fascination of their eyes, perilous for love no less than for witchery.

The appearance of de Lancre and d'Espaignet in Labourd in May of 1609 caused great alarm. Some residents, anticipating the bloodshed that was to come, fled into the mountains, to Spain and to Newfoundland. Most, however, remained in their homes. Initially, those questioned yielded no information. The dam of resistance was broken by a 17-year-old girl, Margarita, who perhaps thought she could save herself by denouncing others. This she did in great detail, enabling the judges to begin hauling in suspects. They were tortured, pricked for insensitive spots and searched for witch's marks (see WITCH'S MARK). Margarita herself participated in some of the tortures. The confessions implicated others, until hardly a family in Labourd had not been denounced for witchcraft.

De Lancre was undiscriminating in his acquisition of evidence. No person was too young, too old or too feeble in body or brain—he believed them all. He relied heavily upon the testimony of children. Some as young as five years old admitted to attending sabbats and riding on broomsticks (see BROOMS) and the backs of goats; some testified against their own mothers. De Lancre collected numerous tales of nocturnal sabbats and the brewing of OINTMENTS and POISONS. On the face of the confessions, the Basque witches were the most active and diabolical of all in Europe. They met weekly, sometimes almost daily, at any hour, even during Mass. Crowds of up to 2,000 attended the four major sabbats held during the year. They danced naked, ate corpses, copulated, said Black Masses (see BLACK MASS) and worshipped the Devil. They made poisons out of TOADS for ru-

ining the crops, including one incredible mixture of grilled toads and clouds, which ruined fruit trees.

D'Espaignet quit his post in June, leaving de Lancre to carry on alone. De Lancre became convinced that some 3,000 persons, including members of the clergy, bore witch's marks. He said the local priests dispatched sailors to Newfoundland, then imported devils from Japan who copulated with the wives left behind.

De Lancre pushed through trials and executions. At intervals in the proceedings, he played the lute from the bench and had the condemned witches dance before him. The first group of witches to be burned named many others, which so infuriated the townsfolk that they attacked the condemned as they were being led in carts to the stakes, crying at them to withdraw their accusations. de Lancre relates that on the sabbat after these first burnings, the cowardly Devil did not show up, nor did he for the next three sabbats, but sent an inferior IMP in his stead. Satan allegedly told his followers that no more witches would be burned, but de Lancre proved him a liar.

At one point, de Lancre became convinced that witches and the Devil attempted an attack on him one night while he slept in a castle in Saint Pe. On the night of September 24, the Devil supposedly entered his bedchamber and said a Black Mass. Witches forced their way under his bed curtains to poison him but could not do so because he was protected by God. The Devil had sex with one of the witches. According to another version of the story, the Devil and the witches could not gain entrance to the bed chamber but said two Black Masses.

According to de Lancre, when the last witch to be tried and executed was set afire, alive, at the stake, a swarm of toads escaped from her head. The spectators responded with a hail of stones, so that the witch was nearly stoned to death before the flames claimed her. One great black toad, however, managed to avoid stones, sticks and flames, and escaped.

At the end of de Lancre's legal tour in 1610, he was granted a leave of absence and went to Rome, Naples and Lombardy. Sometime between 1612 and 1622, he was rewarded for his great service to the state and was made a state counsellor in Paris. He wrote the details of his trials and investigations in three works: *Tableau de l'inconstance des mauvais anges et demons (Description of the Inconstancy of Evil Angels)* (1612); *L'Incredulite et miscreance du sortilege plainement convaincue (Incredulity and Misbelief of Enchantment)* (1622); and *Du Sortilege (Witchcraft)* (1627). He died in Paris in 1630 or 1631.

Laveau, Marie (1794?–1881); (1827–1897) The most famous voodoo queen (only recently have Vodounists dropped the derogatory term *voodoo; see* VODOUN) in North America was actually two people: mother and daughter. As leaders of voodoo worshipers in New Orleans during the 19th century and perhaps into the 20th, both women epitomized the sensational appeal of the religion: magical powers, control of one's lovers and enemies and sex.

Marie Laveau I reputedly was born in New Orleans in 1794 and was considered a free woman of color. She was mulatto, of mixed black, white and Indian blood, and sometimes was described as a descendant of French aristocracy or the daughter of a wealthy white planter. Records of her marriage on August 4, 1819, to Jacques Paris, a free man of color from Saint Domingue (Haiti), report that Marie was the illegitimate daughter of Charles Laveau and Marguerite Darcantel. Marie was tall and statuesque, with curly black hair, flashing black eyes, reddish skin and "good" features (meaning more white than Negroid). She and Paris lived in a house in the 1900 block of North Rampart Street, given to them by Charles Laveau as part of Marie's dowry.

Paris was a quadroon—three-fourths white. Not long after the marriage, he disappeared, perhaps returning to Saint Domingue. About five years later his death was recorded, but there is no certification of interment. Long before, Marie began calling herself the Widow Paris and took up employment as a hairdresser to the wealthy white and Creole women of New Orleans. These women confided their most intimate secrets to Marie, about their husbands, their lovers, their estates, their husbands' mistresses, their business affairs and their fears of insanity and of anyone discovering a strain of Negro blood in their ancestry. Marie listened and remembered their confessions, using them later to strengthen her powers as *Voodooienne.*

A few years later, in about 1826, Marie took up with Louis Christophe Duminy de Glapion, another quadroon from Saint Domingue who moved in with her on North Rampart until his death in June of 1855 (some accounts say 1835). They never married, but he and Marie had 15 children in rapid succession. She quit the business of hairdressing and began to devote all her energies to becoming the supreme Voodoo Queen of New Orleans.

Blacks had been practicing voodoo secretly around New Orleans ever since the arrival of the first boatload of slaves. New Orleans was more French-Spanish than English-American, and the slaves had come from the same parts of Africa that sent blacks to work the French and Spanish plantations in the Caribbean. After the blacks won their independence in Haiti in 1803–1804, Creole planters brought their slaves with them to the friendlier shores of southern Louisiana

from Saint Domingue and other West Indian islands. These slaves were avid practitioners of the ancient cult, and it grew rapidly.

Stories circulated of secret rites deep in the bayous, complete with worship of a snake called Zombi and orgiastic dancing, drinking and lovemaking. Nearly a third of the worshippers were whites, desirous of obtaining the "power" to regain a lost lover, take a new lover, eliminate a bad business partner or destroy an enemy. The meetings became so frequent that white masters feared the blacks were plotting an uprising against them. In 1817 the New Orleans Municipal Council passed a resolution forbidding blacks to gather for dancing or any other purpose except on Sundays and only in places designated by the mayor. The accepted spot was Congo Square on North Rampart Street, now called Beauregard Square, where for more than 20 years the blacks, most of them voodoos, met and danced and sang, overtly worshipping their gods while seemingly entertaining the whites with their African "gibberish."

By the early 1830s, there were many voodoo queens in New Orleans, fighting over control of the Sunday Congo dances and the secret ceremonies out at Lake Pontchartrain. But when "Mamzelle" Marie Laveau decided to become queen, contemporaries reported the other queens faded before her, some succumbing to her powerful GRIS-GRIS and some being driven away by brute force. Always a devout Catholic, Marie Laveau added many facets of Catholic worship—including holy WATER, incense, statues of the saints and Christian PRAYER—to the already sensational voodoo ceremonies.

She first took control of the rites out at the lake, turning them into large spectacles and inviting the police, the press, young New Orleans roués and any other thrill-seekers interested in forbidden fun. Admission fees were charged for the first time, turning voodoo into a profitable business. Other, more secret, orgies were organized for wealthy white men looking for beautiful black, mulatto and quadroon mistresses. Marie presided over those meetings to which no outsiders were privy, but almost every gathering became public. She then gained control of the dances at Congo Square, entering the gated area before any of the other dancers and performing with her snake for the fascinated onlookers.

Eventually, the information learned in Creole boudoirs, her considerable knowledge of SPELLS and her own style and flair made her the most powerful woman in the city. Whites of all classes appealed to her for help in their various affairs and amours, and the blacks acknowledged her as their leader. Judges paid her as much as $1,000 to help them win elections, and even the most insignificant love powders cost whites $10. Few blacks paid for her services. She became so well known that visiting Marie Laveau for a reading became the thing to do while in New Orleans.

Nearly every New Orleanian still alive up to World War II had a story to tell about Marie Laveau, some about the mother and some about the daughter, who strikingly resembled her mother and carried on the dynasty. Most of the tales are no doubt exaggerations and hard to attribute to either mother or daughter, but some of the best are these, as told in *Voodoo in New Orleans* by Robert Tallant and *Mysterious Marie Laveau, Voodoo Queen* by Raymond J. Martinez.

In 1869 Marie Laveau I presided over her last official voodoo conclave, where the assembled worshippers decided she should retire, as she was past 70 years of age. She continued her work at the prison and did not completely retreat from active service until 1875, when she entered her St. Ann Street home and did not leave until her death in 1881. But for the faithful, "Marie Laveau" had not changed since the 1830s, still a tall, beautiful woman with flashing black eyes and the power to control lives. She was Marie Laveau II.

Marie Laveau Glapion was born February 2, 1827, one of the 15 children crowding the St. Ann Street cottage. Whether Marie I designated her daughter to follow her or whether Marie II chose the role herself, no one knows. She was lighter skinned than her mother but just as tall and straight, with curling black hair and fine features. Some accounts tell that the pupils of her eyes were half-moon shaped. She apparently lacked the warm compassion of Marie I and inspired more fear and subservience than her mother had. Like her mother, Marie II started her career as a hairdresser, eventually running a bar and a brothel on Bourbon Street between Toulouse and St. Peter streets.

Marie continued the assignations at "Maison Blanche" (White House), the house her mother had built for secret voodoo meetings and liaisons between white men and black women. One account says that Marie Laveau II was a talented procuress, able to provide whatever men desired for a price. The parties at Maison Blanche offered champagne, food, wine and music, while the young women danced naked for white men only, including politicians and other high officials. The police never bothered her, because they were afraid of crossing her and ending up "hoodooed."

One of the most important events in the New Orleans voodoo calendar was June 23, St. John's Eve. Every year the faithful went out of New Orleans to Bayou St. John to participate in the voodoo gathering, which had started as a religious ceremony but had

become a circus under Marie I. St. John's Day corresponds to the summer solstice, celebrated since ancient times. By the time of Marie II, most St. John's Eve conclaves were led by underling voodoo queens, but Marie II presided more than once.

In a newspaper account of St. John's Eve, 1872, the reporter told that after the arrival of Marie Laveau, the crowd sang to her, then built a large fire to heat a boiling CAULDRON. Into the cauldron went water from a beer barrel, salt, black pepper, a black snake cut in three pieces representing the Trinity, a cat, a black rooster and various powders. Meanwhile, Marie Laveau commanded all present to undress, which they did, singing a repetitive chorus to "Mamzelle Marie." At midnight everyone jumped into the lake for about half an hour to cool off, then came out and sang and danced for another hour. At that time Marie preached a sermon, then gave the celebrants permission for a half-hour's "recreation," or sexual intercourse.

After the rest and recreation, everyone ate and sang some more, until the signal was given to extinguish the fire under the cauldron. Four nude women threw water on the fire; then the contents of the kettle were poured back into the barrel. Marie told everyone to dress again; then she preached another sermon. By now it was daybreak, and everyone went home.

Marie I, as Widow Paris, died in her St. Ann Street home on June 16, 1881. Newspaper accounts painted her in the most glorious terms, describing her as a saintly figure of 98 (she was 87) who had nursed the sick and prayed incessantly with the diseased and the condemned. Reporters called her the recipient "in the fullest degree" of the "heredity gift of beauty" in the Laveau family, who gained the notice of Governor Claiborne, French General Humbert, Aaron Burr and even the Marquis de Lafayette. The obituaries claimed she had lived her life in piety, surrounded by her Catholic religion, with no mention at all of her voodoo past. Even one of her surviving children, Madame Legendre, claimed her saintly mother had never practiced voodoo and despised the cult.

Strangely, Marie II "died" in the public eye with Marie I, seeming to pass into obscurity. Since the public had made no distinction between mother and daughter, the death of one ended the career of the other. Marie II still reigned over the voodoo ceremonies among the blacks and ran the Maison Blanche, but she never regained much notice in the press. Supposedly, Marie II drowned in a big storm in Lake Pontchartrain during the 1890s, but some people claimed to see her as late as 1918.

Death did not diminish the power of Marie Laveau,

however. Though she reportedly was buried in the family crypt at St. Louis Cemetery No. 1, the vault does not bear her name. Instead, the inscription indicates that the tomb is the final resting place for "Marie Philome Glapion, deceased June 11, 1897." The tomb still attracts the faithful and the curious. Petitioners leave offerings of food, money and flowers, then ask for Marie's help after turning around three times and marking a cross with red brick on the stone. The cemetery is quite small, but even so the tomb seems to appear out of nowhere when walking among the crypts.

Others believe Marie II is buried in St. Louis Cemetery No. 2, where another crypt marked "Marie Laveau" bears red-brick crosses and serves as the "wishing vault" for young women seeking husbands. Stories place Marie in cemeteries on Girod Street, Louisa Street and Holt Street as well. Marie still makes personal appearances, according to legend, frequenting the areas around the cemetery, the old French Quarter and her voodoo haunts.

leaf doctors   See WITCH DOCTORS.

Leek, Sybil (1923–1983)   English Witch and astrologer who moved to America in the 1960s and gained considerable fame in publicizing the renaissance of WITCHCRAFT in the Western world. Her trademarks were a cape, loose gowns and a jackdaw named Mr. Hotfoot Jackson, who perched on her shoulder. She always wore a crystal necklace, passed on to her by her psychic Russian grandmother.

Leek was born in Midlands, England. Her family, she said, came from a long line of hereditary WITCHES and could trace its roots in the Old Religion to 1134 in southern Ireland on her mother's side, and to occultists close to the royalty of czarist Russia on her father's side. Leek's mother sported red-gold hair, a color said to be common among witches. Psychic ability ran in all members of her family. Her most famous ancestor, she said, was an English witch named Molly Leigh, who died in 1663. According to Leek, Leigh was buried at the very edge of the local church graveyard. Some time afterwards, the vicar and others went to open Leigh's cottage and were shocked to see Leigh, or an apparition of her, sitting in her chair with her jackdaw perched on her shoulder. The vicar and his company allegedly reopened her grave, drove a stake through her heart, threw the living jackdaw into the coffin and reburied it.

Leek, who said she had an IQ of 164, demonstrated an early gift for writing. She was taught at home by her grandmother until local officials required her to be enrolled in school at age 12. She stayed four years and left at age 16.

Leek was nine years old when she met ALEISTER CROWLEY, a frequent visitor to the household. She remembered him as a good-looking man ("by the usual standards") with penetrating eyes and a tremendous animal magnetism. Crowley would take her out climbing on the rocks, and recite his poetry, which encouraged her to write her own. He also gave Leek instruction in the importance of words of power and the power of sound. According to Leek, Crowley announced to her grandmother that little Sybil would someday pick up where Crowley would leave off in occultism. The last time she saw him was in 1947, shortly before his death.

When Leek was 15, she met a well-known pianist-conductor who was 24 years her senior, and fell in love. They were married shortly after her 16th birthday and traveled about England and Europe. He died when she was 18. Leek returned home.

Later, she was initiated into the Craft in southern France, in George du Loup in the hills above Nice, an area that was populated by Cathars in the Middle Ages. According to Leek, she was initiated to replace an elderly Russian aunt, who had been high priestess of a COVEN and had died (see INITIATION). Returning again to England, Leek went to live in Burley, a village in the heart of the New Forest. She lived among GYPSIES and joined the Horsa coven, which claimed to have existed for 700 years. She eventually became its high priestess. She successfully ran three antique shops. At some point, she married a man named Brian and had two sons, Stephen and Julian, who reportedly inherited the family's psychic gifts.

In the 1950s she experienced a mystical vision one spring day while walking alone in the New Forest. She said she became enveloped in a bright blue light that instilled in her a great sense of peace and the realization that her purpose in life was as an evangelist for the Old Religion. Media publicity turned a spotlight on her, bringing tourists and more media to her village. Business at her antique shop declined in the wake of autograph seekers, and her landlord refused to renew her lease unless she publicly denounced Witchcraft. She refused, closed up the shop and left the New Forest. In the early 1960s she went to the United States to pursue media appearances and decided to become a resident there.

Leek lived first in New York but found it a depressing city, and particularly gloomy during the winter. She moved to Los Angeles, where she became acquainted with Crowley's one-time secretary ISRAEL REGARDIE. In her later years, she divided her time between Houston and Florida.

She worked as an astrologer, becoming editor and publisher of her own astrological journal. In 1968 her first book, *Diary of a Witch*, was published. The book described what it was like to be a "modern woman" practicing Witchcraft, and it unleashed an enormous public response. Leek made frequent appearances on the media circuit, trying to dispel myths and stereotypes about Witches and educate the public. She met with mixed success, as some of her interviewers expected her to reinforce the stereotypes of Witches as evil hags (see HAG). One of her greatest trials, she said, was learning patience and tolerance in dealing with such situations.

In all, Leek wrote more than 60 books, plus an internationally syndicated column. She liked to say that she never "preached" Witchcraft but sought only to explain the holistic philosophy of religion and how it differed from SATANISM. She did not approve of nudity in rituals, a requirement in some Witchcraft traditions, or of drugs. She believed in cursing (see CURSES), which set her apart from most other Witches who joined the neo-Pagan traditions.

Leek wrote and spoke a great deal about reincarnation, guided, she said, by the spirit of Madame Helena P. Blavatsky, cofounder of the Theosophical Society (see REINCARNATION).

Leek had a particular fondness for snakes and birds. A jackdaw (a relative of the raven) accompanied her to all coven meetings until his death in 1969. Leek also had a pet boa constrictor named Miss Sashima.

Leek suffered from illness in her last years and died in Melbourne, Florida, in 1983.

Legba (also Elegguá)

Not the oldest, but perhaps the most important, orisha (god) in the African spirit pantheon is called Legba in VODOUN and Elegguá in SANTERÍA. He is the god of doors and entryways, of gates and paths, of CROSSROADS, SORCERY and trickery. WIthout his permission, the other gods may not come to earth. He has been identified with St. Peter in the Catholic catalogue of saints, since Jesus Christ gave Peter the keys to the Kingdom of Heaven, and like Peter, he serves as the foundation for the cult, or church. He is also associated with a holy guardian angel, St. Michael, St. Martin de Porres or St. Anthony.

In Vodoun, Legba is called Papa, or the Father. He is the solar prototype and magical archetype. Vodoun worships the sun as a life-giving force, and Legba is the Sun, the Orient, the East, the place where life is created and MAGIC is controlled. As such, Legba is called *Legba-Ji,* or "god of the creation." His cardinal point in the magical cross is the east. He is greeted first when welcoming the gods or *mysteres,* so that he can open the door and let the

others enter. *Legba-Ati-Bon* also represents the "good wood," or sacred trees of the African jungle, symbolized by the wooden center post, or *poteau-mitan,* in the Vodoun peristyle. The *poteau-mitan* also acts as a conductor of the spirits into the Vodoun ceremonies. Legba forms one-third of the sacred trinity along with *Danbhalah-Wedo* and *Erzulie.*

As *Legba Grand-Chemin* or *Maitre Grand-Chemin,* Legba is guardian of the crossroads and master of the highways. In occult terms, the crossroads symbolize the joining of the astral vertical forces with the horizontal, so Legba controls the astral-causal magic of the gods. Legba, a cosmic axis, conducts the souls of the faithful to union with the *mysteres* and leads the *mysteres* down through the center post to the crossroads to receive the SACRIFICE of the worshippers. Some Vodounists believe his associations with CROSSES make Legba the Vodoun Christ. But as master of the crossroads, or *Maitre Carrefour,* Legba also governs SORCERY and is the greatest magician.

Drawings of Legba usually depict him as an old man, bent over with age. He is also associated with water bearers, as Legba controls the fluids of the earth, including blood and circulation. Anatomically, Legba represents vertebrae, bones and bone marrow, symbolized by the center post—the backbone of the peristyle. *Veves,* or symbolic drawings, of Legba incorporate an equal-sided cross. His favorite sacrificial animals are lions and white sheep, his sacred animal is the lizard and his special metal is gold.

In Santería, Elegguá controls all gates and entryways, acting as messenger for the gods. After Obatala, father of the gods, Elegguá is the most important; his permission must be gained for any of the other *orishas* to function. Legends tell that Olorun-Olofi, the creator, was ill, and all the efforts of the orishas had had no success. Elegguá, still a child, asked to see Olorun-Olofi and gave him an herb concoction that cured him within a few hours. In gratitude, Olorun-Olofi decreed that Elegguá was the god to be honored first in ceremonies, and he gave Elegguá the keys to all doors and made him owner of the roads.

Elegguá's followers keep his image in their houses, prepared by the Santero according to each individual's temperament and guardian angel. First the Santero gathers earth from a crossroads, an anthill, a churchyard, a hospital, the jail and a bakery, mixing these dirts with herbs sacred to Elegguá, a turtle's head, a stone from an open field and 29 coins of various denominations. This mixture is then added to cement, which has been moistened with wine, honey and *omiero,* a sacred herbal liquid used in initiation ceremonies. Next the Santero forms Elegguá's head, using seashells for the eyes and mouth.

After the cement dries, the Santero buries the head before sunrise at a crossroads to allow Elegguá's spirit to enter and animate the statue. Seven days later, the Santero disinters the head and fills the empty hole with three roosters, whose blood is sprinkled around the inside. Also into the hole go bananas, corn, candies and some of Elegguá's favorite foods, like coconut. He then generously sprinkles rum over the contents and fills the hole with dirt. Back at the house, the Santero sacrifices a mouse or goat; if neither of these animals is available, he substitutes a black chicken. The sacrifice consecrates the statue, and it becomes Elegguá with all his attendant powers.

Devotees keep Elegguá in a small cabinet near the front door. Every Monday, and on the third day of the month, the statue is removed and exposed to the sun for a few hours before noon, then anointed with a special grease called *manteca de corojo* and replaced in the cabinet. The devotee pours a little bit of water three times on the floor in front of the image and then fills his mouth with rum and sprays the stone with it. Next the devotee lights a cigar and blows smoke in Elegguá's face, as the orisha loves cigars, then leaves the lighted smoke by the statue's side. Next, the devotee feeds Elegguá some small pieces of smoked opossum, some coconut and a few grains of corn along with candy. The devotee customarily tells Elegguá—or any orisha, for that matter—what foods he or she is offering the god. A candle is lit by the cabinet door, which is open all day; then the devotee asks Elegguá's protection and help in acquiring a better job, more money or better luck.

Elegguá has 21 different manifestations, some beneficent and some devilish. The oldest Elegguá is Elufe, whose image is carved from a wide, flat stone and kept in the backyard. The guardian Elegguá of cemetery doors is Anagui, who also distributes and adjudicates the work of the other Elegguás. Alaroye lives behind the doors and counts the goddess Oshun among his good friends. Ayeru is messenger to the god Ifá and protector; Baraine is messenger to the god Chango.

But the personae most feared are the Eshus or Echus, considered by many to be incarnations of the Devil. The Eshus live in darkness; on St. Bartholomew's Day, August 24, the Eshus roam the streets and create as much trouble as possible. As a best friend of the god Oggun, Elegguá is called Eshu Ogguanilebbe and is responsible for automobile accidents and railroad derailments. Whenever Oggun is hungry, this Eshu either kills a dog or causes an accident so that bloodthirsty Oggun may feast. Eshu

)ku Oro controls life and death, and Eshu Bi is the king of mischief and stands in corners. Eshu Alayiki brings the unexpected. The colors red and black symbolize all the Elegguás.

Many Santeros believe the dark Eshu represents all 21 of Elegguá's personalities. These manifestations of Elegguá fit the Brazilian concept of *Exus*, horned gods often mistaken for the devil, who symbolize nature's primal forces. The Exus act as messengers to the gods and are responsible for the world's mischief and trickery. No ceremony in Brazil begins without first asking the Exus for protection and permission to call on the other gods. Evil spells, or *despachos*, need the Exus's help to succeed, and the practitioners of *Quimbanda*, or black magic, worship Exu's worst personalities: Exu Mor (death), Exu of the Crossroads and Exu of the Closed Paths.

Legend of the Cape Cod Cranberry   According to an American folklore tale, the story of how the cranberry came to Cape Cod involved a test of religions between a Puritan missionary and a Mashpee shaman. Rev. Richard Bourne was working to convert the Mashpee Indians of Cape Cod to Christianity but was continually stymied in his efforts by the tribe's shaman. Finally, the shaman cast a spell that caused Bourne's feet to become mired in quicksand (see SPELLS). Bourne challenged the shaman to a test of wills and religions: the shaman's magic versus Christian prayer. If Bourne lost, he would serve the shaman; if Bourne won, the shaman would promise to stop harassing him.

For 15 days and nights the two debated the virtues of their religions. They did not eat or sleep. Eventually, the shaman began to weaken. Bourne, however, was sustained by God, who sent a white dove bearing a single cranberry to his lips every time he fell silent. When one berry fell to the ground, the shaman realized what was happening, and attempted, in vain, to stop the dove with MAGIC.

At last the shaman fainted, and the spell on Bourne's feet was broken. Bourne fetched a silver bowl of soup for the shaman. As he drank the last drops, the shaman saw a vision on the bottom of the bowl—a picture of Judgment Day and the unhappy fate of sinners. The vision frightened the shaman into converting to Christianity. The berry that had fallen to the ground in the contest of wills took root and became the first cranberry bush on Cape Cod.

While the legend may have served to bolster Puritan resolve in settling and Christianizing New England, the American Indians most likely were the original discoverers of the medicinal value of the cranberry, which is indigenous to parts of northern Europe and North America. Tea made from the bark of the cranberry, and a related shrub, *V. trilobum*, was used to help ease the pain of childbirth, and menstrual and stomach cramps. Cranberry-bark tea was a staple among early American pioneers as a remedy for cramps.

See also SHAMANISM.

Leland, Charles Godfrey (1824–1903)

American folklorist, lecturer and prolific author whose immersion in Gypsy lore and WITCHCRAFT influenced the revival of the latter in the 20th century.

Leland was born August 15, 1824, in Philadelphia to a family with Puritan roots. His father, Henry, was a descendant of Hopestill Leland, one of the first white settlers in New England. Family lore maintained that one ancestor was a German sorceress, and Leland always believed that he resembled her in an atavistic way.

The young Leland showed an intense interest in occult subjects, Gypsies and high adventure. He was ambivalent about education; though he graduated from Princeton and studied in Munich and Heidelberg, he later freely acknowledged that he had hated school. Once out of college, he began a lifetime of exotic travel and penetration of the mysterious worlds of GYPSIES, WITCHES and voodoo (see VODOUN).

He returned periodically to America, where he had short-lived careers as a lawyer, newspaper editor and article writer. In his thirties he married Isabel Fisher; the marriage lasted more than 40 years, until her death in 1902.

Leland's real love was the occult and folklore, and after his parents died, he took his inheritance and moved to England. From there, he traveled the world. He learned about the Gypsies and also learned to speak their language, Romany. He discovered Shelta, the secret language of the tinkers. The Gypsies took him into their society, calling him a Romany Rye—a non-Gypsy who associates with Gypsies. He collected Gypsy, Witchcraft and voodoo artifacts and books, turning his home into a veritable museum.

In 1879 he returned to Philadelphia, where he established the Industrial Art School. He spent several summers with American Indians, learning their spiritual lore. After four years he returned to England, where he began *The Gypsy Journal*. He wrote extensively about the Gypsies in books and articles.

In 1886, while in Italy, Leland met a Florentine Witch whom he referred to only as "Maddalena." He described Maddalena as a hereditary Witch with ancient Etruscan roots. She was born in Tuscany into a family of Witches and was educated by her grandmother, aunt and stepmother in the ways of the Craft.

Maddalena and Leland became close friends. She introduced him to other Witches and divulged many secrets of the Craft to him. The information Leland gleaned from Maddalena was incorporated into a series of books, the best-known of which is *Aradia, or Gospel of the Witches*, published in London in 1889. *Aradia* attempts to establish the antiquity of Witchcraft as a religion. It was the first book of its kind to record specific Witchcraft spells, incantations, beliefs and lore (see ARADIA).

Leland died on March 20, 1903, in Florence, of pneumonia and heart trouble. He had spent the last seven years of his life in ill health, which was further aggravated by his grief at the death of his wife on July 9, 1902. Leland was cremated, and his ashes were returned to Philadelphia for burial.

Since the publication of *Aradia*, experts in the field have disagreed over its authenticity. Some scholars dismiss it as spurious. Author T. C. Lethbridge comments that *Aradia* may be a collection of beliefs and practices dating back only to the Middle Ages but perhaps drawing on beliefs that may be much older.

Levi, Eliphas (1810–1875)

The pseudonym of Alphonse Louis Constant, a French occultist who was largely responsible for the revival of interest in MAGIC in the 19th century. Levi studied magic and believed in it but was more of a commentator than an adept, though he did claim to practice NECROMANCY on several occasions.

Constant was born in Paris, the son of a shoemaker. He was bright and quick and was sent to the church at St. Sulpice for education. He was intrigued by magic and the occult, and the headmaster's belief that animal magnetism, the vital energy of the human body, was controlled by the DEVIL only incited his curiosity. Nevertheless, he pursued an ecclesiastical career and became a priest. He was thrown out of the church for his left-wing political writings and because he could not observe his vow of chastity. His writings earned him three short jail sentences.

Constant was attracted to an eccentric old man named Ganneau, who claimed to be a prophet and the REINCARNATION of Louis XVII. (Ganneau's wife believed she was the reincarnation of Marie Antoinette.) Constant became one of Ganneau's followers and was drawn deeper and deeper into the world of magic and the occult.

In 1846 he married Noemie Cadot, who was no older than 18. They had one daughter who died while very young. The marriage disintegrated in 1853 and was annulled in 1865.

For a time, Constant made a living from his writing and by giving lessons in the occult. He renamed himself Magus Eliphas Levi, the Hebrew equivalents of his first and middle names.

In 1854 he took a trip to London, where he first tried necromancy. A mysterious woman who claimed to be an adept asked him to conjure the spirit of APOLLONIUS OF TYANA, a renowned magician of ancient times. Levi undertook an enormous preparation that included two weeks of eating a vegetarian diet and a week of fasting, during which he mediated on Apollonius and imagined having conversations with him.

When he felt ready to perform the conjuration, Levi dressed in white robes and entered his magic chamber, where there were MIRRORS on the walls. In the center of the room he placed a table and covered it with white lambskin. He lit fires in two metal bowls and placed them on the table. Then he began his incantations, which went on for 12 hours.

According to Levi's account, he began to feel progressively colder as he went deeper into the ritual. After 12 hours had passed, the floor beneath him began to shake, and he saw an apparition in one of the mirrors. He asked the ghost to appear. At his third request, a grayish spirit appeared in front of him, thin and sad and wrapped from head to foot in a gray shroud. Levi, frightened, felt extremely cold. The apparition touched Levi's ritual sword, and his arm suddenly went numb. He dropped the sword and fainted.

Levi's arm was sore and numb for days after the incident. He said later that though he never spoke his questions, they were in his mind, and the apparition had responded in telepathy. The answers, he said, were "death" and "dead," but he never revealed the questions. Levi remained unconvinced that he had conjured the spirit of Apollonius. In subsequent rituals, however, he claimed he called up Apollonius several times.

His first and most important book, *The Dogma and Ritual of High Magic*, was published in 1861. He followed that with *A History of Magic, Transcendental Magic, The Key of Great Mysteries* and other occult books. His writing was "purple" and highly imaginative—and not very accurate. For example, he believed in the existence of a universal "secret doctrine" of magic throughout history, everywhere in the world.

In *Dogma*, Levi devoted 22 chapters to the 22 trump cards, or Major Arcana, of the TAROT, linking each one to letters of the Hebrew alphabet and to aspects of God. Some experts say this work is significant; others call it ignorant.

Levi also put forth the theory of *astral light*, based on his belief in animal magnetism. The astral light was rather like the ether, a fluidic life force that fills all space and living beings, another popular belief of the 19th century. To control the astral light, Levi said, was to control all things; a skilled magician's will was limitless in power.

Levi acknowledged being influenced by an earlier writer, FRANCIS BARRETT, who had attempted unsuccessfully to revive magic in the early 1800s. In turn, Levi influenced another occultist and writer, Sir Edward Bulwer-Lytton, whom he visited in England in 1861. Bulwer-Lytton, who wrote *The Last Days of Pompeii*, was also the author of some occult books that helped make magic fashionable in the waning days of the 19th century in England. He and Levi joined an occult group—Bulwer-Lytton may have even organized it—and studied SCRYING, magic, ASTROLOGY and mesmerism.

Until his death, Levi made his living from his occult writings and lessons. He was popular and had a cult of followers, some of whom were inspired to write their own books.

Levi's magic was adopted by the HERMETIC ORDER OF THE GOLDEN DAWN, founded in London in 1888. ALEISTER CROWLEY, who was born the year Levi died, claimed he was the reincarnation of Levi.

See also BAPHOMET.

levitation A paranormal phenomenon whereby a body or object is raised up into the air in defiance of gravity. Levitation is frequently reported in cases of bewitchment, hauntings (see GHOSTS, HAUNTINGS AND WITCHCRAFT) and DEMONIC POSSESSION; it also is attributed to saints and holy persons.

In 1550 in Wertet, Brabant, a group of nuns reportedly levitated into the air, climbed trees like cats and were pinched by invisible fingers. A townswoman was tortured into confessing she had bewitched them. In other cases, beds are said to levitate off the floor. In hauntings, WITCHES, poltergeists and FAIRIES have been blamed for levitating people, animals and objects.

Levitation also has been accomplished by Western psychics and mediums and was a common occurrence—often done fraudulently—at séances in the heydey of Spiritualism. The best-known levitating medium was Daniel Dunglas Home (1833–1886), a Scotsman who was expelled from the Catholic Church on charges of SORCERY. Home was reported to levitate many times over a 40-year-period and to control his flights, which were done in trance. On one occasion, witnesses said he flew out of one third-story window in a home and returned through another window.

Home was suspected of trickery, but he was never convicted of any fraud.

See also SIMON MAGUS.

leys Patterns of invisible lines with a complex power which seem to link sacred places and natural magical sites. In modern WITCHCRAFT and NEO-PAGANISM, these patterns and alignments are important for their apparent connection to the forces of the elements, the basis of natural MAGIC.

The original theory of leys was put forth in 1925 by a British amateur antiquarian, Alfred Watkins. Watkins observed that man-made sacred places such as burial mounds, MEGALITHS, churches and pagan worship sites, as well as natural peaks, magical springs and WELLS and other earth features seemed to align with one another. The *leys*, as Watkins named these alignments, were "old straight tracks" found by prehistoric ley hunters, or Dodman surveyors, who mapped the countryside to find power spots for sacred constructions, trade routes and astronomical sites. Although the original mapping allegedly was done by prehistoric societies, Watkins included in his list of ley sites pre-Reformation churches. His theory was quite controversial. It was and still is rejected by scientists but has enjoyed a popular following. Public interest waned in the 1940s but has increased since the 1960s and 1970s, along with the increase in interest in the psychic and occult. Leys also are called *ley lines,* a phrase that some feel is inaccurate.

Not all alignments are true leys. Modern ley-hunters map leys by checking the alignments of various locations according to what else of significance lies in a sight-line within a certain distance: a standing stone, church site, pagan sacred site, burial mound, mountain, etc. Some alignments are astronomical, such as points where the sun rises at Beltane, the solstices or the equinoxes. Some ley-hunters say that five alignments within 10 miles is required to establish a ley, while others maintain that five within 25 miles is sufficient. Dowsers say that in addition, the alignment must be a dowsable energy line (see DOWSING).

Ley centers, places charged with energy, radiate at least seven ley lines and are situated over magnetic fields or blind springs, a primary spiral of converging primary geodetic lines (the shortest lines between two points on a curved surface). It is possible that ancient pagans were aware of this energy radiating up from the earth and situated their sacred sites accordingly.

The energy charge is a vital force classed as either male or female depending on its rate of vibration, and it is present in all living material. In ley centers, the charge may be natural or artificial. Artificial charges may be induced in stones and metals by handling. Whether natural or artificial, the charge dissipates over time unless fixed by hammering, heating or the presence of a magnetic field.

The stones used in the construction of megalithic monuments, churches, holy wells and temples were charged by handling, then fixed by being shaped with the blows of axes and chisels. J. Havelock Fidler, British agricultural scientist and dowser, states that the magnitude of the charge is related to the number of blows and the dimensions of the stones. Therefore, the charge of megaliths would be very great. Cremation pits and burials (such as those at STONEHENGE), sacrificial pits and altars and the burning of wood also fixed the charges. Fidler speculates that some megaliths may have been charged and fixed by witches or pagans who used the CONE OF POWER ritual to raise and direct psychic power. In his own experiments, Fidler found that he could impart greater charges to stones during the full moon, the time of greatest magical and psychic power.

The very ground itself may be charged and fixed with blows. British folklore tells of the ancient custom of "beating the parish bounds," in which the church priest and choirboys would go around the parish perimeter beating the ground with rods. Most likely, this was believed to erect a protective energy barrier around the parish.

Fidler also has found that, while the geomagnetic forces surrounding ley centers emit a beneficial energy, the charge of stones themselves seem to emit an energy detrimental to living things. This apparently is counteracted by the leys themselves, which redirect energy to other centers where it can be neutralized. Also, the charges at one time may have been deliberately masked. Certain woods, such as elm and elderberry; metals such as iron; and mineral substances such as salt, quartz crystals, amethysts, jasper and flint have been shown to mask charged stones. (It is interesting to note that iron, salt, elm and elderberry are all revered in folklore for their protective properties against bewitchment, illness, demons and bad fortune.) The giant bluestones of Stonehenge contain flakes of quartz crystal. These stones were dismantled and re-erected twice during the various construction phases of the monument; perhaps the builders recognized their beneficial properties. Also, quartz chips scattered among charged stones disrupt the power.

Most of the investigating and hunting of leys is done in the United Kingdom, though there is some evidence that leys exist in the United States, France and Peru.

See also AVEBURY; GLASTONBURY.

ligature   See AIGUILLETTE

Lilith   A female demon of the night who flies about searching for newborn children to kidnap or strangle, and sleeping men to seduce in order to produce demon sons. Lilith is a major figure in Jewish demonology, appearing as early as 700 B.C. in the book of Isaiah; she or beings similar to her also are found in myths from other cultures around the world. She is the dark aspect of the Mother Goddess (see DEMONS; GODDESS).

Lilith was the first wife of Adam; the two were created by God as twins joined in the back. Lilith demanded equality with Adam, and, failing to get it, left him in anger. According to Muslim legend, she slept with Satan and created the demonic DJINN.

Adam complained to God that his wife has deserted him. God sent three angels, Sanvi, Sansanvi and Semangelaf, to bring Lilith back to Eden. The angels found her in the Red Sea and threatened her with the loss of 100 of her demon children every day unless she returned to Adam. She refused and was punished accordingly.

Lilith took revenge by launching a reign of terror against women in childbirth, newborn infants—particularly males—and men who slept alone. She was forced, however, to swear to the three angels that whenever she saw their names or images on an amulet (see AMULETS), she would leave infants and mothers alone.

As late as the 18th century, it was a common practice in many cultures to protect new mothers and infants with amulets against Lilith. Male infants were vulnerable for the first week of life, girls for the first three weeks. Sometimes a MAGIC CIRCLE was drawn around the lying-in bed, with a charm (see CHARMS) inscribed with the names of the three angels, Adam and Eve and the words "barring Lilith" or "protect this newborn child from all harm." Sometimes amulets with such inscriptions were placed in all corners of and throughout the bedchamber. If a child laughed in its sleep, it was a sign that Lilith was present. Tapping the child on the nose made the demon go away.

Men who had nocturnal emissions believed they had been seduced by Lilith during the night and that they had to say incantations to prevent the offspring from becoming demons. Lilith was believed to be assisted in her bloodthirsty nocturnal quests by succubi, who gathered with her near the "mountains of darkness" to frolic with her demon lover, Samael, whose name means "left" or "sinister." *The Zohar*, the principal work in the Kabbalah, describes Lilith's powers at their height when the moon is on the wane.

In addition to Jewish folklore, the Lilith demon appears in Iranian, Babylonian, Mexican, Greek, Arab, English, German, Oriental and North American Indian legends. She is sometimes associated with other characters in legend and myth, including the Queen of Sheba and Helen of Troy. In medieval Europe she was often portrayed as the wife, concubine or grandmother of Satan. In the late 17th century she was described as a screech owl, blind by day, who sucked the breasts or navels of young children or the dugs of goats.

Lithobolia of New Hampshire, The   A strange case of LITHOBOLY, or stone-peltings, occurred in the late 1600s in the colony of New Hampshire. The exact date of the incident is not known, but it was recorded in INCREASE MATHER'S *Providences* in 1684 and in an eyewitness account published in 1698.

The stone-peltings took place over a period of several months at the home of George Walton, a wealthy landowner. The suspected source of the trouble was an elderly woman who was a neighbor of Walton's and was believed to be a witch (see WITCHES). She and Walton had a dispute over a piece of land, which Walton claimed belonged to him and which he succeeded in appropriating from her. The bitter woman was overheard to remark that Walton would "never quietly enjoy that piece of ground." Her curse (see CURSES) apparently came true.

One Sunday night in May at about 10 o'clock, Walton and his family, servants and guests were surprised by the clatter of a great number of stones against the roof and all sides of the house. Walton and several persons ran outside to investigate but could see nothing despite the bright moonlight. Walton found his fence gate torn off its hinges. Before he and the others returned inside, they were pelted by a rain of stones.

They ran back inside the house, where everyone was in an uproar. Stones began flying into the house. Everyone withdrew from the outer rooms, yet stones, some of them as large as fists, continued to fly at them and drop from the ceiling. Stones battered the windows from the inside, punching holes in the leaded glass and forcing out the bars, lead and hasps before ricocheting back into the room. Some of the stones seemed to fly out of the fire and were hot. Stones pelted the brass and pewter ware that was out, sending pots and candlesticks crashing to the floor.

By some miracle, no one was seriously injured by the stones. The occupants of the house immediately assumed preternatural causes. For four hours, stones continued to fly about the house and rain down the chimney. One of the guests grew weary and went back to bed, only to awaken when an eight-pound stone crashed through his chamber door.

The next day, Walton's domestics discovered that various household objects were missing. Some turned up in the yard and other odd places, while others abruptly sailed down the chimney or fell into rooms as though dropped from the ceiling. The men who went to work in the fields found the land littered with stones. A black cat was seen in the orchard and was shot at, but got away (see CATS).

That evening, one of the guests began to play a musical instrument. A "good big Stone" came rumbling in the room, followed by an avalanche of more stones. A hand was seen thrusting out from a hall window, tossing more stones upon the porch, at a time when no one was in the hall.

The stone-throwing and the disappearance of household objects went on for weeks, sometimes stopping for a day or two, then renewing with more force. The stones got larger; two stones weighing more than 30 pounds apiece thundered against one of the guest-room doors. The men at work outside continued to be plagued by stones that rained down and then disappeared from the ground, only to rain down on them again.

On Monday, June 28, came one of the worst stone attacks. Members of the household were eating supper in the kitchen when stones hurled down and broke the table into pieces. R. C. Esq. writes in his account, *Lithobolia: or, the Stone-throwing Devil, etc.* (1698):

> . . . many Stones (some great ones) came thick and threefold among us, and an old howing Iron, from a Room hard by, where such Utensils lay. Then, as if I had been the designed Object for that time, most of the Stones that came (the smaller I mean) hit me, (sometimes pretty hard), to the number of above 20, near 30 . . . and whether I moved, sit, or walk'd, I had them, and great ones sometimes lighting gently on me. . . . Then was a Room over the Kitchen infested, that had not been so before, and many Stones greater than usual lumbering there over our Heads, not only to ours, but to the great Disturbance and Affrightment of some Children that lay there.

Walton continued to work in the fields with his men, though they were repeatedly pelted by stones. One day Walton said he was struck by more than 40 of them, which injured him so that he suffered chronic pain for the rest of his life. The corn planted in the fields was mysteriously cut off at the roots or uprooted. No agent of the damage was ever seen by anyone. The men said they heard at times an eerie "snorting and whistling" while they worked.

Other strange things continued to happen. A maid was hit on the head by a falling porringer. Hay baled

one day was found strewn about the ground the next, with some of it tossed into the trees. One night, a "violent shock of Stones and Brickbats" crashed through a window, toppled books off a case and ripped a foot-long hole in a picture.

Finally, on August 1, Walton had had enough and decided to fight WITCHCRAFT with witchcraft. On the advice of someone who claimed to know about such matters, he attempted to cast a spell to punish the witch responsible for the harassment (see SPELLS). A pot containing URINE and crooked PINS was set on the fire. As it boiled, it was supposed to remove the bewitchment and make the witch suffer. But as the urine began to heat, a stone fell into it and spilled it. The Waltons refilled the pot with more urine and crooked pins. Another stone fell in the pot and spilled the contents again. Then the handles fell off the pot, and the pot split into pieces. The Waltons gave up.

The hails of stones went on. Now more than 100 stones fell on the field while Walton and his men worked. Walton found his tools broken and his fences pulled down.

Walton at least complained to the council in Portsmouth, which summoned both him and the elderly woman for interrogation. En route, Walton was struck by three fist-sized stones, one of which "broke his head," a wound that he showed to the president of the council.

The outcome of the affair is not recorded. Most likely, the stone-throwing stopped after the Portsmouth Council became involved. Walton remained on his land, but his health was ruined.

lithoboly Mysterious hails of STONES have been reported from time to time in cases of WITCHCRAFT and possession (see DEMONIC POSSESSION; SPIRIT POSSESSION). Victims claim to be pelted by stones which suddenly rain down from the sky, or appear from nowhere inside a room. In folklore, the hails are credited to lithobolia, or stone-throwing DEMONS.

See also THE LITHOBOLIA OF NEW HAMPSHIRE.

lithomancy A method of DIVINATION using STONES that is popular in the British Isles and Europe. Each stone has its own significance, and the divination is done by casting the stones in lots and interpreting the way they fall.

Thirteen stones are used. The stones are selected from natural surroundings during favorable astrological configurations (see ASTROLOGY) and with the guidance of intuition. Ideally, the stones are smooth and roughly uniform in size and shape. They may be pebbles picked up from the beach or semiprecious stones such as agates or types of crystal.

Seven of the stones represent astrological signs: the sun, moon, Mars, Venus, Mercury, Jupiter and Saturn. The remaining six represent the home, love, life, magic, luck and news (see ASTROLOGY).

Divinatory stones may be stored in a charm bag (see GRIS-GRIS).

loa See VODOUN.

Lord's Prayer A common belief from about the 16th to early 18th centuries was that true WITCHES were incapable of reciting the Lord's Prayer from start to finish. The reasoning was that the prayer, or any passage from the Bible, was offensive to the DEVIL, who would not permit his disciples to repeat it. This test was considered virtually infallible both in formal trials and inquisitions and in informal witch-hunts. If the accused stumbled or omitted even a few words, she failed the test. Since a good many accused witches were old, uneducated women, it was likely that a good number of them did not know the prayer or any other bit of Scripture demanded of them; nor would it be surprising that many of them stumbled or forgot lines out of fear. Some, like FLORENCE NEWTON, tried in Ireland in 1661, said they could not remember because of their bad memory and old age. Sometimes a successful recitation of the Lord's Prayer made no difference. Most of the seven women accused of witchcraft in the Island Magee case in Ireland in 1711 had no trouble reciting the Lord's Prayer, yet all seven were found guilty by a jury (see ISLAND MAGEE WITCHES).

The Lord's Prayer has long been considered a powerful charm against witchcraft and the forces of evil (see CHARMS). The theologian St. Augustine (354–430), in his *Sermon Against Fortune-tellers and Diviners*, stated, "But as often as you have to do anything or to go out, cross yourselves in the name of Christ, and saying faithfully the Creed or the Lord's Prayer you may go about your business secure in the help of God." According to the *MALLEUS MALEFICARUM* (1486), reciting the Lord's Prayer was one of a number of remedies guaranteed to drive away incubi and succubi and nullify bewitchments of men and beasts.

The Lord's Prayer customarily is recited by priests in DEMONIC EXORCISM of DEMONIC POSSESSION. According to European lore, the prayer also helps ward off vampires.

In some black-magic and satanic rituals, the Lord's Prayer is recited backwards. An 18th-century magic textbook, the *Grimorium Verum*, instructs that to harm an enemy, one should drive a coffin nail into his footprint and recite the Lord's Prayer backwards.

See also PRAYER.

Loudun Possessions The DEMONIC POSSESSION of the Ursuline nuns of Loudun by Father Urbain Grandier is probably the most famous case of mass possession in history. Vividly described in Aldous Huxley's *The Devils of Loudun* (1952), the torments of Mother Superior Jeanne des Anges (Joan of the Angels) and the sisters, supposedly inflicted by the handsome Grandier in 1634, resulted in not only the priest's fiery death but also a great debate on the veracity of the nuns' sufferings, the theological probability of WITCHCRAFT and whether one man had not been sacrificed for his political misdeeds.

Appointed parish priest of St.-Pierre-du-Marche in Loudun, a town in Poitiers, France, in 1617, Urbain Grandier cut a quite a figure. Handsome, urbane, wealthy and eloquent, he had no trouble finding women willing to help him bend his priestly vows. Townspeople suspected Grandier of fathering a child by Philippa Trincant, the daughter of the king's solicitor in Loudun, and he openly courted Madeleine de Brou, daughter of the king's councillor, for whom he composed a treatise against the celibacy of priests. Most assumed Madeleine was Grandier's mistress.

Grandier's first serious setback occurred on June 2, 1630, when he was arrested for immorality and found guilty by his enemy, the Bishop of Poiters. But Grandier's own political connections restored him to full clerical duties within the year. Next, Grandier's enemies approached Father Mignon, confessor to the Ursuline nuns at their convent and a relative of Trincant. The plan was for Father Mignon to persuade a few of the sisters to feign possession, swearing that Father Grandier had bewitched them, causing his removal and downfall. The Mother Superior, Jeanne des Anges, and another nun readily complied, falling into fits and convulsions, holding their breath and speaking in hoarse voices.

Contemporaries of Jeanne des Anges, formerly Madame de Beclier (or Becier) before joining the order, described her both as a living saint and as a strange, ambitious woman. Apparently rich and extravagant in her secular life as the daughter of a baron, Jeanne lived devoutly and humbly at the convent, awaiting her chance to become Mother Superior. She reportedly had strange dreams about Father Grandier; appearing to her as a radiant angel, he spoke more like a devil, enticing her to sexual acts and vices. Her hysterical dreams and ravings disturbed the peace of the convent, but after flagellation and penance, Jeanne was no quieter, and other nuns had succumbed to hallucinations and dreams. At this point, some accounts report that Jeanne called for Father Mignon's help, not the other way around.

In any case, Father Mignon and Father Pierre Barre, his aide, saw an opportunity for revenge against

Grandier. The two priests began exorcising the nuns, while Jeanne and the others shrieked, cavorted and suffered convulsive fits. Whether because the rituals added to the performance or caused Jeanne's mind to snap, she swore that she and the others were possessed by two devils, Asmodeus and Zabulon, sent by Father Grandier via a bouquet of roses thrown over the convent walls. Realizing his peril, Grandier appealed to the bailiff of Loudun to have the nuns isolated, but the bailiff's orders were ignored. In desperation, Grandier wrote to the archbishop of Bordeaux; the archbishop sent his doctor to examine the nuns and found no evidence of possession. The archbishop ended the exorcisms on March 21, 1633, and ordered the nuns to confinement in their cells. Peace returned for a while, but the hysteria began again later that year.

Meanwhile, Grandier's enemies continued their efforts to remove him. Jean de Laubardemont, a relative of Jeanne's and a crony of the powerful Cardinal Richelieu, along with a Capuchin monk, Tranquille, brought to the Cardinal's attention a libelous satire of Richelieu that Grandier was supposed to have written in 1618 and reports of the unsuccessful exorcisms. Eager to prove his power in the Church and in France, and also aware of his relative, Sister Claire, in the convent, the Cardinal appointed Laubardemont head of a commission to arrest and convict Grandier as a witch. The exorcisms resumed, this time publicly, led by the Capuchin Father Tranquille, Franciscan Father Lactance and Jesuit Father Jean-Joseph Surin.

Besides the accusations of the nuns, Grandier's former mistresses came forward with stories of adultery, incest, sacrilege and other sins committed not only by a priest but in the holiest places of the church. The dreams and physical responses of the nuns were overtly sexual, providing shocking evidence of Grandier's diabolical nature. Jeanne added a new possessor, Isacaaron, the devil of debauchery, and even went through a psychosomatic pregnancy.

Finally, Father Grandier was forced to exorcise the nuns himself, since he was the apparent cause of their sufferings. To test their knowledge of languages previously unknown to the nuns—a sure sign of possession—Grandier spoke in Greek, but the nuns had been coached, replying that one of the terms of their pact had been never to use Greek. Of course, Grandier failed.

One of the most interesting items from the exorcisms and trial was the written pact between the Devil and Grandier, allegedly stolen from Lucifer's cabinet of devilish agreements by Asmodeus and presented to the court as proof of Grandier's complicity (see DEVIL'S PACT). The pact was signed in blood by Grandier and by various demons, including Asmodeus, who also accommodatingly wrote out a promise to leave one of the nuns he was possessing, as reported by an earlier exorcist, Father Gault:

> I promise that when leaving this creature, I will make a slit below her heart as long as a pin, that this slit will pierce her shirt, bodice and cloth which will be bloody. And tomorrow, on the twentieth of May at five in the afternoon of Saturday, I promise that the demons Gresil and Amand will make their opening in the same way, but a little smaller—and I approve the promises made by Leviatam, Behemot, Beherie with their companions to sign, when leaving, the register of the church St. Croix! Given the nineteenth of May, 1629.

The message is written in Jeanne des Anges's hand. Other demonic "evidence" came from Astaroth, a devil of the order of Seraphims and chief of the possessing devils; from Easas, Celsus, Acaos, Cedon, Alex, Zabulon, Naphthalim, Cham and Ureil; from Asmodeus of the order of thrones; and from Achas of the order of principalities.

Still convinced he could not be convicted of such imaginary crimes, Grandier was thrown in prison at the castle of Angiers on November 30, 1633. Witches' or Devil's marks were quickly found by lancing him in one part of the body, causing pain, and lightly touching him elsewhere, causing none (see DEVIL'S MARK). Observers such as Dr. Fourneau, the physician who prepared Grandier for TORTURE, and the apothecary from Poitiers protested the examiner's hoax and found no such marks. Other voices were raised in Grandier's defense, even from the possessed nuns themselves. But Laubardemont, intent on conviction, simply attributed the nuns' retractions to attempts by the Devil to save one of his own. Jeanne des Anges appeared in court with a noose around her neck, threatening to hang herself if she could not expiate her previous perjury. Such efforts were ignored, and other defense witnesses were either pressured to keep silent or threatened with arrest as accessory witches or traitors to the king. Many had to flee France.

Inevitably, the Royal Commission passed sentence on August 18, 1634: following the first and last degrees of torture, Grandier was to be burned alive at the stake. Even under extreme torture, Father Grandier maintained his innocence, refusing to name accomplices, which so angered Father Tranquille and the others that they broke both his legs and claimed that every time Grandier prayed to God, he was really invoking the Devil. Grandier had been promised he could make a last statement and be mercifully strangled before burning, but the friars who carried him to the stake deluged him with holy water, pre-

Burning of Father Urbain Grandier

God but continually saw visions of devils, black wings and other terrors. In 1645 he tried to kill himself. Only after Father Surin received tender care from Father Bastide, the new head of Surin's Jesuit College at Saintes in 1648, did he begin to recover. Surin finally wrote again in 1657 and walked in 1660. He died at peace in 1665.

Grandier's death did not stop the possessions at Loudun. Public appreciation of the exorcisms had been so great that the convent continued the performances as a type of tourist attraction. Nuns would lift their skirts and coarsely beg for sexual relief. Or the women would beat their heads, bend backwards, walk on their hands, stick out blackened tongues and use language that would, according to one account, "have astonished the inmates of the lowest brothel in the country." Such shows continued until 1637, when the Duchess d'Aiguillon, niece to Cardinal Richelieu, reported the fraud to her uncle. Having satisfied his original aim—to demonstrate his considerable power—Richelieu righteously cut off the performers' salaries and put the convent at peace. Jeanne des Anges, convinced of her saintliness by Father Surin, died also in 1665.

Huxley's account of the madness at Loudun forms the basis of Ken Russell's film version, *The Devils* (1971). Vanessa Redgrave plays Jeanne des Anges, portrayed as a deformed, bitter and sexually repressed woman. Oliver Reed plays the unfortunate Grandier.

venting him from speaking. And the garotte was knotted so that it could not be tightened, leaving Grandier to be burned alive. One monk who witnessed the execution reported that a large fly buzzed about Grandier's head, symbolizing that Beelzebub, the lord of the flies, had come to carry Grandier's soul to hell.

But Grandier had the last word. As he struggled, he told Father Lactance that he would see God in 30 days, and the priest died accordingly, reportedly crying, "Grandier, I was not responsible for your death." Father Tranquille died insane within five years, and Dr. Mannouri, the fraudulent witch-pricker, also died in delirium. Father Barre left Loudun for an exorcism at Chinon, where he was finally banished from the Church for conspiring to accuse a priest of rape on the altar; the blood stains turned out to be from a chicken. Father Surin succumbed to possession by Jeanne's devil of debauchery, Isacaaron.

Like so many other exorcists, Father Surin triumphed over the Devil only to become his victim. For years after Grandier's death, Surin was haunted by the exorcisms, eventually becoming unable to eat, dress himself, walk, read or write. He no longer prayed to

Louviers Possessions   A case of mass DEMONIC POSSESSION, similar to that in Loudun (see LOUDON POSSESSIONS) occurred at a convent in Louviers, France, in 1647. As with the possessions at Aix (see AIX-EN-PROVENCE POSSESSIONS) and Loudun, conviction of the priests involved hinged mainly on the evidence of the possessed demoniacs.

On the promptings of Sister Madeleine Bavent, 18 nuns were possessed, allegedly due to bewitchment by Mathurin Picard, the nunnery's director, and Father Thomas Boulle, vicar at Louviers. Madeleine confessed to authorities that the two clergymen had taken her to a witches' sabbat (see SABBATS), where she married the devil Dagon and committed horrible and obscene acts with him on the altar. During the orgy, she said, babies were strangled and eaten, and two men who had attended out of curiosity were crucified and then disemboweled. Dagon disturbed the peace of some of the other nuns as well, and all showed the classic signs of possession: contortions, unnatural body movements, glossolalia (talking in unknown languages), insults, blasphemies and the appearance of strange wounds which just as suddenly vanished.

A witness to the exorcisms wrote that one young nun "ran with movements so abrupt that it was difficult to stop her. One of the clerics present, having caught her by the arm, was surprised to find that it did not prevent the rest of her body from turning over and over as if the arm were fixed to the shoulder merely by a spring."

Besides seducing them to unspeakable sexual acts, Satan tried to lead the nuns of Louviers down heretical roads as well. According to the account of the proceedings at Louviers published in 1652 by Father Bosroger, the DEVIL—appearing as a beautiful angel—engaged the nuns in theological conversations, cleverly spoken and so charming that the nuns began to doubt what they were taught. Meekly protesting that what the Devil told them had not been revealed by their teachers, Satan replied that he was a messenger of heaven, sent to speak the divine truth and reveal the errors in established dogma.

As in Loudun, the exorcisms were public and became more of a circus than a holy ritual. Nearly everyone was questioned and harassed by the inquisitors, and the whole town of Louviers exhibited hysteria as the cries of the nuns rose with the tortured screams of Father Boulle (see DEMONIC EXORCISM). In the end, the parliament at Rouen passed sentence: Sister Madeleine was imprisoned in the church dungeon, Father Boulle was burned alive and the body of Mathurin Picard, who had died earlier, was exhumed and burned.

Lugh Heroic solar deity of the Irish Tuatha de Danaan, or FAIRIES, who continues to be recognized in the sabbat observance of his festival day, Lugnasadh, on August 1 (see SABBATS). Lugh was born of Ethniu, the daughter of the one-eyed king of giants, Balor, and the Dagda, the "Lord of Perfect Knowledge." Lugh was schooled in all the athletic feats and arts and crafts, which he bore as magical gifts from his place in the "Land of the Living" to the Tuatha. He wore red from sunrise to sunset, and his face was often compared to the sun. The sea god, Mananan, gave him his horse, corselet and magic sword. It was prophesied that Balor would be slain by a grandson, and Lugh fulfilled that prophecy by taking his slingshot and knocking out Balor's eye. The eye and stone went straight out the back of Balor's head and killed three times nine of his men. With Dectera, a Milesian maiden, Lugh sired Cuchulain, an even greater heroic figure in Irish Celtic mythology. Lugh's Welsh counterpart is the solar god, Llew Llaw Gyffes.

See also DANU.

lycanthropy The transformation of a human being into a wolf. There are two types of lycanthropy: a mania in which a person imagines himself to be a wolf and exhibits a craving for blood; and the magical-ecstatic transformation of a person into a werewolf ("man-wolf," from the Old English *wer*, man, plus wolf), usually accomplished with OINTMENTS or magical charm (see CHARMS).

Werewolf lore has existed in numerous countries and civilizations since antiquity. In some legends, the werewolf is a person born under a curse, who cannot prevent himself from his hellish METAMORPHOSIS, which happens on nights of the full moon. The person, usually a man, but sometimes a woman or a child, acquires the shape of a wolf and all its attributes, and roams about the countryside attacking and eating victims. In most tales, the werewolf is wounded, and the wound sympathetically carries over to the human form and reveals the identity of the werewolf. P. E. I. (ISAAC) BONEWITS theorizes in *Real Magic* (1971) that sympathetic wounding actually is a cellular psychokinesis brought on by an extreme telepathic rapport between the human and the animal. The human identifies so much with an animal that he enters the animal and takes over the body. The identification is so strong that any injury sustained by the animal while the human has control of it is carried over by cellular psychokinesis to the human's body.

In other legends, the werewolf is a sorcerer or witch who deliberately transforms himself at will to do evil and lay waste to his enemies. In South America, shamans, like sorcerers, turn into werewolves and attack and drink the blood of their enemies. Sorcerers also turn into other were-animals (man-animals), including serpents, leopards, panthers, jackals, bear, coyotes, owls, foxes and other feared creatures. But it is the wolf who elicits the most universal fear and is the most dangerous of were-animals. The Navajo believe witches become werewolves and other were-animals by donning animal skins, which enables them to travel about at night at great speed. Were-animal witches are said to meet in caves at night, where they initiate new members, plan ritual killings-at-a-distance, practice necrophilia with the corpses of women and eat their victims (see SHAMANISM; SORCERY; WITCHCRAFT).

Werewolf beliefs were particularly strong in medieval times in Europe and the Baltic countries. Later, in the 15th and 16th centuries, it was believed that werewolves, like witches, became servants of the Devil by diabolic pacts (see DEVIL'S PACT), and trials of accused werewolves increased. The cases were characterized by murder and cannibalism. In 1573 in Dole, France, Gilles Garnier was tried and convicted for the murder of several children. He confessed that he killed one victim, a 10-year-old girl, with his teeth and claws, then stripped off her clothing and ate part

Witch turned werewolf attacking travelers (Hans Weiditz, 1517)

of her. He took the rest of her flesh home to his wife. He strangled a 10-year-old boy (he did not specify how a wolf can strangle), then bit off a leg and ate the boy's thighs and belly. He was identified when he attacked another victim but was interrupted by several peasants, who thought they recognized Garnier's face, despite his wolf form. He was sentenced to be burned alive.

Perhaps the most celebrated werewolf trial was that of Peter Stubb (also Stube or Stumpf) in 1589 at Bedburg near Cologne. Put on the rack and threatened with torture, Stubb made a lurid confession. He said that he had practiced the "wicked arts" from the age of 12 years and that the Devil had given him a magic belt that enabled him to change into "the likeness of a greedy deuouring [devouring] Woolf, strong and mighty, with eyes great and large, which in the night sparkled like vnto [unto] brandes of fire, a mouth great and wide, with most sharpe and cruell teeth, A huge body, and mighty pawes." By taking the belt off, he returned to the shape of a man.

Stubb terrorized the countryside at night, stalking children, women, men, lambs, sheep and goats. He was an "insatiable bloodsucker," taking great pleasure in killing. He killed his own son and ate his brains. He killed lambs, kids and other livestock, "feeding on the same most usually raw and bloody." He murdered 13 young children "and two goodly yong women bigge with Child, tearing the Children out of their wombes, in most bloody and sauedge [savage] sorte, and after eate their hartes panting hotte and rawe, which he accounted dainty morsells & best agreeing to his Appetite."

If that weren't enough, Stubb also confessed to incest with his daughter, Beell (Bell) and sexual escapades with various mistresses, including a "gossip," Katherine Trompin. His lust remained unsated, so the Devil sent him a succubus.

Astonishingly, he got away with this behavior for 25 years and finally was exposed when some hunters chased him down in wolf form, and he slipped off his belt and was recognized.

In his trial, his daughter and Trompin were judged accessories in some of the murders. Like many condemned witches in Germany, Stubb was sentenced to a most horrible execution, as described in a pamphlet published in 1590:

Stubbe Peeter as principall mallefactor, was judged first to haue his body laide on a wheele, and with red hotte burning pincers in ten seueral [several] places to haue the flesh puld off from the bones, after that, his legges and Armes to be broken with a woodden Axe or Hatchet, afterward to haue his head strook from his body, then to haue [have] his carcass burnde to Ashes.

Also his Daughter and his Gossip were judged to

be burned quicke to Ashes, the same time and day
with the carkasse of the aforesaid Stubbe Peeter.

One unusual werewolf case resembles that of the
BENANDANTI of northern Italy: the werewolves were
men who left their bodies and in spirit assumed the
shapes of wolves, descending into the underworld
to battle the witches. The case was tried in 1692 in
Jurgensburg, Livonia, an area east of the Baltic Sea
steeped in werewolf lore, and involved an 80-year-
old man named Thiess.

Thiess freely confessed to being a werewolf. He
testified that his nose had been broken by a man
named Skeistan, a witch who was dead at the time
he struck Thiess. His story of how it happened was
this: Skeistan and other witches prevented crops
from growing by carrying seed grain into hell. Thiess
was a werewolf, who, with other werewolves, attempted to protect the crops by descending into hell
and fighting with the witches to recover what was
stolen. Three times a year, on the nights of St. Lucia,
Pentecost and St. John (seasonal changes), the battles
took place. If the werewolves delayed their descent,
the witches barred the gates of hell, and the crops
and livestock, even the fish catch, suffered. The

werewolves carried iron bars as weapons, and the
witches carried broom handles. Skeistan had broken
Thiess's nose with a broom handle wrapped in a
horse's tail.

The judges, naturally, were shocked to hear that
werewolves, who were supposed to be agents of the
Devil, could not tolerate the Devil and fought with
witches. Asked what happened to werewolves at
death, Thiess replied that they were buried like ordinary folk, and their souls went to heaven—another
shock for the judges. Thiess insisted that the werewolves were the ''hounds of God'' who served mankind, preventing the Devil from carrying off the
abundance of the earth. If not for them, everyone
would suffer. He said werewolves in Germany and
Russia likewise fought the witches in their own hells.

Thiess refused to confess that he had signed a
compact with the Devil, despite the efforts of the
judges. Even the parish priest, summoned to chastise
him for his evil ways, failed to sway Thiess. The old
man angrily said he was a better man than the priest
and that he was neither the first, nor would be the
last, werewolf to fight the witches. The judges sentenced him to 10 lashes for acts of idolatry and
superstitious beliefs.

Macbeth Shakespeare's play about intrigue and murder in the royal court of Scotland was perhaps the most influential literary work in establishing the stereotype of WITCHES as evil, ugly hags (see HAG). The play, written around 1603 and published around 1623, is drawn partly on Raphael Holinshed's *Chronicles of England, Scotland and Ireland* (1577).

Three unnamed witches, sometimes called the "Weird Sisters," are consulted for their prophecies. The play opens with the witches gathered on a barren heath; later, in the famous first scene of Act IV, they stir up a CAULDRON full of vile ingredients and conjure the Greek patron goddess of witchcraft, HECATE, and various spirits. Macbeth's ambition to be king, plus the witches' prophecies, spur him to commit murder. He brings about his own undoing and dies cursing the day he met the witches.

Stated MONTAGUE SUMMERS in *The History of Witchcraft and Demonology* (1926):

> There are few scenes which have so caught the world's fancy as the wild overture to *Macbeth*. In storm and wilderness we are suddenly brought face to face with three mysterious phantasms that ride on the wind and mingle with the mist in thunder, lightning, and in rain. They are not agents of evil, they are evil; nameless, spectral, wholly horrible.

Act IV, Scene 1 opens with the three witches stirring in their cauldron. Appropriately, thunder roils outside their cavern:

1st Witch: Thrice the brinded cat hath mew'd.
2nd Witch: Thrice, and once the hedgepig whin'd.
3rd Witch: Harpier cries; 'tis time, 'tis time.
1st Witch: Round about the cauldron go;
In the poison'd entrails throw.
Toad, that under cold stone
Days and night has thirty-one

Swelter'd venom sleeping got,
Boil thou first i' the charmed pot.
All: Double, double, toil and trouble;
Fire burn and cauldron bubble.
2nd Witch: Fillet of a fenny snake,
In the cauldron boil and bake;
Eye of newt and toe of frog,
Wool of bat and tongue of dog,
Adder's fork and blind-worm's sting,
Lizard's leg and howlet's wing,
For a charm of powerful trouble,
Like a hell-broth boil and bubble.
All: Scale of dragon, tooth of wolf,
Witches mummy, maw and gulf
Of the ravin's salt-sea shark;
Root of hemlock digg'd i' the dark,
Liver of blaspheming Jew,
Gall of goat, and slips of yew
Sliver'd in the moon's eclipse,
Nose of Turk and Tartar's lips,
Finger of birth-strangled babe
Ditch-deliver'd by a drab,
Make the gruel thick and slab:
Add thereto a tiger's chaudron.
For th' ingredients of our cauldron.
All: Double, double toil and trouble;
Fire burn and cauldron bubble.
2nd Witch: Cool it with a baboon's blood,
Then the charm is firm and good.
Hecate enters.
Hecate: O, well done! I commend your pains;
And every one shall share in th' gains:
And now about the cauldron sing,
Like elves and fairies in a ring,
Enchanting all that you put in.
Music and song; Hecate exits.

The influence of *Macbeth* on popular opinion about Witches is evidenced in an incident that happened to SYBIL LEEK in the late 1960s. The English Witch had just written her autobiography, *Diary of a Witch*, and was a sought-after guest on the media tour circuit in America. She accepted an invitation to appear on NBC's *Today* show, then hosted by Barbara Walters and Hugh Downs. She expected to have an opportunity to educate *Today's* considerable audience on the Old Religion. Apparently, the NBC programmers expected to entertain viewers with a bit of theater. Leek recounts in her book, *The Complete Art of Witchcraft* (1971):

> I arrived to do the show in the early hours of the morning, to find that I was expected to stir a *cauldron* while mouthing the usual "Double, double, toil and trouble" bit out of Shakespeare, and to look as cackling and as evil as possible.

Leek declined to play the stereotype and managed to salvage some of her appearance on the show with a serious discussion of Witchcraft as a religion (see WITCHCRAFT).

Macumba Macumba is the Brazilian form of VO-DOUN and SANTERÍA, or the worship of the ancient African gods through SPIRIT POSSESSION and MAGIC. Strictly speaking, there is no "Macumba" religion; the word is an umbrella term for the two principal forms of African spirit worship in Brazil: *Candomblé* and *Umbanda*. Macumba sometimes refers to black magic, but that is more properly called *Quimbanda*.

Black slaves transported to Brazil by the Portuguese in the 1550s found their tribal religion had much in common with the spiritual practices of Indian tribes along the Amazon River. Forced to syncretize the worship of their gods, or *orishas*, into the veneration of Catholic saints to escape persecution, the blacks continued to follow the old ways and rituals in secret. By the time the slaves won their independence in 1888, more than 15 generations of Brazilians—black, white and Indian—had heard the stories of the orishas and how their magical intervention had snared a lover, saved a marriage or a sick baby or eliminated a wicked enemy. Today, members of all classes and races in Brazil believe in some sort of ancient spiritual communion with the gods while professing Catholicism in public.

Candomblé. Candomblé most closely resembles the ancient Yoruban religions, as does Santería, and retains the Yoruban names of the orishas. Spellings are Portuguese, not Spanish, so *Chango* becomes *Xango*, *Yemaya* is *Yemanja* or *Iemanja*, *Oggun* becomes *Ogun*, and *Olorun* is *Olorum*. Figures of Catholic saints represent the orishas, although Jesus Christ, also known as *Oxala*, is venerated as a saint on his own.

The term *Candomblé* probably derives from *candombé*, a celebration and dance held by the slaves on the coffee plantations. The first Candomblé center was organized in 1830 in Salvador, the old capital city of Brazil and now the capital of the state of Bahia, by three former slaves who became the cult's high priestesses. The slave women inherited the formerly all-male ceremonial duties when the men were forced to spend their time in slave field labor. The women also served as mistresses to the white Portuguese and claimed that the exercise of their magical rites helped maintain their sexual skill and prowess. These "Mothers of the Saints" trained other women, called "Daughters of the Saints," ensuring that the men were excluded from major responsibilities. Even today, the men perform political rather than spiritual roles.

Candomblé ceremonies follow much the same pattern as those for Santería and Vodoun, with invocations (see EVOCATIONS AND INVOCATIONS) to the gods, PRAYERS, offerings and possession of the faithful by the gods. Afro-Brazilian traditions stress the importance of healing the spirit, and devotees of Candomblé believe the moment of greatest spiritual healing occurs when a person becomes one with his orisha during initiation into the cult. Such possession is often intense, requiring constant aid from the other worshippers. The priest may beg the orisha to treat the initiate gently, offering a pigeon or other SACRIFICE to the orisha in return for his or her mercy. The stronger the orisha—gods like Xango or Ogun are considered the strongest—the more violent the possession.

Instead of asking LEGBA or Elegguá to let the spirits in, followers of Candomblé call on the *Exus*, primal forces of all nature who act as divine tricksters and messengers to the gods. Connections exist between Elegguá/Legba and the Exus, however; some of Elegguá's manifestations in Santería are called *Eshus*. They are the gods of mischief, the unexpected and life and death, as well as messengers to the other orishas.

One of the major celebrations to the orisha Yemanja, "goddess of the waters," takes place every January 1. Brazilian television broadcasts the event in Rio de Janeiro live to the entire country, although smaller ceremonies occur in other coastal and river towns and cities. More than one million celebrants, dressed in white, wade into the ocean at dusk. A priestess, or *mao de santo* (mother of the saint), lights CANDLES and then purifies and ordains other young priestesses. As the sun sinks behind the mountains, celebrants decorate a small wooden boat with candles, flowers and figurines of the saints. Sometimes doves sail on the boat as well. At midnight, the boat is pushed from shore, and all watch eagerly as the craft bobs in the waves. If the boat sinks, the orisha

Yemanja (believed to be the Virgin Mary) has heard her children's prayers and accepts their offering, promising her support and guidance for another year.

Umbanda. Umbanda was not founded until 1904 and has its roots in Hinduism and Buddhism in addition to African tribal religions. The teachings of Spiritism—that communication with discarnate spirits is not only possible but necessary for spiritual healing and acceptance of one's earlier incarnations— also plays a large part in the practices of Umbanda.

The term *umbanda* probably derives from *aum-gandha*, a Sanskrit description of the divine principle. Umbanda incorporates not only worship of the Catholic saints but the beliefs of the Brazilian Indians. The orishas go by their Catholic names and personae, and *Umbandistas* do not call on the gods directly, fearing their intense power. Instead, spirits of divine ancestors act as intermediaries on the worshippers' behalf.

Although followers of Candomblé and Umbanda approach their faiths quite differently, researchers Alberto Villoldo and Stanley Krippner (*Healing States,* 1986) found they share three beliefs:

1. Humans have both a physical and spiritual body.
2. Discarnate entities constantly contact the physical world.
3. Humans can learn to contact and incorporate the spirits for the purposes of healing and spiritual evolution.

Like the devotees of Candomblé, Umbandistas also call on the Exus to protect their temples and let the divine presences enter.

Communication with the spirits of Umbanda resembles very closely the practice of trance channeling. During ceremonies, the Fathers or Mothers of the Saints—either men or women can lead the congregation spiritually in Umbanda—become possessed with a spirit guide, usually of an Amerindian or African, or perhaps of a child who died quite young. The two most popular spirit mediums are the Old Black Man (*Preto Velho*) and Old Black Woman (*Preta Velha*), representing the wise old slaves who perished in toil and torture, taking their African wisdom with them into the spiritual world.

As with possession in Vodoun and Santería, those receiving the spirits assume the characteristics of their possessors, performing medicine dances of the American Indians, smoking cigars and pipes (tobacco was sacred to the Indians) or bending over from advanced age and labor. Any worshipper can receive the spirits, with help from the priest-mediums. Umbandistas believe that healing of the physical body cannot be achieved without healing the spirit; opening the mind to the entrance of a spirit guide via ecstatic trance is essential to spiritual growth. Spirits enter the body through the head—this is true in Candomblé, Santería and Vodoun—and are perceived by the physical body through the "third eye," located in the center of the forehead. Spirits never die but continue on an eternal journey through other worlds, sometimes reincarnating in another physical body. Umbandistas believe the most enlightened spirits teach and heal through the mediums of Umbanda, and mediumship forges a link with these highly evolved minds. Every time a medium receives a spirit guide for teaching and healing, the medium's mind and spirit are raised to another plane of consciousness (see REINCARNATION).

Quimbanda. Umbandista mediums generally refer to "lower" or "mischievous" spirits, rather than "evil" ones, believing that all spirits evolve to higher consciousness. The misbehavers simply need education to set them on the right path.

But the practitioners of *Quimbanda* or *Cuimbanda*— black magic—find that evil spirits suit their purposes quite well. Here again the Exus serve, this time as the tricksters, the gods of WITCHCRAFT and SORCERY. Equated by some with Lucifer himself, "King Exu" receives assistance from Beelzebub and Ashtaroth, known as Exu Mor and Exu of the Crossroads.

Francis X. King, in *Witchcraft and Demonology* (1987), reports that Exu of the Closed Paths inspires the most dread. To sicken or destroy an enemy, the Quimbandista prepares a RED satin cloth adorned with mystical symbols and takes it to a CROSSROADS; the magician places upon it four red-and-black crosses. (Red and black are the Exus' colors, as they are for Legba and Elegguá.) Accompanying the crosses are a COCK, plucked and stuffed with red pepper, and other devilish items. Then the Quimbandista lights 13 candles, intoning the name of the enemy and invoking the powers of darkness to do their work. If the Quimbandista is successful, the unlucky victim will find "all paths closed" and will lose his job, become ill, lose his lover and family and eventually dye if not cured by the powers of the orishas.

magic Magic is the art of effecting change through an external and supernormal force. Man's awareness of magic and his efforts to use it to enhance his place in his environment are ancient and universal and have been a part of all religious systems. The earliest evidence of magic dates from cave paintings of the Paleolithic Age, some of which suggest that magic rituals were employed to secure successful hunts. Various magical systems and philosophies have developed around the world, and volumes of literature have been written on them. The discussion here will

The soul of the world (Robert Fludd, *Utriusque Cosmi Historia*, 1617)

focus on the development of Western magic and its role in SORCERY and modern WITCHCRAFT and NEO-PAGANISM.

The word *magic* comes either from the Greek *megus*, which means "great" (as in "great" science), or from the Greek term *magein*, the science and religion of Zoroaster. Numerous definitions of magic have been offered by many who have practiced and studied it, yet magic eludes precise description. Though systems of magic exist—and some are quite complex—magic remains an individualistic experience. Every person who practices magic sees it in a different way.

Magic, like science, works in conformance to the natural laws of the universe. The *Goetia* portion of the *Lemegeton of King Solomon*, a grimoire (see GRIMOIRES), said to be in existence since around 1500, defines magic as

. . . the Highest, most Absolute, and most Divine Knowledge of Natural Philosophy, advanced in its works and wonderful operations by a right understanding of the inward and occult virtue of things;

so that true Agents being applied to proper Patients, strange and admirable effects will thereby be produced. When magicians are profound and diligent searchers into Nature, they, because of their skill, know how to anticipate an effect, the which to the vulgar shall seem to be a miracle.

ALEISTER CROWLEY gave perhaps the most succinct modern definition of magic as "the science and art of causing change to occur in conformity to the will" (*Magick in Theory and Practice*, 1929). Crowley further postulated that "any required Change may be effected by the application of the proper kind of degree of Force in the proper manner through the proper medium to the proper object." He theorized that "every intentional act is a Magical Act" and that if a magical act failed, it meant the performer had not fulfilled all the requirements for success.

More recently, neo-Pagan P. E. I. (ISAAC) BONEWITS, in *Real Magic* (1971), defined magic in terms of energy, as

. . . a science and an art of comprising a system of concepts and methods for the build-up of human emotion, altering the electrochemical balance of the metabolism, using associational techniques and devices to concentrate and focus this emotional energy, thus modulating the energy broadcast by the human body, usually to affect other energy patterns, whether animate or inanimate, but occasionally to affect the personal energy patterns.

Magic is variously described as *white*, *black* and *gray*, but actually it has no color. Magic is neutral and amoral. It can be bent to good, evil or ambiguous purposes, depending on the intent of the practitioner. The distinction between "white" and "black" magic is fairly modern, according to occultist A. E. Waite, and depends upon sharp contrasts between good and evil spirits. The distinctions were far more obscure in ancient times.

Anthropologist Bronislaw Malinowski (1884–1942) stated that magic has three functions—to produce, protect and destroy—and has three elements—the spell or incantation; the rite or procedure; and the state of the practitioner, who usually undergoes a purification process that alters his state of consciousness (fasting, inhaling fumes, taking drugs, chanting, dancing, and so forth).

The simplest form of magic is mechanical sorcery, in which a physical act is performed to achieve a result. For example, a waxen image is melted over a fire to make a victim die; BLOOD is scattered over a field to ensure a bountiful harvest in the next growing season; KNOTS are tied in a cord to store wind for a sea voyage. Typically, such sorceries, or SPELLS, are performed while reciting magical incantations or

CHARMS, to aid the effectiveness of the act. A higher form of sorcery involves petitioning the help of spirits or deities.

Sorcery, out of which grew witchcraft, forms the bulk of the folk magic practiced on an everyday basis to affect matters of everyday life, such as ensuring that one's cows give milk, that the butter churns, that one's illness is cured or that one's home is protected from lightning and bewitchment.

James G. Frazer, in *The Golden Bough* (1890), theorized that all magic was based on the Law of Sympathy, which holds that all things are linked together by invisible bonds. Sometimes sorcery is called *sympathetic magic*. Frazer further divided sympathetic magic into two types. *Homeopathic magic* holds that like produces like: a melted waxen image causes death. *Contagious magic* holds that things once in contact can continue to exert influence on each other, even at a distance. For example, a wound can be magically cured by rubbing ointment on the sword that caused the wound.

Sorcery is widespread in tribal societies and was practiced extensively in the ancient civilizations of Mesopotamia and the Mediterranean. The ancient Egyptians, Persians, Babylonians, Greeks, Romans and Hebrews had magical systems that greatly influenced later magic in the West. In Egypt, the pharaohs were considered divine kings and were thought to possess innate magical abilities. There were two classes of magicians. The most esteemed were the trained priests, professional magicians who acted as substitutes for the pharaoh, who could not possibly perform all needed magical services. The second class were the lay magicians, the equivalent of folk magicians, healers and WIZARDS. From Egyptian magic came the concept of the power of sacred names, which influenced European magic during the Middle Ages and Renaissance (see NAMES OF POWER).

The Greeks developed both a system and philosophies of magic, which were influenced by concepts imported from Egypt, the Middle East and the East. The Greeks envisioned magic as divided into two classes: high and low. High magic, which calls upon the aid of beneficent spirits, is akin to religion. It is called *theurgy*, from *theourgia*, or "working things pertaining to the gods." Theurgic magic was practiced by the Neo-Platonists, adherents to a philosophical and religious system developed in Alexandria in the 3rd century A.D. that was based on a blend of the doctrines of Plato and other Greek philosophers, Oriental mysticism, Judaism and Christianity. Plato believed in a morally neutral natural magic.

Low magic in Greece, *mageia* (sorcery), had acquired an unsavory reputation for fraud by the fifth

Doctor Faust watching magical disk in his laboratory (Rembrandt Harmensz van Rijn, 1652)

century B.C. Practitioners were not members of the priesthood but individuals who claimed to have magical powers and would help clients for fees. The very lowest form of this magic is *goeteia*, which in the classical world was practiced by persons who cast spells, "howled" incantations and concocted PHILTRES and potions.

The Romans used sorcery and counter-sorcery to defeat rivals and advance themselves politically and materially. Though sorcery was popular with the public, the private practice of it was greatly feared by those in authority, and harsh laws were passed against it. The Cornelian Law proclaimed, "Soothsayers, enchanters, and those who make use of sorcery for evil purposes; those who conjure up demons, who disrupt the elements, who employ waxen images destructively, shall be punished by death."

The Christian Church began separating magic from religion as early as 364 A.D., when the Ecumenical Council of Laodicea issued a Thirty-sixth Canon forbidding clerks and priests from becoming magicians, enchanters, astrologers and mathematicians. In 525 the Fourth Canon of the Council of Oxia prohibited the consultation of sorcerers, augurs and diviners and outlawed DIVINATION by wood or bread. In 613 the Council of Tours instructed priests to teach the public that magic to cure illness would not work. The Church excommunicated diviners in 692 and renewed its prohibitions against divining in 721. Divining is actually not magic, because it attempts to interpret omens and understand the future, not influence it, but the proscriptions against diviners indicate the Church's overall attitude toward magic, which had a great bearing on the prosecution of sorcerers and witches during the Inquisition. While the Church discouraged the private practice of magic, it absorbed both theurgic and goetic magic elements and Christianized them in its own rites and ceremonies. The goetic magic of sorcerers and witches was said to be evil; witches supposedly derived their magical powers from pacts with the Devil (see DEVIL'S PACT).

From about the 7th century to the 17th century, alchemy was in its heyday. Alchemy is not a branch of magic, but many alchemists also were theurgic magicians. Alchemy is based on the HERMETICA and traces its roots to the ancient Egyptians, who, according to the Greeks, believed in the magical properties of metals and alloys and could separate gold and silver from their native matrices.

Alchemists pursued three basic objectives: the transmutation of base metals into gold and silver; the discovery of the elixir of life, which would bestow immortality; and creation of the homunculus, an artificial man. The key to the transmutation and the elixir lay in the discovery of the Philosopher's Stone, an ambiguous material said to be either a stone, powder or liquid that was easy to obtain but recognized only by the initiated. According to some experts, the true purpose of alchemy was mystical and concerned the spiritual regeneration of man.

From about the 8th to 16th centuries, various forms of medieval magic emerged from a renewal of Neo-Platonism, plus Kabbalistic doctrines and Oriental doctrines brought back to Europe by the Crusaders (see KABBALAH). Very little was transcendental. Medieval magic coalesced as a system in the 12th century in Europe. The KNIGHTS TEMPLAR, formed in 1118, developed a magical system learned from the Johannites sect in Jerusalem. Other magicians of Europe were learned men, scholars, physicians and alchemists. Their magic consisted of intricate procedures involving dress, consecrated tools, magical symbols and, most importantly, sacred NAMES OF POWER, which, in incantations, summoned and banished various spirits. The unspeakable name of the Hebrew God, Yahweh, the Tetragrammaton, became the most potent name. The magician worked within a protective MAGIC CIRCLE.

Magicians were not troubled much by the Church until the 13th century, with the beginnings of the

Inquisition. In the 13th and 14th centuries, Aristotelian philosophy gained favor over Platonic philosophy. Under Aristotelian thought, no natural magic exists; therefore, magic must be either divine or demonic.

By the 15th century, magicians—competitors with the Church—were routinely harassed and hounded, though never to the same degree as sorcerers and witches, who were executed by the thousands for heresy.

Medieval magic reached a peak in the Renaissance in the 16th century under AGRIPPA von Nettesheim and PARACELSUS in Europe and JOHN DEE and Robert Fludd in England. Agrippa's *De Occulta Philosophia* dealt with divine names, natural magic and cosmology. Paracelsus stressed the Hermetic doctrine of "As above, so below," which holds that the microcosm of the earth reflects the macrocosm of the universe. Dee, with his partner, Edward Kelly, developed the system of ENOCHIAN MAGIC, a language of calls for summoning spirits and traveling in the astral planes. Fludd, a Kabbalist, attempted to reconcile Neo-Platonic and Aristotelian philosophies and to relate Aristotelianism to the Kabbalah. He wrote in defense of the Kabbalah, magic and alchemy.

The 17th and 18th centuries witnessed a popularity of secret magical orders, such as the Freemasons and Rosicrucians, whose rituals were based on the Hermetica, mystery schools, the Tarot, interpretations of the Kabbalah and ASTROLOGY. Magical grimoires, containing detailed instructions for magical rites, circulated widely. The most important of these, still used today, is the *Key of Solomon*, whose authorship is attributed to the legendary King Solomon, said to be one of the greatest adepts of mystical wisdom. The grimoire was in existence as early as the 1st century A.D.

During the 17th and 18th centuries, modern ceremonial magic, or ritual magic, had its beginnings. Ceremonial magic is a complex art of dealing with spirits. It requires a rigorous discipline and has an intellectual appeal. In ceremonial magic, the magician derives power from God (the Judeo-Christian God) through the successful control of spirits, usually DEMONS, which are believed easier to control than angels. Demons may be good, evil or neutral. In its highest sense, ceremonial magic is a transcendental experience that takes the magician into mystical realms and into communication with the Higher Self. It awakens the magician to the God within.

Magic enjoyed a great revival of interest at the beginning of the 19th century with the publication of FRANCIS BARRETT's *The Magus* in 1801. The revival was greatly influenced by ELIPHAS LEVI, whose explanation of how magic works, in *Dogma and Ritual of High Magic* (1856), has had a lasting impact on the thinking of magicians. Levi put forth three laws of magic. The first law was that of will power, which Levi said was a tangible force, not an abstract concept. The success of magic depends upon the will summoned and directed by the magician. The ceremonial props of medieval magic—the tools, dress, symbols, etc.—had an express purpose: to facilitate the will. The second law was that of astral light, a substance or energy permeating the universe which the magician could access and use to effect changes at a distance. The third law was Levi's interpretation of the Hermetic axiom, "As above, so below." Any force existing in the universe also existed in the soul of man. Magicians could invoke anything from the macrocosm into themselves and evoke anything from within their own souls into their magical triangle. Other factors contributing to the rise of ceremonial magic were Spiritualism and Theosophy, both of which brought public attention to communication with spirits and the dead.

Perhaps the greatest system of Western ceremonial magic was devised by the HERMETIC ORDER OF THE GOLDEN DAWN, founded in England by three Rosicrucians, which had a brief heyday from 1888 to 1896 but lasted into the 20th century. The Golden Dawn expanded upon Levi's writings, adding a fourth law, that of the imagination, without which the will was ineffective.

The Golden Dawn had a great deal of influence on Crowley, said to be the greatest magician of the 20th century. Crowley used both Enochian Magic and Abra-Melin Magic in his explorations of the mystical realms, resulting in a popular interest in both systems that has continued into the present (see ABRAMELIN THE MAGE).

Crowley's greatest contribution to magic is the Law of Thelma: "Do what thou wilt shall be the whole of the law," or do what you must and nothing else.

Another magical group which has influenced modern magic is the Ordo Templi Orientis (O.T.O.), founded around the turn of the 20th century by a German, Karl Kellner, and devoted to sex magic derived largely from Tantra. Sexual energy is ritually aroused; practitioners identify with the gods and goddesses who personify the sexual principle. Crowley contributed to the rituals. Kellner served as head of its British affiliate and, from 1922 until his death in 1947, as head of the outer order of the organization. Following his death, the O.T.O. fractured. There are now two O.T.O. organizations, one based in England and one based in California.

Members of the Golden Dawn and O.T.O. exported their rituals to North America in the early part of the 20th century. Some practices of both groups have been absorbed into some forms of modern Witchcraft.

Components of magic rituals. To be effective, magic must be performed in an altered state of consciousness. Depending upon the practitioner and the type of ritual, the altered state may be a mild one of dissociation or one of trance possession. Sounds, gestures, colors, scents, visual images and symbols all contribute to attaining an altered state. This enables the magician to reach the astral planes, which are inhabited by various entities, and where a good deal of magical work takes place. First, the magician typically undergoes a rigorous and elaborate preparation, first by purifying his body with abstinence. The old magical grimoires give detailed instructions. The magician either fasts or abstains from consuming alcohol, caffeine, meat and other substances that hinder altered states. He also removes himself from distractions and prays, meditates and concentrates on the upcoming ritual. The purification process can last for days. It should be noted that some magicians attempt to achieve an altered state of mind by indulging themselves in food, drink, drugs or sex.

The magician follows the instructions for the ritual to be performed. He bathes and dons his magical robe, a consecrated garment usually decorated with magical symbols. The grimoires recommend white for purity. He consecrates his magical tools, which, ideally, he has made himself according to specific instructions, or, failing that, purchased new, but never used. The principal tools are the wand, sword, knife or dagger, pentacle and chalice, but they can also include a sickle, lancet, hook, lamp, scourge, tripod, cross, spear, crook and other objects. He follows a procedure for drawing and purifying a magic circle. The magician burns incense, the formula of which is appropriate for the ritual. He also uses colors, such as colored CANDLES.

The incantations for invoking spirits are long formulas including names of power, recited in a crescendo of intensity to shrieking, with gesturing of the wand, until the magician directs his entire will and energy into the ritual. When the spirit manifests, he communicates with it and then dismisses it.

The old grimoires specified blood sacrifices of animals and birds, for the release of the life force enhanced the magical power raised (see SACRIFICE). Crowley made blood sacrifices. Many modern ceremonial magicians emphasize the use of ritual magic (sans blood sacrifice) for spiritual illumination. Those who seek to use it for power over others have the wrong purpose and supposedly are doomed to failure or disaster.

Magic in Modern Witchcraft

Neo-Pagan Witchcraft magic is a blend of *theurgy* and *goetia*. It contains elements of folk magic, ceremonial magic and sex magic. (Some Witches in addition have incorporated non-Western elements into their practices.) The Witch works within a magic circle and uses four primary magical tools, which correspond to the ELEMENTS: the athame (or sword)—fire; the pentacle—earth; the chalice—water; and the wand—air. In addition, the Witch uses a censer for the burning of incense and, in most practices, a scourge and cords for tying knots (see WITCHES' TOOLS). Like ceremonial magic tools, the Witch's tools ideally are handmade or purchased new, inscribed with magic SIGILS or RUNES and consecrated in the four elements (water, candle flame, incense and salt). The Witch invokes the forces of nature, the elements and the elemental spirits that rule the elements (see ELEMENTALS) and appeals to the many faces of the GODDESS and God. Most Witches believe very strongly in working only with benevolent beings and deities for good purposes. Many spells are derived from pagan sorcery and folk magic, based upon Frazer's Law of Sympathy. The Witch makes use of colors, scents, sounds, movements, symbols and visual images in ritual. Witches do not use blood sacrifices.

GERALD B. GARDNER, the English Witch credited with reviving modern interest in Witchcraft, the dominant form of which is now known as the Gardnerian tradition, received ritual material from his original COVEN of hereditary Witches. He borrowed from the writings of Aleister Crowley. In addition, he had been made an honorary member of the O.T.O. by Crowley, was a Maosn, and had spent many years living and working in the East as a British civil servant. Gardner stated eight ways to raise power for magic. Many Witches have been inspired also by the occult fiction works of DION FORTUNE, a member of the Stella Matutina splinter group of the Hermetic Order of the Golden Dawn.

Gardner's eight ways to make magic, usually used in combinations, are:

1. Meditation or concentration. This corresponds to the ceremonial magician's preparatory period, in which he or she gains a clear idea of the purpose of the ritual, eliminating all other thoughts and distractions and focusing all attention on the task at hand. Gardner may have learned the efficacy of Eastern meditation techniques, used in magic and in mysticism, during the many years he spent living and working in the East as a British civil servant. Eastern meditation incorporates breath control (*pranayama*), steady and balanced posture (*asana*), finger and hand gestures (*mudra*) and chanting (*mantra*).

2. Chants, spells, invocations. Chants are chanted or sung slowly at first, then increased in tempo to shrieks. When the power is at a peak, the Witch releases it and psychically directs it toward the goal.

Spells are combinations of movement, gesture and chanted rhymes or charms (the stated purpose of the ritual), designed to bring about the desired effect or change. Invocations are invitations or appeals to the deities for help (see EVOCATIONS AND INVOCATIONS).

3. Trance or astral projection. In astral projection, one leaves the body behind and travels in the astral realms in the astral body, or double, a spirit replica of the physical body. The double remains connected to the physical body by a silver cord. It can pass through physical matter and travel at the speed of thought. It is invisible to most people, though psychically attuned persons may sense its presence or see it. While the double is out of body, the physical form appears to be in deep sleep. It is theorized that dreams are astral projections.

Gardner advised Witches not to attempt going out of body until clairvoyance is developed. To go out of body, he advocated assuming a kneeling position with arms strained forward and bound, so as to produce a sensation of being pulled forward. The scourge, a whip made of fabric cords, is applied in a light, dragging motion. By traveling astrally, a Witch can arrive at a distant location quickly, communicate with spirit guides or look into the future. Healing work can be done, including the analysis of a problem and the discovery of its solution; attendance to watch over someone; and the delivery of healing energy. It is also possible to use astral projection to influence others while they sleep or to engage in psychic attack; however, most Witches are strongly opposed to harmful or manipulative actions (see WICCAN REDE).

Witches of centuries past who said they attended nocturnal SABBATS in spirit, after smearing on magical OINTMENTS, may have experienced astral projection. Undoubtedly, some cases of travel-in-spirit were hallucinatory, induced by drugs in the ointments. But in records of numerous trials, witches stated that in traveling in spirit, they left the body behind, and their spirit assumed the form of a mouse, cat, hare or other animal (see METAMORPHOSIS).

Such statements were common in the trials of the *BENANDANTI*, a pagan agrarian cult in Italy in the 16th and 17th centuries, in which certain villagers engaged in nocturnal spirit games and fights with witches over the crops. Paolo Gasparutto, a benandante ordered before inquisitors in 1580, admitted that he went to the annual game-fights "invisibly in spirit and the body stays behind."

Two women witches burned at the stake in 1571 in Lucca said they, too, left their bodies, according to an account in *Night Battles: Witchcraft & Agrarian Cults in the Sixteenth & Seventeenth Centuries* by Carlo Giuzburg (1966; 1985). Polissena of San Marcario said an aunt of hers persuaded her to become a witch. One night, the aunt's voice called to her, "Let's go," and she greased herself with ointment "and was transformed into a cat, left the body at home, descended the stair, and went out by the door." A fellow witch, Margherita of San Rocco, confessed that "the visits to the games which I have made did not take place in person, but in spirit, leaving the body at home."

The accused in the benandanti trials also testified that when left behind, the body could not be roused from its apparent sleep no matter how great the effort, and that if it were taken for dead and buried, the spirit would wander forever, or until the appointed time of the body's death occurred.

4. Incense, wine and drugs. The fumes of incense contribute to the altered state of consciousness, a technique used by both Witches and ceremonial magicians. Gardner said that a moderate amount of wine before and during the ritual aided the raising of power but that too strong or too much drink could cause the Witch to lose control. Some Witches have experimented with drugs.

5. Dancing. Witches join hands and dance around the magic circle, speeding up the tempo until the power is at a peak. When the magic is released, they drop to the floor or ground.

6. Blood control and use of cords. Binding parts of the body with cords restricts blood flow and alters consciousness, which facilitates the opening of the third eye for clairvoyance, and astral projection. Some Witches assert that Gardner learned these techniques while he lived and worked in the East. There are dangers in this practice, for if the bindings are too tight, physical damage can result. Cords also are used in knot magic, which binds and releases magical power (see WITCH'S LADDER).

7. Scourging. Religious mystics have used flagellation for centuries. In Witchcraft, it ideally is light, slow and steady. Scourging is a milder form of blood control, for it draws blood away from the brain. Not all traditions of Witchcraft practice scourging. Its use in those that do has declined since the 1960s.

8. The Great Rite. Ritual sexual intercourse between the high priest and high priestess of the coven is said to release tremendous magical power (see GREAT RITE). It requires keeping the mind focused on the purpose of the ritual and ideally releasing the magical power at the moment of climax. The Great Rite often is performed symbolically rather than in actuality.

Sex has been an integral part of magic and religious rites since ancient times. Many modern Witches find great similarity between Witchcraft and the Tantra of East. Tantra is a complex mystical tradition of psychic liberation and self-enlightenment through enjoy-ment, which includes the union of male and female polarities. Woman and man become personifications of Goddess and God. There are various Tantric sects, whose rituals employ sex, concentration, Yoga, sound (*mantra*), breath control, forms, gestures and postures, and offerings of flowers, incense and other objects.

The object of Tantric sex is to achieve spiritual ecstasy by controlling the climax and the release of semen. The sex act is viewed as neither immoral nor moral but as a mechanism for the raising of the powerful *kundalini* energy. The contained orgasmic energy liberates the kundalini, which rises up through the *chakras* of the body from the root to the crown of the head, resulting in bliss. It is widely believed in both the East and the West that this ritual sex helps maintain youth.

magic circle In WITCHCRAFT, the magic circle provides a sacred and purified space in which all rites, magical work and ceremonies are conducted. It offers a boundary for a reservoir of concentrated power and acts as a doorway to the world of the gods. The circle symbolizes wholeness, perfection and unity; the creation of the cosmos; the womb of Mother Earth; and the cycle of the seasons and birth-death-regeneration. Within the circle it becomes possible to transcend the physical, to open the mind to deeper and higher levels of consciousness.

Circles have had a magical significance since ancient times, when they were drawn around the beds of sick persons and mothers who had just given birth, to protect them against demons. The remnants of stone circles in Britain attest to the importance of the circle in ancient pagan rites.

The Witch enters a magic circle in anticipation of uniting with the gods and the forces of nature in a harmonious relationship. The deities are invited, not commanded, to witness and participate in the rites; all spirits are treated respectfully. Negative energy may be banished prior to casting a circle, sometimes symbolically swept out with a broom by the high priestess. The circle itself serves to keep out unfriendly spirits and negative energies.

The Witches' circle is customarily nine feet in diameter, though bigger circles are cast to accommodate large groups of people. The altar and ritual tools—the wand, pentacle, censer, cauldron, scourge, athame, chalice, cords and other items—are placed inside the circle area. The circle is ritually cast DEOSIL with an athame, though sometimes swords or wands may be used. As the circle is traced on the floor or ground (or laid out with cord), the Witch visualizes the field of energy established. The working space of the circle actually is a three-dimensional sphere, with

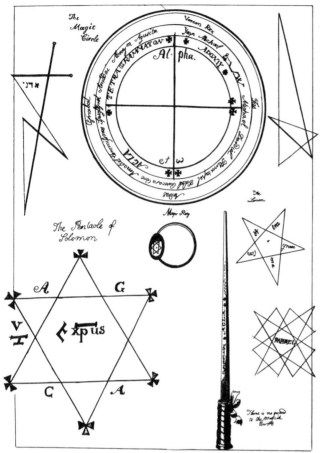

Ceremonial magic circle and Pentacle of Solomon (Francis Barrett, *The Magus*, 1801)

candles placed on the floor or ground at the four quarters, or cardinal points. The coveners are invited inside through a gate, which is then closed. The circle is consecrated with the four elements or symbols of the elements. The guardians of the four quarters and elements, called the Lords of the Watchtowers, or the Mighty Ones, or the Guardians, are invoked. If the ritual takes place outdoors, nature spirits are invited to participate. God and Goddess are invoked through ritual. The purpose of the ritual—such as magic working, a handfasting or sabbat observance—is stated and the work is carried through. The circle may be opened at any time for exit or entry, then closed again. At the close of the rites, food and drink is consecrated, offered to the deities and shared by the coveners. As a final release of energy, the spirits and deities are bid farewell, the candles are extinguished and the circle is ritually banished.

Witches sometimes cast magic circles intended for protection; for example, to ward off psychic attack or protect a home against intruders. Magic circles do not last indefinitely; protective ones must be periodically recharged through ritual.

Witches use the term *circle* as a synonym for their regular meetings. Some covens run *training circles* for individuals who are in training to become witches and be initiated into the coven.

The Four Quarters

Each cardinal point of the magic circle is associated with an element, ritual tool, color and attributes; correspondences may vary among covens or traditions.

North. To ancient pagans, the north was the source of great power. The heavens spun around the North Star, and the ancients aligned their temples and pyramids to this star. North, the cardinal point never touched by the sun, was associated with darkness, mystery and the unknown.

Perhaps because of the pagan reverence for the north, it became associated with the Devil in Christianity. Cemeteries were seldom placed on the north side of a church, which, if used for burial at all, was reserved for unbaptized children, criminals, reprobates and suicides. Many old churches throughout Europe and the British Isles have a north door called "the Devil's door," which was traditionally opened after baptisms in order to allow the exorcised demon to escape. Most of these doors have long since been bricked over.

The north is associated with the element of earth, the new phase of the moon, the pentacle, secrecy and darkness and the colors gold or black. Some traditions of the Craft align their altars to the north. In Masonry, which has parallels with modern Witchcraft, the north represents the condition of the spiritually unenlightened.

East. The quarter of enlightenment, illumination, mysticism and the eternal. It corresponds to the element of air, the athame or sword, the colors red or white. In most traditions of the Craft, the altar is aligned to the east. When a magic circle is cast, the high priestess or high priest leaves an opening, sometimes in the northeast portion, as the gate for other coveners to enter. The northeast is the symbolic dividing line between the path of darkness (north) and the path of light (east). In Masonry, the east represents mankind's highest and most spiritual consciousness.

South. Solar energy, the sun, the element fire, the colors blue or white and the magic wand are associated with the south. This is the quarter of the will, the direction and channeling of the energy forces of nature and the psychic. South-running water has long been held to have magical properties, and it was used in medieval times by wise women and witches in preparing medicine and in anti-witchcraft spells. In Masonry, the south is the halfway meeting point between the spiritual intuition of the east and the rationality of the west. It represents the zenith of intellectuality, as the sun attains its zenith in the southern sky.

West. The quarter of water, creativity, emotions, fertility and courage to face one's deepest feelings. It is associated with the chalice, the symbol of female creative power and fecundity, and the colors red or gray. In Masonry, it represents reason, common sense, and material-mindedness. In ceremonial MAGIC, the magic circle also is ideally nine feet in diameter. However, it acts as a barrier to protect the magician from hostile forces. The magician summons entities to manifest outside the circle (see DEMONS).

See also CONE OF POWER; DRAWING DOWN THE MOON; ELEMENTS; WITCHES' TOOLS.

Magus, The See FRANCIS BARRETT.

maleficia

Malicious acts attributed to WITCHES and sorcerers (see SORCERY) in times past that caused harm or death to humans, animals or crops. Since antiquity, witches, sorcerers and magicians have been said to cast negative SPELLS against others out of revenge, spite or malice. During the medieval witch-hunting craze, *maleficia* implied a pact with the Devil (see DEVIL'S PACT) and was used to explain virtually any natural disaster, accident, illness or personal misfortune. According to popular belief, witches did nothing but think up ways to bring misery to others.

In its narrowest definition, *maleficia* meant damage to crops and illness or death to animals. In its broadest, it included anything with a negative impact upon a person: loss of love, storms, insanity, disease, bad luck, financial problems, lice infestations, even death. Witch-hunters encouraged the blame of accidents and natural disasters upon WITCHCRAFT because it enabled them to round up suspects and get convictions.

If a villager muttered a threat or a wish for calamity upon someone and misfortune of any sort occurred to the victim—*maleficia*. If the local wise woman administered a remedy for an illness and the patient worsened or died—*maleficia*. If a hailstorm destroyed the crop, the cows wouldn't give milk or the horse went lame—*maleficia*. In cases of disease, *maleficia* was especially suspect if an illness came on suddenly and violently or if a patient's condition deteriorated rapidly. *Maleficia* was definitely the cause if a priest administered holy ointment and the patient broke out in a sweat.

Witches were believed to effect *maleficia* through a variety of ways: incantations; powders, potions, OINTMENTS and herbs; effigies stuck with thorns and

Newsletter citing alleged *maleficia* and execution of witch Anna Eberlehrin, Augsburg, 1669

nails; or a HAND OF GLORY. *Maleficia* could be combatted with preventive witchcraft—CHARMS, powders and potions made from certain herbs such as sage or christianwort, and incantations.

Belief in, and the practice of, malefic magic still exists in various cultures in the modern world, especially in tribal societies and rural areas steeped in folk magic. In many cultures various AMULETS and charms are believed to protect one against evil in general, but specific CURSES must be removed with specific remedies, usually by another witch or sorcerer. In neo-Pagan Witchcraft, however, such acts constitute a violation of ethics, which hold that witches should harm no living thing (see WICCAN REDE).

Malleus Maleficarum (The *Witch Hammer*)

A comprehensive witch-hunter's handbook, by far the most important treatise on prosecuting witches to come out of the witch hysteria of the Middle Ages and Renaissance (see WITCHCRAFT). Published first in Germany in 1486, it proliferated into dozens of editions throughout Europe and England and had a profound impact on witch trials on the Continent for about 200 years. MONTAGUE SUMMERS called it "among the most important, wisest, and weightiest books in the world." It was second only to the bible in sales until John Bunyan's *Pilgrim's Progress* was published in 1678.

The *Malleus Maleficarum* was written by two Dominican inquisitors, Heinrich Kramer and James Sprenger. The two men were empowered by Pope INNOCENT VIII in his Bull of December 9, 1484, to prosecute WITCHES throughout northern Germany. The papal edict was intended to quell Protestant opposition to the INQUISITION and to solidify the case made in 1258 by Pope Alexander IV for the prosecution of witches as heretics. It was the opinion of the Church that the secular arm, the civil courts, was not punishing enough witches solely on the basis of MALEFICIA. The effect of both the bull and The *Malleus Maleficarum* spread far beyond the Germany, its greatest influence being felt in France and Italy and, to a lesser extent, in England. It was adopted by both Protestant and Catholic civil and ecclesiastical judges.

The full biographies of Kramer and Sprenger are not known, but it is evident that they distinguished themselves brilliantly in their ecclesiastical careers. Sprenger, born sometime between 1436 and 1438 in Basel, rose rapidly in the Dominican order and was named prior and regent of studies of the Cologne Convent. In 1488 he was named provincial of the Province of Germany. Summers described him as a mystical, "most saintly" man.

Kramer was born in Schlettstadt in Lower Alsace (date unknown) and also rose rapidly to become prior of the Dominican House in his hometown. In 1474 he was appointed inquisitor for the provinces of Tyrol, Bohemia, Salzburg and Moravia. There he employed fraudulent tactics to frame people as witches, and subsequently tortured them. The Bishop of Brixen expelled him.

Both men were prolific writers, and by 1485 Kramer drafted a comprehensive manuscript on witchcraft, which was absorbed into the *Malleus Maleficarum*. The book is based generally on the Biblical pronouncement, "Thou shall not suffer a witch to live" (Exodus 22:18) and draws on the works of Aristotle, the Scriptures, St. Augustine and St. THOMAS AQUINAS as support. It maintains that because God acknowledged witches, to doubt witchcraft is in itself heresy. The sexism of the *Malleus* is unmistakable; the clerics' view of women as inferior, weak and corruptible creatures is emphasized again and again.

The *Malleus Maleficarum* is divided into three parts, each of which raises questions and purports to answer them through opposing arguments. Part I concerns how the Devil and his witches, with "the permission of Almighty God," perpetrate a variety of evils upon men and animals, including tempting them with succubi and incubi; instilling hatred; obstructing or destroying fertility; and the metamorphosis of men into beasts. It is the premise of the authors that God permits these acts; otherwise, the Devil would have unlimited power and destroy the world.

Part II concerns details of how witches cast spells and bewitchments and do their *maleficia* and how these actions may be prevented or remedied. Particular emphasis is given to the DEVIL'S PACT, a key to proving heresy. The existence of witches and their *maleficia* is treated as unassailable fact, and wild stories are presented as truth. Most of the stories of spells, pacts, the sacrifice of children and copulation with the Devil came from the inquisitions conducted by Sprenger and Kramer and from material of other ecclesiastical writers on witchcraft.

Part III set forth the legal procedures for trying witches, including the taking of testimony, admission of evidence, procedures for interrogation and TORTURE and guidelines for sentencing. Judges are instructed to allow hostile witnesses on the reasoning that everyone hated witches. Torture is dealt with matter-of-factly; if the accused did not voluntarily confess, even after a year or so in prison, then torture was to be applied as an incentive. Judges are permitted to lie to the accused, promising them mercy if they confess—it is all done in the best interests of society and the state. The *Malleus* does provide for light sentences of penance and imprisonment in certain cases, but the acknowledged purpose of the authors was to execute as many witches as possible, and most of the instructions on sentencing pertain to death.

Some questions are never clearly answered, and contradictions abound. For example, the authors say that the Devil, through witches, afflicts mostly good and just people; they later say that only the wicked are vulnerable. At one point, judges are said to be immune to the bewitchments of witches; at another, the authors assert that witches cast spells over judges with the glance of an eye, and judges are admonished to protect themselves with salt and sacraments.

The success of the *Malleus Maleficarum* was immediate in Europe. Fourteen editions were published by 1520; another 16 editions appeared by 1669. It became the guidebook by which inquisitors and judges conducted themselves and which subsequent writers used as a foundation for their own works. The book was important in the way it linked witchcraft to heresy.

In England, the book was slower to catch on, perhaps because of the independence of the English Protestant Church. Foreign-language editions surfaced in libraries and among scholars, but no English edition appeared until 1584. Nevertheless, Protestant writers absorbed the material into their own writings.

The emphasis in English witchcraft trials was less on heresy and more on *maleficia*.

Kramer and Sprenger piously maintained that God would never permit an innocent person to be convicted of witchcraft. Yet their collaboration, the *Malleus Maleficarum*, provided the blueprint for condemning thousands of innocent people to horrific torture and death.

mandrake   A poisonous perennial herb that grows in the Mediterranean region and that is reputed to have powerful magical properties (see MAGIC). Mandrake, part of the nightshade family, has a strong and unpleasant odor. It is highly toxic, though it is used in therapeutic remedies and as an aphrodisiac in love PHILTRES. The magic attributed to mandrake is due to the shape of its thick root, which looks like a man or woman, or sometimes a phallus, and to the phosphorescent glow of its berries in the light of dawn. The ancient Arabs and Germans believed a *mandragoras*, a demon spirit resembling a little man with no beard, dwelled in the plant.

According to lore, mandrake shrinks at the approach of a person. Touching it can be fatal. If uprooted, it shrieks and sweats BLOOD, and whoever pulls it out dies in agony. It is safely harvested by digging around all but a small portion of the root, tying a dog to it and leaving. The dog strangles itself pulling out the root in an attempt to follow its master. The death of the dog gives the mandrake root the power to protect against DEMONS. The root also is believed to prophesy the future by shaking its head in answer to questions.

In ancient Greece, mandrake was called the plant of CIRCE, the witch goddess who made a juice of the

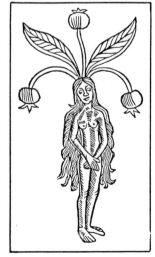

Male and female mandrakes (Johannes de Cuba, *Hortus Sanitatis*)

root and used it to transform Odysseus's men into swine. In Greece and Rome it was used medicinally as an anesthetic before cauterization and surgery.

Medieval WITCHES were said to harvest the root at night beneath gallows trees—trees where unrepentant criminals, evil since birth, were supposed to have died. The root purportedly sprang up from the criminal's body drippings. According to Christian lore, the witch washed the root in wine and wrapped it in silk and velvet. She fed it with sacramental wafers stolen from a church during communion, which placed witches in the DEVIL's camp.

Mandrake is reputed to be an aphrodisiac and a fertility pill and is known as *love apples*. In Genesis, the barren Rachel, wife of Jacob, ate mandrake root in order to conceive Joseph. Mandrake is given to women to ensure large families of boys; Arab men wear the root as an amulet to enhance virility (see AMULETS).

Martello, Dr. Leo Louis   American Witch, hypnotist, graphologist and activist for civil and gay rights, and publicly prominent in modern WITCHCRAFT since the 1960s.

Born in Dudley and raised in Worcester and Southbridge, all in Massachusetts, Martello is a descendant of Sicilian Witches, or *streghe*, a heritage he knew little about as a child, except for his father's references to his resemblance to his grandmother. He was baptized a Catholic and claims that the six worst years of his life were spent in a Catholic boarding school. He had psychic experiences early in life, and in his teens began studying palmistry and the Tarot with a Gypsy. By age 16, he was making radio appearances giving handwriting analyses, and selling articles.

Martello was educated at Assumption College in Worcester, Massachusetts, and Hunter College and the Institute for Psychotherapy, both in New York City. After moving to New York at age 18 he learned about his ancestral heritage from cousins who said they had been watching him for years for his potential in the Old Religion. His grandmother, Maria Concetta, was renowned in her hometown of Enna, Sicily, as the local *strega*, whom people sought for help when the Catholic Church failed them. She was reputed to be a *jettatore*, one who has the ability to cast the evil eye. She was said to have cursed a *Mafiosi* to his death by heart attack, after he beat up her husband and threatened him unless he paid monthly protection money. Secretly, Concetta was a high priestess of the Goddess of the Sikels, who were the founding inhabitants of Sicily.

On September 26, 1951, Martello was initiated into his cousins' secret Sicilian coven, and became a *mago*,

Rev. Leo Louis Martello (courtesy Leo Louis Martello)

a male Witch. The initiation involved a blood oath to keep the secrets of the coven and its members.

In 1955 Martello was awarded a doctor of divinity degree by the National Congress of Spiritual Consultants. He became an ordained minister (Spiritual Independents, Nonsectarian), and served as pastor of the Temple of Spiritual Guidance from 1955–60. He left that position to pursue his interests in Witchcraft, parapsychology, psychology and philosophy, and no longer accepts the theology of the National Congress of Spiritual Consultants.

He also did work in hypnography, the study of handwriting obtained under hypnotic age regression, and has worked professionally as a graphologist, analyzing handwriting for business clients. He was founder and director of the American Hypnotism Academy in New York from 1950 to 1954 and was treasurer of the American Graphological Society from 1955 to 1957.

From 1964 to 1965 he lived in Tangier, Morocco, where he studied Oriental Witchcraft. In 1969 shortly before publication of his first book on Witchcraft, *Weird Ways of Witchcraft,* Martello, with the permission of his coven, decided to go public as a Witch, in order to promote the truth about Witchcraft. Subsequently, he contacted and was initiated into the Gardnerian, Alexandrian and Traditionalist tradi-

tions. He was the first public Witch to champion the establishment of legally incorporated, tax-exempt Wiccan churches; paid legal holidays for Witches; and Wiccan civil rights activities and demonstrations.

To further these goals, Martello founded the Witches Liberation Movement and the Witches International Craft Association (WICA). In 1970, he launched publication of the *WICA Newsletter and Witchcraft Digest,* which had a circulation of about 3,500 by the mid-1980s.

Colorful and outspoken, Martello received much publicity in 1970 for his organization of a "Witch-In" in Central Park on Samhain (All Hallow's Eve). The city parks department at first refused to issue a permit for the Witch-In but relented after Martello secured the aid of the New York Civil Liberties Union and threatened to file a suit for discrimination against a minority religion. The Witch-In, attended by about 1,000 persons, was filmed and made into a documentary. Martello then formed the Witches Anti-Defamation League, dedicated to ensuring Witches' religious rights. By the late 1980s, chapters of the League were being established in every state in the United States.

He drafted a "Witch Manifesto," which called for a National Witches Day Parade; the moral condemnation of the Catholic Church for its torture and murder of Witches during the Inquisition; a $500 million suit against the Church for damages and reparations to the descendants of victims, to be paid by the Vatican; and a $100 million suit against Salem, Massachusetts for damages in the 1692 trials. He foresaw that the Civil Rights Acts of 1964 would enable the establishment of Witchcraft temples and churches.

Martello makes his living primarily as a writer, graphologist and lecturer. He makes numerous public appearances to educate others about the Craft and to speak at major Pagan/Wiccan festivals and gatherings. He compares the Craft to an underground spring which has existed for centuries and predates the Judeo-Christian and Muslim faiths, and occasionally rises to the surface in small streams and lakes. The modern Craft movement reflects a worldwide rising of this underground spring, coming with such force that it cannot be dammed by enemies. The spiritual force behind the renaissance is comprised of the reincarnated souls of those murdered as Witches by the Inquisition. Martello defines a Witch as a wise practitioner of the Craft, a Nature worshipper and a person who is in control of his or her life. He is of the opinion that too many persons enter the Craft with hangups from their Judeo-Christian upbringing, and that there is too much emphasis on personalities in the broad neo-Pagan community. His Sicilian tradition teaches that a wrong must be rectified in this life and not left to "karma" in a future life. The Witch must not permit injustices. His own philosophy, as outlined in *How to Prevent Psychic Blackmail* (1966), is one of "Psychoselfism: sensible selfishness versus senseless self-sacrifice."

Martello has authored numerous magazine articles and books. Other major published credits include: *Witchcraft: The Old Religion; Black Magic, Satanism and Voodoo; Understanding the Tarot; It's Written in the Cards; It's Written in the Stars; Curses in Verses; Witches' Liberation and Practical Guide to Witch Covens; Your Pen Personality;* and *The Hidden World of Hypnotism.*

Mass of St. Secaire   See BLACK MASS.

Mather, Cotton (1663–1728)   "My Hearers will not expect from me an accurate *Definition* of the *vile Thing*," the Reverend Cotton Mather stated once in a sermon on WITCHCRAFT, "since the Grace of God has given me the Happiness to speak without *Experience* of it. But from Accounts both by *Reading* and *Hearing* I have learn'd to describe it so." Thus did Mather, a formidable figure in the Salem witch trials, admit his own limitations in dealing with a highly volatile subject (see SALEM WITCHES). A brilliant, well-educated and esteemed Puritan minister, Boston-born Mather nonetheless was credulous in his beliefs about WITCHES and helped to fuel witch panics in New England.

The son of INCREASE MATHER, a Boston minister and president of Harvard University, Cotton Mather was a precocious student, unimpeded by a stutter he suffered. At age 12 he entered Harvard. By age 25 he had assumed a leadership role in his father's North Church in Boston. He viewed himself as one of those chosen by God to ensure the salvation of the Puritans, "a People of God settled in those, which were once the Devil's Territories."

He had an intense interest in the "dark side," including violent crime, the sins of drink, dance and cursing, natural disasters and hell, writing dozens of books on these and other subjects over the course of his life. With his father, he investigated cases of alleged witchcraft and DEMONIC POSSESSION of young girls, avowing that prayer and fasting were the only methods of treatment.

Mather accepted without question the credulous writings of WILLIAM PERKINS and others attesting to the existence and evil nature of witches. Even witches who professed to be "white witches" were in fact evil, Mather blindly asserted, and used good deeds to wreak havoc later. As for proof of the existence of witches, Mather often cited references in the Bible, especially to the WITCH OF ENDOR, and the "evidence"

amassed at English and European trials, including "voluntary" confessions. A confession, even if unsupported by evidence, was enough to convict, he asserted.

When witchcraft cases began cropping up in New England in the 1640s, Mather defended the trials and executions. He made his case against witches in *Memorable Providences Relating to Witchcrafts and Possessions*, published in 1689. The book perhaps laid the groundwork for the hysteria that was to result from the Salem witch trials in 1692.

Mather was appointed official chronicler of the trials by the colony's governor, Sir William Phips. While Mather did profess doubt about the validity of spectral evidence, heavily relied upon in the trials, he did little to cool or put a stop to the rising hysteria, beyond cautioning the judges not to rely too heavily upon spectral evidence. Instead, he encouraged identification and punishment of all witches.

Mather believed the Salem trials exposed the Devil's plot against New England: the Puritans were so righteous and virtuous as to enrage the Devil and drive him to try to destroy the community. He cited the curse of a New England witch, executed some 40 years earlier, who had announced that a "horrible plot" of witchcraft existed against the populace, which would threaten to pull down all the churches if not discovered. That plot, Mather said, was discovered and destroyed at Salem.

Mather attended the hanging of George Burroughs, one of the convicted "witches." Given the infallible test of reciting the LORD'S PRAYER perfectly, Burroughs did so, shaking the faith of the crowd in his conviction. Mather launched a savage, impromptu speech negating the prayer recital and convincing the crowd to carry on with the execution.

Mather's account of the trials, *On Witchcraft: Being the Wonders of the Invisible World*, appeared in 1693. He wrote it in stages, without the help of court documents (which did not arrive in his possession until most of the book was completed), relying instead on his own colored opinions.

When the public backlash to Salem occurred, Mather entrenched himself even deeper in his beliefs. The backlash was so great that Mather's father, Increase, was moved to speak out against the Salem trials, criticizing the spectral evidence and stating that it would be better to let 10 guilty witches go free than to punish one innocent person.

Cotton Mather, however, continued to fan the fires of hysteria. In September 1693 a Boston woman, Margaret Rule, claimed spectral evidence of witchcraft, and Mather declared she was telling the truth. A new panic nearly broke out but was calmed by more reasoned voices.

The Wonders of the Invisible World.

OBSERVATIONS

As well *Historical* as *Theological*, upon the NATURE, the NUMBER, and the OPERATIONS of the

DEVILS.

Accompany'd with,

I. Some Accounts of the Grievous Moleſtations, by DÆ-MONS and WITCHCRAFTS, which have lately annoy'd the Countrey; and the Trials of ſome eminent *Malefactors* Executed upon occaſion thereof : with ſeveral Remarkable *Curioſities* therein occurring.

II. Some Counſils, Directing a due Improvement of the terrible things, lately done, by the Unuſual & Amazing Range of EVIL SPIRITS, in Our Neighbourhood : & the methods to prevent the *Wrongs* which thoſe *Evil Angels* may intend againſt all ſorts of people among us . eſpecially in Accuſations of the Innocent.

III. Some Conjectures upon the great EVENTS, likely to befall, the WORLD in General, and NEW EN-GLAND in Particular; as alſo upon the Advances of the TIME, when we ſhall ſee BETTER DAYES.

IV. A ſhort Narrative of a late Outrage committed by a knot of WITCHES in *Swedeland*, very much Reſembling, and ſo far Explaining, That under which our parts of *America* have laboured !

V. THE DEVIL DISCOVERED : In a Brief Diſcourſe upon thoſe TEMPTATIONS, which are the more Ordinary *Devices* of the Wicked One.

By **Cotton Mather**.

Boſton Printed by *Benj. Harris* for *Sam. Phillips.* 1693.

Title page of first edition of *Wonders*, Boston 1693

Mather himself came under fire, most notably from Robert Calef, Boston merchant and author of the book, *Another Brand Pluckt Out of the Burning or More Wonders of the Invisible World.* Calef presented caricatures of Cotton and Increase Mather as lecherous men who were titillated by young girls whose possessions had lewd overtones. No publisher in New England was willing to touch *More Wonders;* it finally appeared in 1700 in London and made its way back to the Colonies.

The backlash, the credulity of *Wonders* and the mockery of *More Wonders* helped to tarnish Mather's reputation. He was passed over several times for the presidency of Harvard, which left him bitter and prompted him to influence the founding of Yale University.

Mather defended his views on witchcraft to the end of his life, by which time he was virtually ignored by an increasingly skeptical public.

Mather, Increase (1639–1723) Illustrious Puritan minister and intellectual who viewed WITCHCRAFT

and supernatural happenings as evidence of God's growing displeasure with New England. While his son, COTTON MATHER, became a strident witch-hunter, Increase Mather remained more cautious in evaluating cases and accusations.

Mather was the son of Richard Mather, an English Puritan minister who moved his family to New England in 1635 to escape persecution by the Church of England. Increase Mather was born in Dorchester, Massachusetts. He graduated from Harvard University in 1656 and Trinity College in Dublin in 1658. He worked as a minister for the Church of England until 1661, when, like his father, he returned to Massachusetts for reasons of religious differences. He became pastor of the North Church in Boston and served as president of Harvard from 1685 to 1701.

Mather was an orthodox Puritan, believing firmly in strict fidelity to a covenant with God and strict obeyance of the laws set forth in the Bible. The beginnings of witchcraft cases in the colonies disturbed him; with Cotton, he investigated a number of alleged witchcraft and possession cases.

Mather attributed witchcraft to a decline in religion; he voiced this belief in *An Essay for the Recording of Illustrious Providences,* a collection of supernatural and witchcraft incidents and his views on the subjects in general. Published in 1684, the book was intended to warn people of the need to get their spiritual houses in order, reminding them that as Puritans and Pilgrims, they were players in a cosmic battle between God and Satan for control of the New World and, therefore, of the history of mankind. For reasons known only to God, the DEVIL was permitted to infest the world with legions of DEMONS to test the moral mettle of humans.

Providences immediately captured public interest—perhaps more for its accounts of the supernatural than its moral lectures—and became a best-seller, garnering numerous letters of praise from readers in New England and abroad.

Mather did nothing to prevent the tragedy of the Salem witch-hunt (see SALEM WITCHES), but in the wake of the public backlash to the hysteria, he did speak out for greater caution in his *Cases of Conscience Concerning Evil Spirits Personating Men; Witchcrafts, Infallible Proofs of Guilt in such as are Accused with the Crime* (1693). While he acknowledged that spectral evidence alone was insufficient grounds for convicting accused WITCHES, he supported the Salem convictions on the grounds that other, sufficient evidence was given: the testimony of neighbors and the fact that some of the afflicted girls were relieved of their fits when a concoction of rye paste, water and the hair and nail clippings of the accused witches was mixed together and set afire. Mather did not personally attend any of the Salem trials except for that of George Burr. He would not have acquitted Burr, Mather said, because others testified to his diabolical activities.

See also LITHOBOLIA OF NEW HAMPSHIRE.

maypole A central feature in the festivities of Beltane, one of the major SABBATS observed by modern WITCHES and neo-Pagans, is the maypole, a freshly cut tree stripped of its branches and decorated with ribbons and flowers. Beltane is a fertility sabbat celebrated on May Eve, from which the maypole gets its name. The May rites are most common in the British Isles, Europe, Canada and the United States.

The maypole is a phallic symbol and usually is made from a tree that is associated with fertility, such as the oak, birch, elm or fir. TREES have been worshipped as bringers of life since ancient times. They have played important roles in pagan rites to ensure the fertility of women, cattle and crops. According to tradition, the cutting of the maypole tree is accompanied by much celebration, singing and dancing. In earlier times, the maypole was erected in the center of a village; in contemporary times, it is erected in a clearing or wherever the sabbat is taking place. It is festooned with garlands of flowers and long ribbons, which are fastened at the crown. In the most common tradition, young men and women take ribbons, alternating male and female, and dance around the pole, weaving over and under each other in opposite directions until the ribbons are braided around the pole. In parts of France, only the girls dance around the pole while a boy wrapped in leaves, who is called Father May, is led around it. In Bavaria, the maypole is erected in front of a tavern, and a man called the *Walber*, who is wrapped in straw, dances around it. The dancing and singing are followed by feasting. In Scandinavia, it is traditional to set up many maypoles at each house. The festivities are celebrated in midsummer instead of the beginning of May.

The pole is customarily burned at the end of the year at the autumn sabbat. Ideally, the pole should be a fresh, green tree for every Beltane sabbat, but in earlier times, villagers found it convenient to have permanent maypoles that were decorated anew each year. The Puritans, who frowned on the pagan festival because of its sexual aspects, destroyed the permanent maypoles in many locations throughout England. The Puritan writer Stubbs called the maypole a "stinckyng idoll." After the townspeople set it up, he wrote, "then fall they to banquet and feast, to leape and daunce around it, as the Heathen people did at the dedication of their idolles, whereof this is a perfect pattern, or rather the thyng itself."

Medea In Greek mythology the "Wise One," a powerful witch who was the niece of the great witch CIRCE and a priestess of HECATE the goddess of WITCHCRAFT and *magic*. Herodotus called Medea the Great Goddess of the Aryan tribes of Parthia. Her magic, according to Pliny, controlled the sun, moon and stars.

According to myth, Medea aided Jason, the adventurer who set out to get the Golden Fleece in order to win a kingdom in Greece that was rightfully his but had been taken over by Pelias. The Golden Fleece was possessed by the King of Colchis in Asia Minor. Medea was his daughter. When Jason and his band of Argonauts appeared, Medea fell madly in love with Jason and helped him win the Golden Fleece.

Medea's father set what he thought was an impossible task for Jason: he could have the fleece if he yoked two bulls with bronze hooves and flaming breath, plowed a field and sowed it with dragon's teeth. The teeth would spring immediately into an army of fierce warriors, all of whom had to be slain.

Medea prepared a magic OINTMENT that made Jason and his men invulnerable for a day. The task was accomplished. Then Medea bewitched the serpent who guarded the Golden Fleece, and she and Jason stole it and, with the Argonauts, fled to Greece. To delay the pursuit of her father, Medea cut the throat of her brother and scattered pieces of his dismembered corpse after them. Jason promised to marry her.

In Greece, they discovered that Pelias had forced Jason's father to kill himself, and Jason's mother had died of grief. Once again, Jason turned to Medea for witchcraft so that he could have revenge. Medea demonstrated her magical powers of rejuvenation by cutting up an old ram and boiling it while she recited incantations. A young lamb sprang up out of the cauldron. Medea convinced Pelias's daughters to cut him up so that she could make him young again. This they did, but she vanished without saying the necessary magic words.

Jason and Medea were forced to go to Corinth in exile, where they had two sons. Then Jason fell in love with the daughter of the King of Corinth and married her. Betrayed and enraged, Medea gave the princess a gift of a poisoned robe, and the girl burst into flames as soon as she put it on. Medea killed her two sons and escaped in a dragon-drawn chariot.

Medea was made immortal by Hera, and in Elysium, the afterworld of heroes, she became the wife of Achilles.

See also GODDESS.

megaliths Large stone structures and groups of standing stones, erected in various sites around the world and believed to have religious or sacred significance or to be associated with various pagan rites. The term *megalith* means "great stone" and is derived from the Greek *megas* ("great") and *lithos* ("stone"). In the broadest sense, megaliths include any structure made up of large stones, but the term generally refers to those tombs and circular standing structures built in certain parts of North and South America, Asia, Africa, Australia and Europe.

Who built these structures, how they were built and for what purposes are questions that have tantalized researchers and laypersons alike throughout the centuries. The most widely accepted view is that they were built by Neolithic and early Bronze Age peoples who used them for religious commercial purposes and as burial sites, and as astronomical observatories for the sun and other celestial bodies. Special powers have been attributed to certain stones, and they were apparently believed to be sacred or to have healing, magical, supernatural or electromagnetic forces.

Megaliths fall into two broad classifications: *dolmens* and *menhirs*. Dolmens, also called *chambered tombs*, usually contain one or more stone-built chambers or rooms where the dead lay. Some tombs were long while others were passage-graves, or round tombs with stone passages leading to one or more central rooms. Long tombs are common in parts of Wales, Scotland and England. Passage-graves are most commonly found in Ireland and western parts of Britain. Some tombs are covered with earth, forming mounds or *tumuli* (the plural form of *tumulus*).

Dolmens apparently served as either tombs of collective graves, in which some remains have been found, or as temples for the dead, in which no human remains have been found. The uncovering of bone shards at some sites has led to the theory that sacrificial rites, even cannibalism, might have taken place there. Prehistoric man probably believed that the body's spirit lived in the head; therefore, breaking the head might have been an attempt to free the spirits of the dead. Some investigators believe that the tombs were more than burial sites and were used for religious, social and community gatherings as well.

Menhirs consist of single standing stones, or groups of standing stones, arranged in circles, or *cromlechs*, and henges. Henges are circular arrangements of stone or wood distinguished by a bank or ditch surrounding them, and have one or more entrances.

Standing stones, especially those with holes, were believed to have the power to heal or hurt. The ill person had to climb through the hole of a holed stone to be restored to health. Women hugged stones to stimulate fertility or make a wish come true. The famous Men-an-Tol group of standing stones in Cornwall includes a five-foot-high holed stone that has been reputed for centuries to have healing properties. The stone is nicknamed "The Devil's Eye" and stands between two phallic-shaped boulders. In earlier times, sick children was passed through the hole nine times against the sun to cure them of their illnesses. Women desiring children passed themselves through the hole, as did the sick who wished to be cured (see HEALING).

FAIRIES were said to inhabit some stones, and people left gifts to curry favor with them. Many large, solitary black menhirs have Devil legends associated with them.

Stones reputed to have supernatural forces are associated with WITCHES, who were said to practice the occult arts as they gathered around them. In the 1596 trial of the Aberdeen witches of Scotland, the accused confessed to dancing around a gray stone at the foot of Craigleauch hill. The Hoar Stones in Britain's Pendle Forest were said to be the gathering site of the LANCASHIRE WITCHES in the 17th century. Another such site is the Bambury Stone of Bredon Hill. The ROLLRIGHT STONES of the Cotswolds continued to be used as a nocturnal meeting place of Witches into the 20th century.

Other stones are thought to have earth forces emanating from them. Some psychics fear being near these stones after dark because their strange powers disturb them. Psychic researchers have felt sensations like electric shocks when placing their hands on them, powerful enough to knock them over. Others report feeling tingling and giddiness. Photographs show light radiations emanating from the stones. Dowsers claim that these forces indicate the source of hidden underground water (see DOWSING).

Some stones were believed to move in search of water, and even dance. Legends associated with some stones say that they brought harm to people who uprooted them, and the stones themselves are said to be the petrified remains of people who were punished for dancing or playing on the Sabbath.

The greatest and oldest of all megalithic remains exist in Carnac in the countryside of Brittany, where some 3,000 standing stones are arranged into avenues, dolmens, mounds and cromlechs. It is believed that the stones originally numbered at least 11,000. One dolmen, covered by a tumulus, has been dated at 4700 B.C. The largest stone is the 350-ton Fairy Stone, originally 20 feet high but now lying in pieces on its side at the end of a Neolithic burial site. Most likely, it was felled by lightning or an earthquake. Astronomical calculations show the Carnac megaliths may have been designed for astronomical observations.

See also STONES.

Mendes, Goat of   See BAPHOMET.

Merlin   Archetypal wizard of Arthurian lore, who has, over the centuries, been studied and pondered by historians, occultists and Celtic enthusiasts (see WIZARDS). The name *Merlin* is a Latinized version of the Welsh *Myrddin*. His exact origins are lost in myth; he may have been a god (perhaps a version of Mabon or Maponos, the British Apollo), the divine ruler or guardian of Britain. Some speculate that the name *Merlin* may have been given to a succession of wizards. There is no concrete evidence, but it is likely that a Merlin, who was a prophet or a bard, existed toward the end of the 5th century and has become the basis for the Merlin myths.

Merlin's first appearance in literature occurs in the Latin works of Geoffrey of Monmouth, a 12th-century Welsh cleric. *The Prophecies of Merlin*, written in the early 1130s, comprise verses of prophecies made by an alleged man of the fifth century, named Merlin. Monmouth made up many of the prophecies, which stretched beyond the 12th century. In the *History of the Kings of Britain*, which Monmouth finished around 1135–36 and which laid the foundation for the Arthurian legends, Merlin becomes a character, though Monmouth muddles chronology by placing him in both the fifth and sixth centuries. He is a magical boy, born of a union between a mortal woman and a spirit (a *daemon*, which later Christian writers interpreted as the DEVIL). He has great magical powers of prophecy and matures quickly. Merlin uses MAGIC to bring great stones from Ireland to the Salisbury Plain (STONEHENGE) and arranges for King Uther Pendragon to seduce Ygerna, who bears the infant Arthur. At that point, Arthur vanishes from Monmouth's story. He reappears in a third poetic work, *The Life of Merlin*, in which he has a sister, Ganieda, who also has prophetic vision. *Vita Merlini*, written by Monmouth around 1150, is a biography of the adult Merlin, but it is also a text of Western magical and spiritual enlightenment. It sets down Celtic oral lore of mythology, cosmography, cosmology, natural history, psychology and what are now called archetypes of the human personality.

In 1150 a French poetical version of *History of the Kings of Britain* has Arthur constructing his Round Table under the aegis of Merlin. The best-known portrait of Merlin comes from Sir Thomas Malory's *Le Morte d'Arthur*, published in 1485, a romantic tale in which the infant Arthur is raised by Merlin. Upon

Merlin and Viviane in the Forest of Broceliande (early 15th-century book cover)

the death of Uther Pendragon, Merlin presents the youth Arthur to the knights of the land and has him prove he is heir to the throne by withdrawing the sword Excalibur from the stone in which it is imbedded. Merlin serves as Arthur's magical advisor but disappears from the story early in Arthur's reign. He is brought down by his passion for Nimue, or Viviane, a damsel of the lake who tricks him into revealing the secret of constructing a magical tower of air, which she uses to imprison him.

In contemporary fiction, Merlin usually is presented as a wise old man, despite his youthfulness in early writings. It may be said that he has three aspects: youth, the mature prophet and the wise elder. He has been subject to many interpretations:

magician, mystic, shaman, lord of the earth and animals, seer of all things, embodiment of time and trickster. He appears in the form of Mr. Spock of *Star Trek* and Obi Wan Kenobe of *Star Wars*.

In June 1986 the First Merlin Conference drew capacity crowds in London, who came to hear presentations by numerous Arthurian experts on Merlin's origins, character and continuing influence.

metamorphosis Since ancient times, WITCHES, sorcerers (see SORCERY) and other magically empowered persons have been believed to have the power to transform themselves and other humans at will into animals, birds and insects. In WITCHCRAFT trials during the witch hysteria of the Middle Ages and Renaissance, it was not uncommon for people to testify that the accused witches had appeared before

Demons riding to sabbat (Ulrich Molitor, *Von den Unholden oder Hexen*, 1489)

them or tormented them in some nonhuman shape. For example, in 1663 Jane Milburne of Newcastle, England, did not invite Dorothy Strangers to her wedding supper. Consequently, Milburne alleged, Strangers transformed herself into a cat and appeared with several other mysterious cats to plague Milburne.

In another English witchcraft case in 1649, John Palmer of St. Albans confessed that he had metamorphosed into a toad in order to torment a young man with whom he had had a quarrel. As a toad, Palmer waited for the man in a road. The man kicked the toad. After he returned to the shape of a man, Palmer then complained about a sore shin and bewitched his victim. In areas where witchcraft fears ran high, the sight of nearly any hare or stray dog caused great concern.

Witches were said to transform themselves as they rose up their chimneys on poles and broomsticks to fly off to SABBATS. The most common forms were he-goat, wolf, cat, dog, cow, hare, owl and bat. Many witches actually believed that they had done this, perhaps as the result of the hallucinogenic ingredients in some of the OINTMENTS they rubbed themselves with prior to a sabbat. In 1562 alchemist Giovanni Batista Porta, in his book, *Natural Magick*, told of how hallucinogenic potions caused two men to believe they had metamorphosed into a fish and a goose, respectively:

> . . . the man would seem sometimes to be changed into a fish; and flinging out his arms, would swim on the Ground; sometimes he would seem to skip up, and then dive down again. Another would believe himself turned into a Goose, and would eat Grass, and beat the Ground with his Teeth, like a Goose: now and then sing, and endeavor to clap his Wings.

ISOBEL GOWDIE, a Scottish woman who voluntarily confessed to witchcraft in 1662, said she and her sister witches used incantations to transform themselves into hares, cats, crows and other animals. Sometimes they were bitten by hunting dogs.

Witches, it was believed, used metamorphosis to gain easy entry into a household, in order to cast an evil spell upon an unsuspecting person. An insect crawling on the floor, or a mouse skittering through the door, might be suspect.

Witches also allegedly transformed themselves in order to escape captors. According to one story, a husband tried to prevent his witch wife from attending a sabbat and tied her to the bed with ropes. She changed into a bat and flew off. Another story tells of a witch brought before inquisitors in Navarre in 1547, who was able to smuggle along her magic ointment. She rubbed herself down and turned into a screech owl, escaping certain death.

To torment or punish other humans, witches and sorcerers turned them into beasts. In Greek myth, the sorceress CIRCE turned Ulysses' men into swine. In folktales, wicked sorcerers and witches turned people into frogs or other creatures, who had to wait for the right person to come along and break the evil spell. The magician ALEISTER CROWLEY was reputed to have this power. He was supposed to have once turned the poet Victor Neuburg into a camel.

One of the most feared metamorphoses was that of wolf. Man-eating wolves who terrorized villages were sometimes said to be witches. The man-wolf condition known as LYCANTHROPY, however, is not the same as metamorphosis, since it is involuntary. According to one 17th-century French tale, a hunter was attacked in the woods by an enormous wolf and was able to cut off one of its paws. Howling, the wolf fled. The hunter took the paw to show to a friend. When he took it from his pocket, he was astonished to see that it had changed into a woman's hand with a ring on one finger, which he recognized as belonging to his wife. He sent for his wife, who was missing one hand. She confessed to being a witch and transforming herself into a wolf in order to attend a sabbat. She was burned at the stake. Another version of the same tale has the wife admitting to lycanthropy.

In 1573 Gilles Garnier, an accused wizard of Lyons, France, was condemned to be burned alive for turning himself into a wolf and attacking and killing children, whom he devoured.

Despite the popular belief in the ability of witches to transform themselves and others into beasts, experts disagreed on the matter. While some demonologists such as JEAN BODIN and Joseph Glanvil accepted metamorphosis as fact, others denounced it as fallacy. The MALLEUS MALEFICARUM (1486), the leading inquisitor's guide, stuck to the latter view, citing saints Augustine and THOMAS AQUINAS as saying that metamorphoses were nothing but illusions created by the Devil and demons. Such illusions, said authors Heinrich Kramer and James Sprenger, were the result of God punishing some nation for sin. They pointed to verses from the Bible: Leviticus 26, "If ye do not my commandments, I will send the beasts of the field against you, who shall consume you and your flocks," and Deuteronomy 32, "I will also send the teeth of the beasts upon them." As to man-eating wolves, Kramer and Sprenger said they were true wolves possessed by demons. If a person believed himself to have turned into a wolf, it was the result of a witch's illusory spell.

INCREASE MATHER called the notion of metamorphosis "fabulous" and wondered in awe at the stories that were believed. In *An Essay for the Recording of Illustrious Providences* (1684), Mather says:

> But it is beyond the power of all the Devils in Hell to cause such a transformation; they can no more do it than they can be Authors of a true Miracle. . . . Though I deny not but that the Devil may so impose upon the imagination of Witches so as to make them believe that they are transmuted into Beasts.

Mather recounts a story of a woman who was imprisoned on suspicion of witchcraft and claimed to be able to transform herself into a wolf. The magistrate promised not to have her executed, in case she would turn into a wolf before him. The witch rubbed her head, neck and armpits with an ointment and fell into a deep sleep for three hours. She could not be roused by "noises or blows." When she awakened, she claimed that she had turned into a wolf, gone a few miles away and killed a sheep and a cow. The magistrate investigated and discovered that a sheep and cow in the location described by the witch had indeed been killed. It was evident that the Devil "did that mischief" and that the witch had merely experienced the dreams and delusions created by Satan.

In SHAMANISM, it is an ancient and widespread belief that shamans can metamorphose (shape-shift) into their guardian animal spirits or power animals (animals from whom they derive their chief power). The shape-shifting is a spiritual transformation, accomplished by achieving a transcendent state of consciousness by ecstatic dancing or ingesting hallucinogenic drugs. In dancing their animal spirits, the shamans make the appropriate movements and sounds associated with that animal or bird.

Miracle of Laon   The DEMONIC EXORCISM of Nicole Obry in 1566 served not only to rid the possessed girl of the devil Beelzebub but also to prove to the faithful the power of the Catholic Church in France and the danger of the threat of Huguenot reform.

The central issue dividing French Catholics and Huguenots was transubstantiation, or the Real Presence: whether or not, during communion, the bread and wine actually became the body and blood of Christ. This miracle occurred for Catholics, whereas Huguenots considered such an interpretation idolatry. By exorcising Beelzebub, who claimed the Huguenots as his own, the Catholic Church declared a victory for the power of the Presence.

A teenager and young wife living at Vervins near Laon, Nicole first showed signs of DEMONIC POSSESSION in 1565. One day while praying alone, Nicole was visited by the spirit of her maternal grandfather,

Joachim Willot. Willot entered the girl and explained that since he had died suddenly after supper, he had not confessed his sins nor uttered certain vows. His soul was in purgatory; to let him ascend to heaven, Willot asked Nicole to have masses said in his name, give alms to the poor and make holy pilgrimages, especially to the shrine of St. James.

Nicole's family complied but evaded the pilgrimage to St. James, perhaps because of the expense involved. Her convulsive fits, present since Willot's possession, got no better, and Nicole blamed her family's failure to visit St. James. The family arranged a fake departure for the pilgrimage, but Nicole was not deceived. At this point the family asked the local priest, the schoolmaster and a Dominican monk to conjure the spirit, who admitted he was not the soul of Willot but his good angel. Knowing that to enter a person's body as an angel or his soul was heresy, the priests finally got the spirit to admit he was a devil—Beelzebub.

For two months, Nicole was exorcised daily in front of ever-growing crowds. Originally appearing on a stage in her home town of Vervins, Nicole moved to the cathedral in Laon when Beelzebub complained that a prince of his rank could be expelled only by a bishop in a suitable location. The exorcisms continued on stage in the cathedral for two days but moved to a private chapel to avoid mob chaos. But Beelzebub protested again. In the account of Nicole's exorcism by Hebrew professor Jean Boulaese in 1578, Beelzebub told the priests that "it was not right to hide what God wanted to be manifested and known to all the world" and that he would only leave Nicole in "that great brothel" (the cathedral) and on stage.

The exorcisms increased in frequency to two times a day, during which Nicole gave an impressive demoniacal performance, complete with contortions, horrible noises, blackened tongue, rigidity and LEV-ITATION. During the rituals, the priests tried to use more traditional methods—holy water, relics, the sign of the cross, prayers to the Virgin Mary—but these only succeeded in angering Beelzebub. Only the host, or eucharist—the body and blood of Christ—tamed him. By submitting to the host, Beelzebub confirmed the power of the Real Presence.

Nicole occasionally suffered repossessions as often as 50 times a day, leading to mass consumption of holy wafers. The host came to be regarded as medicine for her spiritual sickness. Although he admitted that he was the father of lies, Beelzebub taunted Huguenot doubters about Nicole's possession, gleefully noting that their lapses of faith made them all the more precious to him. Through Nicole, Beelzebub also pointed out sinners in the masses watching the exorcisms, revealing their secret, unconfessed sins. Many went to be confessed and some rejoined the

Church. As propaganda, Nicole's sufferings were unparalleled.

French theologians did not use the accusations of demoniacs against accused witches until the 17th century (see AIX-EN-PROVENCE POSSESSIONS). But it may have been the possession of Nicole Obry at Laon that planted the seeds of such evidence. As well as identifying secret sinners, Beelzebub, through Nicole, accused some women of WITCHCRAFT while still in Vervins. And according to the account by Barthelemy Faye, a magistrate, Nicole claimed that a Gypsy woman had bewitched her early in her possession. Boulaese claimed it was a man. In addition, the Huguenots continually claimed SORCERY and MAGIC against Nicole's mother, one of the exorcists and a priest, Despinoys, who accompanied Nicole after her expulsion from Laon.

Beelzebub finally left Nicole at 3 P.M. on Friday, February 8, 1566. Following his expulsion, Nicole and her husband remained in Laon until, fearing outright religious war, the Huguenots succeeded in barring Nicole from the city. Still weak, Nicole survived only on eucharist wafers. She made one last bid for celebrity in 1577, when she became blind and was cured, not by the host, but by the holy relic of John the Baptist's head.

The Catholic Church, rejoicing in this miraculous affirmation of transubstantiation, used the accounts of it to their greatest advantage. Future cases of possession and exorcisms relied on the happenings at Laon, and even certain Huguenots—including Florimond De Raemond, a historian of the 16th-century heresy—were converted. Nicole's redemption was celebrated yearly at the Cathedral of Laon on February 8 until the French Revolution at the close of the 18th century.

mirrors   One of the most ancient forms of DIVINA-TION is *crystallomancy* or *catoptromancy*, performed with a magic mirror. The Magi of Persia are said to have used mirrors, as well as the ancient Greeks and Romans. In ancient Greece, the WITCHES of Thessaly wrote their oracles in human blood upon mirrors. (see ORACLES). The Thessalian witches are supposed to have taught Pythagoras how to divine by holding a magic mirror up to the moon. Romans who were skilled in mirror reading were called *specularii*.

In primitive societies, mirrors were and still are believed to reflect the soul and must be guarded against lest the soul be lost. These fears carry over into superstitious customs, such as covering the mirrors in a house after death to prevent the soul of the living from being carried off by the ghost of the newly departed; and removing mirrors from a sickroom because the soul is more vulnerable in times of illness (see GHOSTS, HAUNTINGS AND WITCHCRAFT). According to another superstition, if one looks into a mirror at night, one will see the DEVIL. In Russian folklore, mirrors are the invention of the Devil, having the power to draw souls out of bodies. The Aztecs used mirrorlike surfaces to keep witches away. A bowl of water with a knife in it was placed in the entrances of homes. A witch looking into it would see her soul pierced by the knife, and flee. According to another belief, witches have no souls, and therefore, like vampires, have no reflections in mirrors.

Medieval and Renaissance magicians often used mirrors, bowls of water, polished STONES and crystals for divination, to see the past, present and future. Village WIZARDS frequently employed mirrors to detect thieves. Whatever the purpose, the magicians would stare into the polished surface until they hypnotized themselves into light trances and saw visions that answered the questions that were put to them. JOHN DEE, England's royal court magician in the 16th century, employed both a crystal egg and a mirror made of polished black obsidian, reportedly taken from Mexico by Cortés. CAGLIOSTRO used mirrors, as did AGRIPPA.

According to one legend, Cartaphilus, the Wandering Jew, asked Agrippa in 1525 to produce a vision of his dead childhood sweetheart in his mirror. Agrippa asked the man to count off the decades since the girl had died, and he waved his magic wand at each count. Cartaphilus kept counting far beyond the girl's death. At 149, Agrippa felt dizzy but told him to keep counting. Finally, at 1,150, a vision appeared of the girl in ancient Palestine. Cartaphilus called out to her—in disobedience to Agrippa's admonitions—and the vision dissolved. Cartaphilus fainted. Later, he told Agrippa he was the Jew who had struck Christ as he carried the cross and was condemned to wander the earth.

Even royalty believed in and used magic mirrors. Catherine de Medici, a devout believer in the occult arts, had a mirror that revealed to her the future of France. Henri IV also relied on a magic mirror to discover political plots against him.

The medieval magician ALBERTUS MAGNUS recorded a formula for making a magic mirror: Buy a looking glass and inscribe upon it "S. Solam S. Tattler S. Echogordner Gematur." Bury it at a CROSSROADS during an uneven hour. On the third day, go to the spot at the same hour and dig it up—but do not be the first person to gaze into the mirror. In fact, said Magnus, it is best to let a dog or a cat take the first look.

See also SCRYING.

mistletoe An evergreen shrub believed to possess many occult powers of fertility, HEALING, luck and protection against evil. One of the most important plants of European magic lore, mistletoe is ceremonially cut at the summer and winter solstices. Throughout history, it has been used in potions, powders and teas to control epilepsy, hypertension and palsy, to enhance fertility and cure sterility, as an aphrodisiac and to protect against POISONS. It has been hung in homes, barns and stables as an amulet to protect against WITCHCRAFT, fire, illness and bad luck (see AMULETS). A sprig of mistletoe over a doorway is said to prevent WITCHES from entering.

Mistletoe, which bears white berries, grows parasitically on many deciduous trees in Europe and America. Its seeds are spread by bird droppings and it grows anywhere, even on trees, thus giving the appearance of springing to life from nothing. Some ancient peoples believed it descended from heaven on lightning bolts.

The Celts, who populated Britain and large portions of Europe ca. 8000–2000 B.C., considered mistletoe sacred because it grew on their venerated oak trees. It excited great wonder because it could grow without touching the earth, and it seemed to propagate itself magically. DRUIDS used it in fertility rituals.

The Christmas (winter solstice) custom of harvesting mistletoe and kissing beneath it is a relic of the ancient Druidic fertility rites.

Mistletoe also appears in mythology. In Virgil's *Aeneid*, the hero Aeneus picks a "golden bough" of mistletoe at the gate of the underworld, which ensures his safety as he goes through it. Balder, the Norse god of light and joy, is slain by a spear of mistletoe that is thrown by Hodur at the instigation of Loki, god of darkness and evil. In Sweden, mistletoe is sacred to Thor, the god of thunder.

In Ozark folklore, mistletoe is commonly called *witch's broom* and is said to be used by witches in casting SPELLS. It is also used as an amulet, hung in homes and barns to keep witches away.

In folk medicine, mistletoe is commonly called *allheal*. It has been revered since the times of ancient Greece for its ability to treat nervous conditions and disorders. It also is used as a sedative, to lower blood pressure and as a treatment for tumors. A powder made from the berries is believed to make any man, woman or beast fertile.

Medical data on mistletoe is inconclusive. While the plant may have sedative effects, there is no evidence that it lowers blood pressure. In experiments with animals, it seems to treat tumors effectively. The U.S. Food and Drug Administration considers mistletoe toxic and unsafe for internal consumption.

money In folklore, money that comes from FAIRIES, WITCHES, sorcerers (see SORCERY) and the DEVIL often turns out to be worthless. The victim accepts payment for goods or services and discovers, after it is too late, that the gold coins or currency are actually toads, cat claws, shells, lead or other worthless—and sometimes repulsive—objects.

According to legend, PARACELSUS, the 16th-century Swiss alchemist, roamed about Europe penniless during his last years, paying innkeepers with gold coins that turned into seashells after he departed. Belief in illusory money parallels another folk belief that livestock purchased unwittingly from witches and fairies would disappear or metamorphose into something undesirable: cows would dissolve in running water, horses would turn into pigs, and so forth.

Montaigne, John   See DOCTOR JOHN.

moon   Since ancient times, the moon has been associated with woman and her fertility, monthly cycle, powers of nurturing and powers of darkness. The moon, ruler of the night and the mysteries of the dark, represents wetness, moisture, intuition, emotion, tides, the psychic, moods and madness. It embodies time, for its phases provided mankind with the first calendar. In modern WITCHCRAFT, the moon is the source of WITCHES' power, drawn down from the sky; it is the worker of MAGIC. The Great GODDESS, the Mother Goddess, the All-Dewy-One, is at her most formidable and potent as lunar deity.

In the earliest primitive times, the moon was viewed as the source of fertility of all things. Its light was considered indispensable for abundant harvests, large flocks and herds and human fecundity. It was believed that women were made pregnant by moonbeams. Women who desired children slept under the light of the moon; those who did not resorted to crude CHARMS, such as rubbing their bellies with spittle to avoid swelling like the waxing of the moon.

Since antiquity, lunar phases have governed all facets of life. The waxing moon is auspicious for crop planting and new endeavors, for luck and increasing; the waning moon is a time of diminishing and destruction. In the Renaissance and Reformation, when alchemy, high magic and folk magic were at their peaks, lunar phases governed all manner of magical rituals for the creation and consecration of magical tools, the summoning of spirits, the preparations of remedies and charms and the castings of SPELLS. One cut one's HAIR AND NAILS, entered into marriages and business arrangements, let blood and traveled according to the phases of the moon. The moon was believed to govern the humours, the moisture in the body and brain. In 1660 one English astrologer declared that children born at the full moon would never be healthy. Such children ran the risk of moonstruck madness, or *lunacy*. Folklore beliefs about the moon persist to the present day. The moon still influences magic rites.

The cycle of woman's menstruation is tied to the lunar phases. In many cultures, the words for "moon" and "menstruation" are the same or very similar (see BLOOD).

The moon as person and deity. The moon remained primarily a power and a force until about 2600 B.C., when it became personified in Middle Eastern civilizations as the Man in the Moon or the Great Man. During his waning, the Man in the Moon was eaten by a dragon and went down into the underworld. He rose anew as his son. The moon also was believed to incarnate on earth as a king; some lines of kings claimed to be the representatives of the moon and wore horned headdresses. Eventually, the Man in the Moon was replaced by the deity of the moon, who was first a god, then a goddess. The lunar goddess was the Great Goddess, the giver of all things in her waxing phase and the destroyer of all things in her waning phase. She took on the fertilizing power of the moon and was the protector of women. As destroyer, she could bring storms, particularly heavy rains, and floods.

The lunar gods and goddesses were portrayed with crescent moons, the auspicious symbol of the waxing and lucky moon. The Great Goddess was associated with the cow, goat and bull, whose horns represented the crescent or horned moon.

To the Greeks, the goddess SELENE once was the sole lunar goddess. Selene was replaced by Artemis (DIANA) and HECATE. The true power of the moon resided in Hecate, who ruled the waning and dark moon, the time when the moon slipped into the underworld and ghosts and spirits walked the earth. Hecate became known as the Three-Headed Hecate, whose triple aspects combined Selene, Artemis and Hecate. The witches of Thessaly were said to be able to draw down the power of the moon from the sky. In myth, Aphrodite taught her son, Jason, "how to draw down the dark moon" whenever he needed magic.

The moon in Witchcraft. In modern Witchcraft, worship of the Goddess is associated with the moon. The consort of the Goddess is the HORNED GOD, the god of the woodlands, whose horns represent both the beasts of nature and the horned moon. The activities and magic workings of a Witch or COVEN are timed according to the phases of the moon. Most covens meet at the full moon; some also meet at the new moon. The moon is personified by a triple aspect of the Goddess, usually Diana (the Roman name is more common than the Greek name, Artemis), the Virgin, who rules the new and waxing moon; Selene, the Matron, who rules the full moon; and Hecate, the Crone, who rules the waning and dark moon. Magic for healing, gain, luck and increase is done during the waxing moon. Magical power is greatest on nights of the full moon, particularly at midnight. Magic for binding, banishing and eliminating is done during the waning phase (for those Witches who curse, this is the appropriate time; see CURSES).

The power of the moon also is drawn down for a trance ritual called DRAWING DOWN THE MOON, in which the high priestess invokes the spirit of the Goddess into her so that She may speak to her followers.

Some feminist witches have a ritual of howling at the moon in order to connect with the primitive power of the Goddess within.

The moon is associated with the metal SILVER, favored by Witches for its properties as an amulet (see AMULETS; JEWELRY) and as an enhancer of psychic powers.

Mora Witches   Like the witch hysteria of Salem, Massachusetts (see SALEM WITCHES), the 1669 witch-hunts in Mora, in central Sweden, demonstrate how public fears can run quickly out of control. By the end of the witch-hunt, 85 WITCHES had been executed for allegedly seducing some 300 children and spiriting them away to satanic SABBATS. And, as in Salem, the hysteria of Mora was started by children.

The specter of witches first was raised on July 5, 1668, when a 15-year-old boy in Elfdale, Sweden, accused a 17-year-old girl of stealing children for Satan. Others were also accused. All pleaded not guilty except one 71-year-old woman.

That confession sparked concern, and King Charles XI established a commission to redeem the witches by mass public PRAYER instead of TORTURE or imprisonment. Instead, public fears were ignited, and stories of child stealing and devilish activities increased.

The king's commissioners arrived in Mora on August 12, 1669, to investigate, to the relief of the villagers. The following day, the entire population of about 3,000 persons turned out to church to hear a sermon "declaring the miserable case of those people that suffered themselves to be deluded by the devil." Everyone prayed to be delivered from the scourge.

Children who allegedly had been spirited away to sabbats were assembled and then interviewed one by one. Their stories agreed: they had been snatched sleeping in their beds and spirited away to the most horrid satanic revelries. Some of the children spoke of a white angel who appeared and rescued them, assuring that what was happening to them would not last long but had been permitted "for the wickedness of the people." The children named 70 witches, 15 of whom were other children. Some of them were

from the neighboring district of Elfdale. The accused were rounded up, interrogated and tortured. Twenty-three of them confessed immediately.

The witches said they would meet at a gravel pit by a CROSSROADS, where they put vests on their heads and danced "round and round and round about." They went to the crossroads and summoned the DEVIL to take them to an imaginary place called Blockula. According to Mackay, the Devil "generally appeared as a little old man, in a grey coat, with red and blue stockings, with exceedingly long garters. He had besides a very high-crowned hat, with bands of many-colored linen enfolded about it, and a long red beard that hung down to his middle."

After getting their promise to serve him body and soul, the Devil ordered them to steal children, threatening to beat them if they disobeyed. They said they were able to enter the homes because the Devil first removed the window glass. They took the children, promising them fine clothes and other things, and then flying off with them on the backs of beasts, on men whom they had charmed to sleep or astride posts. They admonished the children not to tell anyone. Some who did were "miserably scourged" to death, according to COTTON MATHER, in his book *On Witchcraft, Being the Wonders of the Invisible World* (1693). The judges did find some children with lash marks on them.

The witches said the Devil carried them all away on the backs of horses, asses, goats and monkeys, over the tops of houses, to Blockula, a house with a gate in an infinite green meadow. In a pledge to service of the Devil, the witches cut their fingers and wrote their names in their own blood in his book (see DEVIL'S PACT). The Devil baptized the witches and bade them sit down at a long table for a feast of broth made of coleworts and bacon, bread and butter, milk, cheese and oatmeal. Sometimes the Devil played a harp or fiddle while they ate. Afterwards, they danced in a ring before the Devil, the witches swearing and cursing "most horribly." Sometimes they danced naked.

The Devil caused a terrible dragon to appear and told the witches that if they confessed anything, he would unleash the dragon upon them. The Devil also swore he would kill the judges. Some of the witches said they had attempted to murder the trial judges but could not.

The witches also said they had attempted to kill the minister of Elfdale. One witch said the Devil gave her a sledgehammer, which she used to try to drive a nail into the minister's head, but the nail would not go all the way in. The minister complained of a terrible headache at about the same time.

The judges asked the witches to demonstrate their

black magic. They were unable to do so, explaining that since they had confessed, they had lost their powers.

All 70 persons accused were condemned to death. The 23 adults who confessed were burned together in one fire in Mora; the following day, 15 children were burned together. The remaining 32 persons were sent to Faluna, where they later were executed.

Milder punishment was meted out to another 56 children who were involved in the escapades. Thirty-six of them, between the ages of nine and 16, were forced to run a gauntlet and were lashed on their hands once a week for a year. Twenty children had their hands lashed with rods for three consecutive Sundays at the church door. Observed Mather, "This course, together with Prayers, in all the Churches thro' the Kingdom, issued in the deliverance of the Country."

The Mora case was long considered to be one of the most convincing pieces of evidence of the prevalence of evil witchcraft.

Morgan le Fay In Celtic lore, a sorceress or fairy (see SORCERY; FAIRIES) who possessed the art of magic herbal HEALING and who was either the sister or half-sister of the legendary King Arthur. According to some legends, she was the mistress of MERLIN, who taught her MAGIC. Malory said she learned her arts in a nunnery.

Morgan, invariably portrayed as evil, plotted against Arthur to steal his talisman (see TALISMANS) sword, Excalibur or otherwise bring him down. Yet she also came to his aid: when Arthur was mortally wounded in the battle of Camlan, she was one of the four queens who spirited him away to the Isle of Avalon, where she used her magic to save his life.

Sometimes described as a goddess, Morgan in fact seems to be a composite character derived from various Celtic myths and deities. In Welsh folklore, she was related to lake fairies who seduce and then abandon human lovers; in Irish folklore, she lived in a fairy mound from which she flew out in hideous guises to frighten people. In English and Scottish lore, Morgan lived either on Avalon or in various castles, including one near Edinburgh that was inhabited by a bevy of wicked fairies. She also is related to the mermaids of the Breton coast, called Morganes, Mari Morgan or Morgan, who enchanted sailors. Depending on the story, the sailor either went to their deaths or were transported to a blissful underwater paradise. In Italy, mirages over the Straits of Messina are still called the Fata Morganas.

Morgan was sometimes portrayed as an evil, old HAG or crone, as in the stories of Sir Lancelot and the Lake and *Gawain and the Green Knight*. She is not, however, the "Lady of the Lake" in the Arthurian legend by that name. Morgan was said to have a prodigious sexual appetite and was constantly capturing knights to satisfy her desires.

According to MARION ZIMMER BRADLEY, a novelist and occultist who has researched the Arthurian legends, Morgan Le Fay was a damsel of the Lady of the Lake, a Druidess who learned dragon magic in a Druid college for priestesses (see also DRUIDS).

Morrigan, the In Irish mythology, one of three war goddesses, the other two being Neman and Macha. She also was the Mighty Queen, viewed either as the Triple Goddess or the death aspect of the Triple Goddess. Robert Graves gave three aspects of the Morrigan: Ana, Babd and Macha.

In legend, the Morrigan protected the Tuatha de Danaan (see FAIRIES) with a cover of fog and rain so that their boats could land upon the shore of Ireland. On battlefields, she appeared as a raven or scald crow, eating the bodies of the dead. She could present a winsome side that hid her secret intentions of destroying someone, or she could be openly vengeful. She fell in love with Cuchulain, the heroic son of LUGH, but was rejected by him. In anger, she harassed him on the battlefield, then tried, in vain, to save his life.

The Morrigan sometimes is associated with the three phases of the moon—waxing, full and waning—and with the maiden, matron and crone aspects of the Triple Goddess.

See also GODDESS.

Morris dance A lively, reel- or jiglike dance of Britain that may be the relic of an old pagan ceremony, still performed around the world at Beltane (May Eve) and midsummer festivals (see SABBATS). The Morris dance is believed to be named after *morisca*, a Moorish dance or play, and is performed solely by men. The dance is believed to bring good luck.

Morris dancing dates back to at least the 15th century; some theories place its origin in Britain at the 14th century. The dance is descended from an old Moorish dance, the *fandango* of Spain. It may also be connected to a secret Moroccan cult, the Dhulqarneni, or "The Two-Horned Ones," who danced in a circle to raise MAGIC power and worshipped the MOON. It is believed to have been introduced to England from Spain by John of Gaunt, son of Edward III (1312–1377), who spent a great deal of time in that country.

According to anthropologist MARGARET A. MURRAY, an old Morris-dance tune, "Green Garters," was the traditional music for the processional dance to the MAYPOLE on May morning. The May games and dances, which were pagan spring festivals and fertility rites, were important to villages, especially during the 16th century, and thus tolerated by the Church. In the 17th century, the Puritans condemned and abolished them. Morris dancing was restored during the Restoration.

There are different versions of the Morris dance, which traditionally is performed by five men and a boy dressed as "Maid Marian," with two musicians. In Lancashire, the Britannia Coconut Dancers, who perform at Easter, blacken their faces and wear black breeches, white barrel skirts and wooden disks fastened to their knees, hands and belts, which are clapped together. The men are led by a Whiffler, who whips away winter and bad luck. Also found in Lancashire is the North-west style, a revival of the dance that led the Rushcart Processions during Wakes Weeks, a former annual British holiday commemorating the dedication of the local church. The dancers wear black breeches, white shirts, bells and wooden clogs. The Cotswold Morris dance is done with bells, handkerchiefs, sticks and hand clapping. In some versions, the Morris dancers are circled by masked dancers representing bulls, stags, hobby horses and dragons.

Mother Redcap (d. 1926)   In the early 20th century, an elderly woman who lived in a village about 14 miles from Cambridge, England, became known as a Witch (see WITCHES). Mother Redcap, as she was called, said she was endowed with her Witch powers in circumstances reminiscent of the DEVIL'S PACT legends of medieval times. According to an article published in the London *Sunday Chronicle* on September 9, 1928:

> One day a black man called, produced a book and asked her to sign her name in it. The woman signed the book and the mysterious stranger then told her she would be the mistress of five imps who would carry out her orders. Shortly afterwards the woman was seen out accompanied by a rat, a cat, a toad, a ferret, and a mouse. Everybody believed she was a witch, and many people visited her to obtain cures.

Mother Redcap's neighbors apparently viewed her new status as an asset and not something evil, and she was not persecuted. Her story is odd, however, for she claimed to sign the mysterious book without asking what it was or why. In traditional stories of the Devil's pact, the person supposedly knows full well the terms of the deal—soul in exchange for earthly gain—which places a moral burden squarely

upon the shoulders of the individual. Mother Redcap appeared not to suffer and to use her alleged supernatural abilities to help others. She died in 1926.

Mother Shipton (1488–?)   A 15th-century English witch and seer who supposedly prophesied scientific inventions, new technology, wars and politics through several centuries, all written in crude rhymes. The books of her "prophecies" are likely the invention of later writers, among them Richard Head, who published a book of her predictions in 1667; an anonymous writer who published the *Strange and Wonderful History of Mother Shipton* in 1668; and a man named Hindley, who apparently authored Shipton predictions in 1871.

More myth and fabulous tales surround Mother Shipton than fact. Reputedly, she was born Ursula Southeil near Dropping Well in Knaresborough, Yorkshire, in 1488, though the dates 1448 and 1486 also are given in various texts. Her mother, who possessed the powers of HEALING, clairvoyance, STORM RAISING and hexing (see HEX), died in childbirth with "strange and terrible noises." Ursula, who inherited her mother's powers, was raised by a local townswoman. Mysterious things happened around Ursula: furniture moved about on its own, and food disappeared from dinner plates. Once, the townswoman left Ursula alone in her cottage. When she returned with several neighbors, they were attacked by strange forces. A woman was hung by her toes from a staff floating in the air, and men were yoked to the same staff. Other women found themselves dancing in circles; if they tried to stop, an IMP in the shape of a monkey pinched them to keep them going.

Ursula fit the classic stereotype of HAG. Head described her as follows:

> ". . . with very great goggling, but sharp and fiery eyes; her nose of incredible and unproportionable length, having in it many crooks and turnings, adorned with many strange pimples of divers colors, as red and blue mixed, which, like vapors of brimstone, gave such a lustre to the affrighted spectators in the dead time of the night, that one of them confessed that her nurse needed no other light to assist her in the performance of her duty.

In art, she is depicted as wearing a tall, conical, brimmed black hat (see WITCH'S HAT).

Despite this incredibly ugly appearance, Ursula married Tobias Shipton at age 24. Her husband then disappeared from all records, and Ursula became known as Mother Shipton. She did not like prying neighbors and once took revenge on a group of them by bewitching them at a breakfast party (see SPELLS).

The guests suddenly broke into hysterical laughter and ran out of the house, pursued by GOBLINS. For this mischief, Mother Shipton was summoned to court, but she threatened to do worse if she were prosecuted. She then said, "Updraxi, call Stygician Helleuei," and soared off on a winged dragon.

The verses attributed to her vary. One of the best-known is:

> Carriages without horses shall go
> Around the world thoughts shall fly
> In the twinkling of an eye
> Iron in the water shall float
> As easy as a wooden boat
> Gold shall be found, and found
> In a land that's not now known
> A house of glass shall come to pass
> In England, but alas!

Her predictions included automobiles, telephone and telegraph, iron-clad boats, the California gold rush and the Crystal Palace in London. Mother Shipton also is credited with predicting the Civil War in England, the Great Fire of London (1666), the discovery of tobacco and potatoes in the New World, World War II and the women's liberation movement.

Her memorial, Mother Shipton's Cave, is in Knaresborough.

Murray, Margaret Alice (1863–1963)

British anthropologist, archaeologist and Egyptologist best known for her controversial theories on the origins and organization of WITCHCRAFT as a religion.

Murray was born July 13, 1863, in Calcutta. She distinguished herself in the British academic world, entering University College in London in 1894. She was named a fellow of the college and specialized in Egyptology. She became a junior lecturer in Egyptology in 1899 and was assistant professor of Egyptology until 1935, when she resigned her post to pursue other studies. She also held other lecturer positions.

Murray did archaeological excavations in Egypt, Malta, Hertfordshire (England), Petra, Minorca and Tell Ajjul in south Palestine. Her interest in witchcraft led her to field studies of the subject throughout Europe, which included an examination of written records of witchcraft trials.

Her first book on witchcraft, *The Witch-cult in Western Europe*, was published in 1921 and caused immediate controversy among her peers. Murray maintained that witchcraft in the Middle Ages and Renaissance was not a phenomenon of Christian heresy but was the remnants of an organized, pagan fertility religion that dated back to Paleolithic times. She also maintained that witchcraft was far more widespread and organized during those centuries than had been generally believed by most historians and anthropologists.

Murray was not the first to put forth this theory. Sir James Frazer had discussed the prehistoric origins of witchcraft rituals and beliefs in his extensive work, *The Golden Bough*, published in 1890. Murray elaborated upon Frazer's work and took her own theories much further.

Murray called witchcraft *the Dianic cult* because of the pagan worship of the goddess DIANA. She believed that most witches were organized into covens that always consisted of 12 members plus a leader, either the DEVIL or a man impersonating the Devil, despite the lack of evidence to support such a belief (see COVEN). She also believed that practitioners of witchcraft came from "every rank of society, from the highest to the lowest." Murray remained convinced of the existence of an organized witchcraft religion, despite the lack of evidence to prove it.

In her second book on witchcraft, *The God of the Witches*, published in 1933, Murray discussed the HORNED GOD, or male pagan deity, tracing its origins back to Paleolithic times as well. She portrayed the Horned God as one of power but not evil. A third book, *The Divine King in England*, published in 1954, was perhaps the most controversial of all her works. In it, she asserted that every English king, from William the Conqueror in the 11th century to JAMES I in the early 17th century, was a secret witch and that many of the country's statesmen had been killed in ritual deaths.

For decades, scholars of witchcraft have argued over Murray's theories. Some of her views have been widely rejected, including most of her material in *The Divine King in England* and her opinion that the term *sabbat* comes from the French term *s'esbettre*, which means "to frolic" (see SABBATS). Nevertheless, she is recognized for her pioneering work in the field of witchcraft and for shedding light on the continuity of ancient pagan practices, not only into the Middle Ages but into the 20th century as well.

Murray's theories gave fuel to a movement in England in the 1950s to rediscover Witchcraft as an organized religion. GERALD B. GARDNER, one of England's most influential white WITCHES, expounded upon her theories in his own book, *Witchcraft Today* (1954), for which Murray wrote the introduction.

Murray died in London on November 13, 1963, shortly after her 100th birthday.

N

nails See HAIR AND NAILS.

names of power In Western MAGIC, powerful words which, when rhythmically chanted by a magician from within a MAGIC CIRCLE, effect the conjuration of spirits and DEMONS or the achievement of SPELLS. The names of power are the secret names of God or deities, or words substituted for these names.

The concept of names of power dates back to the ancient Egyptians, Greeks, Hebrews, Assyrians and Gnostics, who believed that incredible power could be unleashed by the sound vibrations of the words. The Egyptians invented names of power for magical rituals, which were passed into texts that in turn were absorbed into Western culture.

The most powerful of all names of power is the Tetragrammaton, the personal name of God in the Old Testament, usually expressed as YHWH, the transliteration of the Hebrew letters *Yod, He, Vau, He.* The numerical values assigned to these letters add up to ten, which in Hebrew NUMEROLOGY represents the basic organizing principle in the universe. So awesome is the Tetragrammaton that for centuries it was seldom spoken. As early as the time of Jesus, it was whispered only on Yom Kippur by a high priest. In the scriptures, substitute words were used, such as *Adonai, Adonay* or *Elohim.* The exact pronunciation of the Tetragrammaton is not known; the most accepted is "Yahweh." A common variation is "Jehovah."

By using various anagrammatical and numerological formulas (see GEMATRIA), numerous names of power have been created for magical purposes. *Agla,* an abbreviation frequently used by rabbis, comes from the first letters of the Hebrew phrase, *Aieth*

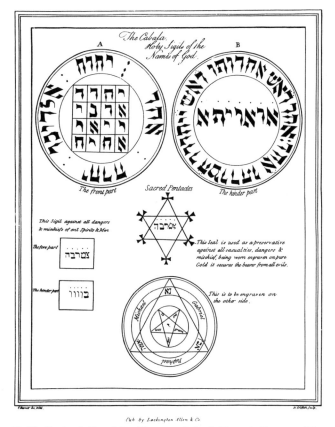

Kabbalistic sigils of the Names of God (Francis Barrett, *The Magus,* 1801)

Gadol Leolam Adonai, which means "Adonai (the Lord) will be great to eternity." *Amen* is a word of power, because in Hebrew it adds up to 91, as does *Jehovah Adonai.*

Some names or words of power are nonsensical, created for their rhythm or their numerical value.

The essence of the power unleashed by the words is not in the words themselves but in their intrinsic occult power and the faith of those using them.

Names and words of power appear in all of the major magical GRIMOIRES. In many cases, the origins and meanings of the words have long been lost. For example, the *Key of Solomon* ends a conjuration of demons with the words:

Aglon, Tetragram, vaycheon, stimulamation, ez-phares, retetragrammaton olyaram irion esytion ex-istion eryona onera orasym mozm messias soter Em-manuel Sbaoth Adonay, *te adoro, et te invoco.* Amen.

Most of the words are unrecognizable, but they probably contribute to the rhythm of the chant, which is important in the attainment of a state of frenzy on the part of the magician.

ALEISTER CROWLEY created AUGMN as an ultimate word of power, which he believed was a mantra of such force that a magician chanting it would be able to control the universe. AUGMN is an expansion of the Buddhist mantra Om, which represents God and the Supreme Reality, the sum total of everything in all creation. The basis for AUGMN is a gematric formula. In Hebrew, the letters of the mantra add up to 100. By breaking down 100 as a sum of 20 and 80, one arrives at the Hebrew letters *kaph* and *pe,* which, transformed into Greek, are the first letters of *kteis* and *phallos,* which correspond to the female and male sexual organs. In *Magick in Theory and Practice* (1929), Crowley describes AUGMN as ''the Magical formula of the Universe as a reverbatory engine for the ex-tension of Nothingness through the device of equi-librated opposites.''

nature spirits   Low-level beings said to exist in all life forms in nature, in the plant, animal and mineral kingdoms. The term *nature spirits* is used synony-mously with ELEMENTALS, the beings who exist in the four ELEMENTS of earth, air, fire and water.

In NEO-PAGANISM and neo-Pagan WITCHCRAFT, na-ture spirits are to be treated with respect, as they can combine in a powerful energy. Their participation and cooperation is sought to enhance rituals and stimulate communication between mankind and Mother Earth. When sites are selected for outdoor rituals, an effort is made to communicate with nature spirits, through meditation, to secure their coopera-tion and seek their guidance. Nature spirits manifest themselves physically, through animal and insect noises, a rising of wind, fox fire, a clearing of sky, the sudden presence of an animal or a flock of birds. Some clairvoyant individuals claim to be able to see them.

necromancy   An ancient art of conjuring the dead for the purpose of DIVINATION. Necromancy dates back to ancient Persia, Greece and Rome and in the Middle Ages was held to be widely practiced by magicians, sorcerers and WITCHES (see MAGIC; SOR-CERY; WITCHCRAFT). It is condemned by the Catholic Church as ''the agency of evil spirits,'' and in Eliza-bethan England it was outlawed by the Witchcraft Act of 1604. Throughout history, necromancy has been feared because of the dangers involved, and is reviled as one of the ugliest and most repugnant of magical rites. Necromantic rites are not practiced in neo-Pagan Witchcraft, but they are in VODOUN.

Necromancy is not to be confused with conjuring DEMONS or the DEVIL. The spirits of the dead are sought for information because they are no longer bound by the earthly plane and therefore supposedly have access to information beyond that available to the living. Conjured spirits are asked about the future and where to find buried treasure.

FRANCIS BARRETT, author of *The Magus* (1801), said necromancy ''has its name because it works on the bodies of the dead, and gives answers by the ghosts and apparitions of the dead, and subterranean spir-its, alluring them into the carcasses of the dead by certain hellish charms, and infernal invocations, and by deadly sacrifices and wicked oblations.''

There are two kinds of necromancy: raising a corpse itself to life and, more commonly, summoning the spirit of the corpse.

The rituals for necromancy are similar to those for conjuring demons, involving MAGIC CIRCLES, wands, TALISMANS, BELLS and incantations, as prescribed by various GRIMOIRES. In addition, the necromancer sur-rounds himself by gruesome aspects of death: he wears clothing stolen from corpses and meditates upon death. Some rituals call for the eating of dog flesh, for dogs are associated with HECATE, the patron goddess of witchcraft, and for consuming unsalted and unleavened black bread and unfermented grape juice, symbolic of decay and lifelessness.

Such preparations may go on for days or weeks. The actual ritual itself may take many hours, during which time the magician calls upon Hecate or various demons to help raise the desired spirit. The ritual customarily takes place in a graveyard over the corpse itself. The objective is to summon the spirit to re-enter the corpse and bring it back to life, rising and speaking in answer to questions posed by the magi-cian. Recently deceased corpses are preferred by nec-romancers, for they are said to speak most clearly. If the person has been dead a long time, necromancers try to summon their ghostly spirit to appear. Once the ritual has been performed successfully, the nec-romancer is supposed to burn the corpse or bury it in quicklime, so that it will not be disturbed again. In the Middle Ages, many believed that necromancers also consumed the flesh of the corpse as part of the ritual.

Some necromancers summon corpses to attack the living. This practice dates back as far as ancient Egypt and Greece and is still done in Vodoun.

One of the best-known necromancers is the WITCH OF ENDOR, whose conjuring of the dead prophet Samuel for King Saul is recorded in the Bible; Samuel foretold Saul's doom. APOLLONIUS OF TYANA gained a great reputation in first-century Greece as a philosopher and necromancer. The 16th-century English magician, JOHN DEE, and his scalawag companion, Edward Kelly, were reputed necromancers, though Dee never recorded any such activities in his diaries. The 17th-century French magician, ELIPHAS LEVI, attempted to conjure the spirit of Apollonius, an experience that left him badly shaken and frightened.

Necromancy techniques were taught in medieval Spain, in deep caves near Seville, Toledo and Salamanca. The caves were walled up by Isabella the Catholic, who considered them evil.

The numbers nine and 13 are associated with necromancy. Nine represents an old belief that there were nine spheres through which a soul passed in the transition from life to death. Thirteen was the number of persons who attended Christ's Last Supper, at which he was betrayed; Christ later rose from the dead.

In Vodoun, corpses are "raised" from graves in rituals in which appeals are made to Baron Samedi, the scarecrowlike god of graveyards and zombies. In Haiti, the rites take place in a graveyard at midnight. They are performed by the person who is the local incarnation of Papa Nebo, father of death, and a group of followers. A grave is selected and white candles are implanted at its foot and lit. A frock coat and a silk top hat, the symbols of Baron Samedi, are draped on the grave's cross (if the grave has no cross, one is made). A ritual is performed to awaken Baron Samedi from sleep. While the god makes no visible manifestation, he signals his presence and approval by moving or flapping the frock coat or hat.

The necromancers pay homage to the Baron and promise him offerings of food, drink and money, then send him back to sleep by tossing roots and herbs. The corpse is unearthed, and the incarnation of Papa Nebo asks it questions. The answers usually are "heard" only by the Papa Nebo representative.

Necronomicon, The A fictitious black-magic grimoire, the idea of which was created by the American occult and horror-fiction writer, H. P. Lovecraft (1890–1937). Lovecraft wrote about the book in his fiction and acquired a cult of followers who believe that it actually exists and that it is based, at least in part, on fact (see GRIMOIRES).

The Necronomicon was born of Lovecraft's fertile imagination in his 1936 essay, "A History of *The Necronomicon*."

The fantasy captured the imagination of some of Lovecraft's fans, and for years a belief persisted that a real grimoire titled *The Necronomicon* existed. Booksellers received requests for it. As of the late 1980s, at least two versions of the "real" *Necronomicon* had been published.

neo-Paganism A broad, eclectic movement, centered in the industrialized West, which is characterized by a return to, or a reconstruction of, pre-Christian Western nature religions. It gained momentum in the 1960s with the flowering of the Age of Aquarius and the environmental movement. Neo-Paganism means different things to different followers: it is a religion, a philosophy and a way of life. As a movement, it is not unified, centralized, structured or highly organized, which is one of the key factors in its appeal. It has no charismatic gurus or proselytizers. Neo-Pagans, like modern WITCHES, are independent and autonomous. Some belong to groups and organizations, while other prefer to remain solitary (see SOLITARIES). All neo-Pagans value choosing their own paths and beliefs. Some neo-Pagans call themselves simply "Pagans."

The word *pagan* comes from the Latin *paganus*, which means "country dweller." As Christianity spread slowly throughout the West, the last pockets to convert from pre-Christian religions were the country folk who were isolated from the mainstream. Like the term *witch*, *pagan* came to have unsavory connotations that have lingered to the present times. As the Christian Church worked to eradicate opposition from heretics in the Middle Ages, Renaissance and Reformation, *pagan* became a derogatory term. It implied that one was unsophisticated and uneducated, and worshipped false gods.

Neo-Pagans find a resonance with the ecstatic and mystery traditions of pre-Christian religions, which they feel are missing from modern mainstream Western religion. Neo-Paganism brings them closer to both nature and the Divine Force. To neo-Pagans, Christianity's God is remote, inaccessible and intangible, and Christians view nature as merely an economic resource to be exploited. The Pagan gods and goddesses are more than deities, they are also archetypes of the collective unconscious.

MARGOT ADLER observes in *Drawing Down the Moon* (1986) that the three key principles of neo-Paganism are polytheism, pantheism and animism. Not all neo-

Pagans believe in all three principles. In the polytheistic view, the Divine Force has not one, but a multitude of faces, personified by various Pagan gods and goddesses. Addressing prayers and rituals to different deities gives neo-Paganism diversity, richness and depth. Neo-Pagans enjoy the creativity of composing poetry, music, songs, rituals and dramas in honor of the many faces of the Divine Force.

Pantheists believe that the Divine Force is immanent in nature; some believe that the Deity is both immanent and transcendent. Mother Nature herself has a persona, and to some, she is a living, sentient being (see GAIA). The neo-Pagan views all life as sacred and interconnected. The pagan religions celebrated fertility and the cycles of Nature. The neo-Pagan seeks to be in harmony with the rhythms of life and the forces of the ELEMENTS. One takes from the earth what one needs for survival, gives thanks and returns energy in another form to the earth.

In animism, all things, even inanimate objects, are imbued with a life-force. States Adler, "At some level Neo-Paganism is an attempt to reanimate the world of nature; or, perhaps more accurately, to reenter the primeval world view, to participate in nature in a way that is not possible for most Westerners after childhood." Neo-Paganism, then, enables the individual to feel like an integral part of a greater whole, of nature and of the cosmos.

In addition to those principles, most neo-Pagans believe in REINCARNATION and adhere to a creed virtually identical to the WICCAN REDE; "An' it harm none, do what ye will." Most observe the eight seasonal SABBATS observed in pagan Europe: the solstices, equinoxes, and four agrarian/pastoral holidays.

While neo-Paganism concerns mostly the pre-Christian religions of Western Europe, some neo-Pagans have integrated into their beliefs elements of Native American Indian religions, Eastern religions, shamanic practices and African and Latin religions.

In terms of sexual beliefs and attitudes, neo-Pagans tend to be more liberal and tolerant than the mainstream population. Some have participated in group marriages. Most believe that sex should be enjoyed and celebrated, not considered a sin. In 1978–79 a movement for gay, male neo-Pagans, the Radical Faeries, began at a gay conference in Arizona, to explore the connections between the Pagan nature religions and gay spirituality.

Many neo-Pagans practice various types of MAGIC in their rituals. Most see magic as a means of using the will to effect change or influence events. They draw upon modern Witchcraft magic, folk magic, ceremonial magic and magic in other religions and traditions. Celtic and Egyptian magic are popular, based upon what is known about those ancient magical systems.

People come to neo-Paganism in a variety of ways. Many arrive at it through study of religions and philosophy. Many are drawn through environmental concerns and politics. Others become interested through friends, classes, seminars or contact with one of the many neo-Pagan journals or networking organizations. Followers cut across all racial, class, economic, educational, occupational and (previous) religion lines. By and large, it appears to be a white, middle-class phenomenon, perhaps because it concerns the reconstruction of ancient European religions. In the United States, it is estimated that about half of the neo-Pagan community (said to range up to 100,000 in number) are Witches.

The first formal neo-Pagan organization in the United States was Fereferia, founded in California in 1957 by Fred Adams, then a graduate student at Los Angeles State College. Adams, an artist, astrologer and student of mythology and ancient cultures, was inspired by utopian authors such as Robert Graves to create his own vision of utopia, a response to a "planet in crisis." Fereferia, which comes from Latin words for "wilderness festival," was an intricate, Goddess- and nature-oriented system that preached an abandonment of technology and a return to a peaceful, loosely organized vegetarian society.

The organization was first known as the Fellowship of Hesperides. From that early group, Fereferia evolved in the 1960s, becoming incorporated in 1967. As the group's charismatic leader, Adams developed his vision by creating virtually all the rituals and writings of Fereferia, including a calendar based on Pagan seasons.

Adams saw a return to worship of the divine female as essential, if mankind was to save itself from itself. He advocated the cultivation of tree crops, which he said were much more productive than the fields; he saw the tree as the Guardian of Life. He coined the term *eco-psychic* in describing how mankind ought to relate to the environment of earth and the heavens.

While many other neo-Pagan groups emphasized the Mother Goddess (see GODDESS), Fereferia emphasized the maiden: Kore, or Persephone or the Goddess of Spring. "Evo Kore!" was the salutation among followers. Adams's maiden was playful, sensuous and erotic. Adams maintained that humans must recapture their sensuality via nature, a connection which has been lost in industrialization.

Adams and his then-partner, Lady Svetlana, envisioned a balanced, perfect planet that supported only 10 to 20 million nonaggressive persons collected in groups of no more than 1,000, living on a diet of fruits, berries, nuts and vegetables. The social structure would be "egalitarian aristocracy." Cities would be replaced by cultural centers, in which people would come together for worship and festivals. The reduction in world population would come about through birth control and natural cataclysms, Adams and Svetlana predicted.

Fereferia rituals, which celebrated nature, were conducted in open-air henges oriented to the four cardinal points and the polestar. The first henge was established in 1959 in the Sierra Madre Mountains.

In the early 1970s Fereferia had only 50 or so active members; Adams was choosy about initiates. The organization was still in existence as of the late 1980s.

In the United States, the two organizations that most influenced the early development and spread of neo-Paganism were the CHURCH OF ALL WORLDS and PAGAN WAY. The Church of All Worlds was incorporated in 1967 in St. Louis, Missouri, by founder Tim Zell (see OTTER ZELL). During the 1970s it emphasized ecology; Zell called upon neo-Pagans to become involved in environmental issues. The Church entered a disorganized and then inactive phase following the departure of Zell and his wife, MORNING GLORY ZELL, in 1976. It has since reorganized under the Zells and is based in Ukiah, California. Pagan Way emerged in 1970 as the result of an international collaboration of a core group of people. Numerous groves were established, and in 1971 the Pagan Front, later renamed the PAGAN FEDERATION was established in Britain. By 1980 Pagan Way was no longer an organization, but its rituals, composed primarily by American ED FITCH, continue to be used by many neo-Pagans.

The Pagan Federation remains active in Britain. The Fellowship of Isis, located in Ireland, was founded in 1976 by Laurence and Pamela Durdin-Robertson and Laurence's sister, Olivia Robertson. In 1986 it claimed more than 6,000 members in 57 countries, including followers of WICCA, African/Latin religions, Christianity, Buddhism, Shinto and Hinduism.

The largest neo-Pagan (and Wiccan) networking organization is CIRCLE SANCTUARY, formed in 1974 near Mt. Horeb, Wisconsin, by SELENA FOX, Jim Alan and a small group of neo-Pagans. Circle offers numerous services, including an international contact service for persons interested in neo-Paganism or the Craft. In 1988 it assisted a group in West Germany in the planning of the first European Pagan festival.

In the 1980s neo-Pagans began to address such issues as providing Pagan-oriented counseling and social services, and paid clergy. Some organizations established social-service programs, but clergy have continued to work on a volunteer basis.

Pagan festivals. Festivals are popular with neo-Pagans and Witches, and a number of large outdoor gatherings take place annually, coinciding with one of the sabbat holidays. For two or more days, participants camp outdoors, live a communal life, attend classes and workshops and take part in rituals. In California, festivals were organized as early as 1968, attended first by small groups and then by hundreds. In the United States, the first great festival, the Pan-Pagan Festival, took place in 1977. The largest festival was organized by the Midwest Pagan Council in 1980, drawing nearly 600 neo-Pagans and Witches. By 1985 there were some 50 regional and national neo-Pagan/Wiccan gatherings around the United States. Most are held on private land.

The largest Pagan festival in the United States is the International Pagan Spirit Gathering (IPSG), which takes place each summer solstice at a private campground in Wisconsin. Organized by Circle Sanctuary, it draws 250 to 500 Pagans, Wiccans, shamans and persons from other religious traditions, including Christianity, Judaism, Buddhism, Shinto and Druidism, all of whom have in common a deep love of nature. The purpose of the event is to help people from different backgrounds and traditions meet, work and learn together, commune with nature and further their spiritual development.

The first IPSG took place in 1981, as an outgrowth of the Pan Pagan Festival. Gatherings are not open; attendance is limited and advance registration is required. Part of the registration fee goes to Circle Sanctuary.

For the weeklong event, a "magical village" is created. Participants camp out and share in the communal responsibilities of running the village. A central fire is lit and tended throughout the Gathering. Each person takes a turn on the festival staff, which oversees child and health care, security, wood gathering, food preparation and arts and crafts activities. The leading of rituals also is shared. Problems are solved by the village as a whole.

The Gathering also includes a Pagan Youth Experience, an ecumenical educational program for children of all ages. Children under 18 cannot attend the Gathering unless accompanied by an adult or given written permission from a parent or guardian.

See also *ÁR NDRAÍOCHT FÉIN;* P. E. I. (ISAAC) BONEWITS; DRUIDS.

New Reformed Orthodox Order of the Golden Dawn (NROOGD)

What began as a college-class experiment in San Francisco in 1968 resulted in a neo-Pagan religious organization (see NEO-PAGANISM). The NROOGD has no connection with the original HERMETIC ORDER OF THE GOLDEN DAWN, a ceremonial MAGIC fraternity. It recognizes the triple aspect of the GODDESS and is organized in covens (see COVEN).

The creators of NROOGD were classmates in a course on ritual magic at San Francisco State College. The group, which included Aidan Kelly and Glenna Turner, created their own rituals for a Witches' sabbat, which they performed for the rest of the class. Intrigued by the occult, the group continued to meet as an informal study group. Another sabbat was held on Lammas Day, August 1, 1968, which drew a crowd of about 40 persons (see SABBATS). A year later, in 1969, the group members decided they had adopted a new religion, and they initiated themselves as WITCHES and formed a coven. From 1972 to 1976 the organization published a periodical, *The Witches Trine.* As of the mid-1980s, active NROOGD covens existed around the United States, frequently hosting large public and semipublic outdoor festivals at sabbats.

Kelly left the organization in the late 1970s and returned to his original religion, Roman Catholicism. He confessed to having doubts about Paganism beginning in 1977; the final break came when he took a teaching position at a Catholic university in San Francisco in 1979.

Turner helped to form the COVENANT OF THE GODDESS, a federation of covens.

Newbury Witch (?–1763) An old woman, probably harmless, who was executed as a witch in 1763 by Cromwell's soldiers, near Newbury in Berkshire. The soldiers reportedly saw the old woman sailing on a plank down the River Kennet—by some accounts, the soldiers claimed she was walking on the water—and captured her as a witch and tried to shoot her. According to a 17th-century pamphlet, "with a deriding and loud laughter at them, she caught their bullets in her hands and chewed them." The soldiers then "blooded" her, a custom of the times in which a witch's forehead was slashed in the belief that the bleeding would drain out her power. One of the men put his pistol under her ear and shot her, "at which she straight sank down and died."

See also WITCHES; WITCHCRAFT.

Newton, Florence (ca. mid-17th century) One of the most important witch trials of Ireland was that of Florence Newton, the "Witch of Youghal," who was tried at the Cork assizes in 1661. Newton was accused of bewitching a young girl, Mary Longdon, into fits, and of bewitching one of her jail sentries, David Jones, to death. Unlike many of the witch trials conducted at the time on the Continent, the trial of Florence Newton involved no TORTURE. Some important people were involved in the trial, including

the mayor of Youghal, who gave sworn testimony, and VALENTINE GREATRAKES, a noted Irish healer.

Newton was arrested and jailed after Mary Longdon, a maid of John Pyne, claimed Newton had bewitched her. Longdon said Newton had become angry when Mary refused to give her some of her master's beef. Newton "went away grumbling."

A week later, Longdon encountered Newton, who threw herself upon the maid and violently kissed her, saying, "Mary, I pray thee let thee and I be friends; for I bear thee no ill will, and I pray thee do thou bear me none." A few days after the encounter, Mary woke up and saw Newton standing beside her bed with a "little old man in silk cloaths," whom she took to be a spirit. The spirit told Longdon to "follow his advice and she would have all the things after her own heart," to which Longdon replied she would have nothing to do with him, her faith being with the Lord.

A month after being kissed by Newton, Longdon fell ill with "fits and trances." She had shaking fits so violent that three or four men could not hold her down. She repeatedly vomited needles, pins, horsenails, stubbs, wool and straw (see ALLOTRIOPHAGY). She was pelted with mysterious showers of stones that followed her from room to room in her house, and outdoors, from place to place (see LITHOBOLY). Most of the stones vanished when they hit the ground. Longdon grabbed one with a hole in it, knotted a leather throng through it and stuck it in her purse. The stone vanished, but the knot remained in the thong.

Longdon said that during her fits, she saw Newton, who stuck pins in her arms do deeply that men had difficulty getting them out. The maid also said she was levitated out of her bed and carried to the top of the house (see LEVITATION).

Newton was summoned by the authorities. Whenever Longdon was in the accused witch's presence, her fits and discomfort grew worse. Newton was removed to Cork for trial. During the proceedings, whenever Newton was restrained "in bolts," Longdon seemed to be fine; if Newton was let out of bolts, Longdon fell ill, even if she were not in the presence of Newton.

Newton at first denied bewitching Longdon, describing herself as "old and disquieted, and distracted with her [own] sufferings." She mumbled about Longdon suffering, supposedly at the exact times the maid was having fits.

There was a prevailing belief at the time that witches could not recite the LORD'S PRAYER, so the court asked Newton to do this. The old woman stumbled over the prayer, omitting "and forgive us our trespasses." She said the omission was due to her bad memory, but the court was skeptical and appointed a man to try and teach her the prayer; however, she was unable to utter the one line.

Nicholas Pyne, a Youghal townsman, testified that he and two other men had visited Newton in jail and she had confessed her crimes to them. She told them she had not bewitched Longdon but overlooked her with the EVIL EYE, and that there was a vast difference between the two. Newton implicated two other Youghal women, whom she said had the same supernatural powers as she, and she suggested that perhaps one of them had harmed the maid.

Pyne testified that during the visit, they heard noises like a person in chains and bolts running up and down the cell but could see nothing. The next day, Newton confessed the noise was made by her familiar, which had the shape of a greyhound and went in and out the window (see FAMILIARS).

The famous healer Valentine Greatrakes and two other men gave Newton a test for WITCHCRAFT. They sat her on a stool and had a shoemaker try to stick an awl into the stool; he could not do so until the third try. When he attempted to pull the awl out, it broke. There was no mark in the stool where it had been pierced. Then they brought in Longdon and put another awl in her hand. ". . . [O]ne of them took the maid's hand, and ran violently at the witch's hand with it, but could not enter it, though the awl was so bent that none of them could put it straight again." Finally, the men lanced one of Newton's hands with a cut 1½ inches long and ¼-inch deep, but the hand did not bleed. Newton's other hand was similarly lanced, and then the two hands bled.

Newton said she was sorry for casting the evil eye on Longdon and causing her harm. The mayor of Youghal rounded up the two women Newton implicated as witches, but before he could subject all three women to the swimming test (see SWIMMING), Newton confessed to overlooking the maid. Longdon said the two women were not guilty, and they were released.

While Newton was in prison, one of her sentries was David Jones, who attempted to teach her the Lord's Prayer. One night she called Jones to her cell and announced she could recite the entire prayer. Once again, she omitted "and forgive us our trespasses." Jones taught the prayer to her again, and Newton, in gratitude, asked to kiss his hand. When Jones went home, he complained to his wife that he had a great pain in his arm and that it was the result of being kissed by the witch.

For the next 14 days Jones grew progressively ill, complaining that the pain was shooting up his arm into his heart, describing symptoms that sound like angina. He told a friend that the hag Newton was pulling off his arm. "Do you not see the old hag, how she pulls me?" Jones said. "Well, I lay my death on her, she has bewitched me." At the end of a fortnight, Jones died.

The surviving records of Newton's trial do not indicate her fate. Longdon apparently recovered.

nightmare An ugly demon, HAG, or *mare*, who sits on a person's chest during the night, causing great discomfort, a sensation of heaviness and suffocation and bad dreams. It also is the term for the bad dream itself—the definition that prevails in current popular usage.

In centuries past, DEMONS were believed to bring erotic dreams as well as terrifying ones, tempting their victims with forbidden lust. *Mare* is Old English for *incubus*, a male demon. The erotic dreams also could be caused by *succubi*, female demons. In the 16th century, the Swiss alchemist PARACELSUS even claimed that menstruation brought on nightmares. More likely, erotic nightmares were a result of repressed sexual desires.

The belief in nightmares as real demons is ancient. The storm god Alu brought nightmares to the Babylonians, while Greeks suffered the onslaughts of the giant, Ephialtes. The *Zohar*, or "Book of Splendor" in the KABBALAH, asserts that succubi did indeed cause nightmares in men. In medieval times, nightmares were sometimes thought to be caused by SPELLS cast by WITCHES or by DEMONIC POSSESSION. People protected themselves against the dreaded demons by reciting CHARMS and PRAYERS and making the sign of the cross before they went to sleep.

Modern research has found the "Old Hag" syndrome to be commonplace around the world; in the United States, it afflicts about 15 percent of the population. The syndrome is characterized by a person awakening to find himself paralyzed and in the presence of a nonhuman entity, sometimes humanoid in shape and with prominent eyes, which often sits on his chest and causes feelings of suffocation. The experience sometimes is accompanied by musty smells and shuffling sounds. Occultists still attribute such attacks to evil spirits. One scientific theory put forward suggests that the Old Hag syndrome might be a side effect of a poorly understood sleep-pattern derangement, such as narcolepsy.

Norse Paganism A branch of NEO-PAGANISM that worships the Norse pantheon of deities and stresses conservative values of honor, honesty, courage and duty to one's family, kin and friends. In the 1970s a number of Norse Pagan groups sprang into existence almost simultaneously, and independently of one another, in America, England and Iceland. This form of Paganism has a small but dedicated following, which belong to various groups. The largest is the Asatru Free Assembly, based in Breckinridge, Texas, formed in 1972 by Stephen McNallen, who at the time was a student at Midwestern University in Wichita Falls, Texas. McNallen found little appeal in WITCH-CRAFT or MAGIC but was drawn to the Vikings and Norse deities. He originally named his organization the Brotherhood and began publishing a quarterly journal, *The Runestone.* The Brotherhood's name was changed to the Asatru Free Assembly (AFA) in 1976.

In Old Norse, *Asatru* means "loyalty to the Aesir." The Aesir are one of two branches of Norse deities, the race of sky gods that includes ODIN and his wife Frigga, Thor, Loki, Balder and others. The second branch is the Vanir, concerned with earth, agriculture, fertility and the cycle of death and rebirth. Norse Paganism, and the AFA, embrace both branches of deities, and most followers of Norse Paganism are pantheistic. Odinism, a form of Norse Paganism, recognizes only the Aesir.

The symbology in Norse Paganism is Norse and Germanic, including RUNES, spears, warriors and the SWASTIKA—an ancient symbol that represents Thor's hammer and the wheel of the sun. While the warrior imagery has a macho appeal to men and the religion is heavily patriarchal, women in Norse Paganism find the Norse goddesses to be strong and assertive. FREYA, the goddess of fertility, does not shrink from a battle; Odin sends his warrior-maiden Valkyries off to the battlefields to bring dead heroes to Valhalla.

Festivals center on the seasonal equinoxes and solstices, and Norse holidays such as Ragnar's Day, March 28, which commemorates Viking Ragnar Lodbrok's sacking of Paris in 845. The AFA holds an annual festival called *Althing.* There is little interest in the magic and meditation that play a much larger role in Witchcraft and other branches of Paganism, though the AFA has a guild on shamanism. Other guilds, which are intended to build skills and foster fellowship, are devoted to artistry and writing, brewing, warrior skills (martial arts), computers and other areas of interest to the membership.

Many adherents to Norse Paganism are attracted by the emphasis on blood ties and genetics, the warrior ethic and the Norse symbology. The religion provides many with a way of identifying with Scandinavian or German ancestral roots. However, Norse Pagan groups constantly face accusations of white-supremacy racism, especially since the Nazis borrowed Norse motifs and probably tainted some forever, particularly the swastika and the rune for the letter S (see RUNES). Neo-Nazis have resurrected these symbols.

In *Drawing Down the Moon* (1986), MARGOT ADLER notes that there are a few extreme right-wing Norse Pagan groups, who believe they have founded a religion upon the Aryan race; some do include neo-Nazis. Most Norse Pagans consider these people a fringe element not connected to their religion.

North Berwick Witches   An alleged COVEN of WITCHES exposed in 1590–91, providing Scotland with its most celebrated witch trials and executions. King James VI (who became JAMES I of England), a believer in WITCHCRAFT, took part in the proceedings himself. The TORTURE applied to the victims was among the most brutal in Scotland's entire history of witch trials.

The North Berwick witches were accused by a maid named Gillis Duncan, who worked for a man named David Seaton in the town of Tranent. Duncan suddenly began to exhibit strange behavior: a miraculous power to cure virtually any kind of sickness. During the night, she would sneak out of her master's house. Seaton suspected that her nocturnal activities, and her miraculous healing power, were related to the Devil.

Duncan was not able to explain to Seaton's satisfaction how she had obtained her power, so he had her tortured. Duncan's fingers were crushed in a vise called the *pillwinkes,* and her head was "thrawed," which consisted of it being bound with a rope that was twisted and wrenched savagely. Still she would not confess to witchcraft. A diligent search of her body was made, and a DEVIL'S MARK was found on her throat. At this incriminating evidence, Duncan confessed to being in league with the Devil.

Duncan was imprisoned and induced to betray others. She named JOHN FIAN, a Saltpans schoolmaster and alleged leader of the coven; Agnes Sampson, a respected and elderly woman of Haddington; Euphemia Maclean and Barbara Napier, two respected women of Edinburgh; and a host of other men and women. Duncan said Maclean had conspired to kill her own husband, and Napier had bewitched to death her husband, Archibald, the last earl of Angus. The suspects were arrested.

Sampson, who had a reputation as a wise woman, was brought before King James and a council of nobles but refused to confess. Her body was shaved, and a Devil's mark was found on her genitals. Then she was tortured. She was pinned to a wall of her cell by an iron witch's bridle, which had four sharp prongs that were forced into her mouth, against her tongue and cheeks. Her head was thrawed, and she was deprived of sleep. Finally, she broke down and confessed to 53 counts against her, most of which concerned diagnosing and curing diseases by witchcraft.

According to *News from Scotland, Declaring the*

Damnable Life of Dr. Fian, a Notable Sorcerer, a pamphlet published in 1591, Sampson confessed to attending a sabbat (see SABBATS) with 200 witches on All Hallow's Eve, and that "they together went to sea, each one in a riddle, or cive [seive] . . . with flagons of wine, making merrie and drinking." They landed in North Berwick and danced and sang, with Duncan playing the Jew's harp. The Devil appeared and chastised them for tarrying so, and ordered each of them to kiss his buttocks as penance (see KISS OF SHAME). This the witches did, said Sampson, and made their oaths of allegiance. They asked the Devil why he hated King James, and he answered that the king "was the greatest enemie hee hath in the world." Then the witches went home.

James, though he believed in witchcraft, doubted the confessions and accused the witches of being "extreme lyars." To convince him she spoke the truth, Sampson took the king aside and whispered in his ear the words he and his queen exchanged on the first night of their marriage in Norway.

Sampson also confessed to hanging up a black toad by the heels and catching the poison that dripped from its mouth in an oyster shell. She obtained from the king's chamber attendant a piece of soiled clothing worn by the monarch and used it with the toad venom to make a charm (see CHARMS) to bewitch the king into feeling "extraordinary pains as if he had been lying upon sharp thorns and endes of needles."

Finally, Sampson revealed to the king how she and the coven of witches had tried to drown James at sea by raising a storm during his journey to Denmark to fetch his bride-to-be. The Devil told them to catch a cat for the storm-raising charm (see STORM RAISING). When the victim they chose proved to be too fleet-footed for Fian, the Devil raised Fian up in the air and enabled him to catch the cat. The witches christened it and bound to each of its paws the limb of a corpse. Then, sailing through the air in their riddles and cives, they threw the cat in the ocean, crying *Hola!* A terrible storm arose and sank a boat traveling from Brunt Island to Leith, but the king's vessel was unharmed.

Sampson said the same cat was responsible for a foul wind encountered by the king's ship on his way back from Denmark, while the other ships in his company enjoyed a fair wind. The king never would have arrived safely if his faith in God had not prevailed against the witches' charm, she said.

She described another witches' sabbat, which took place at 11 P.M. one night in the North Berwick church and was attended by more than 100 witches, men and women. The witches paid homage to the Devil by curtsying and then turning WIDDERSHINS, the men doing this nine times and the women six.

Fian blew open the church doors with his breath. Surrounded by the light of black candles, the Devil mounted the pulpit and preached a sermon, exhorting them to "not spare to do evil; to eat, drink and be merriye, for he should raise them all up gloriously at the last day." Then the company went out to the cemetery, and Satan showed them which graves to open and which corpses to dismember for body parts for charms.

If Sampson had hoped to save herself by making these confessions, she was sadly mistaken. She was condemned, strangled and burned.

John Fian suffered the most extreme torture. He confessed but then recanted. He was strangled and burned in January 1591.

Euphemia Maclean, the daughter of Lord Cliftonhall and the wife of Patrick Moscrop, a wealthy man, possessed her own considerable estate. She was accused of scheming to kill her husband in order to get another man; of conspiring with the other witches to kill the king by destroying a wax image of him; of conspiring to drown a boat between Leith and Linghorne, in which 60 persons drowned; and "many other monstrous points." She was vigorously defended by half a dozen lawyers, but James insisted on a guilty verdict. Maclean was burnt on July 25, 1591, and her lands were forfeited to the king, who gave them to Sir James Sandilands. Maclean's children were relieved of making further forfeitures by an act of Parliament in 1592.

Barbara Napier, wife of Archibald Douglas, was accused of consulting with Richard Graham, a "notorious necromancer," and of killing her husband with witchcraft in 1588. She also was accused of the aforementioned crimes along with the other witches and was condemned to be burnt. According to some accounts, her execution was stayed because she pleaded pregnancy. Later, she was set free.

The witches accused the Earl of Bothwell of conspiring with them to drown the king at sea. Bothwell, a reputed necromancer, was an enemy of the king. He was charged with high treason and was imprisoned in Edinburgh Castle, but he eventually escaped.

Richard Graham was convicted of witchcraft and SORCERY and was burned in February 1592.

In all, approximately 70 persons were accused of witchcraft or treason in the North Berwick trials. All were probably imprisoned, but the records are unclear as to how many of the rest of them were executed, left in jail or released.

Norton, Rosaleen (1917–1979) New Zealand pantheist and artist of the supernatural, whose eerie works of magical consciousness earned her the title of "the Witch of Kings Cross." Norton's surrealistic

Pagan work was greatly misunderstood by the public during her life and was subject to censorship.

Norton was born in 1917 in Dunedin, New Zealand, to a family with conventional religious beliefs. Her father was a captain in the merchant navy. By age three, Norton exhibited artistic talent and was drawing unusual pictures of animal-headed ghosts. At age five, she experienced an apparition of a shining dragon at her bedside.

Her family moved to Lindfield, Australia. Norton was expelled from secondary school in Sydney for her drawings of vampires, werewolves, ghosts and other supernatural beings; the headmistress stated that she had a "depraved nature."

At age 15, she began selling occult short stories. She worked for a while as a cadet journalist and then an illustrator for *Smith's Weekly* but found the work too limiting and left. She studied with artist Rayna Hoff, then took her works to the streets to sell. She supported herself with various low-level jobs. She pursued a study of MAGIC, occultism, metaphysics and psychology.

Norton received her inspiration from what she said were real encounters with Pagan deities, especially those of ancient Greece and Rome. They would appear to her in trance visions, but only if they so desired. In addition to deities, Norton had encounters with Lucifer, BAPHOMET, DEMONS, astral entities and other beings, some of whom she drew as nude half-animal, half-human beings.

In 1949 Norton exhibited paintings at Melbourne University. They shocked and offended many and were treated as obscenities.

In 1952 publisher Walter Glover of Sydney published *The Art of Rosaleen Norton*, a collection of her works accompanied by poems written by Gavin Greenlees, Norton's lover. The book was attacked by critics as "blatant . . . obscenity," and the Post Master General threatened to prosecute Glover for an indecent publication. A magistrate fined the publisher five pounds plus costs for including in the book two illustrations deemed "offensive to public chastity and human decency." The offending works were blacked out of subsequent copies.

Copies shipped to the United States were confiscated and burned by U.S. Customs. Glover had difficulty advertising the book. Serious financial problems developed, and in 1957, Glover declared bankruptcy.

In 1955 Norton's reputation was further damaged by charges that she was "the black witch of Kings Cross" and had participated in Satanic cult activities. The charges were made by a 19-year-old waitress who had been arrested on vagrancy charges and later admitted her accusations against Norton were based on hearsay. Norton attempted to make a public explanation of how PAN, one of her favored deities, was not Satan, but the episode nevertheless was played up sensationally in the press. A month after the arrest of the waitress, Norton and Greenlees were arrested in their basement tenement flat by the vice squad.

Norton and Greenlees endured nearly two years of protracted court hearings, which received a great deal of media attention. The two had been filmed in ceremonial garb performing a ceremonial ritual to Pan. It was alleged that they had engaged in an "unnatural sex act" and that the film supposedly was evidence of a Kings Cross witch cult. There was testimony about the "lewd" and "lustful" nature of Norton's work. Norton and Greenlees eventually were fined 25 pounds each for assisting in the production of obscene photographs.

After the conclusion of the court hearings, Norton retired from public view. She died in 1979.

In 1981 Glover, back in business, received the copyright to Norton's book from the Official Receiver in Bankruptcy. He reissued it in 1982, to a more sympathetic audience.

Nostradamus (1503–1566) French healer, astrologer and prophet whose fame endures because of his predictions, which reach to the year 3797, when, some interpreters say, the world is supposed to come to an end. He is said to have foreseen such major events as the French Revolution, the rise of the British Empire, the rises and falls of Napoleon and Hitler and the assassinations of the Kennedy brothers.

Nostradamus was born Michel de Nostredame in St. Remy de Provence. He was the oldest of five sons in a Jewish family. His parents converted to Catholicism by the time he was nine, but the KABBALAH remained a major influence on him throughout his life. As a boy, he was quick and bright and was encouraged to study languages, mathematics and science, which at the time included ASTROLOGY. He was particularly interested in astronomy and was outspoken in his agreement with Copernicus that the world was round and revolved around the sun. Because this belief was condemned by the Church, Nostradamus's nervous parents sent him away to Montpellier in 1522 to study medicine.

After he earned his degree and his license to practice, Nostradamus dedicated himself to helping victims of the plague, which was ravaging southern France. He earned an outstanding reputation as a healer, even though he refused to follow customary treatments, such as bleeding patients. He also concocted his own medicines.

Nostradamus spent years wandering about the

Dieu se sert icy de ma bouche
Pour t'anoncer la verité
Si ma prediction te touche
Rends grace à sa Divinité

Nostradamus (eighteenth-century French engraving)

method of DIVINATION was SCRYING. He followed a magical ritual said to have been practiced by the ancient Greek oracles of Branchus. At night he retired alone to his study, where he set up a brass tripod and a bowl of water. Using a wand, he touched the tripod and then annointed his robe with a few drops of water. He gazed into the still water until it became cloudy and he saw visions.

He published his first prophecies in a book, *Les Prophéties de M. Michel Nostradamus*, in 1555. The predictions were rhymed quatrains grouped in hundreds, or "centuries," and were written in a polyglot of languages that included French, Greek, Italian, Provençal and Latin. The "centuries" were not composed in any chronological order. Some of the quatrains contained anagrams.

The book was an immediate hit with the aristocracy. Because of one quatrain that seemed to predict the death of King Henry II of France, Nostradamus was invited to court by the king's consort, Catherine de Medici. At court, he earned money by casting horoscopes and reading moles on the body, another popular form of divination. By the time he returned to Salon, his fame as a prophet was well established. He published a second, larger edition of *Prophéties* in 1558.

In 1559 Henry II died a lingering death from a jousting wound. The circumstances seemed to fit Nostradamus's prediction, which boosted his reputation even more. Henry's successor, Charles IX, appointed Nostradamus to a salaried position as physician-in-ordinary. Catherine, now Queen Regent, continued to consult him, even traveling to Salon to visit him.

Nostradamus intended to write one thousand quatrains, or 10 "centuries." He did compose 10 of them but left the seventh incomplete, for reasons unknown. His records indicate that just before his death, he was contemplating adding eleventh and twelfth "centuries."

In 1566 his health declined. He suffered from arthritis, gout and dropsy. He summoned a priest on July 1 for his last rites. He died afterwards, during the night. He was buried upright in a wall of the Church of the Cordeliers in Salon.

In 1791, during the French Revolution, three superstitious soldiers opened his grave. According to legend, the soldiers were intent on testing a story that whoever drank from the skull of Nostradamus would inherit his prophetic powers. They were unmindful of another story that whoever disturbed the grave would die. When the grave was opened, the soldiers were amazed to see a plaque that read *1791* hung around the neck of the skeleton, as though Nostradamus had predicted the year his grave would

country, until he settled in Agen around 1534 and married a woman whose name is not known. They had two children. A few years later, the plague killed his family. To add to his woes, the Church accused him of heresy and summoned him before inquisitors. Nostradamus fled Agen and the Church and drifted around France and Italy for six years, studying and sometimes treating victims of the plague and other illnesses.

Legend has it that during this period, his prophetic vision developed. He experienced visions and flashes and intensified his study of the occult. One of his chief sources was the book *De Mysteriis Egyptorum*, which he quoted in some of his prophecies.

He settled at last in Salon and married a wealthy widow, Anne Ponsart Gemelle, who bore him six children. After 1550 he wrote an annual almanac and then began to work on his ambitious prophecies. His be violated. One of the men poured wine into the skull and drank from it—and was subsequently shot dead by a stray bullet from nearby fighting. Nostradamus's remains were reburied in the Church of St. Laurent, also in Salon.

Nostradamus's writings, and the interpretations of them, have created controversy through the centuries. The Catholic Church condemned them in 1781. Adolf Hitler seized upon them as evidence of his victorious destiny and littered parts of Europe with air-dropped quatrains. In return, the British mounted a massive antipropaganda campaign, air-dropping selected quatrains that claimed the opposite. In the United States, quatrains were used to generate public support for America's involvement in the war.

Dozens of books and analyses have been written about the prophecies. Interpretations vary widely because of Nostradamus's vague language. For many of the quatrains, history must be searched for the circumstances that fit. Many quatrains remain obscure and are believed to refer to events that have yet to occur. Many scholars say some quatrains predict that World War III will be started by a Middle Eastern despot between 1994 and 1999 and will last for 27 years, after which will come a reign of peace for 1,000 years. In the year 3797 the earth will come to an end, according to interpretations of a letter that Nostradamus wrote to his infant son.

Nostradamus was never persecuted as a witch, though he lived during a time of growing witch-hunts in France. Suspected WITCHES included those who had second sight and a magical gift of HEALING. The cry of WITCHCRAFT often went up if the patient of a healer died. Though some of his plague patients undoubtedly died despite his best ministrations, no one ever accused Nostradamus of witchcraft. It is speculated that he used anagrams and a mixture of languages in his prophecies in order to confuse potential witch-hunters.

numerology   "The world is built upon the power of numbers," said the Greek philosopher Pythagoras, who created the system of MAGIC and DIVINATION now known as numerology. In numerology, all words, names and numbers may be reduced to single digits, which correspond to certain occult characteristics that influence one's life. Numerology is used to analyze a person's character; assess weaknesses, strengths and natural gifts; predict one's future and fate; determine the best places to live; and discover the best times to make decisions and take action. Some people also use it to select their partners in life—business, marital and social.

In the 6th century B.C., Pythagoras discovered that the four musical intervals known then could be ex-

pressed in ratios between the numbers 1 through 4. Furthermore, he realized that the numbers one through four added together total 10, a holy number which represents the material and metaphysical totality of the universe, perfection. If the four notes could be expressed in numbers, he reasoned, then perhaps all of creation could be explained numerically as well. The universe is expressed in the numbers one through four which add up to 10, from which everything else springs.

Pythagoras and the philosophers who embraced his system of thought also believed that numbers possessed individual, sublime qualities. The Greeks recorded numbers in dots, arranging them in geometric shapes. Even numbers could be split in two and therefore had feminine "openings," while odd numbers could not be split and therefore had a masculine "generative part." Even numbers represented wholeness, stability or weakness, while odd numbers represented assertion, power and creativity.

The Kabbalists (see KABBALAH) expanded upon the Pythagorean concepts, using numbers in magical squares for various amuletic and talismanic purposes (see AMULETS; TALISMANS) and to create NAMES OF POWER used in magic rituals (see GEMATRIA). With scientific discoveries concerning light, electricity and magnetism in the 19th century, the ancient occult values ascribed to numbers became ascribed to vibrations of energy as well.

The modern system of numerology uses the nine primary numbers, which are assigned to letters in the alphabet:

1	2	3	4	5	6	7	8	9
A	B	C	D	E	F	G	H	I
J	K	L	M	N	O	P	Q	R
S	T	U	V	W	X	Y	Z	

The numerical value of a name or word is totaled, and the digits are added together to create a single number. "John Smith" totals 44, or $4+4$, which is 8. The number 10 is $1+0$, or 1. The numbers 11, 22 and 33 are not reduced further, for they are "master numbers" of high spirituality.

Here are some of the attributes of the nine primary numbers:

One: Creation, unity, intellect, the leader of all, unique. One is associated with God and the sun.

Two: The most evil of numbers, two is duality and the Devil (as represented by his horns). It is female and links these attributes to women. Two is the number of uncleanness, for the Old Testament relates that God commanded the unclean beasts to go into Noah's ark two by two.

Three: Sexual potency and procreation. Three is a

triangle, or the symbol of male genitals. It represents the Trinity, the ultimate creative force in the universe. It is a holy and complete number, for all things consist of three—a beginning, a middle and an end. Complete numbers are important in magic; many rituals require incantations to be chanted three times. In neo-Pagan WITCHCRAFT, three is significant, representing the Triple Goddess aspects of the MOON.

Four: The foundation and root of all numbers, associated with the earth and its four elements, cardinal points and seasons, all of which are important to neo-Pagan Witchcraft. The MAGIC CIRCLE in the Craft is consecrated to the elements and cardinal points. In terms of personality, four is associated with dullness, plodding, toiling and misery.

Five: A number with both male and female elements, the first number comprised of even and odd. It represents male sexuality and, in general, sensuality, pleasure, adventure and impulsiveness.

Six: A number of wholeness, perfection, tranquility, domesticity and female love. As the sum of three plus three, it also expresses creativity.

Seven: The most mystical and magical of numbers, appearing innumerable times in religion and magic. It is aloof, alone, unique. It is associated with the moon, which at one time was believed to be the seventh planet from the sun. The moon, which has four phases of seven days each, controls the flux of life with its waxing and waning, according to primitive belief. In folklore, the seventh son of a seventh son is reputed to inherit incredible magical power. Seven represents wisdom, knowledge, mysticism, secrets, the mystery of time, the occult and the psychic.

Eight: The Pythagoreans called eight the number of justice and fullness. It has a dual nature—two circles—and may bring failure or success. Lying on its side, it represents infinity and has strong Christian associations.

Nine: Another magical number, the symbol of completeness and the highest attainment of mental and spiritual achievements. It also has Christian associations, for Jesus died in the ninth hour upon the cross. In magic and Witchcraft, nine is the ideal diameter for the magic circle.

These basic characteristics are interpreted and amplified by numerologists, who do not always agree on exactly what a number represents. One's character may be determined by reducing the full name given at birth. By adding that to the birthpath number—the reduction of the birth day, month and year—one's destiny is revealed. Numerologists say it is possible to alter one's character and destiny to more favorable numbers by changing one's name. The complete analysis of a person's numerology is called a *numeroscope.*

O

oak apples Oak apples are galls formed on oak trees by the larva of a type of wasp. In folk MAGIC, they are used as a means of divining whether or not a child has been bewitched or struck by the EVIL EYE. To determine bewitchment, three oak apples are cut from a tree and dropped into a bowl or pail of water that is placed beneath the child's cradle. If they float, the child is safe; if they sink, he or she is bewitched. The procedure requires strict silence or it will not be accurate.

See also DIVINATION.

Obry, Nicole See MIRACLE OF LAON.

obsession Although the terms *obsession* and *possession* were and still are used interchangeably, obsession, from the Latin *obsidere*, technically refers to "besieging" or attacking a person or personality from without. Possession, on the other hand, refers to being completely taken over by the DEVIL, DEMONS or other spirits from within. Medieval theologians distinguished between the two states, although in neither case was the victim responsible.

In general, saints could not be possessed but were obsessed by devils and evil thoughts. Usually such torments afflicted monks and hermits who lived ascetic, celibate lives, often in the desert. The *Life of St. Hilary* tells how the saint's "temptations were numerous; . . . how often when he lay down did naked women appear to him." And when St. Anthony tried to sleep, the Devil assumed the form of a woman and tried to seduce him with feminine gestures. Other holy or Biblical figures, such as Saul, also suffered obsessive spirits, not total possession.

In the 17th century a young Spanish nun, Doña Micaela de Aguirre, was obsessed by the Devil. Irri-

tated by Doña Micaela's perfection, the Devil began tormenting her, appearing one night in the shape of a horse. He stood on Micaela with his full weight, kicking and trampling her and leaving her badly bruised. Sometimes the Devil immersed Doña Micaela in the convent well up to her neck, leaving her there all night. In the end, according to her biographer, Doña Micaela triumphed: "Mocking his cunning she bade him fetch an axe and chop wood. And the enemy could not disobey her [for she was a saint]; he took the axe and chopped the wood up with all haste and departed in confusion, roaring with anger at being defeated by a young nun."

In modern psychiatry, obsession means being totally dominated by a fixed idea that controls or affects all other actions, such as constantly checking to see if a door is locked, or believing that deadly germs

Man obssessed by Devil (Johannes Lichtenberger, *Prognosticatio*, 1500)

are everywhere. Most physicians do not believe that a person can become totally possessed by demons from within.

See also DEMONIC POSSESSION.

Odin (also Wotan, Woden) In Norse and German mythology, the one-eyed patriarch of gods and the god of wisdom. He is usually portrayed as tall and thin with long, tangled hair, and wearing a long, dark cloak. In his thirst for forbidden wisdom, he hanged himself from Yggdrasil, the sacred ash tree of the universe, for nine days in a trance. He sacrificed one eye in the process but was able to create a magical runic alphabet (see RUNES).

Odin had an insatiable thirst for knowledge. He created the arts and was a powerful magician, sorcerer and healer. When Mimir, the ocean god who had the power to see into the past and future, was beheaded, Odin preserved his head with CHARMS and herbs and used it as an ORACLE.

Odin could change his shape at will. He loved adventure and flew through the sky on an eight-legged horse. He frequently traveled among mortals disguised as The Wanderer, with a big slouch hat hiding his ruined eye. Odin was not viewed as a vengeful god, though Christians identified him with the DEVIL. The day of the week Wednesday comes from his Germanic name, *Wotan*.

Odin is revered by some neo-Pagans.

See also NORSE PAGANISM.

oils (also anointing oils) Perfumed and floral oils have played an important role in magical and religious rites throughout history. Their efficacy is based on the belief that odors and scents have the power to affect people and objects. In ancient Egypt, magical SPELLS to assure the well-being of the dead called for the magician to anoint himself with certain oils. The Catholic Church uses sacred oils in baptisms, confirmations and the ordination of priests. In neo-Pagan WITCHCRAFT, scented oils are used to perfume the air prior to rituals, to create a pleasing atmosphere for the gods, and scented and plain oils are used in anointing in INITIATION, self-blessings, WICCANING and magical spells. Oils also are common in folk magic and in the magical spells of VODOUN and SANTERÍA.

The formula for oils depends upon their purpose. The oil itself should be pure and virgin; olive oil is ideal, but other vegetable oils are also used. The oils are mixed with various herbs, flowers, roots and essences. As the Witch works, she chants over them a charm related to the oils. The bottles or vials are left in the dark for several days to increase the potency of the oils (see CHARMS).

Anointing oils are rubbed on various parts of the body, such as the palms, forehead, heart, genitals and chakras; are placed in shoes; and are rubbed onto ritual tools. They also are rubbed onto CANDLES, which are then burned in spells and rites; and onto effigies and poppets.

Oils are made for numerous purposes, such as to attract love, money, protection and luck; to ward off negative influences, the EVIL EYE and illness; to cast or break CURSES; to bless, confuse and influence others; to enhance psychic powers and "dream true"; to gain success and win victory in legal disputes.

Examples of formulas are as follows: to attract health, mix two ounces of virgin oil with a single scent, either rose, gardenia, carnation, grated lemon peel or lemon flowers. A blessing oil for ritual tools and altar consists of two tablespoons of a mixture of two parts frankincense and one part benzoin gum, added to two ounces of oil.

See also OINTMENTS.

oils, anointing See OILS.

ointments (also unguents) Grease-based preparations have been used in magical, healing and oracular rites since ancient times. The ancient Egyptians used magical and sacred ointments for numerous purposes, such as embalming mummies and stimulating prophetic dreams. According to the instructions on a third-century magical papyrus, divining dreams could be induced in an elaborate rite, part of which called for the smearing of a magical ointment on the eyes. The ointment was made from the flowers of "the Greek bean," which could be purchased from a garland seller. The flowers were sealed in a glass container and left for 20 days in a dark and secret place. When the container was opened, it would reveal a phallus and testicles inside. The container was resealed for another 40 days, after which the genitals would become bloody. The ointment made from this was kept on a piece of glass in a pot that was hidden, and was rubbed on the eyes when an answer to a question was desired from one's dreams.

In folklore, WITCHES were reputed to use ointments—also called *sorcerer's grease*—for two chief purposes: to enable them to fly (see FLYING), and to kill others. Some ointments also were said to enable witches to shape-shift into animals and birds (see METAMORPHOSIS). Various recipes for ointments have been handed down through the centuries and have been published in magical GRIMOIRES. Typically, the recipes contain vile ingredients such as baby's fat and bat's BLOOD, or bizarre ingredients such as the filings of BELLS. Many also call for herbs and drugs

Witches concocting flying ointment before the sabbat (Hans Baldung Grien, 1514)

that are toxic and/or hallucinogenic, such as belladonna (the "Devil's weed"), hemlock, hellebore root, *cannabis*, hemp, MANDRAKE, henbane and aconite. Such drugs produce dizziness, confusion, shortness of breath, irregular heartbeat, delirium and hallucinations.

According to lore, witches of old brewed the ointments in their cauldrons (see CAULDRON). For FLYING, they rubbed the ointments on themselves and the BROOMS, pitchforks, chairs, poles or beanstalks that they used to ride through the air. Some accused witches confessed in trials that they were given magic ointments by the DEVIL. Five women brought to trial in Arras, France, in 1460 said they had been given such an ointment by Satan, which they rubbed on small poles and "straightway flew where they wished to be, above good towns and woods and waters, and the Devil guided them to that place where they must hold their assembly."

Legends tell of nonwitches who found pots of ointment, rubbed themselves with it and instantly found themselves transported to the scene of wild witch revelries.

While witches often insisted they had indeed flown through the air with the help of their ointments, most demonologists, as early as the 15th century, believed the effects to be imaginary and not real. In some tests conducted by investigators, a witch rubbed herself down with the ointment and then fell into a deep sleep. Upon awakening, she insisted she had been transported through the air to a sabbat, when in fact she had been observed not moving for hours (see SABBATS). In a tale from 1547, a witch summoned before the Inquisition of Navarre secretly brought along a jar of magic ointment, which she managed to rub on herself. In front of the judges, she turned into a screech owl and flew away (see METAMORPHOSIS).

One recipe published in REGINALD SCOT's *Discoverie of Witchcraft* (1584) calls for sium, *Acarum vulgare* (probably sweet flag), cinquefoil, bat's blood, oil and *Solanum somniferum*, combined with fat or lard, which the witches were supposed to rub vigorously into their skin "till they look red and be verie hot, so as the pores may be opened and their flesh soluble and loose."

Scot also offered another flying recipe, which called for the fat of young children to be boiled in water and combined with "eleoselinum" (probably hemlock), aconite, poplar leaves and soot. Still another recipe called for aconite, poppy juice, foxglove, poplar leaves and cinquefoil, in a base of beeswax, lanoline and almond oil.

Like demonologists of his time, Scot believed that the ointments affected the brain and did not really enable witches to fly.

In modern times, Dr. Erich-Will Peuckert of the University of Göttingen, West Germany, tested a medieval flying-ointment recipe on himself and a colleague. The ingredients included deadly nightshade, thornapple, henbane, wild celery and parsley in a base of hog's lard. The ointment caused the two men to fall into a trancelike sleep for 20 hours, during which each had nearly identical dreams of flying through the air to a mountain top and participating in erotic orgies with monsters and demons. Upon awakening, both men had headaches and felt depressed. Peuckert was impressed with the intense realism of the dreams. In light of his experiment, it is probable that medieval witches who used such ointments believed that they actually had such experiences, which accounts for the similarities in many "confessions."

The following killing ointment was recorded by JOHAN WEYER, 16th-century demonologist and student of CORNELIUS AGRIPPA:

> Hemlock, juice of aconite,
> Poplar leaves and roots bind tight.
> Watercress and add to oil
> Baby's fat and let it boil.
> Bat's blood, belladonna too
> Will kill off those who bother you.

It is possible that some medicinal ointments, concocted by village wise women and wise men for deadening pain and healing, contained an imbalance of toxic ingredients that proved fatal.

Another kind of ointment supposedly made witches invisible. Medieval witches were said to rub themselves down with it before leaving their homes for secret sabbats. The chief ingredient was the herb vervain, associated with invisibility, which was crushed and steeped overnight in olive oil or lard, then squeezed through a cloth to remove the leaves. Sometimes mint was substituted for vervain.

GERALD B. GARDNER, the father of modern WITCHCRAFT, said he knew of no 20th-century Witches who used any kind of ointments. Gardner believed medieval witches did use ointments but said such preparations most likely were applied to help keep naked witches warm in outdoor rites or to make them slippery if they were caught. Some ointments, he said, contained perfumes that were released in dancing as the skin grew hot.

See also OILS.

Old Shuck   See BLACK SHUCK.

omen A sign, preferably found in nature, that foretells either good or bad events. The use of omens as a means of prophecy is not universal, nor is it limited to primitive cultures. Many contemporary superstitious beliefs incorporate omens. For example, popular omens of bad luck include having one's path crossed by a black cat (see CATS), spilling SALT and breaking a mirror (see MIRRORS). Seating 13 at a dinner table, according to one superstition, means one person will die within the year. In an old English superstition, seeing a hare is a portent of WITCHCRAFT, since WITCHES were once commonly believed to assume this animal shape (see HARE).

Ancient cultures relied heavily upon omens in making all sorts of personal, business and legal decisions. Typically, nature, with its dependable rhythms, provided many omens in the forms of disruption of rhythms: storms, eclipses, comets and meteor showers. In England, comets remained bad omens well into the 18th century, despite scientific discoveries that comets made regular appearances according to orbits, which had nothing to do with chance. Nevertheless, preachers insisted that even regular appearances were deliberate signs from God that humanity was in store for periodic trouble.

The ancient Sumerians saw omens in nearly everything: dreams, birth defects, the movements of animals, the shapes of clouds, the positions of stars and planets, the direction of the wind—even the symptoms of various diseases. Priests kept detailed omen records written in cuneiform on clay tablets.

The Romans also were keenly interested in omens and elevated augury, or DIVINATION by omens, to a priestly occupation. Roman augurs often interpreted the flight patterns of birds for answers to questions. Examining the livers of various animals for marks was another common method.

Throughout history, birds and animals have remained powerful sources of omens. Birds are though to communicate with the gods or God and communicate messages to humans. Most bird calls are bad omens, foretelling death, illness and disaster, especially if heard after dark. Screech owls are particularly ominous, as are crows and ravens. These three birds are associated with witches and the DEVIL. Dogs generally are good omens, while black cats—another creature associated with witches—are generally unlucky. However, dogs that howl at the full moon portend evil. The root of this superstition goes back to ancient Greece. HECATE, the dreaded goddess of witchcraft and the night, who was also associated with the moon, would roam about in the dark, visible only to dogs. Her approach would set them howling.

In divination, many omens are sought through created circumstances. Diviners cast grains, read tea leaves, roll dice and bones and throw sticks. Around the world, there are countless folk recipes for reading omens, from plucking the petals off a daisy to determine true love to more elaborate concoctions.

Physical characteristics also provide omens. People whose eyebrows meet in the middle have the EVIL EYE; the eyebrows are the warning omen. Shivering, itching and having a ringing in one's ears means someone is talking about one or walking on one's grave.

Omens also are seen in supernatural phenomena such as visions in the sky and the appearance of apparitions and ghostly lights.

Essayist Joseph Addison commented upon the great store placed in omens in the *Spectator* in 1710–11:

> We suffer as much from trifling accidents as from real evils. . . . A screech-owl at midnight has alarmed a family more than a band of robbers; nay, the voice of a cricket has struck more terror than the roaring of a lion. There is nothing so inconsiderable which may not appear dreadful to an imagination that is filled with omens and prognostics. A rusty nail or a crooked pin shoot up into the prodigies.

oracle In antiquity, a revered and sacred form of prophecy was the consultation of an oracle, usually a priestess who entered a trance and served as a medium for a deity. Oracles were regularly consulted by rulers and leaders concerning matters of state and war. In addition to prophecy, advice was sought. The oracle provided illumination as to the best of several alternative courses of action.

Women served as oracles in ancient Babylonia and Egypt, but the most famous and powerful of them were the sibyls of ancient Greece and Rome. The best-known oracle of this type was seated at Delphi, near the foot of Mt. Parnassus, in a temple built in the sixth century (see ORACLE AT DELPHI).

Consulting the oracle was a privilege determined by lot. The enquirer phrased a question and waited in an outer room of the temple while the Pythia entered a lower, inner chamber and went through the ritual of trance. She sat on a tripod, gazed into a flat dish and held a laurel branch, according to ancient art. Her trance was usually frenzied. The answers were so elliptical that they had to be interpreted by priests, who rephrased them in hexameter verse.

Other sibyls were located at Cumae, Phrygia, Libya, Samos, Erythrae, Cimmeria, Marpessa and Tibur.

In ancient Egypt, deities spoke primarily through oracular dreams but also through prophetesses, who were the women of important families. During the New Kingdom (1570–1342 B.C.), cult statues served as the mouthpieces for deities, primarily Amun, god of fertility, agriculture and "the breath of life." The statues were said to be able to nod and talk but probably were manipulated by priests.

Oracles are still consulted in cultures around the world. In Africa, WITCH DOCTORS of the Zande use a type of oracle that is not a human medium but a poisoned chicken. *Benge*, a strychnine-like substance, is carefully harvested from creepers, according to ritual, and administered to the chicken or other fowl. The effects upon the bird are interpreted to derive answers to questions, which usually concern the identity of witches who have bewitched someone with illness or misfortune. If the bird dies, the *benge* is said to be bad. If the answers are inaccurate, the fault lies with the *benge* or is due to mistakes in the ritual. Among the Cape Ngui of South Africa, oracles are women possessed by ancestral spirits. In Tibet, oracles are predominantly men who manifested psychic gifts at an early age and who become possessed by various deities.

A psychic or witch who uses psychic gifts for DIVINATION and prophecy, sometimes in trance, is a type of oracle.

See also AFRICAN WITCHCRAFT.

Oracle at Delphi

The most famous and powerful ORACLE of ancient Greece, the Oracle of Apollo, was located at Delphi, a shrine about 100 miles from Athens near the foot of Mt. Parnassus. Hundreds of correct Delphic prophecies have survived history.

The temple was built in the 6th century B.C., originally for the worship of the earth goddess, Gaia. The name *Delphi* comes from *Delphyne,* the great snake of the Mother Goddess. Snakes, associated with prophecy and wisdom, were in residence at the shrine, and the sacred snake was a spiraling python. Later, the earth goddess gave way to Apollo, when, according to a myth, he slew the sacred python.

GAIA, followed by Apollo, dispensed prophecy and advice through an entranced priestess, the Pythia or pythoness. Enquirers were chosen by lots and paid fees. While the enquirer remained in an outer chamber, the Pythia entered into an inner sanctuary. Her trance ritual included drinking blood, which was supposed to feed the ghosts of the shrine and induce prophecy. According to some accounts, she may also have inhaled smoke or chewed laurel leaves. Ancient art depicts her as sitting on a tripod, gazing into a flat dish and holding a laurel branch. The Pythia's trance was often accompanied by frenzy and strange moanings and sounds. The sounds and obscure answers that issued forth were interpreted by priests and turned into hexameter verses. Originally, the prophecies were given only on the seventh day in a month in spring, but later they were given once a month, except for three months in the winter.

One of the best-known Delphic prophecies was said to have been given to King Croesus of Lydia. After testing a number of oracles for accuracy, he asked the one at Delphi if he should wage war against the Persians. The answer was that if he attacked the Persians, a great army would be destroyed. He did and it was—his own.

There is no evidence of a cave or subterranean room at Delphi, despite the belief of some scholars that the Pythia did her work underground. By the 4th century A.D., the Greeks and Romans believed the Pythia breathed vapors emitted from the rocks in order to enter a trance. However, geologists have determined that the rocks, which are limestone, could not have produced hallucinatory vapors. No clefts have been discovered that might indicate the escape of gases from the earth's interior. Nevertheless, foliage, branches or other substances could have been burned and inhaled. The Pythia is said to have eaten laurel leaves. (Greek laurel leaves are similar to the bay-rum herb of the West Indies.) Some experts believe the prophecies were merely bits of advice written by the Pythia's assistants.

Order of the Garter

The highest order of knights in Great Britain, founded by King Edward III in 1350, it was linked to the witch cult by British anthropologist MARGARET A. MURRAY. Her evidence is rather dubious, though there are some curious aspects to this chivalric Order.

Edward conceived the Order in 1344 and formally created it on St. George's Day, April 23, 1350, in honor of the Holy Trinity, the Virgin Mary, St. Edward the Confessor and St. George, the patron saint of England. The Order is sometimes called The Order of St. George.

According to legend, the Order resulted from an episode at court. While the king danced with the Countess of Salisbury, her garter fell to the floor. The king swooped it up and placed it on his own leg, saying, *"Honi soit qui mal y pense"* ("Shame on him who thinks evil of it"). The remark became the Order's motto. The official emblem was a dark blue ribbon edged in gold, bearing the motto in gold letters; this ribbon was worn below the left knee.

The Order originally numbered 26: 12 knights led by Edward, plus 12 knights led by the Prince of Wales. Beginning in 1786 the Order was opened to admit others. In modern times, the order has a dean and 12 canons.

In *The Witch-cult in Western Europe* (1921), Murray reads a great deal of significance into the numbers of the Order. The original groups of 13—12 plus a leader—equate with the traditional number in a

Witches' COVEN. THIRTEEN is still represented in the modern structure: a dean plus 12 canons. Murray also points out that Edward's mantle, as Chief of the Order, bore 168 garters. He wore another garter on his leg, and the total of 169 equals 13 times 13.

According to witch lore, GARTERS were worn as a secret means of identification. GERALD B. GARDNER, in *Witchcraft Today* (1954), theorizes that the Countess of Salisbury was a witch (see WITCHES) and that Edward immediately recognized her dropped garter as her secret identification and gallantly saved her from being exposed and brought to trial. Garters, however, were in fashion at the time, and it was not unusual for ladies of the court to be wearing them.

Gardner further speculates that a Black Book, containing the Order's original constitution, was spirited away after Edward's death in 1377.

Most likely, the purpose of the Order of the Garter was nothing more than what Edward publicly intended it to be: purely one of chivalry.

orishas   See SANTERÍA.

Osiris   The Greek name for *Ousir,* the Egyptian god who enjoyed his greatest popularity as god of the dead. Originally, Osiris was a NATURE SPIRIT, embodied in the crops that die in harvest and are reborn again each spring. According to the legend of his transformation into the god of death, Osiris was a handsome king of Egypt who married his sister, ISIS. The symbol of Osiris was the sun, while the symbol of Isis was the MOON. In a treacherous plot, his brother, Set, murdered Osiris and hacked his body to pieces. Using MAGIC, Isis reassembled the body and breathed life back into him. In some versions, Set murdered him again. Osiris preferred to remain in the domain of the dead rather than return to his throne. He served as king and judge of the dead; the *Book of the Dead* had about 100 litanies to him. He was often portrayed with Isis and their posthumous son, Horus, in a trinity.

In the Egyptian mysteries of Osiris, a cult of secret teachings relating to the god, his passion, death and resurrection were re-enacted in a fertility drama. The Romans absorbed Osiris's cult and spread it throughout the Roman Empire.

owls   The owl universally has been associated with death, SORCERY and the dark underside of life. To the ancient Egyptians, the owl represented night, death and cold. The Bible (Leviticus) says the owl is an unclean bird. The ancient Greeks, however, viewed it as the sacred symbol of wisdom, for the owl was the constant companion of Athena, goddess of wisdom.

The ancient Romans considered the bird a bad OMEN, presaging death; Caesar's murder was announced by the screeching of owls. Besides death, the hooting of an owl foretells illness, bad weather and the loss of virginity of a village girl. In European and American folklore, various CHARMS could counteract the owl: throwing SALT in a fire, turning one's pockets inside out or tying KNOTS in a handkerchief.

The Aztecs equated owls with evil spirits, including one regarded as the enemy of the human race, whose name was "Rational Owl." In Africa, owls are feared because they are instruments of sorcerers (see AFRICAN WITCHCRAFT). To North American Indians, the owl is a bird of ill omen, either the harbinger of death or a messenger from the dead. The Sauk believe that if an owl is seen at night, it will cause facial paralysis. Chippewa medicine men stuff the skin of an owl with magic ingredients and direct it to fly to a victim's house and cause starvation. Folk healers in Peru use owls to combat negative sorcery. In Peruvian myth, the "owl woman" is associated with shamanistic rituals and magical curing (see SHAMANISM).

In the Middle Ages, DEMONS in the forms of owls attended WITCHES, accompanying them on their broomstick flights and running errands of evil for them. Magicians and healers used owl feathers as a charm to lull people to sleep.

In some cultures, the owl has long been respected. In India, eating owl eyeballs is said to give a person night vision. The Kiowa Indians of North America believe medicine men turn into owls at death.

P

Pagan Federation   A London-based organization that seeks to provide contact between the Craft of the Wise and "genuine seekers of the Old Ways," and to promote harmony among the various European Pagan religions that began re-emerging in the 1980s (see WITCHCRAFT; NEO-PAGANISM). Originally called the Pagan Front, the Federation was founded in 1971 by members of four branches of the Old Religion of Wisecraft. One of the key founders was JOHN SCORE, also known as M, who served for years as editor of the influential periodical, *The Wiccan*, which became the newsletter of the federation.

The Pagan Federation works with institutions, governmental bodies and the public to present accurate information on Pagan religious views and rights. It seeks to uphold Article 18 of the Universal Declaration of Human Rights, to which Britain is a signatory, which states:

> Everyone has the right to freedom of thought, conscience and religion; this right includes freedom to change his religion or belief, and freedom, either alone or in community with others and in public and private, to manifest his religion or belief in teaching, practice, worship and observance.

Members include WITCHES, Pagans and others who agree with the three principles of Paganism:

> 1. *Love for and kinship with Nature,* participation in the cosmic Dance of Goddess and God, Woman and Man, rather than the more customary attitude of aggression and domination over Nature, or suppression of the female principle.
> 2. *The Pagan Ethic,* "Do what you will, but harm no-one." This is a *positive* morality, not a list of thou-shalt-nots. Each person is responsible for discovering

their true nature and is committed to developing it fully in harmony with the world.
> 3. *Reincarnation* in some form, as taught by many religions throughout all time, including DRUIDS and Witches.

See also PAGAN WAY.

Pagan Way   A neo-Pagan movement that emerged in America in 1970 in response to a rapidly rising interest in European Paganism, WITCHCRAFT and MAGIC (see NEO-PAGANISM). Existing Witchcraft covens, with traditional intensive screening programs and "year-and-a-day" probationary periods, were unable to accommodate the large number of inquiries and applicants (see COVEN). Pagan Way provided an alternative with an open, nature-oriented system that emphasized celebration of nature over magic and that had no formal INITIATION or membership requirements.

One of the central figures in the development of Pagan Way was Joseph B. Wilson, an American Witch who founded a popular journal, *The Waxing Moon,* in 1965. While stationed with the U. S. Air Force in England in 1969, Wilson began and coordinated correspondence among 15 to 20 groups and persons interested in establishing an esoteric form of Paganism. Among other key figures were ED FITCH, an American and high priest in the Gardnerian tradition, at the time stationed with the U. S. Air Force in North Dakota; Fred and Martha Adler, American witches and Amtrad (American tradition) leaders in California; JOHN SCORE (also known as M) of England, who wielded considerable influence on both sides of the Atlantic through his newsletter, *The Wiccan;* the leaders of the Regency and Plant Bran covens in

Britain; Tony Kelly, British poet; and Susan Roberts, journalist and author of *Witches U.S.A.*

After four to five months of round-robin correspondence, the founders decided upon basic principles for the new movement and conceived ideas for rituals. Fitch and Kelly began writing introductory materials. Fitch composed group and solitary rituals based on Celtic and European folk traditions, with some Gardnerian influence. In addition, he composed material for an Outer Court, an introduction to Witchcraft. The material first appeared in *The Waxing Moon*, the publication of which Wilson turned over to Fitch and Thomas Giles, of Philadelphia, in 1969.

Fitch and Giles set up mailing centers in Minot, North Dakota, and Philadelphia. The Pagan material was so enthusiastically received that Fitch and Giles approved the establishment of additional, independent mailing centers.

The rituals, lore and background material were never copyrighted but were placed in the public domain in order to gain the widest possible distribution. Over the years, they have been republished several times by various occult houses as *The Rituals of the Pagan Way*, *A Book of Pagan Rituals* and perhaps under other titles as well.

The movement received a strong boost in America from two of Fitch's colleagues, Donna Cole and Herman Enderle, Gardnerian Witches in Chicago. Cole and Enderle adapted Fitch's material and formed the first formal GROVE in Chicago. The organization called itself by different names, including The Temple of the Pagan Way and the Temple of Uranus, before it eventually became known simply as Pagan Way. In Philadelphia, Penny and Michael Novack took over from Giles and formed other groves, which rapidly expanded and spawned more groves in the eastern United States.

In the 1970s Pagan Way groves spread across the United States, primarily in major cities but also in some small communities. Many followers were SOLITARIES. Pagan Way appealed to two main audiences: those just getting started in Witchcraft, and those interested in attending Pagan ceremonies and structuring social and civic activities around them, much like mainstream churches. According to Fitch, the movement never was intended to address the esoteric audience of mystery seekers. Eventually, adaptations were made for those who wanted more esoteric aspects: initiation rites were added by Cole, Enderle and others, and secret, closed Outer Courts were formed which gave more emphasis to magic.

In 1971 Wilson resumed editorship of *The Waxing Moon*; Fitch and Giles renamed their journal *The Crystal Well* and published separately.

Pagan Way groves thrived during the 1970s. The founders and early organizers let the movement take its own course. No central organization was formed; the groves and mailing centers remained autonomous and loosely affiliated. By 1980 what little there was of the organization had fallen apart, and groves dwindled in size and number. An ever-changing scene of new groups emerged out of Pagan Way. The Pagan Way rituals, however, endured, and continue to be used and adapted by numerous succeeding Pagan groups.

Some covens of Witches run Pagan Way groups as training circles for interested persons and potential initiates. Candidates for initiation spend the traditional year and a day in probation, studying the Craft and undergoing evaluation by coven leaders. Not everyone who joins a Pagan Way training circle is initiated into Witchcraft. Those who aren't may remain in Pagan Way as long as they choose; may work as solitaries; or may form their own Pagan Way groups.

In the United Kingdom, the movement evolved separately from the American movement with the founding in 1971 of the Pagan Front, which later changed its name to the PAGAN FEDERATION. The Regency covens, which were involved in the formation of Pagan Front/Pagan Way, became established in the United States under the name Roebuck.

Pagan/Occult/Witchcraft Special Interest Group of Mensa

Among the more than 200 active special interest groups (SIGs) of Mensa is the Pagan/Occult/Witchcraft SIG, an international network of persons interested in WITCHCRAFT, MAGIC, NEO-PAGANISM, Native American Indian traditions, Druidism (see DRUIDS) and other related topics. The group was formed as early as 1976 and perhaps earlier; no records of the exact date exist. The probable founder is Rhuddlwm Gawr, a Georgia man who served as the first coordinator. In 1978 the coordinatorship was passed to Jean Michele Martin, and in 1980 to Valerie Voigt of San Jose.

The Pagan/Occult/Witchcraft SIG has a membership of about 350 to 400 persons who hail from a wide range of religious disciplines, including Gnostic Christians and Discordians, and numerous professions, arts and occupations. Full members must also be members of Mensa, the qualification for which is scoring at least 98 percent on any standard intelligence test (an IQ of roughly 130). Non-Mensans may be associate members.

Networking information on about 8,000 Pagans around the world—most are in the United States—is maintained. The Pagan/Occult/Witchcraft SIG also publishes a newsletter, *Pagana*, under the editorship of Voigt, which is considered one of the best Pagan journals.

Paganing See WICCANING.

palmistry The art of DIVINATION by the reading of hands is, according to legend, one of the oldest Witch skills. In the legend of ARADIA, the daughter of DIANA and Lucifer who was sent to earth to teach WITCH-CRAFT to mortals, "to know the secrets of the hand" was one of the powers bestowed upon WITCHES. Throughout Western history, palmistry has been the special province of village wise women, GYPSIES and witches, all of whom apply their psychic and intuitive gifts to this skill.

The actual origin of palmistry is not known. It is believed to have begun in China or India as far back as 3000 B.C. and then to have spread west into Greek and Roman cultures. In earlier times, it was known as *cheiromancy* or *chiromancy*.

Palmistry has always been a serious art in the East. In the West, during the Middle Ages, it was considered a scientific discipline, infrequently used and tolerated by the Church. With the arrival of the Gypsies in Europe in the 15th century, palmistry, one of the Gypsies' most common forms of divina-

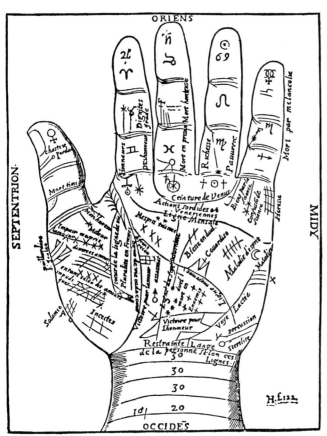

Lines, Zodiac signs in hand (Jean Baptiste Belot, *Oeuvres*, 1640)

tion, grew in popularity. Its widespread use, and the rising deception that accompanied its growth, caused palmistry to be condemned by the Church by the end of the 15th century. By the early 17th century, palmistry had fallen into disrepute as lowly occultism and had been discredited by both the Church and science. It survived as a parlor art; among its adherents was Napoleon Bonaparte, who was mightily impressed by Mlle. M. A. Le Normand, the palm and card reader of his first wife, Josephine.

Le Normand was wildly enthusiastic about the greatness she saw in Napoleon's hand—perhaps she was anxious to secure her position in court—and was also uncannily accurate in describing his character, tastes and his secret intention to divorce Josephine. In a memoir, Le Normand described Napoleon's hand as "brutal and unattractive" at first glance, "but on examining its interior one felt oneself suddenly gripped by keen emotion."

Beginning in the 1960s, palmistry enjoyed a revival of interest in the West, along with other forms of divination. It is practiced by some modern Witches.

What the hand reveals. Palmistry is closely related to ASTROLOGY; the signs and aspects of the heavenly bodies are assigned locations on the hand. A palmist examines the shape and size of the hands and digits, the fleshy mounts and the lines on the palms, wrists and digits. The reading reveals the person's character, life expectancy and destiny. The left hand shows what is intended for a person at birth, and the right hand indicates how that blueprint has been altered by decisions and actions. If the subject is left-handed, the reverse applies.

There are several major lines and innumerable small ones. The major ones include the line of life, the line of the heart (emotions), the line of the head (intellect), the line of Saturn (fate) and the line of health. Among the smaller lines are those of marriage, and the wristlets or bracelets, which denote happiness in life. The mount of Venus, at the base of the thumb, indicates compassion and warmth. The mount of the moon, on the outer palm, reveals psychic ability; a triangular mark here indicates the presence of natural psychic talent. Each digit is associated with a Zodiac sign: thumb = Venus; index finger = Jupiter; middle finger = Saturn; ring finger = Sun; and small finger = Mercury.

Like other forms of fortune-telling, palmistry reveals a portrait and direction at a given time. Choices made through free will may alter these, and palmists say choices will physically change the hands over time, within certain limits.

Pan Greek pastoral deity of flocks and herds, who was half man and half goat, with the legs, horns and beard of a goat. He was the offspring of either HERMES and Penelope, or Hermes and Dryope, daughter of King Dropys, whose flocks he tended. His cult was centered in Arcadia, where he haunted the woodlands, hills and mountains, sleeping at noon and then dancing through the woods as he played the panpipes, which he invented. As a lusty leader of satyrs, he chased the nymphs; he later was incorporated into the retinue of Dionysus. His symbol was the phallus, and he was invoked for the fertility of flocks, or an abundant hunt. Every region in Greece had its own Pan, who was known by various names, and Pan eventually came to symbolize the universal god. He is recognized in NEO-PAGANISM and neo-Pagan WITCHCRAFT and is an aspect of the HORNED GOD.

Paracelsus (1493–1541)

Born Philippus Aureolus Theophrastus Bombast von Hohenheim, Paracelsus was an eminent Swiss alchemist and doctor with a gift for natural HEALING. He believed in natural MAGIC and was far ahead of his time in his conviction that man's body and soul must be treated together in the curing of illness.

Paracelsus was born on or around November 10, 1493, in Einsiedeln, Switzerland, the only son of a poor German doctor and chemist. As a youth, he worked in the mines as an analyst, which laid the foundation for his later work in chemistry and alchemy. He attended the University of Vienna and is said to have earned a bachelor's degree in medicine in 1510, at age 17. He is believed to have earned his doctorate from the University of Ferrara.

Until he graduated from college, Paracelsus went by his given name of Theophrastus. He then created the name *Paracelsus*, which means "above Celsus," a reference to his belief that he was greater than the Roman physician, Celsus.

Though he is often called a magician, Paracelsus was skeptical of "magic" as performed in rituals by magicians and sorcerers. However, he did believe that sorcerers and "wise" women and men often possessed more effective remedies than did the learned physicians of the day (see SORCERY). He believed there existed a natural magic in nature and in all things. This natural magic, he said, is a "power that comes direct from God," and when it is directed to a doctor, it manifests as an ability to heal. Paracelsus gained quite a reputation as a healer, concocting natural remedies using minerals, which worked when conventional treatments did not. He successfully treated syphilis with mercury and cured plague victims by giving them pills that contained minute amounts of their own excrement.

He espoused a revolutionary view toward wounds, asserting that wounds would heal themselves if allowed to drain and prevented from becoming infected. The prevailing wisdom of the day was to pour boiling oil onto wounds to cauterize them, or, if they were on a limb, to allow them to become gangrenous and then amputate the limb.

Paracelsus's natural magic included a belief that the stars and planets influenced life and matter. He had magic TALISMANS which were the signs of planets inscribed upon certain metals; the talismans then became endowed with the astral powers of the planets.

One of his most significant beliefs was that the body and soul were intertwined:

> Man is not body. The heart, the spirit, is man. And this spirit is an entire star, out of which he is built. If therefore a man is perfect in his heart, nothing in the whole light of Nature is hidden from him.

Self-discovery could be achieved, he said, through the power of imagination.

As an alchemist, Paracelsus was the first to describe zinc and the first to introduce chemical compounds into medicine. He was the first to talk about "alkahest," a mysterious burning water that allegedly acted upon the liver and prevented disease from within. He believed in the existence of the *prima materia*, the world soul, or simplicity of heart, which was essential in the creation of gold. Paracelsus said

Paracelsus (Paracelsus, *Astronomica et astrologica opuscula*, 1567)

every person had *prima materia*, though the poor had it more than the rich.

For all of his advanced thinking and his achievements as a healer, Paracelsus was never well liked. He had a short temper, a scorching tongue, no lack of scorn for his contemporaries and a great capacity for bombast. As a result, he was hounded from city to city over a good portion of his adult life. At the University of Basel, where he held the chair of medicine for less than a year, he angered his colleagues by burning the books of such recognized medical authorities as Galen and Avicenna. He was forced out of town after getting into trouble with the law over a physician's fee he sued to collect.

After leaving Basel, he spent about nine years wandering around Europe. During most of this time he was broke. He revised old manuscripts and wrote new ones but had difficulty finding publishers. In 1536 he succeeded in getting *Die grosse Wundartzney* published, a book on his medical theories which enabled him to make a brief comeback in popularity.

In 1541 Paracelsus went to Salzburg at the invitation of the Prince Palatine, the Arch-Bishop Duke Ernsty of Bavaria. In six months, he was dead. The circumstances surrounding his death are mysterious. Legends have it that he was pushed from a cliff or was poisoned at the White Horse Inn.

One of the reasons Paracelsus is often called a magician is because he lived in a time when science and magic were still intertwined, and the pursuit of science meant the study of magic as well. In more modern times, he might have been considered a scientist rather than a magician and alchemist.

Parsons, Hugh (mid-17th century)   One of the few trials in the early American colonies of a man accused of WITCHCRAFT was that of Hugh Parsons, which took place in 1651 in Springfield, Connecticut. A successful sawyer and bricklayer, Parsons enjoyed a reputation as an "honest, sensible laboring" man, according to the records of his trial. He was one of the first settlers in the Springfield area.

Parsons married a young woman, Mary Lewis, on October 27, 1645. Mary had a sharp tongue and did not get along with some of her neighbors. Furthermore, she had swings in mood and temper. At some point in the marriage, Mary accused Goodwife Marshfield of bewitching the children of Mr. Moxon, the settlement's minister. Goody Marshfield sued for libel and won. Parsons made no secret of his opinion that the verdict was due to false testimony, but he paid the fine of 24 bushels of corn plus 20 shillings.

Sometime later, Parsons had another run-in involving Moxon. The dispute concerned an alleged agreement to replace the bricks in Moxon's chimney.

Parsons conceded to Moxon's terms and did the job, muttering that now Parsons "would be even with" Moxon, and "this will be the end of it."

Such incidents stirred up resentment against Parsons and his wife among the townspeople. Furthermore, the area had been plagued since 1641 by bad fortune and mischief attributed to WITCHES. Evidently, the townspeople finally decided to put a stop to their troubles by prosecuting a witch, and Parsons provided them with the ideal victim.

On October 4, 1649, the Parsons had their first child, Samuel, who died a year later. On October 26, 1650, a second son, Joshua, was born. Shortly after the baby's birth, Mary's mental and physical health began to deteriorate. She neglected her baby, which languished and died on March 11, 1651. Mary was declared permanently insane, having been rendered so by witchcraft. Her condition and the deaths of her two infants were taken as legal evidence that both she and Parsons were witches. The records state, "the clamor against the Father increased and he was denounced as a Witch on all Sides."

Parsons was brought to trial in Springfield first. There was no shortage of "evidence" against him, including the testimony of the vengeful Moxon and Goody Marshfield. A jury convicted him of bewitching his second child to death.

Mary was sent to jail in Boston on May 1. She went to trial on May 7 facing two charges: having familiarity with the DEVIL as a witch, and "willfully and most wickedly murdering her owne Child." She was found not guilty on the first charge, due to insufficient evidence. She confessed she was guilty of the second charge and was condemned to death.

On May 27 Mary confessed that she was a witch. The Springfield court reluctantly reversed the verdict against Parsons. He was not, however, a free man. More charges were brought against him of having familiarity with the Devil to hurt "diverse Persons." The jury was convinced that even though Parsons did not bewitch his second child to death, he did practice witchcraft on his neighbors. The incriminating "evidence" was little more than his habits of cutting boiled puddings longitudinally, filing his saws at night and other "amusements." After a long and tedious trial in Springfield, Parsons was sent to jail in Boston. There is no record of his final fate, but he never returned to Springfield.

Passing Rite   SEE RITE OF PASSING.

Pearson, Alison   SEE FAIRIES.

Pendderwen, Gwydion (1946–1982)   Celtic bard whose legacy to the neo-Pagan movement includes a collection of moving writings, rituals, music, songs and poetry; the Faery Tradition, which he cofounded; and two organizations: Nemeton, originally a networking group and Forever Forests, dedicated to reforestation work. Pendderwen devoted much of his life to a spiritual search and artistic expression. He was witty, eloquent and highly respected but also given to outbursts of temper that made some of his personal relationships difficult. He spent some of his later years in a spartan, solitary life in Mendocino County, California, on a homestead called Annwfn, now a Pagan retreat; prior to his death, he was active in the Pagan antinuclear movement (see NEO-PAGAN-ISM).

He was born in Berkeley, California, on May 21, 1946. Pendderwen was 13 when he met Victor Anderson, a Witch, seer and poet with whom he cofounded the Faery Tradition of WITCHCRAFT. He studied with Anderson until he was in his early twenties, learning about the Craft, Celtic folklore and other systems, such as Huna and Haitian and West African VODOUN. He was particularly influenced by Robert Graves's theories of GODDESS as muse and poet as sacred king. Pendderwen and Anderson developed and wrote much of the liturgical material of the Faery Tradition.

Pendderwen's magical practices were based on trance, poetry and communication with NATURE SPIRITS and FAIRIES. He often retired early and spent much of the night in solitude in trance.

He attended California State University at Hayward, where he majored in theater and earned a bachelor of arts degree. He enrolled in the master of fine arts program but apparently did not complete it. He disliked modern theater, preferring *dromenon*, drama in its original form as religious or mystical ritual. He learned Welsh, which led to a long correspondence with a friend in Wales, who interested him in Celtic nationalism. He was active in historically oriented groups, including the Society for Creative Anachronism (SCA), serving as Court Bard for the society's Kingdom of the West.

With Alison Harlow, an initiate of the Faery Tradition and a fellow member of the SCA, Pendderwen founded Nemeton in 1970 in Oakland. Nemeton, which means "sacred grove" in Welsh, originally served as a neo-Pagan networking organization. In 1974 Nemeton published three issues of *Nemeton* magazine, then folded. Regional secretariats of the Nemeton organization spread across the United States, playing a key role in early Wiccan and Pagan networking and growth there. In 1978 Nemeton merged with the CHURCH OF ALL WORLDS and became the Church's publishing arm.

In 1972 Pendderwen's first recording, *Songs of the*

Gwydion Pendderwen (photo by Chas. Clifton; courtesy Church of All Worlds)

Old Religion—songs for each sabbat (see SABBATS), the seasons and love songs to the GODDESS—brought him fame within the Pagan community. He was married briefly, then divorced.

He earned his living working for the Internal Revenue Service and the Department of Health, Education and Welfare but did not enjoy the restrictions of federal bureaucracy. On a vacation to the British Isles, Pendderwen reached a turning point in his life. He met his Welsh correspondent, Deri ap Arthur, and others active in the Wiccan movement, including Alexander Sanders and Stewart Farrar. It is likely that Sanders or other members of the Alexandrian tradition shared an Alexandrian BOOK OF SHADOWS with Pendderwen, for he and Anderson later incorporated Alexandrian material into the Faery Tradition.

At the Eistedffodd in Wales—a regular gathering of bards for artistic competition in Welsh music, poetry and drama—he was profoundly moved by being honored onstage as a foreigner of Welsh descent. In Ireland he experienced a terrifying vision of the MORRIGAN, one of the forms taken by the ancient Irish war goddess, Badb, upon Tara Hill; it made him identify more strongly with the archetypal sacred king.

Pendderwen quit his job upon his return to the United States and began homesteading at Annwfn in Mendocino County. He lived in a cabin with no electricity and only a cat for company. He learned carpentry and gardened, and pursued his artistic work. He began to identify with a new archetype, the GREEN MAN, and started to hold tree plantings every winter on his own and nearby land. The outgrowth was Forever Forests, formed in 1977 to sponsor annual tree plantings and encourage ecological consciousness as a magical process in harmony with Mother Earth.

He emerged from seclusion in 1980 to appear in concert and ritual at the first Pagan Spirit Gathering. He spent the last two years of his life active in public, sponsoring and organizing Pagan gatherings and tree plantings, and participating in antinuclear demonstrations. He was arrested for civil disobedience, along with members of Reclaiming (see STARHAWK), at a demonstration at Lawrence Livermore Laboratory in California in 1982.

Pendderwen tried to establish an extended family on Annwfn, but personal differences with friends and a constant shortage of money impeded him. In the fall of 1982 he was killed in an automobile accident.

Pendderwen's published works, all through Nemeton, include: *Wheel of the Year* (1979), a songbook of music and poems produced with the help of P.E.I. (ISAAC) BONEWITS, Craig Millen and Andraste; *The Rites of Summer* (1980), two musical fantasies performed at the 1979 Summer Solstice gathering at Coeden Brith, a 200-acre piece of wilderness owned by Nemeton and adjacent to Annwfn; and *The Faerie Shaman* (1981), songs of trees, country life, British Isles history and Pendderwen's love for Wales.

Much of his poetry, rituals and liturgical material remains unpublished.

In 1978 Forever Forests merged with the Church of All Worlds (CAW). CAW took over the magical and ritual work in 1987, leaving the activities of Forever Forests limited to tree plantings and environmental and reforestation projects. See also ANODEA JUDITH.

pentacle and pentagram   The pentacle, a five-pointed star with a single point upright, is the most important symbol of WITCHCRAFT. It is both a religious symbol, as the cross is to Christianity and the six-pointed star is to Judaism, and a symbol of the magical craft of Witchcraft. A written or drawn pen-

Pentalpha, sign of recognition used by Pythagoras and disciples (medieval drawing)

tacle is called a pentagram. In Craft rituals and MAGIC, the pentacle is a round disk made of clay, WAX or earthenware (or, in some traditions, copper or silver) which is inscribed with a pentagram and other magical SIGILS and symbols and is used to consecrate the MAGIC CIRCLE, to ground energy and to serve food. In rituals such as DRAWING DOWN THE MOON, the high priestess may assume the pentacle position—standing with arms and legs outstretched—the symbol of birth and rebirth.

Many WITCHES wear a pentacle pendant or ring (see JEWELRY) as a sign of their religion, or as AMULETS or TALISMANS; most are made of SILVER, the metal of the MOON and psychic forces, but some are made of GOLD, the metal of power and energy. Some covens use the pentacle as the sigil of Witches initiated into the second degree (see COVEN).

Pentagrams are drawn in the air with the sword or ATHAME. The methods of drawing a pentagram are precise and vary according to purpose. Pentagrams to invoke are drawn differently than pentagrams to banish. In magic, the pentagram is the Witch's symbol of protection and positive power and is used to control the elemental forces. Pentagrams also are used in Craft meditation exercises, in which each point of the star is associated with a specific quality, attribute, concept, emotion or the name of a Pagan deity.

Magician's pentacle. The magician's pentacle is a round disk or circle inscribed, customarily, with a five-pointed star. It is also called the *Pentacle of Solo-*

mon and is an important and powerful magical symbol of divine power. According to various interpretations, it represents God or man and the four elements of nature; the five senses; the five wounds inflicted on Christ on the cross; and the five points of man in an outstretched position: head, arms and legs. The magician embroiders pentacles on his robes and inscribes them inside and outside the magic circles used in ceremonies and rituals. Pentacles are engraved on rings. As an amulet, the pentacle protects the magician against attack from demons and spirits; as a talisman, it enables him to conjure and command them.

Some pentacles are symbols other than the five-pointed star: circles, semicircles, squares and crosses, inscribed with the names of angels or demons, or the magical names of God (see NAMES OF POWER). These symbols act as talismans to achieve a specific purpose, such as wealth, love or revenge.

Inverted pentacle. The sacred symbol of Witchcraft often is misunderstood because of associations of the inverted pentacle, with single point down and double points up, with the infernal. If an upright five-pointed star represents God or the deity, then the reverse typically represents Satan. In the 19th century, ELIPHAS LEVI erroneously described the inverted pentacle as representing the horns of the goat of the witches' sabbat (see SABBATS). "It is the goat of lust attacking the Heavens with its horns. It is a sign execrated by initiates of a superior rank, even at the Sabbath," Levi said in *Key of the Mysteries.*

The Church of Satan, founded in 1966 in America, adopted as its symbol the BAPHOMET, an encircled inverted pentacle inscribed with a goat's head and Kabbalistic symbols (see KABBALAH) spelling "Leviathan," an infernal serpent associated with the DEVIL (see SATANISM).

In Europe, some Witches have used the inverted pentacle to denote the second-degree rank. This use has declined, because of the association of the symbol with Satanism.

Perkins, William (1555–1602)

Perkins, William (1555–1602) English Puritan and demonologist, a Fellow at Christ's College in Cambridge, whose views on WITCHES and WITCHCRAFT greatly shaped public opinion in the last decade of the 16th century and the beginning of the 17th century.

Perkins's work, *Discourse on the Damned Art of Witchcraft,* was published posthumously in 1608 and surpassed JAMES I's *Daemonologie* as the leading witch-hunter's bible. He accepted completely the witch dogma of other demonologists. He divided witchcraft into two types—"divining" and "working." The sec-

ond type included STORM RAISING, the poisoning of air (which brings pestilence), the BLASTING of corn and crops and the "procuring of strange passions and torments in men's bodies and other creatures, with curing of the same." He said that witches should get a fair trial, but he favored the use of TORTURE.

Of Devil's pacts (see DEVIL'S PACT), Perkins said:

When witches begin to make a league, they are sober and sound in understanding, but after they once be in the league, their reason, and understanding may be depraved, memory weakened, and all the powers of the soul blemished, they are deluded and so intoxicated that they will run into a thousand of fantastical imaginations, holding themselves to be transformed into the shapes of other creatures, to be transported in the air, to do many strange things, which in truth they do not.

Perkins set forth a number of "safe" ways for discovering witches, which COTTON MATHER endorsed and summarized in *On Witchcraft: Being the Wonders of the Invisible World* in 1692. These ways were not sufficient for conviction but raised conjecture that a suspect was a witch:

1. Notorious defamation as a witch, especially by "men of honesty and credit."
2. Testimony by a fellow witch or magician.
3. A cursing, followed by a death.
4. Enmity, quarreling or threats, followed by "mischief."
5. Being the son or daughter, servant, familiar friend, near neighbor or old companion of a known or convicted witch, since witchcraft is an art that can be learned.
6. The presence of a Devil's mark.
7. Unconstant or contrary answers to interrogation.
8. Recovery from scratching [see PRICKING] and SWIMMING.
9. The testimony of a wizard who offers to show the witch's face in a glass.
10. A deathbed oath by a victim that he has been bewitched to death.

The following were deemed sufficient for conviction:

1. A "free and voluntary confession" of the accused.
2. The testimony of two "good and honest" witnesses that the accused has entered into a pact with the Devil or has practiced witchcraft.
3. Other proof of a Devil's pact.
4. Proof that the accused has entertained familiar spirits.
5. Testimony that the accused has done anything to infer entering into a Devil's pact, using enchant-

ments, divining the future, raising tempests or raising the form of a dead man.

philtre Magical potion that causes a person to fall in love with another. Philtres, also called *love potions,* have been common in MAGIC, folk magic and myth since antiquity. They seem to have been important in the Middle Ages, then gradually declined in popularity in the 17th and 18th centuries in favor of SPELLS and CHARMS. Philtres are still brewed in modern times in various folk-magic traditions but not in neo-Pagan WITCHCRAFT.

Traditionally, a philtre consists of wine, tea or water doctored with herbs or drugs. For best results, according to lore, it should be concocted only by a professional witch. When drunk, the philtre supposedly makes the recipient fall in love with the giver, which means great care must be taken that it is administered properly. In the tale of *Tristan and Isolde,* Isolde's mother obtains a philtre that will make her unwilling daughter fall in love with her betrothed, King Mark of Cornwall. Thinking it is poison, Isolde shares it with Tristan, the king's knight who is escorting her to Cornwall. They fall irrevocably in love, which proves fatal to both of them.

There is at least one story of a philtre producing not love but insanity. According to the Roman biographer Suetonius (69–140 A.D.), the Emperor Caligula (12–41 A.D.) went mad after drinking a love philtre administered by his wife, Caesonia.

Throughout history, the most common ingredient in philtres has been the smelly MANDRAKE root, also called "love apples," a poisonous member of the nightshade family. Orange and ambergris added a little flavor and pleasant aroma. Vervain, an herb, was also used a great deal and still is used in the 20th century. Other common ingredients are the hearts and reproductive organs of animals, such as the testicles of kangaroos, used by Australian aborigines, and the testicles of beavers, used by some North American Indians. In India, betel nuts or tobacco are added to philtres. A simple formula from Nova Scotia calls for a woman to steep her hair in water and then give the water to her intended to drink.

Herbs and plants are common additives: briony (similar to mandrake) and fern seed in England, the latter of which must be gathered on the eve of St. John's Day. The Chinese use shang-luh, a plant that resembles ginseng. In Germany, a red gum called dragon blood is used. Some ingredients are ground

Witches brewing magical potions (Hans Weiditz, 1517)

into powders, such as the hummingbird hearts favored by Creoles in the southern United States.

One medieval philtre recipe called for grinding into a powder the heart of a dove, the liver of a sparrow, the womb of a swallow and the kidney of a hare. To that was added an equal part of the person's own blood, also dried and powdered. This was mixed into a liquid and offered as a drink, with "marvellous success" promised.

In the 16th century, Girolamo Folengo offered this formidable recipe in his *Maccaronea*:

> Black dust of tomb, venom of toad, flesh of brigand, lung of ass, blood of blind infant, corpses from graves, bile of ox.

Since philtres depend upon convincing someone to drink a brew that may not taste or smell pleasant, they are no longer as popular as other charms, such as GRIS-GRIS, dolls or poppets and spells. Even in the Middle Ages, the limitations of philtres were recognized. One alternative recipe recommended rubbing the hands with vervain juice and touching "the man or woman you wish to inspire with love."

In neo-Pagan Witchcraft, the concoction of any love charm for the purpose of forcing love or manipulating an unsuspecting person is considered unethical by many Witches. It is acceptable to make love charms to enhance love that already exists between two persons. Love charms also are acceptable if caveats are added, such as "for the good of all," "if they are right for each other" and "if no one is harmed" (see WICCAN REDE).

Pickingill, Old George (1816–1909) A legendary figure in English WITCHCRAFT, Old George Pickingill claimed to be descended from a line of hereditary WITCHES dating back to the 11th century. He was born in 1816, the oldest of nine children, to Charles and Susannah Pickingill, in Hockley, Essex, in East Anglia. Like his father, George was a farm laborer and worked in the Canewdon district. He was viewed by his neighbors as a mysterious, ill-tempered man who practiced magic and employed a fleet of imps (see IMP) to plow his fields for him while he relaxed.

Pickingill claimed his original witch ancestor was a woman named Julia, the "Witch of Brandon," a village north of Thetford in Norfolk. In 1071, according to family legend, Julia was hired to make magical chants to the troops of Hereward the Wake, inspiring them in battle against the enemy Normans. Her chants also were supposed to befuddle the Normans. Nevertheless, the Normans set fire to the village, and Julia was burned to death. Ever since, according to

legend, members of each generation of the Pickingill family served as priests in the Old Religion.

The Pickingill witches worshipped the HORNED GOD. George Pickingill was vehemently anti-Christian and openly advocated the overthrow of the Christian church. To that end, he collaborated with ceremonial magicians, witches, satanists, Rosicrucians and Freemasons, in the hopes of spreading beliefs that would replace the Church. He was influential in the founding of the Rosicrucian Society of England and the HERMETIC ORDER OF THE GOLDEN DAWN, and in the creation of the Golden Dawn rituals.

Over a 60-year period, Pickingill established a group of covens known as the Nine Covens, located in Hertfordshire, Essex, Hampshire, Sussex and Norfolk (see COVEN). He selected leaders who had hereditary connections to the Craft. Initiates included both men and women, but all rituals were performed entirely by women. Pickingill also was said to be the leader who controlled a coven of female witches called the Seven Witches of Canewdon (see CANEWDON WITCHES). He terrorized the local farmers and extorted beer from them by threatening to stop their machinery with magic.

Called a Master of Witches, Pickingill reputedly could make nine secret covens of witches declare themselves simply by whistling. He was known to sit by his hedge and smoke his pipe while his army of imps harvested his fields in half the time it would have taken men. No one went to his house without invitation, and even then they did so in fear. After his death, the imps were seen lurking about his empty bed.

In 1899 or 1900 ALEISTER CROWLEY was said to be initiated into one of the Nine Covens. Crowley's tenure was short-lived, however; reportedly, he did not like being subordinate to women.

Another famous Pickingill pupil was GERALD B. GARDNER, who said he was initiated into one of the Nine Covens in 1939. Gardner, who met Crowley toward the end of Crowley's life, was instrumental in the resurrection of modern Witchcraft.

The descendants of at least some of Pickingill's Nine Covens were claimed to exist as of the 1980s.

pictographs Mysterious drawings of men and animals as well as abstract lines, designs, notations and mazes—some of gigantic proportions—carved into the earth and rock by pagans. Most likely, pictographs were created to portray magical and sacred beliefs and a connection with the power of the earth and heavens; some modern commentators believe they were intended as landing signals to ancient alien astronauts.

Drawings. Most commonly found in England, these

huge depictions of animal and human figures are carved into the chalk earth of hills below earthworks that may have been the site of rites connected with fertility. Hills enabled ancient man to feel closer to his gods and their life-giving forces, to the sun and moon, which he worshipped, and to the stars and planets.

The Uffington White Horse, located outside the town of Swindon, England, is believed to date from 100 B.C., a time when the Celts worshipped Epona, who was personified by a horse. Coins from the Iron Age depict a similar figure, and horses figure in numerous legends and festivities involving horse worship. The figure is 360 feet long and stands between an earthbank enclosure known as Uffington Castle to the right, and a flat-topped mound called Dragon Hill to the left. Until 1857 local inhabitants held a fair and games at the site, at which time they cleared it of grass and weeds.

The drawing is often taken to be a dragon rather than a horse. Legend states that St. George slew a dragon on the top of the mound. Where dragon blood was spilled, no grass would grow; there is a bald spot on the top.

The White Giant of Cerne Abbas is located on Giant Hill near Cerne Abbas, Dorset, England, and is believed to be a fertility symbol. The figure, 180 feet tall, resembles a naked man with an erect phallus and delineated testicles, ribs and nipples. He wields a knobby club 12 feet long. Above the figure is an enclosure where MAYPOLE celebrations were held for centuries. Women hoping to conceive a child would sleep the night lying on its body to draw its power. Some researchers believe that the figure represents Gog in pre-Christian mythology, an ally of the Devil. Numerous legends surround the White Giant, including one that tells of a real giant who terrorized the countryside, killing and eating the locals' sheep, and causing havoc. One day, after devouring some sheep, he lay down on the hill and fell asleep. The locals killed him and carved his outline into the earth.

The Long Man of Wilmington stands on Windover Hill, near Wilmington, Sussex, England. This tall, thin figure with two outstretched arms holding what appears to be a staff in each hand, is 231 feet high and is possibly the largest human-figure pictograph in the world. The figure dates back an estimated 2,000–2,500 years and is associated with sun worship; it may be opening the doors of heaven after subduing the demon of darkness, or holding up sun disks on poles. He also has been identified as a giant, an ancient surveyor, a Roman soldier, Wotan, Thor and St. Paul. The figure was restored in 1874.

A figure similar to the Long Man appears in rock carvings found in Denmark, Sweden and Norway and is believed to represent Wotan and his spear, Gungnir, just as they are described in the Edda, a collection of Norse poems dating from the 13th century.

Designs and notations. These representations are thought to have numerical or astronomical significance. Cup and ring designs are most commonly found in Britain and Scandinavia, but some have been found in North and South America and Asia. Explanations center on their astronomical meanings. The Painted Pebbles of Mas D'Azil, with dots and nature designs, are believed to have been used for calculations. An ancient stone found near Norwalk, Connecticut, appears to have calendric notations.

Mazes. Humankind's fascination with mazes and labyrinths spans an estimated 5,000-year history. Mazes have appeared on coins, pottery and all kinds of implements, and on funerary objects and gravesite markers. They have been carved in the earth and created out of turf and foliage. The maze is symbolic of the archetypal hero's quest and the journey of the soul to the otherworld. It also is linked to fertility rites.

Britain at one time had many turf mazes, often found near earthworks. They may have been used for fertility and rebirth rites during the spring equinox, and Beltane (May 1) festivals. Another theory holds that they were used as astronomical observatories, since some of the patterns suggest stars and planets.

pins Pins are used in some magical SPELLS and in sympathetic MAGIC. Stray pins always should be picked up, according to superstition; otherwise a witch will pick them up and use them in magic. Medieval WITCHES were said to throw crooked pins into their brews to cast evil spells and also to break evil spells. To bless a friend with happiness and prosperity, a witch plucked a lemon at midnight and recited the proper incantation while sticking the fruit full of pins of various colors. To curse an enemy (see CURSES), the witch took the lemon, uttered a different incantation and stuck it with at least several black pins among other colors.

In the WITCHCRAFT trials of earlier centuries, pins were used to prick the bodies of the accused in order to locate spots insensitive to pain. Such spots, called Devil's marks, were considered proof that the accused was a witch (see DEVIL'S MARK).

In English lore, a witch's power could be destroyed by pricking a pigeon with pins or by sticking pins in the heart of a stolen hen.

In cases of DEMONIC POSSESSION, pins are often vomited by the victims, along with other strange objects (see ALLOTRIOPHAGY).

In folk magic, crooked pins are tossed into magic WELLS to help effect both curses and wishes. In VODOUN, SANTERÍA, MACUMBA, folk magic and various tribal and other cultures, pins are stuck into effigies and poppets to cause discomfort, pain and even death. The victim supposedly feels the distress in the part of the body that has been pierced by the pin. Such magic is proscribed by the tenets of neo-Pagan Witchcraft, which hold that magic is not to be used to harm or manipulate others (see WICCAN REDE).

pointing WITCHES and sorcerers (see SORCERY) in various tribal cultures around the world are believed to have a fatal power to kill by pointing. The Malaysian *pawang*, or magician, points his *kris,* a type of dagger with a wavy blade, which begins to drip with BLOOD. Many North American Indian tribes have legends of the killing of animals by pointing. The underlying principle of pointing is the belief that magicians have the power to use their will as a weapon and direct it against others. The deadly, magical energy streams out of their fingers toward the victim. If they send hatred and death, that energy attracts the necessary dark forces to accomplish the goal. If a victim knows he has been pointed at, and believes in the power of the sorcerer, he may bring about his own demise as self-fulfilling prophecy.

See also CURSES.

poisons Dexterity with poisons has been ascribed to WITCHES and sorcerers (see SORCERY) in virtually all cultures since ancient times. The knowledge to kill is the reverse side of the knowledge to heal, and the village sorcerer or wise woman who was skilled with herbs had the power to do both. Sorceresses knowledgeable in herbs and poisons were believed to exist in Cro-Magnon times, according to anthropologists' conclusions based on cave paintings. In classical times, witches were consulted for poisons—the best way to get rid of an enemy—as often as for love potions. In ancient Rome, 170 women were once condemned for poisoning under the pretense of incantation. During the witch-hunts, accused witches were commonly believed to poison humans and animals as part of their ongoing MALEFICIA against Christians. They allegedly poisoned WELLS and barber's flour and smeared lethal OINTMENTS on door handles.

In the modern West, the association of WITCHCRAFT with poisons—the witch stirring up a CAULDRON of deadly brews—causes problems for neo-Pagan Witches. Poisoning, or causing any harm to any living creature, violates the primary law of the Craft (see WICCAN REDE), which holds that Witches must use their skills only for healing and good. Outside of neo-Pagan Witchcraft, in other cultures, particularly tribal ones, illness and death is sometimes blamed on poisoning by witchcraft.

Poisons, used as covert and highly selective weapons, have no peer. They are discreet, hard to trace and can be administered either in deadly doses or in small doses over a period of time, leading to slow illness and death. Some of the most innocuous-looking plants and animals contain fatal poisons, which can be incorporated into OILS, foods or powders. Many poisons have no taste or smell, making them especially insidious.

Plant and animal poisons. Native Africans and Indians of the New World have long been experts in the use of poisons. Curare, the infamous plant poison traditionally used on arrows and darts, acts as a muscle relaxant, causing eventual asphyxiation. Curare's main component, D-tubocurarine, works so well as a muscle relaxant that it now appears in various anaesthetics used in conventional surgery. Strychnine, a poison from the *nux vomica* plant, has the opposite effect, stimulating the nervous system to the point of severe spasms and death. Poisonous mushrooms, containing toxic alkaloids, such as muscarin and phalloidin, also appear in native concoctions.

Plants of the Solanaceous, or nightshade, family—like belladonna, henbane and MANDRAKE—allegedly have been used by witches for centuries, producing hallucinations and death. One particularly effective method for ingesting nightshades is topically, through the moist tissues of the vagina. Other popular witch poisons included hemp and hemlock.

One nightshade, datura, is so highly hallucinogenic and dangerous that even researchers are afraid of it. Also called ''the holy flower of the North Star,'' datura and its derivatives, which produce a very deep sleep, have been the preferred drugs of criminals and black magicians for centuries. The name supposedly originates in ancient India, where bands of thieves called *dhatureas* used the drug to incapacitate their victims. Portuguese explorers to India found that Hindu prostitutes were so adept at using datura that they knew exactly how many seeds were necessary in a dose to keep their clients unconscious for hours. A 17th-century traveler to India reported that Indian women, seething with passion for the light-skinned Europeans but held in check by their husbands, gave the men datura, then made love in front of them while the husbands sat stupefied with their eyes open.

The Yaqui Indians of northern Mexico used to rub a salve containing datura on their genitals, legs and feet and believe they were flying. Wives and slaves of dead kings among the Chibcha Indians of Colombia received doses of datura before being buried alive with their masters. Quechua Indians in Peru called the plant *huaca*, or "grave," because they believe persons intoxicated with the drug can locate the tombs of their ancestors. Togo witch doctors mixed datura with fish poison and administered it to reputed witches to determine guilt. Some West African women still raise beetles, feed the beetles on datura, then mix the beetles' feces in food to eliminate unnecessary husbands or unfaithful lovers.

Animals, too, such as venomous snakes and lizards, provide poisons. Cleopatra died from the bite of a poisonous asp, and as early as Roman times women used poisonous toads to remove unwanted husbands or lovers. [The fungus gets its name because Europeans believed toads ingested their venom by eating poisonous mushrooms, hence *toadstool*.] Medieval soldiers wounded their enemies by discreetly rubbing the secretions of *Bufo vulgaris*, the common toad, into the skin. When boiled in oil, the bufo easily secreted venom which could be skimmed off the top. Sixteenth-century Italians learned how to extract toad poison with salt, which could then be sprinkled on the victim's food. Toad venom was so highly regarded that by the 18th century, weapons makers added it to explosive shells—if the gunpowder and shrapnel didn't kill the enemy, the toad toxin would.

The *Bufo marinus*, or bouga toad, a native of the New World, reached the old one not long after Columbus and was immediately recognized by those familiar with poisons as a handy little beast. The Choco Indians of western Colombia milked poisonous toads by placing them in bamboo tubes suspended over open flames, then collecting the exuded yellow venom into ceramic jars. The main toxic ingredients of the toad's glands are bufogenin and bufotoxin, 50 to 100 times more potent than digitalis and causing death by rapid heart movement leading to heart failure. The *bufo marinus* also contains bufotenine, a hallucinogen.

The Chinese, way ahead of the conquering Europeans in medicine, were most expert with the *bufo marinus*. They collected the venom and condensed it into smooth, dark disks, like pills, called *ch'an su*, dispensing it for the treatment of toothache, canker sores, sinus inflammations and bleeding gums. Taken orally, the pills worked on the common cold. Of course, the toad's toxic properties were not forgotten in labyrinthine Chinese politics.

Other poisonous sea creatures include two varieties of tropical fish, the *fou-fou*, or *Diodon hystrix*, and the sea toad, or *Sphoeroides testudineus*. Both are commonly called blowfish or puffer fish, describing their ability to puff up their spiny bodies to dissuade predators. Such procedures are unnecessary, as the puffer fish contains tetrodotoxin in its skin, liver, ovaries and intestines—a poison 500 times stronger than cyanide, 150,000 times more potent than cocaine. Ancient Egyptians appreciated the puffer fish at least 5,000 years ago, and the presence of deadly puffers in the Red Sea led to the Old Testament injunctions against eating scaleless fish, outlined in the Book of Deuteronomy. The puffer is a modern delicacy in the Orient. Prepared correctly, it is harmless; prepared incorrectly, it is fatal, which turns a puffer fish meal into a sort of Russian roulette.

Poison and justice. Long before the Europeans raided the coasts of Africa looking for slaves, WITCH DOCTORS and certain tribes specialized in the administration of poisons to determine the existence of witches and a suspect's guilt or innocence. The Efik tribespeople along the Niger River became famous for their secret societies, which were responsible for keeping order among their neighbors through various horrible punitive methods. One of the Efik's most powerful weapons was the poison test, in which the accused was forced to drink a potion made from eight seeds of the highly toxic Calabar bean, whose main component is physostigmine. Such a huge dose sedates the spinal cord, causing progressive paralysis from the feet to the waist, and eventually leads to loss of all muscular control and death by asphyxiation.

The victim, after drinking the poison, had to stand before a judicial gathering of the Efik until the poison began to take effect, then walk toward a line drawn ten feet away from the tribunal. If the accused vomited up the poison, he was declared innocent. If he reached the line but had not vomited, he was also innocent and was quickly given an antidote of excrement mixed with water used to wash a female's external genitalia. Most died horribly, however, wracked with convulsions. The guilty did not receive burial, either, but had their eyes gouged out and their bodies cast naked into the forest.

Peoples of nearly all African cultures used poisons to eliminate the guilty. In certain regions chiefs ordered criminals to be executed by pricking their skin with lances or needles dipped in toxic plant juices. In West Africa, the son and heir of a chief had to undergo two poison ordeals to see if he possessed the superhuman qualities necessary to become the new chief; if he failed, the line was broken and another family became royal leader.

To purge communities of witchcraft, WITCH DOCTORS would prepare poisons and force all the citizens to drink them. One witch doctor prepared a concoction containing poisonous bark from the *Leguminosae* tree, along with a powder made from the dried hearts of previous victims, ground glass, lizards, toads, crushed snakes and human remains. This disgusting liquid was left to ferment for a year, at which time the entire village drank a draught during a great festival. Up to 2,000 people died every year. When Africa was carved up into European imperial colonies, such practices were outlawed.

Africans also use poison tests on animals to divine a human's innocence or witch-inspired guilt. The *benge* test involves giving poison to chickens while reading a list of suspects. When a chicken dies at the same instant a name is called, that suspect is found guilty (see AFRICAN WITCHCRAFT).

Witches and poisonous retribution. As Europeans grew more sophisticated with medicines and chemicals, metal-based poisons like lead, arsenic and mercury derivatives became popular. Socially accepted doctors, primarily male, suffered little suspicion about poisoning, but the female midwives, healers and abortionists continually battled indictments as witches. Perhaps the doctors saw such condemnation as a way to eliminate competition.

Nevertheless, the fear of witchcraft was rampant, particularly in the 16th and 17th centuries, when anything unexplainable was attributable to the DEVIL. Midwives were especially vulnerable, since they were blamed for murdering children and for using their bodies to obtain ingredients for poisons. Even high officials were not above suspicion; when the Milanese Commissioner of Health was observed wiping his ink-stained hands on a wall in 1630, he was accused of spreading plague. Intense interrogation and TORTURE gave rise to the Commissioner's full confession and names of accomplices. All involved were torn with hot pincers and burned at the stake.

In the 17th-century French court of Louis XIV, the Chambre Ardente case revealed a ring of poisoners who allegedly supplied witches and abortionists all over France. Poisons and love potions were common at court, used to dispose of unwanted lovers and attract new ones. After an enormous investigation accompanied by torture, evidence surfaced that the poisoners had been the cause of an unknown number of murders, including some 2,500 unwanted babies who were secretly buried in a garden at Villenouve-sur-Gravois. The ringleader, Catherine Deshayes, called La Voisin, and her confederates were accused not only of poisoning but also of Devil-worship and practice of the BLACK MASS. They suffered brutal torture and died at the stake. The entire case would have run on its own hysteria for years if King Louis had not intervened in 1680, outlawing fortune-tellers and mandating legal controls over poisons.

See also FLYING; ALICE KYTELER; ZOMBIE.

popes and sorcery Numerous popes throughout history were associated with SORCERY and were ru-mored to make pacts with DEMONS (see DEVIL'S PACT), and practice black MAGIC and NECROMANCY. The legends undoubtedly arose out of jealousy and political intrigue, as all the "sorcerer popes" were involved in controversies. An accusation of sorcery was not uncommon in fights for control of the papacy. Among the alleged "sorcerer popes and antipopes" were:

Leo I (pope 440–461). Also called St. Leo the Great, he was said to practice sorcery and black magic. He waged a power struggle against his bishops and attacked Manichaeism in Italy.

Leo III (pope 795–816). He was credited with writing a magical GRIMOIRE, the *Enchiridion*, which he sent to Charlemagne, who protected him after Leo III was physically attacked by the family of his predecessor.

Sylvester II (pope 999–1003). A learned man interested in science and the arts, Sylvester II also was a reputed necromancer who won the papacy through SPELLS. He reportedly had a lifelong demon mistress named Meridiana, who satisfied his carnal lust and provided him with material wealth. According to legend, Sylvester II sold his soul to the Devil, who gave him a bronze head that gave oracular responses (see ORACLE). The head predicted that Sylvester would not die, "except at Jerusalem." While giving Mass one day at a church in Rome, the Pope fell ill. Remembering the oracle's prophecy, he asked for the name of the church and was told it was the Holy Cross of Jerusalem. The Pope knew the prophecy had come true, and he died. He was buried in the Lateran, and his tomb reputedly sweats prior to the death of a prominent person. If a pope is going to die, the sweat is so heavy that it turns into a stream and creates a large puddle.

Gregory VII (pope 1081–1084). The Synod of Bressanone pronounced him a sorcerer on June 25, 1080, prior to his becoming Pope. He was an austere reformer, much opposed by cardinals.

Honorius III (pope 1216–1227). Said to have written a new version of a magical grimoire, the *Black Book*.

Boniface VIII (pope 1294–1303). Boniface VIII found his authority seriously challenged by the monarchies of Western Europe. He possessed a keen and superior intellect, which was tarnished by a short temper and an impulsive nature. Philip IV of France, one of his main opponents, whom he intended to excommunicate, used defamation, forgery and intimidation against him, including accusations of sorcery and heresy.

Boniface was charged with making a pact with demons and conjuring them regularly; keeping an IMP in a ring on his finger; infidelity; and, when still a cardinal, sacrificing a cock in a black-magic spell one night in a garden. Furthermore, it was said that when he died, he confessed his demonic pacts on his deathbed, and his moment of death caused, according to one account, "so much thunder and tempest, with dragons flying in the air and vomiting flames, and such lightning and other prodigies, that the people of Rome believed that the whole city was going to be swallowed up in the abyss." Boniface was exonerated of all charges posthumously in 1312.

Benedict XIII (pope 1394–1417). An antipope, Benedict XIII was believed to hold "continuous traffic with spirits . . . [keep] two demons . . . in a little bag . . . and [look] everywhere for books on magic."

John XXIII (pope 1410–1415). An antipope who supposedly enlisted the magical help of ABRAMELIN THE MAGE to save him from the Council of Constance, which deposed him.

Sixtus V (pope 1585–1590). According to legend, Pope Sixtus V sold his soul to the Devil in order to gain the papacy. Born Felice Peretti, he entered the Franciscan order and was sent to Spain in 1565 to investigate the alleged heresy of the Archbishop of Toledo. He stirred up much animosity in Spain, and when he was named pope in 1585, the Spaniards accused him of entering into a pact with Satan. The story goes that the Devil granted Sixtus a six-year reign. After five years, the pope fell gravely ill, and the Devil appeared at his bedside one night to collect his soul. The pope protested that he still had another year remaining in his contract. The Devil said he was reneging on one year, because Sixtus earlier had sentenced to death a young man who was one year too young to be executed, according to law. The pope had no rebuttal, and died.

During his papacy, Sixtus spent huge sums of money on public-works projects, such as the completion of the dome of St. Peter's. He also authorized Philip II of Spain to send his Armada against England. According to legend, the witches of England raised a psychic force to cause storms at sea and help defeat the Armada.

possession, demonic See DEMONIC POSSESSION.

possession, spirit See SPIRIT POSSESSION.

power, cone of See CONE OF POWER.

power doctor In the Ozarks region of the United States, power doctors are backwoods healers who use CHARMS, AMULETS, incantations and MAGIC to cure illness. They are similar to the powwowers of the Pennsylvania Dutch in function, performing services without charging fees but accepting "gifts" and "voluntary offerings" instead (see POWWOWING). Unlike the powwowers, power doctors must learn their craft from a person of the opposite sex who is *not* a blood relative. They believe that they may in turn teach two or three others, but to spread the word to more than that means losing their ability.

Power doctors often are called upon to "charm off" warts, sores and boils and to cure various minor maladies, such as colds, headaches and body aches. Literally hundreds of recipes exist in the lore for charming off warts. One method calls for killing a toad and rubbing its intestines on the offending growth (see TOADS). Another, more exotic, formula requires killing a black cat and taking it to a graveyard at night, where it must be placed on the grave of a person who has been buried the same day (see CATS). If the person led a "wicked life," the wart will disappear that much quicker. Most power-doctor cures prescribe similar measures, all of which must be carried out in secrecy lest the cure will not take effect. Charms must also not be mentioned to others for the same reason.

Each power doctor has his or her own favored charms, methods and incantations. Many incantations come from the Bible or are loosely adapted from it—they are called "old sayin's"—while other incantations are nonsense, such as "bozz bozzer mozz mozzer kozz kozzer." There is no formal handbook as there is in powwowing.

Blood stopping is a service commonly performed by power doctors. Persons who suffer deep cuts and wounds from hunting accidents or from knives and axes used in farm labor are rushed to a power doctor to stop the heavy bleeding.

Rabies may be stopped with madstones, a treatment once common in many parts of the United States. The stones resemble porous volcanic ash, but the hill folk claim they are taken from the entrails of a deer. They are passed down from father to son, never sold, but often lent to someone who is bitten by a rabid animal. The stone is applied to the wound and supposedly draws out the poison. When it falls off, it is immersed in warm milk, which turns green. The stone is applied to the wound repeatedly and immersed in milk until the milk no longer turns green. At that point, the rabies is supposed to be cured.

Some power doctors claim to be able to cure serious disease and illness, such as cancer. In addition to mumbled charms and prescriptions for KNOTS, burned mole feet, pricked beetles and other strange ingredients, the doctors may practice a laying on of hands. Their faith healing is considered different from that of religious faith healers.

powwowing The German settlers who colonized the interior of Pennsylvania in the 1700s and 1800s brought with them their Old World beliefs in WITCH-CRAFT and MAGIC. The Pennsylvania Dutch (*Dutch* is a corruption of the German word for "German," *Deutsch*) clustered in the verdant rural farmland of York, Dauphin, Lancaster, Schuylkill, Carbon and other surrounding counties, which reminded them of their former homeland. They kept to themselves, retained their German language (which became mixed with English over time to form the Pennsylvania Dutch dialect) and remained suspicious of outsiders. The witchcraft practiced became known as *powwow-ing*.

The term was derived from the settlers' observations of Indian powwows, meetings for ceremonial or conference purposes. Much of the Germans' witchcraft centered around cures and HEALING. The settlers enlisted the help of the Indians in finding native roots and herbs that could be used in their medicinal recipes. They discovered that, like themselves, the Indians used CHARMS and incantations. They were intrigued by the powwows conducted to drive out evil spirits. They adopted the term *powwow* to apply to their own magical healing.

Powwowing has survived into the late 20th century. Some of the charms and incantations used date back to the Middle Ages, probably to the time of ALBERTUS MAGNUS, a magician, alchemist and prolific author whose feats were often called witchcraft. Powwowing also includes Kabbalistic and Biblical elements (see KABBALAH).

As is typical in witchcraft around the world, the most skilled practitioners of the craft are born into it and inherit such paranormal abilities as clairvoyance, precognition and the ability to heal by a laying on of hands. The ability may be inherited by either males or females; in fact, some of the most powerful Pennsylvania Dutch witches are men. According to tradition, the SEVENTH SON OF A SEVENTH SON inherits unusually marked witch powers. The offspring of witches are schooled verbally in the lore only by family members of the opposite sex, as is customary in many witchcraft practices around the world. The apprentice witches may "try for" their first cures while still children. Other names for the witches are hex doctor, powwower, *hexenmeister* and *braucher*. Powwowers consider themselves staunch Christians who have been endowed with supernatural powers, both to heal and to harm. "Divine Truth" is considered the active ingredient in all healing.

Powwowing is officially against the law in Pennsylvania, but most powwowers operate quietly, attracting clients by word of mouth. Many run their powwowing as a side business, seeing clients in the evenings and weekends; others work at it full-time. It is considered unethical for powwowers to charge

fees. Instead, they accept "voluntary offerings" and suggest certain amounts for various kinds of services. They will help clients who cannot afford to pay anything, perhaps in the certainty that the grateful clients are bound to return when funds are available.

Most of a powwower's business concerns minor health complaints, such as removing warts, "stopping blood" (stopping bleeding by touch) and relieving a host of infections, aches and pains. Other common complaints include a malady called "the liver grow'd" and opnema, a wasting away usually due to malnutrition. Some powwowers treat cancers and diseases of the organs.

Powwowers also offer charms for protecting the household, livestock and crops from misfortune, witchcraft and evil spirits, and for success in virtually every kind of endeavor, from hunting to games to lawsuits to love.

Another oft-requested activity is the casting and removing of hexes (see HEX) or SPELLS. In superstitious areas such as Pennsylvania's "hex belt" (as the areas heavily populated by Pennsylvania Dutch are called) it is common to blame bad crops, illness, bad luck and other misfortunes on hexes, or CURSES cast by enemies. A person who believes he has been hexed consults a powwower, who must first identify the person responsible for the hex and then offer a charm for breaking the spell. The power of the hex rises and falls in direct proportion to the reputed power of the witch who casts it. A powerful spell can only be broken by a powerful witch. Typically, several visits to a witch are required before a spell can be broken.

Most of the charms used by powwowers come from or are related to two books, the "bibles" of powwowing. The more important book is *Pow-wows, or Long Lost Friend* (1820), a slim volume written by John George Hohman, a powwower who lived near Reading. Hohman and his wife, Catherine, immigrated to Pennsylvania from Germany in 1802. He was a devout Roman Catholic and a great believer in faith healing, but he proved to be mediocre as a practitioner of it. He also failed at farming. He finally achieved modest financial success by collecting various charms and herbal remedies that had existed for centuries in oral tradition and publishing them as a sort of handbook. The *Long Lost Friend*, as it became known in powwowing country, was not a book of hexes, Hohman emphasized. It was for healing, not destroying. While the book did not make him rich, it remains in print to the present day.

The *Long Lost Friend* mixes magic and healing formulas from a variety of sources dating back to antiquity, including Germany, the British Isles and Egypt. It also includes wisdom from the GYPSIES and the

Kabbalah. Hohman includes his own testimonials of successfully cured persons and notes in his introduction:

> There are many in America who believe neither in a hell nor in a heaven; but in Germany there are not so many of these persons found. I, Hohman, ask: Who can immediately banish the wheal, or mortification? I reply, and I, Hohman, say: All this is done by the Lord. Therefore, a hell and a heaven must exist; and I think very little of any one who dares deny it.

Hohman also promises his readers:

> Whoever carries this book with him, is safe from all his enemies, visible or invisible; and whoever has this book with him cannot die without the holy corpse of Jesus Christ, nor drowned [sic] in any water, nor burn up in any fire, nor can any unjust sentence be passed upon him. So help me.

To prevent witches from bewitching cattle, or evil spirits from tormenting people in their sleep at night, Hohman offers the following charm, to be written down and placed either in the stable or on the bedstead:

> Trotter Head, I forbid thee my house and premises; I forbid thee my horse and cow-stable; I forbid thee my bedstead, that thou mayest not breathe upon me; breathe into some other house, until thou hast ascended every hill, until thou hast counted every fence post, and until thou hast crossed every water. And thus dear day may come again into my house, in the name of God the Father, the Son, and the Holy Ghost. Amen.

To stop blood, Hohman recommends consulting the first book of Moses, second chapter, verses 11–13, for the names of the four principal waters of the world which flow out of Paradise—Pison, Gihon, Hedekial and Pheat—and writing them down. "You will find this effective," he states.

The second common "bible" of powwowing is the anonymous *Seventh Book of Moses*, also known as the *Sixth and Seventh Books of Moses*. It is a mishmash of wisdom from the Talmud, Kabbalah and Old Testament. According to this book, one may break a hex by wearing a special amulet that consists of herbs wrapped in specially prepared parchment inscribed with Bible verses or charms (see AMULETS). Another method directs the hexed to avoid direct sunlight, stay indoors when the moon is full, hold the ears at the sound of a bell and absolutely never listen to the crowing of a cock (see BELLS; COCKS).

One does not have to be a powwower to possess or use these two books. They were once a staple in virtually every Pennsylvania Dutch household. But the charms were believed to be most effective when prescribed and recited by a bona fide powwower, followed by the requisite three signs of the cross.

Powwowers use a variety of techniques in their craft. Some clients may require only a laying on of hands, a murmured incantation and the sign of the cross. Others may be given special potions or powders. A well-reputed powwower at the turn of the century, Charles W. Rice, who lived in York, specialized in curing blindness with "sea monster tears," which he dispensed at $2.50 per drop.

One of the most common charms is the *Himmelsbrief ("heaven letter")*, a verse or guarantee or protection which the powwower writes on a piece of parchment or paper, to be hung in the house or barn or carried on the person. *Himmels-briefs* protect homes against fire, lightning and pestilence, and persons against murderers, robbers, mad dogs and all assaults with a deadly weapon, in war or peace. Doubters are told, "Whosoever doubts the truth of this may attach a copy of this letter to the neck of a dog and then fire upon him, and he will be convinced of its truthfulness." *Himmels-briefs* may cost anywhere from $25 to hundreds of dollars, depending on the reputation of the powwower and the purpose of the charm. They were popular with soldiers in World War I, who carried them into battle hoping for protection from injury and death.

Faithful clients swear by the efficacy of powwowing, and undoubtedly some powwowers do possess a true gift for faith healing. The danger lies in clients who prefer to seek powwowers when they are really in need of medical care. Burning an egg tied to a piece of woolen string, a common powwow cure for a cold, is not likely to be effective for pneumonia, for example, which requires antibiotics.

Some powwowers have been known to advocate violence, even murder, as the way to break a hex when charms and doses of dove's blood fail. A number of murders in the history of Pennsylvania have been attributed to witchcraft, even the murders of witches themselves, such as the 1928 case of Nelson Rehmeyer, the "Witch of Rehmeyer's Hollow," and the 1934 case of Susan Mummey, "the Witch of Ringtown Valley."

See also JOHN BLYMIRE; POWER DOCTOR.

prayer As part of its efforts to stamp out rival pagan religious practices in the Middle Ages, the Church Christianized and absorbed many of them. One such practice was the use of magical CHARMS, or little prayers, verses and incantations recited to achieve a goal, cure illness or ward off evil. Charms were associated with MAGIC, and the WIZARDS, sorcerers (see SORCERY), WITCHES, and cunning men and women who practiced magic. The Church inveighed against using magical charms but sanctioned the use of Christian prayer in their place for the same purpose.

It was acceptable and proper to recite Christian prayers—but not pagan or folk-magic charms—while gathering medicinal herbs in order to enhance their effectiveness, and in the application of medicine for illness. The Christian prayer became an all-purpose spiritual shield: for example, a nine-day regimen of holy bread or water accompanied by the recitation of three Paternosters and three Aves in honor of the Trinity and St. Herbert would protect against all disease, WITCHCRAFT, mad dogs and Satan.

Historian Keith Thomas, in *Religion and the Decline of Magic* (1971), suggests that by muddying the distinction between magical charms and Christian prayers, the Church may have made it more difficult to abolish the former. Many magical healers used Christian prayers or debased versions of Christian prayers as their own charms, but the Church claimed that the source—the magician—rendered such charms ineffective. It was not always a successful argument; to be on the safe side, many people relied both on magic and the Church.

During the witch-hunts, Christian prayer was said to be one of the best defenses against the Devil and his demons and witches. Prayers said every morning would protect a person against witchcraft throughout the day. Witches were supposed to be unable to recite certain prayers, especially the LORD'S PRAYER; this was used as a test in many witch trials. Prayers are part of the Catholic Church's ritual of DEMONIC EXORCISM of DEMONIC POSSESSION.

pricking A common method of discovering WITCHES in the 16th and 17th centuries was to prick their skin with needles, pins and bodkins, daggerlike instruments for drawing ribbons through loops or hems, or punching holes in cloth. It was believed that all witches had a WITCH'S MARK, a patch of skin or blemish that was insensitive to pain or that would not bleed when pricked. The discovery of such a spot alone was not sufficient proof to convict a person but was added to the evidence against her. Pricking was done throughout Europe but was most widespread in England and Scotland.

It was not uncommon for professional witch finders, who earned good fees by unmasking witches from town to town, to use fake bodkins in order to falsify evidence. Some of these instruments had hollow wooden handles and retractable points, which gave the appearance of penetrating the accused witch's flesh up to the hilt without pain, mark or blood. Other specially designed needles had one sharp end and one blunt end, which was used by sleight of hand to draw blood in "normal" spots and have no effect on "witch's marks."

MATTHEW HOPKINS, England's notorious witch-hunter of the 17th century, used pricking as one of his methods. In 1650 the officials of Newcastle-on-Tyne offered another witch-hunter 20 shillings for each witch he uncovered. The man, not named in the records, examined and pricked suspects, and succeeded in getting one man and 14 women executed. One woman was saved by Lieutenant-Colonel Hobson of Newscastle, who ordered her repricked.

The pricker had forced the woman to stand in front of a group of witnesses, naked to the waist. Then he ordered her to pull her skirt up over her head while he appeared to ram a pin in her thigh. It drew no blood. Hobson suspected the woman had no reaction to the pin out of fright and shame, and because the blood was rushing to another part of her body. He had her brought to him and the test was done again. This time, the wound bled, and the woman was released.

The pricker collected his fees and left Newscastle but later was discovered to be a fraud. He fled England for Scotland but soon was captured and sentenced to hang. He confessed he had falsely caused the deaths of 220 persons in order to collect fees ranging from 20 shillings to three pounds.

Q

Qabalah   See KABBALAH.

Quimbanda   See SANTERÍA.

quirin (also quirus)   In folklore, a stone said to have the powers of a truth serum and highly valued by WITCHES and magicians. When placed beneath a pillow, the quirin causes a person to talk in his sleep and confess his "rogueries." The stone allegedly is found in the nests of either the lapwing or the hoo- poe, two Old World species of birds often confused in earlier centuries. The lapwing, a species of plover, exists in Europe and Asia, while the hoopoe, related to the kingfisher, lives in Europe, Asia and Africa. Both are crested but they are differently colored: the lapwing is predominantly gray and white, while the hoopoe is orange-gold, black and white.

See also STONES.

quirus   See QUIRIN.

R

Rais, Gilles de (1404–1440)   Gilles de Laval, Baron de Rais, one of the wealthiest noblemen of Europe, whose spectacular military career ended ignominiously in execution for alleged ritual child murder and Devil worship.

As a young man, Gilles distinguished himself in the military. He took up the side of the Dauphin Charles in Charles's dispute with the English over the French throne and was assigned to JOAN OF ARC's guard. He fought several battles with Joan and accompanied her to Reims for the coronation of the victorious dauphin as Charles VII. The king named him marshal of France. After Joan was captured by the British and executed in 1431, Gilles returned to his family lands in Brittany.

He had enormous wealth—besides his inheritance, he had married a wealthy woman in 1420—and began to live in a more lavish style than the king himself. He employed hundreds of servants, hired 200 knights as bodyguards and threw extravagant parties. Gilles spent all his money and went deeply in debt. He began selling off lands to pay his creditors and finance his high-style living. In 1435 Charles officially prohibited him from selling or mortgaging more land.

Desperate, Gilles turned to alchemy and began invoking DEMONS in an attempt to get more riches. Rumors began to circulate that Gilles was involved in far more than alchemy: he was kidnapping children for sexual abuse and ritual torture and murder (see SACRIFICE). It should be noted that the Duke of Brittany and his chancellor were interested in acquiring Gilles's lands. They may have seized upon the rumors as a way to get Gilles convicted as a heretic, which would enable them to confiscate his property. Gilles was arrested in September 1440 and charged with abducting and murdering more than 140 children in BLACK MASS rituals. He was brought to trial in Nantes before both an ecclesiastical and a civil court.

The church inquisitors brought 47 charges against Gilles. Among them were accusations that he sodomized boys and girls; hanged them until they were nearly dead, raped them and then cut their heads off; and burned, tortured and dismembered them. He was alleged to have let many bleed to death slowly, having intercourse with them while they died or after they were dead. He supposedly cut out their eyes and organs with a dagger and offered them to the DEVIL. He was accused of gloating over their pain and suffering.

Gilles refused to plead to the charges, which he said were not true. He was threatened with excommunication and so pleaded not guilty. The ecclesiastical trial lasted 40 days. Gilles was tortured until he confessed not only to the crimes but to enjoying committing them as well. Several of his servants and alleged accomplices also were tortured.

In the civil court, parents of missing children testified that their children had disappeared in the vicinity of Gilles's castle. Gilles's personal attendants testified that they had witnessed Gilles defiling and murdering children and had counted their heads.

Gilles was condemned for heresy, sodomy and sacrilege, and found guilty of murder. The civil court sentenced him to death. On October 26, 1440, Gilles was executed. By some accounts, he was hanged. By other accounts, he was strangled and set to burn, the common punishment for witches and sorcerers (see WITCHCRAFT), and his family was permitted to remove his body and bury it in a Carmelite church.

red   The color of blood, health, vigor, sexual passion and aggression, red has had magical significance since the time of ancient Egypt. Egyptians linked red

278

to death and to an evil dragon, Typhon; they mocked redheaded men in certain religious rites. Red is the color of the Greek and Roman phallic god, Priapus, and the god of war, Mars. The Old Testament links sin to the color scarlet: "Though your sins be scarlet . . ." (Isaiah 1:18). Because it is the color of BLOOD, red is commonly used in the trappings of ritual blood SACRIFICE.

Red is also associated with WITCHES. It is a widespread folk belief that witches have red hair, perhaps because red hair is unusual. In some places, it is unlucky to see people with red hair: fishermen in Scotland and Ireland believe they will catch no fish if they spot a red-haired woman on the way to their boats. In old Irish lore, witches were believed to don red caps before flying through the air to their SABBATS. They could turn pieces of straw into red pigs, which they sold at the market to unsuspecting customers. If the pigs crossed running water as they were driven home, they changed back into straw. According to another folk belief, a witch's soul pops out of her mouth in the form of a red mouse.

Red works in CHARMS against witches. The Pennsylvania Dutch draw red lines around barns to keep witches out (see HEX). In Bohemia, it is believed that a charm tied in a red cloth and hung around the neck will protect one from bewitchment. Other charms to repel witches include red-painted carts and wreaths of rowan tied with red threads. Braided red cords or ropes hung in stables force witches to stop and count each thread before they can harm animals, according to one popular folk belief.

With its Biblical association with sin, red figures prominently in old tales of witches' sabbats and Black Masses (see BLACK MASS). Abigail Williams, one of the accused SALEM WITCHES in 1692, said witches consumed "red drink and red bread" at their sabbats. The priests who officiated at blasphemous Black Masses often wore red garments and slippers and read from red-and-black books. In 1895 Prince Scipio Borghese of Italy was discovered to have a chamber in his palace which was devoted to satanic masses, furnished with crimson-and-gold chairs and scarlet-and-black silk curtains (see SATANISM).

In neo-Pagan WITCHCRAFT, red is associated primarily with health, vigor and passion. In healing it is called "the great energizer" and is said to stimulate the blood. Red CANDLES and cords (see KNOTS) are used in magic SPELLS.

Regardie, Francis Israel (1907–1983)

Occultist and one-time secretary of ALEISTER CROWLEY, whose writings continue to have a wide audience among occultists, neo-Pagans and neo-Pagan WITCHES.

Born in England on November 17, 1907, Francis Israel Regardie (he dropped the use of his first name later on) spent most of his life in the United States, emigrating there at age 13. He became fascinated with occultism and the activities and writings of Crowley, and managed to secure a position as Crowley's secretary in 1928. From that year to 1934, Regardie traveled around Europe with Crowley. It is said that no one person knew "the Beast," as Crowley called himself, better than Regardie. Nevertheless, like many of Crowley's friends and associates, Regardie eventually suffered a falling out with him.

Regardie wrote numerous books on occultism, the first of which were *The Tree of Life* and *The Garden of Pomegranates*, both of which were published in 1932. In 1934, the year of his falling-out with Crowley, he joined the Stella Matutina temple of the HERMETIC ORDER OF THE GOLDEN DAWN. He left after a few years and violated his oath of secrecy by publishing the complete rituals of the Golden Dawn, which appeared in a four-volume encyclopedia, *The Golden Dawn: an Encyclopedia of Practical Occultism*, between 1937 and 1940. The work has been revised and reissued several times, including a single-volume edition in 1986. Regardie broke his oath because he believed the teachings of the Golden Dawn should be revealed to the public. The Stella Matutina, no longer a secret society, began to decline. Golden Dawn material has been incorporated into numerous neo-Pagan WITCHCRAFT rituals.

Regardie became a chiropractor. He served in the U.S. Army during World War II, then settled in southern California, where he worked as a psychotherapist. He authored perhaps the definitive biography of Crowley, *The Eye in the Triangle*, and coauthored, with P. R. Stephensen, another Crowley associate, *The Legend of Aleister Crowley*, both of which appeared in 1970. Regardie always acknowledged Crowley's faults but defended Crowley as "a great mystic, sincere, dedicated and hard working."

Regardie's other books include: *My Rosicrucian Adventure* (1936; 1971); *Middle Pillar* (1945; 1970); *The Romance of Metaphysics* (1946); *The Art of Healing* (1964); *Roll Away the Stone* (1964); *Tree of Life; A Study in Magic* (1969); *What is the Qabalah?* (1970); *To Invoke Your Higher Self* (1973); and *Twelve Steps to Spiritual Enlightenment* (1975).

Rehmeyer, Nelson See JOHN BLYMIRE.

reincarnation

Most neo-Pagans and neo-Pagan Witches believe in reincarnation: that the soul lives a series of lives in the flesh, as part of a process of spiritual development that ends when perfection is achieved and the soul merges with the Divine Consciousness, or advances from human form to god form, or some other plane of existence (see NEO-

PAGANISM; WITCHCRAFT). The concept of reincarnation has existed for thousands of years, flourishing in nearly every part of the world. It is not accepted in most forms of Christianity. Reincarnation has never been proved scientifically, though thousands of cases exist of people possessing unexplainable knowledge connected to other lives in the past.

Reincarnational beliefs have existed in the West since ancient times. The Egyptians originally believed that reincarnation only applied to advanced souls who were destined to be great leaders of humankind. Gradually, this belief changed to apply to all souls. Zoroaster, the Persian prophet who lived around the sixth century B.C., taught reincarnation. Ancient Greek philosophers such as Pythagoras and Plato also believed in reincarnation. Belief in reincarnation was common in Judaism until about the 18th century. Stories of reincarnation appeared in the writings of early Christians but disappeared when the doctrine of pre-existence of the soul was anathematized in 553.

Some modern Witches say their belief in reincarnation comes from the Celts. The Celts, however, believed in rebirth—not the same as reincarnation—in which the soul passed from earthly life into the otherworld and was reborn. According to W. Y. Evans-Wentz, the Celtic esoteric doctrine of rebirth did not conceive of personal immortality, however, but of immortality of an unknown principle that evolved as a whole and was expressed in individual reincarnations. The Celts also believed it was possible for humans to evolve into gods, who then would re-enter the earth as great, divine teachers to help the advancement of the human race. The DRUIDS, the priestly caste of the Celts, appeared to believe in literal personal immortality—again, not the same as reincarnation. The Romans and Greeks, who wrote most of what little is known about the Druids, were particularly struck by this belief. The Greek writer, Diordus Siculus (writing ca. 60–30 B.C.), said that the Druids believed "the souls of men are immortal, and that after a definite number of years they live a second life when the soul passes to another body." The Greek philosopher Strabo (ca. 63 B.C.–21 A.D.), observed that the Druids believed that "men's souls and the universe are indestructible, although at times fire and water may prevail."

Reincarnation as a doctrine of neo-Pagan Witchcraft most likely came from GERALD B. GARDNER, the namesake of the dominant tradition in the Craft, who spent part of his life in the East and was exposed to Eastern religions. Among neo-Pagans and neo-Pagan Witches, beliefs about reincarnation vary. Generally, reincarnation is seen as part of nature's wheel of life, the ongoing cycle of birth-death-rebirth, and is one of the chief means of spiritual learning for all souls. Some lean more toward the Hindu concept of reincarnation, in which the personality remains intact and a soul's spiritual advancement is tempered by karma. According to the doctrine of karma, every act has a consequence, either in the present life or in a future life. Good acts beget good karma and speed the soul's development; bad acts beget bad, or negative, karma and slow the soul's progress. Gardner was a strong believer in karmically controlled reincarnation. Magical techniques exist for controlling the speed of karma.

Few neo-Pagans, however, believe in the Hindu concept that a human can be reborn in an animal body, in a regression caused by bad karma. Most neo-Pagans do believe that animals and other life forms reincarnate in accordance with their own spiritual destinies.

Some Witches believe the Buddhist concept of rebirth, in which the individual personality disintegrates at death, sending off sparks that reignite in new incarnations. The personality does not reincarnate, but its attributes, achievements and flaws pass into a pool from which new personalities are formed.

Odinism, a form of Paganism tied to the Norse pantheon of deities, holds that reincarnation takes place within the boundaries of race, tribe or family, and that characteristics are passed down through generations in this way (see NORSE PAGANISM).

A widespread belief in neo-Paganism is that after death, the soul passes into a state in the astral plane called the Summerland, the first three subdivisions of the astral plane in the etheric world. The Summerland is a restful plane of illusion, a self-created reality that reflects the pleasures of earthly life without its problems. Eventually, the soul withdraws from this state to another, where preparation is made for the next incarnation.

Many neo-Pagans have explored past-life recall, through guided meditation, dreams and, occasionally, hypnotic regression. Many Witches say they recall previous lives as a healer, Witch or priestess/priest, including episodes in which they believe they were persecuted or executed in the Inquisition.

SYBIL LEEK, who spoke and wrote about the validity of reincarnation, believed she was guided by the spirit of Madame Helena P. Blavatsky, cofounder of the Theosophical Society. After moving to the United States in the 1960s, Leek prepared one night to give a talk on psychic phenomena to an audience of the Theosophical Society in St. Louis. As she reached the lectern, she was overcome with a shining light, in which she could see the face of an elderly woman. The light seemed to penetrate into Leek. She began her talk, but it was not her original speech; instead, it was on reincarnation. She said later that she had no awareness of what she was saying.

Afterward, Leek saw a photograph of Blavatsky and recognized her as the woman in her vision. For the rest of her life, Leek said, she felt that Blavatsky had become part of her, using her as an instrument to finish her own work and educate others on reincarnation.

See also THREEFOLD LAW OF RETURN.

Remy, Nicholas (1530–1616) French lawyer, demonologist and determined witch-hunter who claimed to have sent 900 WITCHES to their deaths over a ten-year period in Lorraine. So convinced was Remy of the evil doings of witches that he compiled his "facts" into a book, *Demonolatry*, which became a leading handbook for witch-hunters.

Remy was born in Charmes to a family of distinguished lawyers. He followed the family tradition and studied law at the University of Toulouse. He practiced in Paris from 1563 to 1570, when he was appointed Lieutenant General of Vosges, filling a vacancy created by his retiring uncle. In 1575 he was appointed secretary to Duke Charles III of Lorraine. Besides being a lawyer, Remy also was a historian and poet and wrote several works on history.

As a youth, Remy had witnessed the trials of witches, which may have shaped his later opinions. It was not until 1582 that he took up his own personal crusade against witches. Several days after refusing to give money to a beggar woman, his eldest son died. Remy was convinced the woman was a witch and successfully prosecuted her for bewitching his son to death. Like his contemporary JEAN BODIN, Remy believed in Devil's pacts (see DEVIL'S PACT), wild SABBATS and *MALEFICIA* against men and beasts. He was credulous, believing the most fantastic stories about DEMONS raising mountains in the blink of an eye, making rivers run backwards, putting out the stars and making the sky fall. Like Bodin and other authorities, he also believed that witches should suffer and be burned as punishment.

In 1592, after a decade of prosecuting witches, Remy retired to the countryside to escape the plague. There he compiled *Demonolatry*, which was published in 1595 in Lyons. The book includes notes and details from his many trials and his assertions about witches' black MAGIC and SPELLS, the various ways in which they poisoned people (see POISONS) and their infernal escapades with demons and the DEVIL. He devoted much space to describing satanic pacts and the feasting, dancing and sexual orgies that took place at sabbats. He described how the Devil drew people into his service, first with cajoling and promises of wealth, power, love or comfort, then by threats of

disaster or death. He backed up his statements with "evidence" obtained from confessions, such as the following:

> At Guermingen, 19th Dec., 1589, Antoine Welch no longer dared oppose the Demon in anything after he threatened to twist his neck unless he obeyed his commands, for he seemed on the very point of fulfilling his threat. . . . Certainly there are many examples in pagan histories of houses being cast down, the destruction of the crops, chasms in the earth, fiery blasts and other such disastrous tempests stirred up by Demons for the destruction of men for no other purpose than to bind their minds to the observance of some new cult and to establish their mastery more and more firmly over them.
>
> Therefore we may first conclude that it is no mere fable that witches meet and converse with Demons in very person. Secondly, it is clear that Demons use the two most powerful weapons of persuasion against the feeble wills of mortals, namely, hope and fear, desire and terror; for they well know how to induce and inspire such emotions.

Remy's claim of sending 900 witches to their deaths cannot be corroborated by existing records; he cites only 128 cases himself in his book. Nevertheless, his accumulated "facts" seemed reasoned and beyond refute. *Demonolatry* was an immediate success and was reprinted eight times, including two German translations. It became a leading handbook of witch-hunters, replacing the MALLEUS MALEFICARUM in some parts of Europe.

While he influenced the unhappy fate of countless innocent victims, Remy continued in the comfortable service of the Duke until his death in 1612, secure in the righteousness of his work.

See also WITCHCRAFT.

resquardos See GRIS-GRIS.

rings Rings are AMULETS of power, strength, divinity, sovereignty and protection. In legend, they are also TALISMANS of MAGIC, enabling their wearers to perform supernatural feats or become invisible. The origins of magic rings are not known, but they appear in ancient mythology. Marduk, the champion of the Babylonian gods, holds a ring in his portrayal as a warrior; in Greek myth, Jove released the Titan Prometheus from his chains but required him to wear one link on his finger.

The legendary King Solomon had a magic ring, etched with a hexagram and the real name of God, which enabled him to conjure the DJINN (demons) and force them to work for him. One of Satan's fiercest demons, Asmodeus, craftily convinced Solomon to lend him the magic ring, whereupon Asmodeus threw Solomon out of Jerusalem and set himself up as king. He threw the ring into the sea. Solomon recovered it from a fish's belly and restored himself to his throne. He imprisoned Asmodeus in a jar.

Ancient Egyptians and Hebrews used signet rings, which were inscribed with names or magic words or phrases (see NAMES OF POWER). The signet ring is still a symbol of authority in both church and state. In the Middle Ages, rings inscribed with magic formulas were popular amulets to ward off illness. In England, from the early Middle Ages to the 16th century, "cramp rings" were popular as cures for epilepsy and related disorders. Originally, the rings were fashioned from the coins given by the monarch in Good Friday devotions. Later, rings were simply made and then blessed and rubbed by the monarch. Some cramp rings were exported to Europe. In World War I, German soldiers wore rings inscribed with RUNES as protection against wounds and death.

Rings set with semiprecious and precious STONES, cast in a precious metal, are amulets bearing the particular properties of the stone (see GOLD; SILVER; BRASS). Red jasper, for example, is associated with BLOOD, and soldiers in ancient times wore rings of red jasper to prevent bleeding to death from wounds. AMBER is one of many stones that protect against the EVIL EYE, while cat's eye and ruby protect against WITCHCRAFT. Many stones are medicinal amulets that protect against various diseases and disorders.

Many modern Witches wear silver rings bearing runic inscriptions, the names of deities, a pentacle, a crescent moon, images of the GODDESS or other representations of the Craft.

See also JEWELRY.

Rite of Death   See RITE OF PASSING.

Rite of Passing (also Rite of Death, Passing Rite, Crossing the Bridge)   All traditions of NEO-PAGANISM and neo-Pagan WITCHCRAFT have ceremonies and rituals for observing the death of a Witch or Pagan. The decorations of the MAGIC CIRCLE and altar (see ALTAR), the ritual and music all vary according to individual custom. The rite celebrates death as a rebirth, not only on a spiritual plane but as preparation for return to earth in another life (see REINCARNATION). It is common to say that the deceased has passed into the Summerland, a Spiritualist term to denote heaven, or the afterlife. In neo-Paganism, it denotes an intermediate stage in the astral plane where the soul rests before moving on to prepare for another incarnation.

The rite of passing may include the Spiral Dance, a symbol of death/rebirth and initiation/rebirth, or the Legend of the Descent of the Goddess into the Underworld. The legend was composed by GERALD B. GARDNER, who may have borrowed some of it from other sources, as an epilogue to the second-degree INITIATION ritual; various versions are extant. It resembles the story of ISHTAR, who risked the perils of the underworld to rescue her lover, Tammuz.

According to the legend, the GODDESS meets a challenge to enter the underworld, where Death is overwhelmed by her beauty and requests her to stay. She demurs but submits to a gentle scourging (whipping) by Death, in which she experiences the pangs of love. Death gives her a necklace, the circle of rebirth, and teaches her all his mysteries. The Goddess, in turn, teaches Death her mystery of the sacred cup, the cauldron of rebirth.

The Rite for the Dead, a Pagan Way ritual composed by ED FITCH, calls for a simple altar with four CANDLES set about a central white candle, a picture of the deceased and a bough of evergreen. After a short meditation, the high priest or high priestess light the four candles, and begin the rite.

The rite honors the deceased, offers comfort to loved ones and recognizes that the soul will return again to earth. Toasts of wine are made to the Goddess, God and the deceased. The rite ends with the old tradition of making merry. Ideally, the candles are allowed to burn until they extinguish themselves.

Rite of Release   A neo-Pagan rite, originally from the PAGAN WAY rituals composed by ED FITCH, in which the soul of an animal is helped across the threshold of death. In NEO-PAGANISM, including neo-Pagan WITCHCRAFT, all life is sacred, and all sentient beings are considered to have souls. Fitch was inspired to write the Rite of Release to help animals that had been killed in highway accidents, whose bewildered souls remained by their corpses, visible to clairvoyant persons. The rite also is of benefit to pets, who sometimes feel such a strong attachment to their owners that they may be reluctant to leave the earth plane upon death.

The rite begins by making the sign of the pentagram (see PENTACLE AND PENTAGRAM) with the right hand and the sign of the horns (hand clenched except for index and third fingers raised) with the left. The person visualizes breathing pure white light in and out and says aloud a prayer to help the animal's spirit cross over to the Summerland (see REINCARNATION). The person visualizes a glowing door to the west of the corpse, opening to woodlands or whatever environment most suits the creature. The animal is blessed and bid farewell.

Rituale Romanum, The   The *Rituale Romanum,* or priest's service manual, contains the only formal exorcism rites sanctioned by an established church.

First written in 1614 under Pope Paul V, the ritual remained untouched until 1952, when two small revisions were made in the language.

As early as its publication in the 17th-century, the *Rituale* strongly cautioned priests against exorcism when no true possession existed (see DEMONIC EXORCISM; DEMONIC POSSESSION). And as medical science further defines illnesses previously thought to be the result of demonic interference—hysteria, multiple personality, schizophrenia, paranoia, sexual dysfunction and other neuroses brought on by childhood terrors and obsessions—determining true possession has become increasingly difficult. The 1952 revisions changed the wording that symptoms of possession *"are signs of the presence of a demon"* to *"might be."* States other than possession, originally described as "those who suffer from melancholia or any other illness," became "those who suffer from illness, particularly mental illnesses." Many devout Christians have turned away from the idea of possessing demons at all.

Others continue to believe in demonic possession. If the victim exhibits paranormal capabilities, shows superhuman strength and, most importantly, manifests knowledge of previously unknown languages, then he or she is a possible candidate for demonic exorcism. If such symptoms accompany extreme revulsion for sacred texts and objects, then the church may deem the victim possessed. With permission from a bishop, the exorcist begins the ancient ritual.

Exorcism is not a sacrament but a rite and is not dependent on rigid adherence to a set of actions; exorcism relies on the authorization of the Church and the faith of the exorcist. The exorcist is free to vary the procedure, substituting his own favorite prayers, altering the sequence of events or speaking in his own language (see PRAYER). Most exorcists have found, however, that Latin particularly bothers evil spirits. The *Rituale* provides instructions for exorcism, exorcism of people possessed by the DEVIL and exorcism of places infested with the Devil or other DEMONS.

The *Rituale* exhorts the exorcist to make sure that the victim is possessed and not suffering from mental illness. Even during exorcism, the priest should continue to question the victim about his mental and spiritual state. Under no circumstances should the exorcist offer medicine to the victim, leaving such work to a medical practitioner. If the possessed is a woman, the exorcist should be assisted by a strong woman, preferably from the possessed's family, to avoid the hint of scandal. The possessed should hold a crucifix during the exorcism, and the exorcist is encouraged to use holy water and relics, recite passages from the Bible and liberally make the sign of the cross over the victim. Finally, the exorcist should speak in a commanding voice, only questioning the Devil about his name, the number of demons in possession, where they came from and how they got there. In keeping with its 17th-century origins, the *Rituale* asks the exorcist to find out whether the evil spirits were sent because of a sorcerer's magic spell or other occult documents. Unnecessary questions about future events or the conditions of past loved ones only put the exorcist in the power of the Devil.

Before beginning, the priest should make confession. Then, donning a surplice and a purple stole (required dress for an exorcizing priest), the exorcist stands before the possessed and recites the Litanies of the Saints, the Pater Noster (commonly known as the LORD'S PRAYER) and Psalm 53. He calls upon the spirit to name itself, followed by more scripture readings, then a laying on of hands. The exorcist calls for the demon to leave, then enjoins the spirit to succumb to Jesus Christ and depart.

Each recitation is accompanied by more prayers, including the *Ave Maria* (Hail Mary), the *Gloria Patri* (Glory be to the Father), the *Anima Christi* (Body of Christ) and the *Salve Regina* (Save us, merciful Mary), the sign of the cross and scripture readings. The demon is enjoined a second time; the exorcist repeats each of these acts until the demon leaves for good.

The victim, released from evil, is then encouraged to profess faith in Christ and refrain from evil thoughts and actions so as to provide no haven for devils in the future. More prayers are said, and then finally the exorcist asks the Lord's help in protecting the victim from further harm.

Exorcizing demonic infestation of a place rather than a person follows a shorter ritual. The priest begins by invoking the archangel Michael to intercede with Christ on behalf of the Church and to crush the Serpent. This call is followed by a formal announcement of the exorcism, prayer and then an address to Satan and his legions to leave the place and harm it no longer. The priest offers more prayers, always accompanied by the sign of the cross, and finally blesses the place with holy water.

Because of modern beliefs that scoff at demonic possession, the Catholic church has become less active in exorcisms.

Rollright Stones   In the Cotswolds in England are the Rollright Stones, a group of prehistoric standing stones (see MEGALITHS), probably connected to pagan rituals but associated in popular legend with a witch (see WITCHES). The stones, which are estimated to be older than STONEHENGE, are located between Chipping Norton and Long Compton, on a high, windy ridge overlooking Long Compton. The area has a long history of WITCHCRAFT activities.

According to legend, an unnamed Danish king

and his army once invaded England. At Rollright, they encountered a witch, and the king sought her supernatural knowledge, asking if he would conquer England. She told him to walk seven strides to the top of the ridge. If he could see the village of Long Compton below, then he would become king of England.

The king eagerly followed her instructions. But at the seventh step, he discovered that the view of the village was blocked by a barrow. At that instant, the witch cried,

> Sink down man, and rise up stone!
> King of England thou shalt be none.

The king and all his men were suddenly turned to stone. The king became the solitary King Stone. Nearby, his soldiers formed a cromlech, or circle, called the King's Men. The witch prepared to turn herself into an elder tree, but before she did, she backtracked to four of the king's knights, who had lagged behind, whispering and plotting against the king. She turned them to stone, and today they are called the Whispering Knights.

Originally, the King's Men numbered 11 stones, but some have been broken into pieces. The cromlech measures about 100 feet across. The stones are believed to date to the Bronze Age; the Whispering Knights are most likely part of a burial mound.

Legend has it that at midnight, the stones come alive and turn into men again. They join hands and dance, and anyone unfortunate enough to gaze upon them either goes insane or dies. According to 18th-century lore, village maidens would go to the Whispering Knights one by one on Midsummer's Eve and listen carefully, hoping to hear in the whisperings their future and fate.

Until 1949 the Rollright Stones were regularly used as the site of Witches' meetings and SABBATS. Sometimes local people liked to sneak up and spy on the Witches. One such person was CHARLES WALTON, who was murdered in 1945 in what appeared to be a ritual killing. In 1949 a sabbat was observed by two outsiders, and the resulting press publicity forced the Witches to go elsewhere. In 1964 a London COVEN held a special gathering at the Rollright Stones for a magazine article. The stones have been vandalized by teenagers, and access to them is now restricted to daylight hours.

root doctors   See WITCH DOCTORS.

Rosemary's Baby   Ira Levin's 1967 novel about Devil-worshipping WITCHES perpetuates numerous stereotypes about WITCHCRAFT, but ironically, it interested many people in the Craft. It was published during a time of high interest in the occult and during the initial expansion of neo-Pagan Witchcraft. These stereotypes have left witches with the ongoing task of educating others on the distinctions between neo-Pagan witchcraft and SATANISM.

The novel was made into a popular film in 1968, starring Mia Farrow as the victim, John Cassavetes as her opportunistic husband and Ruth Gordon and Stanley Blackmer as the old Witches. Ralph Bellamy starred as a doctor and member of the COVEN. Much of the shooting was done at the Dakota, New York's brooding, Gothic dwelling at 72nd Street and Central Park West (and the site where, in 1980, John Lennon was fatally shot).

Levin's plot deals with Devil-worshipping satanists who call themselves Witches. They follow the DEVIL's instructions to arrange for him to rape the woman the Devil has chosen to conceive and deliver the Antichrist.

The story takes place in New York City in 1966. Rosemary and Guy Woodhouse are young newlyweds in search of a new apartment. Guy is a mediocre actor struggling to succeed but barely making it in bit parts and commercials. At the sinister-looking Branford building, Rosemary falls in love with an apartment and persuades Guy to rent it. The apartment belonged to a mysterious old woman who grew herbs and died in a coma. After taking the apartment, the Woodhouses learn from a writer friend, Edward Hutchins ("Hutch") that the Branford has a long and dark history of crime and strange happenings, including cannibal sisters and a dead baby found in the basement. It was home to the notorious Adrian Marcato, a self-proclaimed Witch who, in the 1890s, claimed to be able to conjure up the Devil. The Woodhouses laugh these stories off.

The couple meet their odd neighbors, Minnie and Roman Castevet, following the suicide of a young girl who was living with the Castevets. Unbeknownst to Rosemary, the Castevets seduce Guy with promises of professional success in exchange for a satanic rape of Rosemary. Rosemary is drugged by a chocolate mousse dessert made by Minnie but remains conscious enough during her hideous ordeal to know that it is not a dream. The naked witches stand around her chanting while an inhuman monster with animal eyes, leathery skin and a huge penis rapes her. The following morning, she decides it was a dream, after all. Guy tells her he made love to her while she was asleep.

Rosemary becomes pregnant, and the Castevets convince her to see a Dr. Abraham Saperstein. Saperstein prescribes a daily "vitamin" drink made by Minnie, supposedly containing fresh herbs but which in fact contains a mysterious and vile-smelling "tanis root.'' This root, which is more like a fungus, also is contained in a silver amulet necklace the Castevets give Rosemary to wear—the same necklace worn by the girl who committed suicide.

The pregnancy does not go well. Rosemary loses weight and suffers constant pain, which Saperstein tells her is not unusual. When Hutch visits and hears of the tanis root, he becomes alarmed and does some research. He attempts to tell Rosemary of his findings but is felled by a coma and dies before he is able to do so—the handiwork of the Witches. At his funeral, a woman gives Rosemary a book that Hutch had wanted her to have, along with the message that ''the name is an anagram.''

The book, *All of Them Witches,* tells of a fungus known as ''Devil's pepper,'' used in rituals, and profiles various infamous witches, among them Adrian Marcato. Rosemary gets out her Scrabble set to try to decipher the anagram in the book's title, but nothing makes sense. Then she notices that the name of Marcato's son, Steven, is underlined in the book. ''Steven Marcato'' rearranges to ''Roman Castevet.'' Rosemary buys books on Witchcraft, which tell her that witches cast malevolent spells upon people to maim and kill them, and use blood in their rituals—particularly baby's blood—as well as human flesh. She surmises that the Witches want her baby to use in their rituals.

From that point, the dark forces close in on Rosemary, despite her attempts to save herself. She appeals to Guy, then discovers he's part of the conspiracy. The same thing happens with Saperstein. She attempts to escape, but the Witches trap her in her apartment, and she is delivered of the baby. She is told the baby was stillborn, but she discovers the witches are keeping it in the Castevets' apartment.

The coven convenes to hail the birth of the Antichrist, who has been named Adrian Steven. Rosemary, armed with a knife, appears. She is told how the Devil chose her for her role. When she first sees the infant, swaddled in black in a black bassinet, she is horrified and can hardly bear to look upon the golden-yellow animal eyes, the orange-red hair, the tail and the budding horns. His little hands, which have ''tiny, pearly'' claws, are encased in black mittens so that he doesn't scratch himself. Rosemary decides she will kill the creature and commit suicide but then becomes fascinated with it; it is, after all, hers. With the Witches' encouragement, she begins to mother it, holding on to a naive hope that she will be able to exert a good influence over it.

runes A magical alphabet of symbols used for HEALING, DIVINATION and in a variety of CHARMS and invocations (see EVOCATIONS AND INVOCATIONS). The runes were spread through Britain, Europe and Russia by the Saxons, Norse, Danes and Vikings and were at their height of usage during the Middle Ages (ca. 400–1400 A.D.).

According to myth, the runes were created by the Norse god ODIN (also Woden or Wotan), the one-eyed chief of gods and god of wisdom and war. Odin gained the forbidden, mystical knowledge of the runes by impaling himself with his own spear to Yggdrasil, the World Tree, for nine days and nights. Runic symbols have been discovered in rock carvings and dating back to the prehistoric Neolithic and Bronze Ages. The early DRUIDS may also have been familiar with runes.

In Western Europe during the Dark Ages, the runes were believed to possess potent magical power. They were the tools of magicians, who passed on their knowledge to initiates by word of mouth. Runic symbols were inscribed—never in the light of day—on wands made of HAZEL, ash or yew, swords, chalices and stone tablets to accomplish whatever the magician desired: victory in battle, HEALING, safe journeys, protection from the EVIL EYE, the opening of psychic power, cursing, love, fertility or blessings for SACRIFICE. They were used in legal contracts and pacts. As TALISMANS, runes were inscribed on swords to ensure more pain and death to the enemy. As AMULETS, they were inscribed on personal JEWELRY

The Kensington Runestone (U.S. Library of Congress)

or on objects displayed in one's home. Runes could ward off grave robbers; however, they could not be inscribed upon IRON for this purpose, for iron was believed to scare away spirits. Runes also symbolized the forces of nature, the sun and moon and the names of the gods and goddesses.

One important use of runes was for divination. In that respect, the runes were associated with the Norns, the Norse Three Fates of past, present and future. Runic rods or stones were cast by tossing, in the fashion of the I CHING, and their patterns were interpreted by the adept.

During the slow conversion of Europe to Christianity, the use of runes coexisted with the new religion for centuries. CROSSES, coffins, swords and other objects show runic inscriptions with Christian elements. But when the Inquisition began in earnest in the 14th century, runes, along with other pagan practices, were nearly snuffed out of existence.

Interest in runes was revived in the late 19th and early 20th centuries by German occultists who associated runes with racial supremacy. When the Nazis came to power, they adopted two runes that became the most feared and hated symbols on earth: the SWASTIKA, the rune of the Earth Mother and the hammer of Thor, Norse god of thunder; and the sig or S rune, which was the trademark of Heinrich Himmler's *Schutzstaffel*, or SS.

In the 1980s rune stones became popularized as a means of divination, to be cast like the *I Ching* or laid out in crosses or wheels like TAROT cards.

Some modern WITCHES use runes to inscribe their names or magical SIGILS on ritual tools (see WITCHES' TOOLS), wedding bands and other RINGS and personal objects, which imbues the objects with the Witch's magical power. Norse neo-Pagans have attempted to reclaim the swastika, with little success.

See also NORSE PAGANISM.

S

sabbats The belief that WITCHES convened in sabbats, assemblies characterized by obscene behavior, is a product of the Christian witch-hunts. It appears to have emerged in Europe during the 14th and 15th centuries. The origins of the sabbat seem to be a blend of seasonal pagan rites still in existence—most notably the great Druidic festivals of Beltane (observed April 30) and Samhain (observed October 31)—and the well-established idea that heretics held obscene rites. The sabbat also may be related to the Bacchanalian and Saturnalian rites of the ancient Greeks and Romans. The term *sabbat* is Old French and is derived in part from the Hebrew *Shabbath*, "to rest," pertaining to the seventh day of the week designated by the Ten Commandments as the day of rest and worship.

Some historians theorize that *sabbat* as it was applied to heretics and witches was anti-Semitic, for Jews were among the heretics. Similarly, heretics, and sometimes witches, were said to meet in *synagogues*, a term that also was used synonymously with *sabbats*. The sabbat became much more prominent in continental Europe during the witch-hunts than it did in England, where there is no record of a witch sabbat prior to 1620, except for an innocuous feast that was termed a *sabbat* in the Lancaster witch trials of 1612 (see LANCASTER WITCHES).

The assemblies of heretics were described as including sexual orgies, gluttonous feasting, worship of the DEVIL, blasphemous and diabolical rites and copulation with DEMONS. As WITCHCRAFT became heresy, these activities were attributed to witches.

The first mention of a sabbat in a trial of the Inquisition occurred in Toulouse in 1335. The term *sabbat* (also *sabbath*) for these meetings was not applied regularly until about the mid-15th century. Once

the sabbat appeared in trials, however, it quickly assumed a regular form. Sabbats invariably took place at night in remote locations, such as mountains, caves and deep forest areas. The best-known gathering place for sabbats was the Brocken in the Harz Mountains of Germany, where the greatest activity took place on WALPURGISNACHT (Beltane), April 30. To get to a sabbat, witches flew through the air, sometimes on the backs of demons that had metamorphosed into animals, or astride broomsticks or poles (see FLYING). The witches themselves sometimes changed into animals (see METAMORPHOSIS) and were accompanied by their FAMILIARS. The Devil usually appeared in the shape of a he-goat, ugly and smelly, though at times he was said to arrive as a toad, crow or black cat. He presided over the sabbat while sitting on a throne. The witches took off their clothes and paid homage to him by kissing his backside (see KISS OF SHAME). Unbaptized infants were offered up in SACRIFICE. New witches were initiated by signing his black book in BLOOD, renouncing Christianity, taking an oath and trampling upon the cross (see INITIATION). The Devil marked his initiates with his claw (see DEVIL'S MARK). There followed a great feast, with much drinking and eating, although demonologists often noted that the food tasted vile and that no SALT was present, for witches could not abide salt. If infants had been sacrificed, they were cooked and eaten. After the feasting came dancing and indiscriminate copulation among the witches and demons. On occasion, the witches would go out into the night and raise storms or cause other trouble (see STORM RAISING). The witches flew home before dawn. The nights of the sabbats varied. Some witches said they attended weekly sabbats, while others said they went only once or twice a year.

Witches' sabbat meal (Ulrich Molitor, *Von den Unholden oder Hexen,* 1489)

In 1659 a French shepherdess gave this description of a sabbat that occurred on the summer solstice, observed by her and some companions:

> [They] heard a noise and a very dreadful uproar, and, looking on all sides to see whence could come these frightful howlings and these cries of all sorts of animals, they saw at the foot of the mountain the figures of cats, goats, serpents, dragons, and every kind of cruel, impure and unclean animal, who were keeping their Sabbath and making horrible confusion, who were uttering words that were most filthy and sacrilegious that can be imagined and filling the air with the most abominable blasphemies.

It is doubtful that such organized, malevolent activities took place. Most likely, the witches' sabbat was a fabrication of the witch-hunters, who seized upon admission of attendance at a gathering, meeting or feast and twisted it into a diabolical affair. Victims who made such confessions were pressed to name others who had attended the sabbats. In this manner, sometimes entire villages became implicated in Devil-worship.

Sabbats in Modern Witchcraft

The concept of diabolical witches' sabbats has become ingrained in popular witch lore. Modern Witches—and many neo-Pagans—observe eight holy days a year that once were pagan seasonal festivals. These sabbats revolve around the changing of seasons and agricultural observances and have nothing to do with the Devil or diabolical rites.

A system of greater and lesser sabbats was long in existence when GERALD B. GARDNER joined a COVEN of hereditary Witches in England in 1939. The celebration of the sabbats by both Witches and neo-Pagans has provided opportunities for creative expression through poetry, music, dance, song and drama. Rites contain both old pagan customs of Europe and the British Isles, especially Celtic traditions, and newer elements of the modern Craft and NEO-PAGANISM. The sabbats honor GODDESS, God (see HONNED GOD) and Nature and provide a means for giving thanks for the bounties of the Earth. They are festivals, times of rejoicing, feasting, dancing and gaiety. Generally, sabbats are held outdoors and may last over two or more days. If sabbats must be held indoors, rituals are changed to suit the circumstances.

Not all traditions observe each of the eight sabbats; each tradition follows its own customs and rituals. Some observe the sabbats skyclad, or nude, while others are robed or dressed in re-created pagan garb. Some traditions have emphasized reconstructing ancient Celtic customs, while others emphasize creating new practices. Beltane and Samhain are the most universally observed.

The Greater Sabbats and their observance dates are: Oimelc (also Imbolc, Imbolg), February 2; Beltane (also Bealtaine, Walpurgisnacht), April 30; Lughnasadh (also Lammas); July 31; and Samhain, October 31. The Lesser Sabbats fall on the solstices and equinoxes: winter solstice, December 22; spring equinox (Ostara), March 21; Summer solstice, June 22; and autumn equinox, September 21.

Winter solstice. The winter solstice marks the longest night of the year. The Goddess awakens from her sleep and finds she is pregnant with the Sun God. Solstice rituals, for both winter and summer, are universal and are intended to help the sun change its course in the sky. The winter solstice has been Christianized as Yule or Christmas.

Oimelc. A winter purification and fire festival, often called the Feast of Lights, Imbolc or Imbolg (pronounced "im mol' g"), which means "in the belly" and signifies the growing of life in the womb of Mother Earth. It celebrates Brigid (Brigit), Irish Celtic goddess of fire, fertility, crops, livestock, wisdom, poetry and household arts. Oimelc provides the first glimmers of life in the darkness of the Earth. The Goddess prepares for the birth of the Sun God. Candlemas is the Christian name for this festival, which also is known as St. Brigid's Day. In Christianity, the festival is observed with candlelight processionals and commemorates the Presentation of Christ in the Temple (Eastern Church) or the Purification of the Virgin Mary (Western Church). Oimelc coincides with Groundhog Day, the popular litmus test for the arrival of spring.

Spring equinox. A solar festival, in which day and night, and the forces of male and female, are in equal balance. The spring equinox, the first day of spring, marks the birth of the infant Sun God and paves the way for the coming lushness of summer. Dionysian rites are performed. The Christian version of this sabbat is Easter.

Beltane. One of the great Celtic solar festivals, observed in earlier times with bonfires. Beltane rites celebrate birth, fertility and the blossoming of all life, personified by the union of the Goddess and Sun God, also known in Christianized lore as King Winter and Queen May. Celebrants jump over broomsticks and dance around maypoles (see MAYPOLE), both symbols of fertility. Beltane begins at moonrise on Beltane Eve. It is bad luck to be out late at night on Beltane Eve or to sleep outside, for witches and FAIRIES roam the countryside in great numbers and hold wild revelries. Beltane bonfires were believed to bring fertility to crops, homes and livestock. People danced DEOSIL, or clockwise, around the fires or crept between fires for good luck and protection against illness. Cattle were driven through fires for protection against illness. In Druidic times, the DRUIDS lit fires on hillsides as they uttered incantations. Beltane was Christianized by the Church, which replaced pagan rites with a church service and processional to the fields, where a priest lit the fires.

Summer solstice. One of the most important and widespread solar festivals both in Europe and throughout the world. In European tradition, the night before the solstice, Midsummer's Eve, is a time of great MAGIC, especially for love CHARMS. Certain herbs picked at midnight will bring luck and protect against lightning, fire, witchcraft, disease and ill fortune. Witches and fairies roam about on Midsummer's Eve, as they do on the eve of Beltane; a bit of madness is in the air. Great bonfires are lit to help the sun change its course in the sky, and rites resemble those for Beltane. Burning wheels are rolled

downhill, and burning disks are hurled at the sun. The peak of power of the Sun God is manifested in the flourishing of crops and livestock. Celebrants jump over fires. The Christian Church absorbed the holiday as St. John's Day (for St. John the Baptist).

Lughnasadh. A great festival of games and dance, named for LUGH, the Irish Celtic solar god. The word *Lughnasadh* is related to words meaning "to give in marriage" and was once associated with marriage contracts. Nine months away is the next Beltane, the birth of summer and life. According to medieval legend, the festival celebrates Lugh's marriage to "the Sovranty of Ireland," the goddess Eriu. A hag, Eriu is transformed into a beauty by the marriage and personifies the land of Ireland. First harvests are made, accompanied by thanksgivings and rites to ensure the bounty of the next year's crops. Some traditions observe the death of the Sacred King as a sacrifice to ensure the fertility of next year's crops. In old pagan customs, the blood of a cock would be scattered on the fields.

Lammas, from the Old English terms for "loaf" and "mass," is a Christianized name for an old Saxon fruit-and-grain festival applied by the early English church. The holiday celebrated the ripening of apples and winter wheat, the latter of which, according to tradition, was made into loaves and blessed in the church. Lammas Day also was a day of accounts. In Scotland, tenant farmers took their first grain harvests to their landlords on August 1 to pay the rent.

Autumn equinox. Once again, day and night and male and female forces are equal. The autumn equinox is the time of second harvests. Traditionally, the Eleusinian mysteries are observed in rites and dramas. The mysteries concern the myth of DEMETER and her daughter Kore (Persephone), and of the attainment of immortality through adoration of them.

Samhain. An ancient Celtic festival that celebrates the beginning of winter, marked by death, and the beginning of the Celtic New Year. *Samhain* means "end of summer." In ancient Ireland, the Druids sacrificed to the deities by burning victims in wickerwork cages. All other fires were to be extinguished and relit from the sacrificial fire. In Ireland and Scotland, the custom of extinguishing one's home fire and relighting it from the festival bonfire has continued into modern times, without sacrificial victims. Samhain marks the third and final harvest and the storage of provisions for the winter. The veil between the worlds of the living and the dead is at its thinnest point in the year, making communication easier. The souls of the dead come into the land of the living. Samhain is a time for getting rid of weaknesses, a time when pagans once slaughtered weak animals that were unlikely to survive the winter. A common ritual calls for writing down weaknesses on a piece of paper or parchment and tossing it into the fire. Cakes are baked as offerings for the souls of the dead. In Christian terms, Samhain is known as All Hallow's Eve or Halloween, and a multitude of customs have evolved in its observance. It is possible that the custom of trick-or-treating originated with an old Irish peasant practice of going door-to-door to collect money, breadcake, cheese, eggs, butter, nuts, apples and other food in preparation for the festival of St. Columb Kill. APPLES appear in many rites, especially as ingredients in brews. Apple dunking may once have been a form of DIVINATION.

sacrifice An offering of a gift, especially to a deity or being, in petition, thanksgiving or appeasement. The most common offerings are food, drink, the fruits of harvest and the blood sacrifice of animals and fowl. The highest sacrifice is that of human life, a practice now rare. In various religions sacrifices also are made to the ELEMENTS, the sun and moon, the cardinal points, sacred landmarks (mountains, lakes, rivers and so on), ghosts and supernatural beings (see GHOSTS, HAUNTINGS AND WITCHCRAFT).

In neo-Pagan Witchcraft and NEO-PAGANISM, sacrifices (usually called offerings) are nonbloody and consist of cakes, drinks, fruits, flowers, poems, handicrafts, incense, nuts and other items. Blood sacrifice is considered an abomination and unnecessary for worship. In Witchcraft rituals and at SABBATS, an offering of food and drink is presented at the altar or sprinkled about the outdoors as an offering (see ALTAR). The modern DRUIDS of *ÁR NDRAÍOCT FÉIN* give burnt offerings at sabbats: flowers, nuts, small, handmade crafts, sheets of poetry and such are presented and thrown on a fire.

Blood sacrifice. Ritual blood sacrifice is an ancient custom of propitiation to the gods. Animals, fowl and humans have long been sacrificed in various religious rites to secure bountiful harvests and secure blessings and protection from deities. BLOOD consumed in ritual sacrifice is believed to give the drinker the soul and attributes of the blood of the deceased, whether it be human or animal. The Celts and DRUIDS drank the blood of their sacrificed human victims, whose throats were slashed over cauldrons, or burned their victims alive in wickerwork cages. The Aztecs cut the hearts out of human sacrifices with flint knives; the still-beating heart was held aloft by the priest, then placed in a ceremonial receptacle. The body was often dismembered and eaten in an act of ritual cannibalism. The Khonds of southern India impaled their victims on stakes and cut off pieces of their backs to fertilize the soil.

The sacrifice of first-born children was once a common custom in various cultures, particularly in times of trouble. During the Punic Wars, the nobility of Carthage sacrificed hundreds of children to Baal by rolling them into pits of fire.

The early Hebrews practiced blood sacrifices of animals. The book of Leviticus in the Old Testament lays out instructions for all kinds of sacrifices, including animals and fowl. In Genesis, Cain offers the fruits of his harvest, which does not please the Lord, and Abel offers one of his flock, which does please the Lord. Also in Genesis, God tests Abraham by instructing him to sacrifice his son. Abraham is stopped at the last moment, and a ram is substituted.

The Paschal Lamb, eaten at Passover, is a sacrifice commemorating the deliverance of the Israelites from Egypt. Christ obviated the need for blood sacrifice by shedding his own blood on the cross, thus securing eternal redemption for mankind. The Eucharist and communion services are nonbloody sacrifices, in which bread and wine or grape juice substitute for the body and blood of Christ.

Mythologies are replete with divine sacrifice: for example, Osiris, Dionysus and Attis are dismembered in sacrifice for rebirth.

During the witch-hunts of the Renaissance and Reformation, witches were said to sacrifice COCKS and unbaptized children to the DEVIL. They also were charged with cannibalism of infants and children. The cock sacrifices most likely relate to the pagan custom of sacrificing cocks as the corn spirit in harvest festivals, or in folk-magic SPELLS, in order to ensure an abundant crop the following year. The accusations of sacrifice and cannibalism of children were most likely the result of the TORTURE applied during inquisitions and trials of accused WITCHES. It also is in keeping with the historical trend of similar accusations leveled by one religious group against another. The Syrians accused the Jews of human sacrifice and cannibalism, much as the Romans accused the Christians and the Christians accused the Gnostics, Cathars, Waldenses and Albigenses.

In ceremonial MAGIC, blood sacrifice releases a flash of power, which the magician uses for a spell or conjuration. The old GRIMOIRES call for killing animals and using their skins to make parchment used in drawing the magical symbols needed. Animals offered to God or various demons should be young, healthy and virgin, for the maximum release of energy. The letting of blood, and the fear and death throes of the victim, add to the frenzy of the magician.

ALEISTER CROWLEY, in *Magick in Theory and Practice* (1929), said that "The ethics of the thing appear to have concerned no one; nor, to tell the truth, need they do so." Crowley routinely sacrificed animals and fowl in his rituals, within a MAGIC CIRCLE or triangle, which prevented the energy from escaping. He considered the torturing of the animal first, in order to obtain an elemental slave, as "indefensible, utterly black magic of the very worst kind," although in the next breath he said that he had no objection to such black magic if it was "properly understood." Crowley also noted that a magician could effect a blood sacrifice without the loss of life by gashing himself or his assistant.

Animals are sacrificed in various tribal religions and in VODOUN and SANTERÍA. The animal sacrifices of Santería—usually fowl and sometimes lambs or goats—have raised much opposition in America from animal-rights groups and offended individuals who consider the custom barbaric. The issue has been exacerbated by the practice of some Santeríans of leaving their beheaded and mutilated sacrifices in public places for others to find. Charges of stealing pet dogs and cats for sacrifice have been levied against the groups. In September 1987 the city of Hialeah, Florida, which has a large population of Santeríans, banned animal sacrifices. Santeríans counter that the Constitution protects their right to worship as they see fit. They defend animal sacrifice by pointing to its ancient roots.

Satanic groups, which are not connected to neo-Pagan Witches, also practice blood sacrifice, of both animals and humans, according to reports from ex-cult members (see SATANISM). Human victims include kidnapped runaways, children and derelicts. Torture or sexual abuse is sometimes applied first. In some rites, the blood of the victim is drunk, and sometimes part of the flesh is consumed. The remainder of the corpse is burned.

See also BLOOD.

St. Secaire, Mass of   See BLACK MASS.

Salem "Old Witch" Jail   The jail that housed the accused SALEM WITCHES during the witch hysteria of 1692–93 was a cold, foul, rat-infested dungeon located near the North River. It was used to house Indians, pirates and criminals, most of whom were condemned to die; the conditions in which such persons spent their last days were of little concern. It also housed debtors: people jailed because they could not pay their debts and those who were unable to pay the fees levied for keep in the jail.

Construction of the dungeon was approved in 1683 by the town of Salem. It succeeded two earlier prisons, one built in 1663 on the seized lands of Quakers, and another built in 1669. The new jail, built in 1684, was constructed of large, hand-hewn oak timbers and siding, and measured 70 by 280 feet. There were

no bars, for Puritan prisoners accepted their punishment. Those who did not and managed to escape were either caught or killed by Indians or wild animals.

The prisoners were fed salted foods and drink mixed with herring-pickle, for which they had to pay. This caused a constant, dreadful thirst, which made them more likely to confess in order to get relief.

Despite its grim conditions, the jail was a sort of social gathering place. The jailkeeper sold grog to visitors who came in the evenings to play chess and other games. For a bond of one pound, a prisoner was released during the day to visit family and friends, and then returned at night.

During the witch hysteria of 1692, the jail housed four lots of accused victims. The jailers routinely stripped the women of their clothing to examine and prick them in search of witch's marks (see PRICKING; WITCHES' MARK). They—and members of their families—were tortured for confessions (see TORTURE). One of the accused, Elizabeth Cary, was locked in leg irons and placed in a room with no bed. "The weight of the irons was about eight pounds," wrote her husband, Captain Nathaniel Cary. "These irons and her other afflictions, soon brought her into convulsion fits, so that I thought she would die that night." Cary bribed the jailer with his life's savings in order to get his wife freed.

Elizabeth Cary was not the only accused witch to suffer convulsions; many of the other victims suffered hysterical fits from the conditions and their treatment at the hands of the jailers. Two victims, Sarah Osborne and Ann Foster, died in jail. Foster's son was assessed a fee of two pounds, 16 shillings for permission to remove his mother's body for burial.

The salaries and expenses of the sheriff and his staff, the magistrates, the hangman and all persons concerned with the court were paid by the accused, who were each assessed one pound, 10 shillings. In addition, the prisoners were billed seven shillings and sixpence for their fetters, chains and cuffs, and an extra fee for being searched for witch's marks. The hangman's substantial fee was charged to the victims' estates or families. Those who had money fared the best. Captain John Alden, jailed on witchcraft charges, escaped by bribing the jailkeeper five pounds; he hid in New York until 1693, when the hysteria ended.

After victims were condemned, they were taken from the jail by oxcart out to GALLOWS HILL. Their corpses, swaying from the limbs of the locust trees, could be seen from the center of town.

In 1764 the jail was expanded with the addition of

second and third stories. It was discontinued as a jail in 1813 and subsequently passed into private ownership and was used as a residence. In 1863 it was purchased by Abner Cheney Goodell, state historian; it was later acquired by his son, Abner Cheney Goodell, Jr.

The jail was given little historical attention until 1934, when Mrs. Goodell, Jr., found in an old sealed closet a jailer's bill for the keep of paupers, some of whom were victims in the Salem trials. In response to public inquiries about the dungeon, the Goodells opened the jail to the public in 1935. The original jail was closed sometime later and re-created in a museum, the Salem Witch Dungeon.

See also WITCHCRAFT.

Salem Witches One of the last outbreaks of WITCHCRAFT hysteria, and certainly the largest in the New World, occurred in Salem, Massachusetts, from 1692 to 1693. During the course of the trials, 141 people were arrested as suspects, 19 were hanged and one was pressed to death. Those afflicted by the WITCHES were mostly young girls, yet their "child's play" led not only to the deaths of innocent people but also to total upheaval in the colonial Puritan church.

Scores of studies have examined the causes of the Salem witchcraft trials, some dealing with the political and social problems of Salem Village (now Danvers, Massachusetts); others with repressed sexual, generational or racial hostility; revolt by the disenfranchised; repression of women; regional feuds brought over from England; or ergotism, a food poisoning in the bread flour that may have led to hallucinations. Some studies have concentrated solely on the overly zealous nature of the parishioners. Whatever the reasons, there is little doubt that all those who were involved believed totally that witchcraft posed a serious threat to the health and spiritual well-being of the colony.

Divisions in the town. The Puritans who left England and settled in Salem in 1626, under the leadership of Roger Conant, hoped they would find peace in the new land. The settlement originally was named *Naumkeag*, the Indian term for "land of three rivers." Sometime before July 24, 1629, the name was changed to *Salem* from the Hebrew term *shalom*, meaning "peace." By 1692, however, peace was far from the order of the day.

For years, the community of Salem Village had chafed under the administration of neighboring Salem Town, which held legal, church and taxing authority over the more rural village. Villagers were required to attend services in the Town, although the distance for some residents was more than 10 miles. As early as 1666, Village residents petitioned the Town and the colony's General Court for permission to build a meetinghouse and hire a minister, which they finally accomplished in 1672.

That permission alone did not make them a full-fledged community, however, but more a parish within the jurisdiction of Salem Town. The 17th-century Puritan "church" was not the building, minister or attendees but an "elect"—those select few who had been filled with divine grace, given testimony to God's power and were allowed to receive communion. Church members attending services in Salem Village still had to travel to their real churches

Witch flying over Salem (Bert Poole, 1895; Essex Institute)

for communion. Continued discontent among Salem Villagers about their situation, coupled with disputes over who in the village had the power to select ministers, was described as a "restless frame of spirit"—a moral defect in the villagers' characters—instead of a legal issue. By the time Samuel Parris arrived to be the fourth minister in Salem Village in 1689, the community was irreparably split between those who wished to maintain ties with Salem Town and those who believed the Village was best served by autonomy. Parris vocally supported the separatist interests. Eventually, the Village divided between those who stood behind Parris and those who did not.

Beginning of the hysteria. In some ways, Rev. Parris caused the witch hysteria, however unknowingly. Before becoming a minister, Parris had worked as a merchant in Barbados; when he returned to Massachusetts, he brought back a slave couple, John and Tituba Indian (Indian was probably not the couple's surname but a description of their race). Tituba cared for Parris's nine-year-old daughter Elizabeth, called Betty, and his 11-year-old niece, Abigail Williams. Especially in winter, when bad weather kept the girls indoors, Tituba most likely regaled the girls with stories about her native Barbados, including tales of voodoo (see VODOUN).

Fascinated with a subject that the Puritans found shocking, the girls soon became dabblers in the occult. Joined by other girls in the Village who ranged in age from 12 to 20—Susannah Sheldon, Elizabeth Booth, Elizabeth Hubbard, Mary Warren, Mary Walcott, Sarah Churchill, Mercy Lewis and Ann Putnam, Jr. (Ann Putnam, Sr. was her mother)—they began telling each other's fortunes. Making a primitive crystal ball by floating an egg white in a glass of water, the girls tried to ascertain the trades of their future husbands. One reportedly saw the likeness of a coffin, representing death; what had begun as a fun game had now turned into dangerous magic.

The girls, beginning with Betty Parris in January 1692, began having fits, crawling into holes, making strange noises and contorting their bodies. It is impossible to know whether the girls feigned witchcraft to hide their involvement in Tituba's magic or whether they actually believed they were possessed (see DEMONIC POSSESSION). In any case, Rev. Parris consulted with the previous Salem Village minister, Rev. Deodat Lawson, and with Rev. John Hale of nearby Beverly. In February he brought in Dr. William Griggs, the Village physician and employer of the now-afflicted Elizabeth Hubbard. Griggs had no medical precedent for the girls' condition, so he diagnosed bewitchment.

Seventeenth-century Puritans believed in witch-craft as a cause of illness and death. They further believed the accepted wisdom of the day that witches derived their power from the Devil. So the next step was to find the witch or witches responsible, exterminate them and cure the girls. After much prayer and exhortation, the frightened girls, unable or unwilling to admit their own complicity, began to name names.

Right before this, Mary Walcott's aunt, Mary Sibley, tried to use magic to find the witches. She requested that Tituba make a witch cake out of rye meal mixed with the urine of the afflicted girls. The cake, taken from a traditional English recipe, was then fed to the dog. If the girls were bewitched, one of two things were supposed to happen: either the dog would suffer torments too, or he would identify the witch as her FAMILIAR. Rev. Parris furiously accused Mary Sibley of "going to the Devil for help against the Devil," lectured her on her sins and publicly humiliated her in church. But the damage had been done: "the Devil hath been raised among us, and his rage is vehement and terrible," said Parris, "and when he shall be silenced, the Lord only knows."

Crying out against the witches. The first accused, or "cried out against," were Tituba herself, Sarah Good and Sarah Osborne. Goodwife (usually shortened to Goody; Mistress or Mrs. was reserved for women of higher rank) Good's husband William did not provide for his family, and she defiantly begged and looked out for them herself. Goody Osborne, old and bedridden, had earlier caused a scandal by allowing her servant to live in her house before she married him. Tituba was a natural suspect. Suspicious neighbors were not surprised that any or all three were witches, and none was a member of the church.

Warrants for their arrest were issued, and all three appeared in the ordinary, or public house, of Nathaniel Ingersoll before Salem Town magistrates John Hathorne and Jonathan Corwin on March 1. The girls, present at all of the interrogations, fell into fits and convulsions as each woman stood up for questioning, claiming that the woman's specter was roaming the room, biting them, pinching them and often appearing as a bird or other animal someplace in the room, usually on a particular beam of the ceiling. Hathorne and Corwin angrily demanded why the women were tormenting the girls, but both Sarahs denied any wrongdoing.

Tituba, however, beaten since the witch cake episode by Rev. Parris and afraid to reveal the winter story sessions and conjurings, confessed to being a witch. She said that a black dog had threatened her and ordered her to hurt the girls, and that two large cats, one black and one red, had made her serve them. She claimed that she had ridden through the air on a pole to "witch meetings" with Goody Good and Goody Osborne, accompanied by the other women's familiars: a yellow bird for Good, a winged creature with a woman's head and another hairy one with a long nose for Osborne. Tituba cried that Good and Osborne had forced her to attack Ann Putnam, Jr., with a knife just the night before, and Ann corroborated her statement by claiming that the witches had come at her with a knife and tried to cut off her head.

Most damningly for Salem, Tituba revealed that the witchcraft was not limited to herself and the two Sarahs: that there was a COVEN of witches in Massachusetts, about six in number, led by a tall, white-haired man dressed all in black, and that she had seen him. During the next day's questioning, Tituba claimed that the tall man had come to her many times, forcing her to sign his Devil's book in blood, and that she had seen nine names already there (see DEVIL'S PACT).

Such a story, frighteningly real to the Puritans because of rumors that had circulated a few years earlier that a conspiracy of witches would destroy Salem Village, beginning with the household of the minister. Hathorne, Corwin and Rev. Parris were pushed to begin an all-out hunt for the perpetrators of such crimes. All three women were taken to prison in Boston, where Good and Osborne were put in heavy iron chains to keep their specters from traveling about and tormenting the girls. Osborne, already frail, died there.

The politics of witchcraft. Complicating the legal process of arrest and trial was the loss of Massachusetts Bay's colonial charter. Massachusetts Bay was established as a Puritan colony in 1629 and was enjoying self rule when the English courts revoked its charter in 1684–85, restricting the colony's independence. The high-handed Sir Edmund Andros, the first royal governor, was overthrown in 1688 when William and Mary of Orange took away the English throne from James II in the Glorious Revolution. Since that time, Massachusetts Bay had had no authority to try capital cases, and for the first six months of the witch-hunt, suspects merely languished in prison, usually in irons (see SALEM "OLD WITCH" JAIL).

But more than the legal ramifications, the loss of Massachusetts's charter represented to the Puritans a punishment from God: the colony had been established in covenant with God, and prayer and fasting and good lives would keep up Massachusetts's end of the covenant and protect the colony from harm. Increasingly, the petty transgressions and factionalism of the colonists were viewed as sins against the covenant, and an outbreak of witchcraft seemed the ultimate retribution for the colony's evil ways. Published sermons by COTTON MATHER and his father, INCREASE MATHER, and the long-winded railings against witchcraft from Rev. Parris's pulpit every Sunday, convinced the villagers that evil walked among them and must be rooted out at all cost.

More witches are named. Relying on the spectral visions of the afflicted girls, the magistrates and ministers pressed them to name more witches if they could, and Ann Putnam, Jr., with the help of her vengeful mother, cried out against Martha Corey, a member of the Salem Village congregation and wife of local landowner Giles Corey. Before arresting her, Ann's uncle Edward Putnam and Ezekiel Cheever rode to the Corey home to speak with Martha. The men pressed Ann to reveal what clothes Martha was wearing, hoping to prove that such a godly churchwoman was innocent. Ann claimed she could not, as Martha had temporarily removed her spectral sight.

When the men arrived, Martha calmly said she knew why they had come and even taunted them by asking, "Does shee tell you what cloathes I have on?" They were shocked to think Martha had preternatural knowledge of the earlier conversation. And when Martha visited the Thomas Putnam home to see young Ann, the girl fell into terrible fits, claiming she saw Martha's specter roasting a man over a fire. Mercy Lewis said other witches joined Martha's specter, urging her to sign the Devil's book. Martha steadfastly maintained her innocence later before the magistrates, but the girls' torments and anguish in court convinced the judges she was a witch. Every time she said something or made a gesture, the girls mimicked her. If she bit her lip, the girls shrieked in pain, showing teeth marks on their arms and hands. Even her husband, Giles, testified against her and asked her to confess to witchcraft.

The next woman named as a witch was Rebecca Nurse, one of the most outstanding people of her community and a church member. If the girls had named Rebecca Nurse or Martha Corey as witches first, instead of Sarah Good and Sarah Osborne, their accusations probably would have been dismissed as folly. But by now, the magistrates were willing to believe anything the girls claimed. Even close family members of the accused believed in the women's guilt, refusing to believe that the magistrates or girls would accuse anyone who was not a witch.

Rebecca's accuser was Ann Putnam, Sr., who had joined the ranks of "the afflicted," as the accusing girls were known, by claiming that the specters of Corey and Nurse had come to her and tortured her hellishly, urging her to sign the Devil's book. Abigail Williams, Mary Walcott and Elizabeth Hubbard agreed that Nurse had come to them, too, wanting them to

The Wonders of the Invisible World:

Being an Account of the

TRYALS

O F

Several Witches.

Lately Excuted in

NEW-ENGLAND:

And of several remarkable Curiosities therein Occurring.

Together with,

I. Observations upon the Nature, the Number, and the Operations of the Devils.

II. A short Narrative of a late outrage committed by a knot of Witches in *Swede-Land*, very much resembling, and so far explaining, that under which *New-England* has laboured.

III. Some Councels directing a due Improvement of the Terrible things lately done by the unusual and amazing Range of *Evil-Spirits* in *New-England*.

IV. A brief Discourse upon those *Temptations* which are the more ordinary Devices of Satan.

By *COTTON MATHER.*

Published by the Special Command of his EXCELLENCY the Governeur of the Province of the *Massachusetts-Bay* in *New-England.*

Printed first, at *Boston* in *New-England* ; and Reprinted at *London*, for *John Dunton,* at the *Raven* in the *Pultry.* 1693.

Title page of London edition of Cotton Mather's witch pamphlet, 1693

sign. Rebecca was old and ill, but she was forced to stand before the magistrates and the girls. Ann Putnam, Jr. claimed Nurse's specter had beaten her, and Ann Sr. cried out that Nurse had brought the "black man" with her. Rebecca defended herself as best she could, but she too was sent to prison.

Joining Rebecca in prison was four-year-old Dorcas Good, whom the afflicted girls had claimed was a witch, learning her evil trade from her mother Sarah. Dorcas was chained like all the others.

The next victims of witch hysteria were John and Elizabeth Proctor, tavern-keepers and vocal opponents of the proceedings. Mary Warren, one of the original afflicted girls and Proctor's maid, earlier had been "cured" of her fits when Proctor threatened to beat her if she persisted. Knowing of the Proctors' opposition, the girls were eager to eliminate any who would dispute them.

But before the Proctors were arrested, Sarah Cloyce, the sister of Rebecca Nurse, stormed out of church in disgust when Rev. Parris's sermon implied the guilt of her sister and all the other accused witches.

Such a display of anger made her a convenient target, and the girls cried out against Cloyce and Elizabeth Proctor together. John Proctor accompanied his wife to support her before the magistrates, who had moved the proceedings to the Salem Town meetinghouse and were joined by Deputy Governor Thomas Danforth and Captain Samuel Sewell. Tituba's husband John had joined the afflicted, and he, along with Mary Walcott, Abigail Williams, Ann Putnam, Jr. and Mercy Lewis all claimed that the witches' specters tortured them, urging them to sign the Devil's book and drink victims' blood. During the interrogation, Abigail and Ann, Jr., saw John Proctor's specter sitting on a ceiling beam and tormenting the girls.

Abigail accused Elizabeth Proctor of forcing her maid, Mary Warren, to sign the Devil's book, a shrewd defense against Mary's reluctance to testify against her employer. By doing so, the girls named Mary a witch and gave notice to the other afflicted that hesitation or denial would result in their being named witches. During her own interrogation, Mary had no choice but to confirm the girls' accusations and rejoin their ranks.

Arrested along with Mary Warren were Giles Corey, Bridget Bishop and Abigail Hobbs. Bishop entertained people in her home with liquor and games to all hours, dressed in flashy red outfits and had scandalized Salem for years. Accusations of witchcraft were not far behind. Abigail Hobbs, mentally unbalanced, readily confessed to witchcraft and told Hathorne of her bargain with "the old boy" that allowed him to appear to the afflicted girls in her shape. Instead of dismissing her story as that of an insane person, the magistrates believed every word and found vindication in it for the girls' spectral attacks.

Eighty-year-old Giles Corey, Martha's husband, described as powerful and brutal, resolutely denied any involvement with witchcraft. But the girls' usual performance, claiming spectral pinching and other torments, sealed his fate as a wizard.

On April 21 Abigail Hobbs's wild tales led to the arrests of nine more people: a very old man named Nehemiah Abbot; Abigail's parents, William and Deliverance Hobbs; Bridget Bishop's stepson Edward and his wife Sarah; Mary Esty, sister of Rebecca Nurse and Sarah Cloyce; a Negro slave named Mary Black; Sarah Wilds; and Mary English, wife of the wealthy Salem merchant Philip English. Up to now, all the accused had lived in the Salem vicinity, but five of these suspects were from Topsfield. Eventually, witches were sought in 22 other communities.

The interrogations before Hathorne and Corwin followed the usual pattern, with the magistrates badgering the accused and the girls throwing fits and claiming spectral violence. But for the first time, they recanted their accusations against a victim, and Nehemiah Abbot was acquitted. If their change of heart was intentional, it was judged a shrewd move: the girls would not charge an innocent person and could tell witches from godly people.

The others were not so lucky. Edward and Sarah Bishop were guilty by association with his mother. Deliverance Hobbs first denied involvement but then succumbed to the magistrates' bullying and confessed signing the Devil's book, brought to her by Sarah Wilds. Such confessions brought the girls temporary relief. Her husband obdurately held onto his innocence but was carried off to prison just the same. Mary Black, the slave, denied pricking dolls and said she just pinned her collar. But when the magistrates asked her to pin her collar, the girls screamed in pain, and Mary Walcott appeared so badly pricked that she bled. Sarah Wilds's meek denials did not save her, either.

Villagers considered Mary Esty a likely witch since her sisters were already accused. But her adamant protestations of innocence impressed even Hathorne, leading him to demand of the girls that they be sure. Naturally, spectral evidence found Goody Esty guilty. When Hathorne, angry at what he thought was Esty's lying, asked her if she believed the girls bewitched, she is reported to have replied, "It is an evil spirit, but wither it be witchcraft I do not know." Over the next few weeks, the girls—all but Mercy Lewis—began to doubt they had seen Esty's specter, and she was freed. But then Mercy fell into terrible convulsions and claimed that Esty's specter was choking her because she alone maintained the woman was a witch. Esty was returned to prison.

On April 30 six more people were arrested: Sarah Morey, Lydia Dustin, Susannah Martin, Dorcas Hoar, merchant Philip English and Rev. George Burroughs. Morey was eventually acquitted, and Dustin died in prison. Dorcas Hoar and Susannah Martin, independently minded, had long been accused of witchcraft; Martin even had the temerity to laugh at the antics of the girls. Philip English escaped to Boston with his wife Mary, also accused, until the affair died down. He saved their lives but lost most of his property.

Rev. Burroughs, however, had been brought to Salem from his home in Wells, Maine. A minister at Salem Village before Parris, he had alienated many of the parishioners, especially Ann Putnam, Sr., and witchcraft was a convenient vehicle for her vengeance. Ann, Jr., actually first accused Burroughs, screaming that a minister was offering her the Devil's book. The specter told young Ann that his name was Burroughs, that he had murdered several people

while in Salem and that "he was above witch for he was a conjurer." All agreed that Burroughs was the coven leader that Tituba had described.

Given Burroughs's station and occupation, the magistrates decided a more discreet examination would be in order. He was interrogated at Ingersoll's ordinary by Hathorne, Corwin, Captain Sewall and William Stoughton, a man vigorously in favor of rooting out witchcraft. After the private questioning, various citizens stepped forth and accused Burroughs, a small man, of feats of superhuman strength and cruelty, and the girls writhed as always. The magistrates sighed collectively at the capture of the witches' ringleader.

Unfortunately, Burroughs still had followers unapprehended. John Willard, who had earlier helped in the arrests, was himself accused and caught after he refused to issue any more warrants. His damning evidence was his inability to recite the LORD'S PRAYER, viewed as certain proof of the Devil's handiwork; only the godly can recite the Lord's word. George Jacobs, an early opponent of the proceedings, was arrested with Willard and Jacobs's granddaughter Margaret. Jacobs could not recite the Lord's Prayer either, and his maidservant, Sarah Churchill, said she had seen his name in the Devil's book.

Like Mary Warren, Churchill had second thoughts about the girls' games when Jacobs, her employer, stood accused. But the girls turned on her as well, saying she had signed. She confessed, but later recanted. Haunted by her false confession, Churchill complained that everyone believed her accusations, but no one believed her when she said someone was innocent. None of this impaired her qualifications as an accuser of others, and Churchill remained in company with the other afflicted girls.

Prosecution, condemnation and execution. As noted earlier, no trials could be held until Massachusetts obtained a new charter, and so all the accused remained in prison without a formal trial. Finally, in May of 1692, the new royal governor, Sir William Phips, arrived with a charter. Unwilling to concern himself with the witchcraft mess, Phips established a Court of Oyer and Terminer ("to hear and determine") to try the witches. Sitting on the court were now Lt. Governor William Stoughton as chief justice, Bartholomew Gedney, Jonathan Corwin, John Hathorne, Nathaniel Saltonstall, Peter Sergeant, Wait Still Winthrop, Samuel Sewall and John Richards. All were among the most respected men in the colony, but many were the same men already sending accused witches to prison.

By May's end, approximately 100 people sat in prison based on the girls' accusations. Three of the more memorable were Elizabeth Cary, Martha Carrier and John Alden, the son of John and Priscilla Alden of Plymouth. Judge Gedney was shocked to find Alden, a respected sea captain, accused of witchcraft, but when the girls shrieked and cried out in pain, Gedney pressed Alden to confess. He refused and was led away; he later escaped to New York. Elizabeth Cary came of her own free will to the court when she heard she had been accused, and she learned that her specter did no harm to the girls until they were sure it was she.

Martha Carrier was the first accused from Andover, Massachusetts, which eventually named 43 witches in its citizenry. Defiantly, Carrier denied tormenting the girls or seeing any black man, but the more she stood firm, the more the girls writhed. Finally, Carrier's hands and feet were bound to keep her specter from torturing the girls further, for the wisdom of the day said a witch in bondage could harm no one.

The Court of Oyer and Terminer first sat on June 2 and lost no time in trying and sentencing the accused witches. Bridget Bishop was first on the docket and was found guilty. Chief Justice Stoughton signed her death warrant on June 8, and she was hanged two days later. The body was casually placed in a shallow grave on Salem's GALLOWS HILL, for witches did not deserve Christian burial. Justice Saltonstall resigned from the court not too long thereafter, disgusted at the entire affair and uncomfortable at the total reliance on the girls' spectral evidence. His opposition later earned him an accusation of witchcraft.

The question of spectral evidence had dominated the proceedings from the beginning. The problem was not whether the girls saw the spectral shenanigans but whether a righteous God could allow the Devil to afflict the girls in the shape of an innocent person. If the Devil could not assume an innocent's shape, the spectral evidence was invaluable against the accused. If he could, how else were the magistrates to tell who was guilty? Turning to the colony's clergy, the Court asked for an opinion, and on June 15 the ministers, led by Increase and Cotton Mather, cautioned the judges against placing too much emphasis on spectral evidence alone. Other tests, such as "falling at the sight," in which victims collapsed at a look from a witch, or the touch test, in which victims were relieved of their torments by touching the witch, were considered more reliable. Nevertheless, the ministers thanked the Court for its diligence and pushed for "the vigorous prosecution of such as have rendered themselves obnoxious."

Chief Justice Stoughton firmly believed until his death that God would not allow the Devil to assume an innocent's shape, and so the Court pressed on.

The next to appear were Susannah Martin, Sarah Good and Rebecca Nurse. Martin and Good were condemned, but Nurse was originally acquitted. The girls, present as always, went into terrible fits at the news, and Stoughton calmly asked the jury if it was certain of her innocence. The jury reconsidered and found her guilty. Again, Nurse's friends tried to save her, petitioning Governor Phips to reprieve her. He did but later rescinded his order.

On June 30 the Court tried and condemned Sarah Wilds and Elizabeth How. How, of Topsfield, had cured John Indian's fits by touching him, and others accused her of bewitching their children and animals. Interestingly, during the trials one of the afflicted accused Rev. Samuel Willard, pastor of the Old South Meeting House in Boston. Because he was minister for three of the justices, the court protected Willard, reprimanded the accuser and explained to the public that she had meant John Willard, already imprisoned.

The executions of Nurse, How, Martin, Sarah Good and Sarah Wilds took place July 19. Rev. Noyes, present as a witch-hunter from the beginning, urged Sarah Good to confess, but she defiantly cursed him, saying, "I am no more a witch than you are a wizard, and if you take away my life, God will give you blood to drink." Noyes died in 1717, supposedly of an internal hemorrhage, choking on his own blood. All but Nurse remained in the shallow grave on the hill; her family secretly removed the body that night to give it a decent burial.

Witchcraft in other communities. By now the girls' power was so great that they were celebrities in the colony and believed invincible. Consequently, citizens of neighboring towns requested that the girls look at their communities with their spectral vision and find the witches responsible for whatever problems existed: illness, poor crops, dead livestock. Most affected was the town of Andover, which the girls found to be crawling with witches. The problem with these later hotbeds of witchcraft was that the girls knew no one by name and had to identify the criminals by fits in front of individuals or the touch test. Many confessed to witchcraft in Andover, because all had realized that those who confessed were spared execution. Lying was preferable to hanging.

The girls began naming very prominent people as witches, including Andover's justice of the peace, Dudley Bradstreet, the son of the colony's former governor. His brother John was also accused. The brothers and their wives fled the colony before they could be arrested. Two dogs were executed as witches in Andover as well. One man accused by the girls, described as a "worthy Gentleman from Boston," turned the tables on them and issued a warrant for

Trial of George Jacobs (Essex Institute)

their arrest for slander, demanding £1000 in damages. The afflicted balked and quickly went on to scrutinize other towns.

The executions continue. The next group condemned by the Court of Oyer and Terminer consisted of Elizabeth and John Proctor, John Willard, George Burroughs, George Jacobs and Martha Carrier. The Court granted Elizabeth Proctor a stay of execution because she was pregnant, a delay that saved her life. Carrier's own sons confessed to witchcraft, but their confessions were obtained after torture. Jacobs's granddaughter Margaret also testified he was a wizard but later retracted her testimony. No one believed her, but she was later acquitted.

Willard, Jacobs, Carrier, Burroughs and John Proctor went to Gallows Hill on August 19. Before Burroughs died, he shocked the crowd by reciting the Lord's Prayer perfectly, creating an uproar. Demands

for Burroughs's freedom were countered by the afflicted girls, who cried out that "the Black Man" had prompted Burroughs through his recital of the prayer. It was generally believed that even the Devil could not recite the Lord's Prayer, and the crowd's mood grew darker. A riot was thwarted by Rev. Cotton Mather, who told the crowd that Burroughs was not an ordained minister and that the Devil was known to change himself often into an angel of light if there was profit in doing so. When the crowd was calmed, Mather urged that the executions proceed, and they did. As before, the bodies were dumped into a shallow grave, leaving Burroughs's hand and chin exposed.

Fifteen more witches were tried and convicted in September. Of those, four confessed and escaped execution to save their souls. Three more avoided death either by pregnancy, confession or outright escape from prison. The remaining eight—Martha Corey, Mary Esty, Alice Parker, Ann Pudeater, Margaret Scot, Wilmott Redd, Samuel Wardwell and Mary Parker—were hanged on September 22.

Alice Parker, Ann Pudeater and Wilmott Redd were all hanged based on the spectral evidence of the girls. Mary Parker of Andover had passed the touch test in court and had caused a pin to run through Mary Warren's hand and blood to run out of her mouth. Samuel Wardwell, completely intimidated, confessed to signing the Devil's book for a black man who promised him riches. He later retracted his confession, but the Court believed his earlier testimony. Wardwell choked on smoke from the hangman's pipe during his execution, and the girls, ever-present, claimed it was the Devil preventing him from finally confessing.

Giles Corey was pressed to death on September 19 for refusing to acknowledge the Court's right to try him. A landowner, Corey knew that as a convicted witch his property would be confiscated by the Crown. He reasoned that if he did not acknowledge the right of trial, he could not be tried and convicted, and without conviction his property remained his. In frustration, the Court sentenced Corey to a "punishment hard and severe." He was taken to a Salem field, staked to the ground and covered with a large wooden plank. Stones were piled on the plank one at a time, until the weight was so great his tongue was forced out of his mouth. Sheriff George Corwin used his cane to poke it back into Corey's mouth. Corey's only response to the questions put to him was to ask for more weight. More stones were piled atop him, until finally he was crushed lifeless. Ann Putnam, Jr., saw his execution as divine justice, for she claimed that when Corey had signed on with the Devil, he had been promised never to die by hanging.

The hysteria subsides. The crowd didn't know it in late September, but these were the last executions. The colony's ministers, long skeptical of the spectral evidence, finally took a stand against such proof, casting doubt on the decisions of the Court. The number of accusers had grown to more than 50 people, leading even dedicated witch-hunters like Rev. John Hale to question such large numbers of witches and bewitched in so small a colony. And the afflicted girls, giddy with power, had gone so far as to accuse Lady Phips, wife of the royal governor. That was the last straw; on October 29 Governor Phips dissolved the Court of Oyer and Terminer.

But the prisons were still overflowing with accused witches, so Governor Phips asked the General Court to establish a Superior Court to finish the business. Sitting on the Superior Court in January 1693 were William Stoughton, again as chief justice, John Rich-

ards, Wait Still Winthrop, Samuel Sewall and Thomas Danforth. All but Danforth had been on the Court of Oyer and Terminer, but except for Stoughton, they had confided to the governor their uneasiness over the convictions and their desire to try again. He agreed. The trials were no longer held exclusively in Salem but traveled to the seat of each witch's county. Most importantly, spectral evidence was no longer admissible.

Without spectral evidence, juries acquitted most of the accused. Only three were convicted, and Stoughton quickly signed their death warrants and those for five more convicted in September. But Governor Phips, tired of Stoughton's intransigence, reprieved all eight. The Superior Court again sat on April 25 and for the last time on May 9; all those tried were acquitted, and Massachusetts's witchcraft nightmare was over. Tituba was released from jail in May and was sold as a slave to cover her prison expenses.

The aftermath. Throwing out spectral evidence placed the colony in a grave dilemma: either the state admitted it was wrong and had committed murder, threatening the political system, or the men involved confessed their sins before God and protected their Puritan covenant. If spectral evidence was inadmissible, could witchcraft ever be proven?

Eventually, the prosecutions were seen as one more trial placed on God's covenant with New England—not so much a judicial miscarriage as a terrible sin to be expiated. Those who had participated in the proceedings—Cotton and Increase Mather, the other clergy, the magistrates, even the accusers—suffered illness and personal setbacks in the years following the hysteria. Samuel Parris was forced to leave his ministry in Salem, while Ann Putnam, Jr., publicly begged forgiveness before the Village in 1706. Long before that, the Puritan clergy had called for an Official Day of Humiliation on January 14, 1697, for fasting and public apology. Samuel Sewall heard his confession of guilt read that morning from the pulpit of his church.

By 1703 the Massachusetts colonial legislature began granting retroactive amnesties to the convicted and executed. Even more amazing, they authorized financial restitution to the victims and their families. In 1711 Massachusetts Bay became one of the first governments ever to compensate voluntarily persons victimized by its own mistakes.

As early as 1693 Increase Mather wrote in *Cases of Conscience Concerning Evil Spirits Personating Men* that finding a witch was probably impossible, because the determination rested on the assumption that God had set humanly recognizable limits on Satan, but Satan and God are beyond human comprehension. Summing up, Rev. John Hale, an early supporter of the witch-hunt, wrote in his *Modest Enquiry into the Nature of Witchcraft* (1697) that "I have had a deep sence of the sad consequence of mistakes in matters Capital; and their impossibility of recovering when compleated." He went on to say that the people involved meant well, but "such was the darkness of that day, the tortures and lamentations of the afflicted, and the power of former presidents [precedents], that we walked in the clouds, and could not see our way."

Giles Corey, who died the most unusual death of the Salem victims, was memorialized in a ballad:

> Giles Corey was a Wizzard strong,
>   And a stubborn Wretch was he,
> And fitt was he to hang on high
>   Upon the Locust Tree.
>
> So when before the Magistrates
>   For Triall did he come,
> He would no true Confession make
>   But was compleatlie dumbe.
>
> "Giles Corey," said the Magistrate,
>   "What hast thou heare to pleade
> To these that now accuse thy Soule
>   Of Crimes and horrid Deed?"
>
> Giles Corey—he said not a Worde,
>   No single Worde spake he;
> "Giles Corey," sayeth the Magistrate,
>   "We'll press it out of thee."
>
> They got them then a heavy Beam,
>   They laid it on his Breast;
> They loaded it with heavie Stones,
>   And hard upon him prest.
>
> "More weight," now said this wretched Man,
>   "More weight," again he cryed,
> And he did no Confession make,
>   But wickedly he died.

One interesting footnote to the Salem witch hysteria is that the American author NATHANIEL HAWTHORNE, a descendent of magistrate John Hathorne, added the *w* to his name to expunge some of the Puritan guilt by association. The trials also served as an allegory for the Communist purges in America during the 1950s; the most notable example of this is Arthur Miller's play, *The Crucible*.

Modern Salem's legacy. The witchcraft hysteria of 1692 still attracts many tourists to Salem and the neighboring town of Danvers each year. Gallows Hill, the once remote site where the victims were executed and buried in shallow graves, has long been built over with residential dwellings. Legend has it that the ghosts of the victims haunt the area. The Witch House, the restored Salem home of Judge Jonathan Corwin, is open for tours; visitors see the small upper chamber where the magistrates subjected nervous townsfolk to the questioning that determined whether or not they would be charged and tried. The original jail no longer exists, but the dungeon has been re-created in the Witch Dungeon Museum. The entire witch episode is re-created in a narrated, multisensory presentation in the Witch Museum, located in a former church, which draws more than 140,000 visitors a year.

See also LAURIE CABOT.

salt   Pure in its whiteness, long linked to life and health, salt is held to be anathema to DEMONS and evil. As a preservative, salt is contrary to the corrupting nature of demons. In neo-Pagan WITCHCRAFT, salt is used as an agent of purification, to ward off negative influences. It represents the element earth and is a staple in MAGIC and worship. A small dish of it is consecrated and is used, along with the other ELEMENTS—water, fire and air (incense)—to consecrate the MAGIC CIRCLE and magical tools (see WITCHES' TOOLS). Salt is used in various other rituals as well.

According to folklore, however, witches are supposed to be repelled by salt, which is therefore supposed to protect one against witchcraft, the EVIL EYE, WITCHES and demons, as well as break evil SPELLS. In medieval times, it was believed that witches and the animals they bewitched were unable to eat anything salted. Inquisitors who interrogated accused witches were advised by demonologists first to protect themselves by wearing a sacramental AMULET that consisted of salt consecrated on Palm Sunday and blessed herbs, pressed into a disk of blessed wax. One means of torturing accused witches was to force-feed them heavily salted food and deny them water (see TORTURE).

An old recipe for breaking an evil spell calls for stealing a tile from a witch's roof, sprinkling it with salt and URINE and then heating it over fire while reciting a charm (see CHARMS). Such antidotes were still in use in the 20th century in rural parts of Europe to remove spells from stables and homes and to cure illness. In American Ozark lore, women who complain of food being too salty are suspected of being witches. One Ozark method of detecting a witch is to sprinkle salt on her chair. If she is a witch, the salt will melt and cause her dress to stick to the chair.

In Christianity, salt is symbolic of incorruptibility, eternity and divine wisdom. Church sites were traditionally consecrated with salt and holy water. The Catholic ritual of the benediction of salt and water ensures physical health and the exorcism of evil spirits. Salted holy water is used in baptisms. As an extra precaution against demons, some people put salt in a newborn baby's cradle until the infant can be baptized. At death, salt is often left in a coffin to help protect the soul from demons during its transition from earth to the spirit world.

In alchemy, all things, including the four elements, were believed to be composed of a divine trinity that included salt, mercury and sulphur. Salt represented the body, female and earth aspects, and was a crucial ingredient in alchemic recipes for making gold. One 17th-century formula for potable gold, believed to be an antidote for POISONS, a curative of heart disease and a repellent of the DEVIL, included GOLD, salt, red-wine vinegar, the ashes of a block of tin burnt in an IRON pan, wine and honey.

Salt is supposed to be avoided in magic rituals designed to conjure demons. Medieval necromancers avoided salted food before performing their ceremonies to summon the spirits of the dead (see NECROMANCY).

Even today, it is considered bad luck to spill, borrow or run out of salt, perhaps because in times past, salt was a valuable and scarce commodity. Spilling salt makes one vulnerable to the Devil; the bad luck may be negated by tossing a pinch of salt with the right hand over the left shoulder.

Salt Lane Witches   According to English folklore, two white WITCHES once lived in Castle Street, Worcester, in medieval times. They were considered white witches because instead of bewitching others to their harm, they used their MAGIC to free the carts that frequently became stuck in the mud near their cottages. For sixpence, one witch would stroke and bless the horse while the other would stroke the cartwheels.

One day a wagoner tried to bargain with the witches and noticed a piece of straw on his horse's back. Thinking it was part of their magic, he cut it in half. Immediately, the witch who was stroking the horse screamed and fell dead, severed in two. The cart was freed, and the wagoner fled. The second witch lived on and later turned a troop of soldiers into stone, when they appeared in town to collect taxes. According to legend, their petrified figures once stood at what is now the main road that passes through Worcester. A local merchant tried to break the spell of the figures, but one of the stones turned into a giant horse which reared up and pawed the air, frightening him off.

Sanders, Alexander (1926–1988)   Self-proclaimed "King of the Witches" in his native England, Alexander Sanders rose to fame in the 1960s, founding a major tradition that carries his name: Alexandrian. A gifted psychic with a flamboyant style, he was for some years the most public Witch in Britain, gaining headlines for his reputed sensational acts of MAGIC. Some called him the *enfant terrible* of British WITCHCRAFT, whose life was surrounded by more myth than fact.

Sanders was born in Manchester, the oldest of six children. His father was a music-hall entertainer and suffered from alcoholism. By Sanders's own account, he was seven when he discovered his grandmother, Mary Bibby, standing naked in the kitchen in the middle of a circle drawn on the floor (see MAGIC CIRCLE). She revealed herself as a hereditary Witch (see WITCHES) and initiated him on the spot (see INITIATION). She ordered him to enter the circle, take off his clothes and bend down with his head between his thighs. She took a knife and nicked his scrotum, saying, "You are one of us now."

According to Sanders, Mary Bibby gave him her BOOK OF SHADOWS, which he copied, and taught him the rites and magic of Witches. He discovered his own natural psychic gifts for clairvoyance and healing by touch.

He worked as an analytical chemist at a laboratory in Manchester, where he met and married a 19-year-old co-worker, Doreen, when he was 21. They had two children, Paul and Janice, but the marriage rapidly disintegrated. Doreen took the children and left Sanders when he was 26.

Sanders then entered a long period of drifting from one low-level job to another, drinking and indulging in sexual flings with both men and women, according to his account of his life. He decided to follow the "left-hand path" and use magic to bring him wealth and power. For a time, he worshipped the Devil. He also studied Abra-Melin magic (see ABRAMELIN THE MAGE). He apparently attracted people who supported him financially. He formed his first COVEN, began getting media attention, attracted more followers and by 1965 claimed to have 1,623 initiates in 100 covens, who then "persuaded" him to be elected King of the Witches.

Sanders boasted about his alleged feats of magic. He claimed to create a flesh-and-blood "spiritual baby" in a rite of ritual masturbation, with the help of a male assistant. Sanders said the baby disappeared shortly after its creation and "grew up" as a spirit which took him over in his trance channeling. Michael, as the spirit was called, supposedly was responsible for "forcing" Sanders to carry on at wild parties, insult others and otherwise act abominably. Eventually, Sanders claimed, Michael simmered down and became a valuable spirit familiar (see FAMILIARS), offering advice in healing matters. Sanders also channeled another familiar, Nick Demdike, who said he had been persecuted as a witch in the Lancaster trials of the 17th century. No existing records of those trials mention a "Nick Demdike" (see LANCASTER WITCHES).

Sanders reportedly got rid of warts by "wishing them on someone else, someone who's already ugly, with boil marks I can fill up with the warts." He claimed to cure a man of heroin addiction and to cure cystitis in a woman by laying his hands on her head and willing her affliction away. He also said he cured a young woman of stomach cancer by sitting with her in the hospital for three days and nights, holding her feet and pouring healing energy into her.

He effected other cures by POINTING at the troubled spots on the body and concentrating. Pointing, he said, never failed. He claimed he gave magical abortions by pointing at the womb and commanding the pregnancy to end.

One of Sanders's more famous alleged cures concerned his daughter, Janice, who was born in dry labor with her left foot twisted backwards. Doctors shook their heads, saying nothing could be done until the child was in her teens. Sanders received an "impression" from Michael to take olive oil, warm it and anoint Janice's foot. Sanders did so, then simply twisted Janice's foot straight. The foot remained corrected; Janice walked normally, except for a slight limp in cold, damp weather.

In the 1960s, Sanders met Maxine Morris, a Roman Catholic 20 years his junior, whom he initiated into the Craft and handfasted (see HANDFASTING). Maxine became his high priestess. In 1967 they married in a civil ceremony and moved to a basement flat near Notting Hill Gate in London, where they ran their coven and taught training classes. They attracted many followers and initiated people into the Craft. Their daughter, Maya, was born the same year.

Sanders was catapulted into the national public spotlight by a sensational newspaper article in 1969. The publicity led to a romanticized biography, *King of the Witches*, by June Johns (1969), a film, "Legend of the Witches," numerous appearances on media talk shows and public-speaking engagements. Sanders enjoyed the publicity and was adept at exploiting it, to the dismay of other Witches, who felt he dragged the Craft through the gutter press.

Curiously, Sanders usually appeared robed or clad in a loincloth in photos of himself in rituals, while the other Witches with him were naked. He explained this by saying that "Witch law" required the elder of a coven to be apart from the others and easily identifiable.

Sanders's accounts of his initiation into the Craft by his grandmother, his magical escapades and the extent of his "kingdom" are dubious. Years after his

publicity peaked, it was revealed that he passed off the writings and teachings of others as his own. Stewart Farrar, a journalist who was initiated by Sanders, said Sanders used material from the Gardnerian book of shadows, written by GERALD B. GARDNER and DOREEN VALIENTE, and either took credit for it himself or passed it off as inherited material. He also passed off material written by ELIPHAS LEVI and Austrian occultist Franz Bardon as his own, sometimes after making slight changes in it and other times not bothering to make any changes at all. Even his name, "Alexander Sanders," was not his own, but one that he had assumed.

According to other Witches, Sanders created his Alexandrian tradition after he was refused initiation into various Gardnerian covens. He apparently obtained a copy of the Gardnerian book of shadows and used it as the basis for his own tradition. The Alexandrian tradition closely follows the Gardnerian tradition.

In 1971 Sanders and Maxine separated. Sanders moved to Sussex, where he entered a life of retirement and seclusion, away from the limelight. Maxine remained in the London flat, where she continued to run a coven and teach the Craft. In 1972 a son, Victor, was born.

Sanders remained in seclusion for the rest of his life. He died on April 30, 1988 (Beltane Eve), after suffering from lung cancer. At his funeral, a tape recording was played in which he declared that Victor should succeed him as "King of the Witches." According to Maxine, Victor had no desire to do so and had gone to live in the United States. A "Witchcraft Council of Elders," which claims to have an incredible 100,000 members in Britain alone, said no other successor would be elected. (Note: In all other traditions no king or queen of the Craft is ever elected. Some witches say the council is a "fabrication" of followers of Sanders. It is highly unlikely that there are 100,000 witches total in Britain, not to mention members of a council.)

The Alexandrian tradition was exported to other countries, where it continues to be practiced, as well as in the United Kingdom. In the United States, it never gained as wide a following as the Gardnerian tradition and was hurt by negative publicity about Sanders. As of the 1980s none of the U.S. Alexandrian covens had any connection with Sanders himself. The tradition is much stronger in Canada, where it was more firmly established prior to Sanders's fall from grace.

Despite Sanders's media grandstanding, he is recognized for contributing to the overall evolution of modern Witchcraft. Following Sanders's death, Stewart Farrar observed: "Alex was a born showman; but the fact remains that he made a major contribution to the Craft, in his own often bizarre way, and many people (including ourselves [Stewart and wife Janet Owen Farrar]) might never have been introduced to it but for him."

See also STEWART AND JANET FARRAR.

Santería Similar in practice to VODOUN, Santería centers around the worship of the ancient African gods who have been assimilated as Catholic saints. *Santería* comes from the Spanish word *santo*, meaning "saint"; practitioners are called *Santeros* (female: *Santeras*).

Like Vodoun, Santería came to the Americas with the millions of black slaves from West Africa, principally from the Yoruban tribes along the Niger River. Forced to convert to Catholicism, the slaves continued their religion in secret, passing along ancient traditions either orally or in handwritten notebooks that came to be called *libretas*. Gradually, the Yorubans began to see what they believed were the incarnations of their gods in the Catholic saints and syncretized the two faiths. The slaves' Spanish and Portuguese masters eventually grew fascinated with Yoruban magic and began to practice it themselves. Today, any city with a large Hispanic population probably boasts as many Santeros as devout Catholics, since many of the devotees practice both. New York, Miami, Los Angeles and the nations of Cuba and Jamaica are all Santería strongholds. Brazilians also practice Santería but under the names of *Candomblé*, *Umbanda* and *Quimbanda* (see MACUMBA).

The orishas. In the ancient Yoruban tongue, gods were called *orishas*, and that is the term still used today. Just like the Vodoun *loa*, the orishas have complex human personalities, with strong desires, preferences and temperaments. When they possess their "children," the devotees assume the orishas' supernatural characteristics, performing feats of great strength, eating and drinking huge quantities of food and alcohol and divining the future with great accuracy.

Santeros also believe there was a supreme creator of heaven and earth, but like the *Gran Met* in Vodoun, he is unapproachable. In the beginning was Olodumare, a being incomprehensible to mortals, who was composed of three spirits: Nzame, Olofi (also called Olorun) and Baba Nkwa. Nzame created all the stars, planets, earth, plant and animal life, then made Omo Oba, a man, at the suggestion of the other two, to rule over all creation. Such power went to Omo Oba's head, causing Olodumare to order Nzalam, the lighting bolt, to destroy the earth in flames. But Omo Oba's immortality saved him; he hid deep underground, changed his name to Olosi and only resurfaces to tempt men to break Olodumare's laws—much like the story of Lucifer as a fallen angel. Afterward, Olodumare took pity on the scorched earth, and so Nzame, Olofi and Baba Nkwa again gave it life, this time creating a mortal man, Obatalá. At this second creation, Olofi took over provenance of earth, and the other two went off to create life elsewhere. As the first ancestor, Obatalá is the father of the gods and the first orisha.

Depicted as a white man on horseback, Obatalá is associated with all things white and represents peace and purity. His wife, Oddudúa, is a black woman who is usually shown breastfeeding an infant and represents maternity. Obatalá and Oddudúa had two children: a son Aganyú and a daughter Yemayá. Aganyú and Yemayá married and had a son Orungán, who was so handsome that Aganyú died of envy. Orungán forced himself incestuously upon his mother, a beautiful woman of yellow skin who is the goddess of the MOON and womanhood. She cursed him and he died. Completely overcome with her sorrows, Yemayá climbed a mountain, where she delivered 14 gods conceived by Orungán in a single birth and then died. The waters released when her abdomen burst caused the deluge—the Flood—and the place where she died became the holy city of Ile Ife, the same sacred place worshipped in Vodoun.

Tragic Yemayá remains a popular goddess in Santería, whose colors are light blue and white. The 14 deities born to Yemayá include Changó, the god of fire, thunder and lightning. Young, virile and handsome, Changó also governs the passions. His colors are red and white, and he is one of the most popular deities in Santería. His wife, Oba, is goddess of the Oba River. Continually jealous and suspicious of her philandering husband, she follows him and has him watched.

Oyá, goddess of the Niger River, is wife of the god Oggún, but also is Changó's favorite concubine. She gives him power over fire, which is holy to her. Oyá controls memory and is the patroness of justice. She also governs death and cemeteries, and maroon is her favorite color. Alefi, the wind, is Oyá's messenger. Oshún, the goddess of the Oshún River, also enjoys Changó's favors. She is the goddess of love and marriage and loves fans, mirrors and seashells. Also the goddess of gold and money, Oshún prefers the color yellow. Pumpkins are sacred to her. She is a very popular deity.

Ochosi is the god of hunters, birds and wild animals and also watches over jails, perhaps as cages for humans. He likes lavender and black and chooses the bow and arrow as his symbols. Olokun lives on the ocean floor with the mermaids, watching over the seas. He is a hermaphrodite and has very long hair. His favorite mistress is Olosa, who aids fishermen and employs the crocodile as her messenger. Orisha-Oko governs the fields and harvests and brings fertility to land and families. Oke rules over the mountains and protects those who live in high places.

Chankpana, the god of smallpox, appears as an old man nursing a lacerated leg. He uses flies and mosquitoes as his messengers. Dada governs unborn children and gardens. Ayé-Shaluga rules fortune and good luck. The last two of the 14, Orun, god of the sun, and Ochu, goddess of the moon, have few followers.

Other important orishas include Elegguá (called LEGBA in Vodoun), the god of entrances, doorways and roads, who allows the other orishas to enter the sphere of man. All homes keep an image of Elegguá behind the door as he is the most powerful orisha after Obatalá. One of Elegguá's best friends, Oggún, governs war and iron, all weapons (including sacrificial knives) and the treatment of tumors and skin diseases. He prefers black dogs as sacrifices (see SACRIFICE) and has many followers in Santería. Orúnla owns the Table of Ifá, the sacred system of DIVINATION, and also shares great friendship with Elegguá. Babalu-Ayé is patron of the sick. Symbolized by a pair of crutches, he appears as an old man accompanied by two dogs.

Aroni is the god of medicine, while Osachin is the patron god of doctors. Ayé or Ayá is the midget goddess of the jungle, and Oyé rules storms. Ochumare serves as goddess of the rainbow. Homes come under the protection of Olarosa, while Olimerin guards the entire village. The twin gods Ibeyi watch over infants. Ifá is the patron of impossible things and the god of fertility and palm trees. He was the first owner of the Table of Ifá. Chiyidi controls nightmares and used to be an evil entity (see NIGHTMARE). Iku is the spirit of death. Rounding out this partial list is Bacoso, the king and founder of the Yoruba dynasty and the holy city of Ife. Each of the orishas appears in many forms, and only the priest best knows what manifestation to invoke, depending upon the situation. Extremely difficult cases may necessitate calling upon the Seven African Powers, a combination of Obatalá, Elegguá, Orúnla, Changó, Oggún, Yemayá and Oshún.

Saints identified with the orishas may be of either sex and not necessarily of the same gender as the orisha. Santeros do not dare question such arrangements, explaining the situation by saying that after the gods' mystical deaths, they were reincarnated in new bodies. A partial list of the saints identified with the orishas of Santería follows:

Olorun/Olofi, God the Creator	The Crucified Christ
Obatalá	Our Lady of Mercy
Oddudúa	Saint Claire
Aganyú	Saint Joseph
Yemayá	Our Lady of Regla
Orungán	The Infant Jesus
Changó	Saint Barbara
Oyá	Our Lady of La Candelaria; also St. Theresa and St. Catherine
Oshún	Our Lady of La Caridad del Cobre
Ochosi	Saint Isidro
Dada	Our Lady of Mount Carmel
Ochumare	Our Lady of Hope
Oggún	Saint Peter, St. Anthony or Joan of Arc
Babalú-Ayé	Saint Lazarus
Elegguá	Holy Guardian Angel, St. Michael, St. Martin de Porres, St. Peter
Orúnla	Saint Francis of Assisi
Ifá	Saint Anthony of Padua
Bacoso	Saint Christopher

Rites and practices. Although all worshippers of Santería could be called Santeros, the term usually refers to the priests or priestesses. The highest order of priest is a *babalawo*, who has power not only to heal the sick and punish the unjust but to divine the future through the Table of Ifá. All babalawos are male, as Orúnla, god of the Table of Ifá, is male. Within the order of babalawo are various degrees, ranging from high priest to the one responsible for a particular orisha's sacrifice. Following the babalawo are the priests of orishas who govern the sick or healing, and the priests or priestesses of Orisha-Oko, the god of agriculture. Priests consecrated to lesser orishas or human deities also fall in this third category. The power of the babalawo is limitless, as he wears the hats of healer, diviner, judge, pastor, matchmaker and magician.

The babalawo's second-most important duty is sacrificing animals as offerings to the orishas. Common sacrificial animals include all types of fowl—chickens, roosters, pigeons, doves and other birds—goats, pigs and occasionally bulls. In Cuba, Santeros may obtain government meat-ration cards because they have to buy so many live animals. In some parts of the United States, animal-rights groups oppose ritual sacrifice on the grounds that animals may be tortured and pets may be stolen and slaughtered. The Santeros counter that animal sacrifice, if done humanely, is legal in many states; they deny that cats and dogs are sacrificed. Those practicing black MAGIC, however, reputedly use cats and dogs as ingredients for evil SPELLS.

Reading the seashells (los caracoles) of the Table of Ifá is the paramount divination procedure in Santería. Santeros who specialize in Table readings are called *italeros* and are often babalawos consecrated to the service of Orúnla. Reading the Table is also known as *diloggun* or *mediloggun*. The Table has 18 shells, but the italero uses only 16. The shells may be bought in any *botanica* (a store where Santería and Vodoun paraphernalia and herbs are sold) by anyone, but uninitiated users, *aleyos*, may use only 12. The smooth, unbroken sides of the shell are filed until the serrated sides appear, showing what appears to be a tiny mouth with teeth. As such, the shells are the "mouthpieces" of the orishas.

During a consultation, called a *registro*, the italero prays to the gods, rubs the 16 shells together, then throws them onto a straw mat (*estera*). The shells are read according to how many of them fall with their top sides, or "mouths," uppermost. The italero interprets the pattern in which they fall, called an *ordun*, then repeats the procedure four times. Each ordun has a name and number and "speaks" for one or more of the orishas. Like the Chinese system of I CHING, the divinations rely on ancient proverbs associated with each ordun and require the italero to interpret for the particular situation.

Very often the babalawo finds the questioner has been put under an evil spell, or *bilongo*, by an enemy. Such action requires placing an *ebbo*, or counteracting spell, on the guilty party. If the ebbo does more damage to the enemy than the enemy's original spell, it only increases the prestige of the babalawo. The greater the babalawo's accuracy in divination and response, the larger his clientele. Remedies range from herbal baths to complicated spells involving various oils, plants and intimate waste products of the intended victim. Babalawos commonly prescribe a *resguardo*, or protective talisman. A typical resguardo is a small cloth bag filled with various herbs, spices and other ingredients, dedicated to a certain orisha, which will keep the owner from harm.

Another popular divinatory method, normally used to consult Elegguá, is called *darle coco al santo* ("give the coconut to the saint"), or reading coconut meat. Coconuts are used in all major Santería ceremonies and form the main ingredient for several spells. To prepare a coconut for divination, the reader must break its shell with a hard object, never cracking the nut on the floor, as that would offend Obi, the coconut's deity. The meat—white on one side and brown on the other—is then divided into four equal pieces. The pieces are thrown on the floor, and one of five patterns results.

Readings of the Table of Ifá by the babalawo help determine all of the important characteristics of a person's life and how he or she should deal with each event as it occurs. Upon the birth of a child, the parents consult the babalawo to find the infant's assigned orisha, plant, birthstone and animal. In Santería, birthstones have no relation to the birth month. Good-talisman animals include goats, elephants and turtles; noxious ones are many reptiles, venomous insects, some types of frogs, all birds of prey, rats, crocodiles, lizards and spiders.

WATER has great spiritual powers as a defensive measure for the Santero, as it does in other religions and magical systems. Since evil spirits dissolve in water, all devotees keep a small receptacle of water under their beds to clean away evil influences, which must be changed every 24 hours. The "dirty" water must never fall onto the floor or go down the kitchen sink.

Other protective agents against evil are GARLIC and brown sugar. To be really safe, a Santero burns brown sugar and garlic skins in a small pan over hot coals. The thick smoke, called *sahumerio*, fills the house, seeping even into closets and corners where evil spirits can hide. Evil beings also dislike black rag dolls.

Healing and magic. All Santeros are accomplished herbalists, since plants, and especially herbs, are sacred to the orishas. Most plants serve dual purposes, as curatives and as magic ingredients, and can be obtained in any good botanica. Garlic lowers high blood pressure, coconut water acts as a diuretic, anise seed alleviates indigestion, sarsaparilla cures rheumatism, nerves and syphilis and indigo works on epilepsy. *Higuereta*, which produces castor oil, has been used by the Santeros on cancerous tumors for centuries with amazing results.

Cuttings from *escoba amarga* bushes are used in purifying baths and to drive away the *abikus*, mischievous spirits that reincarnate in a child who dies very young. According to the older Santeros, the only way to drive out an abiku is to beat it with a branch of the bush, usually on a Wednesday. If a child dies young, the Santero makes a mark on its body, often by cutting off a piece of the child's ear before burial. Following the birth of another child, the Santero searches for the mark, which he claims he often finds. To keep the abiku from taking the second child, the baby is "tied" to the earth by placing a small chain on its wrist or ankle. The chain is not removed until the child is well past puberty.

The *bombax ceiba* tree, or five-leaf silk-cotton tree, gives the Santero curative or magical powers from almost every part. Sacred to Santería, the ceiba is worshipped as a female saint; worshippers will not even cross the tree's shadow without first asking permission. Teas from the ceiba's roots and leaves aid in curing venereal disease and urinary tract infections. The leaves also work on anemia. Ceiba-bark tea helps cure infertility. The tree trunk and the ground around it help cast evil spells; if a Santero wishes harm upon someone, he must walk naked around the ceiba tree several times at midnight and brush the trunk with his fingertips, softly asking the tree to help him against his enemy. Even the shade attracts spirits, giving strength to spells cast there.

Santería has been described as African magic adapted for the West and for city life. It is ruled by the laws of similarity (that like produces like) and contact (that things that have been in contact with each other continue to affect one another even after contact has been broken). The magic of similarity is *homeopathic,* or *sympathetic.* The Santero can affect situations by acting out the scene beforehand or by using natural objects in alliance with or resembling the intended victim; e.g., a wax doll. Another common sympathetic practice is to take a small stone and name it after the victim, then kick it under a bed and concentrate very hard on the named person.

Magic by contact is *contagious.* The magician procures items that have been in contact with the victim—clothing, nail parings, hair clippings (see HAIR AND NAILS), even dirt from under the feet (see FOOT-PRINTS) or air from the victim's home—and uses them to effect the spell.

The Santero wields enormous power, having knowledge that can change a person's life either through his own skill or by the help of the orishas. The decision to use that power for good or evil rests with the Santero alone.

Santeros fear the EVIL EYE, knowing that the eye's harmful magic can come from anyone. Children wear a tiny jet hand and a bit of coral on a gold bracelet to protect them; adults may be similarly protected or wear a small glass eyeball pinned to the chest (see AMULETS).

Black magic. Most magic in Santería comes under the "white" classification: spells for wayward lovers, good luck, money and cures. Santeros who deal exclusively in black magic—*brujería* or *palo mayombe*—come primarily from Congo tribal ancestry and are called *mayomberos,* or "black witches." In her book, *Santería: African Magic in Latin America* (1981), author Migene Gonzales-Wippler describes the mayomberos as "people of unparalleled malignancy, specializing in revenge, necromancy and the destruction of hu-

man life." She says ethics never come under consideration, because the mayombero lives in a world "outside of reality"—magic is merely a means of survival in a hostile environment. Retribution can be avoided by magic and by "paying" the demonic forces through offerings of food, liquor, money and animal sacrifice.

Gonzales-Wippler says that before a novice can become a full-fledged mayombero, he must sleep under a ceiba tree for seven nights. At the end of the week, he takes a new set of clothes and buries them in a previously chosen grave in the cemetery. While his clothes are buried, the novice takes a series of purifying herbal baths; at the end of 21 days, or three successive Fridays, the candidate digs up his clothes, puts them on and goes with his teacher back to the ceiba tree. Other mayomberos join them there as witnesses, invoking the spirits of the dead and that of the ceiba to approve the initiation. The candidate is crowned with ceiba leaves, which represent the spirits of the dead taking possession of the new mayombero. Finally, the mayomberos place a lighted candle in a white dish in the initiate's hands and give him his scepter, or *kisengue:* a human tibia bone wrapped in black cloth. He is now ready to call on the powers of darkness.

Making the nganga. Once the mayombero has been initiated, his next project is the making of the *nganga,* or cauldron, that contains all his magical potions and powers. When the moon is right—no WITCHCRAFT can be accomplished during a waning moon, since that period signifies death—the mayombero and an assistant return to the cemetery to a preselected gravesite. The chosen grave is usually fairly recent, since the mayombero desires a corpse with a brain still inside the skull, no matter how decayed. The mayombero also knows the identity of the corpse, called the *kiyumba.* Choice kiyumbas were violent persons in life, preferably criminals or the insane. The still-extant brain helps the kiyumba to think and better act on the mayombero's evil purposes. The bodies of whites are also favored, since some mayomberos believe whites take instruction better than blacks. Other mayomberos hedge their bets by taking a brain from corpses of both races, ensuring that their evil spells will work on either.

The mayombero sprinkles rum in the shape of a cross over the grave, then opens it. The corpse is raised, and the mayombero removes the head, the toes, the fingers, ribs and the tibias of the kiyumba, wrapping them in black cloth and taking them home. Once there, the mayombero lies on the floor, and his assistant covers him with a sheet and lights four tapers around the body as if the mayombero were dead. A knife is placed near the mayombero, and on the blade are seven little heaps of gunpowder called *fula*. As the kiyumba takes possession of the mayombero, he becomes rigid and then goes into convulsions. The assistant asks the kiyumba if it will do the bidding of the mayombero; if the answer is yes, the gunpowder ignites spontaneously. If no, the body parts must be returned to the cemetery.

If the spirit agrees, the mayombero writes the kiyumba's name on a piece of paper and places it in the bottom of a big, iron CAULDRON together with a few coins in payment to the kiyumba. He adds the remains, along with some earth from the gravesite, then cuts a small incision in his arm with a white-handled knife and lets a few drops of blood fall into the cauldron to "refresh" the kiyumba. Some mayomberos sacrifice a rooster to the kiyumba instead, fearing the spirit could become too fond of the mayombero's blood and turn into a vampire.

To the blood, the mayombero adds wax from a burned candle, a cigar butt, ashes, lime and a piece of bamboo sealed at both ends with wax. The bamboo contains sand, seawater and quicksilver, to give the kiyumba the speed of quicksilver and the persistence of the ever-moving tides. Next, the mayombero puts in the body of a small black dog to help the kiyumba track its victims, along with various herbs and tree barks. The rest of the recipe calls for red pepper, chili, garlic, onions, cinnamon, rue, ants, worms, lizards, termites, bats, frogs, Spanish flies, a tarantula, a centipede, a wasp and a scorpion. If the mayombero plans to create good spells from his nganga, a splash of holy water is added at the end. If the cauldron will be used for both good and evil, no baptism is necessary.

After combining all these ingredients, the mayombero takes the cauldron back to the cemetery, where it is buried and left for three successive Fridays. At that time, the mayombero disinters the cauldron and reburies it beside a ceiba or other magical tree for another three Fridays. At the conclusion of the 42 days, the mayombero hauls the cauldron home, where he adds some rum with pepper, dry wine, Florida water (a popular cologne in the Caribbean) and fresh blood. The nganga is ready.

Occasionally the mayombero does not use a cauldron, choosing instead to place the ingredients, called *boumba*, in a sheet and then tie it up in a burlap sack. The sack, known as a *macuto*, then hangs from a ceiling beam in the darkest room of the mayombero's house. The nganga or macuto forms a small world completely at the bidding of the mayombero, with the kiyumba controlling the animals and plants inside the nganga with it and obeying the orders of the mayombero like a faithful slave, always willing and ready.

The nganga must pass two tests before the mayombero trusts its powers. For the first trial, the mayombero buries the nganga under a tree and tells the kiyumba to dry all the tree's leaves within a certain length of time. If the nganga passes, then the mayombero orders the kiyumba to kill a specific animal. If the kiyumba succeeds again, the mayombero takes the nganga home.

There are two other types of ngangas: the *zarabanda* and the *ndoki*. The mayombero makes a zarabanda in the traditional manner but invokes the spirit of the Congo deity Zarabanda to work directly with the kiyumba. The ndoki ranks as perhaps the most infernal preparation in the mayombero's repertoire. First, a black cat is tortured and boiled alive. The mayombero then buries the cat for 24 hours. Upon disinterment, he adds a few of the cat's bones to seven phalanx bones from the little fingers of seven corpses, along with the dust from seven graves. These ingredients are placed in the cauldron with garlic and pepper; then the mayombero sprinkles rum over the pot and blows cigar smoke over it. The cauldron stays in the woods overnight, and then it is ready. Considered the property of the DEVIL, the ndoki is used to kill and destroy its victims in the most fearsome and horrible ways.

Gonzales-Wippler notes that Santeros fear the nganga's powers so much that they will not even speak of them except in whispers. Making a nganga is illegal, needless to say, punishable with a fine or imprisonment, but few mayomberos worry about trifles like legal codes or police officers. They operate with impunity, wielding death and destruction on behalf of anyone for a price.

See also AFRICAN WITCHCRAFT; GRIS-GRIS; ZOMBIE.

Satanism The worship of Satan, or the DEVIL, the god of evil in Christianity. During the Renaissance, WITCHES, along with heretics, were accused of worshipping the Devil. Many confessed to it, probably coerced by TORTURE. In popular lore, witches are still believed to worship the Devil. (In modern NEO-PAGANISM and WITCHCRAFT, or WICCA, as it is often called, there is no belief in nor worship of the Devil.)

Satanism has been far less common throughout history than many would believe. The inquisitors and witch-hunters of earlier centuries tried to persuade the populace that Devil-worshippers were everywhere and posed a serious threat to their well-being. For about 250 years, from the mid-15th century to the early 18th century, the height of the witch-hunts, that argument worked. It is possible that some Devil-worship may have actually existed in those times, as an act of defiance among those who opposed the authority of the Christian Church.

Satanism as an organized activity did not exist much before the 17th century. As early as the seventh century, however, the Catholic Church was condemning priests who subverted the magical powers of the Holy Mass for evil purposes. The *Grimoire of Honorious*, a magical textbook first printed in the 17th century (but perhaps older), gave instructions for saying masses to conjure DEMONS. In the 17th century, satanic activities were conducted by Christians who indulged in the magical/sexual rites of the BLACK MASS, presided over by defrocked or unscrupulous priests. The most notorious of these escapades took place in France during the reign of Louis XIV, engineered by the king's mistress, Madame de Montespan, and led by an occultist named La Voisin and a 67-year-old libertine priest, the Abbé Guiborg.

There is no reliable evidence of satanic activity in the 18th century. In England, the Hellfire Club, a society founded by Sir Francis Dashwood (1708–1781), has often been described as satanic, but in actuality it was little more than a club for adolescent-like men to indulge in drinking, sexual play with women called "nuns" and outrageous behavior. The Hellfire Club, or the "Medmenham Monks," as they called themselves, met regularly between 1750 and 1762 in Dashwood's home, Medmenham Abbey. The members were said to conduct Black Masses, but it is doubtful that these were serious satanic activities. Similar groups were the Brimstone Boys and Blue Blazers of Ireland.

Perhaps the most famous satanist of the 19th century was the Abbé Boullan of France, who became the head of an offshoot of the Church of Carmel and allegedly practiced black magic and infant SACRIFICE. The Church of Carmel was formed by Eugene Vintras, the foreman of a cardboard box factory in Tilly-sur-Seulles. In 1839 Vintras said he received a letter from the archangel Michael, followed by visions of the archangel, the Holy Ghost, St. Joseph and the Virgin Mary. He was informed that he was the reincarnated Prophet Elijah, and he was to found a new religious order and proclaim the coming of the Age of the Holy Ghost. The true king of France, he was told, was one Charles Naundorf.

Vintras went about the countryside preaching this news and acquiring followers, including priests. Masses were celebrated that included visions of empty chalices filled with blood and blood stains on the Eucharist. By 1848 the Church of Carmel, as the movement was known, was condemned by the Pope. In 1851 Vintras was accused by a former disciple of conducting Black Masses in the nude, homsexuality and masturbating while praying at the altar.

Shortly before his death in 1875, Vintras befriended Boullan, who formed a splinter group of the Church of Carmel upon Vintras's death. He ran the group for 18 years, until his death, outwardly maintaining pious practices but secretly conducting satanic rituals.

Boullan seems to have been obsessed with Satanism and evil since age 29, when he took a nun named Adele Chevalier as his mistress. Chevalier left her convent, bore two bastard children and founded with Boullan The Society for the Reparation of Souls. Boullan specialized in exorcising demons by unconventional means, such as feeding possessed victims a mixture of human excrement and the Eucharist (see DEMONIC EXORCISM). He also performed Black Masses. On January 8, 1860, he and Chevalier reportedly conducted a Black Mass in which they sacrificed one of their children.

By the time Boullan met Vintras, Boullan was claiming to be the reincarnated St. John the Baptist. He taught his followers sexual techniques and said the original sin of Adam and Eve could be redeemed by sex with incubi and succubi. He and his followers also were said to copulate with the spirits of the dead, including Anthony the Great.

Boullan's group was infiltrated by two Rosicrucians, Oswald Wirth and Stanislas de Guaita, who wrote an exposé, *The Temple of Satan*. Boullan and de Guaita supposedly engaged in magical warfare. Boullan and his friend, the novelist J. K. Huysmans, claimed to be attacked by demons. When Boullan collapsed and died of a heart attack on January 3, 1893, Huysmans believed it was due to an evil spell cast by de Guaita, and said so in print. De Guaita challenged him to a duel, but Huysmans declined and apologized.

In his novel, *La-bas*, Huysmans included a Black Mass, which he said was based on his observations of one conducted by a satanic group in Paris, operating in the late 19th century. He said the Mass was recited backwards, the crucifix was upside down, the Eucharist was defiled and the rite ended in a sexual orgy.

By the early 20th century, ALEISTER CROWLEY was linked to Satanism. Although he called himself "the Beast," used the words "life" "love" and "light" to describe Satan and once baptized and crucified a toad as Jesus, he was not a satanist but a magician and occultist.

Modern Satanism

The largest movement of modern Satanism began in the 1960s in the United States, led by Anton Szandor LaVey, a shrewd, intelligent man with a charismatic persona and an imposing appearance. LaVey founded the Church of Satan in San Francisco in 1966, the activities of which became the object of great media attention.

Born April 11, 1930, in Chicago, LaVey claimed an ancestry of Alsatian, Georgian and Romanian blood, including a Gypsy grandmother from Transylvania (see GYPSIES). As a child, he studied music and became interested in the occult. He learned to play the piano at 10 and at 15 became an oboist for the San Francisco Ballet Symphony Orchestra. He dropped out of high school in his junior year and joined the Clyde Beatty Circus as a cage boy. He had a gift for working with the big cats and became assistant trainer. It was in the circus, working with lions, he later said, that he learned about inner power and magic. On the side, he investigated haunted houses. At 18, he left the circus and joined a carnival as a magician's assistant and a calliope player. In 1948 he met Marilyn Monroe and played as her accompanist.

He married his first wife, Carole, in 1951; they had one daughter, Karla. He studied criminology at City College in San Francisco and spent three years as a crime photographer with the San Francisco Police Department. Disgusted with the violence he saw, he quit and returned to playing the organ in nightclubs and theaters. He began holding classes on occult subjects. From these classes evolved a magic circle, which met to perform rituals LaVey had devised or re-created from historical sources on the KNIGHTS TEMPLAR, the Hellfire Club, the HERMETIC ORDER OF THE GOLDEN DAWN and Aleister Crowley. LaVey apparently enjoyed the theatrics of the rituals; he dressed in a scarlet-lined cape and kept skulls and other odd objects about. Magic-circle members included actress Jayne Mansfield and filmmaker Kenneth Anger.

LaVey divorced Carole in 1960 and married Diane, a 17-year-old who worked as an usherette at his Friday-night occult sessions. They had a daughter, Zeena. From 1960 to 1966 he developed his elitist satanic philosophy. He viewed the Devil as a dark force hidden in nature, ruling earthly affairs. Man's true nature, he claimed, is one of lust, pride, hedonism and willfulness, attributes that enable the advancement of civilization. Flesh should not be denied but celebrated. Individuals who stand in the way of achieving what one wants should be cursed (see CURSES).

On WALPURGISNACHT (April 30) in 1966, LaVey shaved his head and announced the founding of the Church of Satan. He shrewdly recognized the shock value of using the term *church* for worshiping the Devil and recognized people's innate need for ritual, ceremony and pageantry. He performed satanic baptisms, weddings and funerals, all of which received widespread media coverage. He used a nude woman (partially covered by a leopard skin) as an altar. His wife, Diane, became high priestess of the Church. He baptized Zeena. Karla began giving lectures on Satanism at universities and colleges.

LaVey preached antiestablishmentarianism, self-indulgence and all forms of gratification and vengeance. Enemies were to be hated and smashed. Sex was exalted. He opposed the use of drugs, saying they were escapist and unnecessary to achieving natural highs. He also deplored the use of black magic in criminal activity. He did not include a Black Mass in his rituals, because he believed the Black Mass to be out of date.

The Church of Satan organized into grottoes. A reversed pentacle containing a goat's head, called the BAPHOMET, was chosen as the symbol. LaVey used Enochian as the magical language for rituals and espoused the Enochian Keys used by Crowley (see ENOCHIAN MAGIC).

The Church attracted an international following. Most were middle-class and included occultists, thrill seekers, the curious, racists and political right-wingers. At its peak, it was said to have about 25,000 members (years later, ex-members said the figures were exaggerated). Followers included celebrities, among them Jayne Mansfield, who became an active member.

Mansfield's involvement with LaVey deeply disturbed Sam Brody, Mansfield's attorney and lover. Brody feared word would leak out to the press and that she would be damaged by negative publicity. In 1967 Brody attempted to scare off LaVey by threatening to publish stories about him that would label him a fraud. LaVey responded by putting a curse on the lawyer, who suffered a minor car accident shortly thereafter. LaVey also warned Mansfield that she should sever her relationship with Brody.

In June 1967 LaVey reportedly told Mansfield he had a premonition that Brody would be involved in another car accident, and if Jayne were with him, she might be injured. She dismissed the warning. On June 29 she was riding with Brody in his car when it collided with a truck. Both she and Brody were killed, Mansfield by decapitation.

Film director Roman Polanski hired LaVey for his film version of Ira Levin's novel of Devil-worshippers, ROSEMARY'S BABY, released in 1968. LaVey portrayed Satan and advised Polanski on satanic ritual details.

LaVey turned much of his organizational activities over to others in the Church and began writing books. *The Satanic Bible* was published in 1969, followed by *The Satanic Rituals* in 1972. A third book, *The Compleat Witch*, was published in Europe.

In 1975 the Church suffered a serious loss of members, who left to form a new satanic organization, the Temple of Set. In the mid-1970s the Church of Satan reorganized as a secret society and dissolved its grottoes. The headquarters remain in San Francisco. LaVey is no longer active. Membership began to rise again in the 1980s.

The Temple of Set also is based in San Francisco and had several hundred members as of the mid-1980s. Key founders were Michael A. Aquino, Lilith Sinclair (Aquino's wife) and Betty Ford (not the former First Lady, wife of President Gerald Ford). It is an initiatory society devoted to the Egyptian god Set (also known as Seth), whom members do not consider evil but merely the prototype of Satan. According to the Temple, Set has, over the millennia, altered human genetics in order to create people of superior intelligence for the next level of evolution. Three major phases have occurred: the first in 1904, when Crowley received *The Book of the Law;* the second in 1966, when the Church of Satan was formed; and the third in 1975, when the Temple of Set was formed.

In his writings, Aquino has prophesied an apocalypse in which only the "elect," or members of the Temple of Set, will survive. Aquino, a lieutenant colonel in the U.S. Army Reserve, has an interest in Nazi Pagan rituals practiced during World War II but says he does not sympathize with Nazi politics.

A number of other satanic groups formed in the United States in the 1970s were defunct by the 1980s. Nevertheless, satanic activities remain widespread on both sides of the Atlantic; some experts believe they were on a rise as of the 1980s. The extent of Satanism is impossible to gauge, because of the great secrecy of many organizations. There is evidence of small "family traditions" of Satanism, passed down from one generation to another. Some satanists are associated with neo-Nazi organizations or sex-magic orders. Some satanic cults are alleged to be involved in drug, prostitution and pornography trade and to have real estate holdings. Members are said to include white-collar professionals.

Michelle Remembers (1980), by Michelle Smith and Lawrence Pazder, M.D., recounts the terrors Smith experienced as a child of five in satanic rituals in Victoria, British Columbia, in 1954–55. She said her mother yielded her to satanists, who used her as a living pointer in rituals. She witnessed the ritual killings of animals and infants and was shut in coffins that were put into graves and into which were thrown dead animals. She also watched the cult members attempt to bring to life a white statue of a man with horns. She said she was tricked into defecating on the cross and was asked to renounce God. Smith describes instances in which, during rituals, she witnessed the Devil emerge from the fire, a man-animal with a whipping, snakelike tail that struck her on the neck and seared her flesh. Fire shot from his fingertips and filled his mouth. He had clawlike hands, steaming nostrils and odd toenails. His shape constantly changed, and he appeared to be a part of the fire. Smith was able to purge her memories in psychiatric therapy at age 28.

Perhaps most dangerous of all are small cults whose members call themselves satanists and practice ritual murder and animal mutilation. Such groups are said to kidnap runaway children and the homeless and use them as sacrificial victims. Ex-satanic cult members have reported gruesome rituals in which hearts are cut out of living victims. Others report that victims are sexually abused before being killed; then their blood is drunk and their flesh is eaten. Women "breeders" produce babies for the "ultimate" and "ideal" human sacrifice. Former breeders report witnessing their babies skinned alive, eaten, burned, poured in concrete, and cut up and thrown in the ocean. Ritual tools are made from their bones.

In 1985 a 10-year-old boy in Bakersfield, California, said he and about two dozen other children were taken to a "bad church" by some 40 adults, who took off their clothes while chanting prayers to Satan. The children were forced to throw knives at a living baby, which was killed and dismembered. The children were then forced to drink its blood. Then, the boy said, the adults molested the children. Similar cases were reported throughout California, but authorities found little evidence to support the claims. In 1987 a report issued by the Alberta Royal Canadian Mounted Police suggested that Satanism might be related to unsolved cases of missing children. Satanists also are believed to be responsible for some grave desecrations and robbings.

Satanism has been linked to certain oppressive heavy-metal rock music and teenage suicides and murders. Some troubled teens apparently turn to Satanism when they feel powerless and abandoned by their families, the world and God. They join cults that encourage, or require, them to carry out acts of violence to prove their homage to Satan. Drug abuse is common. The ritual violence gives them a sense of power.

Author Maury Terry, in *The Ultimate Evil* (1987), asserts that David Berkowitz, the convicted "Son of Sam" killer who terrorized New York neighborhoods in the late 1970s, was a member of a satanic cult that operates in Westchester County and planned the Son of Sam murders. Terry states the cult is linked to a network of cults across the country, with a primary headquarters near Los Angeles, and that Charles Manson may also have been involved with it. The cult reportedly is an offshoot of a satanic group in England.

Neo-Pagan Witches and neo-Pagans often are wrongly blamed for satanic activities. Several organizations carry on public relations and education programs for the media and members of the law-enforcement community to counteract such accusations.

Satanic religious organizations, such as the Church of Satan and Temple of Set, say they do not condone the violent blood sacrifices of the cults and are not associated with them. According to Aquino, the Temple of Set emphasizes "rational self interest" and taking responsibility for one's own intellectual and ethical decisions.

Sator square   See AMULETS.

School of Wicca   See CHURCH AND SCHOOL OF WICCA.

Score, John (d. 1979)   Also known as M, John Score was an influential figure in Britain during the formative years of the re-emergence of Paganism (see NEO-PAGANISM) and WITCHCRAFT, the latter of which Score preferred to call the Old Religion of Wisecraft.

Score, of Wimborne, Dorset, served in the Royal Air Force from 1931 to 1946, retiring with the rank of Flight Lieutenant (Signals). In 1948 he organized and directed the telecommunications for the Olympic Games, held in London that year, work that earned him a bronze medallion.

In 1968 he became editor of *The Wiccan.* Under his direction, *The Wiccan* rose to prominence in both Britain and the United States as one of the leading Pagan journals. With a group of persons from Britain and America, Score played a role in the formation of the PAGAN WAY in America. In 1971 he was a key founder of the Pagan Front in Britain, which evolved separately from the American group, later changing its name to the PAGAN FEDERATION. *The Wiccan* became the newsletter of the Pagan Front/Federation.

In establishing the Pagan Front, Score sought to defend the religious freedom of all Pagans and to protect Paganism from undesirable exploitation and the infiltration of black-MAGIC elements. To these ends, he was often controversial.

Throughout his life, Score maintained a deep interest in the occult and what he called the Ancient Wisdom. He delved into all forms of natural healing and earned a Naturopathic Doctor degree in the United States. He studied REINCARNATION and experienced memories of his own past lives in ancient Egypt and Atlantis. He also researched ways to use his technical knowledge with help from his spirit guides to develop an instrument for communicating with spirits without the need for a human medium.

His work was done independently of other researchers in what eventually became known as the "electronic voice phenomenon," the recording of spirit voices directly onto magnetic tape. Score believed he achieved some success on his own, but poor health forced him to leave his work incomplete.

Score suffered from ill health through much of his life, particularly in his later years. He died in December 1979, survived by his wife and two sons.

Scot, Michael (ca. 1175–1234)   Reputed Scottish magician whose life is surrounded by as much legend as fact. Scot was respected as a mathematician, physician, astrologer and scholar. He was outspoken in his condemnation of MAGIC and NECROMANCY, yet he seemed to know so much about these subjects that most of his peers considered him both a sorcerer (see SORCERY) and a necromancer. Legends grew up around him, transforming him into a magician with great supernatural powers.

Little is known about Scot's early life, including his exact birthplace. It is believed that he may have come from Balwearie in Fife. His family evidently was affluent, for he studied at Oxford.

After Oxford, Scot traveled to various centers of learning in Europe: the Sorbonne in Paris; Bologna; Palermo; Toledo and Sicily. In Sicily, he was an astrologer to King Ferdinand II, whose court included many adepts in magic, alchemy and the occult arts.

Scot entered the clerical order at some point in his life and enjoyed great esteem in the eyes of the Pope. In 1223 the Archbishopric of Cashel in Ireland became vacant, and the Pope nominated Scot to fill it. He declined because he did not know the Irish language.

In 1230 Scot went to England, where he is erroneously credited with having introduced the works of Aristotle, which he translated.

He wrote extensively, mixing science and the occult. His book on physiognomy, the study of man's face, held that the stars and planets marked life's events upon the face. His book on astronomy included astrological prayers and conjurations (see ASTROLOGY). As was typical of the time, Scot believed in alchemy, DIVINATION and the magical properties of precious STONES and herbs as sciences.

Scot also wrote extensively on magic and necromancy, fully describing practices and rituals. The publication of such magic acts customarily was prohibited out of fear that people would be encouraged to perform them. It was said that Scot performed them himself, disguising his magic rituals as scientific experiments.

According to legend, Scot commanded a retinue of FAMILIARS, which he dispatched to raid the kitchens of the Pope and French and Spanish royalty, and transport their food back to him by air (see FLYING). He also was said to ride through the sky on a demonic horse; to sail the seas in a demonic ship; and to ride on the back of some fantastical sea beast. He supposedly could make the BELLS of Notre Dame ring with a wave of his magic wand.

The DEVIL was said to help Scot in his philanthrophic undertakings, such as the building of a road in Scotland within a single night.

A recipe for making GOLD that is attributed to Scot calls for "the BLOOD of a ruddy man and the blood of a red owl," mixed with saffron, alum, URINE and cucumber juice.

Dante called Scot a fraud and placed him in eternal torment in the eighth circle of the *Inferno*. He is said to be buried in Melrose Abbey in Scotland. According to legend, a "wondrous light" burns within his tomb to chase away evil spirits and will continue to burn until the day of doom.

Scot, Reginald (ca. 1538–1599)

During the darkest days of the witch persecutions, Reginald Scot was among the few voices of reason to be heard. In 1584 he self-published a massive book, *The Discoverie of Witchcraft*, in which he refuted many of the beliefs concerning the power of WITCHES and denounced their persecution as the "extreme and intolerable tyranny" of the Inquisition (see WITCHCRAFT).

Reginald Scot was drawn to the subject of witchcraft not by profession—he was not a judge, scholar or demonologist—but by his own sense of personal outrage at the TORTURE and execution of people he considered to be innocent of any wrongdoing. In the 1886 edition of *Discoverie*, Dr. Brinsley Nicholson writes in the introduction that Scot saw himself

> . . . engaged in a righteous work, that of rescuing feeble and ignorant, though it may be too pretentious and shrewish, old women from false charges and a violent death, and in a noble work endeavoring to stem the torrent of superstition and cruelty which was then beginning to overflow the land.

Scot was born to the genteel family of Sir John Scot near Smeeth in Kent, in or around 1538. He was sent to Oxford at age 17 but left school without earning a degree and returned to the family lands. He was thoughtful, bright and reflective, and he enjoyed studying "obscure authors that had by the generality of Scholars been neglected," according to Nicholson. He worked for a time as a subsidies collector for the government, served a year in Parliament and tended to hop gardening, which was the subject of his first book, *The Hop Garden*, published in 1574.

He married in 1558, but his wife, Jane, died and left him childless. A second marriage also yielded no children. Scot was supported by his cousin, Sir Thomas Scot, whose estate he managed.

In composing *Discoverie*, Scot drew upon his knowledge of superstition in rural life, the law and literature. He also drew upon the writings of numerous scholars, theologians and experts in various fields, even those who disagreed with his own views. He was heavily influenced by the writings of JOHANN WEYER, a German physician who opposed the witch-hunts.

Scot's book became a compendium of the beliefs of the day, a classic in witchcraft literature, covering such topics as ghosts (see GHOSTS, HAUNTINGS AND WITCHCRAFT), DEMONIC POSSESSION, CHARMS, OMENS, DIVINATION, FAIRIES, SPELLS, MAGIC, witchcraft itself and the practices of the DEVIL.

Scot defined four basic categories of witches:

1. the falsely accused innocent;
2. the deluded and crazy who convinced themselves they were in a pact with Satan;
3. the true, malevolent witch who harmed by poisoning but not by supernatural power; and
4. imposters who collected fees for false spells, cures and prophecies.

Scot allowed that the last two categories were those that the Bible had said should not be suffered to live. But he resolutely denied that any witch derived supernatural power from the Devil, whom he said had no physical power of his own.

Scot also maintained, among his various arguments, that the manifestations of spirits were delusions due to mental disturbances in the beholder and that the incubus was a natural disease. He denounced the Pope, who "canonized the rich for saints and banneth the poor for witches."

He included his own beliefs, such as the healing powers of unicorn horns and precious gems, and the power of a carp's head bone to staunch bleeding.

Scot was not alone in his condemnation of the witch persecutions; his writing was part of a continuing skepticism about witchcraft that persisted in England. *Discoverie* did have a favorable impact upon the clergy in England, but King JAMES I was violently opposed to it. He ordered copies burned and wrote his own refutation, *Daemonologie*.

See also WITCH OF ENDOR.

scrying

The ancient art of clairvoyance achieved by concentrating upon an object—usually one with a shiny surface—until visions appear. Magicians (see MAGIC) and WITCHES of all ages have practiced scrying.

The stereotypical version is the Gypsy woman fortune-teller, who gazes into a crystal ball in a dark room and sees her client's future (see GYPSIES).

The term *scrying* comes from the English word *descry*, which means "to make out dimly" or "to reveal." The services of a scryer typically are sought for predictions of the future, answers to questions, solutions to problems and help in finding lost objects and in identifying or tracking down criminals. In the Middle Ages, a typical scryer was a wise woman or wise man—perhaps also called a witch—who was naturally gifted with second sight.

Scrying is not limited to crystal balls but includes virtually any smooth and shiny object that makes a good speculum. Many early scryers simply gazed into the still water of a lake or pond at night. Most scryers use objects with reflective surfaces, such as mirrors, polished STONES or metals and bowls of liquid. Egyptian scryers have used ink, BLOOD and other dark liquids for centuries. In the 16th century, NOSTRADAMUS used bowls of water to see the visions from which he produced his famous prophecies. JOHN DEE, the royal court magician in 16th-century England, used a crystal egg and a piece of obsidian said to have been brought from Mexico by Cortés. Like many other magicians, ALEISTER CROWLEY used a precious gem for scrying. Crowley's speculum was a topaz set in a wooden cross of six squares, painted vermilion.

Few witches throughout history have used crystal balls, which are very heavy and expensive. In England, glass-ball fishing floats are commonly used, as are WITCH BALLS, colored glass balls intended to be hung in homes to keep out witches and the EVIL EYE. The favored speculum is the magic MIRROR, preferably one with a concave side painted black. Witches may make magic mirrors themselves, painting and decorating them with magic SIGILS during the waxing of the moon and consecrating them in rituals like other working tools (see WITCHES' TOOLS). GERALD B. GARDNER practiced scrying with an old picture frame he found in a London junk shop. The glass was slightly curved and had been coated gray-black on the concave side.

Another scrying tool used by witches is a CAULDRON painted black on the inside. The witch fills the cauldron with water and drops in a silver coin to represent the moon in the night sky.

As in other magic work, witches scry within a MAGIC CIRCLE. The best results are obtained at night, when the reception of psychic vibrations is believed to be clearer. Methods vary, but after a period of concentration upon the speculum, the scryer either sees visions upon its surface or receives mental images and impressions. Sometimes the visions are symbolic and must be interpreted. Practice is necessary to learn the meanings behind the symbols seen.

See also DIVINATION.

sea witches The sailing trade in Britain has been steeped for centuries in folklore, including belief in sea WITCHES, who allegedly have the power to control a man's fate out on the waves. Sea witches are said to lurk up and down the coast, ready to curse ships and cause them to wreck upon the rocks or founder in a storm. Some sea witches are phantoms, the ghosts of dead witches (see GHOSTS, HAUNTINGS AND WITCHCRAFT). According to legend, Sir Francis Drake sold his soul to the DEVIL in order to become a skilled seaman and admiral. The Devil sent Drake phantom sea witches, who helped him raise a storm at sea and defeat the Spanish Armada in 1588 (see STORM RAISING). The witches are still said to haunt the land near where the battle took place: Devil's Point, which overlooks Devonport.

Seal of Solomon (hexagram) Also called the *Shield of David* and, in more recent times, the *Star of David*, this symbol is a six-sided star with powerful amuletic and talismanic properties (see AMULETS; TALISMANS). It appeared as early as the Bronze Age as a decoration on lamps, seals and artifacts, and on friezes along with pentacles (see PENTACLE AND PENTAGRAM) and SWASTIKAS. In Arabic legend, the hex-

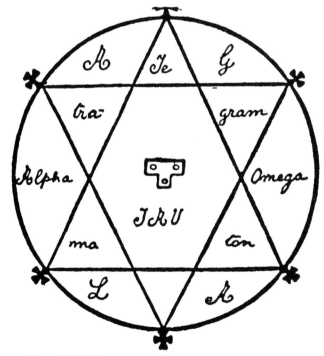

Doble seal of Solomon

agram and the real name of God were etched on the magic ring of King Solomon, which enabled him to command an army of demons, the DJINN.

As an amulet, the Seal of Solomon protects against the EVIL EYE and LILITH, the terrible Hebrew demon who steals children during the night. The seal was not widely used in amulets until the early Middle Ages, when it appeared in Kabbalistic prescriptions for inscribed amulets, medallions or pieces of parchment bearing the hexagram and various inscriptions, SPELLS or PRAYERS (see KABBALAH). In the late Middle Ages, the symbol was popular as an amulet against fire.

In alchemy, the seal became the symbol of the Philosopher's Stone, because it joined the symbol of fire, an upright triangle, with the symbol of water, an inverted triangle.

The most important use of the Seal of Solomon is in MAGIC, as a talisman to control the DEMONS and spirits conjured by the magician. The magicians' GRIMOIRES, or handbooks, give instructions for drawing the Seal of Solomon inside or outside the MAGIC CIRCLE. The Tetragrammaton, or name of God, was usually inscribed in the middle of the symbol (see NAMES OF POWER).

The magician was to follow strict instructions for creating the seal. According to *The Magus* (1801) by FRANCIS BARRETT, it was to be made in the day and hour of Mercury upon virgin kidskin parchment or pure white paper, with the letters written in GOLD. The magician then had to consecrate it and sprinkle it with holy water.

Selene   A Greek goddess of the MOON, Selene is a winged, silvery woman who presides over night skies, sailing along in her chariot pulled by shining, winged white horses, cows or bulls (whose horns represent the crescent moon). Sometimes she sits astride a bull, horse or mule. In WITCHCRAFT, Selene is one aspect of the Triple Goddess, along with DIANA (Artemis) and HECATE.

Selene's role in Greek mythology is minor. Generally, she is believed to be the daughter of Theia and Hyperion. In other myths she is the daughter of Theia and Helios, the sun god, and is the sister of Phoebus Apollo, who succeeded Helios as the sun deity. Other names for Selene include Phoebe and Mene, the latter of which refers to her changing shape during the course of the lunar month.

The Greeks worshiped Selene at new and full moons, believing her to influence the fecundity of all life forms on earth. During the Hellenistic era, Selene (the moon) was the destination of the souls of the dead.

The most significant myth of Selene is that of her fascination with her lover, Endymion, a magnificent youth who is variously recorded as a king, hunter and shepherd. In the version recorded by Theocritus, a 3rd-century poet, Endymion falls asleep on Mount Latmus and is observed by Selene, who falls in love with his beauty. She comes down from the sky and kisses him, bewitching him into immortal, deathless sleep so that she can visit him night after night into eternity. In other versions, Endymion wakes and is equally enchanted with Selene. He begs Zeus to grant him immortality so that he can continue to love Selene, and Zeus does so on the condition that Endymion remain asleep forever.

Selene has a more important role as an aspect of the Triple Goddess in neo-Pagan WITCHCRAFT. She presides over the full moon, a seven-day period that lasts from three days before fullness to three days after, when certain kinds of MAGIC are at their greatest strength. It is Selene's aspect that is invoked in the DRAWING DOWN THE MOON ritual. WITCHES sometimes call upon her in magic related to finding solutions to problems.

See also GODDESS.

self-blessing   In feminist or Dianic WICCA, the self-blessing ritual provides a Witch with an opportunity to affirm herself, her power as a woman and Witch, to recognize the GODDESS within her and to seek to improve her life (see WITCHES). It is a recognition of a woman's ties to the MOON and its natural influence upon her cycle of ovulation and menstruation. Self-blessings are timed to phases of the moon. The new moon is a time for beginnings, for clearing the body and meditating upon the chakras, whirlpools of energy connected to the body which are said to absorb a life energy that exists in the universe. The full moon is a time for giving thanks for one's bounties and for making affirmations. The dark of the moon is a time for banishing the unwanted and negative. Self-blessings may be done alone or with a group of close friends. The ritual is preceded by a bath enhanced with herbs, candlelight and incense, then is performed skyclad (nude) before a Craft altar (see CANDLES; ALTAR).

sending   Sorcerers in many cultures send animals, birds, insects, spirits, animated objects and allegedly even bewitched corpses to carry out CURSES—usually of death—against victims (see SORCERY). The animal may be the sorcerer's own familiar (see FAMILIARS) or a creature suited to the curse. Navajo and Hindu sorcerers often use dogs, but if the curse calls for destroying crops, they will send grasshoppers, locusts, caterpillars and other insects. The Chippewa lay a curse of starvation by stuffing an owl skin with magical substances and causing it to fly to the victim's home. Shamans send familiars—usually in the form of an animal or bird—out to battle for them, but if the familiar dies, so does the shaman (see SHAMANISM). New Guinea sorcerers favor snakes and crocodiles for sending, while in Malay, the familiar is usually an owl or badger passed down from generation to generation. New Guinea sorcerers also send disease-causing objects, such as pieces of magical bone and coral, to lodge in bodies. In Africa, the Kaguru witches send anteaters to burrow under the walls of their victims' huts, and the Gisu send rats in pairs to collect hair and nail clippings of victims for use in black-magic spells (see AFRICAN WITCHCRAFT; HAIR AND NAILS).

Spirits dispatched on magical errands may be DEMONS or entities summoned by the sorcerer, or they may be artificial ELEMENTALS, also called *thoughtforms*, created by MAGIC. Rather than relying on familiars, the sorcerer may send his or her own *fetch*, or astral body, which is projected out from the physical body.

The Zulus' familiars are said to be corpses dug up and reanimated with magic; they are sent out on night errands to scare travelers with their shrieking and pranks. Corpses also are sent in VODOUN, with an invocation to St. Expedit, whose image is placed upside-down on the altar:

> Almighty God, my Father, come and find (name) that he may be disappeared before me like the thunder and lightning. Saint Expedit . . . I call on you and take you as my patron from today, I am sending you to find (name); rid me of . . . his head, rid me of his memory . . . of all my enemies, visible and invisible, bring down on them thunder and lightning. In thine honour Saint Expedit, three Paters.

Sending is most common among tribal societies of the Pacific islands, Africa, Siberia and North America but also is known among the folk witches of Scandinavia, Iceland and the Baltic countries. In European and English lore, WITCHES were believed to send their familiars, usually CATS, dogs, TOADS, HARES or OWLS, to carry out evil spells against their neighbors.

seventh son of a seventh son   Seven is the most mystical and magical of numbers, and in the lore of folk MAGIC, the seventh son of a seventh son is believed to be born with formidable magical and HEALING powers: he is clairvoyant, capable of casting powerful SPELLS, and possesses the ability to heal by a laying on of hands.

The Pennsylvania Dutch hold in high regard the seventh son of a seventh son who is born into a family of WITCHES or *brauchers*: his spells are considered more powerful than those of other witches and more difficult to break (see POWWOWING).

The seventh daughter of a seventh daughter is accorded no comparable prestige, however, except among the GYPSIES, who believe she can always predict the future accurately.

shadows, book of   See BOOK OF SHADOWS.

shamanism   Perhaps the oldest system of HEALING in the world, shamanism is prevalent in tribal cultures which, though isolated from one another, have developed beliefs and techniques with startling similarities. The shaman is an individual who enters an ecstatic altered state of consciousness, which enables him to communicate with guardian and helping spirits and draw upon sources of enormous power. The primary purpose of shamanism is the healing of body and mind. It also is used for DIVINATION and to ensure good hunts and prosperity for a tribe or village.

Shamanism is a complex phenomenon and is often erroneously equated with MAGIC, SORCERY and WITCHCRAFT. An ecstatic trance, communication with spirits or the ability to heal or divine do not necessarily make a shaman.

According to archaeological and ethnological evidence, shamanism has been practiced for some 20,000 to 30,000 years. It may be much older, perhaps as old as the human race. It is found all over the world, including very remote portions of the Americas, Siberia and Asia, Australia, northern Europe and Africa. According to some modern theories, the Celts and DRUIDS may have practiced a form of shamanism, which provided a source for the development of European sorcery and witchcraft.

Shamanic systems vary greatly, but there are basic similarities in most systems. The shaman must function comfortably in two realities; the ordinary reality of the everyday, waking world, and the nonordinary reality of the shamanic state of consciousness. The nonordinary reality is attained in a trance, which varies from very light to deep coma and enables the shaman to see and do things that are impossible in ordinary reality. Once in trance, the shaman enters the lowerworld by slipping into a hole or opening in the earth. In the lowerworld, he sees the cause of disease in a patient and knows its cure, and sees his guardian spirit and spirit helpers. He can shape-shift into these spirits and fly through the air (see METAMORPHOSIS). He performs his cures and can see into the future. When his shamanic work is done, he re-emerges from the lowerworld back into ordinary reality. Shamans are also said to ascend to the sky in spirit boats or astride the spirits of sacrificed horses.

The nonordinary reality is as real to the shaman as is the ordinary reality. The things he sees are not hallucinations but are externalized. The shamanic state of consciousness is induced through drumming, rattling and dancing or, in some societies, by ingesting hallucinogens.

Shamans tend to be men, though women also can become shamans; some women shamans are extraordinarily powerful. In some cultures, shamans are involuntarily chosen by the spirits; they realize their calling in a transformational experience, often a serious illness that brings them close to death and is self-cured. In other cultures, persons with natural shamanic gifts are selected at a young age, trained and initiated (see INITIATION).

The shaman must obtain a guardian spirit, which is the source of his spiritual powers. The guardian spirit also is called a *power animal, tutelary spirit, totemic animal* or *familiar.* A common method of discovering and connecting with the guardian spirit is the vision quest, a solitary, all-night vigil outdoors. The guardian spirit usually manifests as an animal, bird, fish or reptile but may also appear in human form. It is both beneficent and beneficial and brings to the shaman the powers of an entire species. The shaman invites the guardian spirit into his body; it protects him from illness and from unfriendly forces in the lowerworld. Guardian spirits change over the years as the shaman's needs change.

After a guardian spirit is acquired, healing and divination may be performed. Healing techniques vary. A shaman may collect spirit helpers, which are the causes and cures of illness. Spirit helpers are represented by plants, insects, small objects, worms and the like. When the shaman sees, in trance, the cause of an illness, he places one of these objects in the back of his mouth and one in the front. He then begins to suck the illness out of the body of the patient. The energy that causes the illness is absorbed by the spirit helpers in his mouth who protect the shaman from absorbing the illness himself. The helper in the back of the mouth acts as a backup, in case the illness gets past the helper in front.

In other techniques, the shaman descends to the lowerworld, or the realm of the dead, to bring back the soul of a patient or to retrieve a patient's guardian spirit. Some shamans exorcise disease-causing spirits in séancelike procedures or by invoking or cajoling them to leave the patient.

Western interest in shamanism has been rising since 1951, when Mircea Eliade published his landmark study, *Shamanism.* An increasing amount of literature has been written since about shamanic systems and the uses of hallucinogenic drugs. (*Note:* not all shamanic systems use psychedelics.) Since the 1970s many neo-Pagan Witches and neo-Pagans have blended shamanic techniques with their religious and magical ceremonies. One of the earliest neo-Pagan churches to do so was the Church of Seven Arrows, of Wheatridge, Colorado, founded in 1975 as a Universal Life Church congregation with a shamanic tradition. The CHURCH OF ALL WORLDS, of Ukiah, California, has developed its own methods of transcendence through drumming, chanting and dancing, fasting and vision quests and the acquiring of totemic spirits.

See also CHANTING; WICCAN SHAMANISM.

shamrock The three-leafed clover—the national emblem of Ireland and symbol of St. Patrick's Day (March 17)—is an ancient sacred symbol associated with the sun. According to legend, St. Patrick used the shamrock to explain the Holy Trinity to the Celts. However, the clover has much older pagan associations. It was worshipped by the mythical Tuatha de Danaan (see FAIRIES); to the Irish DRUIDS, it symbolized the spring equinox. The shamrock is associated with the Celtic sun wheel, used in spring and summer SABBATS. As a trefoil, it is associated with the magical number three, the Triple Goddess and the three-leaved wand of HERMES. ISIS and OSIRIS wore shamrocks on their heads; at the moment of Osiris's death, the shamrock fell off his head.

The shamrock appears in Christian art and symbolism. Medieval artists portrayed angels presenting the shamrock to the Virgin Mary. It became the badge of the Order of St. Patrick with the order's founding in 1783 and became the Irish national symbol in 1801.

Several types of plants produce the three-leafed clover, including the shamrock, sour trefoil and wood sorrels, and opinions vary as to which is the true shamrock. In Scottish herbal lore, shamrocks have pain-relieving properties and must be gathered in silence with the left hand. Wood sorrel is used in herbal remedies as a diuretic, for kidney and bladder problems, although excessive doses can cause kidney failure, hemorrhaging and other problems. Sorrel also is used by herbalists in lotions for skin infections. A vase of fresh wood sorrel placed in a sickroom is believed to have restorative powers for the patient.

shape-shifting See METAMORPHOSIS.

Sheila-na-Gig A Celtic fertility-goddess figure that once adorned all Irish, and some British, church doorways as an amulet (see AMULETS). The Sheila-na-Gig, or "merry Sheila," is a carving of a naked woman squatting with her genitals displayed. Sometimes her mouth is open, which represents the birth ecstasy. Her vulva is in the shape of the *vesica piscis*, or "vessel of the fish," a sacred geometric shape used by the ancient Egyptians in construction of the pyramids, by the ancient builders of various megalithic sites and by the Masons. The *vesica piscis* is an oval formed by two intersecting, equal circles. It represents equilibrium between equal forces and the interpenetration of heaven and earth, and spirit and matter. In its association with the vulva, it is also a symbol of creation.

The Sheila-na-Gig was carved over all Irish church doors before the 16th century and is found on some British doorways as well. Considering Christianity's historically negative attitude toward sex and women, female genitalia seem a curious symbol for a church doorway. However, the Sheila-na-Gig is indicative of the way Christianity and paganism coexisted for quite some time. Representations of female genitalia were widely used by the Celts as doorway amulets. Most of the Sheila-na-Gigs were taken down by the Victorians in the 19th century.

The Sheila-na-Gig is similar to the *Mahadevi*, or Mother Goddess, figure worshipped in Tantra as creatrix of all things and to the death-goddess aspect of the Hindu KALI. A modern survivor of the Sheila-na-Gig is the HORSESHOE, a female symbol commonly used as an amulet against bewitchment and bad luck.

Shuck, Black   See BLACK SHUCK.

Shuck, Old   See BLACK SHUCK.

sigils   In Western MAGIC, symbols linked to sets of ideas, by which spirits or deities may be called into awareness and controlled. The term comes from the Latin *sigillum*, which means "seal." A sigil in and of itself does not call forth spirits but serves as a physical focus through which the magician achieves a desired state of mind. Sigils represent the secret names of spirits and deities, which reveal themselves differently to each magic practitioner. Once a spirit or deity has been summoned in magic, it may be controlled, if necessary, by subjecting its sigil to fire or thrusts with the magical sword. Sigils also represent complex concepts. The pentacle (see PENTACLE AND PENTAGRAM) is the most powerful sigil for neo-Pagan WITCHCRAFT. Sigils are also used as identifying logos of organizations. An individual may adopt a sigil, such as a runic or Theban letter (see RUNES), to inscribe on magical tools (see WITCHES' TOOLS). Sigils may serve as AMULETS, TALISMANS or meditational tools.

Sigils may be geometric shapes, astrological signs, alchemical symbols, CROSSES and signs associated with deities. The best sigils are created through intuition and inspiration, by meditating or gazing into a crystal or smoke patterns (see SCRYING). Another technique is to ask the spirits for a sigil by placing a plate of polished SILVER, BRASS, GOLD, glass or other shiny material on the altar (see ALTARS). It is said

A Table, shewing the names of the Angels governing the 7 days of the week, with their Sigils, Planets, Signs, &c.

Sunday	Monday	Tuesday	Wednesday	Thursday	Friday	Saturday
Michael	Gabriel	Camael	Raphael	Sachiel	Anael	Caffiel
name of the 4.th Heaven	name of the 1.st Heaven	name of the 5.th Heaven	name of the 2.d Heaven	name of the 6.th Heaven	name of the 3.d Heaven	the Angels ruling above the 6.th Heaven
Machen.	Shamain.	Machon.	Raquie.	Zebul.	Sagun.	

Sigils of the angels of the week, in column below names (Francis Barrett, *The Magus*, 1801)

that the deities or spirits will inscribe a sigil upon the surface in dew. The sigil is then magically imbued with power.

silver   The favored metal of WITCHES for its associations with the GODDESS, moon MAGIC, the female principle and the Goddess in winter. Silver reputedly possesses protective powers against negative influences and evil spirits and has been used since ancient times for AMULETS. The metal also is said to enhance psychic faculties. Some Witches prefer to wear all silver JEWELRY; many who wear GOLD also wear at least one piece of silver at the same time.

Silver, which appears in nature in a pure state and is an excellent conductor of electromagnetic energy, has always been valued in various societies and has long been used for magical and sacred purposes. The ancient Egyptians revered silver more than gold, for silver is not found in Egypt. The god Ra was said to have bones of silver. Egyptians used the metal to make scarabs, RINGS and other objects used in magical SPELLS.

Silver has always been associated with the MOON. The Incas considered silver to be a divine quality rather than a metal substance. They associated silver with the luster of moonlight and called it the tears of the moon. In alchemy, the symbol of silver is a crescent moon; alchemists called the metal Luna or DIANA, after the Roman goddess of the moon. In China, the moon is called the silver candle and the Milky Way is called the silver river.

Silver nails in a coffin prevent the spirit of the corpse from escaping. Silver amulets repel evil spirts from persons, houses and buildings. In the folklore of parts of France, couples who are going to be married encircle themselves in a silver chain in order to avoid being bewitched en route to the church.

In the folklore of other cultures, silver bullets are required to kill vampires, werewolves, ghosts, sorcerers, witches, giants and persons who lead charmed lives.

Simon Magus (1st century)   Simon the Magician, or Simon the Sorcerer, as he was sometimes called, was a Gnostic wonder-worker who became the prototype of a heretic and black magician (see MAGIC; SORCERY). He came from Samaria, where he was worshipped as a god for his occult powers, which may have included mediumistic ability. He was attracted to Christianity and the miracles associated with it and was converted to the faith by Philip the Deacon, whose magic impressed Simon.

According to Acts 8:9–24, the apostles Peter and John were sent to Samaria to deliver the Holy Spirit into the population by a laying on of hands. When

Simon witnessed their supernatural work, he offered the apostles money: "Give me this power, that any one on whom I lay my hands shall receive the Holy Spirit." The apostles, angry that Simon should expect to buy holy power, had him thrown out of the church. Peter told him, "Your silver perish with you, because you thought you could obtain the gift of God with money." Simon's name gave rise to the term *simony*, the sin of buying or selling a church office.

Undaunted, Simon traveled to Rome, where he impressed people with his occult ability, and then to Egypt, where he allegedly learned such magical skills as making himself invisible, levitating himself and transforming himself into a animal (see LEVITATION; METAMORPHOSIS). He is said to have created a man out of thin air and then boasted that he was part of the Holy Trinity. He conjured a woman he said was Helen of Troy, but his critics claimed the woman was a prostitute from Tyre. Simon said he was God and Helen was his "Thought of God."

In Rome again, Simon impressed Nero and was named court magician. His feats, which also included the moving of heavy furniture without touching it (psychokinesis) and passing through fire unharmed, probably were illusions or the result of hypnosis. He convinced one of Nero's guards that he had cut off his own head, when actually he had decapitated a ram. Thus, he claimed to Nero that he had risen from the dead.

Peter came to Rome to challenge Simon and expose him as a fraud. Simon conjured huge dogs and ordered them to attack Peter and tear him to shreds; Peter made the dogs vanish by holding out a loaf of holy bread. Simon said he would offer ultimate proof of his ability by ascending bodily into heaven. He went to the top of the Roman forum and levitated. Peter fell to his knees and prayed to God to stop the deception, whereupon Simon crashed to earth, broke both legs and died.

Simon is credited with founding a Gnostic sect that became known as the Simonians. The Simonians recognized Simon as the first God, sometimes worshipped as Zeus, and his consort Helen as the goddess Athena. Gnostics, who believed that spirit was good, matter was evil, and salvation lay in the attainment of esoteric knowledge (sophia), were branded heretics by the Roman Catholic Church. Most of their records were destroyed.

six-six-six (666)   The number of "the Beast," or Antichrist, according to the book of Revelations in the Bible. It remains associated with the DEVIL and SATANISM but has nothing to do with neo-Pagan WITCHCRAFT or NEO-PAGANISM.

Revelations was authored by John the prophet in

the first century and was based upon a series of remarkable visions he had on the island of Patmos, near Asia Minor, where he had been exiled for failing to worship the image of Emperor Domitian. In one of John's apocalyptic visions, a beast rose up from the sea. It had seven heads, ten horns and ten crowns; the heads bore the name of blasphemy. One of the heads had been wounded to death but had healed. A voice said, "Let him that hath understanding count the number of the beast: for it is the number of a man; and his number is six hundred threescore and six."

Throughout history, attempts have been made to look for the Beast in names or things that added up to 666. ALEISTER CROWLEY, who believed himself to be the Antichrist, often signed his name as *The Beast 666* or *TO MEGA THERION* which equals "The Great Beast" in Greek, or 666.

Slater, Herman

American Wiccan high priest (see WICCA) and occult-bookstore proprietor and publisher, whose flamboyant style and outspokenness have earned him both admirers and critics. He views his role as "telling the truth about WITCHCRAFT and NEO-PAGANISM within the context of today's life-styles."

A Depression baby, Slater grew up in a lower-middle-class Jewish neighborhood of New York. At an early age, he became aware of anti-Semitism on the part of the Catholic Church, which became one of the influences that led him to Witchcraft. He also was influenced to become politically active after seeing Frank Sinatra portray a politically strong figure in *The House I Live In.*

Slater studied business administration at New York University, liberal arts at Hunter College and traffic management at the Traffic Management Institute in New York. He completed a full course at the United States Navy Personnel School in Bainbridge, Maryland.

From 1958 to 1969 he worked in a series of business jobs in management, traffic expediting and insurance-claims investigation. In 1969 he was forced to quit work because he was suffering from tuberculosis of the bone, which cost him a hip bone and required three years of recuperation.

Slater began experiencing paranormal phenomena, including clairvoyance and a mysterious LEVITATION. The levitation occurred during his recuperation, in which he spent one year in bed in a body cast that weighed 300 pounds. One morning, he awoke and found himself, in his cast, stretched across a chair on the opposite side of the room. His paranormal experiences led him to the Craft, and in 1972 he was initiated (see INITIATION) into the New York Coven

Herman Slater (courtesy Herman Slater)

of Welsh Traditional Witches, of which Ed Buczynski was high priest.

Slater and Buczynski became public advocates for Witchcraft and opened a bookstore in Brooklyn, the Warlock Shop. For several years they published a periodical, *Earth Religion News.* Through an affiliate organization, Friends of the Craft, they presented awards to the Inquisitional Bigot of the Year. In 1972 Slater presented the award to NBC during a guest appearance on the *Today* show, for an episode of *Macmillan and Wife* that had taken Witchcraft rituals and corrupted them into Devil-worship rituals for the plot. The outraged *Today* crew had Slater physically removed from the set.

In 1974 Slater was initiated into the Gardnerian tradition (see GERALD B. GARDNER). He assumed leadership of the COVEN in the late 1970s and moved it and the bookstore to Manhattan. The coven was renamed Earthstar Temple, practicing a blend of Welsh and Gardnerian traditions. The bookstore was renamed the Magickal Childe.

Slater has devoted a great deal of time to educating others about Witchcraft. He is a frequent guest lecturer in area colleges. He stars in his own video, *An Introduction to Witchcraft and Satanism,* in which he appears in his ceremonial robe and antler headdress, along with his familiar (see FAMILIARS), a snake named Herman. In 1987 he began hosting a weekly cable television show aired in Manhattan, *The Magickal Mystery Tour*, which features interviews, rituals, music, occultism and magic instruction. Slater loosely defines it as an "Earth religion 700 Club" because it spreads the word on the Old Religion and asks for donations to continue doing so.

A conservative who opposes drugs, promiscuity and love magic, he is also blunt in his criticism of the actions of fellow Witches and neo-Pagans, such as those who have used Witchcraft as an excuse for drugs and sex—practices that began to wane in the 1980s. He acknowledges that such bluntness has made him unpopular but feels compelled to tell the truth the way he sees it.

Slater is the author of *A Book of Pagan Rituals, The Magickal Formulary* and *The Magickal Formulary II.* He divides his time between Manhattan, where he lives with three dogs, a cat and the snake, and Ft. Lauderdale, Florida. His Craft name is Govannan.

solitary   A neo-Pagan Witch who practices the Craft and worships alone rather than as a member of a COVEN. During the early growth of neo-Pagan WITCHCRAFT (the 1960s into the 1970s), membership in covens was emphasized. To be considered a Witch, one had to be initiated by another Witch, and that usually meant joining a coven (see INITIATION). As Craft traditions changed and became more liberal, it became acceptable to initiate one's self. Some Witches feel initiations are ceremonial only and are not necessary to becoming a Witch. Many solitaries have belonged to various covens and have decided they prefer being alone; others opt to be solitaries to protect their privacy. The number of solitaries is not known, but it is estimated that they comprise most neo-Pagan WITCHES.

Solomon, Seal of   See SEAL OF SOLOMON.

sorcery   The distinction between sorcery and WITCHCRAFT is at best murky. Both have been nearly universal throughout history and have been defined with different shades of meaning. In many cases, the terms *sorcery* and *witchcraft* have been used interchangeably. During the Renaissance witch hysteria in Europe, however, *witchcraft* was regarded as quite different than *sorcery.*

The word *sorcery* comes from the French *sors*, for "spell," and refers to the casting of SPELLS or the use of CHARMS to influence love, fertility, luck, health and wealth. The French word for "witch" is *sorcier.* In many societies, the assumption is made that these spells have an evil purpose and that sorcerers cast

spells against others for whom they have an unjustified hatred. Conversely, sorcery provides protection against other sorcery, and counter-sorcerers, WITCH DOCTORS or medicine men may be sought out to cast protective spells against the evil spells of other sorcerers, or to break evil spells.

Sorcery fulfills various needs in society, such as protecting people and livestock against disaster, outsiders and enemies; redressing wrongs and meting out justice; controlling the environment; and explaining frightening phenomena.

Sorcery is low MAGIC: it is not a set of beliefs, like high magic, but is mechanistic and intuitive. Some societies still make distinctions between sorcery and witchcraft. Many African tribes view witchcraft as thoroughly evil, while sorcery is close to religion. It is benevolent when performed for the good of society, such as protecting a village or tribe from the evil of enemy sorcerers or from natural disasters, but it is evil if performed for the gain of one individual at the expense of another. The Lugbara, however, view sorcery as more evil than witchcraft, for sorcerers use medicines against others, while witches direct only hostile emotions against others (see AFRICAN WITCHCRAFT). The Navajo associate witchcraft with death and the dead and sorcery with enchantment by spells; sorcerers, however, also kill others and participate in witches' SABBATS.

DIVINATION is related to sorcery. In some societies it is viewed as completely separate—performed by oracles, card readers, palm readers and the like—while in others it is considered a form of sorcery and is performed by sorcerers or WITCHES.

Sorcerers, like witches, have long been accused of other evil, offensive behaviors: holding orgiastic nocturnal sabbats, conjuring the dead (see NECROMANCY), shape-shifting (see METAMORPHOSIS), cannibalism, night riding (see NIGHTMARE), owning and having sex with FAMILIARS and vampirism.

Anthropologists have attempted to distinguish sorcery from witchcraft by defining sorcery as harmful magic, usually illegitimate, that is performed by a professional, the sorcerer. The witch, on the other hand, is a person, usually female, who is believed to be inherently evil, born with the power to commit evil against others, and filled with anger and envy. Such a person has some physical characteristic to distinguish her as a witch, such as a mark, a substance within the body or the EVIL EYE. This definition stems from E. Evans-Pritchard, an anthropologist who did one of the first systematic studies of sorcery, among the Zande of Africa, in the early 20th century. The definition does not hold up for sorcery and witchcraft in all societies, and it has no bearing at all upon the definition of Witchcraft held by modern hereditary and neo-Pagan Witches in Western cultures.

In its simplest form, sorcery is magic by the manipulation of natural forces and powers to achieve a desired objective. Neolithic cave paintings depicting rituals for successful hunts give evidence that primitive peoples had a grasp of magic and practiced sorcery. One of the most famous examples is the *Sorcerer of Trois Frère* cave painting in France, a depiction of an antlered half-man half-beast or man in animal costume performing a ritualistic walk or dance. The figure may represent a sorcerer preparing for a hunt or the god spirit of the forests or animals. The ancient Greeks believed that sorcerers called upon *daimones*, intermediary spirits between heaven and earth, to help them in their magic. Originally, *daimones* were neither good nor evil but could be swayed to either purpose (see DEMONS). Demons began to take on the aspects of evil with Plato's pupil, Xenocrates, who believed that the gods embodied good and *daimones* embodied evil.

By the sixth century B.C., sorcery was associated with fraud. As Christianity developed, sorcery became entangled with demonology, the system of demons who served the DEVIL.

European witchcraft grew out of sorcery, the casting of spells and divination. Until the Inquisition, sorcery was considered a civil crime, punishable under civil law. By the 14th century, the Church succeeded in linking sorcery to heresy, making sorcery an ecclesiastical crime. The most odious form of heretical sorcery was witchcraft, the performing of MALEFICIA in service to the Devil. The *MALLEUS MALEFICARUM* (1486), the leading witch-hunter's handbook of the Inquisition, further strengthened the connection between sorcery and heresy and attributed most witchcraft to women.

During the late Middle Ages and Renaissance, the term *sorcerer* was also applied to men of high learning, such as alchemists and physicians, some of whom were believed to derive their knowledge from supernormal sources. Their conjuring of demons for knowledge or riches was not considered the same as a witch's conjuring of demons for *maleficia*. Royalty and popes were reputed to practice sorcery.

The European view of witchcraft as Devil-worship sorcery has lasted to present times and has become firmly ingrained in the Western cultural notion of witchcraft. Modern Witches, who define their Witchcraft as GODDESS worship and benevolent magic for the good of others, have sought to re-educate the public, which has proved to be a difficult task.

See also WIZARDS.

sorrel See SHAMROCK.

Spare, Austin Osman (1886–1956) English magician with a bizarre occult vision, which he expressed in strange and sometimes frightening artwork. His talent for art was widely acknowledged and even called genius. He could have pursued a conventional artist's career but instead chose to devote himself to creating images of DEMONS and spirits raised up from deep levels of consciousness.

The seeds for Spare's offbeat life were sewn early in childhood. Alienated from his mother, he gravitated toward a mysterious old woman named Mrs. Patterson. She claimed to be a hereditary witch (see WITCHES) descended from a line of SALEM WITCHES who escaped execution during the witch trials of 1692—a rather unlikely claim, considering that the Salem incident was a fraud perpetrated by hysterical children. The young Spare referred to her as his "witch-mother."

Mrs. Patterson taught Spare how to visualize and evoke spirits and ELEMENTALS, and how to reify his dream imagery. The witch-mother also initiated Spare in a witches' sabbat. Spare said he attended (see INITIATION; SABBATS).

Spare's strange artwork is best known for its atavisms, the reifying of primal forces from previous existences, drawn from the deepest layers of the human mind. This, too, was credited to his education from Mrs. Patterson. Some of his work appears in two quarterly art-review magazines he edited, *Form* and *Golden Hind*. He wrote three books that were published: *The Book of Pleasure (Self-love)*, *The Psychology of Ecstasy* (1913), and *The Focus of Life* (1921), both of which dealt with his magic system; and *A Book of Automatic Drawing*, published posthumously in 1972.

Spare spent most of his life as a recluse, living in poverty in London. He was a follower of ALEISTER CROWLEY. Remote and detached, he preferred the company of his CATS to that of human beings.

Spee, Friedrich von (1591–1635) German Jesuit and poet who, in the course of serving as confessor to WITCHES during the trials in Würzburg, became revolted by the TORTURE and execution of innocent people. Spee wrote and anonymously published *Cautio Criminalis*, an exposé of the fraud in witch trials, which may have influenced the decline of witch-hunts in subsequent years (see WITCHCRAFT).

Spee was born in Kaiserwerth. He was educated at the Jesuit College in Cologne and entered the order in 1611. Further studies included philosophy in Würzburg and theology in Mainz. In 1624 Spee was sent to Paderborn as a preacher; in 1627 he was sent back to Würzburg, where he worked as a professor.

During the 1620s the witch hysteria was reaching its peak in Germany, especially in the communities of Bamberg, Würzburg, Mainz, Cologne, Baden and Brandenburg. The prince-bishops of Würzburg and Bamberg were particularly zealous about hunting down and burning witches and, encouraged by the Jesuits, they executed about 1,500 persons between them (see BAMBERG WITCHES).

It was Spee's duty to serve as confessor to the condemned in Würzburg. He began his job believing that real witches, servants of the DEVIL, did exist. But in the course of watching one after another victim be condemned with no hope of a fair trial, Spee began to change his views. While he continued to believe that a few witches did exist, he became convinced that none of them had been found in Würzburg. The flimsy evidence and brutal torture sickened him. By the time he was 30, his hair was nearly white—"through grief," he explained, "over the many witches whom I have prepared for death; not one was guilty."

Spee observed that the slightest hint of witchcraft was sufficient to condemn a person to death and that once the accusation was made, there was no hope of escape. If the accused had led an impious life, she was certainly a witch; if she had led a good life, she also was a witch, because witches deceived others by appearing to be virtuous. If the defendant broke down readily under torture, it was proof of witchery; if she didn't, that was proof, too. If she died under torture, it was said that the Devil broke her neck, and that also was proof. Spee said:

> Often I have thought that the only reason why we are not all wizards is due to the fact that we have not all been tortured. And there is truth in what an inquisitor dared to boast lately, that if he could reach the Pope, he would make him confess that he was a wizard.

Spee also was concerned about the ever-widening ripple effects of the trials. Victims were always forced to name accomplices, and Spee feared that, as the trials mounted, "there is nobody in our day, of whatsoever sex, fortune, rank, or dignity, who is safe, if he have but an enemy and slanderer to bring him into suspicion of witchcraft."

In 1631 Spee anonymously published *Cautio Criminalis* ("Precautions for Prosecutors"), in which he savagely attacked the witch-hunters and exposed their methods. He pointed out that there was great incentive among the inquisitors to condemn as many persons as possible, since they were paid a fee per witch burned, plus whatever they could confiscate from the victims' assets. He exposed the claims of confessions without torture as lies; "no torture" in fact meant light torture, and while that in itself was severe, it was nothing compared to the torture that would follow if a victim persisted in a claim of innocence. Spee wrote:

> She can never clear herself. The investigating committee would feel disgraced if it acquitted a woman; once arrested and in chains, she has to be guilty, by fair means or foul.
>
> Meanwhile, ignorant and headstrong priests harass the wretched creature so that, whether truly or not, she will confess herself guilty; unless she does so, they say, she cannot be saved or partake of the sacraments.

Although *Cautio Criminalis* was published anonymously, Spee's authorship was generally known within Jesuit circles, and the book was denounced by many of his order. Despite attempts to suppress it, the book was translated into French, Dutch and Polish and disseminated throughout the Continent. Witch trials continued at a fevered pace for some 30 years after the book's first appearance, then began to abate.

Spee was sent to Treves as a parish priest. He died on August 7, 1635, just 44 years old, a victim of the plague.

spells   A spell is a spoken or written formula that, in an act of MAGIC, is intended to cause or influence a particular course of events. Belief in and use of spells have been universal since ancient times and have been an integral part of religious practices. Methods vary according to culture, but all spell work is based on a ritual of some sort.

Spells are closely related to PRAYER, which is a ritual consisting of a petition to a deity or deities for a desired outcome, and which involves visualization of the goal, statement of desire for the goal and ritualized movements or body positions (e.g., bowing of head, folding or clasping of hands, closing of eyes). Spells are also closely related to various methods of mind power such as "creative visualization," "positive thinking" and "positive imaging," all of which emphasize mental images, identification with mental images, a clear goal, repetition of one's intent to achieve this goal, projection of will and invocation of the aid of spirits, deities or the Divine Force.

Spells may be beneficial or harmful, and they may be worked on man and beast alike. The purposes are limitless and include healing, love, money, success, fertility, longevity, protection from disaster, ill fortune and evil, exorcism of ghosts and spirits (see SPIRIT EXORCISM), victory in battle, truth in DIVINATION, weather control and accomplishment of supernatural feats. When directed against enemies, spells are used to cause illness, destruction, loss of love, impotence, barrenness, failure and even death. One may cast a spell for oneself, or one may direct a spell against another person. A positive spell is a *blessing*. Archaic terms for spells include *bewitchment* and *en-*

chantment; negative spells generally are called *hexes* or *curses.* A *binding* spell is one intended to prevent harm or disaster, or to stop someone from performing a particular act: for example, stopping murder or rape, as in the case of serial criminals, or something as innocuous as stopping the spread of gossip.

In most cultures, WITCHES, sorcerers (see SORCERY), WITCH DOCTORS and other magically empowered persons cast both beneficial and harmful spells, according to need. In neo-Pagan WITCHCRAFT, however, a set of ethics exists that prohibits curses. Neo-Pagan Witches are divided as to the acceptability of binding spells (see WICCAN REDE).

Anatomy of a spell. An act of magic requires a magician, witch or sorcerer; a ritual; and a spell. The spell consists of words or incantations (sometimes called a CHARM or RUNE); the ritual is a set of actions done while the words are being spoken. The ancient Egyptians believed words were so powerful that speaking them would bring about the desired goal. Words and NAMES OF POWER were vital to Egyptian magic and had to be pronounced correctly and with the proper intonation. In Western ceremonial magic, the ultimate name of power is the Tetragrammaton, YHWH (Yahweh), the sacred name of God.

A spell-casting ritual raises power through a combination of visualization, meditation, identification, body movement, incantation (statement of goal), petition to deities and projection of will. The success of a spell rests on the power and will raised and the skill with which they are focused and projected. Words, chants, songs, movements and use of objects such as ritual tools, effigies, poppets, cords, candles or nail clippings facilitate spell casting.

In ancient India, many spells were sung. The bodhisattvas combined reciting spells with meditation. Ancient Jain wizards had numerous spells named after various animals and fowl; presumably by uttering a spell, a wizard could change a person into that animal or bird. The Indians of South America use powerful chants in virtually every magical ritual; certain spells are believed to assume human shape and carry out orders.

In neo-Pagan Witchcraft, there is less emphasis on the precision of words and more emphasis on the power and will that go into the ritual of spell work. Spell casting is done within a MAGIC CIRCLE, or comparable, psychically-protected space, regardless of whether the spell is cast by a SOLITARY or by a COVEN. Most covens work spells as part of their regular meetings, and each coven is likely to have its own techniques. The goal of the spell is stated; some Witches write it down. The act of writing down a desired goal, which is emphasized in positive-thinking techniques, helps to bolster the will to achieve the goal. Any necessary preparations are made for the ritual, such as the lighting of colored CANDLES or the mixing of magical OILS. In a healing or love ritual, an herb-filled poppet, or cloth doll, may be used. The doll is identified with the person who is the object of the spell so that it *becomes* the person during the ritual. To aid the identification, the doll may be marked with the person's name or astrological sign or have attached to it hair clippings from the person. Photographs also are used. If there is no object, a thought-form, or mental image, is created. If the spell is cast by a group, all must agree upon the image and hold it firmly in their minds.

Power is raised in various ways, including CHANTING, dancing, tying KNOTS in cords or hand clapping. Drums and rattles may be used. Witches invite higher forces to work with them in implementing the spell, usually an aspect of the GODDESS or HORNED GOD, and the forces of the ELEMENTS. An aspect of the deity is chosen that best fits the nature of the spell. For example, a spell for money might be addressed to Math, the Welsh Celtic god of wealth and increase.

The words of incantations used in a spell usually are spontaneous and created to serve the purpose at hand; rhyming words or verses help the rhythmic buildup of energy. Numerous spells and charms are contained in many books on Witchcraft, folk magic and magic. While they may be effective, most Witches feel that words composed from the heart are best. The recitation of a chant or charm alone will not cast a spell.

While performing the ritual, the Witch focuses intense concentration and will in achieving the goal, visualizing it and believing it is already accomplished. When the psychic power is at its peak, it is released and directed toward the goal. The spell work ends with a psychic cleanup ritual to banish remnants of psychic energy. The Witch thanks the deity and forces of the elements.

spider In folk MAGIC, a black spider eaten every morning between two slices of buttered bread will endow one with great strength and power. According to lore, medieval WITCHES could raise storms at sea by catching spiders in pots (see STORM RAISING).

Spiders are ingredients in numerous folk remedies around the world. Spiders caught while weaving are considered all-around AMULETS against disease. In England, it is believed that a spider carried in a silk bag around the neck will help ward off contagious diseases. Old ague remedies prescribed ingesting live spiders that were rolled in either butter, molasses or cobwebs.

The weaving of the spider is associated with creativity, imagination, destiny and the waxing and waning of the MOON. In some myths, the moon is portrayed as a spider.

In some cultures, it is considered very unlucky to kill spiders. Tahitians believe spiders are the shadows of gods and take great care never to harm them.

spirit exorcism   In accordance with the idea that possession is not an evil situation but merely a spiritual one, exorcism is not a religious expulsion but a firm good-bye, sending the spirit out of its living host and on to its proper realm (see SPIRIT POSSESSION). Such techniques of persuasion involve the use of psychic force.

Spirit exorcists may perform several "persuasive departures" in one day, depending on the intuitive ability and strength of the exorcist. Working with spirits, the exorcist comes to realize the sensations associated with such restless entities, usually described as vibrations or a feeling of cold. Some entities emit odors, like stale flowers or worse.

The late Dr. Carl A. Wickland and Anglican clergyman Canon John D. Pearce-Higgins are two of the most famous Western practitioners of persuasive exorcism. Wickland believed that possession occurred when a discarnate entity blundered, confusedly, into a living person's aura and became trapped. Using the services of his wife Anna, a medium, Wickland coaxed the spirit out of its victim and into his wife, through whom he communicated with it.

Canon Pearce-Higgins agrees with Wickland that possession is not demonic but a manifestation of confused, earthbound spirits. He refuses to call himself an exorcist, since in Christian tradition exorcism implies condemning a demonic possessing spirit to eternal damnation (see DEMONIC EXORCISM). Instead, Pearce-Higgins uses religious services and simple conversation to persuade the spirit to leave. Like his colleague and fellow "exorcist" Dr. Martin Israel, Pearce-Higgins feels the spirit needs as much help and consolation as the possessed victim.

WITCHES are often called upon to perform exorcisms of ghosts and remnants of unwanted psychic or spiritual energy (see GHOSTS, HAUNTINGS AND WITCHCRAFT). Spirit exorcisms, as cures to illness and solution to a wide range of personal problems, are common in Africa, Latin America, the Middle East, the Orient and among tribal cultures (see AFRICAN WITCHCRAFT; MACUMBA; SHAMANISM).

spirit possession   Unlike DEMONIC POSSESSION, in which a person is taken over by devils or evil spirits for harm, spirit possession is a voluntary, culturally sanctioned displacement of personality. The spirits—which may be deities, angels, DEMONS, advanced entities or the dead—are invited to enter a human being to educate or communicate with the living or merely because they are unaware they are dead and need help to pass into the next realm.

In some cultures, spirit possession is practiced by oracles and prophets, who go into trance and become possessed by deities in order to see the future (see ORACLE). In certain shamanic traditions, shamans become possessed for prophecy and in healing, the latter of which involves driving or sucking evil spirits out of the sick. Most shamans, however, control spirits rather than allow themselves to become possessed by them (see SHAMANISM).

In neo-Pagan WITCHCRAFT, the rituals of DRAWING DOWN THE MOON and Drawing Down the Sun are a form of spirit possession. The rituals involve the invoking of the GODDESS (moon) into the high priestess and the God (sun) into the high priest, who then speak in trance. Depending on the individuals and circumstances, actual spirit possession may not always take place, but when it does, its effects reportedly can linger for days afterward.

For many people in the Caribbean, the Middle East, India and Africa, the concept of possession by various gods serves as an important part of religious worship. To be possessed means that the god has found a person worthy to receive the spirit of the god. In Hindu India, possession by spirits permeates daily life. Most often the possessed person is a woman, who attributes all sorts of personal problems—menstrual pain, the death of children, barrenness, miscarriage, her husband's infidelities—to the intervention of the spirits. In many cases the woman has little family support and perhaps suffers harsh treatment from her husband, father or brothers, and so possession by a spirit gains her sympathy instead of condemnation for her troubles.

Besides being female, most possessed people in Eastern or African cultures are humble laborers or servants. Possession gains these people stature. They can control their relatives, large crowds, and even gain for themselves gifts of money, food or liquor. In some cases, subservient women use the possessed state to castigate their husbands and make them act more kindly. In such cultures, possession provides liberation for the women, allowing them to ask for more material goods and attention, air grievances, be more sexual and achieve some parity in their male-dominated societies (see AFRICAN WITCHCRAFT).

In the Caribbean and in many parts of Africa, ancient VODOUN worship involves the possession of the faithful by the various gods. Such possession is called "mounting the horse"—the horse being the victim who "manifests" the spirit, who "rides" him or her. Spirit possessions usually last only as long as the ceremonies, brought on by the feverish excitement of fast-beating drums and chanting. Similar possessions take place in SANTERÍA and MACUMBA.

In Haiti, if someone becomes recurrently possessed, at any time and any place, he or she is not considered to be filled with the spirit of the gods but to be psychologically unbalanced.

Spirit possession also occurs in Christianity. The word *enthusiastic* originally meant being filled with the holy spirit. After the crucifixion and resurrection of Jesus Christ, on the first day of Pentecost, the apostles were said to be possessed by the Holy Spirit. Fire appeared above their heads, and they spoke in different languages, or tongues, than those they knew. Speaking in tongues in an ecstatic state characterized early Christian worship, but by the Middle Ages it represented demonic possession more often than saintly enthusiasm.

In modern Christian worship, the Pentecostal movement has revived interest in speaking in tongues and ecstatic communion with God. The movement began on January 1, 1901 (the first day of the 20th century), when a group of Bethel College, Topeka, Kansas, reportedly received the Spirit. Various sects have sought communication with the Lord in this manner, with the so-called Holy Rollers being perhaps the most famous in the first part of this century. Worshippers rolled and writhed on the floor, putting themselves in a state of self-induced hypnosis, and prayed that the Spirit would come to them. The congregation considered those who received the Spirit as blessed, much like the worshippers during a Vodoun rite praise those who have been mounted by a god. Earlier critics of such worship would have found the participants possessed. The largest group of Pentecostals in the United States is the Assemblies of God, with thousands of members worldwide.

In Spiritualism, some trance mediums allow themselves to be possessed by spirits who speak through them. In some Spiritualist churches, spirit-possessed mediums deliver sermons in trance, as well as messages from the dead to members of the congregation. *Channeling*, a New Age term for a sort of spirit possession, involves the invoking of highly evolved entities, who "possess" the medium in order to speak to a human audience.

Trance mediums and channelers do not fear such encounters, believing that such possession is a temporary state. The "exorcism" of such a transient spirit is not a religious ritual but more a conversation to sent the spirit on its way. In most modern Western cultures, few people besides mediums experience spirit possession.

See also SPIRIT EXORCISM.

spittle According to witch lore, WITCHES effected evil SPELLS or CURSES against others with their own spit. Some spit on STONES, which they rubbed while reciting curses. In Lapland, witches could bring all sorts of illness and misfortune upon a person by spitting three times upon a knife and then rubbing the knife on the victim. Another Lapland witch charm for dooming someone to destruction called for tying three KNOTS in a linen towel in the name of the DEVIL, spitting on them and naming the victim.

The practice of spitting in spells still exists, especially in tribal societies. Marquesan sorcerers spit into leaves and bury them while reciting incantations against enemies. Malay sorcerers place spit, blood, urine and excrement on clay effigies, which they roast to curse a victim to death (see SORCERY). Necromancers sometimes spit as part of their rituals for conjuring the spirits of the dead (see NECROMANCY).

In other MAGIC, the saliva of the victim is believed to boost the power of the spell. Therefore, some people believe it is unwise to spit indiscreetly, as it enables DEMONS to capture one's saliva and use it for evil purpose. Among the tribes of East Africa, South Africa and New Zealand, spittle is hidden lest it fall into the hands of a sorcerer.

During the Middle Ages and Renaissance, European witch-hunters believed that witches could not shed tears but would try to fool inquisitors by smearing their cheeks with spittle (see WITCHCRAFT).

In folk magic, spitting is a universal defense against the EVIL EYE, bad luck, illness and witchcraft. Practices that date back to early Roman times include spitting in the right shoe every morning; spitting into the toilet after urination; spitting on the breast or on the ground three times; and spitting while passing any place where danger might exist. Pliny records the effectiveness of spittle against various disorders, such as boils, eye infections, epilepsy and leprosy.

Spittle is especially potent in protecting infants and children against fascination, (another term for evil eye). In Italy, persons who are suspected of overlooking children (casting the evil eye on them) are asked to spit in their faces to nullify the harm done.

The custom of spitting into the hands before a fight in order to make the blows stronger dates back to early Roman times.

Sprenger, James See *MALLEUS MALIFICARUM, THE*.

Stacker Lee (also Stagolee, Stackerlee, Stackalee) In American folklore, a black man who entered into a pact with the DEVIL, which brought about his own undoing (see DEVIL'S PACT). By selling his soul, Stacker Lee obtained a magical Stetson hat, which enabled him to metamorphose into various shapes, from animals to mountains (see METAMORPHOSIS); to have great prowess with women; and to have mastery over fire: he could walk on hot slag and eat flames. But the supernatural powers swelled Stacker Lee's ego to the point where even the Devil found him to be unbearably obnoxious, and so the Devil arranged for him to lose his hat. The hat was stolen in a barroom by Billy Lyon (also Billy Lion or Billy Galion). In a rage, Stacker Lee shot Billy to death and ultimately went to hell himself.

Stackerlee   See STACKER LEE.

Stagolee   See STACKER LEE.

Stamford Witches   While the witch hysteria gripped Salem, Massachusetts, in trials and executions in 1692–93 (see SALEM WITCHES), cooler heads prevailed in Stamford, Connecticut, where a servant girl accused six women of afflicting her with fits. Nevertheless, two of the accused came close to being put to death on slender "evidence," in the zeal of officials to avoid a panic of the type that had occurred at Salem.

The ordeal of the Stamford Witches began in the spring of 1692, when Katherine Branch, a 17-year-old French servant of Daniel Wescot, was seized with severe fits. It is possible that she suffered from epilepsy, but such fits commonly were blamed on WITCHCRAFT at that time.

In late April, Branch had been out gathering herbs when she experienced a "pinching and pricking at her breast," according to case records. She went home and burst into tears. Upon Wescot's questioning, she said she had seen a cat who had promised her "fine things" if she would go with it. Several days later, she saw ten cats who threatened to kill her for telling about her experience in the fields.

Visions and fits continued for 13 days, until Branch denounced Goodwife Elizabeth Clauson as a witch who was causing Branch's troubles. Clauson was a highly respected pillar of the community but had been involved in a long, ongoing dispute with Mrs. Wescot over a quantity of spun flax.

Wescot summoned a midwife, who said Branch's fits might be due to a natural cause. But when the girl did not respond to treatments, which included burning feathers under her nose and bleeding, the midwife became convinced she was bewitched.

Thus encouraged, Branch cried out against five other women: Mercy Disborough, Mary and Hannah Harvey, Mary Staples and Goody Miller. Wescot's wife suspected Branch of fabricating elaborate lies; nevertheless, a court of inquiry into the matter began hearings on May 27, 1692.

The accused women emphatically denied that they were witches. Goody Miller fled to New York Colony in order to avoid being arrested. The two prime suspects, Clauson and Disborough, were searched more than once for witch's marks (see WITCH'S MARK).

Nothing was found on Clauson save a wart that was judged normal, but Disborough exuded several "unnatural" excrescences that were held in evidence against her. Meanwhile, Branch continued having her fits.

The matter was deemed serious enough for a special trial, and the women were jailed while testimony was gathered. Two ministers questioned Branch, who cried out against Clauson, "You kill me, you kill me."

The trial opened on September 14, and Clauson and Disborough were swiftly indicted by a grand jury which proclaimed, "by the law of God and the law of the Colony, thou deseruest [deserve] to dye." The two women pleaded not guilty.

Staples and the two Harvey women were considered to be only under suspicion of witchcraft. The court invited people to step forward and testify against them, but only two persons did, and the three were acquitted.

Disborough insisted on being given the swimming test, which was not commonly administered in American witchcraft trials. She and Clauson were bound and thrown into water. Both floated "like a corck," a sign of guilt (see SWIMMING).

The prosecution presented numerous depositions it had collected, all against the two accused, which was not surprising in light of the prevailing belief that to testify on behalf of an accused witch meant being in league with the Devil as well. However, two longtime neighbors of Clauson's did step forward and testify in her favor.

Perhaps encouraged by this bravery, others stepped forward in Clauson's defense. Seventy-six Stamford residents signed a petition attesting to her good character and behavior.

The jury deliberated long and hard and was unable to reach a verdict. A committee of five prominent ministers was called in to examine the trial records and evidence. In their formal opinion, they stated that swimming was sinful and unlawful and could not be used as evidence; that Disborough's excrescences should not be allowed as evidence unless so decreed by "some able physitians"; that they suspected Branch of lying; and that Branch's fits might be related to the same condition that afflicted her mother.

The jury was reconvened in Fairfield on October 28 and heard additional testimony. By this time, 19 accused witches had been hanged in Salem, 100 were in jail and some 200 more had been accused of witchcraft, all of which must have had some effect on everyone concerned in the trial. The jury convicted Disborough and sentenced her to die but did find Clauson not guilty. Clauson was set free from jail and returned to Stamford, where she lived with her family until her death, at age 83, in 1714.

After the trial, friends of Disborough petitioned the court, claiming the second part of the trial was illegal because one of the original jurors had been missing. An investigating committee reprieved Disborough.

Starhawk (1951–)   American Witch, feminist and peace activist whose popular books are credited with influencing thousands of persons to discover their inner power and spirituality and to join the Craft (see WITCHCRAFT).

Starhawk was taught Witchcraft while she was a college student; among her teachers was Z. BUDAPEST, a founder of feminist Dianic Witchcraft. Much of Starhawk's knowledge was derived from dream and trance experiences.

Starhawk remained a SOLITARY for years before forming her first COVEN, Compost, from a group of men and women who attended a class in Witchcraft that she taught at the Bay Area Center for Alternative Education in the San Francisco area. After organizing, the coven performed a formal INITIATION ceremony. Later, Starhawk was confirmed as the coven's high priestess.

She was initiated into Victor Anderson's Faery Tradition, which was based upon the legendary "little people" of Stone Age Britain. She formed another coven, Honeysuckle, comprised entirely of women. Rituals for both covens were based on the Faery Tradition (see VICTOR ANDERSON).

Starhawk works with Reclaiming, a feminist collective in San Francisco, of which she was founder, and which offers classes, workshops and public rituals in Witchcraft. She also teaches at several Bay Area colleges and travels internationally to lecture and give workshops. She and other members of Reclaiming participate in demonstrations against nuclear power plants and military bases.

Her first book, *The Spiral Dance: A Rebirth of the Ancient Religion of the Great Goddess* (1979), was based on the Faery Tradition and was widely acclaimed throughout the Witch and Pagan communities. Though feminist, her rituals include men and have been influential in the increasing contact between feminist women and men in Witchcraft and NEO-PAGANISM.

Her other published credits include *Dreaming the Dark* (1982) and *Truth or Dare: Encounters of Power, Authority and Mystery* (1987).

Stonehenge   Rising above the chalk plain of Salisbury in Wiltshire, England, is one of the most awesome and mysterious of ancient megalithic sites:

Stonehenge (see MEGALITHS). Experts throughout history have been unable to say for certain exactly why Stonehenge was constructed. The name *Stonehenge* means "hanging stones" and was given by the Saxons; medieval writers called it the "giant's dance." What remains of Stonehenge today are a henge and horseshoe of sarsen sandstones and bluestones, some of which weigh as much as 26 tons. Some of the sandstones are topped by lintels and are thus called *trilithons*. They represent an exceptional engineering feat for a civilization without cranes and hydraulic lifts. It is estimated that the entire construction of Stonehenge required a staggering 1,497,680 man-days of physical labor, not including logistics and planning.

Built in three major phases from about 3500 to 1100 B.C., Stonehenge actually may have served a variety of changing purposes, including religious, magical, political and scientific activities. By the 12th century, its true origins and purposes were lost in legend. As a religious site, it may have been a temple of the sun or the serpent. For centuries, local peoples have believed the STONES to possess magical healing properties that could cure virtually any ailment. As a political site, Stonehenge is variously said to be the tomb of Boadicea, the pagan queen who fought the Romans; a gallows on which defeated British leaders were hanged in honor of the Saxon god Woden (see ODIN); and a monument for men slain in battle against the Saxons.

Most modern experts, including those from the National Aeronautics and Space Administration (NASA), believe Stonehenge was either a planetarium or an astronomical model of the planets; a calendar in stone for the measurement of the solar year; or, most likely, a celestial observatory and computer for predicting eclipses.

Human and animal remains found in excavations at Stonehenge show that it, or the general area, did serve as a cemetery for a time. It may have begun as a burial place, becoming by the early Bronze Age a focal point for seasonal festivals, trade, marriages and ceremonies of death and fertility. Animal remains include ox skulls, suggesting that the bull was worshipped here, as it evidently was elsewhere in Britain, as well as in Greece and northern Europe. Nearly 350 burial mounds have been found within a few miles of Stonehenge.

The construction of Stonehenge. Stonehenge I, built circa 3500 to 2300 B.C. by late Stone Age people, consisted of a ditch with two banks, three standing stones, four wooden posts and a ring of 56 holes, known as Aubrey Holes, named after the 17th-century English antiquarian John Aubrey. The holes measured from 2.5 feet to 6 feet in width, and 2 to 4 feet in depth; they were filled with chalk, then dug out and refilled. They may have been burial pits for the remains of cremated human bones, bits of pottery, animal bone pins, chips of flint and other Stone Age relics. Stonehenge I featured the first standing stone, the Heel Stone, measuring 20 feet long by 8 feet high by 7 feet wide, placed outside the earthwork's entrance and surrounded by a ditch. The Heel Stone was first named by Aubrey, who noted that it bore an indentation like a heel mark. According to a legend that grew up around it the Heel Stone, also called the Friar's Heel, a friar and the Devil were fighting. At the moment of sunrise, the Devil was forced to run, and the stone struck the friar on the heel.

The Beaker people, who lived during the construction of Stonehenge II, ca. 2150 to 2000 B.C., did not believe in cremation. During this phase a double circle of giant bluestones was built within the henge. The entrance was broadened, and an avenue was created linking Stonehenge to the River Avon about two miles away. The 80 blocks of bluestones were taken from the Prescelly Mountains of South Wales, and probably were transported by sea and river and overland, a process that might have taken some 100 years. In Arthurian legend, MERLIN is credited with magically transporting the stones, which were magical healing stones that had been brought to Ireland by giants. Aurelius Ambrosius wanted to honor the noblemen killed during a Saxon invasion. Merlin advised him to send men to Kildare, whereupon the party defeated the Irish in battle and took possession of the stones. After Merlin transported them to Salisbury Plain, they were erected as a monument to the fallen men.

Work on the second phase of Stonehenge was abandoned, possibly because the Wessex people, powerful and rich craftsmen, took over and drove out the Beaker people. The bluestone circle was dismantled.

The final building phase included three subphases. During Stonehenge III A, ca. 2100 to 2000 B.C., Stonehenge was altered to its present shape. The unfinished double circle of bluestones was dismantled and replaced in a different pattern by sarsens from Marlborough Downs in northern Wiltshire, the same location where the Heel Stone had been obtained. Thirty sarsens were placed in a carefully spaced ring around a horseshoe of five sarsen trilithons in the center. A lone upright sarsen was placed far outside even the original line of the double bluestone ring. It now lies on its side and is known as the Slaughter Stone—an apparent misnomer, for there is no evidence that it played a role in executions or sacrifices of any sort.

During Stonehenge III B, ca. 2000 to 1550 B.C., some 20 or more of the dismantled bluestones were re-erected in an oval within the horseshoe; the single Altar Stone in the middle may have been erected. The Altar Stone is of pale green sandstone, apparently from the Cosheston Beds at Milford Haven, Wales. Two holes, called the Y and Z holes, were dug and filled with chalk and fine dirt, containing shards of pottery, flints and other relics. Then the bluestone oval was dismantled. In Stonehenge III C, ca. 1550 to 1100 B.C., the bluestones were once again re-erected, and a bluestone horseshoe of 19 stones was constructed within the trilithons; the remains still stand. A circle of bluestones was placed between the sarsen horseshoe and the sarsen circle. Carvings of bronze axes and daggers, symbols of the sun, were made in the sarsens. "Boats of the Dead" were hammered into the faces of the western stones.

Modern investigations and theories. In popular thought, Stonehenge often is associated with the DRUIDS, though no evidence exists that the Druids built or used the monument. JAMES I, who was mystified by Stonehenge, dispatched architect Inigo Jones to the site to investigate it; Jones declared it not to be the work of the Druids nor of ancient Britons. Aubrey, however, believed Stonehenge was a Druid temple and psychic power center. William Stukeley, 18th-century English antiquarian and archaeologist, concurred with Aubrey. Stukeley believed that the Druids were serpent worshippers and that Stonehenge and AVEBURY were serpent temples of Dracontia.

Stukeley found two distinct astronomical alignments with the sun and moon over four burial stones called the Four Stations, and the Heel Stone. He reasoned that they either served a scientific purpose or had some association with the dead. The Four Stations have their short sides directed toward the midsummer sunrise and the long sides focused to the setting of the moon. These associations with the heavens and death are consistent with the perceived purposes of the long burial mounds around Stonehenge. Four out of five of the mounds have their burial ends facing either moon- or sunrises, or toward the east, where both sun and moon rise in spring and autumn.

Other researchers have explored the relationship between religion and astronomy at Stonehenge. Sir Norman Lockyer, a British astronomer at the turn of the century, determined that Stonehenge had been built to point exactly to midsummer sunrise; he estimated the dates of construction much later, between 1880 and 1480 B.C. Lockyer also believed that early priests had observed the stars by creating a stone circle with a stone or barrow indicating the direction of the place on the horizon at which the star would rise as seen from the center of the circle.

Gerald Hawkins, a modern British astronomer, endorses Lockyer's theory of summer solstice. In the 1960s he theorized that the monument was used as an observatory and that the Aubrey Holes were counting devices to predict celestial movements and solar and lunar eclipses.

Hawkins used a computer to make mathematical calculations of 165 positions and alignments of the sun and moon rising and setting at different times of the year, as seen through the various stones and spaces between the trilithons. He found that the Four Stations marked the winter and summer sun, parallel to the line from the center to the Heel Stone, and also marked the moon and all turning points of the 56-year moon cycle. The sunrises, moonrises, sunsets and moonsets are framed by the archways of the sarsen circle as viewed through the trilithons. Midwinter sunset appears through the great trilithon, and other stones mark the full moon at midwinter, midsummer, winter sunrise and winter sunset. The Great Trilithon, the tallest stone near the center, was found to be aligned with the midwinter sunset. Hawkins estimates Stonehenge was constructed between 1900 and 1600 B.C..

Another modern investigator, John Michell, used a computer and GEMATRIA to conclude that Stonehenge was chiefly a solar temple. In the mid-1970s, Alexander Thom stated that Stonehenge was the center of an observatory for studying lunar movements and that the megalithic calendar consisted of 16 months. Thom also said that the monument might have served as an example for the building of other such observatories in other parts of Britain. He developed the megalithic yard, a unit of measure 2.72 feet in length, which supposedly was used in building stone circles in different parts of the world.

Ceremonies and festivals. Until 1985 season festivals on the solstices and equinoxes were observed at Stonehenge by diverse groups including the modern Druids, who have no connection to the ancient Druids, NEO-PAGANS, WITCHES, Morris dancers (see MORRIS DANCING) and other spiritual pilgrims, all of whom performed their own rituals of CHANTING, dancing and incantation. The Druids' ceremony involved the playing of trumpets and harps, salutations to the stones, chanting, the raising of oak leaves and the burning of incense. Public festivals were banned in 1985 to protect the stones from vandalism and damage.

stones Stones have been long been credited with many MAGIC, HEALING and lucky properties. For centuries, semiprecious stones have been used in AMULETS to ward off the EVIL EYE, illness and death, to bring the wearer good luck and fortune or to cure various ailments. Sardonyx and cat's eye, for example, are considered protection against WITCHCRAFT, while coral wards off the evil eye and prevents sterility.

In folk magic, stones with certain shapes and characteristics are considered supernatural or lucky. Legend has it that Coinneach Odhar, a 17th-century Scottish seer, got his gift of second sight with the help of a stone with a hole in it. While cutting peat one day for a farmer, he stopped to take a nap and woke up with the stone on his chest. He looked through the hole and saw a vision of the farmer's wife bringing him a poisoned meal. When the woman did bring him his meal, he fed it to a dog, which died.

Stones with holes in them are female symbols and have been used in many fertility rites throughout history. In witch lore, a stone with a hole in it is a special sign of the favor of the goddess DIANA and will bring the finder good fortune and luck. A round stone, large or small, is also considered lucky, but only if the finder recites an incantation and throws the stone in the air three times. To give such a stone away brings disaster upon the finder. In India, a holed dolmen has healing power (see MEGALITHS).

In the Ozarks, a stone with a hole in it found in running water is especially lucky, to be collected and placed in a box beneath the front porch or doorstep.

Oval or round stones found in parts of Ireland are called *cursing stones* and are turned counterclockwise (WIDDERSHINS) in cursing SPELLS. The famous Blarney Stone in southern Ireland, a four-foot block of limestone, was a gift of a witch, according to some legends. Kissing the stone is believed to endow one with a great gift of oratory. The real origin of the stone is unknown. Another legend holds that the stone was brought to Ireland from the Holy Land.

Small stones or pebbles scattered about on a floor are said to prevent WITCHES from entering a house. In cases of DEMONIC POSSESSION and CURSES, hails of stones reportedly have rained down on the accursed, following them wherever they go. The stones seem to come from nowhere, even raining down from ceilings inside rooms (see LITHOBOLY).

Stone circles—of which there are more than 3,000 in the British Isles—are remnants of pagan sacred sites. Many stone circles also are associated with witches' meetings and FAIRIES.

See also AVEBURY; ROLLRIGHT STONES; STONEHENGE.

storm raising According to medieval popular belief, tempests, hailstorms and lightning usually were caused by WITCHES. By whipping up the elements of nature, they struck homes and crops, sank ships and

Witches raising storm at sea (Olaus Magnus, *Historia de gentibus septentrionalibus*, 1555)

killed men and animals, all allegedly with great delight. Church authorities said God permitted the DEVIL and witches to do these MALEFICIA as punishment upon the world.

After a sabbat (see SABBATS), witches were said to mount their BROOMS and fly out to sea, where they would stir up a tempest by dumping the vile contents of their cauldrons into the water (see CAULDRON) or by throwing their hair into the sea. From their brooms, they would hurl lightning bolts at ships. If they raised a storm over land, they would throw lightning at men, animals and buildings on the ground (see FLYING).

Witches also caused storms by stirring water poured into holes in the ground, urinating into holes, reciting magical formulas, drawing magical diagrams and shutting up toads and spiders in pots. Spanish witches caused hailstorms to destroy fruit crops by scattering a magic powder over the fruit.

Witches brought on rain by sacrificing COCKS in their cauldrons. Witches could control wind by tying three KNOTS in a rope or whip and unloosing them one by one. One old Scottish recipe for storm raising called for dipping a rag in water and beating it three times on a stone in the name of Satan, while reciting the following:

I knock this rag upon this stone
To raise the wind in the devil's name
It shall not lye till I please again.

Control of the elements, including the ability to raise storms and cause rain, has been attributed to magicians, shamans, sorcerers and witches since ancient times around the world (see MAGIC; SHAMANISM; SORCERY). In ancient Egypt, magicians used waxen images and spells to raise winds and storms against enemy invaders. As early as 700 A.D., the Church was prosecuting sorcerers for causing storms, sentencing them to penance.

During the height of the witch hysteria in the Middle Ages and Renaissance, virtually every natural disaster was attributed to witchcraft, and many people were blamed, tried and executed for being the alleged cause. In Ratisbon (now Regensburg), Germany, in the 15th century, a violent hailstorm destroyed all the crops, fruits and vines in a mile-wide swath. The townsfolk blamed the storm on witches and demanded an official inquiry. There was no shortage of suspects, but the field was narrowed to two women, who were separately imprisoned and interrogated. At first, both denied responsibility. They were tortured—one was hung by her thumbs—until they confessed not only to being witches and causing the storm but to copulating with incubi for 18 and 20 years, respectively. The day after they confessed, they were burned at the stake.

In the village of Waldshut on the Rhine, there lived a witch who was so despised by the townsfolk that she was pointedly not invited to a wedding celebration, as was nearly everyone else. Angry, she conjured up a devil and asked for a hailstorm to pelt the merrymakers. He raised her up and transported her to a hill near the town, where she was seen by shepherds. She made a trench, urinated into it and stirred the urine with her fingers. The devil lifted the liquid up and turned it into a violent hailstorm which pelted the dancers and wedding party and guests. The shepherds told the bewildered villagers about the witch, whereupon she was arrested. She confessed she had caused the storm because she had not been invited to the wedding. For this and other alleged acts of witchcraft, she was burned.

The most famous storm attributed to witches was recorded in the trial of Scotland's JOHN FIAN in 1591. He and his COVEN of NORTH BERWICK WITCHES were accused of raising a sea tempest to try to drown JAMES VI and Queen Anne on their way from Denmark. A storm did arise and slowed the ship down, but no one was drowned.

Remedies against storm raising. The medieval Church prohibited superstitious remedies against witchcraft such as storm raising, because of their pagan associations. What the Church recommended, however, was little more than superstition with a sacrament thrown in, and rituals that replaced magic incantations with Christian ones. In essence, they were pagan remedies trussed up with Christian window dressing.

PRAYER, sacraments and the invocation (see EVOCATIONS AND INVOCATIONS) of the name of God were all said to be the most effective weapons. If a person had faith in God and kept the commandments, revered the rites of the Church and protected himself with the sign of the cross, (see CROSSES), then he would be immune from storms and tempests.

The *MALLEUS MALEFICARUM* (1486) reports the testimony of one witch who was asked by a judge what could be done to stop a storm. She said the townspeople should recite:

> I adjure you, hailstorms and winds, by the five wounds of Christ, and by the three nails which pierced His hands and feet, and by the four Holy Evangelists, Matthew, Mark, Luke and John, that you be dissolved and fall as rain.

But most peasants were loath to give up their superstitions, and the Church also sanctioned such remedies as the ringing of church bells during a storm, which was supposed to drive the storm devils away, and the placing in fields of CHARMS made from flowers consecrated on Palm Sunday. If a storm struck, the charm would protect the owner's crops, even though the surrounding land and crops would be damaged.

Another remedy was throwing three hailstones into a fire during the storm. This had to be accompanied with an invocation of the Holy Trinity, the LORD'S PRAYER and the Angelic Salutation, all repeated two or three times, followed by the Gospel of St. John, "In the beginning was the word." The sign of the cross had to be made in each of the four directions, and then "The Word was made Flesh" was repeated three times. Finally, the ritual was ended with, "By the words of this Gospel may this tempest be stopped." Church officials said that while it was the holy words that really did the job, casting the hailstones into the fire added further torment to the DEVIL.

Weather control. Like medicine men, shamans, WITCH DOCTORS and witches in various cultures, modern neo-Pagan Witches perform rituals aimed at changing weather conditions. But while a tribal sorcerer, for example, would not hesitate to raise a storm to destroy an enemy, such an act is proscribed in neo-Pagan Witchcraft (see WICCAN REDE). Under certain circumstances, and depending on the views of the individual Witch, a weather ritual that binds an enemy might be acceptable (see SPELLS). Neo-Pagan Witches sometimes perform weather rituals on request, to help solve problems, such as alleviating droughts or floods or moderating excessively hot or cold temperatures. Neo-Pagan Witches do not believe in using weather magic to cause harm or suffering.

See also TEMPESTARII.

striga (also *stria, strix*) A blood-drinking night spirit of classical antiquity, which became known as a witch (see WITCHES) in folklore. The *striges* (plural) were said to be terrible women who could turn themselves into dreadful birds of prey, with huge talons, misshapen heads and breasts full of poisonous milk. Like the LAMIA and succubi, they preyed upon un-

protected sleeping men and children. With men, they turned into women, had sexual intercourse, then drank the men's blood. To children, they offered their poisonous milk. They were associated with screech OWLS, birds of SORCERY whose feathers are used in magical spells in classical myth (see OWLS).

Ovid proposed three theories as to the origin of *striges:* they were born that way; they were enchanted; they were hags who had been put under a spell (see HAG). Petronius claimed that *striges* were wise women of the night who possessed the power to overthrow the natural order of things.

After the fall of the Roman Empire, *striges* endured in folklore, and the term became low Latin for "witch." As Christianity spread, the *striges,* along with other pagan spirits, became associated with demonolatry. The Synod of Rome in 743 outlawed offerings to such spirits. In 744 a "List of Superstitions" drawn up at the Council of Leptinnes renounced "all the works of the demon . . . and all evil beings that are like them." Various laws were passed forbidding belief in *striges* and other pagan spirits, such as one in Saxony in 789, which punished such belief with execution.

By the Middle Ages, the *striges* were entrenched in Christianity as servants of Satan and his DEMONS. They were defined as women witches who practiced sorcery and flew through the air. The *striges'* association with screech owls gave rise to the term *owl-blasted,* which referred to the effects of a wasting-away spell cast upon a man (see BLASTING). This expression remained in popular use in Britain through the 16th century.

Stuff, Peter See LYCANTHROPY.

Summers, Montague (1880–1948) English author who wrote extensively on WITCHCRAFT, demonology, vampires and werewolves (see LYCANTHROPY). He believed that Satan and his DEMONS were real and that they exerted a powerful hold over WITCHES, who were evil. He has been criticized by some historians and authors as too credulous of the dark, supernatural worlds he explored. Nevertheless, his books, some of which were still in print in the late 20th century, offer an interesting look at popular stories and beliefs of earlier times.

Summers was born Alphonsus Joseph-Mary Augustus Montague Summers on April 10, 1880, in Clifton, near Bristol. He was the youngest of seven children in a family headed by a banker and justice of the peace. He was raised an Anglican but later converted to Catholicism.

Early in life, Summers was drawn to drama and literature, subjects on which he wrote books later in life. He studied at Trinity College in Oxford and then at Lichfield Theological College. He earned both bachelor and master of arts degrees by 1906.

While working as a curate in Bath, he and another clergyman were charged with pederasty. Summers was acquitted and the charges were dropped.

In 1909 he entered the Roman Catholic Church and became a priest. From 1911 to 1926 he taught at various schools and wrote books on literature, drama, WITCHCRAFT and the supernatural. In his later years he lived at Oxford, studying the thousands of books he had collected over the years. He was considered an odd man by his peers.

Summers devoted more than 30 years to an intense study of witchcraft, which he felt had been neglected by serious English historians. He reviewed the works of older demonologists, men such as JEAN BODIN, NICHOLAS REMY, Francesco-Maria Guazzo and many others. He translated into English the MALLEUS MALEFI-CARUM, first published in 1486 and the most influential guide in the persecution, TORTURE and execution of alleged witches during the entire witch hysteria. He exalted the book's authors, James Sprenger and Heinrich Kramer, as brilliant men. He also translated or edited the works of leading demonologists, including Henri Boguet, Francesco Guazzo, NICHOLAS REMY, REGINALD SCOTT, Richard Bovet and Ludovico Sinistrari.

While Summers believed in witches and felt they deserved the punishment they got, he disagreed with British anthropologist MARGARET A. MURRAY in her theory that witchcraft was an organized religion in the Middle Ages. That, said Summers, was "a most ingenious . . . but wholly untenable hypothesis."

In his book *The History of Witchcraft and Demonology* (1926), Summers maintained that witchcraft was not necessarily a product of the Middle Ages but did rise up at that time with sufficient force to threaten the very peace and salvation of mankind. He believed the confessions of witches to be not the products of hysteria and hallucination but "to be in the main hideous and horrible fact."

Summers embraced every belief about the evil and vileness of witches. In the introduction of *History*, he told his readers:

In the following pages I have endeavored to show the witch as she really was—an evil liver; a social pest and parasite; the devotee of a loathly and obscene creed; an adept at poisoning, blackmail and other creeping crimes; a member of a powerful secret organization inimical to Church and State; a blasphemer in word and deed; swaying the villagers by terror and superstition; a charlatan and a quack sometimes; a bawd; an abortionist; the dark counsellor of lewd court ladies and adulterous gallants; a minister to vice and inconceivable corruption; battening upon the filth and foulest passions of the age.

Summers wrote *The Geography of Witchcraft* (1927) and *A Popular History of Witchcraft* (1937). His books on vampires and werewolves—which some critics say are filled with unsubstantiated old wives' tales—are *The Vampire: His Kith and Kin* (1928); *The Vampire in Europe* (1929); and *The Werewolf* (1933).

Summers died on August 10, 1948, the same year in which a new edition of his translation of the *Malleus Maleficarum* was issued.

swastika A potent sacred symbol of ancient and pagan cultures all over the world and the most nearly universal of all religious symbols. It became tainted in the 20th century as the sinister symbol of the Nazi party.

The swastika, a cross with bent arms of equal length appearing to rotate in the same direction, probably originated with the ancient Aryans (see CROSSES). It appears in the artifacts of the ancient cultures of Troy, Greece, Egypt, China, India, Persia, Central and South America and Scandinavia. The word *swastika* is derived from Sanskrit and means something close to "fortunate." The Chinese called it "thunder-scroll," and the Hindus called it "all is well." Pagans associated it with the Mother Goddess; the Norse believed it was the hammer of the thunder god, Thor. In China and Japan, it has symbolized Buddha since about 200 B.C. In the Iron Age, it symbolized the supreme deity; the Anglo-Saxons called it "fylfot," or "many-footed," cross. In the Middle Ages, the swastika was a solar wheel that represented the movement of the sun across the heavens. It appears among the symbols in Hermetic magic (see HERMETICA) and among various Native American Indian tribes. The Navaho use it in the healing ceremonies of sand painting. Its division into quadrants has been interpreted as symbolic of the four directions on a compass and the four corners of the earth; the center of the cross is sometimes viewed as symbolic of the center of the cosmos.

There are two kinds of swastikas; right-handed, which represents the vernal sun, and left-handed (*swavastika*), which represents the autumnal sun. It is the right-handed swastika that has held mystical associations for so many centuries. But around the turn of the 20th century, the swastika's purity began to tarnish.

Just before World War I, secret racist groups sprang up in Germany and were attracted to the swastika as an emblem of might. They attached it to their occult philosophies of Germanic supremacy. The emblem of one of these groups, the *Germanen Orden*, created in 1912, was a bronze pin designed as a shield, on which two spears crossed a swastika. The bent cross was also the emblem of the Thule Society, whose purpose was to study the supposed occult meaning and symbolism of the German alphabet. The magical rune symbol of the Thule Society was Aarune (Aryan), which was associated with the sun and the center of the universe. It was believed that the sun dispersed rays of esoteric knowledge along with light and heat, and this knowledge could be learned by the initiates.

An occult ferment spread throughout Germany, fueled in part by interest in magical fraternities such as the HERMETIC ORDER OF THE GOLDEN DAWN and esoteric groups such as the Theosophical Society. The swastika was a major symbol of the Golden Dawn, and Crowley wrote a pamphlet about it in 1910. Later, he said the Nazis stole the idea for the swastika from him. The Theosophical Society was formed by H. P. Blavatsky, a Russian-born mystic, in 1875 in New York City, and was dedicated to spreading Eastern esoteric thought throughout the West. The swastika was a mystical symbol to Blavatsky, who wore one as a brooch.

In 1920, as Adolf Hitler was nurturing his growing Nazi party, he seized upon the swastika as the perfect emblem to express what the party stood for and appeal to the masses. He put a black swastika inside a white circle against a red background. In his autobiography, *Mein Kampf*, he exulted, *"A symbol it really is! In red we see the social idea of the movement, in white the nationalist idea, in the swastika the mission of the struggle for the victory of the Aryan man."*

Hitler put the emblem on the armbands of his SS storm troopers and party members. By 1922 the swastika was on flags and standards displayed at all Nazi gatherings and meeting places.

William L. Shirer observes in *The Rise and Fall of the Third Reich*:

This may not have been "art," but it was propaganda of the highest order. The Nazis now had a symbol which no other party could match. The hooked cross seemed to possess a mystic power of its own, to beckon to action in a new direction the insecure lower middle classes which had been floundering in the uncertainty of the first chaotic postwar years. They began to flock under its banner.

By the end of World War II and the defeat of the Nazis, the swastika had become synonymous with horrific cruelties and barbarism. Some modern neo-Pagan groups that worship the Norse and Teutonic deities have sought to restore the swastika to its original symbolism, without much success (see NORSE PAGANISM). The swastika does not appear in neo-Pagan WITCHCRAFT symbolism.

See also RUNES.

swimming An ancient test of guilt or innocence for WITCHES was trial by water, or swimming, a method that was used up until the 19th century. Accused witches were bound and thrown into water to see if they would float or sink. It was believed that the guilty floated while the innocent sank.

Trial by water was used by Hammurabi (1792–1750 B.C.), king of Babylonia, whose laws comprised one of the great ancient codes. Hammurabi declared that if a person was accused of black MAGIC but not proven guilty, he was to be plunged into a river. If he drowned, his accuser got his property. If he survived, his accuser would be executed, and he would take over the dead man's property.

Swimming, or *ducking*, as trial by water came to be known in some WITCHCRAFT trials, appeared in Europe, the British Isles and America in the 16th through 18th centuries but never gained widespread acceptance among judges as irrevocable proof of guilt or innocence. Technically, swimming had been declared illegal in England in 1219 by Henry III, but that didn't stop witch-hunters from doing it.

The accused witch was bound by either the right thumb to the right toe, or right thumb to left toe ("cross bound") and plunged into a river or lake. Innocence seldom mattered, for the victim often sank and drowned before he or she could be pulled out. Sometimes the accused had no chance at all to survive, because he or she was sewn into a sack before being tossed into the water.

Swimming was endorsed by JAMES I of England, who stated in *Daemonologie* (1597) "that God hath appointed (for a supernaturall signe of the monstrous impietie of Witches) that the water shall refuse to receive them in her bosome, that have shaken off them the sacred Water of Baptisme, and wilfully refused the benefite thereof." England's leading witch-hunter, MATTHEW HOPKINS, "swam" many of his accused victims, though he said he never used it as evidence in trials. In Europe, the chief champion of swimming was a Hessian schoolmaster named William Adolf Scribonius, who wrote a book in 1588 on how to identify and punish witches.

In the American colonies, two accused witches in Hartford, Connecticut, were "swum" in 1633 and were judged guilty because they floated; they were hanged. In 1706 a Virginia woman named Grace Sherwood agreed to be swum to prove her innocence. In chronicling the case in *Annals of Witchcraft* (1869), Samuel Drake stated that "few more disgraceful Scenes were ever enacted in the Prosecutions for Witchcraft" in the Colonies.

Sherwood was accused of witchcraft by a man and his wife; a warrant was issued for her to appear before court. Sherwood failed to show, was arraigned and was searched for witch's marks (see WITCH'S MARK). Two "things like Titts on her private Parts, of a black coller, being blacker than ye Rest of her

Body," were found, along with several other "Spots." However, the court had no specific crime with which to charge Sherwood, merely suspicion of witchcraft. Reluctant to acquit her, the court decided to use the "old English Test" of water. Sherwood, who had little to say in her own defense, agreed. Ironically, the court ordered the sheriff to take care not to expose her to rainy weather before she was "swum," as "she might take cold." Sherwood floated in the test, was plucked out and examined again for marks. Surviving records do not tell what became of the unfortunate woman. The place where the water trial took place, an inlet of Lynnhaven Bay in Princess Anne County, became known as "Witch Duck."

Swimming failed to become an ironclad means of unmasking witches because it could be manipulated by either accuser or accused. Many witch-hunters found ways to make certain their victims floated; some victims succeeded in sinking themselves long enough to be declared innocent. The records of various witch trials show that some victims requested the swimming test in order to clear their names, and some of them, unfortunately, floated despite their most valiant efforts to sink.

INCREASE MATHER strongly disapproved of swimming and railed against it in his book, *An Essay for the Recording of Illustrious Providences* (1684). Mather tore apart King James's argument that WATER, being an instrument of baptism and therefore holy, would reject witches, by saying that such a notion would apply only to those who were baptized. That meant anyone who was not baptized would float, regardless of whether or not he or she was a witch, Mather said.

Furthermore, Mather said, morality had nothing to do with body weight. He cited cases of the guilty going free and the innocent being condemned. Some people who were "swum" more than once both floated and sank.

Local jurisdictions throughout the Continent and the British Isles prohibited swimming. It was outlawed throughout all of England in 1712, and those who did it faced murder charges if their victim drowned. Nevertheless, it continued to be employed in lynch-mob situations. Swimming eventually died out in the 19th century.

In Russia, swimming was used in a different way. Persons suspected of witchcraft were taken to the deep side of a river, tied around the waist with rope and lowered in. If they sank, they were quickly pulled out. If they floated, they were hauled out and branded with a red-hot iron in the shape of a cross to warn others that they were witches. It was believed that the branding nullified the witches' power.

T

talismans Objects that possess magical or supernatural power of their own and transmit them to the owner. Talismans often are confused with AMULETS, objects that passively protect their wearers from evil and harm. Talismans usually perform a single function and enable powerful transformations. The magic wand of a sorcerer or fairy, King Arthur's sword Excalibur, seven-league boots and Mercury's helmet of invisibility are all talismans.

A talisman can be any object, but according to MAGIC, it can be endowed with supernatural power only by the forces of nature, by God or the gods or by being made in a ritualistic way. Precious stones have always been considered talismans, for example, each having its own magical or curative powers endowed by nature.

Talismans are found among all cultures in all periods of history. They were common in ancient Egypt and Babylonia, where they were used to try and alter the forces of nature. In the Middle Ages, holy objects were valued as talismans for their ability to cure illness. WITCHES and thieves made talismans out of the severed hands of criminals (see HAND OF GLORY).

Alchemists followed elaborate rituals to make talismans: they waited for auspicious astrological signs (see ASTROLOGY), then recited incantations to summon spirits who would imbue the talismans with power. The most sought-after talisman was the elusive Philosopher's Stone, which alchemists believed would transform base metals into gold and silver.

The GRIMOIRES offer instructions for making talismans of engravings upon stones or parchment under auspicious astrological signs. There are talismans for making fortunes, winning in gambling, preventing sudden death, improving memory and even making good speeches.

Magick Seals, or Talismans.

Talismanic seals (Francis Barrett, *The Magus*, 1801)

Catherine de Medici, queen consort of Henry II of France, always carried with her a talisman that was a medal allegedly made from metals that had been melted together under astrologically favorable signs, plus human and he-goat BLOOD. The original was broken upon her death, but a copy exists in the

335

Bibliothèque Nationale in Paris. One side of the medal is engraved with the god Jupiter, the eagle of Ganymede and a demon with the head of the Egyptian god, Anubis; the other side bears a Venus figure believed to be Catherine, which is flanked by the names of demons. The queen believed the talisman conferred upon her clairvoyance and sovereign power.

See also SEAL OF SOLOMON.

Tarot A DIVINATION system comprising a deck of 78 pictorial cards, the symbolism of which embodies the Western esoteric tradition. The Tarot is one of the most valued and oft-used divinatory tools of modern WITCHES and occultists.

The term *tarot* is French; in Italian, the cards are known as *tarocchi*. The exact origin and purpose of the Tarot are not known; the cards may have evolved out of the HERMETICA of ancient Egypt and Greece. There is no record of the cards' appearance prior to the late 14th century in Europe. Beginning in the 15th century, the GYPSIES spread Tarot use wherever they roamed in Europe. The Gypsies claimed they inherited the cards from ancestors who had obtained them in Egypt or Chaldea. Occultists have put forth

other theories. Court de Gebelin, a French archaeologist of the 18th century, believed they were fragments of an ancient Egyptian book. In the 19th century, ELIPHAS LEVI, English occultist, believed the cards were the legendary Egyptian "Book of THOTH." A. E. Waite, a member of the HERMETIC ORDER OF THE GOLDEN DAWN, believed the Albigenses created the cards in the 12th century.

The deck. The Tarot is two decks within one: a Major Arcana (*arcana* is Latin for "secrets"), which consists of 22 cards, each of which appears to represent an archetype of the human psyche; and a Minor Arcana, which consists of 56 cards and is the prototype of today's ordinary playing cards. The Minor Arcana has four suits: Wands, which corresponds to clubs in today's playing cards; Cups, to hearts; Pentacles, to diamonds; and Swords, to spades.

Interpreting the cards. Each of the 22 Major Arcana has its own symbolic meaning. The suits of the Minor Arcana have numerous correspondences, such as to the elements, the cardinal points, the four letters of the Tetragrammaton, Yod He Vau He (see NAMES OF POWER), the four seasons, endeavors, emotions and so on. The primary associations are: Wands, endeavor or enterprise; Cups, love and happiness; Pentacles, money and finances; and Swords, strife and animosity. The numbers of the Minor Arcana, from one to 10 plus four court cards of page, knight, queen and king, add further shadings to the meanings of each card (see NUMEROLOGY).

Dozens of Tarot decks are in existence, each with its own presentation of symbols and meanings represented by each card. Waite's own deck, known as the "Rider-Waite" pack, created in 1910, is considered the primary standard from which most other decks are derived. ALEISTER CROWLEY created a "Thoth" deck; there also are WITCHES', Mayan, Aztec, Native American Indian, feminist, Aquarian and New Age decks, to name but a few. Numerous interpretations have been written for each deck and for the Tarot in general; they are but guides, for in the final analysis, the cards must be interpreted on an individual, intuitive level.

To read the cards to obtain an answer to a question, one lays them out in various patterns. Rituals for reading can be quite elaborate, and involve lit candles, silken cloths of certain colors and invocations to a deity for the revelation of Truth. The cards are read according to whether they are rightside up or upside down, and how they relate to other cards in the spread. In addition to divination, the Tarot is used for meditation and to plumb one's own spiritual depths. Tarot practitioners spend years perfecting their art.

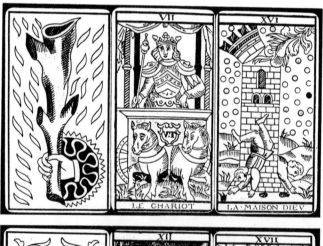

Nineteenth-century Tarot trumps

tasseography   See TASSEOMANCY.

tasseomancy   Also called *tasseography*, tasseomancy is the divinatory art of reading tea leaves and coffee grounds (see DIVINATION). Like PALMISTRY, it is particularly associated with WITCHES and GYPSIES, who popularized it. The roots of tasseomancy date back to the Middle Ages, when diviners interpreted the symbols formed by blobs of melted max, molten lead and other substances. In the 17th century, tea was introduced from the Orient to the West by the Dutch, and tea drinking quickly became a widespread habit. The shapes and symbols formed by the dregs in the bottom of the cup seemed natural for divination.

In a tea-leaf reading, the client drinks a cup of tea, preferably made from coarse leaves in a cup that is broad and shallow. A tiny amount of liquid is left in the cup, just enough to swish the dregs around. The cup is upturned on the saucer. The reader picks up the cup and examines the dregs, which may form letters, numbers, geometric patterns, straight or wavy lines or shapes that resemble animals, birds and objects. Various symbols have certain meanings; for example, straight lines indicate careful planning and peace of mind, while a cup shape indicates love and harmony. Time frames are estimated by the proximity of the leaves to the rim. Dregs closest to the rim and the handle represent the immediate future, while those at the bottom indicate the far future. Some readers say they can predict only 24 hours into the future.

Coffee grounds are less commonly used for divination. Italians in the 18th century claimed to have invented coffee-ground divination, and they believed the prophecies were caused by demons. Diviners who used this method recited incantations during the procedure, such as *"Aqua boraxit venias carajos,"* *"Fixitur et patricam explinabit tornare,"* and *"Hax verticalines, pax Fantas marobum, max destinatus, veida porol."* If the incantations were done incorrectly, the reading would be inaccurate.

Tasseomancy is still done in England, Ireland and Europe. In America, it is done primarily in large cities, in "Gypsy tearooms" and restaurants that have a back room for fortune-telling services.

tattoos   Pigmented markings etched into the skin which serve a variety of purposes: ornamental, religious, mystical, fertility- and health-enhancing and as a means of magical protection against evil spirits and the EVIL EYE. Tattooing is found primarily among tribal societies in Asia, Africa and the Pacific islands.

It is found to a lesser extent in parts of India and Tibet. It is not a practice in neo-Pagan WITCHCRAFT.

The custom of tattooing may be associated with the Arab proverb, "blood has flowed, the danger has passed." A tattoo serves as an initiatory means of identification and represents a sacrifice to an ideal, group or order on the part of the wearer.

The term *tattoo* (also *tatu*) comes from the Tahitian *tatau*. Tattoos were introduced to the West by Captain James Cook, following his exploration of Tahiti. The custom of tattooing is ancient; the pre-dynastic Egyptians (ca. 3500 B.C.) did it, while the Egyptians of the New Kingdom (ca. 1570–332 B.C.) tattooed their breasts and arms with names and symbols of deities. The priestess of the goddess Hathor tattooed three lines across her belly. Tattooing was known to the Greeks and Latins, who did not practice it, and to the Gauls, some of whom did. In Western culture, it died out during the Middle Ages. In present times, it is done primarily for ornamentation and sometimes for luck and protection. Sailors' tattoos of anchors, ships and naked women are believed to bring good luck and protection. In imitative magic, a tattoo of a scorpion, for example, is said to ward off real scorpions.

In other cultures, tattooing takes on various ritual and spiritual meanings. Tattoos are tribal marks of rank, scorecards for warriors and badges of the rites of initiation. In Iraq, they are believed to enhance fertility for women. In Burma and elsewhere, they protect against evil spirits and demons. The Polynesians and Ainus of Japan believe the gods tattoo themselves, and so they tattoo their own bodies accordingly.

There are two basic ways to tattoo skin: by using a chisel or adzlike instrument to groove the skin, and then rubbing in pigment, or by running a needle and soot-covered thread under the skin. Related to tattooing is *cicatrization*, the artificial creation of scars by cutting, scratching, piercing or burning the skin. Painting the skin is an artificial form of tattooing.

tears   According to folk belief, WITCHES are unable to shed tears. The origins of this belief may be found in the tears shed over the crucifixion of Christ and a statement by St. Bernard (1091–1153) that the tears of the humble could penetrate heaven and conquer the unconquerable. Therefore, the reasoning went, tears were an offense to the DEVIL, who would do whatever was necessary to prevent his witches from crying.

This "truth" was repeated in medieval witch-hunters' guides such as the MALLEUS MALEFICARUM (1486) and by leading demonologists of the 16th century, such as JEAN BODIN. In *De la Demonomanie des Sorciers*

(1580), Bodin states that witches and WIZARDS can neither cry nor look a man directly in the eye. JAMES I of England (James VI of Scotland) wrote in *Daemonologie* (1597):

> . . . threaten and torture them [witches] as ye please, while first they repent; (God not permitting them to dissemble their obstinacie in so horrible a crime,) albeit the woman-kind especially be able otherwise to shed teares at every light occasion, when they will, yea, although it were dissembingly, like the crocodiles.

An accused witch's inability to cry during her interrogation, TORTURE, or trial was taken as proof that she was a witch. The possibility that a person might be beyond tears due to terror or pain was never considered; a defendant was damned if she didn't cry, and damned if she did. The *Malleus Maleficarum* instructs judges to take particular note of tears:

> For we are taught both by the words of worthy men of old and by our own experience that this is a most certain sign, and it has been found that even if she be urged by solemn conjurations to shed tears, if she be a witch she will not be able to weep.

Judges were warned that witches, knowing that the absence of tears as proof of their guilt, might try to fake crying by smearing their cheeks with SPITTLE. Defendants were to be watched closely at all times for this trick.

The *Malleus Maleficarum* notes that while witches may not cry in the presence of judges, or during their interrogation, they may weep while in their cells. This was not to be taken seriously, however, because it was most likely a trick of the Devil, "since tearful grieving, weaving and deceiving are said to be proper to women."

If an accused witch was able to cry, she was supposed to be discharged, unless there still existed a "grave suspicion" that she was indeed a witch. Naturally, many defendants who cried were nonetheless convicted of witchcraft, as there were plenty of other ways to prove guilt.

In passing sentence, a judge might give a defendant one last chance to prove her innocence by crying. According to the *Malleus*, he would place his hand upon her head and pronounce:

> I conjure you by the bitter tears shed on the Cross by our Saviour the Lord Jesus Christ for the salvation of the world, and by the burning tears poured in the evening hour over His wounds by the most glorious Virgin Mary, His Mother, and by all the tears which have been shed here in this world by the Saints and Elect of God, from whose eyes He has now wiped away all tears, that if you be innocent you do now shed tears, but if you be guilty that you shall by no means do so. In the name of the Father, and of the Son, and of the Holy Ghost. Amen.

By the time sentence was passed, many victims *were* incapable of tears. Some had been tortured to the point where they were barely conscious; others had had their will to live broken. Crying might only mean a return to torture; refusal to cry could bring a speedier, and therefore merciful, death.

Tedworth, Drummer of   See GHOSTS, HAUNTINGS AND WITCHCRAFT.

Tempestarii   In medieval lore, the Tempestarii were WITCHES who specialized in STORM RAISING for the mythical dwellers of a land in the sky called Magonia. When huge storm clouds rolled over the land, they were said to be the ships of the Magonians. The Tempestarii aided the Magonians by whipping up the wind and creating lightning and thunder. By maliciously dumping their cargoes overboard, the Magonians sent hail to pelt the crops below. Then they would land their ships and, with the further help of the Tempestarii, steal the beaten-down crops. Often they would streak back into the sky without paying the Tempestarii and the WITCHES would give chase, which the peasants below saw as the wispy clouds in the sky that follow a storm.

Theophilus (ca. 538)   One of the most popular legends of the Middle Ages concerning a pact with the Devil (see DEVIL'S PACT) was about the monk Theophilus, bursar of the church of Adana in northern Cicilia. Unlike the legend of FAUST, the story of Theophilus has a happy ending. It was written in various languages and read at many churches, and was made into a drama, *Le Miracle de Theophile*, by Ruteboeuf, a 13th-century *trouvère* (a type of medieval French poet similar to the troubadour).

Theophilus, so the story goes, was offered a bishopric. A modest man, he declined because he was afraid he couldn't do the job. The man who did become bishop took a perverse interest in tormenting and harassing Theophilus, even accusing him of SORCERY. Theophilus lost his job as a result.

In revenge, he went to see Salatin, an "evil old Jew," who took Theophilus to a CROSSROADS and conjured the DEVIL in an exotic language. The Devil offered revenge and the bishopric in exchange for Theophilus's soul. Theophilus agreed, renounced Jesus and Mary and signed a pact in his own blood.

According to *Le Miracle de Theophile*, the pact read:

> To all who shall read this open letter, I, Satan, let know that the fortune of Theophilus is changed in-

deed, and that he has done me homage, so might he have once more his lordship, and that with the ring of his finger he has sealed this letter and with his blood written it, and no other ink has used therein.

As Satan promised, the church realized there was no evidence against Theophilus. The bishop was thrown out of office, and Theophilus was installed in his stead. But Theophilus was not happy; he began to worry about spending eternity in hell. He started praying unceasingly to the Virgin Mary for help. She took pity on him and interceded with God, obtaining God's pardon. The relieved Theophilus burned his pact, made a public confession and lived the rest of his life piously and in peace.

thirteen The number of bad luck and evil power. According to lore, Witches' covens always number 13 members, although there has never been any evidence in history to substantiate it (see COVEN). That myth was given fuel by British anthropologist MARGARET A. MURRAY, who stated in her book *The Witch-cult of Western Europe* (1921) that WITCHES in the Middle East formed in groups of 12 plus 1 leader. In support of her theory, she cited trial records that mentioned a mere 18 covens with 13 members between 1567 and 1673: five in England, nine in Scotland and one each in France, Germany, Ireland and America. The data were discredited by other scholars, who said the number 13 had been obtained by TORTURE or arrived at by error. In some cases, it was the number of witches arrested; far more than 13 were then implicated in the trials. Some accused witches claimed to have 13 members in their covens, such as ISOBEL GOWDIE, tried in Scotland in 1662, and Ann Armstrong, of Newcastle-on-Tyne, England, tried in 1673. Some modern covens may have 13 members, but most range in size from four to 20 members. Covens usually conduct their meetings at the full moon, which occurs 13 times a year.

Thirteen has been considered an unlucky number since ancient times. It is an unstable number, being just one beyond the number 12, which is the divine number of grace and perfection: there are 12 signs in the Zodiac, 12 hours in the day and 12 tribes of ancient Israel. In Christianity, 13 is a parody of the Last Supper, at which Christ and his apostles totaled 13. (Judas the betrayer was the first to rise from the table.) It is still considered unlucky to have 13 people to dinner.

So unlucky is 13 that it is omitted from addresses and floors of buildings. In the case of the latter, people may live or work on the 13th floor but feel better because it is called the 14th floor. The fear of the number 13 is called *triskaidekaphobia*. It is not uncommon for superstitious people to cancel trips on the 13th day of the month.

Friday the 13th packs a double wallop of bad luck, since Friday, the day Christ was crucified, traditionally is an unlucky day to enter into contracts, start new ventures or get married. In 1969 a 13-year-old Eton schoolboy, S. R. Baxter, proved mathematically that the 13th day of the month was more likely to fall on Friday than any other day. There is at least one Friday the 13th every year; the most that can occur is 3, as happened in 1987.

In the 19th century, the Thirteen Club was formed by 13 men in New York City to flout the bad-luck lore of the number. Appropriately, the charter dinner meeting took place on Friday the 13th, January 1882, in room 13 of Knickerbocker Cottage, from 13 minutes past eight until the 13th hour (1 A.M.). The members decided to dine on the 13th of every month. Lifetime membership in the club cost $13; the initiation fee was $1.13, and monthly dues were 13 cents. At the meetings, the members thumbed their noses at other superstitions, such as spilling SALT and breaking MIRRORS. The club was so successful that a sister club was formed in London.

In the Major Arcana of the TAROT deck, the 13th key, or card, is Death. If the card appears rightside-up, it signifies transformation. Upside-down, it signifies disaster, upheaval, inertia and anarchy.

A positive meaning of the number 13 may be found in GEMATRIA, the Kabbalistic system for interpreting words by converting letters to numbers and adding them together (see KABBALAH). Thus, 13 means "love of unity," because the Hebrew words for "love" and "unity" both total 13.

Despite its bad-luck associations, 13 represents an ideal size as a ritual unit for the raising of psychic force fields. Christ, as mentioned earlier, had 12 apostles. In early Christianity, emotional release was sought in the Agape, a group of 13 that sat in a circle and created a psychic field of an altered state of consciousness. King Arthur had 12 knights, and Robin Hood had a merry band of 12 followers. As late as the 19th century in Europe and the British Isles, Beltane festivities included a dance by a group of 13.

Neo-Pagan Witches consider 13 a lucky, propitious number.

See also NUMEROLOGY; ORDER OF THE GARTER.

Thoth (also Toth) The Egyptian god who created the universe and all mystical wisdom, MAGIC, learning, writing, arithmetic and ASTROLOGY. Called "The Lord of the Divine Books" and "Scribe of the Company of Gods," Thoth usually is portrayed as an ibis-headed man with a pen-and-ink holder. The exact symbolic meaning of the ibis has not been discovered, though it is believed to be associated with HEALING. Sometimes Thoth is portrayed as a baboon-headed man holding a crescent moon.

As a healer and magician, Thoth restored the eye of Horus, which was torn to pieces when Horus battled his evil uncle Seth (Set) to avenge the death of his father, OSIRIS. The eye of Horus, also known as the *udjat eye*, became a funerary amulet and magical, all-seeing eye (see AMULETS). Because of his restoration of the eye, Thoth became the patron god of oculists in ancient Egypt. Thoth also was petitioned in many of the spells contained in the Egyptian *Book of the Dead*, such as the opening-of-the-mouth spell to reanimate a corpse, which was spoken over a mummy by the high priest.

The Greeks associated their god HERMES so closely with Thoth that the two blended together. Thoth/Hermes became identified with the HERMES TRISME-GISTUS, a mythical figure who was the patron of magicians and thaumaturgists and the alleged author of the Hermetic books on occult, philosophical and religious subjects (see HERMETICA).

According to legend, Thoth/Hermes gave to his successors the *Book of Thoth*, or the "Key to Immortality," which contained the secret processes for the regeneration of humanity and for the expansion of consciousness that would enable mankind to behold the gods. The *Book of Thoth* was kept in a temple in a sealed golden box and was used in the ancient Mysteries, or secret occult teachings. When the Mysteries declined, it was carried to another, unknown land, where, legend has it, it still exists safely and leads disciples to the presence of the Immortals. Some say the *Book of Thoth* is in reality the TAROT deck.

Threefold Law of Karma See THREEFOLD LAW OF RETURN.

Threefold Law of Return (also Threefold Law of Karma) An ethic, more than a law, of uncertain origin that emerged in the Gardnerian tradition (see GERALD B. GARDNER) of modern WITCHCRAFT and that has been adopted by some WITCHES in other traditions. It is derived from the Eastern concept of karma.

Karma is the cosmic principle of cause and effect, which holds that for every action in life, there is a reaction; good is returned by good, evil is returned by evil. Karma is the sum total of causes set in motion through a series of incarnations, and it influences the spiritual progress of the soul toward Divine Consciousness (see REINCARNATION). Karma is not a law of punishment, though it has been interpreted as such by some schools of Western esoteric thought, such as Theosophy.

The Threefold Law of Return, however says that an action is not returned in equal measure but magnified three times, which defies the known laws of the universe. According to this concept, a Witch who uses her powers for good gets triple good in return. The law is a significant incentive not to use magic to curse others or even manipulate them, for the evil will return in triple strength as well. Some Witches go so far as to say the return is sevenfold.

The origin of the Threefold Law of Return in Witchcraft is not known. References to returning persecution twofold appear in the legend of ARADIA, as recorded in the late 19th century by CHARLES GODFREY LELAND. In the legend of DIANA, the Greek goddess and patroness of witches, sends her daughter, Aradia, to earth to teach witches their art. Diana instructs Aradia:

> And when a priest shall do you injury
> By his benedictions, ye shall do to him
> Double the harm, and do it in the name
> Of me, *Diana*, Queen of witches all!

Gerald B. Gardner, the namesake of Gardnerian Witchcraft, was a believer in karma and promoted the ethic that Witches must not use their power for anything that brings harm to another. There is no evidence that he conceived of the threefold return, though P. E. I. (ISAAC) BONEWITS notes that Gardner did specify threefold return in ritual scourging (light whipping). Three may have gotten attached to the concept of karma simply because it is a magical number; incantations often are repeated three times ("three times is the charm"). Three is perfect and lucky, and in Witchcraft it is associated with the Triple Goddess (see GODDESS).

The first known reference in print to the Threefold Law of Return appeared in 1970 in *Witchcraft Ancient and Modern*, by RAYMOND BUCKLAND, who was initiated into the Craft by Gardner and was instrumental in introducing Gardnerian Witchcraft into the United States. Buckland observes that with the retribution under the Threefold Law, "there is no inducement for a Witch to do evil."

The law of cause and effect is watched over by higher entities called the Lords of Karma, a concept from Theosophy that is drawn from the Hindu *lipikas*, the "scribes," whose job it is to record karma, and the *devarajas*, who rule over the cardinal points (and also are associated with the elements) and are said to be karmic agents during a person's life on earth. According to Stewart Farrar (see STEWART AND JANET FARRAR), the Lords of Karma do not override the law of karma but can help push people in the right karmic direction.

Most neo-Pagan Witches believe in reincarnation

and the cause and effect of karma, but some do not take the Threefold Law of Return literally in terms of a triple return. They believe in using their powers for good and not evil (see WICCAN REDE).

toads Toads are associated with WITCHES both as ingredients in brews and as FAMILIARS. Toad skins are covered with glands that secrete a thick, white poison when the toad is provoked or injured. The poison, *bufotenin*, also called *toads' milk* in popular lore, is hallucinogenic. Depending on the species of toad, the poison may simply taste bad or it may kill (see POISONS).

Toad lore. Since the time of Zoroaster, ca. 600 B.C., toads have been linked to evil; Zoroaster declared that for this reason, they should all be killed. The toad is the infernal opposite of the frog, which for the ancient Egyptians symbolized fertility and resurrection. In medieval and later times, toads were regarded as satanic creatures. Witches were believed to be able to disguise themselves as toads. Toads also were familiars, housing DEMONS who were assigned by the DEVIL to be servants to various witches. Witches were said to send their toad familiars out to poison others and cause mishaps and mayhem. Toads also accompanied them to SABBATS.

Toads were common ingredients in various magical recipes. According to lore, witches decapitated and skinned them and then threw them into their cauldrons along with other bizarre ingredients (see CAULDRON). A lotion made of toad's SPITTLE and sowthistle sap could make a witch invisible. In folk-MAGIC remedies, the ashes of a burned toad mixed with brandy was believed to be an effective cure for drunkenness.

Toads also were used as CHARMS in NECROMANCY and black magic. To kill an enemy, a witch or sorcerer baptized a toad with the enemy's name and then tortured the toad to death. The victim supposedly suffered the same fate.

It was believed that toads carried a jewel, called a *toadstone*, which would detect poison by becoming hot in its presence. The toadstone was either extracted from the toad's head or was vomited up by the toad. As a poison amulet (see AMULETS), it was most effective when set in RINGS.

In fantastic tales of witches' sabbats during the Middle Ages and Renaissance, witches were said to bite, mangle and tear apart toads in their worship of the Devil. By stamping his foot, the Devil could send all toads into the earth.

Toads in modern Witchcraft. Some modern Witches consider toads good familiars, noting that the creatures are intelligent, easy to tame and easy to care for. They also are said to have psychic qualities.

Reportedly, Witches have methods of collecting toad's milk without harm to the toad.

See also CHARLES WALTON.

tools, witches' See WITCHES' TOOLS.

torture During the height of the witch-hunts, a period of about 200 years between the mid-14th and mid-16th centuries, the cruelest, most savage torture was used against accused WITCHES in order to make them confess and name accomplices. The MALLEUS MALEFICARUM (1486) observes, "common justice demands that a witch should not be condemned to death unless she is convicted by her own confession." To that end—confession and execution—torture was considered an acceptable means.

By the time the Inquisition added WITCHCRAFT to its list of heresies in 1320, torture was an ancient institution. It was legal under Roman law and over the centuries had been regularly applied to criminals of all sorts. Numerous devices and procedures had been invented to inflict the most exquisite pain and torment without killing the victim. Many of these were turned upon accused witches.

Between about 1435 and 1484, the hunting down of witches spread like a plague throughout Europe. At least 28 treatises on the evil of witchcraft were written by clerics and demonologists. With Pope INNOCENT VIII's issuance of his papal bull against witches in 1484, the persecution of witches went into high gear. The worst tortures and wholesale exterminations occurred on the Continent, particularly in Germany, as well as in France, Italy and Switzerland, at the hands of both Catholic and Protestant inquisitors. Scotland, during the reign of King James VI (see JAMES I), was also witness to brutal tortures. Torture was far less prevalent and extreme in England, Ireland, and Scandinavia and was eventually outlawed in England. It was virtually nonexistent in the American colonies; the accused in the Salem trials in 1692 were tortured, but mildly compared to what was done on the Continent.

An inestimable number of victims were tortured and executed during the 16th and early 17th centuries. The inquisitors generally followed procedures and guidelines set forth in books such as the *Malleus Maleficarum*, written by Heinrich Kramer and James Sprenger, the Dominican inquisitors of Pope Innocent VIII. At first, the accused was urged to confess. She was stripped naked, shaved, pricked for insensitive spots and examined for blemishes that could be construed as Devils' marks (see DEVIL'S MARK). The *Malleus* cautions that most witches, at this point, would not confess. Then they had to be put to the "engines of torture."

Before torture began, the torturer usually took the victim aside and explained the torture and the effect it would have. He urged the victim to confess. Sometimes, the threat of torture was enough to induce a confession, which was ballyhooed about as voluntary and added weight to the Inquisition's case against the prevalence of witches. Sometimes the victim broke down after light torture, which was also considered a "voluntary" confession.

The *Malleus* notes that a witch who refused to talk, even under torture, was being aided by the Devil, who had the power to render her "so insensitive to the pains of torture that she will sooner be torn limb from limb that confess any of the truth. But torture is not to be neglected for this reason, for they are not all equally endowed with this power."

While the victim was tortured, the inquisitor repeated questions, while a clerk recorded what was said. The potential for error was great, especially if an uneducated victim spoke and understood only dialect. In many cases, clerks resorted to *etc.* instead of recording all details. Sometimes the victim's exact response was not recorded at all, but questions, usually accusatory, were noted merely as *affirmed*.

The torture went on until the victim confessed. The torturer had to take great care not to kill the victim but to relent when she was spent and beyond comprehension. She was taken back to her cell, where she was allowed to rest and regain sufficient strength to endure another round of torture in a few hours or the next day. Each subsequent round of torture was more brutal than the last. For this the torturer and other court officials were paid, usually out of seized funds belonging to the victim. If the victim had no money, her relatives were forced to pay the costs, which included not only the actual torture but the torturer's meals, travel expenses, "entertainment" and hay for his horse. If he had assistants, those were paid as well.

While the hapless victims screamed, the torturers and other court officials carried on like children frightened of the dark. They sprayed their instruments of torture with holy water and inscribed them with the words *Soli Deo Gloria* ("Glory be only to God"), which supposedly would protect them from being bewitched. They wore AMULETS of blessed wax and herbs and constantly crossed themselves, lest the witch harm them with evil magic. They forced the victims to drink witch broth, a concoction made of the ashes of burnt witches, which was supposed to prevent the victims from harming their torturers.

If a victim endured an exceptional amount of torture without confessing, court officials looked for the Devil's intervention. The *Malleus* cites an example of a witch in the town of Hagenau, Germany, who was able to maintain silence with the help of a powder she had made by killing a newborn, first-born male child who had not been baptized, roasting it in the oven with certain other ingredients and grinding it all to powder and ash. Any witch or criminal who carried such a powder was unable to confess crimes.

The exact methods of torture varied according to locale. The *rack*, for example, was not used in Scotland or England but was applied on the Continent, especially in France. In 1652 in Rieux, France, Suzanne Gaudry was stretched horribly on the rack while she "screamed ceaselessly" that she was not a witch, according to records. She finally confessed and was hanged and burned. Her torturer was paid four *livres*, 16 *sous*.

Victims were routinely horsewhipped. The spider, a sharp iron fork, was used to mangle breasts. Red-hot pincers were used to tear flesh, even breasts, off the body. Red-hot irons burned flesh and were inserted up vaginas and rectums. In extreme cases, the *Malleus* recommended the red-hot-iron test, in which a witch was forced to grab the hot iron; if she could hold it, she was guilty. Often by the time this test was administered, the victim was insensitive even to excruciating pain.

A device called the *turcas* was used to tear out fingernails. In 1590–91 JOHN FIAN was subjected to this and other tortures in Scotland. After his nails were ripped out, needles were driven into the quicks.

The *boots*, also called *bootikens* (*cashielaws* in Scotland), was a savage device of wedges that fitted the legs from ankles to knees. The torturer used a large, heavy hammer to pound the wedges, driving them closer together. At each strike, the inquisitor repeated the question. The wedges lacerated flesh and crushed bone, sometimes so thoroughly that marrow gushed out and the legs were rendered useless.

Similarly, the *thumbscrews*, or *pinniewinks*, did the same damage to thumbs and toes, crushing them at the roots of the nails so that blood spurted out. In 1629 a woman in Prossneck, Germany, was left to suffer in the thumbscrews from 10 A.M. to 1 P.M., while the torturer and other court officials went out to lunch.

Other tortures included *thrawing*, in which the head was bound with ropes and jerked from side to side; the application to armpits and groins of burning feathers dipped in sulphur; immersion of fingers and hands in pots of boiling oil and water (it was believed that witches, protected by the Devil, would be unharmed by this, but if they were, it was due to deception by the Devil); and the gouging out of eyes with irons. Alcohol was poured on the head and set afire. Bodies were broken on the wheel. One common procedure was to *blood* the victim by cutting the flesh above the nostrils. Blooding was believed to nullify a witch's power.

The *water torture* involved forcing great quantities of water, sometimes boiling, down the throat of the victim, along with a long knotted cloth. The cloth was then violently jerked out, which tore up the bowels. In another form of water torture, victims were fed only salted foods and briny water.

One of the most vicious torture methods, usually reserved for last, was the *strappado,* in which the victim's hands were bound behind her back and attached to a pulley. She was drawn to the ceiling and then dropped, and the jerk of the rope dislocated the shoulders, hands and elbows. This method was made more severe with the addition of weights to the victim's feet, increasing the pain and dislocating the hips, feet and knees as well. In France, stones weighing 40 to more than 200 pounds were used; one case involved 660-pound weights.

In many instances, there was no limit to the savagery of the torture used against accused witches. Anything was allowed as long as it got the desired results, and some inquisitors were openly sadistic. It was no wonder that many victims confessed in order to avoid great suffering.

After confession, however, came more torture as part of the sentence. Victims were usually condemned to death; in rare instances, they were released or banished. En route to the gallows or stakes, the condemned were flogged, burned, branded, squeezed with red-hot tongs and subjected to the hacking off of fingers and hands and the cutting out of tongues. The severed body parts were nailed to gallows, a grisly chore that netted the executioner an extra fee.

One insidious means of torture was to torture the victim's family while the victim watched helplessly. In 1594 Alison Balfour of Orkney was forced to watch her aged husband, son and seven-year-old daughter be tortured; she quickly confessed.

In England, painful physical torture was more isolated than widespread; instead, *induced torture* was employed. One of the most common methods was *watching* or *waking,* in which the victim was deprived of sleep until a hallucinatory state set in and the victim confessed. *Walking* also was common and was a favorite technique of England's most famous witch-hunter, MATTHEW HOPKINS. The victim was walked to and fro to the point of utter exhaustion. When witch-hunters could get away with it, they subjected victims to SWIMMING, in which they were bound hand and foot and thrown in water to see if they floated or sank. Floating meant guilty. If the innocent victim sank and drowned, it was simply too bad. Swimming was also employed on the Continent; a few cases were recorded in the American colonies.

In the mid-17th century, the wholesale torture and execution of witches began to collapse. Horrified at the excesses, dukes, princes and government officials moved to stop or at least limit torture and commute death sentences to life in prison or banishment. In Germany, the Duke of Brunswick and the Archbishop and Elector of Menz were so shocked at the cruelty of the torturers, and the fact that judges accepted confessions made under torture, that they abolished torture in their dominions and influenced other rulers to do the same.

To demonstrate the barbarism and absurdity of such procedures, the Duke of Brunswick invited two Jesuit priests to hear the confession of an accused witch who was incarcerated in a dungeon. Both priests were strong opponents of witchcraft; one was FRIEDRICH VON SPEE. Unknown to the priests, the duke had instructed the torturers to induce a certain confession from the woman. When the priests and the duke arrived, the torturers began applying pain and questions. In anguish, the woman at last broke down and confessed to attending many SABBATS on the Brocken, a notorious mountain rendezvous of witches. Furthermore, she claimed she had seen two Jesuit priests there, who had shocked even the witches with their abominations. The priests had assumed the shapes of goats, wolves and other animals and had copulated with the witches, who bore up to seven children at a time, all with heads like toads and legs like spiders. Asked to name the Jesuits, she said they were the two men in the torture room, watching.

Spee and the other priest were profoundly upset. The Duke of Brunswick then explained how he had arranged the confession to demonstrate how torture would induce a person to admit to anything suggested by questions. Spee was so affected that he became a strident critic of the witch trials, exposing their horrors in *Cautio Criminalis* ("Precautions for Prosecutors"), published anonymously in 1631.

Other critics and skeptics spoke out against the witch mania, including REGINALD SCOT and Thomas Hobbes in England, Michel de Montaigne in France and Alfonso Salazar de Frias, the grand Inquisitor of Spain. Laws against torture were passed in 1649 in Scotland; 1654 in Brandenburg; 1652 and 1662 in England; and 1682 in France. From the second half of the 17th century on, witch panics died down to sporadic bursts.

Toth See THOTH.

transvection see FLYING.

trees Reservoirs of immense life energy and longevity, trees are associated worldwide with considerable spiritual, religious and magical lore. Trees are the haunts of WITCHES and FAIRIES and sometimes the ghosts of people who have met violent or tragic ends, such as a man hanged from a particular tree (see GHOSTS, HAUNTINGS AND WITCHCRAFT).

Since antiquity, trees have been associated with the beginning of all life, fertility and mystical wisdom. Trees embody the universe: their branches represent the heavens, their trunks the earth, their roots the underworld. The immortal Tree of Life exists in the religions and myths of many parts of the world and is perhaps best known as the ash tree, Yggdrasil, in Scandinavian lore. Sacred trees have long been worshipped as the dwelling places of deities and nature spirits. In some cultures, trees are believed to be animated themselves and to have souls. To cut a limb from them or fell them is to wound them and make them bleed. The person who injures a tree will suffer the same wound or death.

The magical and sacred properties ascribed to trees vary according to culture and locale. Much of the lore surrounding trees comes from Europe, where peasants through the centuries practiced a wide range of tree-worship customs.

The ancient Celts, DRUIDS and early Germans had a strong affinity with trees and used clusters and groves as sites of worship. The oak was sacred to the Druids. Greek deities are associated with various trees: Artemis with cedar, laurel, myrtle, HAZEL and WILLOW; Athena with olive; and Apollo with laurel. The ancient Romans revered the fig tree, whose roots entangled and saved the city's mythical founding twins, Romulus and Remus, as they floated down the Tiber River.

As either animate beings with souls or the dwelling places of gods, trees have been regarded as oracles (see ORACLE). Early Germans would go into oak groves to ask questions and listen for the answers in the whispering and rustling of the leaves. Tribes in South Australia believe that the souls of the dead inhabit trees and may be consulted for their advice and wisdom.

With their power to bring forth fertility, trees play a central role in seasonal rituals and festivals throughout the world. In parts of Eurasia, barren women roll on the ground beneath apple trees in order to conceive. In an old Swedish custom, pregnant women hugged a lime, ash or oak tree in order to ensure an easy delivery. In parts of Africa, pregnant women dress in clothes made out of sacred tree bark in order to protect themselves against the hazards of delivery.

The most common fertility rites involving trees take place on Beltane (May Eve), a seasonal festival with ancient pagan roots observed throughout the British Isles and continental Europe (see SABBATS). According to tradition, trees are cut and stripped onto poles, which are decorated with ribbons and used as the center of dances (see MAYPOLE). Houses and stables are decked with branches of cedar, sycamore, hawthorne, oak, birch, fir and other trees associated with fertility, an activity that is intended to multiply people, ensure good crops and induce the cows to give more milk. Trees are dressed in human clothes or personified in dolls or poppets. Trees and dolls are cast into water or burned in bonfires to represent the departure of the winter of death and the coming of summer. In some rites, people represent the trees by dressing in wicker forms covered with boughs. They step out of the forms before the forms are destroyed in symbolic sacrifice. Sometimes the trees, as rulers of the vegetable kingdom, are represented by a human King and Queen of May. In Scandinavia, the festivals associated with May Eve usually are performed on St. John's Eve, (the summer solstice).

Trees that protect against evil and misfortune. Certain trees are believed to repel witches, fairies and evil spirits and are fastened on doors, about houses and in stables: ash, rowan, birch, hazel, holly, oak, hawthorne and bay. Oak, olive, bay laurel, elm and holly offer protection against lightning. Birch and fir protect new construction from accidents.

Yew and rowan are planted in graveyards in order to keep spirits from wandering about at night. In Russia, aspen laid on the grave of a witch will prevent her spirit from riding out at night to terrorize people.

Trees associated with witches, fairies and spirits. Witches are said to congregate around thorn and elder trees. The thorn is probably associated with witches because it grows alone, has an odd, gnarled shape and is a bad-smelling wood. Witches are said to disguise themselves as elder trees. To burn one is to invite the Devil or ghosts into one's home. If a person cuts an elder branch, he is likely later to see an old woman walking about with her arm in a sling. In Scotland, elder branches are used to keep evil spirits out of houses, while in parts of the United States, burning an elder branch on Christmas Eve will reveal all witches in the locale. Elderberries make a strong wine; elder flowers are used by herbalists in remedies for colds; and elder branches are used in many CHARMS. To cut anything from an elder is bad luck, however, unless one first asks the permission of the spirits that dwell in the tree. Elder wood is sometimes used to make magic wands and as an amulet (see AMULETS) against evil and witchcraft. Fairies are said to congregate around elder and in copses that include oak, ash and thorn.

Some trees are believed to attract evil spirits, particularly cherry and blackthorn.

In England, oaks are believed to have their own personalities. Oak groves are dangerous places at night, because oaks that have been cut will avenge themselves upon humans. In some areas, oaks are haunted by oak-men spirits.

See also APPLES; MISTLETOE.

U

Umbanda   See SANTERÍA.

unguents   See OINTMENTS.

urine   Like nail clippings and hair (see HAIR AND NAILS), urine is considered a potent ingredient in magical CHARMS and counter-charms. Its potency is attributed to its personal connection to an individual and to the belief that urine influences health.

As early as the 16th century, physicians recognized that symptoms of disease showed up in a patient's urine, which would appear cloudy, discolored or foul-smelling. Some physicians believed they could diagnose illness solely by urine, without having to see the patient himself. Astrologers also made medical diagnoses from urine, based on the positions of the planets and stars at the time the urine was voided or delivered to them for examination.

Alchemists used urine in their experiments as well. PARACELSUS, the 16th-century Swiss alchemist, wrote that urine, BLOOD, hair, sweat and excrement retained for a time a vital life essence called *mumia*. These ingredients could be used to make a *microcosmic magnet*, which, through the *mumia*, would draw off disease.

The WIZARDS and cunning men and women who flourished during the 16th and 17th centuries, practicing their magical remedies, used urine both for diagnosing and curing illnesses—especially those caused by WITCHCRAFT.

A handbook published in England in 1631 gave this means of diagnosing a patient's prospects for recovery: take a urine sample and immerse a nettle in it for 24 hours. If the nettle remains green and healthy, the patient will live. If the nettle drys up, the patient will die.

In folk MAGIC, boiling a person's urine helps determine if and how bewitchment has occurred. Urine is then used to effect cures, usually by boiling, baking, burying or throwing it upon a fire. Ann Green, a witch or cunning woman of northeast England, said in 1654 that she cured headaches caused by bewitchment by putting a clipping of the victim's hair in his own urine, boiling it and throwing it on a fire. The fire was supposed to destroy the spell.

Boiled urine also was said to cure nephritis. Urine boiled in a pot containing crooked PINS was a common remedy for bewitchment.

A case in Yorkshire in 1683 involved a sick man whom a doctor said suffered from bewitchment. To break the spell, the doctor prescribed a cake made of the patient's urine and hair, combined with wheat meal and horseshoe stumps. The cake was to be tossed in a fire.

Edible "witch's cakes" were baked in the early American colonies in the 17th century to cure smallpox. Ingredients included rye, barley, herbs, water and a cup of baby's urine. The cake was fed to a dog, and if the dog shuddered while eating it, the patient would recover.

One of the most effective counter-charms against witchcraft was to secure the witch's own urine: if it was bottled and buried, the witch would be unable to urinate. During the Salem witch trials of 1692 (see SALEM WITCHES), a local doctor named Roger Toothaker claimed his daughter had killed a witch with urine. The daughter spied on the witch until she saw the woman go to her outhouse. The daughter collected the witch's urine and boiled it in a pot until the foul-smelling smoke blocked the chimney flue. The next morning, the witch was dead. In another case cited during the Salem trials, a Mrs. Simms of Marblehead said she had been cursed by her witch neighbor, Wilmot "Mammy" Reed, never to urinate again. Mrs. Simms testified she had been unable to urinate for weeks after being cursed. Reed was hanged on September 22, 1692.

In Ozark superstition, it is unlucky to eat while urinating, because it is "feeding the Devil and starving God."

See also WITCH BOTTLES.

V

Valdenses See VAUDOIS.

Valiente, Doreen English high priestess, considered one of the most influential modern WITCHES. She helped GERALD B. GARDNER reshape numerous rituals, which in turn influenced the evolution of modern WITCHCRAFT.

Gardner was initiated by Valiente in 1953 (see INITIATION). Gardner had taken the rituals given him after his initiation into a hereditary COVEN in 1939 (which he published in novel form in 1949 in *High Magic's Aid*) and fleshed them out with material from ALEISTER CROWLEY. Valiente, a poet, removed much of Crowley's material and added her own (see BOOK OF SHADOWS).

Some of Valiente's poetic works are considered the most beautiful in the Craft and have passed into common usage, most notably "The Charge of the Goddess," an address customarily delivered in the DRAWING DOWN THE MOON rite, and "The Witches' Rune," a chant. Unfortunately, some of Valiente's works have been plagiarized and misquoted.

Valiente hived off from Gardner's coven in 1957 and formed a daughter coven. In 1964 she was initiated by Robert Cochrane into a traditional, hereditary branch of Witchcraft.

In 1980 Valiente initiated a search for OLD DOROTHY CLUTTERBUCK, the high priestess whom Gardner said initiated him in 1939. So little was known about Clutterbuck that historian Jeffrey B. Russell implied in his book, *A History of Witchcraft* (1980), that Clutterbuck may never have existed at all. Valiente made a diligent search through records, and in 1982 she triumphantly discovered Clutterbuck's birth and death records and her will.

Valiente is the author of numerous articles and three books about Witchcraft: *Natural Magic* (1975); *An ABC of Witchcraft Past and Present* (1973; 1984; 1986), an encyclopedia; and *Witchcraft for Tomorrow* (1978; 1983; 1985). The last title was in part a response to years of plagiarism and distortion of her contributions to Gardnerian rituals. In addition to an overview of Witchcraft, the book includes *Liber Umbrarum: The Book of Shadows*, a new and simplified book of shadows for persons interested in initiating themselves and organizing a coven.

Valiente lives in Sussex, the last county in England to become Christian, where she practices the Craft. She is a widow. During World War II, Valiente met and married a refugee from the Spanish Civil War, who had gone on to fight with the Free French Forces, was wounded and sent to England to recuperate.

Vaudois The Vaudois area of the Alps was a hotbed of Catholic heresy in the 12th century. Hardly satanists, these "heretics," or Valdenses (Waldenses), were followers of Peter Valdo (Waldo): early Protestants against Catholic ritual and for the purity of the Biblical gospel. Both the Dominican order of friars and the Inquisition had been organized to root out this supposed abomination, and during the fight the inquisitors believed that the heresy was accompanied by the practice of WITCHCRAFT, making the religious crime one against both God and nature.

By the 15th century, the Valdenses were no longer a theological threat, having been eliminated, but the connection with witchcraft remained: in the Alps, in the Lyonnais region and in Flanders, witches are called *Waudenses* and their gatherings are known as *Valdesias* or *Vauderye*.

vervain An herb sacred since the days of the DRUIDS and used in both WITCHCRAFT and antiwitchcraft CHARMS, PHILTRES and potions. Vervain grows throughout Eurasia and North America. It was revered by the Druids because it resembles the oak, which was sacred to them. Druids gathered it on moonless nights in the spring when the Dog Star, Sirius, rose in the sky, being careful not to touch it as they collected it into IRON containers. The ancient Greeks and Romans considered vervain sacred as well. In Rome, it was consecrated for the purification of homes and temples and was used in medicinal remedies for a variety of ailments. Early Christians called vervain "herb-of-the-cross" because it was believed to have staunched Christ's blood as he hung on the cross.

Because of its association with Christ, vervain was said to be an effective charm against WITCHES, evil SPELLS, DEMONS and incubi. In the Middle Ages, people hung it in their homes, over their stable doors, among their crops and around their necks. Nevertheless, witches used it freely in their potions, ointments and brews and in the preparation of a HAND OF GLORY.

In Italian witch lore, vervain is sacred to DIANA, patron goddess of witches. Neo-Pagan witches use it as an ingredient in ritual purification baths.

Vervain is a common ingredient in folk-magic love philtres, because of the belief that its undiluted juice can bring about any wish. Vervain also reputedly can bestow immunity to disease, the gift of clairvoyance and protection against bewitchment.

Among its many medicinal uses are as a cure for toothaches, ulcers, heavy menstrual flow, gout, worms, and jaundice. Early Americans wore vervain around their necks and touched it for good cures and good health.

See also HEALING.

Vodoun (also Voodoo) The cult of Vodoun, recognized today as a legitimate religion, bears little resemblance to the lurid snake-and-sex orgies, complete with pin-stuck dolls and zombielike followers, depicted in the movies. An estimated 50 million worshippers worldwide believe that the work of the gods appears in every facet of daily life and that pleasing the gods will gain the faithful health, wealth and spiritual contentment. The gods "speak" to their devotees through SPIRIT POSSESSION but only for a short time during ceremonies. Vodoun is almost synonomous with Haiti, but the rites also flourish in New Orleans, New York, Houston and Charleston, South Carolina.

Etymologists trace the origins of the word *vodoun* to the term *vodu*, meaning "spirit" or "deity" in the Fon language of the West African kingdom of Dahomey, now part of Nigeria. Eighteenth-century Creoles (whites born in the New World, usually of Spanish or French ancestry but perhaps having some mixed blood), masters of the Dahomean slaves, translated the word into *vaudau*. The Creole language derives from French, with definite African patterns of phonetics and grammar. Eventually, the word became *voudou, voudoun, vodoun, voodoo* or even *hoodoo*. Most current practitioners of the ancient rites regard the terms *voodoo* and *hoodoo* as pejorative, however, preferring one of the other spellings. To the faithful, Vodoun is not only a religion but also a way of life.

Vodoun came to the New World—especially to the Caribbean islands of Jamaica and Saint Domingue, now divided into the nations of Dominican Republic and Haiti—with the millions of black African slaves, encompassing members of the Bambara, Foula, Arada or Ardra, Mandingue, Fon, Nago, Iwe, Ibo, Yoruba and Congo tribes. Their strange religious practices perhaps first amused their white masters, but soon fearful whites forbade their slaves not only from practicing their religion but also from gathering in any type of congregation. Penalties were sadistic and severe, including mutilation, sexual disfigurement, flaying alive and burial alive. Any slave found possessing a FETISH (a figurine or carved image of a god) was to be imprisoned, hanged or flayed alive.

To save the blacks from the "animal" nature they were believed to possess, the masters baptized the slaves as Catholic Christians, which only forced native practices underground. In front of whites, blacks practiced Catholicism, but among each other, the gods of their ancestors were not forgotten. Rites held deep in the woods, prayers transmitted in work songs and worship of saints while secretly praying to the gods preserved the old traditions while giving them a new twist.

What evolved was syncretism: the blending of traditional Catholic worship of saints and Christ with the gods of Africa. Blacks could beg for intercession from St. Patrick, who banished the snakes from Ireland, and really be calling on their serpent god, *Danbhalah-Wedo*. Fetishes became unnecessary: even the masters tolerated a "poor idiot slave" keeping a tame snake or lighting candles for the "saints." Vodounists do not view such blending as profaning Christianity or Vodoun but as enrichment of their faith.

Serving the loa. The Vodoun pantheon of gods, called *loas* or *mystères*, is enormous and can accommodate additional local deities or ancestral spirits as needs arise. Vodounists acknowledge an original Supreme Being, called *Gran Met*, who made the world, but he has long since finished his work and returned to other worlds or perhaps to eternal contemplation. His remoteness precludes active worship. Devotees are those "who serve the *loa*," and depending on the rites observed, the *loas* can be kind, beneficent, wise, violent, sexual, vindictive, generous or mean.

The "father" of the *loas* is *Danbhalah-Wedo*, or the Great Serpent (also called *Danballah* or *Damballah*), which brought forth creation. Prior to the days of slavery, Africans worshipped a large python, called *Danh-gbwe*, as the embodiment of gods. The snake was harmless to humans, and devotees believed that any child touched by the serpent had been chosen as a priest or priestess by the god himself. After transportation to the Americas, the blacks found a substitute in a type of boa. Danbhalah is the oldest of the ancestors and does not speak, only hisses. *Langage*, the sacred language of Vodoun, which represents long-forgotten African liturgy, originated with Danbhalah's hissing. Danbhalah governs the waters of the earth and is also associated with LEGBA, the god of the sun and the way of all spiritual communion.

Aida-Wedo, the Rainbow, which arose from the waters of earth serves as the many-colored way of the gods' message to earth and is Danbhalah's wife. She, too, is a serpent: a short coiled snake who feeds upon bananas and lives mainly in the water. Her bright spectrum decorates Vodoun temples, especially the central support pole. Aida-Wedo is only one manifestation of the goddess *Erzulie*, the deity of beauty, love, wealth and prosperity. Normally referred to as *Maitresse Erzulie*, she is the lunar wife of Legba, the sun. And as the moon, Erzulie is pure, virginal. Contact with her heated husband burned her skin, so Erzulie is usually depicted as a beautiful, dark-skinned Ethiopian. There are many different Erzulies, encompassing not only the better virtues of love and good will but also the vices of jealousy, discord and vengeance. She can be vain, likes pretty jewelry and perfume and angers easily.

According to the creation myth, Danbhalah, the Serpent, and Aida-Wedo, the Rainbow, taught men and women how to procreate, and how to make blood sacrifices so that they could become the spirit and obtain the wisdom of the Serpent.

Although Danbhalah represents the ancestral knowledge of Vodoun, no communion of god and worshipper can take place without the offices of Legba. He is the Orient, the East, the sun and the place the sun rises. He governs gates, fences and entryways; no other deity may join a Vodoun ceremony unless Legba has been asked to open the "door." He controls the actions of all other spirits. Depicted both as a man sprinkling water and as an old man walking with a stick or crutch, Legba personifies the ritual waters and the consolidation of Vodoun mysteries. He is called *Papa*, and through syncretization has become identified with St. Peter, the gatekeeper of heaven and the man to whom Christ gave the keys to the Kingdom. Others see Legba *as* Christ, a mulatto man born of the sun and the moon. Legba also guards CROSSROADS, and as *Maitre Carrefour* (master of the four roads, or crossroads) is the patron of SORCERY.

Other important deities—all of whom have various manifestations—include *Ogou Fer* or *Ogoun*, the god of war and armor, iron and metalworking, wisdom and fire, who is associated with St. James; *Agwe* or *Agoueh*, the spirit of the sea, who presides over all fish and sea life and those who sail upon it; *Zaka*, the god of agriculture, who manifests himself in the clothes and coarse speech of the peasant; and *Erzulie Freda*, the goddess's most feminine and flirtatious persona. As Venus was Mars's lover, so Ogou takes Erzulie Freda. The total pantheon of Vodoun *loas* encompasses hundreds of gods and goddesses and grows each time the spirit of an ancestor becomes divine.

A separate classification of *loas* are the *Guedes*, the various spirits of death and dying, debauchery and lewdness, graveyards and grave diggers. As sexual spirits, the Guedes also govern the preservation and renewal of life and protect the children. Depictions of the Guedes, usually referred to as *Guede Nibbho* or *Nimbo, Baron Samedi* (Saturday, the day of death) or *Baron Cimetiere* (cemetery), show the *loa* in a dark tailcoat and tall hat like an undertaker. His symbols are coffins and phalluses. Those possessed by Baron Samedi tell lewd jokes, wear dark glasses and smoke cigarettes or cigars. They eat voraciously and drink copious amounts of alcohol. Entire cults of Vodoun revolve around the worship of the Guedes.

Rites and practices. Each tribal rite, whether Rada (Arada), Congo, Petro, Ibo, etc., has its own manifestations of the *loas* and different rituals and ceremonies, although most of the primary *loas* appear in each one. The Guedes, using many names to hide their true personalities or intents, move freely among each Vodoun division. The two main rites of Vodoun worship are *Rada* and *Petro* or *Pethro*. Rada rites follow more traditional African patterns and emphasize the gentler, more positive attributes of the *loas*. Devotees wear all-white clothing for the ceremonies. Animals sacrificed—the "partaking of the blood"—include chickens, goats, and bulls (see SACRIFICE). Three oxhide-covered drums provide the rhythms for the CHANTING, representing three atmospheres of the sun, or Legba: the largest, called *Manman*, related to the chromosphere; the next, called simply *Second*, related to the photosphere; and the smallest one, called *Bou-Lah,* which is the solar nucleus. These drums provide the most resonant combinations of musical rhythm of any rite and are struck with drumsticks. The drummers are called *houn'torguiers.*

The Petro rites appear to have originated in Haiti during the slavery days. The name *Petro* allegedly comes from Don Juan Felipe Pedro, a Spanish Vodoun priest and former slave who contributed a rather violent style of dance to the ceremonies. Many of the Petro practices, including more violent worship services and the use of red in ceremonial clothing and on the face, come from the Arawak and Carib Indians who then lived on Saint Domingue. Petro *loas* tend to be more menacing, deadly and ill-tempered than other *loas;* many of their names simply have the appellation *Ge-Rouge* (Red Eyes) after a Rada name to signify the Petro form. Pigs are sacrificed for the benefit of Petro *loas.*

Petro devotees use only two drums, and they are covered in goatskin and struck only with the hands. Rigaud reports that the drums are considered cannibalistic, even demonic, and their syncopated rhythms are difficult to control in MAGIC operations, rendering them dangerous. The first drum is identified with thunderbolts and their patron, *Quebiesou Dan Leh;* the second and smaller with *Guinee,* or the extremity of the world that receives the thunderbolt.

Guinee, or *Ian Guinee* or *Ginen,* represents the symbolic homeland of the Africans in diaspora. The sacred city of Guinee is Ifé, the Mecca of Vodoun. An actual Ifé exists in southern Nigeria, but the Ifé of Vodoun is a legendary place where the revelations of the *loas* descended unto the first faithful. Vodoun devotees refer to themselves as sons or daughters of Guinee: "ti guinin." Vodounists believe all aspects of life—administrative, religious, social, political, agricultural, artistic—originated in Ifé, but most especially the art of DIVINATION. Since Africa is east of the New World, Ifé represents the celestial position of the sun. Devotees gain spiritual strength from Ifé; when the sacred drums need divine refreshment, they are "sent to Ifé" in a very solemn ceremony signifying death, burial and resurrection.

Some aspects of Vodoun worship appear fairly constant, with local alterations, for all rites. The temple, which can be anything from a formal structure to a designated place behind the house, is called a *hounfour, humfo* or *oum'phor.* Within the temple, also known as the "holy of holies," are an altar (see ALTAR) and perhaps rooms for solitary meditation by initiates. The altar stone, called a *pe,* is covered in candles and *govis,* small jars believed to contain the spirits of revered ancestors. Offerings of food, drink or money may grace the altar, as well as ritual rattles,

charms, flags, sacred STONES and other paraphernalia. Years ago, the sacred snakes symbolizing Danbhalah lived in the *pe's* hollow interior, but no longer.

The walls and floors are covered in elaborate, colored designs symbolizing the gods, called *veves.* These drawings can be permanent or created in cornmeal, flour, powdered brick, gunpowder or face powder just before a ceremony. They are quite beautiful and incorporate the symbols and occult signs of the *loa* being worshipped: a *veve* for Legba shows a cross, one for Erzulie a heart, Danbhalah a serpent, and Baron Samedi a coffin. Usually drawn around the center post or the place of sacrifice, the *veve* serves as a ritual "magnet" for the *loa's* entrance, obliging the *loa* to descend to earth.

Ritual flags may hang on the walls or from the ceiling. There are usually pictures of the Catholic saints, believed to be incarnations of lower Vodoun deities. Most *hounfours* even display photographs of government officials. Since every chief of state is the gods' representative on earth, portraits of former dictators Papa Doc and Baby Doc Duvalier used to occupy important positions. A model boat completes the decorations, representing Maîtresse Erzulie and the ritual waters.

Outside the main temple is the *peristyle,* the roofed and sometimes partially enclosed courtyard adjacent to the holy of holies. Since the *hounfour* probably cannot accommodate all the Vodoun participants and onlookers, most ceremonies are conducted in the open-air peristyle, as is treatment of the sick. A low wall encircles the area, allowing those who are not dressed properly or are merely curious to watch less conspicuously. The peristyle's floor is always made of hard-packed earth without paving or tile.

Holding up the peristyle is the *poteau-mitan,* or center post. The *poteau-mitan* symbolizes the center of Vodoun, from the sky to hell, and is the cosmic axis of all Vodoun magic. Usually made of wood and set in a circular masonry base called the *socle,* the post bears colorful decorations and designs representing the serpent Danbhalah and his wife Aida-Wedo. The *poteau-mitan* also symbolizes *Legba Ati-Bon* ("wood of justice," or Legba Tree-of-the-Good), the way of all Vodoun knowledge and communion with the gods. Geometrically, the placement of the center post forms perfect squares, circles, crosses and triangles with the *socle* and the roof of the peristyle, adding to its magical powers. All Vodoun temples have a *poteau-mitan,* or center, even if the post exists only symbolically.

Outside the peristyle, the trees surrounding the courtyard serve as sacred *reposoirs,* or sanctuaries, for the gods. Vodoun devotees believe all things serve the *loa* and by definition are expressions and extensions of God, especially the trees. They are revered as divinities themselves and receive offerings of food, drink and money. Like cathedrals, they are places to be in the presence of the holy spirit; banana trees are particularly revered.

Calling the loas. True communion comes through divine possession. When summoned, the gods may enter a *govi* or "mount a horse"—assume a person's mind and body. The possessed loses all consciousness, totally becoming the possessing *loa* with all his or her desires and eccentricities. Young women possessed by the older spirits seem frail and decrepit, while the infirm possessed by young, virile gods dance and cavort with no thought to their disabilities. Even facial expressions change to resemble the god or goddess. Although a sacred interaction between *loa* and devotee, possession can be frightening and even dangerous. Some worshippers, unable to control the *loa*, have gone insane or died.

The *loas* manifest to protect, punish, confer skills and talents, prophesy, cure illness, exorcise spirits, give counsel, assist with rituals, and take sacrificial offerings.

The priest or priestess, called *houngan* and *mambo*, respectively, acts as an intermediary to summon the *loa* and helps the *loa* to depart when his or her business is finished. The *houngan* and *mambo* receive total authority from the *loas*, and therefore their roles could be compared to that of the Pope, says Rigaud. Indeed, the *houngan* is often called *papa* or *papa-loa*, while the mambo is called *manman*, or *mama*. The *houngan* and *mambo* serve as healers, diviners, psychologists, musicians and spiritual leaders.

Like a ruler's scepter, the most important symbol of the *houngan's* or *mambo's* office is the *asson*, a large ritual rattle made from the calabash, a type of squash with a bulbous end and a long handle. Symbolically, the *asson* represents the joining of the two most active magic principles: the circle at the round end and the wand at the handle. The handle also symbolizes the *poteau-mitan*, or vertical post. Inside the dried calabash are sacred stones and serpent vertebrae, considered the bones of African ancestors. Eight different stones in eight colors are used to symbolize eight ancestor gods (eight signifies eternity). Chains of colored beads, symbolizing the rainbow of Aida-Wedo, or more snake vertebrae encircle the round end of the calabash. When the vertebrae rattle, making the *asson* "speak," the spirits come down to the faithful through Danbhalah, the oldest of the ancestors. Once the *houngan* has attracted the *loa* through the deity's symbol, or *veve*, appealed to Legba for intercession and performed the water rituals and prayers, shaking the *asson* or striking it upon the *veve*

releases the power of the *loas* and brings them into the ceremony.

Other important members of the worship service include *la place* or *commandant la place*, the master of ceremonies, who orchestrates the flag-waving ceremonies, the choral singing and chanting and the drum beating. *La place* carries a ritual sword made of the finest iron and sometimes decorated with geometric designs and symbols. The sword's name is *ku-bha-sah*, which means "cutting away all that is material." Brandishing his sword from east to west during the ceremonies, *la place* cuts away the material world, leaving the faithful open for the divine presences. *La place's* sword also symbolizes the *loa Ogou*, god of iron and weaponry.

The chorus or *canzo*, composed of fully initiated Vodoun members called *hounsihs* or *hounsis*, performs under the direction of the *hounguenicon* or *hounguen-ikon*, usually a woman and the second-most powerful member after the *houngan* or *mambo*. By sending the chants to the *loas* in the astral plane, the *hounguenicon* calls the *loas* and demands their presence on earth.

Novices not yet completely in the *loas'* power are called *hounsih bossales*. The initiate who obtains the sacrificial animals is the *hounsih ventailleur*, and the sacrificial cook is the *hounsih cuisiniere*. The *hounguen-icon quartier-maitre* oversees distribution of sacrificial food not reserved for the loas.

Vodoun and magic. Magic, for both good and evil purposes, is an integral part of Vodoun. Unlike the dichotomy of good and evil expressed in Judeo-Christian philosophy, evil in Vodoun is merely the mirror image of good. The magic of the spirits is there to be used, and if that is for evil, then so be it. A *houngan* more involved in black-magic sorcery than healing is known as a *bokor* or *boko*, or "one who serves the *loa* with both hands."

Dating back to the days of slavery and probably beyond to the tribal kingdoms of Africa, the real Vodoun power resided in the secret societies. Membership in the societies means total commitment to Vodoun and complete secrecy about its practices and rituals. Oaths are made in BLOOD, and like the Sicilian code of *omerta*, or silence, transgressors can expect death if they reveal any of the society's secrets.

The most feared secret society is the Bizango, a sect that dates back to the bands of escaped slaves, called Maroons, hiding in the mountains. Also called *Cochon Gris* (Grey Pigs), *Sect Rouge* and *Vrinbrindingue* or *Vin'Bain-Ding* (Blood, Pain, Excrement), the Bizango reputedly meet at night, secretly, recognizing the other members through elaborate rituals and passwords. All through the night, according to some reports, Bizango initiates travel through the countryside, picking up members as they go, then hold frenzied dances dedicated to Baron Samedi, the *loa* of the graveyard. A nocturnal traveler who cannot give the password supposedly becomes the sect's human sacrifice—a "goat without horns"—or a candidate for zombification. Some members of these red sects believe that Legba, the Vodoun Jesus, died upon the cross to serve as an edible human sacrifice, symbolized by the sacraments, "This is My Body . . . This is My Blood. Take and eat in remembrance of Me."

Politics and Vodoun. Few understood the political nature of the Vodoun societies better than Haitian dictator François (Papa Doc) Duvalier, a physician who was president of Haiti from 1957 until his death in 1971. Allying himself with the *houngan,* he used the trappings of Vodoun to secure his power base, such as changing the Haitian flag to red and black, the Bizango colors, from its original red and blue. Papa Doc dressed in black suits with narrow black ties, the traditional clothing of Baron Samedi, until the people began to believe he *was* the *loa.* Stories circulated that Papa Doc could read goat entrails, that he slept in a tomb once a year to commune with the spirits and that he kept the head of an enemy on his desk.

When a Graham Greene story about Haiti, "The Comedians," was made into a movie in 1967, Papa Doc reputedly stuck pins into effigies of actors Richard Burton, Elizabeth Taylor and Alec Guinness because he hated the film's discussion of his role in Haiti and Vodoun. One story says that Papa Doc sent an emissary to collect a pinch of earth, a withered flower and a vial of air from John F. Kennedy's grave at Arlington National Cemetery so that he could capture the late President's soul and control U.S. foreign policy. Even Papa Doc's secret police, the *Tonton Macoutes,* depended on folk tales and fears of the spirits: children were told that unless they were good, their uncle, or *ton ton,* would carry them off in his *macoute,* or knapsack. Thousands of people were spirited away to be tortured and never seen again.

When Papa Doc died in 1971, his son Jean-Claude, called Baby Doc, declared himself President for Life and managed to hold on until his overthrow in February 1986. Because the Duvaliers had such intricate ties to the Vodoun societies, many *houngan* and *mambos* were murdered or forced to publicly recant their beliefs and become Christians following his departure. Yet many Haitians believe that the societies finally grew sick of Baby Doc and his excesses; when they turned the spirits against him, he had no other options but to go. One of the new junta's first acts was to reinstate the old red and blue flag.

See also GRIS-GRIS; MARIE LAVEAU; SANTERÍA; MACUMBA; ZOMBIE.

Voodoo   See Vodoun.

W

Waldenses   See VAUDOIS.

Walpurgisnacht   In German witch lore, the greatest of the pagan festivals celebrating fertility and one of the major SABBATS observed by WITCHES. Walpurgisnacht is the same as Beltane or May Eve and is celebrated on the night of April 30 in observance of the burgeoning spring. Walpurgisnacht became associated with Saint Walburga, a nun of Wimbourne, England, who went to Germany in 748 to found a monastery. She died at Heidenheim on February 25, 777. She was enormously popular, and cults dedicated to her quickly sprang into existence. In Roman martyrology, her feast day is May 1.

In the Middle Ages, Walpurgisnacht, or Walpurgis Night, was believed to be a night of witch revelry throughout Germany, the Low Countries and Scandinavia. Witches mounted their BROOMS and flew to mountaintops, where they carried on with wild feasting, dancing and copulation with DEMONS and the DEVIL. MONTAGUE SUMMERS observes in *The History of Witchcraft and Demonology* (1926), ''There was not a hill-top in Finland, so the peasant believed, which at midnight on the last day of April was not thronged by demons and sorcerers.''

In Germany, the Brocken, a dominant peak in the Harz Mountains, was the most infamous site of the witch sabbats. The Harz Mountains are in a wild region of northern Germany (now part of the German Democratic Republic), a fitting locale for the reputed witch gatherings. So common was the belief in the sabbats that maps of the Harz drawn in the 18th century almost always depicted witches on broomsticks converging upon the Brocken.

St. Walpurga was a gentle woman who lived a life of exceptional holiness. Yet the festival that carries her name, like other sabbats celebrated by witches, became associated with diabolic activities.

Modern Witches observe the holiday with traditional pagan festivities of dancing, rituals and feasting, none of which are associated with the Devil.

Walsh, John   See FAIRIES.

Walton, Charles (1871–1945)   A man with second sight who was renowned as a witch in his village of Lower Quinton, England, Walton was brutally murdered in 1945 in what was labeled a ritual witch killing, despite the lack of evidence that witches or occultists were responsible (see WITCHES). The murder was never solved, despite the efforts of Scotland Yard.

The village of Lower Quinton lies in Gloucestershire in the Cotswolds, an area of England with a long history of witches and WITCHCRAFT. Nearby are the ROLLRIGHT STONES, strange, ancient monoliths said to be a Danish king and his army that were stricken by a local witch. The area is rife with superstitions.

Walton was an odd, reclusive man who worked as a field laborer and lived in a thatched cottage with his niece, Edith Walton. He was widely known to have clairvoyant powers and claimed he could talk to birds and direct them to go wherever he wanted, simply by pointing. He also claimed to have a lesser control over animals, except dogs, which he feared. He bred large toads of a type called *natterjack*, which runs rather than hops.

Walton's clairvoyance began in his youth, and it changed his personality from extrovert to introvert. For three nights running, he saw a phantom black dog running on nearby Meon Hill, a particularly

Witch riding he-goat Devil to Walpurgisnacht sabbat, goaded by *amoretti* (Albrecht Dürer)

"witchy" site. On the third night, the dog changed into a headless woman, and the following day, his sister died.

For the remainder of his 74 years, Walton withdrew into himself. He worked for meager wages, seldom drank in public and was left alone by his neighbors. It was whispered by the villagers that he would steal out to the mysterious Rollright Stones nearby and watch witch rituals.

On the morning of February 14, 1945, Walton arose early and set out into the fields with a stick, a pitchfork and a bill hook. He had been hired by a farmer whose land lay near Meon Hill. About midday, the farmer saw Walton at work, trimming hedges with the bill hook.

But Walton never returned home. His worried niece contacted her uncle, and the two of them, along with the farmer, set out to search for the old man.

They found his body lying faceup beneath a willow tree on Meon Hill. A pitchfork had been driven through his throat with such force that it had nearly severed his head; the prongs were embedded about six inches into the earth. A cross-shaped wound had been slashed on his chest with the bill hook, which was stuck into his ribs. Walton's face was contorted in terror. A few days later, a black dog was found hanged on Meon Hill.

Scotland Yard sent Detective Superintendent Robert Fabian to investigate. Fabian expected to solve the case quickly. However, he received little cooperation from the residents of Lower Quinton, who insisted Walton had been killed by some unknown person because he was a witch.

The witchcraft aspects of the case attracted a great deal of attention, including that of anthropologist MARGARET A. MURRAY, who said she believed Walton had been killed in a blood-sacrifice ritual. The case also was investigated by a writer, Donald McCormick, who wrote a book on it, *Murder by Witchcraft*. Despite the lack of evidence, some odd facts and stories came to light.

The date of Walton's murder, February 14, was the date that ancient DRUIDS made blood-sacrifice rituals for good crops, in the belief that if life force is taken out of the earth, it must be returned. (According to the Druid calendar, which is two weeks behind the Julian calendar, the old date was February 1.) The crops of 1944 had been poor, and the spring of 1945 did not look promising, either. Walton was known to harness his huge toads to toy ploughs and send them running into the fields. In 1662 a Scottish witch, ISOBEL GOWDIE, confessed to doing the same in order to blast the crops (see BLASTING). Perhaps someone thought Walton was using witchcraft to blast his neighbor's crops.

Significantly, Walton's blood had been allowed to drain into the ground. According to old beliefs, a witch's power could be neutralized by "blooding." Many accused witches bled to death from cutting and slashing, usually done to the forehead. The practice was not uncommon in certain parts of England from the 16th century up to the 19th century (see BLOOD).

In 1875 a suspected witch in Long Compton, not far from Lower Quinton, was killed in almost the exact manner as was Walton. The murderer was the village idiot, John Haywood, who was convinced that 75-year-old Ann Turner was one of 16 witches in Long Compton, and had bewitched him. The local crops were poor as well. Haywood confessed to pinning the old woman to the ground with a pitchfork and, with a bill hook, slashing her throat and chest in the form of a cross.

For Fabian, the case grew even more mysterious. He saw a black dog run down Meon Hill, followed by a farmhand. The dog ran out of sight. Fabian asked the farmhand about the dog, but the terrified man claimed there had been no dog. Later the same day, a police car ran over a dog. The next day, a heifer died in a ditch.

Fabian and his men took 4,000 statements and 29 samples of hair, clothing and blood, and still came to a dead end. The murderer of Charles Walton was never discovered.

Warboys Witches   The story of the Throckmorton (also Throgmorton) children in Huntington, Essex, England, in 1589, is the first well-known case of allegedly possessed young people and the successful destruction of WITCHES based on the evidence of minors (see DEMONIC POSSESSION).

Squire Robert Throckmorton of Warboys and his wife had five daughters: Joan, Elizabeth, Mary, Grace and Jane. As a wealthy landowner, Throckmorton supported many of his poorer neighbors, among them the Samuels. Alice Samuel and her daughter Agnes frequently visited the Throckmorton household and were well known to the girls.

In 1589 the youngest, Jane, began having sneezing fits and convulsions and fell into a trance. Her frightened parents consulted a Cambridge physician, Dr. Barrow, and a Dr. Butler. Looking only at Jane's URINE, both doctors diagnosed bewitchment. When the 76-year-old Alice Samuel came to offer her sympathies, Jane cried out against her, accusing the old woman of WITCHCRAFT. Within two months, all the other sisters were suffering hysterical fits, and the eldest, Joan, predicted that there would eventually be 12 demoniacs in the house. Sure enough, the maidservants fell victim to the SPELLS; if any left Squire Throckmorton's employ, their successors also became possessed. All pointed to Mrs. Samuel as the source of their torments.

Like other demoniacs, the girls shrieked and contorted if the parson attempted prayer or read from the Bible, especially the beginning of the Gospel of St. John. Such actions are generally accepted as the signs of true possession but may also have been a convenient way for the girls to avoid pious exercises. In the only account of the Throckmorton possession, probably written by the girls' uncle, Gilbert Pickering, Elizabeth would throw fits to avoid religious lessons, only to come out of a tantrum if someone played cards with her, and to clench her teeth unless she ate outdoors at a particularly pretty pond.

Squire and Mrs. Throckmorton doubted the girls' possession, since they had only lived in the area a short time and no one had any motive for bewitching the family. They ignored the girls' accusations and tauntings of Mrs. Samuel.

In September 1590 the Throckmortons were visited by Lady Cromwell and her daughter-in-law. Lady Cromwell was the wife of Sir Henry Cromwell (grandfather of Sir Oliver Cromwell), the richest commoner in England. When she saw Mrs. Samuel, who was one of the Cromwells' tenants, Lady Cromwell angrily ripped the old woman's bonnet from her head, denounced her as a witch and ordered her hair burned. Horrified, Mrs. Samuel beseeched Lady Cromwell, "Madame, why do you use me thus? I never did you any harm, as yet."

Back home, Lady Cromwell experienced a terrible nightmare, in which she dreamed that Mrs. Samuel had sent her cat familiar (see FAMILIARS) to rip the flesh from her body. Lady Cromwell never fully recovered; her health gradually declined, and she died a lingering death 15 months later, in July 1592.

By this time, the girls were afflicted, only when Mrs. Samuel was absent, not present. Mrs. Samuel then was forced to live with the Throckmortons for several weeks in order to determine her effect on the children. Mrs. Samuel, her daughter Agnes and another suspected witch also were scratched by the girls, a custom similar to PRICKING. The girls constantly exhorted Alice to confess her dealings with the Devil and delivered pious speeches that moved onlookers to tears. Giving in to the constant pressure, Alice confessed just before Christmas 1592.

Not too long after Christmas, however, Mr. Samuel and Agnes convinced Mrs. Samuel to recant, and she again claimed her innocence, only to reconfess before the Bishop of Lincoln and a justice of the peace in Huntington on December 29. All three Samuels were jailed, although Agnes was released on bail to allow the girls to extract incriminating evidence from her through more scratchings. Mrs. Samuels confessed to having familiars, devils who were far inferior to the princes Beelzebub or Lucifer. She identified them as Pluck, Catch and White and the three cousins Smackes. The demons often appeared as chickens.

The Samuels were not connected to the death of Lady Cromwell until the Throckmorton children accused Mrs. Samuel of bewitching her to death, thus placing her in jeopardy of capital punishment as a murderer under the Witchcraft Act of 1563.

The Samuels were tried on April 5, 1593, on charges of murdering Lady Cromwell by witchcraft. The court accepted the testimony of the Throckmorton girls, as well as several other persons who claimed that the Samuels had bewitched their livestock to death over the years. The jury took only five hours to convict all three.

Mrs. Samuel, Agnes and Mr. Samuel were hanged, and afterwards the Throckmorton girls returned to perfect health. Since Lady Cromwell had allegedly died due to the black offices of Alice Samuel, her husband, Sir Henry Cromwell, received all of the Samuels's goods. He used the money to establish an annual sermon at Queens' College, Cambridge, to "preache and invaye against the detestable practice, synne, and offence of witchcraft, inchantment, charm, and sorcereye." The sermons lasted until 1812.

The Warboys case had a significant impact on public belief in witchcraft and the EVIL EYE. The case was widely publicized, in part due to the impressionable judge, Edward Fenner, who, in collaboration with several others, produced a broadsheet, *The Most Strange and Admirable Discoverie of the Three Witches of Warboys*, published in 1593. The case also left an impact on the governing class. The Cromwells served in the Parliament of JAMES I, who gained the throne in 1603. In response to public pressure for more stringent actions against witches, the Parliament passed a new Witchcraft Act in 1604, which stiffened punishment for some witchcraft offenses.

Compare to SALEM WITCHES.

warlocks A term for male WITCHES, though most men in WITCHCRAFT prefer to be called Witches or Wiccans like their female counterparts. The word has negative connotations; it stems from the old Anglo-Saxon word, *waerloga*, which means traitor, deceiver

Warlock riding to sabbat (Ulrich Molitor, *De lanijs et phitonicius mulieribus*, 1489)

or liar. Traditionally, a warlock is a sorcerer or wizard (see SORCERY; WIZARDS) who has gained supernatural power and knowledge through a pact with DEMONS or the Devil (see DEVIL'S PACT). (Such pacts are not part of contemporary Witchcraft, which does not share Christianity's belief in the DEVIL.)

Since the revival of Witchcraft in the 1950s, few Witches have referred to male Witches as warlocks; SYBIL LEEK once commented that use of the word was a rarity, except among outsiders. In SATANISM, some men who belong to the Church of Satan call themselves warlocks.

washes Herb and water mixtures with magical properties, used to wash or sprinkle about the floors and walls of homes, businesses and other places, in order to attract certain energies and influences. Washes have numerous purposes: in a business location, they are used to attract luck, customers and money, while in a home, they may promote tranquility or exorcise unwanted energies. A wash is made with a pint of water in which herbs are steeped for several days in a dark place. As in the making of magical anointing OILS and OINTMENTS, incantations or CHARMS related to the purpose are said over the wash. Washes are common among, but not limited to, practitioners of VODOUN and SANTERÍA.

water Water has ancient associations with the pure and holy. The Celts were particularly fascinated by its powers of life, HEALING, cleansing, regeneration and destruction and established numerous water deities and cults of rivers, streams, lakes and wells. Many water deities are female; water is linked to the MOON, a female force that governs the tides and female body fluids, and the moisture of wombs and birth. These positive associations of water with the female force are honored in neo-Pagan WITCHCRAFT; yet, in centuries past, water was used as a weapon against WITCHES by the Catholic Church and zealous witch-hunters of both Catholic and Protestant faith.

From the Middle Ages to the 19th century, suspected witches were bound and thrown into water to see if they would float or sink. It was believed that water, the medium of holy baptism, would reject an agent of the DEVIL; witches would float (see SWIMMING). According to another popular belief, witches and DEMONS were unable to cross running streams. If one was pursued by a witch or "fiend," the safest thing to do was cross a stream (see FORTRESS OF DUMBARTON).

Holy water—water mixed with SALT and blessed by a priest—was considered one of the Catholic Church's most powerful weapons against "the Fiend" and his subjects, who are supposed to be allergic to it. During the Middle Ages and Renaissance, holy water was sprinkled on houses to drive away evil spirits and "pestilential vapours," on crops to promote fertility and protect them from being blasted by witches and on farm animals to protect them from bewitchment (see BLASTING). The holy-water carrier came by regularly like a medieval milk man, making sure that no one was ever caught short of divine protection. When storms hit—stirred up by witches, no doubt—villagers raced to the local church to get extra holy water to protect their homes against lightning and to drive the witches away.

Inquisitors in the medieval witch-hunts were advised to keep holy water at hand to fend off SPELLS and evil looks. Holy water was also touted as protection against vampires; both vampires and witches supposedly recoiled at contact with the blessed liquid. This myth still lingers; in popular fiction and film, witches and vampires sizzle and burn if touched with holy water. In the classic film, *The Wizard of Oz*, the Wicked Witch of the West melts away into nothing when doused with ordinary water.

In medieval times, holy water was reputed to have miraculous medicinal powers. A dose of it would prevent one from being stricken by the plague. It was poured down the throats of sick animals who were diagnosed as suffering from a witch's curse and taken by humans for virtually all illnesses and diseases. Ironically, holy water was frequently prescribed by the very people often accused of witchcraft—the village wise women or healers. One such witch in 15th-century England prescribed a diet of holy bread and holy water for horses to prevent them from being stolen.

In the medieval stories about blasphemous witches' SABBATS and Black Masses (see BLACK MASS), holy water was replaced by URINE; sometimes the Devil was said to urinate into a hole in the ground then dip it out and sprinkle it on his witches and demons.

Protestant reformers challenged the supernatural power of holy water, saying it was good for cooking but little else. By the end of the 16th century in England, the Church of England had abolished it from all rituals, along with most other Catholic sacraments.

Holy water is still used in Catholic rites of exorcism (see RITUALE ROMANUM).

In MAGIC, holy water is used to purify the MAGIC CIRCLE and to consecrate the tools of the magician, such as the sword, wand and knife (see WITCHES' TOOLS).

In neo-Pagan Witchcraft, salted water is used in rituals to anoint participants and to consecrate and purify objects, tools and the boundaries of the magic circle itself. The element of water is associated with fecundity, nurturing, emotions, love and compassion.

Weinstein, Marion American Witch, author, entertainer and media spokesperson for the Craft, who has used her visibility to disseminate the truth about WITCHCRAFT and teach positive applications of MAGIC.

Marion Weinstein has known from early childhood that she is a Witch. Born in New York City on a new moon in the sign of Taurus (with the moon in Gemini), she has always felt an affinity with DIANA, the aspect of the GODDESS who rules the new and waxing moon. As a young child, Weinstein called her dolls "witches." She knew instinctively the basics of magic: that reality can be changed by specific, intense concentration. She felt a profound connection to Halloween (Samhain) that went beyond a child's interest in trick-or-treating; to her, this most mysterious of pagan holidays was filled with magic and beauty.

The oldest of three daughters in a Jewish family, Weinstein became interested in Jewish mysticism but was disappointed to find the KABBALAH closed to women. At an early age, she realized she had a psychic link with her mother; this encouraged her to develop her intuition.

In school, she was fascinated by fairy tales, certain they were truth that had become fictionalized. Her discovery at age 15 that Mother Goose was originally Charlemagne's mother-in-law, the "webfooted queen," launched her on a lifelong pursuit of her Witchcraft heritage.

In early adulthood, Weinstein began to piece her intuitions and research together. At age 19, she visited Pompeii and felt a strong, instinctive connection to classical paganism.

She graduated from Barnard College with a bachelor's degree in English literature. Witchcraft played a prominent part in her creative life. She wrote a Rodgers-and-Hart-style musical comedy about Witchcraft, "The Girl from Salem," which was produced on campus. After graduation, she took several courses in film at Columbia University, then went to Los Angeles to work as a commercial artist and animator. After two years, she returned to New York, studied acting, dance and voice, and joined an improvisational theater troupe.

At the same time, she pursued her spiritual research and formed a group of persons interested in magic and Witchcraft. The group quickly recognized itself as a COVEN, with an eclectic tradition, meeting regularly on the Witchcraft holidays and devoted to—among other traditional goals—sending positive energy toward world peace and nourishment of the planet.

In 1969 Weinstein connected with WBAI-FM radio

Marion Weinstein (courtesy Marion Weinstein)

in New York City. Her audition tape became the Halloween show that same year. That led to "Marion's Cauldron," her own program, which aired regularly and (usually) live. Weinstein interviewed occult experts, taught occult techniques, conducted group rituals and discussed topics such as psychic phenomena and dream research—and of course, Witchcraft. Her popular show lasted 14 years, until she concluded her work at WBAI-FM as she had begun, on Halloween.

During 20 years of research, Weinstein compiled a treasury of material on Witchcraft and magic, which she integrated into her first book, *Positive Magic* (1978; 1981). *Positive Magic* gained a reputation as a solid, clear textbook on nonmanipulative, practical magic and occult techniques, useful to anyone regardless of personal spiritual beliefs.

While she was working on *Positive Magic,* her own personal theology crystallized into a system of working with five aspects of the Deity—Diana, SELENE and HECATE as the Triple Goddess, complemented by Kernunnos (CERNUNNOS) and PAN—which she correlates with the five points of the pentagram, the religious symbol of Witchcraft (see PENTACLE AND PENTAGRAM). This work resulted in a second book, *Earth Magic: A Dianic Book of Shadows* (1979). Weinstein initially self-published *Earth Magic,* intending it

primarily for an audience of Witches. Later she revised and expanded it for the general public, and it was commercially published in 1986.

Witchcraft, Weinstein says, is a religion, a philosophy and a way of life, springing from a personal inspiration that comes from within. She encourages people to develop their own groups and traditions in accordance with their inner guidance, rather than to follow rules set by someone else. Her own system of Dianic Witchcraft evolved before the term became synonymous with feminist Witchcraft and relates to her affinity with Diana. She believes it is helpful for women to identify with one particular aspect of the Goddess and embody the attributes associated with that deity, and for men to align similarly with the God.

Weinstein began working professionally as a stand-up comic in nightclubs in 1978, using the Craft, and being a witch, as part of her routines.

In 1979 she formed Earth Magic Productions, an umbrella organization for creative and educational projects related to the positive aspects of Witchcraft and magic. By the mid-1980s, her focus was on the media, with frequent appearances on radio and television talk and news shows, sharing occult information, entertaining and working toward the goal that no one should have to explain that Witchcraft is not Devil-worship. In 1988 Earth Magic Productions launched a quarterly newsletter, *The Earth Magic Times.*

Weinstein lives in New York City with six CATS and two dogs; three of these animals are her FAMILIARS. She spends part of her year on Long Island, where she writes and gardens. She also lectures and conducts workshops on the Craft and related subjects and writes fiction and screenplays. Other book credits include *Racewalking* (1986), an exercise guide to the sport, written in collaboration with William Finley, with photographs by her mother, Sylvia Weinstein, and *Remember the Goddess,* a nonfiction book on the Goddess (1989).

Weinstein's guiding belief about Witchcraft is that a Witch's job is to help the community. Her personal definition of magic is transformation. Thus, she spreads information about personal self-transformation, always for the good of all and according to free will, as an ongoing way to help the individual self and the global community. A self-avowed "city Witch" in a modern world, she believes the ancient traditions translate well to fulfill current needs. Her guiding tenet is the karmic law of Return.

Weir, Thomas (ca. 1600–1670)

One of the most respected citizens of Edinburgh, Scotland, Major Weir shocked the entire city in 1670 by voluntarily confessing to black MAGIC. For all 70 years of his life,

Weir had been a model citizen: a devout Presbyterian, a soldier who served Parliament in the Civil War and a respected civil servant. His secrets could have gone to the grave with him, yet for some unfathomable reason—perhaps overwhelming guilt—he was suddenly seized with the need to unburden himself before the public. Like ISOBEL GOWDIE eight years before, he voluntarily confessed to activities largely sexual in nature.

Weir said he had long practiced black magic and owned a black-magic staff. His chief crime was incest with his sister, Jean, with whom he had sexual relations from the time she was a teenager until she was about 50. Then, disgusted with her wrinkles, he had turned to other young girls: Margaret Bourdon, the daughter of his dead wife, and Bessie Weems, a servant. He had also committed sodomy with various animals, including sheep, cows and his mare.

Despite public disbelief, Weir continued to broadcast his confessions, forcing the Lord Provost of the city to order an investigation.

Weir and his sister were brought to trial on April 29, 1670, charged with sexual crimes. While in prison, Weir cursed the doctors and clergy who tried to help him, and said, "I know my sentence of damnation is already sealed in Heaven . . . for I find nothing within me but blackness and darkness, brimstone and burning to the bottom of Hell." Weir was convicted of adultery, incest, one count of fornication and one count of bestiality. He was condemned to be strangled at a stake between Edinburgh and Leith on Monday, April 11, 1670, and his body burned to ashes.

Jean voluntarily confessed to incest. Perhaps in an effort to save herself, she laid the blame on her brother's WITCHCRAFT. He and she had signed a pact with the DEVIL, she said (see DEVIL'S PACT). She described going to a meeting with the Devil in Musselburgh on September 7, 1648, traveling in a coach drawn by six horses. She also confessed to consorting with WITCHES, FAIRIES and necromancers (see NECROMANCY) and to having a familiar (see FAMILIARS) who spun huge quantities of wool for her and helped her carry out various evil acts.

Jean was sentenced to be hanged on April 12 in the Grassmarket in Edinburgh. To the end, she was contemptuous of the court and the citizenry.

The shocked citizens of Edinburgh were inclined to think the Weirs merely insane. But, in the climate of the times, stories of the Weirs's witchcraft easily became embellished. Weir's house, Bow Head, was said to be haunted, and sounds of spinning could supposedly be heard there at night.

wells Since pre-Roman times, wells have been associated with supernatural powers and spirits and used by diviners, healers, WITCHES and ordinary folk for various purposes. In Bronze- and Iron-Age Europe, wells played an important role in water rituals and the worship of various deities who were thought to live in or guard the well waters. WATER, as a life source, was closely allied with fertility and HEALING. The Celts revered wells and erected shrines and ALTARS at them. In the Christianization of the Western world, the Church was unable to stamp out many pagan beliefs and so absorbed them into the new religion: pagan well deities were replaced by saints, and supernaturally endowed wells became "holy" wells.

Such wells acquired reputations for having special powers. Some were strictly for healing, while others were for CURSING, wishing, DIVINATION or baptism. A few wells were multipurpose. Some wells were believed to be guarded by eels, dragons, serpents, monster fish or vindictive spirits who had to be placated and protected, lest disaster or epidemic sweep the local population.

In order to invoke the powers of a well, rituals were necessary. The pilgrim usually tossed in coins, the idols of deities, PINS or other offerings, while reciting PRAYERS, incantations or simply a wish. In Ireland, it was common practice to decorate supernatural wells with yarn and ribbons, especially on certain holidays. Some rituals were quite elaborate, involving bathing in the well waters at certain hours, sacrificing animals (see SACRIFICE) and circling the well a certain number of times.

One of the most renowned cursing wells was located at St. Elian's Church in Llanelian-yn-Rhos, Clwyd, Wales. Pilgrims from all over the British Isles frequented this popular well up to the late 19th century. The victim's name was written on a piece of paper, which was pierced with a crooked pin. Then the victim's initials were scratched onto a stone, which the well custodian—for a fee—tossed into the water (see STONES). As long as the stone remained in the water, the curse was in effect, causing anything from aches and pains to illness to death. Victims could remove the curse by going to the well and paying the custodian a higher fee than that paid by the curser. The well was so popular that the church rector had it destroyed in the late 1800s to discourage malicious superstition.

Methods of divination varied from well to well. For example, if a stone were tossed into the water, the appearance and quantity of bubbles that arose determined whether or not something would come to pass. At St. Gybi's Well in Llangybi, Gwynedd, Wales, maidens threw rags into the water to determine if their lovers were faithful. If the rag floated south, the answer was yes; if it floated north, no.

Supernatural wells acquired their reputations either

by natural properties or by myth. Healing waters are rich in minerals, chemicals and metals. Other magic wells rise and fall in accordance with—or in contradiction to—the tides. Some are said to be the sites where saints or kings were slain.

Witches were said to use supernatural well water in some of their CHARMS, especially those for inflicting and curing disease. In 1622 in Eastwood, Scotland, one accused witch was said on Halloween to draw water from a well "which brides and burials passed over" for her SPELLS.

Mineral-rich wells and springs renowned for their curative powers, such as Our Lady of Lourdes in France, are still visited by thousands of hopeful pilgrims. The practice of tossing coins into fountains and making a wish is related to the ancient pagan beliefs about supernatural wells.

Weschcke, Carl (1930–)

Magician, Tantric, Pagan and former Wiccan high priest, Carl Llewellyn Weschcke presides over Llewellyn Publications, one of the largest publishers of New Age and occult books in the United States. Weschcke played a leading role in the growth of Wiccan and Pagan religions during the formative years of the 1970s. In the late 1970s he dropped out of WITCHCRAFT to devote more time to his family and to his publishing enterprise.

Weschcke was born September 10, 1930, in St. Paul, to a Roman Catholic family. Early on, he was exposed to metaphysics and the occult. He was fascinated by astronomy, religion and the occult and was most influenced by his paternal grandfather, who was vice-president of the American Theosophical Society and believed in REINCARNATION. When Weschcke turned 12, his present from his grandfather was his own astrological chart (see ASTROLOGY). Weschcke's parents practiced mind reading, which they often discussed. And one of their houses was full of thumpings, which they attributed to the ghost of the deceased former owner.

Weschcke graduated from St. Paul Academy in 1948 and went on to attend business school at the Babson Institute in Massachusetts. Upon graduating, he went to work in the family pharmaceuticals business, but he found it unfulfilling. Instead, he wanted to be a publisher. He returned to school to study for a doctorate in philosophy at the University of Minnesota—which he did not have time to complete—and began looking for publishing opportunities.

During the 1950s and into the early 1960s, Weschcke was very active in the civil rights and civil liberties movements, holding office in the St. Paul branch of the National Association for the Advancement of Colored People (NAACP) and the Minnesota Civil Liberties Union. He played a major role in bringing about fair-housing legislation in St. Paul.

Carl Weschcke (courtesy Carl Weschcke)

In 1960 he purchased Llewellyn Publishing Co., a small mail-order house selling three astrology books and calendars, based in Los Angeles. The founder, Llewellyn George, had died six years earlier. Weschcke moved the business to St. Paul and began building a complete line of astrology and occult books. He purchased titles from all over the world, at one time carrying 3,000 of them.

In 1964 Weschcke bought a large, stone mansion on Summit Avenue in St. Paul as both home and place of business. The house was reputed to be haunted, and Weschcke had numerous odd experiences there. He was awakened by cold drafts coming in open windows that had been closed when he had gone to sleep, and he heard footsteps. He saw apparitions of a man and a woman, which he believed were not true ghosts but the vibrations of former occupants which had been recorded in the woodwork of the house (see GHOSTS, HAUNTINGS AND WITCHCRAFT).

A newspaper story about the hauntings created an avalanche of public attention, paving the way for his media prominence in the emerging Witchcraft/NEO-PAGANISM movement.

Weschcke opened the Gnostica Bookstore in Minneapolis in 1970. It was a popular gathering place for persons interested in the occult and alternative religions. A year later, a local convention manager suggested that Minneapolis could benefit from a Woodstock-style festival, and Weschcke took the opportunity to host it.

The first of several annual festivals was held in 1971. Initially called The First American Aquarian Festival of Astrology and the Occult Sciences, and later called Gnosticon, the festivals drew WITCHES, neo-Pagans, magicians, astrologers, Christians and others from all over the world. Witchcraft rituals were conducted. Weschcke led meditations for peace and the healing of the earth. Some attendees came costumed. At times, the festivities got a little wild, such as in 1974, when a group of about 20 Pagans leaped into the hotel swimming pool at midnight to go skinny-dipping.

Weschcke himself was initiated (see INITIATION) into the American Celtic tradition of Witchcraft in 1972 by LADY SHEBA. He rose to high priest and held COVEN meetings in his Summit Avenue home.

In 1972 Weschcke married Sandra Heggum, a priestess in the same tradition, in a heavily publicized HANDFASTING ceremony conducted under a full moon. They wrote their own vows from old Witch rituals. Guests drank from a large CAULDRON filled with fruit, wine and flowers.

Weschcke remained open about his Witchcraft faith and activities, which brought him constant publicity. He published a popular Pagan journal, *Gnostica*, edited for a time by P. E. I. (ISAAC) BONEWITS. In the fall of 1973 Weschcke helped organize the COUNCIL OF AMERICAN WITCHES and then became its chairperson. For the council, he drafted "The Thirteen Principles of Belief" statement, one of his proudest accomplishments in the Craft. The statement was later incorporated into the U.S. Army's handbook for chaplains.

In the mid-1970s Weschcke began to wind down his activities. In 1973 his son Gabriel was born. His publishing business was stagnating, and Weschcke thought his media publicity was one of the reasons why. He sold the haunted house, moved to the country and began to devote more time to his family. He restructured his business by closing the bookstore, dropping *Gnostica* and the festivals and increasing the number of book titles published. During the same period, he adopted *Llewellyn* as a middle name, to use both in business and in magic. By the late 1980s Llewellyn was publishing 30–50 titles a year, plus audio and video tapes, computer software and

a popular "catazine," a combination magazine and catalog, *The New Times*.

The Weschckes decided to raise their son in the Unitarian church and became inactive in the Craft; however, Weschcke retains ties to the Wiccan and neo-Pagan communities through his publishing business and active research, practice and writing in the area of magic. He holds two honorary doctorates, one in magic. Weschcke also is Grandmaster of Aurum Solis, an international magical order established in Great Britain in 1897, now based in St. Paul.

Weyer, Johann (1515–1588) A German physician, Weyer became so moved by the brutal persecution of accused WITCHES that he spoke out strongly against the witch-hunters. Most witches, he said, were merely mentally disturbed, melancholic women who were incapable of harming any creature.

Weyer was born to a noble Protestant family in Brabant. He was a student of AGRIPPA, who had successfully defended an accused witch and earned a bad reputation for doing so. Weyer studied medicine in Paris and became a physician, serving as a court physician to the Duke of Cleves in the Netherlands.

Weyer became moved by the mounting persecutions and brutal tortures of accused witches. He believed in the DEVIL and his legions of DEMONS but denied that the Devil gave witches power to inflict harm upon mankind. He thought belief in WITCHCRAFT was caused by the Devil and that the Church was playing into Satan's hands by promoting belief in the evil power of witches.

Weyer set down his views in his book, *De Praestigiis Daemonum*, published in 1563. In it, he said most witches were deluded old women, the outcasts of society, who were fools, not heretics. Some might wish harm on their neighbors but could not carry it out. If harm occurred coincidentally, they believed, in their delusion, that they had brought it about.

Weyer acknowledged that there were witches who made pacts with Satan (see DEVIL'S PACT) but said that Satan, not the witches, caused harm. If such a witch killed cattle, for example, she did so by poison, not by supernatural means. He acknowledged that there were sorcerers who entered into demonic pacts for their own personal gain, but he believed that they were not the same as the helpless outcasts who were being persecuted by the Church.

Witches, he said, should be forgiven if they repented, or, at the most, fined. He deplored the tortures and executions of victims (see TORTURE) and said that their confessions of SABBATS, FLYING through the air, STORM RAISING and such were meaningless.

Weyer was able to discourage witch-hunting in

VINCE   TE IPSVM.

EFFIGIES IOANNIS WIERIANNO
ÆTATIS LX·SALVTIS M·D·LXXVI.

Johannes Weyer (Ioannis Wieri, *De Lamiis Liber*, 1577)

much of the Netherlands for a while, until he was forced out by the Catholic governor, the Duke of Alba. While he intended to inject a voice of reason into the witch hysteria, his book, unfortunately, had almost the opposite effect. Weyer was savagely denounced by critics such as JEAN BODIN and JAMES I, who believed in evil witches and advocated their extermination. Bodin said copies of Weyer's book should be burned. Books were written in refutation of Weyer and helped to stimulate further witch-hunts.

In 1568 Weyer had published the *Pseudo-Monarchy of Demons,* an inventory and description of Satan's legions. Weyer claimed that there were 7,405,926 devils and demons organized in 1,111 divisions of 6,666 each. Later, the Lutheran church thought his estimate way too low and raised the census of the demonic population to 2,665,866,746,664.

See also REGINALD SCOT.

Wheel of the Year

In neo-Pagan WITCHCRAFT and NEO-PAGANISM, the life cycles of continual birth, death and renewal as expressed in the changing seasons. The Wheel of the Year is marked by eight SABBATS which celebrate high points of the seasons: the solstices and equinoxes. The sun, which rules the seasons, is symbolized by a wheel. Solar wheels, or *wheels of fire,* are used in spring and summer festivals; wheel symbols are placed on ALTARS and flanked by CANDLES or fire in some form.

Wicca

An alternate, and often preferred, name for the religion of neo-Pagan WITCHCRAFT. Many WITCHES prefer to call themselves Wiccans rather than Witches and say they practice Wicca, rather than Witchcraft, because the words do not carry the negative stereotypes attached to *Witch* and *Witchcraft.* The terms *Wicca* and *Wiccan* distinguish practitioners of neo-Pagan Witchcraft from practitioners of folk MAGIC and other forms of witchcraft. They signify an organized religion with a set of beliefs, tenets, laws, ethics, holy days and rituals.

Some Wiccans believe that *Wicca* is derived from the Old English terms *wita,* which means "councilor," or *wis,* which means "wise." In fact, *Wicca* is Old English for "witch," as is the Old English term *wicce. Wiccian* means "to work sorcery" and "to bewitch." Still another Old English term, *wican,* means "to bend." In the sense that Witches use magic to influence events, *Wicca* and *Wiccan* are therefore appropriate terms.

Wicca, Church and School of

See CHURCH AND SCHOOL OF WICCA.

Wicca, Church of

See CHURCH AND SCHOOL OF WICCA.

Wicca, School of

See CHURCH AND SCHOOL OF WICCA.

Wiccan Rede

The creed of modern neo-Pagan WITCHCRAFT is expressed simply:

> Eight words the Wiccan Rede fulfill;
> An' it harm none, do what ye will.

The Wiccan Rede acknowledges the right of all people to choose their own paths, as long as their choices do not bring injury to another. The term *Wiccan Rede* is derived from the Old English terms *wicca* ("witch") and *roedan* ("to guide or direct"). *An* is Old English, short for *and.* Some Witches erroneously believe it is an archaic term for *if.*

The exact origin of the Wiccan Rede is uncertain. According to GERALD B. GARDNER, the creed is derived from the legendary Good King Pausol, who declared, "Do what you like so long as you harm no one," and apparently was adhered to by successive generations of witches. It is possible that the Rede has more recent origins, dating to the 1940s and 1950s, the early years of what was to become the "Gardnerian tradition" of modern Witchcraft. P. E. I. (ISAAC) BONEWITS theorizes that Gardner, who borrowed from the writings of ALEISTER CROWLEY, composed the Wiccan Rede by modifying Crowley's Law of Thelema: "Do what thou wilt shall be the whole of the Law." Crowley believed that if people knew their true wills and followed them, they would attune themselves to a harmony with the universe.

The Rede may originally have been intended to help make modern Witchcraft more acceptable to the public. It has since become interpreted very conservatively by most Witches and influences the casting of SPELLS. Some Witches feel the Rede should be interpreted more liberally.

Generally, neo-Pagan Witches have a deep and abiding respect for the sanctity and free will of all living creatures and do not believe they should use their powers to interfere in that free will. They believe it is unethical to use magic to harm or manipulate; even a love spell is manipulative if it is an attempt to sway affections against one's free will. Rather than cast a love spell aimed at a particular person, for example, a Witch casts a spell directed at attracting the right and perfect love, for the good and free will of all. Many Witches believe they should not cast any sort of spells on others without first obtaining their permission—even HEALING spells.

Violators of this interpretation of the Wiccan Rede will suffer a karmic boomerang effect and bring negativity or evil upon themselves, it is believed.

This interpretation of the Rede seems extreme to some in the Craft, for it means that spells should not be cast against wrongdoers: a Witch could make no effort to stop a rapist or a crime magically, because that would be manipulation of the criminal's free will. Those who favor the conservative interpretation argue that they can instead cast spells to protect victims.

Other Witches get around the issue by casting "binding" spells; that is, spells that stop or prevent evil. A binding spell on a serial murderer, for example, would not be a curse (see CURSES) upon the murderer but would be aimed at getting him caught. One celebrated binding spell was cast in 1980 in the San Francisco Bay Area, against the Mt. Tam Murderer, a serial killer who ambushed and shot joggers, most of them women. A group of Witches led by Z. BUDAPEST conducted a public "hexing" (their term for binding) ritual, calling for the murderer, who had been at large for nearly three years, to bring himself down through his own evil and mistakes. Within three months, the killer made enough mistakes to lead to his arrest; he was later convicted and given the death sentence.

Many Witches also cast binding spells to help causes, such as antinuclear movements, environmental concerns and animal welfare—to stop the killing of whales, for example. Binding spells are also cast against troublemakers, destructive gossips and annoying, meddlesome persons. In some of these situations, judgment, of course, is subjective. Casting a binding spell upon a co-worker with whom one is having conflicts may be considered ethical by some Witches but probably not so by most. In an effort to be ethically consistent, some Witches cast spells that are directed not at persons but at situations. For example, instead of binding a troublesome person in order to solve a problem, the Witch casts a spell directed at solution of the problem by unspecified means "for the good of all." Or, instead of casting a love spell on a specific individual, the Witch casts a spell to attract "the right and perfect love."

Still other Witches feel the interpretations of the Wiccan Rede have become too convoluted and have stripped Witches of their magical effectiveness, reducing them to a harmless level of "Bambi magic." Bonewits argues that if it is morally responsible to stop a crime physically, it is morally responsible to stop it magically. A minority of Witches do practice cursing when they feel it is warranted, but are quiet about it.

The entire issue is integral to the struggle of neo-Pagan Witches to be accepted by mainstream society. In other cultures where witchcraft plays a different role, the issue simply would not exist: a magician or sorcerer who refused to curse an enemy would be useless to society. Modern Witches also are fighting age-old negative beliefs about Witches. Despite occasional allowances for "white witches" in popular lore, the witch universally has been perceived throughout history as one who uses supernatural forces and powers, especially for evil. Neo-Pagan Witches have defined themselves differently, as agents of good and as healers.

See also THREEFOLD LAW OF RETURN.

Wiccan Shamanism A religion that is a blend of WITCHCRAFT and SHAMANISM, created by SELENA FOX, high priestess of CIRCLE SANCTUARY near Mt. Horeb, Wisconsin. Wiccan Shamanism is a contemporary form of the Wiccan religion with an ecumenical and multicultural focus; that is, it combines Wiccan ways, humanistic psychology and a variety of shamanistic practices from tribal societies around the world.

Rituals usually are held out of doors at sacred nature locations. They are designed to help the individual connect with the Divine through nature. Though structured, they are flexible and can be adapted to different needs.

Ceremonies have elements resembling those of African and Native American tribal societies, such as drumming, ecstatic dancing and use of rattles, which help participants achieve an altered state of consciousness. Meditation is also used. Though some shamanic traditions permit the use of hallucinogenic drugs, Wiccan Shamanism uses only legal methods of achieving higher consciousness. In addition to drums and rattles, other ceremonial tools include feathers, crystals, herbs and natural objects such as stones, gems, tree bark and acorns. Participants usually wear ceremonial garb and/or jewelry, though many worship in everyday clothing.

Rituals are performed within a MAGIC CIRCLE that has been consecrated to five elements: earth at the north cardinal point, air at the east, fire at the south, water at the west, and spirit at the center. The circle represents the wheel of life in seasons and in stages of aging: north the winter and death-rebirth; east the spring and youth; south the summer and adulthood; and west fall and old age. The center represents the entire year. Color associations are: north—green; east—yellow; south—red; west—blue; spirit—white.

Wiccan aspects include recognition of the eight witches' SABBATS and some of their traditional activities, such as MAYPOLE dancing at Beltane (May Eve), the hanging of MISTLETOE at the winter solstice (Yule) and the exchange of eggs at the spring equinox (Easter or Ostara). The Divine is honored in both male and female principles.

Healing is an important facet of Wiccan Shamanism and may be done through group ritual in healing circles or in one-on-one sessions. Healing tools and skills blend ancient magical practices with contemporary psychology and include therapeutic touch, crystals, herbs, TAROT, past life regressions, creative visualization and guided imagery, sound and music and movement.

The WICCAN REDE of harming none is observed. Consequently, no energy, even of a healing nature, is directed toward an individual without that person's permission.

Shamanic elements include the discovery of one's personal relationship with the spirits of nature and finding one's power animals and plants, which become allies in healing. Respect is paid to one's genetic and spiritual human ancestors, to all life forms and to the earth. The INITIATION is a vision quest, a night spent alone in nature without fire, shelter or food. The vision quest, undertaken only after a period of training, brings the individual face to face with deep, primal fears and provides for an intense self-exami-

nation. The initiate uses the Wiccan technique of casting a protective circle of light around the body; the appropriate spirits of nature are summoned for the night's test. The vision quest usually heralds a major life change. Many quests take place on CIRCLE SANCTUARY land, where training classes are taught.

Wiccan Shamanism also includes training in dreamcraft, in which the individual learns how to use dreams to access higher planes; herbology; and positive magic.

Wiccaning A Wiccan birth rite similar to a christening in Christianity (see WICCA). The newly born infant of WITCHES is ritually blessed and given a secret Craft name, which is intended to be used until the child is old enough to select his or her own name, if so desired. Godparents, who may or may not be members of the Craft, may also participate in the ceremony, pledging to help and watch over the child. Unlike a Christian christening, in which an infant is committed by the parents to the Christian faith, Wiccaning does not commit a child to Wicca or any other faith but allows for the child to choose his or her own path when the appropriate time comes.

Wiccaning is conducted by the coven's high priestess and high priest from within a consecrated MAGIC CIRCLE and in accordance with the coven's tradition (see COVEN). The child is presented to the four ELEMENTS, also called the Lords of the Watchtowers. The God and GODDESS are asked to bestow their divine blessings and protection upon the child. The infant is anointed with OIL and/or salted WATER and passed through the smoke of mild incense. The ceremony ends with CAKES-AND-WINE, and gift-giving.

A similar neo-Pagan rite is called *Paganing* (see NEO-PAGANISM).

widdershins (also withershins) A counterclockwise, circular movement used in the casting of binding and banishing SPELLS and CURSES, and in the casting of some MAGIC CIRCLES. The term *widdershins* comes from the Anglo-Saxon term *with sith*, "to walk against." The Irish equivalent is *tuatal* or *tuathal*, which means "a turning to the left"; it is the "unholy round" in Irish folklore. The opposite of widdershins is DEOSIL, moving clockwise.

Widdershins refers to walking against the sun and generally represents the unnatural and negative. In the casting of a black magic spell against the occupants of a house, for example, a witch or sorcerer would walk around the house counterclockwise. Widdershins motions and movements also are used in spells to get rid of negative spells or undesirable situations. It is used in necromantic rituals (see NECROMANCY).

In neo-Pagan Witchcraft, once a magic circle is cast deosil, a small section of it may be opened for access and egress with a widdershins motion with a sword or athame (see WITCHES' TOOLS), then reclosed deosil. In Australia, some Witches normally cast their magic circles widdershins, matching the southern hemisphere counterclockwise movement of the sun through the sky.

Wild Hunt In Celtic and Germanic folklore, a furious bunch of ghosts of the restless dead, which ride through the sky on their phantom horses, accompanied by their spectral hounds, shrieking and making wild noises (see GHOSTS, HAUNTINGS AND WITCHCRAFT). The hounds and horses are black, with hideous eyes. In various medieval versions of the Wild Hunt, WITCHES join the phantoms, and the ghostly train is led by pagan goddesses-turned-devils (by Christianity), including DIANA, HOLDA, Herodias, HECATE and Berchta. A Cornish version of the Wild Hunt, Devil's Dandy Dogs, is the most diabolical of ghostly packs, hunting the countryside for human souls. The Sluagh, or the Host, is a band of the unforgiven dead of the Highland fairy folk (see FAIRIES). Diana's night train punished the lazy and wicked but were generous on occasion: if a peasant left out food for them, they ate it and magically replenished it before they left.

In the English countryside, the Wild Hunt has been reported as late as the 1940s, flying over the terrain on Samhain, All Hallow's Eve.

will-o'-the-wisp See JACK-O'LANTERN.

willow The bark of the willow contains salicin, which has analgesic properties. These properties, which were discovered by the DRUIDS, make willow bark an important ingredient in the herbalist's pharmacopoeia. In ancient Greece, the willow was highly revered by WITCHES and was sacred to the goddesses HECATE, CIRCE and Persephone. In folklore it is called "witches' aspirin" and the "tree of enchantment" and is associated with the MOON. Modern Witches use it in HEALING rituals; the soft branches are knotted (see KNOTS) in the casting of SPELLS. Willow also is used to bind birch twigs onto an ash branch to form a "Witch's broom," also used in rituals. A willow planted in the garden, especially if it is near a spring or river, will bring the blessings of the moon to the occupant and will guard the home. In some parts of England, the willow has a dark side: it is said to stalk travelers at night, muttering low noises.

Wilson, Monique Modern English Witch known as Lady Olwen, high priestess with GERALD B. GARDNER, the namesake of the Gardnerian tradition of revivalist WITCHCRAFT. In 1964 she initiated RAYMOND BUCKLAND into the Craft; Buckland became the chief proponent of the Gardnerian tradition in the United States.

Upon Gardner's death later in 1964, Wilson and PATRICIA C. CROWTHER were designated the chief heirs to his estate. Wilson was the prime beneficiary, inheriting Gardner's Witchcraft Museum (the Witches' Mill) in Castletown on the Isle of Man, his collection of swords, daggers and magical tools and objects, his notebooks and papers and the copyrights to his books. For a few years, Wilson and her husband, "Scotty," an ex-pilot, held weekly coven meetings at Gardner's cottage in Castletown, ran the museum and kept up an international correspondence with Witches.

Wilson then sold the museum to Ripley's International, a move that earned her the undying disfavor of many Witches. Ripley's dispersed the contents in museums in Canada and the United States, including the Ripley Museum of Witchcraft and Magic on Fisherman's Wharf in San Francisco. Many Witches feel the exhibits sensationalize and cheapen Witchcraft and are not a fitting end to Gardner's possessions.

witch See WITCHES.

WITCH One of the manifestations of the counterculture and feminist movements in America was WITCH, an organization that sprang briefly into existence in the late 1960s and flourished among young women at college campuses across the country. WITCH originally stood for Women's International Terrorist Conspiracy from Hell, though on occasion the name changed to fit various political activities. The organization was formally launched in 1968 on Samhain, All Hallow's Eve, the sabbat most strongly associated with WITCHES in the public mind (see SABBATS). The year was a peak for protest movements: civil rights, the war in Vietnam and women's liberation. In that year, Martin Luther King and Robert Kennedy were assassinated. College campuses were hotbeds of demonstrations against the military, big business, big government and authority in general. Interest in mysticism, the occult and WITCHCRAFT was high.

WITCH was strongly feminist and viewed itself as a political, revolutionary, guerrilla organization. Witches and GYPSIES, the WITCH literature stated, were the original guerrilla fighters against the oppression of women and of the oppression of all. Dressed in rags and pointed, conical hats, and carrying brooms, members of WITCH conducted demonstrations.

Some outsiders saw the group as more comic than

serious. Andrew Greeley, Roman Catholic priest, novelist, lecturer on sociology at the University of Chicago and program director of the National Opinion Research Center at the university, called WITCH "a combination of the put-on and the serious, the deliberately comic and the profoundly agonized, of the bizarre and the holy." When three members of WITCH appeared in the university's social-science building to shriek curses upon the sociology department ("A hex on thy strategy!"), Greeley himself responded in comic fashion by offering to sprinkle holy water in the departmental office. His offer was turned down.

As an organization of Witches, WITCH was not regarded as legitimate by many other Witches. WITCH maintained that any woman could become a Witch by saying "I am a Witch" three times and thinking about it—rather than being initiated by another Witch (see INITIATION)—and that any woman could start a COVEN of Witches simply by declaring so.

witch balls Decorative glass balls made in England from the 18th century onward, often hung in windows to ward off witch's SPELLS or ill fortune. They appeared in America in the 19th century. Witch balls measure up to seven inches in diameter and are predominantly green or blue, though some are decorated in enameled swirls and stripes of varying colors. Others are silvered to act as convex mirrors. Because they are similar to the glass balls used by fishermen on nets, witch balls are associated with many sea superstitions and legends.

In the Ozarks, a witch ball is made of black hair rolled with beeswax into a hard pellet about the size of a marble. It is used in CURSES. If a witch wishes to harm or kill someone, she makes a hair ball and tosses it at the victim. In Ozark folklore, it is said that when someone is killed by a witch's curse, the witch ball is always found near the body.

Witch ball is also a term for a puffball fungus found in parts of America, which burns for a long time. Indians have used it to carry fire from one camp to another. -

See also AMULET.

witch bottles Charms used to counteract witches' SPELLS that were prevalent in Elizabethan England, especially in East Anglia, where superstitions and beliefs in WITCHES were strong (see CHARMS). Witch bottles were little bellarmine flasks into which was put victim's URINE, or hair or nail clippings (see HAIR AND NAILS). When the flask was buried, the spell was nullified and the witch supposedly suffered great discomfort. Sometimes the bottles were thrown into a fire; when they exploded, the spell was broken or the witch supposedly was killed. If urine was used

as a counter-charm, then the witch became unable to urinate; thus, she was exposed for her MALEFICIA. Witch bottles also were hung in chimneys as charms to prevent witches from FLYING down them and entering a house.

witch boxes In Britain, CHARMS placed in the house to protect the occupants from witch's SPELLS and to prevent WITCHES from entering. Witch boxes were popular in the 16th and 17th centuries. They usually consisted of a small wooden box with a glass front, filled with herbs, bits of rowan, pieces of human bone and odds and ends, over which a magic spell of protection had been cast. The boxes often were sold by witch-hunters, who went from town to town whipping up hysteria about witches (see WITCHCRAFT).

Witch of Endor According to the story related in Samuel I of the Old Testament, the Witch of Endor was a pythoness and necromancer who raised the spirit of Samuel at the request of King Saul of Israel (see NECROMANCY). Theologians and demonologists have disagreed over whether the witch actually conjured Samuel or tricked Saul by ventriloquism.

The Bible relates that Saul was afraid of an impending attack by a mighty army of Philistines, who had been joined by his rival, David. He gathered up the Israelites and camped at Mount Gilboa. He sought advice from prophets and divination by sacred lot and from the Lord, but he received no answer as to his fate or the action he should take.

Saul instructed his servants, "Seek me a woman that hath a familiar spirit, that I may go to her, and enquire of her." His servants directed him to the pythoness at Endor, whose name is never given.

Saul disguised himself and went to the witch the same night. At first, she was frightened that he had come to expose her as a witch: "Behold, thou knowest what Saul hath done, how he hath cut off those that have familiar spirits, and the wizards, out of the land: wherefore then layest thou a snare for my life, to cause me to die?"

Saul assured the woman he meant her no harm and instructed her to conjure Samuel from the dead. She performed her ritual and claimed to see gods rising out of the earth, followed by a spirit like an old man, wrapped in a robe. Saul, who could see nothing, believed the old spirit was Samuel and prostrated himself on the ground.

Samuel was not pleased to be disturbed from the grave. Saul said he faced war and had been abandoned by God. But Samuel's reply was not what Saul wanted to hear: that God was displeased with Saul for his disobedience and had torn his kingdom from

Witch of Endor conjuring Samuel for Saul (Joseph Glanvil, *Saducismus Triumphatus*, 1681 ed.)

his hand and given it to David. "Moreover, the Lord will also deliver Israel with thee into the hand of the Philistines: and tomorrow shalt thou and thy sons be with me: the Lord shall also deliver the host of Israel into the hand of the Philistines."

Upon hearing this condemnation, Saul fell into a faint. The spirit of Samuel vanished. The witch went to Saul and offered him food for strength, but he refused. His servants and the witch helped him get up. The witch killed a fatted calf she had and cooked it, and made some unleavened bread. Before he left, Saul relented and ate the meal she offered him.

The next day, the Philistines attacked the Israelites, who fled in terror and were slain. Saul's sons Jonathan, Abinadab and Malchishua were slain, and Saul was badly wounded. Saul ordered an armor-bearer to kill him with his sword, but the soldier refused. Saul took his sword and fell upon it.

When the Philistines found his body, they cut off the head, fastened his body to the wall of Beth-shan and put his armor in the temple of ASTARTE. His headless body was removed by the inhabitants of

Jabesh-gilead, who burned the body and buried the bones. David succeeded Saul as King of Israel.

Among those who considered the conjuration of Samuel to be a hoax was REGINALD SCOT, the 16th-century English writer who attempted to debunk beliefs about witchcraft in his book, *The Discoverie of Witchcraft*. Scot devoted several chapters to a discussion of the story, asserting that the distraught Saul was taken for a fool by a clever woman whose familiar was a "counterfeit":

> When Saule had told hir, that he would have Samuel brought up to him, she departed from his presence into hir closet, where doubtles she had hir familiar; to wit, some lewd craftie preest, and made Saule stand at the door like a foole (as it were with his finger in a hole), to hear the cousening [deceitful] answers, but not see the counsening [sic] handling thereof, and the couterfetting [sic] of the matter.

The witch, Scot said, knew who Saul was despite his disguise. She played out her incantations, lied about seeing gods or angels ascending from the earth and about seeing the spirit of old Samuel. Scot discounts that such a spirit could have been Samuel, for it was clothed in a new mantle such as he was buried in and surely would have been rotted by the time he was conjured.

Theologians such as Augustine and Tertullian, and the French demonologist, JEAN BODIN (a contemporary of Scot's), felt a spirit was conjured, but it was the DEVIL, not Samuel. Scot disagreed, saying the Devil would have been banished by the word "God" or "Jehovah," spoken five times during the conjuration. Furthermore, Scot said, the Devil would not appear to rebuke and punish someone for evil but to encourage them to do more evil.

The witch, said Scot, was a ventriloquist, "that is, Speaking at it were from the bottome of her bellie, did cast herself into a transe [sic] and so abused Saule, answering to Saule in Samuels name, in his counterfeit hollow voice."

witch pegs In rural areas of the Ozarks, CHARMS for keeping WITCHES away from a home, made from cedar pegs with three prongs, driven into the ground in the path to the door. Folklore belief holds that the prongs are associated with the Trinity. It is considered bad luck to step on or disturb a witch peg.

witchcraft Belief in witchcraft is universal, but there is no universal definition of *witchcraft*, for the term has different meanings in different cultures and has had different meanings at different times in history. It has both negative and positive connotations. In a neutral sense, witchcraft is SORCERY, the magical manipulation of supernormal forces through the casting of SPELLS and the conjuring or invoking of spirits. Such spells may be for either good or bad purposes. MAGIC and sorcery have been used by mankind since prehistoric times in an effort to control the environment and enhance daily life. In most societies, however, witchcraft has been considered the harmful branch of sorcery. Anthropologists define witchcraft as an innate condition—the use of malevolent power by psychic means without need for ritual or charm. This definition applies to some tribal societies, but in Western witchcraft, the witch works magic through spells.

Witchcraft also involves the use of supernormal powers, such as invisibility, shape-shifting (see METAMORPHOSIS), FLYING, the ability to kill at a distance, clairvoyance and astral projection.

During the Renaissance, witchcraft was defined as evil magic, heresy and Devil-worship. The associations with evil and the DEVIL linger in modern Western culture. Revivalist Witches in the West have redefined Witchcraft as a neo-Pagan religion that worships the GODDESS and HORNED GOD and has no connection with Christianity or the Devil. In addition, neo-Pagan Witchcraft stresses the use of magic only for benevolent purposes, never for harm. Neo-Pagan Witchcraft, which has developed since the 1950s, represents but a small portion of the types of witchcraft still practiced by others, both in the West and elsewhere in the world. Most witchcraft is spell casting. It is usually regarded with fear and uncertainty by the public, though it provides a necessary social function by enabling others to seek redress of wrongs and grievances, and alleviation from stress and troubles.

Evolution of Western Witchcraft

The Inquisition. The Christian Church's determined campaign to eradicate heretics, beginning at the start of the 13th century, was turned on WITCHES by the middle of the 15th century. For nearly 250 years, witches were hunted down and executed as heretics, accused of worshipping the Devil. Most of the witch-hunts in Europe were conducted by the Church, both Catholic and Protestant; in Britain, witchcraft was considered largely a civil crime, and witches were prosecuted by the secular arm. The number of victims of the Inquisition is unknown; estimates have ranged from 30,000 to nine million, an incredibly high figure. In 1598 Ludovicus á Paramo figured that 30,000 witches had been burned in 150 years. Most modern historians estimate that 150,000 to 200,000 victims were executed and that approximately 100,000 of them came from Germany.

The association of witches with heresy occurred slowly over a period of centuries. Prior to the Middle Ages, witchcraft and sorcery were considered essentially the same. Sorcery was a civil crime, and witches and sorcerers were punished under civil law, which usually called for fines, imprisonment and banishment. Heresy, on the other hand, was punishable by death under civil law as early as 430 A.D., even though such laws were not rigorously enforced. Under Roman law, distinctions were made between white witchcraft or sorcery and black witchcraft. White witchcraft, which consisted largely of magical HEALING and DIVINATION, was not considered a crime, while black witchcraft, or harmful magic, was a crime. White witchcraft was tolerated and usually considered beneficial; it served a useful function in society and was defended by the public. White witchcraft could become black witchcraft, however, if a cure resulted in the death of a patient. Under canon law, the distinctions between white and black witchcraft began to disappear, until both were punished as heresy.

From the eighth century on, sorcery was increasingly associated with harmful witchcraft, and witchcraft was increasingly associated with heresy. Beginning in the 11th century, heretics were sentenced with increasing frequency to death by burning. The Church directed its efforts against the religious sects of the Albigenses, which flourished in eastern Europe and southern France; the Cathars, which spread over much of Europe; and the Waldenses (VAUDOIS), which appeared in the late 12th century in southern France. These religious sects were also accused of sorcery, holding SABBATS and Devil-worship. In 1184 the Church's efforts became more formal with the direction of Pope Lucius III to bishops to investigate all deviations from Church teachings. The papal Inquisition was established between 1227 and 1233. In

Witch and wizard riding to sabbat (Ulrich Molitor, *Hexen Meysterey*, 1545)

Devil seducing witch (Ulrich Molitor, *Von den Unholden oder Hexen*, 1489)

1233 Pope Gregory IX issued a bull that decreed that inquisitors would be Dominicans and would be answerable only to the pope.

During the same period, however, ecclesiastical belief in witchcraft was at a low due to the CANON EPISCOPI, which held that witchcraft was an illusion and belief in it was heresy. This was reversed by a series of papal bulls against sorcery and the influence of the writings of demonologists and theologians, who became increasingly obsessed with witchcraft. One of the most influential theologians was THOMAS AQUINAS, who in the 13th century refuted the *Canon Episcopi* and endorsed beliefs that witches copulated with DEMONS, flew through the air, shape-shifted, raised storms (see STORM RAISING) and performed other MALEFICIA. Aquinas believed such acts implied a pact with the Devil. He also believed heretics should be burned.

The demonification of witchcraft received an additional boost by the growing favor in the 13th and 14th centuries of Aristotelian philosophy over Platonic philosophy. Platonic philosophy provides for the existence of natural magic which is neither black nor white, but morally neutral. Under Aristotelian thought, no natural magic exists; therefore, magic must be either divine or demonic (see MAGIC).

As early as 1320, the Church was trying persons accused of heretical sorcery; by 1335 heretical sorcery included SABBATS, Devil-worship and FLYING. Numerous bulls against sorcery and witchcraft were issued through the mid-15th century, some of which instructed inquisitors to distinguish between sorcery/witchcraft and heresy. Sorcery was linked to heresy by Sixtus IV in bulls issued in 1473, 1478 and 1483. The bull that turned the full force of the Inquisition against witches—as heretical sorcerers—was that of INNOCENT VIII in 1484. Two years later, the Inquisitors Heinrich Kramer and Jacob Sprenger published the *MALLEUS MALEFICARUM*, which carried the bull as an introduction and set forth rules for identifying, prosecuting and punishing witches. The *Malleus* quickly spread throughout Europe and was considered the primary witch-hunter's reference as the Inquisition picked up steam. By this time, the characteristics of witchcraft had been established as a DEVIL'S PACT; secret, orgiastic sabbats; infanticide and cannibalism; renunciation of Christianity; and desecration of the cross and Eucharist.

In 1522 Martin Luther called sorcerers and witches "the Devil's whores" and criticized lawyers for wanting too much proof to convict them. In 1532 the *Carolina*, the criminal code enacted under Charles V for the Holy Roman Empire states, distinguished between white and black witchcraft but provided punishment for both. Injurious witchcraft was punishable by death by burning, as was homosexuality

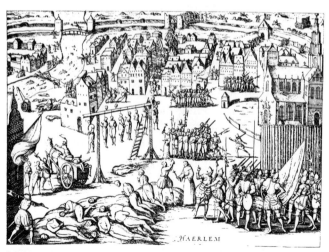

Mass executions of Haarlemites as Devil-worshippers, under Fernando Alvarez de Toledo, Duke of Alba, after conquest of Haarlem, 1573 (Michael Aistinger, *De leone Belgico*)

Devil carrying witch off to hell (Olaus Magnus, *Historia de gentibus septentrionalibus*, 1555)

and sex with animals. Witchcraft that did not cause injury or damage was punished according to the magnitude of the crime. Fortune-telling by sorcery or other magical arts called for torture and imprisonment. In 1572 a Saxon law code was enacted which called for the death penalty for all forms of witchcraft.

Accusations of witchcraft usually started with simple sorceries: spells perceived to harm others. The accused usually had had an argument with a neighbor or had been overheard muttering complaints or curses. They were often tortured, sometimes in the most cruel and barbaric manner, until they died or confessed to black witchcraft and worshipping the Devil. Invariably, the inquisitors also forced them to name accomplices (see TORTURE). In this manner, whole villages were sometimes implicated, and mass executions took place. The most common form of execution in Europe was burning at the stake. If the victim was lucky, he or she was strangled first. Many were burned alive.

Some trials apparently were motivated by the desire of the inquisitors to seize the properties of the accused. This appears to have been a factor in areas that suffered the most savage persecutions, such as Germany. The majority of victims, however, were of the lower classes—poor and often beggars. Most also

were women; the *Malleus Maleficarum* had firmly linked women to witchcraft. Many were social outcasts.

The Inquisition against witches was confined to the Continent. The activities of the Inquisition were strongest in Germany, France and Switzerland in the 15th and 16th centuries, spreading a little into Scandinavia in the 16th and 17th centuries. Few Inquisitional activities against witches took place in Spain or Portugal, where distinctions were made between sorcery (largely divination) and witchcraft (Devil-worship and crimes associated with it). The circumstances that touched off witch-hunts in various areas cannot be generalized. Political and social unrest were factors; trials increased in Germany and elsewhere in Europe during the Thirty Years War from 1618 to 1648. Bad crops years, plagues and infectious illnesses that spread throughout villages also contributed to searches for scapegoats.

Beginning in the 16th century, the witch hysteria was countered by demonologists, such as JOHANN WEYER, who questioned the validity of beliefs about witches and opposed the tactics of witch-hunters. The witch hysteria peaked between 1560 and 1660, then tapered off over another 90 years.

Witchcraft in Britain and the American Colonies. Witch-hunting in Britain took a different form than that of

Newsletter concerning burning of three witches at Derneburg, October 1555

the Inquisition in Europe, and bloomed much later. Throughout the witch hysteria, witchcraft was treated largely as a civil crime in Britain. The emphasis was not on a witch's heresy by virtue of a pact with the Devil but upon her power to bring misery to others with her spells and curses.

Prior to 1542 witchcraft was considered sorcery in England, punishable by various secular and ecclesiastical laws as early as 668 A.D. Witches usually were tried by the church and given moderate punishment by the state. If nobles were involved in charges of sorcery or witchcraft, the crime had the potential of becoming a charge of treason, if sorcery had been used against the throne or to divine the political future. In 1542 Henry VIII passed the first Witchcraft Act, which provided for witches to be tried and punished by the state. The statute of 1542 made a felony of the conjuring of spirits, divining and casting of false or malicious spells and enchantments. Such offenses were punishable by "death, loss and forfeiture of their lands, tenants, goods and chattels." Records exist of only one case brought to trial under the law; the accused was pardoned. The law was repealed in 1547 by Edward VI.

A second Witchcraft Act was passed in 1563 under Elizabeth I. This act was largely the result of eccle-

siastical pressure upon the state to address rising public fears of witchcraft. It increased penalties: death for murder by witchcraft; a year in jail and the pillory for less serious witchcraft; and forfeiture of property for second convictions of divination, attempted murder and unlawful love spells.

A similar act was passed in Scotland the same year. During the reign of James VI (r. 1567–1625), brutal witch-hunts took place in Scotland, involving barbaric torture and burning at the stake (see NORTH BERWICK WITCHES). Though James feared witches and permitted the witch-hunts, he did act to cool the hysteria when it threatened to get out of hand. In 1603 he became JAMES I of England and ruled the united kingdoms of England and Scotland until his death in 1625. In 1604 the Elizabethan Witchcraft Act was repealed, and a third and tougher act was passed for England and Scotland. It called for death by hanging for the first conviction of malefic witchcraft, regardless of whether or not a victim had died. The penalty for divining, destroying or damaging property, and concocting love philtres remained a year in jail plus the pillory. The act also made it a felony to conjure, consult, entertain, covenant with, employ, feed or reward any evil spirit for any purpose, thus introducing Devil's pacts into the law.

The Act of 1604 remained in force until 1736. England's witch hysteria peaked under its force in the 1640s, also a time of political and social strife caused by the Civil War. Witch-hunting was a profitable profession, and witch finders such as MATTHEW HOPKINS made good fees by identifying witches by PRICKING them and discovering the DEVIL'S MARK. Convicted witches in England were hanged, not burned.

Most of the witch trials in England and Scotland concerned accused black witches. The white witches—the cunning men and cunning women, wizards, diviners and healers—were seldom prosecuted by the common-law courts, despite the fact that their sorceries were illegal. The church courts prosecuted them, for their magical miracles were in direct competition with the clergy, many of whom also practiced white witchcraft. Punishments usually were light, in marked contrast to the European trials.

The *Malleus Maleficarum* made little impact in England. It was not translated into English until 1584, 98 years after it had been written. England had its own Protestant demonologists in the 17th century who wrote treatises on identifying and punishing witches, including WILLIAM PERKINS, John Cotta, Thomas Potts, Richard Baldwin and other learned men. These opinion shapers held that white witches were far more dangerous than black witches and deserved to be prosecuted all the more.

Ireland remained free of much of the witch hysteria. Only about eight trials are recorded between 1324 (see ALICE KYTELER) and 1711 (see ISLAND MAGEE WITCHES). Except for the Kyteler trial, they all involved Protestants against Protestants. A law against witchcraft was passed in 1587 and was repealed in 1821.

Witch problems in the American colonies did not begin until the 1640s, just as the hysteria was peaking in England, and they never reached the magnitude of the witch-hunts elsewhere. The first hanging of a convicted witch occurred in 1647 in Connecticut. INCREASE MATHER and COTTON MATHER, leaders in Massachusetts, were influenced by the demonologists of England—Cotton Mather cited Perkins in his own treatises on witchcraft—and believed that a conspiracy of witches who were in league with Satan threatened the survival of New England. The mass trials in Salem in 1692, the most spectacular witch case in America, were tried under the 1604 statute (see SALEM WITCHES). Elsewhere in the colonies, trials were scattered. Besides the Salem victims (31 condemned and 150 accused), there are records of only a dozen or so executions of witches in New England, plus a number of lighter punishments of whippings and banishment. Pennsylvania law under William Penn was tolerant, thus making it possible later for the German immigrant powwowers (wizards or cunning folk) to establish their culture (see POWWOWING).

The end of the witch hysteria. Church and state persecutions of witches largely came to a halt in Europe, Britain and America by the 1730s, though scattered cases occurred for several more decades. The last trial occurred in 1711 in Ireland, resulting in sentences of jail and the pillory. In England, Jane Clarke and her son and daughter were the last to be indicted as witches, in 1717; despite the willingness of 25 persons to testify against them, the case was thrown out of court. In Scotland, Janet Horne was the last to be tried and burned, in 1727. In the American colonies, Grace Sherwood of Virginia was accused of witchcraft in 1706 and was swum (see SWIMMING), but the case may have been dropped. In Jura, the border area between France and Switzerland, a beggar woman was burned as a witch in 1731. Persecutions lingered in France and Germany, where the greatest witch-hunting had taken place during the height of the Inquisition. In France, the last executions took place in 1745. In Bavaria, Anna Maria Schwagel was the last accused witch to be executed in 1775 by beheading.

Political and social changes, and backlash reactions to the persecutions, made witch-hunting both undesirable and unnecessary. In Germany, the threatened destruction of entire populations necessitated a cooling of accusations and trials. Throughout Europe, the evolution from feudalism to capitalism during the 17th and 18th centuries changed attitudes toward the instability created by the threat of heresy and the subsequent confiscations of property. In England, the Civil War drastically changed society by establishing a republican commonwealth, paving the way for a middle class and improving religious tolerance. In the American colonies, public disgust was so great after the Salem debacle that leaders criticized the methods of the court. Salem colony repented, and in 1711 the General Court restored the civil rights of 22 of the 31 persons convicted in 1692 (the rights of the remaining victims were not restored until 1957).

The industrial revolution and Age of Science brought shifts to urban population centers, changes in livelihood and more education. Among the learned men, the skepticism of science took hold, and it became unfashionable to believe in witchcraft and magic. One influential critic was Francis Hutchinson, an English clergyman who wrote his sharply critical *Essay Concerning Witchcraft* (1718), which exposed the false accusations, evidence and political motivations of many trials.

In 1736, under George II of England, the Witchcraft Act of 1604 was repealed and replaced with a new statute that removed penalties for witchcraft, sorcery, enchantment and conjuration. However, the new law punished those who pretended to use witchcraft, sorcery, enchantment and conjuration in fraudulent fortune-telling and divining. Punishment was a year in jail with quarterly appearances in the pillory.

Witchcraft receded as heresy and returned to its former state of sorcery and folk magic. The public still perceived a "witch" as a malevolent person in league with the Devil but continued to rely heavily upon cunning folk, powwowers, witch doctors, sorcerers, white witches and the like for healing, fertility, luck and prosperity charms and divination. White witchcraft flourished during the 18th century and most of the 19th century. Among rural, uneducated populations, antiwitch sentiment continued. In England, Europe and even America, there were outbreaks of violence against suspected witches all through the 19th century, and into the early 20th century (see JOHN BLYMIRE; CHARLES WALTON). The violence sometimes was turned on white witches whose magic failed to work. Stories in the press cropped up periodically about witches, magical charms and rumors of nocturnal meetings in forests.

In the latter half of the 19th century, Spiritualism spread quickly on both sides of the Atlantic. In England, the Witchcraft Act of 1736 and the Vagrancy Act of 1824 were used to prosecute mediums on charges of conjuring spirits and fradulent fortune-telling. A campaign to rescind the 1736 statute was mounted by Spiritualists in 1950, after the law had been used against a medium who defrauded a widow. In 1951 the the Witchcraft Act of 1736, and a section of the Vagrancy Act of 1824, were replaced by the Fraudulent Mediums Act. For the first time in more than 300 years in Britain, witchcraft was no longer a crime.

Witchcraft, women and misogyny. The odious witchcraft defined and attacked by church and state during the witch craze focused almost exclusively on women. Christianity holds women accountable for sin, so it was naturally presumed that they were predisposed to the evils of witchcraft and Devil-worship. The *Malleus Maleficarum* is replete with misogyny. Authors Heinrich Kramer and Jacob Sprenger, Dominican inquisitors, stated that "all witchcraft comes from carnal lust, which in women is insatiable." They added that men are protected from succumbing to witchcraft because Jesus was a man. Furthermore, they stated that women are "chiefly addicted to Evil Superstitions" because they are feeble-brained, "intellectually like children," weak in body, impressionable, lustful, have weak memories and are by nature liars. Much of the offensive behavior attributed to witches was sex-related: uninhibited copulation with demons and FAMILIARS, sexual attacks upon men in the form of succubi, the causation of impotency and infertility and, incredibly, the theft of male sexual organs.

Most of the women accused of witchcraft were social outcasts, beyond the immediate control of men: they were spinsters and widows. The patriarchal societies of Europe and Britain were openly hostile to such women. The hostility was only exacerbated by old age, poverty, handicaps and ugliness. Mary Daly, American theologian, philosopher and feminist, theorizes in *Gyn/Ecology: The Metaethics of Radical Feminism* (1978) that spinsters and widows were subject to male hostility because they were "women free from invasion by the 'member,' women who might even find the 'Male Organ' laughable, unaesthetic, and, perhaps more importantly, uninteresting."

The women of this period had no rights of their own and no say in their own destiny. Most went from being the property of a father to the property of a husband. The masses were stuck in lives of grinding poverty and misery. It is possible that women were more likely to turn to sorcery in an effort to improve their sorry plights or redress their grievances—which would make them more vulnerable to accusations of witchcraft. The tales of imaginary flights to sabbats seem more like desperate attempts to relieve boredom and unhappiness than intents to indulge in evil (see ISOBEL GOWDIE).

In non-European societies, witchcraft is commonly, but not always, associated with women. Most African

tribes believe that witchcraft is inherited and can be passed to either sex; the Tellensi of northern Ghana believe that witchcraft is passed only by the mother. The Navajo associate more men with witchcraft than women, but women witches are invariably old or childless, which corresponds to the European portrait of spinsters and widows.

Ancient legends among the Ona and Yahgans of Tierra del Fuego bear a chilling resemblance to the European witch-hunts. According to Ona legend, witchcraft and the magical arts were known only to women in the old days of Ona-land. The women kept their own Lodge, which was closed to men. They had the power to cause sickness and death, and the men lived in total fear of them. Finally, the men decided they had had enough tyranny and that a dead witch was better than a live witch. They massacred all the women and adolescent girls. They spared only the smallest girls who had not yet begun their training in witchcraft, so that the men eventually would have wives again. To prevent the girls from banding together and reasserting their power when they grew up, the men formed a secret society and Lodge, protected by fierce demons, which excluded women. The men kept their dominance over women from then on.

The Yahgans, neighbors of the Ona, also have a legend of the ancient rule of men by women who used witchcraft and cunning. The Yahgan men also deposed the women, not through massacre but apparently by mutual consent.

The rise of modern Witchcraft. Since the 1950s, Witchcraft has been revived as a neo-Pagan religion, centered on the worship of the Goddess and sometimes her consort, the Horned God, and the practice of benevolent magic. It has nothing to do with the Devil or Christianity. The father of this revival was GERALD B. GARDNER, an English civil servant whose interest in the occult led to his INITIATION in 1939 into a COVEN of witches in England. It is difficult to say whether Gardner intended to create a new religion or whether it grew spontaneously from public interest in his writings. Historians contend both: that Gardner was a creative genius who borrowed from folklore, mythology, ancient pagan rites, literature and ceremonial magic to invent a new religion; or, that he unwittingly planted a few seeds which others cultivated to fruition.

The coven that Gardner joined claimed to be descended from a long line of hereditary Witches, who practiced both a magical craft and a Pagan religion, commonly called "The Craft of the Wise" and "The Old Religion." Other covens scattered about England have claimed the same; most remain rather secretive, and it is not known exactly how far back their lineages go or exactly what has constituted "witchcraft" over the centuries.

In the latter part of the 19th century, American folklorist CHARLES GODFREY LELAND claimed to discover hereditary witches in Tuscany, who worshipped ARADIA, daughter of DIANA. In the 1920s, British anthropologist MARGARET A. MURRAY advanced the theory that the witches who were persecuted during the witch mania were members of organized pagan religious cults who worshiped the Horned God. Both Leland and Murray have been criticized subsequently by historians. It is now acknowledged that no evidence exists in support of Murray's theory of organized witches.

Isolated groups and cults did keep alive various pagan rites and customs, especially those related to health and fertility, such as seasonal festivals and orgiastic dances (see SABBATS). There is evidence of a flourishing cult of Diana in western and central Europe in the 5th and 6th centuries, which apparently survived to the Middle Ages. The BENANDANTI, an agrarian cult of nocturnal witch fighters, survived in northern Italy to the 16th or 17th centuries. The *strigoi* of Romania, witches both living and dead, possessed supernatural powers and fought each other at night (see STRIGA). Another Romanian cult, the Călușari, was a secret society of cathartic dancers whose patronness was the Queen of the Fairies, or Diana/Herodia/Aradia.

At the time of Gardner's initiation, Murray's theory had not been put to rest. Gardner accepted her theory of a European witch cult. He feared that Witchcraft was in danger of dying out because of a lack of young members, and he wanted to publicize it. He had been given a framework of rituals, including initiations and a system of Greater and Lesser Sabbats, by his coven. Because the Witchcraft Act of 1736 was still in effect, his coven allegedly discouraged him from writing openly about Witchcraft. Instead, he wrote a novel, *High Magic's Aid*, under the pseudonym *Scire*, published in 1949. The book contained the rituals and beliefs Gardner had been given by his coven.

After the repeal of the Witchcraft Act in 1951, Gardner broke away from the coven and formed his own coven. To flesh out his rituals, he apparently borrowed from Leland; ALEISTER CROWLEY, whom he met in 1946; the Ordo Templi Orientis (OTO) and Masonry, both of which he was a member of; the HERMETIC ORDER OF THE GOLDEN DAWN; Rosicrucianism; folklore; and mythology. Gardner, who spent many years in the East, may also have borrowed from Eastern magic and mysticism; there is disagreement in the Craft as to whether or not he did. In 1953 he initiated DOREEN VALIENTE, with whom he collaborated in writing and revising the rituals. According to Valiente, Gardner's material showed heavy influence by the OTO and Crowley, which she removed and rewrote in simpler form. Gardner never acknowledged Crowley's exact role in his rituals.

Gardner wrote two nonfiction books about Witchcraft, *Witchcraft Today* (1954) and *The Meaning of Witchcraft* (1959), which described the Craft as he saw it and put forth the Murray theory. The books captured the public's fancy and revived an interest in Witchcraft. In 1957 Valiente "hived off" to form her own coven.

Some historians have credited Valiente with increasing the emphasis on the Goddess. She states that this is not so and that the Goddess was part of the Craft at the time she joined it. Apparently, the presence of the Goddess was neither supreme nor uniform throughout the Old Religion. The Canewdon witches of OLD GEORGE PICKINGILL, who died in 1909, worshipped the Horned God. Pre-Gardnerian covens, while comprised of both men and women, generally were led by a man, called the magister or master. *High Magic's Aid* does not mention the Goddess. In following Murray, Gardner at first emphasized the role of the Horned God. The Goddess gradually assumed more importance, thus elevating the role of the high priestess to leader of the coven.

During the 1950s, Craft laws and ethics took shape. The WICCAN REDE, "An' it harm none, do what ye will," stipulates that Witches may use their magical powers only for good, never to harm any living thing. The actual age of the Rede is not known. It was in force when Gardner joined the Craft, but he may have given it emphasis as a way of making Witchcraft more acceptable to a public that still associated Witches with evil. Some modern Witches and neo-Pagans feel the Rede's conservatism has been carried to an extreme. The need was seen for a set of written rules, and "Ned," who left Gardner's coven with Valiente, is said to have drafted a proposal that was not adopted. Gardner apparently revised it in a false archaic English. The 161 "Ancient Craft Laws," said to date back to the 16th century, cover conduct, secrecy, coven meetings and territories and discipline. Valiente has never considered the document to be authentic. The laws have been published in various versions.

The greatest growth of neo-Pagan Witchcraft took place in the 1960s and 1970s, during a general revival of interest in occultism. Most converts were women and came from the ranks of the white, middle-class, followed by those in creative arts, academia and the professions. Gardner's revival of Witchcraft spread to other countries, including the United States, where it took root in Canada, Australia, France, Germany and Japan.

In the initial boom, there suddenly were more would-be Witches than covens to initiate them. (Initiation was required in order to consider oneself a Witch.) Many persons were attracted for the wrong reasons: the desire to join in a fad or to acquire magical power for the manipulation of others. Most of these persons eventually dropped out of the movement; some splintered off in their own directions. Gardner's Witchcraft became known as Gardnerian, and other "traditions" were created or came to light. ALEXANDER SANDERS, an Englishman who claimed to be a hereditary Witch but who most likely was refused admission to the Gardnerian tradition, founded the Alexandrian tradition, based heavily on the rituals of Gardner. Some traditions claimed ancient, hereditary lineages; some of these claims were soon proved to be false. Numerous traditions were born, lived brief lives and died, while others grew, survived and evolved. Emphasis on the Goddess appealed to many women who were caught up in the feminist movement and to many others who simply felt short-changed and disenfranchised by Christianity and other mainstream religions.

The greatest activity and ferment has taken place in the United States, which afforded the most open atmosphere for a new religion, despite public fears and prejudices about witchcraft. At the same time revivalist Witchcraft was growing, so was the broader neo-Pagan movement of nature religions (see NEO-PAGANISM).

The neo-Pagan Witchcraft movement has not been unified or cohesive by any means. It has been fraught with dissension, disagreement and personality conflicts. It is axiomatic, however, that the history of any religion is full of strife. Autonomy is fiercely protected in the Craft, and unification may never occur. Diversity and change within various frameworks of tradition remain desirable.

Neo-Pagan Witches still find themselves the victims of prejudice, hate and fear. They are often confused with satanists and practitioners of VODOUN, SANTERÍA and other African and Latin religions. Many remain secretive about their involvement in the Craft. Others feel it is essential to seek publicity in order to gain acceptance by society. Organizations and networks have been formed to help educate the media and public and to fight for civil rights (see CHARLES ARNOLD; CIRCLE SANCTUARY; COVENANT OF THE GODDESS; HELMS AMENDMENT; LEO LOUIS MARTELLO; WITCHES LEAGUES FOR PUBLIC AWARENESS).

Some Witches feel that Gardner committed a serious mistake by referring to revivalist Witchcraft as *Witchcraft*, a word tainted over the centuries and nearly universally associated with malevolence and evil. Neo-Pagan Witchcraft is part religion and part magical craft. It cannot be equated with the witchcraft and sorcery of other cultures nor with the witchcraft persecuted during the Middle Ages and Renaissance. Some Witches have abandoned the word *Witchcraft* in favor of *Wicca,* an Old English term for "witch" that is free of stereotype (see WICCA).

By the 1980s most neo-Pagan Witches no longer believed that the Craft was an unbroken religious tradition since pagan times. Many feel they are observing ancient rites and beliefs that have been reconstructed to suit modern times; in this way, they preserve an ancient heritage.

Modern Traditions of Witchcraft

Neo-Pagan Witchcraft is an autonomous religion. There is no central authority or liturgy; various traditions have their own rituals, philosophy and beliefs. Most are derivative of the dominant tradition, Gardnerian. Traditions have undergone continual evolution, multiplying, changing, even dying, in accordance with prevailing religious needs. Some have added elements from Eastern, Native American Indian, aboriginal and shamanic systems; others have injected politics into their traditions. New rituals, songs, chants and poetry are continually created. Critics say that as a result, Witchcraft is an unstable religion. Witches view the change and flexibility as positive, a guarantee that their religion will never grow stale with obsolete ideas.

All modern Witchcraft traditions share a deep respect for nature and all living things. Most Witches are pantheists, believing the Divine Force to be immanent in nature, and are polytheists, believing the Divine Force manifests in multiple forms, recognized as Pagan deities. The Goddess generally is given supremacy over the Horned God. Rituals are colorful, creative and energizing. Witches believe in enjoying sensual and sexual pleasures without guilt. Magic, whether performed individually or in a coven, should be directed toward a good purpose, not to harm.

Within traditions, covens are autonomous, some fiercely so. Each customarily has a secret BOOK OF SHADOWS, which includes the tradition's laws, ethics, rituals, administrative rules and other material, including personal material and material relating just to the coven. Most traditions have formal INITIATION procedures. It has become increasingly acceptable to initiate oneself into the Craft and to practice alone rather than as part of a coven (see SOLITARY).

Some of the traditions are:

Gardnerian. The revived Witchcraft named after Gerald B. Gardner remains the dominant tradition worldwide but no longer holds a monopoly in the Craft. It has been subject to much criticism and reinterpretation. It is centered on worship of the Goddess and her consort, the Horned God, represented in the coven by the high priestess and high priest. It emphasizes polarity in all things manifest in the universe; fertility; and the cycle of birth-death-rebirth. This would seem to preclude homosexuality as being against the natural, heterosexual order, yet many homosexuals practice the Craft. (In the past, opinions were divided as to whether homosexuals fit in the Craft, but they are now generally accepted in Witchcraft and neo-Paganism.)

Nature is honored, and one accepts oneself and all other living things as part of her. Eight seasonal Pagan sabbats are observed. The Wiccan Rede of harming no living thing is the guiding principle.

Formal initiation into a coven by a high priest or high priestess is stressed, though there are rituals for self-initiation. One enters the Craft in "perfect love and perfect trust," which means complete trust of fellow coveners. A woman must be initiated into a coven by a man, and vice versa. Initiates trace their lineage back to Gardner or Lady Olwen (see MONIQUE WILSON) his high priestess. Many receive lineage papers.

The Gardnerian hierarchy has three degrees of advancement, traditionally separated by a minimum of a year and a day. Only a third-degree witch may become a high priestess or high priest. The high priestess is the titular head of the coven. Some covens emphasize the Goddess more than the Horned God, while others put the male and female aspects on a par. The deities are called by a multitude of Pagan deity names, depending on the coven and the rituals being performed. Rituals are performed within a MAGIC CIRCLE. Witches work with a set of tools: an *athame* or ritual knife; wand; sword; cords; censer; pentacle and chalice (see WITCHES' TOOLS).

One of the hallmarks of the Gardnerian tradition is worship in the nude, or *skyclad*, a term Gardner may have borrowed from India. Gardner had become an aficionado of nudist camps in England and believed that nudity was healthy. Gardnerians hold that worshipping in the nude brings them closer to nature and keeps all coveners equal. Some Gardnerian covens have broken away from this practice and worship robed.

Another hallmark of Gardnerian Witchcraft is ritual *scourging*, the light flogging of coveners with cords as a means of purification and symbolic suffering.

This practice has declined in American Gardnerian covens.

Gardner also espoused sexual acts between high priestess and high priest. The sex act, usually called the GREAT RITE, is, as of the 1980s, more commonly performed symbolically than in actuality.

Magic in the tradition is theurgic, that is, performed with the aid of beneficent spirits such as ELEMENTALS and the Guardians of the Watchtowers, and with the deities themselves.

Scourging and sex magic are two of eight ways in which Gardner advocated the raising of power. The others are: meditation or concentration; chants, spells and invocations (see CHANTING; EVOCATIONS AND INVOCATIONS); astral projection; incense, drugs and alcohol; dancing; and blood control through binding parts of the body with cords (see MAGIC). They are all similar to techniques employed by Eastern mystics. Many Witches also practice Tantric sex magic. Some are also Masons; there are similarities in the rituals and symbolisms of both "Crafts," which is not surprising in light of Gardner's Masonic membership.

The Gardnerian tradition was introduced to the United States in the 1960s by Raymond and Rosemary Buckland (see RAYMOND BUCKLAND), natives of England who were initiated into the Craft in 1964 by Gardner's high priestess, Lady Olwen. The Bucklands moved to America and established a coven and museum on Long Island. After the Buckland's divorce in 1973, the coven was turned over to Theos and Phoenix.

Alexandrian. Named after its founder, Alexander Sanders, the British self-proclaimed "King of the Witches," the Alexandrian tradition was the second largest tradition to come out of England. It is based heavily on the Gardnerian tradition, with greater emphasis on cord magic and ceremonial magic. Worshipping is done skyclad. The Alexandrian tradition went into decline with Sanders's retirement from the limelight in the 1970s. The number of covens in the United States has steadily dropped; those remaining no longer have any association with their original founder. Alexandrian Witchcraft is stronger in Canada, where it gained more of a foothold.

Dianic. A broad tradition that includes covens that are feminist and/or strongly matriarchal in orientation. The name is taken from Diana, Greek goddess of the moon and the hunt, and one of the principle names for the Goddess in Witchcraft. The Goddess is worshipped virtually exclusively. The emphasis is on rediscovering and reclaiming female power and divinity, and consciousness raising. Some covens are all-female while others admit men. Some covens are lesbian. The Dianic tradition sets itself somewhat apart from the mainstream Craft. It espouses a feminist spirituality and sisterhood that must struggle against an oppressive, patriarchal society in an effort to bring about positive social and political changes for all.

Dianic Witchcraft is largely a phenomenon of the United States, where it has emerged as an outgrowth of the feminist consciousness movement. One of the first Dianic covens was formed in Dallas, Texas, by Morgan McFarland and Mark Roberts, in the late 1960s. Originally, McFarland had no name for her coven; the name *Dianic* came to her later. Rituals revolved around the phases of the moon and were steeped in ancient matriarchal myth and power. Some years later, McFarland and Roberts split, but the Dianic tradition was continued by other covens. Among the most notable leaders who have shaped Dianic Witchcraft are Californians Z. BUDAPEST and STARHAWK. Budapest, a founder of the Susan B. Anthony coven in 1971, once said Dianic Witchcraft was a "Wimmin's Religion" not open to men. Starhawk, an initiate of the Faery Tradition, has integrated men into Dianic Witchcraft. Rituals are eclectic; some are derived from the Gardnerian and Faery traditions, while others have been created anew. Most feminist covens do not have a handed-down book of shadows.

Many Dianic Witches are political activists for women's and civil rights, pro-environmental issues, peace and antinuclear issues. Efforts by some American Dianic Witches to establish the tradition in Canada have met with limited success.

Celtic. A category of traditions based on ancient Celtic myth, magic, rites and beliefs. Most rituals resemble Gardnerian rituals; covens may be organized differently than Gardnerian ones. Deities are known by Celtic names.

Hereditary and Traditional. Two overlapping, secretive forms of Witchcraft which predate the Gardnerian revival. Most Hereditary and Traditional Witches are found in the British Isles and Europe, though covens in those traditions have been established elsewhere. Traditional Witches are those who follow practices established before Gardner. Hereditary Witches also follow old practices and claim an ancestor or a lineage of ancestors who were initiated Witches. They are likely to be born with psychic gifts. Hereditary witches may be initiated into the Craft by their family members. Unlike the Gardnerian tradition, mothers may initiate daughters and fathers may initiate sons. Hereditary and Traditional Witches work robed. Covens generally are led by the high priest, not the high priestess. Some consider Gardner

a "heretic" and say he was never lawfully initiated into the Craft.

Some modern American Witches claim a Hereditary tradition of a different sort, saying they are descended from families steeped in rural folk-magic traditions, in which members may or may not have been called "witches" (see VICTOR ANDERSON). The Pennsylvania Dutch *hexenmeisters* and "power doctors" also have a Hereditary heritage, which falls outside revivalist Witchcraft.

Some Witches feel the only "true" Witches are hereditary. Others, however, hold that there are many legitimate paths to the Craft, and those who are meant to be a part of it will find their way to it, whether through family, friends, books or spiritual transformations. Many Witches who recall past lives say they have been Witches, adepts or spiritual leaders in other times.

Faery Tradition. An ecstatic and magical Craft religion founded and developed by Americans Victor Anderson and GWYDION PENDDERWEN. *Faery* is spelled in various ways, including *Faerie* and *Fairy*, the latter of which is preferred by Anderson. Initially small and secretive, many of the fundamentals of the Tradition have reached a wide audience through the writings of Starhawk, a Faery Tradition initiate.

Like all Craft traditions, the Faery Tradition honors nature and reveres the deities (the names of which are secret) that personify the forces of nature, life, fertility, death and rebirth. It is polytheistic rather than dualistic, and while it recognizes the male-female and other polarities it does not emphasize polarities as much as the Gardnerian tradition. Rather, it emphasizes pragmatic magic, self-development and theurgy.

There is no standard secret book of shadows but instead an approach to working the Craft and living life. (Several books of writings existed as of the late 1980s, but there was no single canon.) Some aspects remain very secretive, but most are taught openly. Like most of the English traditions, the Faery Tradition provides for a passing of power upon initiation, which links the initiate to the power of the group and those who have gone before.

The Tradition identifies different currents of energy within the universe, which are used in magic. *Faery power* is an ecstatic energy of attunement that is beautiful and sensual but goes beyond the senses: one fills the senses with beauty to go beyond the senses. There is an awareness of the unseen reality, a respect for the wisdom of nature and acceptance of oneself and others as part of nature, and a sensual mysticism that involves a celebratory embracing of life and a love of beauty.

A certain body of material is handed down in the Tradition—metaphysical teachings and secret words and names. Two key teachings center on the iron and pearl pentagrams, meditational tools to bring oneself into balance with the universe and to explore the self. The points of the iron pentagram represent Sex, Self, Passion, Pride and Power. The points of the pearl pentagram represent Love, Wisdom, Knowledge, Law and Power (see PENTACLE AND PENTAGRAM).

The Tradition permits eclecticism. Anderson's own wide-ranging interests in various Pagan religious and magical systems have been reflected in Faery rituals. Rituals are offerings of beauty to the gods. Most initiates are in the arts and incorporate their own poetry, music and invocations into rituals.

It is estimated that there are fewer than 200 Faery Tradition initiates who can trace their initiatory lineage directly to Anderson or Pendderwen. Thousands, however, are estimated to practice neo-Faery Traditions as outgrowths from Starhawk's book, *The Spiral Dance* (1979).

Seax-Wica. A tradition founded in 1973 in America by Raymond Buckland, former high priest in the Gardnerian tradition. Seax-Wica has a Saxon basis but is not a continuation or re-creation of the original Saxon religion. An erroneous rumor circulated that Buckland had started the tradition as a "joke." However, Buckland had for some time been dissatisfied with rituals and with the corruption he saw in certain covens: a system of rank that encouraged ego and power trips. He developed Seax-Wica to answer those concerns.

Seax-Wica is more egalitarian and democratic than the Gardnerian tradition, with only one degree of rank, not three. The coven is led by a high priestess and/or high priest, who are chosen in annual elections. The high priest and male deity are equal to the high priestess and female deity in importance. There is no ritual scourging or binding, and covens decide for themselves whether to worship clothed or skyclad.

The rituals, written by Buckland, are not secret but are published in *The Tree: Complete Book of Saxon Witchcraft* (1974). The tradition is open to anyone and provides for self-initiation as well as initiation by a coven, and for solitary practice.

Autonomous Seax-Wica covens exist throughout the United States and several foreign countries.

Witchcraft As a Science. This tradition, founded in 1955 by LAURIE CABOT of Salem, Massachusetts, holds that Witchcraft is a science as well as a religion and an art. As a science, it may be applied to harness and expand psychic potential. The key to extrasensory perception is the harnessing of light energy and sensitivity to alpha waves, which are part of the aura surrounding every living thing. Cabot says her method of controlling alpha waves is based an ancient Pythagorean method of using colors and numbers.

Witchcraft As a Science teaches that each individual is responsible for all of his or her thoughts and actions. The Wiccan Rede, which Cabot gives as "An' it harm no living thing, do what you will," is extended to defending oneself against evil energy or psychic attack. While other traditions hold that it is acceptable to boomerang psychic attack back to the sender, Witchcraft As a Science considers this a violation of the Rede. Instead, practitioners are taught to erect a psychic neutralizing shield, which enables them either to transform the energy so that it can be used in a positive fashion or to disintegrate it so that it harms no one, including the sender.

Witchcraft As a Science includes practitioners of all other traditions; therefore, rituals are eclectic. Practitioners wear black, which the tradition considers to be the traditional witch's color. Cabot notes that black absorbs light while white reflects it; this absorption of light facilitates psychic power. To further augment power, practitioners of Witchcraft As a Science wear gold jewelry for psychic strength, usually in the form of a pentacle pendant. At least one piece of silver jewelry is worn for its psychic power properties (see GOLD; SILVER).

In addition to Craft basics and history, instruction in Witchcraft As a Science includes parapsychology; physiology; astrology; geometric structure; sociology; anthropology; meditation; aura reading, balancing and healing; the use of crystals; and the psychic arts. Witchcraft As a Science traces the origins of the Craft to the Celts. The tradition teaches past-life regression and Cabot's theory of the root races of humankind, which holds that humans come from other planetary systems. According to Cabot, alpha waves store all knowledge of the universe, and a person who enters an alpha trance may pickup on vibrations from the past.

As of 1988, more than 10,000 students had gone through Witchcraft As a Science courses. Upon completion of training, witches are initiated into the tradition in a ritual similar to Cabot's own initiation into the Craft. There are more than 2,000 Witchcraft As a Science initiates in the Salem area and thousands more across the country.

witch doctors   Witch doctors, also called *jujumen, obeahmen, root doctors, conjure men* and *leaf doctors,* serve as priests and physicians to African tribal members and to believers in VODOUN, SANTERÍA, the MA-

CUMBA cults in Brazil and those who seek the healing powers of herbs.

As their name suggests, witch doctors in Africa treat patients for witch-induced sickness, divining the witch responsible for a victim's illness or misfortune and curing the patient by sending a counteracting spell (see SPELLS). As their power grows, the witch doctors often control entire villages, convincing members they know the sources of evil and how to use them. Among the old Zulu and Ashanti tribes, women often served as witch finders, adorning themselves in feathers and furs and smearing paint and white clay for fierceness on their faces. After reaching a hysterical frenzy brought on by drum beating and CHANTING, the witch finders would point to the witch perpetrators, resulting in the condemned's immediate execution (see also AFRICAN WITCHCRAFT).

A witch-doctor general practitioner is called a *nganga*, the same word used by the black WITCHES in Santería for their evil-spirit cauldrons (see CAULDRON). The nganga divines the source of a victim's misfortunes by casting the *hakata*, or bones (the "bones" may be seeds, dice, shells or actual bones), interpreting the lay of the throws and offering prophecies of good health or evildoing (see DIVINATION). Ngangas supposedly use their power only for good, but they must be familiar with WITCHCRAFT's evil practices in order to combat them. If a witch (see WITCHES) sends a *ngozi*, or grudge-bearing spirit, to harm someone, then the witch doctor must know how to send an even more powerful ngozi to the witch.

POISONS provide powerful weapons for the witch doctor, used to detect witches and perform spells. In a poison test, the witch doctor administers a poisonous drink to a suspect; if he sickens and vomits, he is innocent, but if he tolerates the drink, he is an evil witch. Unfortunately, many suspects die during the ordeal, but their deaths are viewed as divine justice. A variation on the ordeal is the *benge*, in which poisons are given to chickens as the suspects' names are read; if a chicken dies while a name is called, that suspect is guilty.

Used in spells, poisons can bring about the desired effects promised by the witch doctor. One famous case involved a *root doctor*, or specialist in herbal medicines, named Dr. Bug. For $50, Dr. Bug guaranteed his patients that they would fail their physicals when drafted into the armed services. The willing clients took a potion and then suffered from "hippity-hoppity heart syndrome," thereby escaping the draft. Doctors were amazed to find so many sufferers of the condition, until one draftee took a double dose to make sure he would fail the physical and died. His autopsy showed the potion contained a mixture of oleander leaves, which contain digitalis, rubbing alcohol, mothballs and lead.

Witch doctoring did not die with the modernization of Africa. Now often called "traditional healers" to remove the negative connotations of "witch doctor," native practitioners dispense herbal medicines, divine futures and seek alternative methods of treatment for their clients, many of whom have embraced other Western styles and attitudes. In some cases, the healers, also called *jujumen* (from the African *juju*, or FETISH), have scored remarkable successes, especially for chronic illnesses like high blood pressure, asthma, mental illness and venereal disease. The traditional healers' association of Zimbabwe boasts 27,000 members, and the government has begun issuing licenses to them. No certification of technique is necessary or possible, since the healers keep their practices secret. To obtain a license, the healer must simply have the community's agreement that he has been successful.

Some jujumen claim they have cured AIDS as well. In Uganda, one of the African countries suffering most from the disease, witch doctors use animal sacrifices, chants and charms to combat the affliction (see SACRIFICE). One witch doctor says the disease is hereditary, and nearly all Ugandan healers believe that by sacrificing an animal and leaving it for passersby to discover, the victim can transfer his disease to the bystander. With that in mind, Ugandans avoid dead sheep and goats left at intersections (see CROSSROADS).

In the Deep South region of the United States and in Haiti, healers are known as *root doctors, conjure men* or *leaf doctors* (*dokte feuilles* in Creole French). These people practice herbal medicine, administering potions and preparations to cure a variety of diseases, especially the more mundane ones: colds, aching joints, headaches, gastrointestinal complaints and minor "female complications." Although well respected for their knowledge, the leaf doctors have no special access to the gods and cannot treat the more serious illnesses brought on by spirit intervention, spiritual disharmony and witchcraft.

The most famous conjure man in America was DOCTOR JOHN, a free black witch doctor in 19th-century New Orleans. One of MARIE LAVEAU's early mentors, Doctor John controlled most of the blacks and a good deal of the whites in the city with his powders, love potions and amazing knowledge about their lives—usually gained through a network of well-placed spies. He amassed a large fortune by dispensing GRIS-GRIS but ended his life in poverty after losing his property through fraud. His peers said Doctor John had been "fixed," or been the victim of spells greater than his.

In his research on Jamaican native healers, called *obeahmen*, Joseph K. Long asked why many people prefer witch doctors to trained physicians. In some cases, he postulated, witch doctors seem more sympathetic, gearing their treatments to the societal norms of the community. In others, the disease may be more a form of community hysteria, and once fears are calmed, the disease dissipates. Ultimately, however, he found that among peoples who believe in MAGIC, magic works.

In rural Appalachia, a witch doctor is one who breaks the spells of witches. If one is troubled by bewitchment, one seeks out the witch doctor, just as one would go to a medical doctor for a physical ailment.

witches Practitioners of WITCHCRAFT, the meaning of which varies from culture to culture. Generally, witches are skilled in SORCERY and the magical arts (see MAGIC). Through rituals, CHARMS, SPELLS and the conjuring and invoking (see EVOCATIONS AND INVOCATIONS) of spirits, they manipulate forces for either good or evil purposes. They are said to possess supernormal abilities, such as invisibility, FLYING, shape-shifting (see METAMORPHOSIS), clairvoyance, weather control (see STORM RAISING), killing at a distance and (sometimes) HEALING by touch. Belief in witches, sorcerers and magicians has existed universally since prehistoric times. A witch can be either male or female, but in Western culture over the centuries, the term has come to apply almost exclusively to women.

The word *witch* comes from the Old English *wicce*, pronounced "wiche," and *wicca*, which are in turn derived from the root *wikk-*, which applies to magic and sorcery. Many Witches say *witch* means "wise" or "wisdom," so a Witch is a wise person, and Witchcraft is the Craft of the Wise.

Wicce, however, comes from the Germanic root *wic*, which means "to bend" or "to turn"—which does apply to witchcraft, in the sense that witches bend or control forces in order to effect changes. The masculine of *wicce* is *wicca* (see WICCA).

Most witches throughout history have been universally feared and abhorred because they were believed to be vindictive, cast evil spells upon others and consort with evil spirits. The Western concept of witches has evolved from sorcery and magic beliefs dating back to the ancient Assyrians, Babylonians, Akkadians, Hebrews, Greeks and Romans. An ancient Assyrian tablet speaks of the bewitching powers of witches, wizards, sorcerers and sorceresses. In ancient Greece and Rome, witches were renowned for their herbal knowledge, magical potions and supernatural powers. Thessaly, a region in Greece,

The four witches (Albrecht Dürer, 1497)

was particularly "notorious for witchcraft" and "universally known for magic incantations," according to Apuleius, Roman poet of the 2nd century. Thessalian witches reputedly had the power to bring the moon down from the sky (see DRAWING DOWN THE MOON). Pythagoras is said to have learned from them how to divine by holding up a polished silver disk to the moon. So potent was their power that the Roman poet Horace of the 1st century B.C. asked, "What witch, what magician will be able to free you from Thessalian sorceries?"

Roman poets Ovid and Statius described witches as having long, flowing hair and going about barefoot. In *Amores*, Ovid describes a "certain old hag" named Dipsas:

She knows the Black Arts and the spells of Aenea [CIRCE] and by her skill turns back the waters to their source.

She knows what herbs, what the threads twisted by the magic circle, what the poison of the loving mare [a love PHILTRE] can do. At her will, the clouds mass in the entire heavens. At her will, the day shines in the clear sky. I have seen the stars dripping with blood—if you may believe me—and the face of the moon glowing red with blood. I suspect that she flits through the shades of night, and that her aged body is covered with feathers. She summons from the ancient tombs her antique ancestors, and makes the ground yawn open with her incantation.

In his novel *Metamorphoses,* Apuleius describes Meroe, an old witch who owns an inn:

She is capable of bringing down the sky, suspending the earth, making springs dry up, sweeping away mountains, conjuring the spirits of the dead. She can weaken the gods, put out the stars, light up Hell itself.
    When a neighboring inkeeper would not return her love, she changed him into a frog. A lawyer who prosecuted her she turned into a ram.

Classical witches often were said to possess the EVIL EYE. Pliny wrote of those who killed by looks; Tully wrote of women who had two "apples" in one eye; and Ovid and Plutarch wrote of poison in the eyes.

Witchcraft, witches, sorcerers, "them that have familiar spirits," charmers and wizards "that chirp and mutter" are mentioned numerous times in the Bible (see WITCH OF ENDOR). The most famous Biblical quotation cited by the witch-hunters of the Middle Ages and Renaissance was Exodus 22:18: "Thou shalt not suffer a witch to live." However, it was pointed out as early as 1584 (by REGINALD SCOT in *Discoverie of Witchcraft*) that the Hebrew words that were translated as "witch" usually referred to diviners, astrologers, poisoners and jugglers (manipulators) and not "witches" as defined by Christian demonology. According to historian Henry Charles Lea, the "witchcraft" denounced most often by the Bible was merely DIVINATION. The Hebrews practiced magic and sorcery, which included herbal formulas, conjurations, the evil eye, AMULETS and TALISMANS, NECROMANCY and divination, but they did not consider them inherently diabolical or malevolent, as the Christians later did. Hebrew demons, which included evil spirits, were absorbed into Christian demonology (see DEMONS; LAMIA; LILITH).

During the European witch craze, which began in the mid-15th century and ended by the 18th century, witches were defined as heretics who worshipped the DEVIL and engaged in abominable practices, such as MALEFICIA, shape-shifting, orgiastic dances, copulation with demons, cannibalism, vampirism and flying through the air. "The Scriptures assert that there are devils and witches and that they are the common enemy of mankind," asserted INCREASE MATHER in *Cases of Conscience* in 1693. John Wagstaffe, a writer well known in England and New England in the late

17th century, defined witches in terms of Jezebel, the Phoenician princess who, according to the Bible, married King Ahab in the 9th century B.C. and promoted the worship of her own gods, Baal and Asherah (ASTARTE). A disgusted priest threw her out a window to her death, and God's only recourse was to destroy the house of Ahab. Stated Wagstaffe, "Thus you shall often meet in the Bible with fornication and witchcraft joined together. By fornication and whoredom is meant idolatry and by witchcraft the art of engaging men in it. The whoredom of Jezebel was her idolatry, and her witchcraft was the maintaining of Baal's priests."

Demonologists divided witches into classes. Witches also were called diviners, consulters with familiar spirits, wizards, necromancers, charmers and enchanters. GYPSIES, exorcists, astrologers, numerologists and other fortune-tellers were also classed as witches (see FAMILIARS; WIZARD; SPIRIT EXORCISM; ASTROLOGY; NUMEROLOGY). William West wrote in 1594:

A witch or hag is she which being eluded by a league made with the devil through his persuasion, inspiration, and juggling, thinketh she can design what manner of things soever, either by thought or imprecation, as to shake the air with lightnings and thunder, to cause hail and tempests, to remove green corn or trees to another place, to be carried of [by] her familiar which hath upon him the deceitful shape of a goat, swine, calf, etc. into some mountain far distant, in a wonderful space of time. And sometimes to fly upon a staff or fork, or some other instrument. And to spend all the night after with her sweetheart, in playing, sorting, banqueting, dalliance,and diverse other devilish lusts, and lewd desports and to show a thousand such monstrous mockeries.

West said other kinds of witches included enchanters and charmers, jugglers, soothsaying wizards, divinators and magicians.

Some distinctions were made between "white" witches and "black" witches. White witches were those who cured illness, divined lost property, exposed thieves, enhanced fertility and drove away bad weather. Black witches were those who used their magic only for the harm of others. White witches often went by other names, such as cunning folk, wise folk, wizard, sorcerer and witch doctor.

Witch-hunters did not prosecute white witches—chiefly the healers and diviners—with the same fervor as black witches, for they were perceived as serving a vital need in the community. As much as the public feared bad witches as a menace to body and soul, they clung to the village sorcerer who would cure their sicknesses and help them in times of trouble.

As the witch mania intensified, demonologists, witch-hunters and the learned men who shaped public opinion began calling for the prosecution of white witches as well. It was said that good witches really were a menace because of their capability of doing evil; their supernatural gifts did not come from God but from the Devil. In England, WILLIAM PERKINS and Thomas Cooper of Oxford were among those who believed good witches were far more dangerous than bad witches and that both needed to be extirpated. This view was endorsed by COTTON MATHER in Massachusetts. George Gifford, an Oxford preacher, wrote in the late 16th century that all witches should be put to death not because they kill others but because they deal with devils. "These cunning men and women which deale with spirites and charmes seeming to do good, and draw the people into manifold impities, with all others which have familiarity with devils, or use conjurations, ought to bee rooted out, that others might see and feare," Gifford stated.

It was believed that witches could be identified by certain telltale signs: insensitive spots or marks on the body (almost any mole qualified); the inability to shed tears; and supernumerary teats or excresences for suckling imps (see WITCH'S MARK). The evil eye was a sign but was not infallible, said Increase Mather. Others described witches as invariably ugly and deformed (see HAG). Many of the accused witches were outcasts or on the fringes of society, looked down upon by their neighbors because of their unmarried status, handicaps, homely appearances, ill temper or poverty. Not all victims were such: some were married, young and prosperous.

"Witch" was a devastating accusation. If arrested and taken before a court or inquisitor, one often was assumed to be guilty. Torture often was applied until one confessed to the presumed guilt (see TORTURE). Families of accused witches were shunned, and it was not uncommon for them to abandon the victim to save themselves. Such was the pathetic case of a woman burned at the stake in 1649 in Lauder, Scotland. As she faced death, she declared to the crowd:

All you that see me this day! Know ye that I am to die as a Witch, by my own Confession! And I free all Men, especially the Ministers and Magistrates, from the guilt of my Blood, I take it wholly on my self, and as I must make answer to the God of Heaven, I declare that I am as free from Witchcraft as any Child, but being accused by a Malicious Woman, and Imprisoned under the Name of a Witch, my Husband and Friends disowned me, and seeing no hope of ever being in Credit again, through the Temptation of the Devil, I made that Confession to destroy my own Life, being weary of it, and shusing [sic] rather to die than to Live.

Modern Western society thus has inherited a powerful, negative stereotype of the witch: a hag with a large, warty nose, a pointy chin, scraggly hair and a cone-shaped black hat, who lives alone with her animals—usually black cats—who casts evil spells on others and who is in league with the Devil. This stereotype has been reinforced for centuries in literature, drama, the popular press and film and television. It poses an enormous problem for Witches in the neo-Pagan religion of Witchcraft (also called Wicca), who are the complete opposite of this stereotype—they *do not* worship the Devil (or even believe in the Devil), sacrifice animals or babies, shed blood in any way, renounce Christianity or any other religion or dedicate themselves to destroying others.

Neo-Pagan Witches define themselves as healers, servants of the community and servants of the Goddess and (usually) the Horned God, whom they worship in their religion. They believe in respecting the sanctity of all life and being in harmony with all living things and with the forces of the universe. Ideally, they strive to attune themselves to nature and the elements, forces they control in the working of magic. They develop their psychic abilities and seek to raise their spiritual consciousness through study, worship, the practice of their Craft and observance of a moral and ethical life-style, in accordance with Craft laws and tenets. "Witches, on the whole, enjoy ritual—and they are naturally joyous people," state English Witches STEWART AND JANET FARRAR in *Eight Sabbats for Witches* (1981). "Like worshippers of other religions, they find that appropriate ritual uplifts and enriches them."

English Witch SYBIL LEEK defined a Witch as "a woman who has unusual powers of good and evil. These powers bear a direct relationship to one's understanding of religious truths. How these powers that come from a higher force are to be used depends entirely on the intentions of the person." Most neo-Pagan Witches believe quite strongly in using magic only for good, never for harm. Some Witches make judicious use of the power to curse (see CURSES; WICCAN REDE).

Since the rise of neo-Pagan Witchcraft in the 1950s, Witches have worked to eradicate the negative stereotype and re-educate the public, with limited success. Some feel strongly that the word *Witch* must be reclaimed, while others feel the word is lost forever as a positive label and should be substituted with *Wicca*. American Witch STARHAWK, who favors reclaiming *Witch*, wrote in *The Spiral Dance* (1979):

The word "Witch" carries so many negative connotations that many people wonder why we use the word at all. Yet to reclaim the word "Witch" is to reclaim our right, as women to be powerful; as men, to know the feminine within as divine. To be a Witch is to identify with 9 million victims of bigotry and hatred and to take responsibility for shaping a world in which prejudice claims no more victims. A Witch is a "shaper," a creator who bends the unseen into form, and so becomes one of the Wise, one whose life is infused with magic. [Note: the 9 million refers to the estimated number of victims put to death during the witch craze. Most historians estimate the actual number at 150,000 to 200,000.]

American Witch MARGOT ADLER observes in *Drawing Down the Moon* (1986) that "the very power of the word lies in its imprecision. It is not merely a word, but an archetype, a cluster of powerful images."

The task of reclaiming *Witch* and re-educating the public has been made very difficult by the fact that not all witches are neo-Pagan Witches, and not all witches conform to the ethics and laws of the Craft. The average layperson who knows little about witchcraft or Witchcraft lumps all witches together under the stereotype. Witches try to distinguish themselves from satanists, who do worship the Devil, yet some satanists refer to themselves as "witches" (see SATANISM).

Neo-Pagan Witches may be but a small percentage of all those who call themselves witches. P. E. I. (ISAAC) BONEWITS divides American witches into seven categories:

Neo-Pagan (10 percent)—half feminist Witches and half Witches who follow the various revivalist traditions.

Neo-Classical (70 percent)—those who practice a folk magic with pagan and Christian roots, without much regard for Witchcraft as a religion.

Classical (1–2 percent)—the village healers, wise women, etc., found in most societies, especially rural areas, who practice nonreligious folk magic.

Neo-Gothic (1–2 percent)—practitioners of Satanism, which is based on the "gothic" witchcraft of the witch-hysteria era.

Family Traditions, also called "Fam-Trads" (1–2 percent)—families which, over generations, preserved classical witchcraft traditions but did not necessarily call themselves Witches, until the present. Fam-Trad claims were common in the 1960s, during the initial expansion of revivalist Witchcraft, before the "Murray myth" was discredited (see MARGARET ALICE MURRAY).

Immigrant Traditions (1–2 percent)—ethnic folk-magic practices preserved in cultural pockets, such as the Pennsylvania Dutch (see POWWOWING).

Other: VODOUN, SANTERÍA, Native American Indian, etc. (10 percent)—magical practices of other religions.

It is not known exactly how many Witches and witches exist in modern times. Neo-Pagan Witchcraft attracts persons of both sexes from all ages and a wide spectrum of racial, economic, educational and occupational backgrounds; the majority are white middle-class women. Historian Jeffrey Burton Russell estimates in *The History of Witchcraft* (1980) that the number of modern Witches worldwide is less than 100,000. Estimates of the number of neo-Pagan Witches in the United States range from about 10,000 to 50,000. The PAGAN/OCCULT/WITCHCRAFT SPECIAL INTEREST GROUP OF MENSA as of 1988 maintained a network of about 8,000 persons worldwide, most in the United States, but not all Witches. From 1965 to 1988, the School of Wicca in New Bern, North Carolina, enrolled about 50,000 persons in its correspondence courses, but most were not graduated or were initiated by the Church of Wicca, which runs the school (see CHURCH AND SCHOOL OF WICCA). It is not known how many have gone on to practice the Craft on their own. Estimates of neo-Pagan Witches in Canada range from 5,000 to 10,000, most of whom live in urban areas such as Victoria, Vancouver, Toronto and Montreal; another 5,000 persons may be practicing secretly. An estimated 10,000 Witches populate the British Isles. These estimates do not include those who practice folk magic and may or may not call themselves Witches.

Witches in non-Western cultures. Outside of the West, witches, both male and female, generally are viewed as evil persons. The Navaho believe that men and women become witches to gain wealth, hurt others out of envy and wreak vengeance. Initiation into *Witchery Way* requires killing a person, usually a sibling. Witches rob graves, shape-shift into animals, hold nocturnal sabbats, eat corpses and shoot alien substances into the bodies of victims which cause illness. They then charge the victims a fee for a cure. More men than women are witches, but the women are usually old or childless. Among the Shawnee, Fox and other tribes of eastern North America, male and female witches organize into societies with their own rites, which include cannibalism.

African beliefs about witches are similar. Most societies believe witches are at the least unsociable and irritable, and at the worst thoroughly evil. Mandari witches dance on the graves of their victims, while Lugbara witches dance naked—the ultimate outrageous behavior. Lugbara witches also engage in other extraordinary behaviors, such as walking on their hands instead of their feet. The Dinka believe witches have tails. Some tribes, such as the Mandari, Nyak-yusa and Zande, believe that witchcraft is inherited and that a person cannot help committing the anti-social and evil acts that are part of witchcraft (see AFRICAN WITCHCRAFT).

See also COUNCIL OF AMERICAN WITCHES; MAGIC.

Witches, Council of American   See COUNCIL OF AMERICAN WITCHES.

Witches League of Public Awareness

An international organization, based in Salem, Massachusetts, which works to end prejudice and bigotry against WITCHES and WITCHCRAFT. The Witches League of Public Awareness (WLPA) was organized in 1986 by Salem witch LAURIE CABOT, who serves as cochair with Christine Dumas, to protest the filming of John Updike's novel, THE WITCHES OF EASTWICK. The novel concerns three "witches" who are involved with the DEVIL, a gross misrepresentation of the Craft. The League networks with major Witch groups around the world. It also works with the American Civil Liberties Union and with police departments dealing with occult crime, much of which is blamed on Witches but is perpetrated by satanists and others not connected to the Craft (see SATANISM). One of its major accomplishments was exposing "File 18," a secret newsletter compiled by a police officer which constituted an "occult hit list" for police, falsely naming individual Witches and Craft organizations as those who could be suspected of occult crimes. The WLPA does not handle individual discrimination cases.

witches' light

Among tribal societies, it is commonly believed that the presence of WITCHES at night may be detected by lights they either emit or carry. The belief is similar to one prevalent in Europe in the Middle Ages: that witches flew at night on BROOMS lit by CANDLES.

The Azande of Africa believe that a witch releases a spirit to murder others while they sleep, much as medieval witches were believed to dispatch DEMONS in the shape of animal FAMILIARS. This spirit, or essence of WITCHCRAFT, may be seen at night, glowing like sparks kicked off from a fire. In daytime, the light is visible only to those who are witches or WITCH DOCTORS.

Effutu witches of southern Ghana use a spiritual "web" or "wire" by which they travel in search of victims. As they move across this web at night, they are visible as bright flashes of light (see also AFRICAN WITCHCRAFT).

The Pueblo Indians of Mexico, and the Bantu and Gusii of Africa, maintain that witches travel by night,

carrying lights that alternately flare up and down. The Gusii say the changes in brightness are due to the witches removing and replacing the lids of the fire-pots which they carry with them.

Among the Dobu Islanders of the western Pacific, the *kainana*—the fire emitted by the pubes of flying witches—may be seen at night. To ward off danger, the villages gather together around fires which are kept burning all night. No one returns home until dawn.

Witches of Eastwick, The

A novel by John Updike (1984) that describes and perpetuates stereotypes about WITCHCRAFT in the characters of three women living in a rather sleepy, small Rhode Island town.

Alexandra Spofford, a sculptress, Jane Smart, a cellist, and Sukie Rougemont, a reporter for the local newspaper, all dabble in the slightly black arts since losing their husbands through death or divorce. A few SPELLS—such as willing shoes to untie, pearl necklaces to break or storms to appear—or collecting herbs and animal leavings while "skyclad" (naked), or FLYING late at night—help relieve the tedium of raising unwanted children and going from one unfulfilling lover to another. Each has found a third teat, possibly a wart, on her body, supposedly one of the signs of a witch (see WITCH'S MARK), and each has a large dog, or familiar (see FAMILIARS). Just living in New England puts them in the area where American witchcraft beliefs traditionally have been strongest.

Drawn to the mischief, a dark, wealthy, mysterious stranger, Darryl Van Horne, moves to Eastwick and occupies a large, old estate. No one else lives with him but his servant, Fidel. As in medieval descriptions of the DEVIL, he is ugly, with a hairy body, and he easily seduces Alexandra, Sukie and Jane into sexual liaisons, both singly and together. Also like the Devil, his body fluids are cold, and he asks the women to kiss his backside (see KISS OF SHAME).

The witchey women add Van Horne to their COVEN, joining him and Fidel for parties with exotic food, plenty of alcohol and still more sex. Such get-togethers are referred to as SABBATS, like the alleged orgies of earlier Devil-worshippers, and the women seem to know when to congregate at Van Horne's without being invited. They share with him their opinions about the wives of the other men they sleep with, especially Felicia Gabriel, the wife of Sukie's boss and editor, Clyde. To punish Felicia for her strident, narrow opinions of Sukie and the others, the witches cast a spell on her, causing Felicia to suffer ALLOTRI-

OPHAGY and spit up feathers, pennies, thumbtacks, eggshells and pieces of insects. Their MALEFICIA, or evildoing, yields more evil: Clyde can take Felicia's ranting no longer and kills her with a poker before hanging himself.

The longer the witches are influenced by Van Horne, the easier evildoing becomes. Alexandra wills a barking dog to death. She no longer feels any sexual desire, nor do some of the witches' lovers. They appear to be victims of the AIGUILLETTE, or the knot: a device used by witches to bring illicit lovers together, cause impotence in men and barrenness in women and foment general discontent. Once started in a community, Alexandra notes, witchcraft eventually runs on its own, out of anyone's control.

When Van Horne marries Jenny Gabriel, Felicia and Clyde's daughter, the women take revenge. Like a medieval sorcerer, Jane flies to the Van Horne mansion, shrinks herself and collects pieces of Jenny (tissues with lipstick stains, hair, used dental floss, hairs left in the tub after shaving her legs) so that the women can make a charm. The wax figurine is given a female shape, adorned with Jenny's hair and stabbed with tacks. Incantations are recited, and the women ask that Jenny die of cancer. The witches are later struck with some guilt and attempt to undo the spell, but Jenny dies, anyway. Van Horne, for all his sexual encounters and rhetoric on the importance of women, takes Jenny's brother Chris as his lover and disappears.

In the movie version of *The Witches of Eastwick* (1987, directed by George Miller), the women—played by Cher as Alexandra, Susan Sarandon as Jane and Michelle Pfeiffer as Sukie—are not witches but merely bored women before Darryl Van Horne, played by Jack Nicholson, arrives in Eastwick. He introduces them to magic and orgies, which the women enjoy immensely until their witchy dabbling culminates in Felicia Gabriel's murder. Before her death, Felicia vomits enormous quantities of cherry seeds, which Van Horne and the women were spitting out of their mouths at a party. The more they eat, the more seeds she excretes.

Jenny Gabriel is not part of the movie plot at all, and the only wax figurine that figures in the story is one of Van Horne himself, made by the three women in an attempt to purge the Devil from their lives. He has impregnated all three, and they wish him gone before the babies are born. They succeed, and he leaves with horrifying special effects.

One interesting note about the filming of the movie: the producers originally planned to shoot the outdoor scenes in Rhode Island, as in the novel, but local protest by practicing Witches and others moved the location to Cohasset, Massachusetts. The protests were led by LAURIE CABOT, prominent Salem Witch and cochair of the WITCHES LEAGUE OF PUBLIC AWARENESS. The League objected to the book for portraying numerous, inaccurate stereotypes about Witches, who neither believe in nor worship the Devil.

Witches' tools The basic magical working tools of most neo-Pagan WITCHES are associated with the forces of the four ELEMENTS. The tools and their uses are derivative of some Hermetic magical practices (see HERMETICA). Before they can be used in rituals, all magical tools must be consecrated in rites that involve exposure of the tools to all four elements, by immersing or sprinkling them with salted WATER; passing them through or over a flame; passing them through incense smoke; and touching them with a disk of earth or baked clay, or plunging them into the earth. The consecration rituals are similar to those in *The Key of Solomon*, a magical grimoire attributed to the legendary King Solomon (see GRIMOIRES) and translated into English in 1888, to which Pagan elements have been added.

Magical tools customarily are inscribed with RUNES, SIGILS and symbols. Ideally, the tools are handmade, for the act of construction helps to imbue them with the Witch's personal power. However, most Witches buy their tools and personalize them through inscription, consecration and ritual. Magical tools serve a variety of purposes in rituals and are used in the consecration of MAGIC CIRCLES and of other magic tools.

Athame. A Witch's personal, magical knife, traditionally double-bladed with a black hilt, and fashioned of steel or iron. The blade may be magnetized. Magical knives were said to be used by witches in the Middle Ages.

According to the Gardnerian tradition of neo-Pagan WITCHCRAFT, the athame is used only for ritual purposes, such as casting the magic circle, and never for cutting. Other traditions call for using the knife as much as possible in the belief that its power increases with use. In some rituals, the athame takes on phallic symbolism; it is plunged into a chalice filled with juice or wine, signifying the union of male and female forces (see GREAT RITE).

The athame is associated with the element of fire (in some traditions, with air). In some traditions, it is interchangeable with the sword.

Among some hereditary Witches in England, metal is never used in ritual tools because it interferes with ley energy in the earth (see LEYS). Athame blades are therefore made of flint.

Some Witches use a white-hilted knife for cutting and inscribing. Knives are never used for sacrifices, which are not condoned in neo-Pagan Witchcraft.

Censer. A small dish or container used to burn incense, herbs, chemicals, wood or other substances, to cleanse and purify the air before rituals. Censing, which represents the element of air, exorcises and keeps unwanted energies away from the magic site; offers sweet air to the GODDESS and God; raises vibrational rates and summons energies; relaxes the senses; and contains and concentrates power. The formulas used depend on the purpose of the ritual. The burning of incense as protection and offering is an ancient religious practice found around the world.

Cup (also chalice, goblet). The cup is associated with the female forces in the universe: fertility, beauty, the womb, earth, emotion, love, compassion, receptivity, instinct, intuition and the subconscious mind. It is the receptacle of spiritual forces. It is associated with the element of water. Held upright, the cup is an open womb, ready to receive. Held inverted, it symbolizes birth and realization. The chief purpose of the cup in neo-Pagan Witchcraft is to hold wine, which is consecrated and used in rituals or shared among coveners (see COVEN).

Pentacle. Symbol of the earth, the pentacle is a disk or square of metal (usually copper or silver), wax, baked clay, earthenware or wood, and is inscribed with Craft symbols. It is generally associated with female energy. Among its uses are to ground energy and to serve food shared at the end of a coven's working session. See also PENTACLE AND PENTAGRAM.

Sword. Not all Witches use a sword; some covens have a single sword for the entire group. The sword serves the same function as the athame, used for ritual purposes such as casting the circle but not for cutting. It is considered more authoritative than the athame. The sword is associated with the element fire (in some traditions, with air). Gardner made his own swords.

Wand. The wand is the instrument of invocation of spirits. It represents the element of fire (in some traditions, air) and symbolizes the life-force within the Witch. The wand dates back to prehistoric times and is mentioned in the Bible; both Moses and Aaron use rods to bring the plague to Egypt. The Greek god HERMES is represented with a caduceus, a wand entwined with snakes and winged at the top, a symbol of power, wisdom and healing.

HAZEL has always been considered the best wood for wands, followed by ash, rowan and willow; 18 inches is considered a good length. The wood should be cut when the moon is waxing or full. In certain Witchcraft rituals, tipped phallic wands are used. Some Witches use wands made of crystal, silver, carved ivory or ebony, and gold. In some cases, a wand may be used to cast magic circles.

Other Tools

Some traditions of neo-Pagan Witchcraft also employ the following tools:

Cords. Cords of silk, other natural materials or nylon are used primarily in the Gardnerian and Alexandrian traditions. A single, nine-foot red cord is used in a Witch's initiation into the Craft (see INITIATION). In magic work, cords are knotted by Witches either individually or in a group, while they chant a spell (see KNOTS; SPELLS). The knots are tied in certain patterns or orders and are left tied until the right moment for untying, which releases the magic energy and effects the spell. A system of colors is used for different spells. Cords also are used in binding parts of the body to reduce blood circulation, as a means of achieving an altered state of consciousness in the raising of psychic power.

Scourge. Light scourging (beating) with a scourge made of knotted strands of silk or other light materials is done primarily in the Gardnerian and Alexandrian traditions. It was favored by Gardner in initiations, to symbolize the need to learn through suffering and as a potent way to raise psychic power and gain "the Sight" (clairvoyance). For the latter purpose, Gardner said scourging excites both body and soul but allows one to retain control over the power raised. The scourging should not be strong enough to break the skin but should be strong enough to draw blood to that part of the body and away from the brain. If done long enough, it induces drowsiness.

In the evolution of neo-Pagan Witchcraft since the 1950s, scourging has fallen out of favor with many Witches but remains an issue of controversy. Some covens have abandoned the practice, while others scourge so lightly that they might as well not do it at all. Others in the Gardnerian tradition support scourging.

witching hour The hour of midnight on the night of the full MOON. This is a time of transformation and change and the height of WITCHES' spell-casting powers. The roots of this notion go back to ancient times, to the worship of goddesses associated with the moon, fertility and WITCHCRAFT. As the moon waxes in its phases, so do the powers associated with it and its deities, until they culminate at the full moon.

witch's butter In old Swedish lore, the yellow vomit of WITCHES' cats found in gardens. In centuries past, it was believed that the DEVIL gave witches CATS, called *carriers.* The witches sent the cats out into the neighborhood to steal food. The cats were wont to gorge themselves on the stolen food, which they then vomited in their neighbors' yards.

Witches' butter also refers to a genus of the lowest group of freshwater algae, *Nostoc,* also called *star spittle.* After summer rain, *Nostoc* swells suddenly to a gelatinous mass, giving the appearance of having fallen from the sky.

witch's cradle   During the witch-hunts of the Middle Ages and Renaissance, one method of torturing accused witches was to tie them up in a sack, string the sack over a tree limb and set it swinging. The rocking motion of this witch's cradle, as it was called, caused profound disorientation and helped induce confessions. Most subjected to this also suffered profound hallucinations, which surely added color to their confessions (see TORTURE).

In a contemporary context, the term *witch's cradle* also applies to sensory-deprivation techniques and devices used to induce altered states of consciousness and help develop psychic powers and achieve astral projection. Shamans and dervishes suspend themselves with ropes tied around their waists.

Metal swings called witch's cradles are used in paranormal experiments. The subject is strapped in a standing position, blindfolded and given ear plugs.

witch's hat   The stereotypical image of a witch (see WITCHES) is that of an ugly, old HAG wearing a tall, black, pointed hat with a broad brim. There are different theories as to the origin of this stereotype, none of them certain. Most likely, the hat is a fairly modern artist's creation. In medieval woodcuts, witches are shown wearing various costumes of the times, including headscarves and hats of different fashions. Many are shown bareheaded, with locks flying in the wind.

It is possible that the witch's hat is an exaggeration of the tall, conical "dunce's hat" that was popular in the royal courts of the 15th century or the tall but blunt-topped hats worn by Puritans and the Welsh. No matter what the fashion, pointed hats were frowned upon by the Church, which associated points with the horns of the DEVIL.

Brimless, conical hats have long been associated with male WIZARDS and magicians. Goya painted witches with such hats. It is possible that an artist, somewhere along the way, added a brim to make the hats more appropriate for women. One theory holds that the stereotypical witch's hat came into being in Victorian times or around the turn of the century, in illustrations of children's fairy tales. The tall, black, conical hat and the ugly crone became readily identifiable symbols of wickedness, to be feared by children.

According to another theory, the witch's hat may go back to antiquity. Ancient Etruscan coins from the city of Luna have a head on one side which may be the goddess DIANA, who is associated with witches. The head wears a brimless, conical hat.

Neo-pagan Witches do not wear hats in their rituals; most go bareheaded. Some wear headbands with a crescent moon or other religious symbol positioned on the forehead. In certain rituals in which the GODDESS and HORNED GOD are represented, the high priestess may wear a headband crown, and the high priest a helmet with horns or antlers. Horned headdresses were worn by prehistoric shamans in their hunting rites (see SHAMANISM).

witch's ladder   A string of 40 beads or a cord with 40 KNOTS, which some WITCHES use in MAGIC. The beads or knots enable a Witch to concentrate on repetitive chants or incantations without having to keep count. This enables the Witch to focus will and energy on the desired goal.

According to one earlier formula, a witch's ladder was a rope or cord of nine knots. It was believed that witches of old could cast a death spell over a person by tying the knots and then hiding the cord.

Witch's ladders are used frequently in self-healing work.

See also WITCHES' TOOLS.

witch's mark   In witch lore, an extra teat or nipple on WITCHES for suckling FAMILIARS and IMPS, who were said to crave human BLOOD. Extra nipples appear naturally in a small percentage of the population, but in medieval times, they had an infernal association. In fact, virtually any wart, mole, tumor, protuberance or discoloration of the skin was thought to be a witch's mark, particularly if it secreted any liquid or blood. When accused witches were arrested, their bodies and cavities were searched for any irregularities. Red spots, bumps under the tongue and fleshy bumps and folds in the vagina were considered paps for familiars.

In witchcraft trials, "prickers" pricked the skin of the accused to determine insensitive areas (see PRICKING), which also were called witch's marks. Out of fear, some people cut off their warts, moles and lumps, but the resulting scars were also taken as proof of being a witch—and trying to hide it. The term *witch's mark* is often used interchangeably with DEVIL'S MARK, which was considered proof of a covenant with Satan.

Witch's marks also are described as unusual birthmarks. SYBIL LEEK believed in witch's marks and said she and other women in her family line were born with them.

INITIATION rituals in some traditions of modern Witchcraft call for symbolic witches' marks in an X-shaped cross to be made with anointing OILS on the body of the candidate. According to the BOOK OF SHADOWS for the Gardnerian tradition, the crosses are traced over the third eye, the heart and the genitals, symbolizing the freeing of mind, heart and body.

In rural Appalachia, a *witch mark* is a star, similar in shape to a Maltese cross, that is etched or drawn over the doorway of a home or barn, to keep witches away. It is also carved out of wood and nailed over the door.

withershins   See WIDDERSHINS.

wizards   A term used in various periods of history for magicians, sorcerers or witches but seldom used in modern times (see MAGIC; SORCERY; WITCHCRAFT). The word *wizard* is derived from the Middle English term *wis*, which means "wise." It first appeared in 1440 and was synonymous with *wise women* and *wise men*. In the 16th and 17th centuries—the height of popularity of the village magician—it applied to a high magician but also to various popular magicians, who were known by other names as well: cunning men, cunning women, charmers, blessers, sorcerers, conjurers and WITCHES. After 1825, *wizard* became almost exclusively synonymous with *witch*, but its usage has died out during the 20th century. Modern Witches do not use the term.

Virtually every village or town in Britain and Europe had at least one wizard, who usually was respected and feared by the local folk. The wizard specialized in a variety of magical services, such as fortune-telling; finding missing persons and objects; finding hidden treasure; curing illnesses in people and animals; interpreting dreams; detecting theft; exorcising ghosts and fairies; casting SPELLS; breaking the spells of witches and FAIRIES; making AMULETS; and making love PHILTRES. Because he was deemed the diviner of the guilty in crimes, the word of the wizard often carried great weight in a village or town (see DIVINATION). The wizard's CHARMS were part folk magic and part Christian in origin.

Wizards were "commonly men of inferior rank," as Sir Thomas Browne described them in 17th-century England. Most earned paltry fees from their services and worked at other jobs to make a living. Typically, they claimed to get their powers from God, the archangels, ancient holy men of the Bible or the fairies. Thomas Hope, a Lancashire wizard, said in 1638 that he had gotten his healing powers from being washed in special WATER at Rome.

In England, wizards were prosecuted for crimes by both the state and the Church. The Witchcraft Acts of 1542, 1563 and 1604 made felonies of popular forms of magic, such as fortune-telling, divination to find lost or stolen goods, conjuring spirits and making love charms. Prosecution by the state was erratic, due in part to the defense wizards enjoyed from their clientele, their lack of records and the general popularity of folk magic. Wizards suspected or accused of harmful magic were prosecuted as witches. The Church proscribed sorcery and divination as diabolical acts for the Devil.

The wizard as high magician was an intellectual who pursued alchemy, the Hermetic wisdom (see HERMETICA) and the doctrines of CORNELIUS AGRIPPA, PARACELSUS, JOHN DEE, the Neoplatonic philosophers and others. They read the GRIMOIRES, invoked spirits in ceremonial rituals, and scryed in crystals (see SCRYING).

In the 17th century, wizardry of both folk and high magic began to decline in prestige, retreating from urban population centers to the countryside. In the 19th century, FRANCIS BARRETT and ELIPHAS LEVI helped to revive interest in high magic. Folk-magic wizardry continued to be predominantly a rural phenomenon.

Woden   See ODIN.

Women's International Terrorist Conspiracy from Hell   See WITCH.

Wookey Hole   A series of limestone caves near Wells, England, which were carved away over time by the River Axe. In pagan times, the winter death rites of the GODDESS were probably celebrated here. Such rites, performed on the sabbat of Samhain (observed October 31), included the sacrifice of oxen in observance of the dying of the earth (see SABBATS). The Goddess was represented by a high priestess.

The cave also may have been used to initiate women into the pagan priesthood (see INITIATION). In 1912 excavations at the site uncovered the bones of a Romano-British woman. Nearby were the bones of a goat and a kid, as well as a comb, dagger and a round stalagmite that resembled a crude crystal ball.

According to legend, a bloodthirsty "Witch of Wookey" lived in the cave. In one version, the witch had once been spurned in love and in revenge cast SPELLS on the villagers of Wookey and demanded human SACRIFICE. The terrified villagers appealed to the Abbot of Glastonbury, who dispatched a monk to confront the witch in the depths of the cave. Her evil spells were of no avail against the monk. The witch tried to escape, but the monk succeeded in sprinkling her with holy water, turning her into stone. In another version, the witch directed her *MALEFICIA* against lovers throughout Somerset. She cast a spell that ruined one couple's wedding plans. The would-be groom took holy vows and became a monk. He exacted revenge by sprinkling the witch with holy water and turning her to stone.

A 20-foot-high stalagmite inside the cave is said to be the preserved remains of this witch.

words of power   See NAMES OF POWER.

Wotan   See ODIN.

Z

Zell, Morning Glory (1948-   ) Priestess and vice-president of the CHURCH OF ALL WORLDS, Morning Glory Zell has followed a mystical path to the Craft and Paganism (see WITCHCRAFT; NEO-PAGANISM). She describes her life as the story of a shaman: one who, by virtue of physical weakness or other characteristics, does not fit into society, undergoes a struggle for identity that goes into the realm of spirit, and emerges stronger and with a new identity. She is a practitioner of Celtic Pagan Shamanism, and has dedicated herself to working for a pantheistic, ecology-conscious, "Living Goddess" world.

Zell was born Diana Moore in Long Beach, California, on May 27, 1948, to a lower middle-class family with Irish and Choctaw Indian blood. Her parents were from Mississippi and moved to California during World War II so that her father could work in an aircraft factory. Three of her great-grandmothers were Choctaws who married white men in order to avoid the Trail of Tears when the Choctaw reservation was abolished in 1908. One of her grandmothers was an Irish milkmaid who immigrated to America during the Irish potato famine and married a well-to-do Southern planter.

Zell believes she was, or at least a portion of her was, an Indian child who died young in a previous life. She had early memories of walking the Trail of Tears, being hungry and seeing nothing but red dust. When she learned to talk, she told her mother she was not her real mother, that her real mother was somewhere in Oklahoma. Also at an early age, Zell began to experience clairvoyant dreams, which earned her the sobriquet of "witch" as she grew older.

Her mother, a devout Pentecostal who married young, came from a family of 13 children and wanted a large family herself; she was able only to have one child. She was a devoted mother, and raised her daughter in what Zell jokingly describes as "totalitarian Christianity." Zell says that she and her mother suffered abuse from her father, who was ill with industrially caused emphysema and was given experimental drugs that affected his behavior.

On Zell's father's side, one grandfather was a Methodist minister and a supporter of the Ku Klux Klan. At a young age, Zell would debate the Bible with him. A lover of dinosaurs, she was a Darwinist at an early age, and defended evolution. As a child, she attended Methodist services by herself, though her mother did not approve. Between the ages of 10 and 12 she became disenchanted with the Methodists and became deeply involved in the Pentecostal church.

In an effort to remedy the abuse at home, Zell visited her Pentecostal pastor to seek help and advice. She says she was told that she and her mother were subordinate to men, that this was the destiny of women, that they must be obedient to the will of God, and that if they bore their suffering with fortitude, they would "get a gold crown in heaven some day."

This unsatisfactory and offensive attitude sent Zell, a budding feminist, off on a comparative religion quest between the ages of 13 and 16. She found the various denominations of Christianity to be the same in one respect: women were not in positions of power and were not accorded the right of controlling their own destiny. She studied Buddhism and Zen Buddhism and joined the Vedanta Society, but she found that they also had a predominantly male perspective on the order of the cosmos. The Vedanta Society did introduce her to the GODDESS, and she still maintains an altar (see ALTAR) to various Hindu goddesses, most importantly the Mother Goddess, LAKSHMI.

She made her formal break with Christianity at about age 14, following a dialogue with her Methodist minister grandfather, who insisted that animals have no souls and did not go to heaven. As an animal lover, who had spent much of her free time with both domestic animals and wild creatures of the woods, Zell could not accept this. Her comparative religion search had included Greek mythology, which connected her to Paganism and her namesake, DIANA. At night, Zell would go outside and sing to the moon and try to call it down. She felt the Goddess, as huntress and protectress of all wild things, was speaking to her. The Goddess entered her life as a vital force, and Zell became a Pagan.

Around age 17, Zell read SYBIL LEEK's autobiography, *Diary of a Witch*, which made a tremendous impact upon her; she knew she *was* a Witch and felt she had been one in various lives since ancient times. Following graduation from high school she undertook a 30-day wilderness vision quest in Big Sur. For three weeks, she fasted, and for one week she lived off the land. The quest ended with a self-initiation into the Craft, in which Zell dove off a cliff into a pool of water and recognized herself as a Witch as she swam out (see INITIATION).

At the time it was widely believed that the only true Witches were hereditary ones, who could claim a family lineage of Witches. Like others who wanted to join the Craft but had no hereditary pedigree, Zell made up stories about a fictitious family history so that she would be accepted in Craft circles. She came to believe the stories, and clung to them as truth until the early 1980s, when she was able to let go of them during a vision quest.

During her teen years, Zell suffered from epilepsy, and finally was able to bring it under control with biofeedback. Throughout much of her life, she suffered other disorders due in part to blood sugar and chemical imbalances: she was prediabetic and had pancreatic problems; she suffered nervous disorders, extreme mood swings and schizophrenic breakdowns, in which she did not know who or where she was. She has been able to stabilize herself with diet changes.

She changed her first name to Morning Glory at age 19. In her studies of Diana, she learned that as the Greek Artemis, the Goddess had demanded great personal sacrifices from her human daughters, including celibacy. Zell wanted someday to marry and have children, and felt that keeping her given name might be a negative influence.

Zell enrolled in a community college but dropped out after one semester, following Timothy Leary's advice to "turn on, tune in and drop out." With her pet boa constrictor, she traveled to Eugene, Oregon, to join a commune and fell in love with a hitchhiker, Gary, whom she met enroute. Gary went to the commune with her, and they were married when she was 21. A year later, a daughter, Rainbow (now Gail), was born. The marriage, which was open, lasted about four years, until Zell met her present husband, OTTER ZELL (formerly Tim Zell).

Around 1971 Zell had a clairvoyant dream that she was going to meet a man who would change her life; she saw the man clearly in her dream. She told Gary about it. In 1973 she attended the Gnosticon Aquarian festival in St. Paul and listened to Tim Zell give the keynote address. When she saw him, she recognized him as the man in her prophetic dream. "The universe parted, bells rang and lights lit up" when she and Tim looked at each other, she recalls. After the talk, she approached him, and both knew they had found their soul mate. In Morning Glory's words, "It was like electric lightning. We had this silent communion. We held hands and looked into each other's eyes and telepathically conveyed our entire lives. It was powerful and indescribable. We knew we would never be separated."

Morning Glory called Gary from the festival and told him she had finally met the man in her dream. She took her daughter and went to live with Zell in St. Louis, and obtained a divorce. (Rainbow eventually returned to Eugene to live with her father.) In 1974, Morning Glory and Otter were married.

Morning Glory Zell trained for the traditional year and a day to become a priestess of the Church of All Worlds (CAW). In 1974 she became co-editor of the Church's flagship publication, the *Green Egg*, until it went out of print in 1976. When the publication was revived in 1988, she resumed co-editorship, which she shares with Otter.

The Zells left St. Louis and the central nest of the CAW in 1976, and spent a number of years traveling, living in monastic retreat, and undertaking exotic adventures. In 1985 they settled in Ukiah, California. In 1988 Morning Glory Zell became vice president of a revamped CAW.

In addition to her role in the CAW, Morning Glory Zell oversees one of its subsidiaries, the Ecosophical Research Association, which she founded in 1977. Both she and Otter volunteer for Critter Care, a wildlife animal rescue organization. She says she serves the aspect of the Goddess known as Potnia Theron, Our Lady of the Beasts.

Since dropping out of college, Morning Glory Zell has educated herself by pursuing studies in mythology, history, comparative third world religions, zoology, natural history, ethnobotany and the magical and psychic arts. She has collected more than 100 Goddess figures from cultures around the world, which she uses in presentations on the Goddess. She gives lectures, workshops and classes on numerous topics, works with crystals and practices astral travel, aura reading and projection, Tarot, "true dreaming" and other forms of divination, herbalism and spell-work.

Morning Glory Zell also is a writer of nonfiction, fiction and poetry. Her sword-and-sorcery fiction has been published in a fantasy anthology edited by MARION ZIMMER BRADLEY. She has written numerous pamphlets and articles on neo-Pagan theology, including "Firelight and Moonshadows: A Summary of Wiccan Lore," "Whither Wicca," "The Lord of Light," "Who on Earth is the Goddess," "Glossary of Witchcraft, Shamanism and Pagan Religions" and "The Elements of Ritual" (the latter three are collaborations with Otter Zell). She also has written numerous poems and invocations on the goddesses and gods of nature for an anthology, *Moondrops from Morning Glory.*

Zell, Otter (1942–   )

Visionary American Pagan and founder of the CHURCH OF ALL WORLDS, who has played a leading role in the growth and direction of NEO-PAGANISM. A self-described modern Renaissance man, Otter Zell has worn many hats in his career: transpersonal psychologist, naturalist, metaphysician, mystic, shaman, theologian, teacher, author, artist, lecturer, and ordained Priest of the Earth-Mother, Gaea (see GAIA).

He was born on November 30, 1942, in St. Louis, Missouri. His birth was inspired by World War II; his father decided to join the armed services, and the Zells decided to have a child in case he did not return. While the elder Zell went off to fight in the South Pacific, Mrs. Zell moved to St. Louis to live with her family and wait.

A year before his birth, Zell's maternal grandfather died at home. Zell believes he reincarnated aspects of his grandfather's personality. As a child, he experienced dreams of dying and going into a void. He exhibited many personality characteristics of the man he never knew, and at an early age he developed a love for spending time in the woods with nature—just as his grandfather had loved to do (see REINCARNATION).

After his father's return from the war, the Zell family moved to Clark Summit, a small town outside Scranton, Pennsylvania. The backyard of their home blended into woods, a perfect setting for young Zell. His father worked as a traveling salesman for a greeting card company (no longer in business) and spent a good deal of time away from home.

As a child, Zell kept to himself and spent virtually all of his free time in the woods. He would sit

Morning Glory and Otter Zell (courtesy Morning Glory and Otter Zell)

motionless and let the wildlife come around him. According to Zell, his primary childhood friends were the animals and birds; he recalls that he always had at least one girlfriend. He manifested psychic gifts in the form of telepathy, and could hear the thoughts of those around him. As a consequence, he shunned large groups of people, because the telepathic commotion was too much to handle. A large part of his early years were fraught with serious illness and at one point, a nervous breakdown. It was a ghastly period, he says, in which the illnesses erased and reprogrammed his mind several times. His continual memories begin at about age 10; he has few recollections of earlier years. At some point—he does not remember when or how—the reincarnational dreams and the telepathy ceased.

During Zell's teenage years, his father was promoted and the family moved to Crystal Lake, northwest of Chicago, Illinois. Zell took naturally to the lake, as he had to the woods. He learned instinctively to swim "like an otter," folding his arms by his side and wiggling through the water. "Otter" became his nickname. He was introspective, read a wide range of literature, and delved into science fiction and fantasy.

He enrolled at Westminster Fulton College in St. Louis, where, in the early 1960s, he met Richard Lance Christie, an association which eventually led to the formation of the Church of All Worlds. Zell shaped the Church to his personal vision: Religion should not be concerned with personal salvation, a goal overwhelmingly insignificant within the total context of the cosmos, but should be focused on connecting with all time and space, the life flow of the universe, and the oneness of all things.

Under Zell's leadership, the Church, which filed for incorporation in 1967 and was formally chartered in 1968, attracted a wide following of intellectuals. It and Zell played major roles in the coalescing and networking of the budding neo-Pagan movement and the alliance of Paganism with the environmental movement. Zell edited the Church's journal, the *Green Egg,* and made featured appearances at Pagan festivals and science fiction conventions. Sometimes he carried his pet boa constrictor, Histah, on his shoulders as he gave addresses.

In 1963, Zell married his first wife, Martha, with whom he had a son, Bryan, his only child. That relationship ended in 1971.

Between 1965 and 1968 Zell earned undergraduate degrees in sociology/anthropology and clinical psychology, a teaching certificate and a doctor of divinity from Life Science College. He entered, but did not complete, the doctoral program in clinical psychology at Washington University.

In 1970 Zell formulated and published "the thealogy [sic] of deep ecology," which later became known as The Gaea Hypothesis, the concept of Mother Earth as a sentient being who, in order to survive, needs the harmonious balance of all things on the planet.

Zell was invited to give a keynote address at the 1973 Gnosticon Pagan festival in Minneapolis on "Theagenesis: The Birth of the Goddess," his ideas about Oneness with Earth. In the audience was Morning Glory Moore Ferns (see MORNING GLORY ZELL). In a dramatic moment, the two recognized each other as soul mates, and experienced a profound, telepathic intimacy. Zell took Morning Glory back to his home in St. Louis. Six months later, they were legally married in a spectacular Pagan handfasting ceremony at the 1974 Gnosticon festival at Easter. They have an open marriage. Around 1987 they added a third primary partner, Diane Darling, to their relationship.

In 1976, the Zells decided to leave St. Louis and the central nest of the Church of All Worlds. They bought an old school bus and drove it to Illinois, where they converted it into a mobile home. They then headed southwest and west, stopping for awhile at Coeden Brith in Mendocino County, California, land belonging to Alison Harlow, a cofounder of the neo-Pagan organization, Nemeton (see GWYDION PENDDERWEN). From there, they went north to Eugene, Oregon, where they taught WITCHCRAFT, SHA-

MANISM, and Third World religions at a local community college.

In the fall of 1976 Zell underwent a profound mystical vision quest that proved to be a watershed in his life. For two weeks, he fasted alone in the wilderness near a hot spring by the Mackenzie River, with no clothes and only a knife and a sleeping bag. He learned to be completely in tune with nature, meditated, kept a journal and smoked marijuana. He emerged from the experience transformed: his old identity as an urban social psychologist had been obliterated, and he was now a mountain man, ready to embark on new paths, live in the woods and became a priest of Gaea. With Morning Glory, he performed a ritual baptism, and initiated himself into the Eighth Circle of the Church of All Worlds.

For the next eight years, Zell dropped out of public sight. In 1977 he and Morning Glory returned to Coeden Brith and shared with Harlow their secret: that they had discovered how to create unicorns from baby goats. Harlow offered them a contract to live on the land as caretakers. They created a monastic homestead and a Pagan retreat, conducted seminars in the community, raised wild animals and ran the Church of All Worlds as an umbrella organization for several Pagan subsidiaries. Through one subsidiary, the Ecosophical Research Association, they embarked on various projects, including the breeding of unicorns and a hunt for mermaids off Papua New Guinea.

In 1979 Zell decided to change his first name. He had been dissatisfied with it since leaving St. Louis. He tried to forge new names without success. In March of that year, he and Morning Glory sat by the banks of the river that flows through Coeden Brith and discussed the situation. Morning Glory suggested his nickname, Otter. Zell rejected it, saying he wanted a name with more "flash" that would be taken seriously by those with whom they planned to do business with the unicorns. Morning Glory then suggesting asking the Mother for a sign, which Zell did. At that moment, an otter popped up out of the water, climbed on a rock, looked at them, twirled around and dove back into the water. Zell had never before seen a live, wild otter and has not seen one since. "I hear and obey," said Zell. He changed his last name to G'Zell, as a contraction of "Glory" and "Zell," a style borrowed from science fiction. For a time, the Zells were known as Otter G'Zell and Morning G'Zell, then reverted to the original "Zell."

In 1985 Harlow asked the Zells to leave Coeden Brith to make way for other plans; they moved to Ukiah, where they live with their animals and extended family near a bend in the Russian River. Family members include Zell's son, Bryan, and Darling and her son, Zack. Zell emerged from retreat to resume public appearances, lectures, workshops and classes. He and Morning Glory reactivated the Church of All Worlds, which had shrunk to a small, mostly California base. The *Green Egg* was resurrected at Beltane 1988.

Zell works as a freelance graphic artist and computer operator. Since the late 1960s, he has illustrated fantasy and science fiction magazines and books and has designed posters, record album covers and T-shirts. He also sculpts an ongoing series of ancient Goddess figures and prehistoric and mythological creatures.

Zell, Tim See OTTER ZELL.

zombie A zombie is a dead person brought back to life by a magician, but not to the life the person previously knew. Believed dead by all who knew him, and by himself as well, the zombie becomes more like a robot than a human being, staring ahead and blindly following the magician-leader, doing his every bidding.

The word *zombie* probably comes from the African Congo word *nzambi*, which means "the spirit of a dead person." Yet a truly dead person—one who has lost bodily functions, whose cells have decayed—cannot be returned to life. To unlock the mystery of zombies Harvard ethnobotanist Wade Davis went to Haiti in 1982. Davis reasoned that the zombie ("zombi," as he preferred to spell it) was a person buried alive, who only seemed dead. Such a person had to be drugged to appear dead, exhibiting no life at all, but could come out of his trance and resume living. He talked to two people who claimed to be zombies: a man named Clairvius Narcisse and a woman known as Ti Femme. They told how they died, how they witnessed their burials and how the *bokor*, or black-magic Vodoun *houngan* (priest) lifted them from the grave.

After months of study and conversations with various *hougans*, Davis confirmed his suspicions. The "zombies" were created by the administration of a powerful poison to an open wound or into the victim's food, guaranteeing its entrance into the bloodstream. The poison contains various pharmacologically active plants and animals and usually ground human remains, but the most important ingredient is the puffer fish, which contains *tetrodotoxin*. These fish, of the species *Sphoeroides testudineus* and *Diodon hystrix*, are so poisonous that a tiny drop of tetrodotoxin is fatal. Most importantly, tetrodotoxin exhibits two very strange characteristics: the body becomes completely paralyzed, the eyes glazing over and becoming completely unresponsive, mim-

icking death; and one can recover from a highly controlled dose without any aftereffects. Even trained doctors cannot tell if the victim has truly died from the poison.

The ingredients of zombie poison as determined by Davis are as follows:

First a bouga toad (*Bufo marinus*) and a sea snake are buried in a jar until they "die from rage," say the Vodoun preparers; or in other words, the toad secretes venom from its glands in its desperate state. Then ground millipeds and tarantulas are mixed with plant products: *tcha-tcha* seeds, or *Albizzia lebbeck*, which causes pulmonary swelling; consigne seeds, from a tree in the mohagany family with no known poisonous attributes; leaves from *pomme cajou*, or the cashew nut (*Anacardium occidentale*); and *bresillet* leaves (*Comocladia glabra*). The last two plants are in the poison ivy family and cause severe dermatitis. All of these plant and animal products are ground into a powder, placed in a jar and buried for two days.

Next the preparer adds *tremblador* and *desmembre*, plants that Davis was unable to identify botanically. At the third stage, the preparer adds four more plants that produce severe topical irritations. The itching from these plants could cause the sufferer to break the skin while scratching, making it easier for the applied "zombie powder" to enter the bloodstream. To work, the poison must enter through an open wound or be ingested into the stomach. These plants are *maman guepes* (*Urera baccifera*) and *mashasha* (*Dalechampia scandens*), both members of the stinging nettle family. The hollow hairs on the plants' surface act like syringes, injecting a chemical similar to formic acid (the compound responsible for ant-bite stings) into the skin.

Also included is *Dieffenbachia seguine*, known as "dumbcane," which contains oxalate needles that act like ground glass. During the nineteenth century, masters forced slaves to eat *Dieffenbachia* leaves, which irritated the larynx, making breathing difficult and speaking impossible, hence the appellation "dumb." The fourth plant is *bwa pine* (*Zanthoxylum matinicense*), used for its sharp spines.

The animals added at this point complete the poisonous picture. Skins of the white tree-frog (*Osteopilus dominicencis*) are ground with two species of tarantulas, then added to another bouga toad and four species of the deadly puffer fish: *Sphoeroides testudineus, Sphoeroides spengleri, Diodon hystrix* and *Diodon holacanthus*. For dramatic effect, the powder can be mixed with ground human remains, preferably a skull.

Once the *bokor* raises the zombie from his tomb, the victim is force-fed a concoction of cane sugar, sweet potato and *Datura stramonium*, or "zombie's cucumber," which causes hallucinations and disorientation. The *bokor* announces the zombie's new name and new "life," and completely confused, the zombie follows the *bokor* wherever he leads him. Tribal Africans believe that slothful persons in life risk being made zombies after death, condemned to work for the *bokor* into eternity.

Traditionally, zombies work the fields, although some believe they are responsible for other work performed at night, like baking bread. A few zombies reportedly have served as bookkeepers, and even shopclerks. Becoming a zombie was a slave's worst nightmare, since death provided no release from unremitting labor. Zombies require little food, but care must be taken not to give them SALT. Considered a magical, purifying substance since medieval times, salt can give the zombie back his powers of speech and taste, releasing a homing instinct that calls the zombie back to his grave. Once there, he burrows deep into the ground, away from the *bokor's* influence, and resumes his eternal rest.

There is no antidote to "zombie poison," since too many of its components have no recourse. But the Vodoun preparers make what they call an antidote, made of various leaves from plants with no pharmacological properties, the liquor clairin, ammonia and lemon juice. Other possible ingredients include mothballs, seawater, perfume, rock salt and a mysterious liquid available from Vodoun apothecaries known as *magic noire*, or "black magic."

Although making a zombie requires detailed knowledge of the poisons—and cannot work without tetrodotoxin's peculiar properties—the entire process requires belief in magic and the faith that zombies are real. In Vodoun, zombies are made by sorcerers, who have captured the soul—the *ti bon ange* ("little good angel") of the deceased. When a person dies, the Vodounist believes the *ti bon ange* hovers about the cadaver for seven days, during which time the soul is most vulnerable to sorcery. If the *bokor* captures it, he can make not only a zombie of the flesh, as described above, but a "zombie astral": a ghost or spirit who wanders at the command of the *bokor*.

Through SORCERY, the *bokor* controls those who were alive either in the body or the spirit. To guard against such a fate, relatives of the deceased "kill" the body again, stabbing a knife through the heart or decapitating it. Others place a dagger in the deceased's coffin to stab the *bokor* or sew up the deceased's mouth so he cannot answer the *bokor* when he calls. Another trick is to place seeds in the coffin, which the *bokor* must count before taking the body. Such a tedious task can take too long, and dawn could break before the *bokor* can remove the body. And no black magic is performed during daylight.

Davis, who wrote *The Serpent and the Rainbow* (1985), also found that zombification was no random act of evil or criminality but a means of capital punishment. Dating back to the secret Maroon societies—groups of escaped slaves hiding in the mountains of Saint Domingue—and beyond to the secret tribal societies of Africa, blacks have always established their own judicial tribunals for keeping their communities under control. By means of poisons, magic and extreme secrecy, these organizations surrounded their neighbors with a cloak of fear, administering swift retribution to any who broke the codes. In the days of slavery, blacks used poisons to fight back against their white masters. Poisons worked well, too, against any black who betrayed his brother or sister slaves. Stories of people who banded together to eat human flesh, to dance in cemeteries and raise the dead inspired enough dread to cause any lawbreaker to think twice.

Zugarramurdi Witches   As part of their efforts to stem public hysteria over WITCHES and sorcerers (see SORCERY), Spanish inquisitors conducted mass trials of accused witches in the Basque village of Zugarramurdi from June 10 to November 8, 1610. For all the hue and cry mounted by the local folk and the lurid testimony given at the lengthy trials, only six persons went to the stake.

Zugarramurdi, a Navarre town on the border of the Labourd region, where the infamous witch-hunter PIERRE DE LANCRE was scouring the countryside for witches, provided a rich setting for superstitious villagers. Nearby was a large, subterranean cave, cut through by a river called the *Infernukeorreka*, or "stream of Hell," a perfect place for witches to gather and practice their alleged cult of Satan and various pagan rites.

The Supreme Inquisition appointed Don Juan Valle Alvarado as inquisitor in charge of the investigation at Zugarramurdi. Alvarado spent several months gathering testimony, which cast suspicion of WITCHCRAFT crimes upon nearly 300 persons, not counting children. The testimony of wild diabolical activities was accepted without question. Alvarado determined that 40 of the suspects were obviously guilty. He had them arrested and taken to Logrono for trial before three judges.

According to the testimony given at the trials, the Zugarramurdi witches were organized in a hierarchy. At the top were senior sorcerers and witches, followed by second-grade initiates who served as tutors of novices. First-grade initiates were responsible for making POISONS and casting SPELLS. Child recruits included those under the age of five who were taken to SABBATS by force; those from age five or six up who were induced to attend sabbats with false promises or goodies; older novices who were preparing to renounce Christianity; and neophytes who had made their renunciation. The entire lot of them were said to worship an ugly, gargoylelike DEVIL.

Detailed descriptions were given of renunciation ceremonies. The novice was presented to the Devil and formally renounced God, the Blessed Virgin, the saints, baptism and confirmation, parents and godparents, Christianity and all those who follow it. The novice kissed the Devil's hind end (see KISS OF SHAME). The Devil marked the novice with his claw, drawing blood, which was caught in a bowl or cup, and also marked the novice in the pupil of the eye with a shape of a toad (see DEVIL'S MARK).

The novice, now an initiate, was bound over as a slave to a master or mistress, who was paid in silver by the Devil. According to testimony, the silver vanished if not spent within 24 hours (see MONEY). The initiate was given a toad (see TOADS) as his or her familiar (see FAMILIARS), which had been tended by a master or mistress, and instructions for evildoing. After a satisfactory trial period, the initiate was given complete control of the toad and was allowed to make POISONS.

Child recruits were bound over to instructors and given many toads to care for.

The witches were said to meet every Friday night and to hold special masses on the night before major Christian holy days. On these occasions, the Devil preached sermons.

The Zugarramurdi witches also were accused of the usual MALEFICIA attributed to witches elsewhere:

METAMORPHOSIS. They changed into animals in order to frighten and hurt others.

SPELLS. They sabotaged flourishing crops with powders and poisons made from snakes, lizards, toads, newts, slugs, snails and puffballs. The witches metamorphosed into animals and, led by the Devil, sprinkled their poisons over the crops while intoning, "Powder, powder, ruin everything," or "Let all [or half] be lost with the exception of anything that belongs to me." These spells usually were cast during an early autumn southerly wind called *sorguin aizia* or "the wind of the witches." The witches also raised storms (see STORM RAISING) to destroy crops. They allegedly poisoned animals and murdered human beings by administering poisonous powder or OINTMENTS which caused people to become ill and die.

Vampirism. Villagers claimed witches stole children out of their beds at night, carried them off and ate them. Some cases of vampirism of adults also were given at court.

Of the 40 accused witches, 18 confessed and tearfully asked for mercy, and were reconciled with the Church. Six were burned at the stake, including Maria Zozaya, an elderly woman who was said to be one of the senior witches. Five of the accused died during the trials; effigies of them were burned along with the six who were executed. The remaining 11 presumably were not convicted.

Bibliography

Adler, Jerry, with Pamela Abrahamson and John Whitinger. " 'The Second Beast of Revelation.' " *Newsweek*, November 16, 1987, 73.

Adler, Margot. *Drawing Down the Moon*, rev. ed. New York: Viking, 1986.

Anchor/Doubleday. *Foxfire 2*. Garden City, N.Y.: Anchor Books/Doubleday, 1973.

———. *Foxfire 6*. Garden City, N.Y.: Anchor Books/Doubleday, 1980.

Anglo, Sydney, ed. *The Damned Art: Essays in the Literature of Witchcraft*. London: Routledge & Kegan Paul Ltd., 1977.

Ashe, Geoffrey, ed. *The Quest for Arthur's Britain*. New York: Frederick A. Praeger, 1969.

Ashley, Leonard R. N. *The Wonderful World of Magic and Witchcraft*. New York: Dembner Books, 1986.

Baker, Sherry, "Witches Without Broomsticks," *Atlanta*, October 1986.

Baldwin, Richard. *A Revelation of Several Hundreds of Children & Others that Prophesie and Preach in Their Sleep, etc.* London: 1689.

Barber, Chris. *Mysterious Wales*. London: Granada Publishing, 1983.

Baroja, Julio Caro. *The World of the Witches*. Chicago: University of Chicago Press, 1975 (first published 1961).

Barrett, Francis. *The Magus*. London: Lackington, Allen and Co., 1801.

Bias, Clifford. *Ritual Book of Magic*. York Beach, Me.: Samuel Weiser, Inc., 1981.

Blatty, William Peter. *The Exorcist*. New York: Bantam Books, 1971.

Bonewits, P. E. I. *Real Magic*. New York: Coward, McCann & Geoghegan, 1971.

Bonfanti, Leo. *The Witchcraft Hysteria*, vols. I & II. Wakefield, Mass.: Pride Publications Inc., 1971, 1977, respectively.

Bord, Janet and Colin. *Ancient Mysteries of Britain*. Manchester, N.H.: Salem House Publishers, 1986.

Bourne, Lois. *Witch Amongst Us*. New York: St. Martin's Press, 1985.

Boyd, Mildred. *Man, Myth & Magic*. New York: Criterion Books, 1969.

Boyer, Paul and Stephen Nissenbaum. *Salem Possessed: The Social Origins of Witchcraft*. Cambridge, Mass.: Harvard University Press, 1974.

Bradley, Marion Zimmer. *The Mists of Avalon*. New York: Alfred Knopf, 1983.

Brier, Bob. *Ancient Egyptian Magic*. New York: William Morrow, 1980.

Briggs, K. M. *The Fairies in Tradition and Literature*. London: Routledge & Kegan Paul, 1978.

Briggs, Katherine. *An Encyclopedia of Fairies*. New York: Pantheon, 1976.

Broderick, Robert C., ed. *The Catholic Encyclopedia*. Nashville: Thomas Nelson, Inc., 1976.

Brown, David C. *A Guide to the Salem Witchcraft Hysteria of 1692*. Self-published, 1984.

Brown, Peter Lancaster. *Megaliths, Myths and Men*. New York: Taplinger, 1976.

Buckland, Raymond. *Anatomy of the Occult*. New York: Samuel Weiser, 1977.

———. *Buckland's Complete Book of Witchcraft*. St. Paul: Llewellyn Publications, 1986.

———. *A Pocket Guide to the Supernatural*. New York: Ace Books, 1969.

———. *The Tree: The Complete Book of Saxon Witchcraft*. St. Paul: Llewellyn Publications, 1974.

———. *Witchcraft Ancient and Modern*. Secaucus, N.J.: Castle Books, 1970.

———. *Witchcraft from the Inside*. St Paul: Llewellyn Publications, 1971.

———. *Witchcraft from the Inside*, 2nd ed. St. Paul: Llewellyn Publications, 1975.

Budapest, Zsusanna. *The Holy Book of Women's Mysteries*, vol. I (revised) and vol. II. Oakland, Cal.: 1986, 1980, respectively.

Budge, E. A. Wallis. *Amulets and Superstitions*. New York: Dover Publications, 1978 (first published 1930).

——. *Egyptian Magic*. New York: Dover Publications, 1971 (first published 1901).

Bulfinch, Thomas. *Bulfinch's Mythology*. New York: Avenel Books, 1984.

Burl, Aubrey. *Rings of Stone*. New York: Ticknor & Fields, 1979.

——. *Rites of the Gods*. London: J. M. Dent & Sons Ltd., 1981.

Cahill, Robert Ellis. *The Horrors of Salem's Witch Dungeon*. Peabody, Mass.: Chandler-Smith Publishing House, 1986.

——. *New England's Witches and Wizards*. Peabody, Mass.: Chandler-Smith Publishing House, 1983.

Calef, Robert. *Another Brand Pluckt out of the Burning or More Wonders of the Invisible World*. London: 1700.

Call, Max. *Hand of Death: The Henry Lee Lucas Story*. Lafayette, La.: Prescott Press, 1985.

Campbell, Joseph. *The Masks of God*, vol I: *Primitive Mythology*. New York: Viking Penguin, 1959.

——. *The Masks of God*, vol. II: *Oriental Mythology*. New York: Viking Penguin, 1962.

——. *The Way of the Animal Powers*, vol. I: *Historical Atlas of World Mythology*. London: Times Books, 1984.

Carroll, David. *The Magic Makers*. New York: Arbor House, 1974.

Case, Paul Foster. *The Tarot*. Richmond, Va.: Macoy Publishing Co., 1947.

Cavendish, Richard. *The Black Arts*. New York: Putnam, 1967.

——. *A History of Magic*. New York: Taplinger, 1977.

——. *The Powers of Evil*. New York: G. P. Putnam's Sons, 1975.

Cavendish, Richard, ed. *The Encyclopedia of the Unexplained*. New York: McGraw-Hill, 1974.

Cavendish, Richard, ed. in chief. *Man, Myth & Magic: The Illustrated Encyclopedia of Mythology, Religion and the Unknown*. New York: Marshall Cavendish, 1983.

Chippindale, Christopher. *Stonehenge Complete*. Ithaca, N.Y.: Cornell University Press, 1983.

Cirlot, J. E. *A Dictionary of Symbols*. New York: Philosophical Library, 1971.

Clifton, Chas. S., "The Craft Meets the Craft," *Gnosis*, 6(Winter 1988), 28–29.

Cohen, Daniel. *A Natural History of Unnatural Things*. New York: E. P. Dutton, 1971.

Cooper, Nancy, with Ron Moreau, "Haiti's Voodoo Witch Hunt," *Newsweek*, May 26, 1986.

Cooper, Nancy, with Anne Underwood, "Strange Tales from the Duvaliers' Voodoo Dynasty," *Newsweek*, February 17, 1986.

Cornett, Larry, "Finding a Sacred Grove for Druid Initiation," *The Druids' Progress*, Report Number Two, 1985, 49–53.

Covina, Gina. *The Ouija Book*. New York: Simon & Schuster, 1979.

Crabtree, Adam. *Multiple Man: Explorations in Possession and Multiple Personality*. New York: Praeger, 1985.

Cranston, Sylvia and Carey Williams. *Reincarnation: A New Horizon in Science, Religion and Society*. New York: Julian Press, 1984.

Crookall, Robert. *Out-of-the-Body Experiences: A Fourth Analysis*. Secaucus, N.J.: University Books, 1970.

Cross, F. L., ed., and E. A. Livingston. *The Oxford Dictionary of the Christian Church*, 2nd ed. London: Oxford University Press, 1974.

Crowley, Aleister. *Magick in Theory and Practice*. New York: Dover Publications, 1976 (first published 1929).

Crowther, Arnold and Patricia. *The Secrets of Ancient Witchcraft, with the Witches' Tarot*. Secaucus, N.J.: University Books, 1974.

Crowther, Patricia. *Lid Off the Cauldron: A Wicca Handbook*. York Beach, Me.: Samuel Weiser, 1989 (first published 1981).

——. *Witch Blood!* New York: House of Collectibles, Inc., 1974.

Cunningham, Scott. *Cunningham's Encyclopedia of Crystal, Gem & Metal Magic*. St. Paul: Llewellyn Publications, 1987.

——. *Cunningham's Encyclopedia of Magical Herbs*. St. Paul: Llewellyn Publications, 1985.

——. *Earth Power*. St. Paul: Llewellyn Publications, 1983.

——. *Magical Herbalism*. St. Paul: Llewellyn Publications, 1982.

Cunningham, Scott and David Harrington. *The Magical Household*. St. Paul: Llewellyn Publications, 1987.

Curry, Patrick, "The Astrologers' Feasts," *History Today*, 38(April 1988), 17–22.

Daly Mary. *Beyond God the Father*, rev. ed. Boston: Beacon Press, 1985.

———. *The Church and the Second Sex*. Boston: Beacon Press, 1985.

———. *Gyn/Ecology: The Metaethics of Radical Feminism*. Boston: Beacon Press, 1978.

Dames, Michael. *The Avebury Cycle*. London: Thames and Hudson, 1977.

David-Neel, Alexandra. *Magic & Mystery in Tibet*. Baltimore, Md.: Penguin Books, 1971.

Davies, J. G., ed. *The New Westminster Dictionary of Liturgy and Worship*. Philadelphia: The Westminster Press, 1986.

Davis, Rod, "Children of Yoruba," *Southern*, February 1987.

Davis, Wade. *The Serpent and the Rainbow*. New York: Simon & Schuster, 1985.

Deacon, Richard. *Matthew Hopkins: Witch Finder General*. London: Frederick Muller, 1976.

Demos, John Putnam. *Entertaining Satan: Witchcraft and the Culture of Early New England*. New York: Oxford University Press, 1982.

Devillers, Carole, "Of Spirits and Saints," *National Geographic*, March 1985.

Devlin, Judith. *The Superstitious Mind: French Peasants and the Supernatural in the Nineteenth Century*. New Haven: Yale University Press, 1987.

Di Stasti, Lawrence. *Mal Occhio: The Underside of Vision*. San Francisco: North Point Press, 1981.

Douglas, Alfred. *The Tarot: The Origins, Meaning and Use of the Cards*. New York: Taplinger, 1972.

Drake, Samuel G. *Annals of Witchcraft in New England and Elsewhere in the United States, from Their First Settlement*. Boston: W. Elliott Woodward, 1869.

Drury, Neville. *Dictionary of Mysticism and the Occult*. New York: Harper & Row, 1985.

Ebon, Martin. *The Devil's Bride, Exorcism: Past and Present*. New York: Harper & Row, 1974.

Eliade, Mircea. *From Primitives to Zen: A Thematic Sourcebook of the History of Religions*. San Francisco: Harper & Row, 1977.

———. *Occultism, Witchcraft and Cultural Fashions*. Chicago: University of Chicago Press, 1976.

———. *Shamanism*, rev. and enlarged ed. Princeton: Princeton University Press, 1974.

Eliade, Mircea, ed.-in-chief. *The Encyclopedia of Religion*. New York: Macmillan, 1987.

Ellis, Bill, "The Varieties of Alien Experience," *The Skeptical Inquirer*, 12:3(Spring 1988), 263–69.

Elworthy, Frederick Thomas. *The Evil Eye*. Secaucus, N.J.: University Books/Citadel Press, facsimile of the 1895 ed.

Endicott, K. M. *An Analysis of Malaysian Magic*. Oxford: Oxford University Press, 1970.

Evans-Pritchard, E. E. *Witchcraft, Oracles and Magic Among the Azande* (abridged). Oxford: Clarendon Press, 1983.

Evans-Wentz, W. Y. *The Fairy-Faith in Celtic Countries*. Secaucus, N.J.: University Books, 1966 (first published 1911).

Farrar, Janet and Stewart. *A Witches Bible Compleat*. New York: Magickal Childe, 1984 (first published as *Eight Sabbats for Witches* [1981] and *The Witches' Way* [1981]).

Farrar, Stewart. *What Witches Do: A Modern Coven Revealed*, 2nd ed. Custer, Wash.: Phoenix Publishing Co., 1983.

Farren, David. *Living with Magic*. New York: Simon & Schuster, 1975.

———. *The Return of Magic*. New York: Harper & Row, 1972.

———. *Sex and Magic*. New York: Simon & Schuster, 1975.

Fidler, J. Havelock. *Earth Energy: A Dowser's Investigations of Ley Lines*, 2nd ed. Wellingborough, Northamptonshire, England: The Aquarian Press, 1988.

Finucane, R. C. *Appearances of the Dead: A Cultural History of Ghosts*. Buffalo, N.Y.: Prometheus Books, 1984.

Fitch, Ed and Janine Renee. *Magical Rites from the Crystal Well*. St. Paul: Llewellyn Publications, 1984.

Fortune, Dion. *Psychic Self-Defense*, 6th ed. York Beach, Me.: Samuel Weiser, 1982.

Fox, Judy, Karen Hughes, and John Tampion. *An Illuminated I Ching*. New York: Arco Publications, 1984.

Frayser, Suzanne G. *Varieties of Sexual Experience: An Anthropological Perspective on Human Sexuality*. New Haven, Conn.: HRAF Press, 1985.

Frazer, Sir James G. *The Golden Bough.* New York: Avenel Books, 1981 (first published 1890).

Freesoul, John Redtail. *Breath of the Invisible: The Way of the Pipe.* Wheaton, Ill.: Quest Books, 1986.

French, Peter J. *John Dee: The World of an Elizabethan Magus.* London: Routledge & Kegan Paul, 1972.

Fristcher, John. *Popular Witchcraft Straight from the Witch's Mouth.* Bowling Green, Ohio: Bowling Green University Press, 1972.

Frost, Gavin and Yvonne. *Astral Travel.* York Beach, Me.: Samuel Weiser, 1986 (first published 1982).

———. *The Magic Power of Witchcraft.* West Nyack, N.Y.: Parker Publishing, 1976.

Gandee, Lee R. *Strange Experience: The Autobiography of a Hexenmeister.* Englewood Cliffs, N.J.: Prentice-Hall, 1971.

Gardner, Gerald B. *The Meaning of Witchcraft.* New York: Magickal Childe, 1982 (first published 1959).

———. *Witchcraft Today.* New York: Magickal Childe, 1982 (first published 1954).

Gauld, Alan and A. D. Cornell. *Poltergeists.* London: Routledge & Kegan Paul, 1979.

Gibson, Walter B. *Witchcraft.* New York: Grosset & Dunlap, 1973.

Gibson, Walter B. and Litzka B. Gibson. *The Complete Illustrated Book of Divination and Prophecy.* Garden City, N.Y.: Doubleday, 1973.

Gilbert, Henry. *King Arthur's Knights.* London: Bracken Books, 1985 (first published 1911).

Gilbert, R. A. *Golden Dawn: Twilight of the Magicians.* Wellingborough, Northhamptonshire, England: The Aquarian Press, 1983.

Ginzburg, Carlo. *Night Battles: Witchcraft & Agrarian Cults in the Sixteenth & Seventeenth Centuries.* New York: Penguin Books, 1985 (first published 1966).

Givens, Ron, with Janet Huck, "California: Devilish Deeds?" *Newsweek,* September 16, 1985, 43.

Glanvil, Joseph, Rev. *Saducismus Triumphatus: Full and Plain Evidence Concerning Witches and Apparitions.* London, 1689 (first published 1668).

Glass, Justine. *Witchcraft, the Sixth Sense.* No. Hollywood, Cal.: Melvin Powers Wilshire Book Co., 1965.

Gleason, Judith. *Oya: In Praise of the Goddess.* Boston: Shambhala Publications, 1987.

Godwin, John. *Occult America.* Garden City, N.Y.: Doubleday, 1972.

Gonzales-Wippler, Migene. *Santería: African Magic in Latin America.* New York: Original Products, 1981.

Goodell, Alfred P. "The Story of the Old Witch Jail." Undated manuscript, Essex Institute, Salem, Mass.

Graves, Robert. *The White Goddess,* amended and enlarged ed. New York: Farrar, Straus and Giroux, 1966 (first published 1948).

Gray, Eden. *A Complete Guide to the Tarot.* New York: Bantam Books, 1970.

Green, Marian. *The Gentle Arts of Aquarian Magic.* Wellingborough, Northamptonshire, England: The Aquarian Press, 1987.

Green, Michelle and Civia Tamarkin, "A Boy's Love of Satan Ends in Murder, A Death Sentence—and Grisly Memories," *People,* December 1, 1986, 155–61.

Green, Miranda. *The Gods of the Celts.* Gloucester, England: Alan Sutton, 1986.

Grilley, Virginia. *On a Salem Lane.* Salem, Mass.: The Seven Gables Shop, 1959.

Grillot de Givry, Emile. *Witchcraft, Magic and Alchemy.* New York: Dover, 1971 (first published 1929).

Grossman, Richard. *The Other Medicines.* Garden City, N.Y.: Doubleday, 1985.

Guirand, Felix, ed. *New Larousse Encyclopedia of Mythology.* New York: Crescent, 1986 (first published 1959).

Gummere, Amelia Mott. *Witchcraft and Quakerism: A Study in Social History.* Philadelphia: The Biddle Press, 1908.

G'Zell, Otter, "Theagenesis: The Birth of the Goddess," *Green Egg* 2, 81 (Beltane 1988): 4–7 + (first published 1971).

Haining, Peter. *The Anatomy of Witchcraft.* New York: Taplinger, 1972.

Hall, Manly P. *The Secret Teachings of All Ages.* Los Angeles: The Philosophical Research Society, Inc., 1977 (first published 1925).

Hamilton, Edith. *Mythology.* Boston: Little, Brown, 1942.

Hansen, Chadwick, "Andover Witchcraft and the Causes of the Salem Witchcraft Trials," in *The Occult in America,* John Godwin, ed. Garden City. N.Y.: Doubleday, 1982.

———. *Witchcraft at Salem.* New York: New American Library, 1969.

Harding, M. Esther. *Women's Mysteries Ancient and Modern*. New York: Harper & Row, 1971.

Harner, Michael. *The Way of the Shaman*. New York: Bantam, 1982.

Harrison, G. B., ed. *The Trial of the Lancaster Witches*. New York: Barnes & Noble, 1971 (first published 1929).

Hawkins, Gerald S. *Beyond Stonehenge*. New York: Harper & Row, 1973.

———. *Stonehenge Decoded*. New York: Dorset Press, 1965.

Hayden, Brian, "Alliances and Ritual Ecstasy: Human Responses to Resource Stress," *Journal for the Scientific Study of Religion*, 26:1(1976), 81–91.

———, "Old Europe: Sacred Matriarchy or Complementary Opposition?" in *Archaeology and Fertility Cults in the Ancient Mediterranean*, Anthony Bonanno, ed. Amsterdam: B. R. Gruner Publishing, 1986.

Hayden, Brian, M. Deal, A. Cannon, and J. Casey, "Ecological Determinants of Women's Status Among Hunter/Gatherers," *Human Evolution*, 1:5(1986), 449–74.

Head, Joseph and S. L. Cranston, eds. *Reincarnation in World Thought*. New York: Julian Press, 1967.

Heinlein, Robert. *Stranger in a Strange Land*. New York: Putnam, 1961.

Hill, Douglas and Pat Williams. *The Supernatural*. London: Aldus Books, 1965.

Hitchcock, Helyn. *Helping Yourself with Numerology*. West Nyack, N.Y.: Parker Publishing, 1972.

Hitching, Francis. *Earth Magic*. New York: William Morrow and Co., 1977.

Hoffman, Paul, "Friday the 13th," *Smithsonian*, February 1987.

Hohman, John George. *Pow-wows or Long Lost Friend*. Brooklyn, N.Y.: Fulton Religious Supply Co., n.d. (first published 1820).

Holzer, Hans. *The Directory of the Occult*. New York: Henry Regnery, 1974.

———. *The Truth About Witchcraft*. Garden City, N.Y.: Doubleday, 1969.

Hope, Murry. *Practical Celtic Magic*. Wellingborough, Northamptonshire, England: The Aquarian Press, 1987.

Hori, Ichiro. *Folk Religion in Japan*. Chicago: University of Chicago Press, 1968.

Howard, Michael. *The Magic of the Runes*. Wellingborough, Northamptonshire, England: The Aquarian Press, 1980.

Howell, Alice O. *Jungian Symbolism in Astrology*. Wheaton, Ill.: Theosophical Publishing House, 1987.

Huebner, Louise. *Never Strike a Happy Medium*. Los Angeles: Nash Publishing, 1971.

Hueffner, Oliver Maddox. *The Book of Witches*. Totowa, N.J.: Rowman & Littlefield, 1973 (first published 1903).

Hufford, David J. *The Terror That Comes in the Night*. Philadelphia: University of Pennsylvania Press, 1982.

Hughes, Pennethorne. *Witchcraft*. New York: Penguin Books, 1965.

Hunt, Roland. *The Seven Keys to Color Healing*. San Francisco: Harper & Row, 1982 (first published 1971).

Hunt, Stoker. *Ouija: The Most Dangerous Game*. New York: Harper & Row, 1985.

Huson, Paul. *Mastering Witchcraft: A Practical Guide for Witches, Warlocks & Covens*. New York: G. P. Putnam's Sons, 1970.

Huxley, Aldous. *The Devils of Loudun*. New York: Harper & Brothers, 1952.

Hyatt, Victoria and Joseph W. Charles. *The Book of Demons*. New York: Simon & Schuster, 1974.

Iglehart, Hallie Austen. *WomanSpirit*. San Francisco: Harper & Row, 1983.

Johns, June. *King of the Witches: The World of Alex Sanders*. New York: Coward-McCann, Inc., 1969.

Jong, Erica. *Witches*. New York: Harry N. Abrams, 1981.

Judith, Anodea. *Wheels of Life*. St. Paul: Llewellyn Publications, 1987.

Jussim, Daniel, "An Attack on Witchcraft," *Maclean's*, November 25, 1985.

Kalweit, Holger. *Dreamtime & Inner Space: The World of the Shaman*. Boston: Shambhala Publications, 1984.

Kaplan, Stuart R. *The Encyclopedia of Tarot*. New York: U. S. Games Systems, Inc., 1978.

Karlsen, Carol F. *The Devil in the Shape of a Woman: Witchcraft in Colonial New England*. New York: W. W. Norton & Co, 1987.

Katz, Susan, "A Pantheon of Spirits," *Newsweek*, February 24, 1986.

Kerr, Howard and Charles L. Crow, eds. *The Occult*

in America: New Historical Perspectives. Urbana, Ill.: University of Illinois Press, 1983.

King, Francis X. *Witchcraft and Demonology*. New York: Exeter Books, 1987.

Kittredge, George Lyman. *Witchcraft in Old and New England*. Cambridge: Harvard University Press, 1929.

Kluckhorn, Clyde. *Navaho Witchcraft*. Boston: Beacon Press, 1967 (first published 1944).

Kors, Alan C. and Edward Peters. *Witchcraft in Europe: A Documentary History 1100–1700*. Philadelphia: University of Pennsylvania Press, 1972.

Krieger, Delores. *The Therapeutic Touch*. Englewood Cliffs, N.J.: Prentice-Hall, 1979.

Laberis, Bill, "Laurie Cabot: An Interview," *Essex Life*, 2:2(Fall 1982), 88–93.

Ladurie, Emmanuel Le Roy. *Jasmin's Witch*. New York: George Braziller, 1987.

Lady Sheba. *Book of Shadows*. St Paul: Llewellyn Publications, 1971.

Larner, Christina. *Enemies of God*. London: Chatto & Windus, 1981.

LaVey, Anton Szandor. *The Satanic Bible*. New York: Avon Books, 1969.

Lea, Henry Charles. *Materials Toward a History of Witchcraft*. Philadelphia: University of Pennsylvania Press, 1939.

Leach, Maria, ed., and Jerome Fried, assoc. ed. *Funk & Wagnall's Standard Dictionary of Folklore, Mythology and Legend*. New York: Harper & Row, 1972.

Leadbeater, C. W. *Ancient Mystic Rites*. Wheaton, Ill.: Theosophical Publishing House, 1986 (first published 1926).

———. *The Science of the Sacraments*. Wheaton, Ill.: Theosophical Publishing House, 1980 (first published 1920).

Leek, Sybil. *The Complete Art of Witchcraft*. New York: World Publishing Co., 1971.

———. *Diary of a Witch*. New York: NAL Signet Library, 1968.

———. *Reincarnation: The Second Chance*. New York: Stein and Day, 1974.

———. *The Sybil Leek Book of Fortune Telling*. New York: Macmillan, 1969.

———. *Sybil Leek's Book of Curses*. Englewood Cliffs, N.J.: Prentice-Hall, 1975.

Leland, Charles Godfrey. *Aradia, the Gospel of the Witches*. London, 1889.

Lewis, Arthur H. *Hex*. New York: Pocket Books, 1970.

Lissner, Ivar. *Man, God and Magic*. New York: G.P. Putnam's Sons, 1961.

Llewellyn Publications. *The Truth About Witchcraft*. St. Paul: Llewellyn Publications, 1987.

Lockhart, J. G. *Curses, Lucks and Talismans*. Detroit: Single Tree Press, 1971 (first published 1938).

Loewe, Michael and Carmen Blacker. *Oracles and Divination*. Boulder, Colo.: Shambhala Publications, 1981.

Lovelock, J. E. *Gaia*. New York: Oxford University Press, 1979.

Lugh. *Old George Pickingill and the Roots of Modern Witchcraft*. Charlottesville, Va.: Taray Publications, 1984 (first published 1982).

Lutes, Chris, "Suicide Blamed on Music's Satanic Spell," *Christianity Today*, March 18, 1988.

McBride, Robert & Co. *The Encyclopedia of Occult Sciences*. New York: McBride, 1939.

McDowell, Bob. *Gypsies: Wanderers of the World*. Washington, D.C.: National Geographic Society, 1970.

MacGregor-Mathers, S. L. *The Book of the Sacred Magic of Abra-Melin the Mage*. Wellingborough, Northamptonshire England: The Aquarian Press, 1976.

Mackay, Charles, L. L. D. *Extraordinary Popular Delusions and the Madness of Crowds*, 2nd ed. New York: L. C. Page, 1932 (first published 1841).

Mahr, August C., "Origin and Significance of Pennsylvania Dutch Barn Symbols," *The Ohio State Archaeology and Historical Quarterly*, Jan.–Mar. 1945.

Mair, Lucy. *Witchcraft*. New York: McGraw-Hill World University Library, 1969.

Malinowski, Bronislaw. *Magic, Science and Religion*. Garden City, N.Y.: Doubleday Anchor Books, 1948.

Maltin, Leonard, ed. *Leonard Maltin's TV Movies and Video Guide, 1987 Edition*. New York: Signet Books, 1986.

Maple, Eric. *The Dark World of Witches*. New York: A. S. Barnes & Co., 1962.

Marcus, Ronald. *"Elizabeth Clawson, Thou Deservest to Dye."* Stamford, Conn.: Communication Corp., 1976.

Markham, Ursula. *Fortune-Telling by Crystals and Semi-*

Precious Stones. Wellingborough, Northamptonshire, England: The Aquarian Press, 1987.

Marlbrough, Ray L. *Charms, Spells & Formulas*. St. Paul: Llewellyn Publications, 1987.

Marriott, Alice and Carol C. Rachlin. *American Indian Mythology*. New York: Thomas Y. Crowell, 1968.

Martello, Dr. Leo Louis. *Weird Ways of Witchcraft*. New York: HC Publishers, 1969.

———. *Witchcraft: The Old Religion*. Secaucus, N.J.: University Books, 1973.

Martin, Malachi. *Hostage to the Devil*. New York: Harper & Row, 1976.

Marwick, Max, ed. *Witchcraft and Sorcery*. New York: Viking Penguin, 1982 (first published 1970).

Masters, R. E. L. *Eros and Evil: The Sexual Psychology of Witchcraft*. New York: Julian Press, 1962.

Mather, Cotton. *On Witchcraft: Being the Wonders of the Invisible World*. Mt. Vernon, N.Y.: The Peter Pauper Press, 1950 (first published 1693).

Mather, Increase. *Cases of Conscience Concerning Evil Spirits Personating Men; Witchcrafts, Infallible Proofs of Guilt in such as are Accused with that Crime*. Boston: 1693.

———. *An Essay for the Recording of Illustrious Providences*, with introduction by James A. Levernier. Delmar, N.Y.: Scholars' Facsimiles and Reprints, 1977 (first published 1684).

Matthews, John, ed. *At the Table of the Grail*. London: Arkana, 1987 (first published 1984).

May, Herbert G. and Bruce M. Metzger, eds. *The Oxford Annotated Bible with the Apocrypha*, rev. standard version. New York: Oxford University Press, 1965.

Melton J. Gordon. *The Encyclopedia of American Religions*, 2nd ed. Detroit: Gale Research Co., 1987.

———, "Witchcraft: An Inside View," *Christianity Today*, October 21, 1983, 22–25.

Michelet, Jules. *Satanism and Witchcraft*. Secaucus, N.J.: Citadel Press, 1939 (reprint).

Michell, John. *The New View Over Atlantis*. San Francisco: Harper & Row, 1986.

Mickaharic, Draja. *A Century of Spells*. York Beach, Me.: Samuel Weiser, 1988.

Miller, Kay, "Words from Other Worlds," *Minneapolis Star and Tribune Sunday Magazine*, May 11, 1986, 8–13+.

Monter, E. William. *Witchcraft in France and Switzerland*. Ithaca, N.Y.: Cornell University Press, 1976.

Monter, E. William, ed. *European Witchcraft*. New York: John Wiley & Sons, Inc., 1969.

Moore, R. Laurence. *In Search of White Crows*. New York: Oxford University Press, 1977.

Murray, Margaret A. *The God of the Witches*. London: Sampson Low, Marston and Co., Ltd., 1933.

———. *The Witch-cult in Western Europe*. London: Oxford University Press, 1921.

Nauman, St. Elmo, Jr. *Exorcism Through the Ages*. Secaucus, N.J.: Citadel, 1974.

New York Times, "Updike Movie Dismays Followers of Witchcraft," *The New York Times*, August 31, 1986.

Oxford University Press. *Washburn College Bible, The, King James Version*. New York: Oxford University Press, 1979.

Paulsen, Kathryn. *The Complete Book of Magic and Witchcraft*, rev. ed. New York: Signet/New American Library, 1980.

Peerman, Dean, "Voodo and Violence in Post-Duvalier Haiti," *The Christian Century*, July 16–23, 1986.

Peffer, Randall, "Return of the Salem Witch," *Gloucester*, 2:2(1979), 41–45.

Pepper, Elizabeth and John Wilcock. *Magical and Mystical Sites*. New York: Harper & Row, 1977.

Piggott, Stuart. *The Druids*. London: Thames and Hudson, 1975.

Pillsbury, Mark, "Cabot Quits Mayor's Race," *Salem Evening News*, August 11, 1987, 1+.

Potter, Carole. *Knock on Wood and Other Superstitions*. New York: Bonanza Books, 1984.

Prescott, William H. *The Conquest of Mexico*. New York: Bantam Books, 1964 (first published, 1843).

R. C. Esq. *Lithobolia: or, the Stone-throwing Devil, etc.* London: 1698.

Randolph, Vance. *Ozark Magic and Folklore*. New York: Dover Publications, 1964 (first published 1947).

Rawcliffe, D. H. *The Psychology of the Occult*. London: Derricke Ridgway Publishing Co., 1952.

Reader's Digest Association. *American Folklore and Legend*. Pleasantville, N.Y.: Reader's Digest Association, 1978.

———. *Facts & Fallacies*. Pleasantville, N.Y.: Reader's Digest Association, 1988.

————. *Into the Unknown*. Pleasantville, N.Y.: Reader's Digest Association, 1981.

————. *Magic and Medicine of Plants*. Pleasantville, N.Y.: Reader's Digest Association, 1986.

————. *Mysteries of the Ancient Americas*. Pleasantville, N.Y.: Reader's Digest Association, 1986.

————. *Mysteries of the Unexplained*. Pleasantville, N.Y.: Reader's Digest Association, 1982.

————. *Out of This World*. Pleasantville, N.Y.: Reader's Digest Association, 1976.

Reader's Digest Association Ltd. *Folklore, Myths and Legends of Britain*. London: Reader's Digest Association Ltd., 1977.

Regardie, Israel. *Ceremonial Magic: A Guide to the Mechanisms of Ritual*. Wellingborough, Northamptonshire, England: The Aquarian Press, 1980.

————. *The Golden Dawn*, 5th ed. St. Paul: Llewellyn Publications, 1986.

————. *What You Should Know About the Golden Dawn*, 3rd ed. Phoenix: Falcon Press, 1983.

Rhodes, H. F. T. *The Satanic Mass: A Sociological & Criminological Study*. New York: Citadel Press, 1955.

Rigaud, Milo. *Secrets of Voodoo*. San Francisco: City Lights Books, 1985 (first published 1953).

Roads, Michael J. *Talking with Nature*. Tiburon, Calif.: HJ Kramer Inc., 1985.

Robbins, Rossell Hope. *The Encyclopedia of Witchcraft & Demonology*. New York: Bonanza Books, 1981 (first published 1959).

Roberts, Henry C. *The Complete Prophecies of Nostradamus*. New York: American Book-Stratford Press, 1969.

Roelofsma, Derk Kinnane, "Exorcism and Rites of Deliverance," *Insight*, September 28, 1987.

Royston, Richard. *An Advertisement to the Jury-men of England Touching Witches. Together with a Difference Between an English and Hebrew Witch*. London: 1653.

Rush, John A. *Witchcraft and Sorcery*. Springfield, Ill.: Charles C. Thomas, 1974.

Russell, Jeffrey Burton. *The Devil*. Ithaca: Cornell University Press, 1977.

————. *A History of Witchcraft*. London: Thames and Hudson, 1980.

————. *Lucifer: The Devil in the Middle Ages*. Ithaca: Cornell University Press, 1984.

————. *Witchcraft in the Middle Ages*. Ithaca: Cornell University Press, 1972.

Salem Evening News, "Gov. Dukakis Unwittingly Gives 'Witch' Her Wish," *Salem Evening News*, April 28, 1977.

Saletore, R. N. *Indian Witchcraft*. Atlantic Highlands, N.J.: Humanities Press, 1981.

Savramis, Demosthenes. *The Satanizing of Woman: Religion Versus Sexuality*, translated by Martin Ebon. Garden City, N.Y.: Doubleday & Co., Inc., 1974.

Scholem, Gershom. *Kabbalah*. New York: New American Library, 1974.

Schueler, Gerald J. *An Advanced Guide to Enochian Magick*. St. Paul: Llewellyn Publications, 1987.

————. *Enochian Magick: A Practical Manual*. St. Paul: Llewellyn Publications, 1987.

Scobey, Joan, "Witchcraft," *New Woman*, September 1987, 104–110.

Scot, Reginald. *The Discoverie of Witchcraft*. Yorkshire, England: E. P. Publishing, Ltd., 1973 (from the 1886 ed.; first published, 1584).

Scott, Sir Walter. *Letters on Demonology and Witchcraft*. New York: Citadel Press, 1968 (first published 1830).

Seligmann, Kurt. *The Mirror of Magic*. New York: Pantheon Books, 1948.

Seven, Richard, "Today's Just One of Those Days," *Seattle Times*, February 13, 1987.

Seymour, St. John D. *Irish Witchcraft and Demonology*. Dublin: Hodges, Figgis & Co., 1913.

Sharpe, C. K. *A History of Witchcraft in Scotland*. Glasgow: Thomas D. Morison, 1884.

Shepard, Leslie A., ed. *Encyclopedia of Occultism and Parapsychology*, 2nd ed. Detroit: Gale Research Co., 1984.

Shirer, William L. *The Rise and Fall of the Third Reich*. New York: Simon & Schuster, 1959.

Sjoo, Monica and Barbara Mor. *The Great Cosmic Mother*. San Francisco: Harper & Row, 1987.

Sklar, Dusty. *Gods & Beasts: The Nazis and the Occult*. New York: Thomas Y. Crowell, 1977.

Smith, Michelle and Pazder, Lawrence, M.D. *Michelle Remembers*. New York: Congdon & Lattes, Inc., 1980.

Smith, Susy. *Today's Witches*. Englewood Cliffs, N.J.: Prentice-Hall, 1970.

Soman, Alfred, "Witch Lynching at Juniville," *Natural History*, November 1986.

Southern, R. W. *Western Society and the Church in the Middle Ages*. Harmondsworth, Middlesex, England: Penguin Books, 1970.

Spence, Lewis. *An Encyclopedia of Occultism*. Secaucus, N.J.: Citadel Press, 1960 (first published 1920).

Starhawk. *The Spiral Dance: A Rebirth of the Ancient Religion of the Great Goddess*. San Francisco: Harper & Row, 1979.

———. *Truth or Dare: Encounters with Power, Authority, and Mystery*. San Francisco: Harper & Row, 1987.

Starkey, Marion L. *The Devil in Massachusetts*. New York: Alfred Knopf, 1950.

Stein, Diane. *The Women's Spirituality Book*. St. Paul: Llewellyn Publications, 1987.

Stephensen, P. R. and Israel Regardie. *The Legend of Aleister Crowley*. St. Paul: Llewellyn Publications, 1970.

Stewart, R. J. *Living Magical Arts*. Poole, Dorset, England: Blandford Press, 1987.

Stoller, Paul and Cheryl Olkes. *In Sorcery's Shadow*. Chicago: University of Chicago Press, 1987.

Stone, Merlin. *Ancient Mirrors of Womanhood*. Boston: Beacon Press, 1984 (first published 1979).

———. *When God Was a Woman*. San Diego: Harcourt Brace Jovanovich, 1976.

Stover, Leon E. and Bruce Kraig. *Stonehenge: The Indo-European Heritage*. Chicago: Nelson-Hall, 1978.

Stutley, Margaret. *Ancient Indian Magic and Lore*. Boulder, Colo.: Great Eastern Book Co., 1980.

Summers, Montague. *The Geography of Witchcraft*. London: Kegan Paul, Trench, Trubner & Co. Ltd., 1927.

———. *The History of Witchcraft and Demonology*. London: Kegan Paul, Trench, Trubner & Co. Ltd., 1926.

———. *The Werewolf*. New York: Bell Publishing, 1967 (first published 1933).

Summers, Montague, ed. *Malleus Maleficarum*. New York: Dover Publications, 1971 (first published 1928).

Suster, Gerald, ed. *John Dee: Essential Readings*. Wellingborough, Northamptonshire, England: Crucible, 1986.

Symonds, John and Kenneth Grant, eds. *The Confessions of Aleister Crowley, an Autobiography*. London: Routledge & Kegan Paul, 1979.

Teilhard de Chardin, Pierre. *The Phenomenon of Man*. New York: Harper & Row, 1959 (first published 1955).

Terry, Maury. *The Ultimate Evil*. New York: Doubleday, 1987.

Thomas, Keith. *Religion and the Decline of Magic*. New York: Charles Scribner's Sons, 1971.

Tompkins, Peter. *Secrets of the Great Pyramids*. New York: Harper & Row, 1971.

Trigg, Elwood B. *Gypsy Demons & Divinities*. Secaucus, N.J.: Citadel Press, 1973.

Tyson, Donald. *The New Magus*. St. Paul: Llewellyn Publications, 1988.

Updike, John. *The Witches of Eastwick*. New York: Alfred A. Knopf, 1984.

Upham, Charles. *History of Witchcraft and Salem Village*. Boston: Wiggin and Lunt, 1867.

Ussher, Arland. *The Twenty-Two Keys to the Tarot*. Dublin: Dolmen Press, 1970.

Valiente, Doreen. *An ABC of Witchcraft Past and Present*. Custer, Wash.: Phoenix Publishing, 1986 (first published 1973).

———. *Witchcraft for Tomorrow*. Custer, Wash.: Phoenix Publishing, 1985 (first published 1978).

von Hagen, Victor Wolfgang. *The Aztec Man and Tribe*. New York: Mentor/New American Library, 1958.

———. *Realm of the Incas*. New York: Mentor/New American Library, 1957.

Waite, A. E. *The Book of Black Magic and of Pacts*. York Beach, Me.: Samuel Weiser, 1972 (first published 1899).

———. *The Pictorial Key to the Tarot*. Secaucus, N.J.: Citadel Press, 1959.

Walker, Barbara G. *The Crone*. San Francisco: Harper & Row, 1985.

———. *The Woman's Encyclopedia of Myths and Secrets*. San Francisco: Harper & Row, 1983.

Walker, Benjamin. *Encyclopedia of Metaphysical Medicine*. London: Routledge & Kegan Paul, 1978.

Walker, D. P. *Unclean Spirits: Possession and Exorcism in France and England in the Late Sixteenth and Early Seventeenth Centuries*. Philadelphia: University of Pennsylvania Press, 1981.

Ward, Charles A. *Oracles of Nostradamus*. New York: Dorset Press, 1986.

Wedeck, Harry E. *A Treasury of Witchcraft*. Secaucus, N.J.: Citadel Press, 1961.

Weinstein, Marion. *Earth Magic: A Dianic Book of Shadows*, rev. ed. Custer, Wash.: Phoenix Publishing, 1986.

————. *Positive Magic*, rev. ed. Custer, Wash.: Phoenix Publishing, 1981.

Weisman, Richard. *Witchcraft, Magic and Religion in Seventeenth-Century Massachusetts*. Amherst: The University of Massachusetts Press, 1984.

Weltfish, Gene. *The Lost Universe: The Way of Life of the Pawnee*. New York: Ballantine Books, 1965.

Westwood, Jennifer, ed. *The Atlas of Mysterious Places*. New York: Weidenfeld & Nicolson, 1987.

Wilhelm, Richard and Cary F. Baynes, translators. *The I Ching*, Bollingen Series XIX. Princeton, N.J.: Princeton University Press, 1969.

Williams, Howard. *The Superstitions of Witchcraft*. London: Longman, Green, Longman, Roberts & Green, 1865.

Williams, Selma R. and Pamela J. Williams. *Riding the Nightmare: Women and Witchcraft*. New York: Atheneum, 1978.

Wilmhurst, W. L. *The Meaning of Masonry*. New York: Bell Publishing Co., 1980 (reprint of 5th ed., 1927).

Wilson, Colin. *Mysteries*. New York: Perigee/G.P. Putnam's Sons, 1978.

————. *The Occult*. New York: Vintage Books, 1971.

Wood, Chris, "Suicide and Satanism," *Maclean's*, March 30, 1987, 54.

Yeats, W. B. *Irish Fairy and Folk Tales*. New York: Dorset Press, 1986 (first published 1892).

Yewdale, J. H. and Sons. *Encyclopedia of Superstitions, Folklore, and the Occult Sciences of the World*. Chicago: Yewdale, 1903.

Ywahoo, Dhyani. *Voices of Our Ancestors*. Boston: Shambhala Publications, 1987.

Index

409